Engaging Videos explore a variety of business topics related to the theory students are learning in class. **Exercise Quizzes** assess students' comprehension of the concepts in each video.

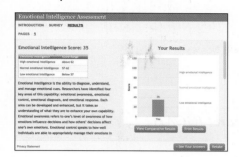

Personal Inventory Assessments is a collection of online exercises designed to promote **self-reflection** and engagement in students, enhancing their ability to connect with management concepts.

"I most liked the Personal Inventory Assessments because they gave me a deeper understanding of the chapters. I would read about personalities and then find out which category I fit into using the assessment."

WITHDRAWN

— Student, Kean University

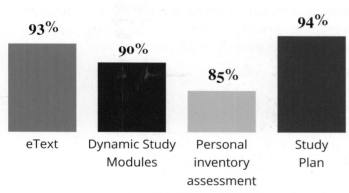

% of students who found learning aid helpful

Dynamic Study Modules use the latest developments in cognitive science and help students study chapter topics by adapting to their performance in real time.

Pearson eText enhances student learning with engaging and interactive lecture and example videos that bring learning to life.

The **Gradebook** offers an easy way for you and your students to see their performance in your course.

86%

of students would tell their instructor to keep using MyLab Management

For additional details visit www.pearson.com/mylab/management

COVENTRY UNIVERSITY LONDON
University House
109 - 117 Middlesex Street, London. E1 7JF
Tel: 024 7765 1016
www.coventry.ac.uk/london

To my family: Laura, Dana, Jennifer,
Jim, Mallory, Judi, David, and Lad

Steve

....

To healing and restoration and faithfulness…
And to my Thursday night girls…you know who you are! IGGATG

Mary

....

To my wife of 35 years, for her love and encouragement.
To my children, Mark, Meredith, Gabriella, and Natalie, who have given me
so much through the years. And now my two precious prides and joy—my grandsons,
William Mason Evans and Lucas Daniel Daley. How you two have changed my life!

Dave

Fundamentals of Management

ELEVENTH EDITION

GLOBAL EDITION

STEPHEN P. ROBBINS

San Diego State University

MARY COULTER

Missouri State University

DAVID A. DECENZO

Coastal Carolina University

Pearson

Harlow, England • London • New York • Boston • San Francisco • Toronto • Sydney • Dubai • Singapore • Hong Kong
Tokyo • Seoul • Taipei • New Delhi • Cape Town • Sao Paulo • Mexico City • Madrid • Amsterdam • Munich • Paris • Milan

Vice President, Business, Economics, and UK Courseware: Donna Battista
Director of Portfolio Management: Stephanie Wall
Specialist Portfolio Manager: Kris Ellis-Levy
Editorial Assistant: Amanda McHugh
Content Producer, Global Editions: Sudipto Roy
Acquisitions Editor, Global Editions: Ishita Sinha
Senior Project Editor, Global Editions: Daniel Luiz
Media Producer, Global Editions: Abhilasha Watsa
Manufacturing Controller, Production, Global Editions: Kay Holman
Vice President, Product Marketing: Roxanne McCarley
Senior Product Marketer: Carlie Marvel
Product Marketing Assistant: Marianela Silvestri
Manager of Field Marketing, Business Publishing: Adam Goldstein
Field Marketing Manager: Nicole Price

Vice President, Production and Digital Studio, Arts and Business: Etain O'Dea
Director, Production and Digital Studio, Business and Economics: Ashley Santora
Managing Producer, Business: Melissa Feimer
Senior Content Producer: Claudia Fernandes
Operations Specialist: Carol Melville
Design Lead: Kathryn Foot
Manager, Learning Tools: Brian Surette
Learning Tools Strategist: Michael Trinchetto
Managing Producer, Digital Studio and GLP: James Bateman
Managing Producer, Digital Studio: Diane Lombardo
Digital Studio Producer: Monique Lawrence
Digital Studio Producer: Alana Coles
Full Service Project Management, Interior Design: Integra Software Services Pvt Ltd.
Cover Designer: Lumina Datamatics, Inc.
Cover Art: vector-RGB/Shutterstock

Microsoft and/or its respective suppliers make no representations about the suitability of the information contained in the documents and related graphics published as part of the services for any purpose. All such documents and related graphics are provided "as is" without warranty of any kind. Microsoft and/or its respective suppliers hereby disclaim all warranties and conditions with regard to this information, including all warranties and conditions of merchantability, whether express, implied or statutory, fitness for a particular purpose, title and non-infringement. In no event shall Microsoft and/or its respective suppliers be liable for any special, indirect or consequential damages or any damages whatsoever resulting from loss of use, data or profits, whether in an action of contract, negligence or other tortious action, arising out of or in connection with the use or performance of information available from the services.

The documents and related graphics contained herein could include technical inaccuracies or typographical errors. Changes are periodically added to the information herein. Microsoft and/or its respective suppliers may make improvements and/or changes in the product(s) and/or the program(s) described herein at any time. Partial screen shots may be viewed in full within the software version specified.

Microsoft® and Windows® are registered trademarks of the Microsoft Corporation in the U.S.A. and other countries. This book is not sponsored or endorsed by or affiliated with the Microsoft Corporation.

Pearson Education Limited
KAO Two
KAO Park
Hockham Way
Harlow
Essex
CM17 9SR
United Kingdom

and Associated Companies throughout the world

Visit us on the World Wide Web at: www.pearsonglobaleditions.com

© Pearson Education Limited 2020

ISBN 10: 1-292-30732-3
ISBN 13: 978-1-292-30732-9

British Library Cataloguing-in-Publication Data

A catalogue record for this book is available from the British Library

10 9 8 7 6 5 4 3 2 1

Typeset in Times LT Pro by Integra Software Services Pvt Ltd.

Printed and bound by Vivar in Malaysia.

Brief Contents

Contents

Content highlighted in purple indicates that it is presented via a visual spread.

Part 5 Controlling

Preface

This Eleventh Edition of *Fundamentals of Management* covers the essentials of management in a way that provides a sound foundation for understanding the practical issues facing managers and organizations. The focus on knowing and applying the theories of management remains, while now also highlighting opportunities to develop employability skills. *Fundamentals of Management* offers an approachable, streamlined, realistic emphasis around what works for managers and what doesn't—with the ultimate goal to help students be successful.

To improve student results, we recommend pairing the text content with *MyLab Management*, which is the optional teaching and learning platform that empowers you to reach every student. By combining trusted author content with digital tools and a flexible learning platform, MyLab personalizes the learning experience to help your students learn and retain key course concepts while developing skills that future employers are seeking in potential employees. Learn more at **www.pearson.com/mylab/management**.

New to This Edition

- *New chapter on entrepreneurship.*
- *All new Experiential Exercises*. Each chapter's new Experiential Exercise is a hands-on activity in which students typically collaborate with other students to complete a task, such as writing a personal mission statement.
- *Employability skills highlighted throughout book*. Introduced in Chapter 1, these employability skills include critical thinking, communication, collaboration, knowledge application and analysis, and social responsibility. Each chapter is loaded with opportunities for students to use and work on the skills they'll need to be successful in the twenty-first-century workplace.
- *Material on early twentieth-century contributors: A diversity perspective*. Because management history is the result of the contributions of many diverse individuals, we added a section to the Management History Module highlighting some noteworthy contributors.
- *Module on professionalism and employability*. Expanded version of the module on Careers now focuses on professionalism and employability.
- *Diversity material added to managing human resources chapter.*
- *Managing operations material presented in a modular format.*
- *Several new examples throughout*, including Facebook's public scrutiny over what it was doing and not doing to protect its community of users, BMW's sustainability actions, digital currency use in Sweden, European "zombie" companies, Hootsuite's culture, the global cashew industry, Fox Sports World Cup advertising challenge, the organizational redesign at *The Wall Street Journal*, and many others.
- *New and updated content*, including current issues in organizational culture, anti-globalization, stumbling blocks to creativity, revision bias, crisis planning, digital tools as strategic weapons, managing disruptive innovation, remote work, multicultural brokers, inclusion, generational differences in the workplace, emotions and communication, alternate reality, toxic bosses, having civil conversations in the workplace, and workplace design.
- *Making Ethical Decisions in the Workplace*. This element has been renamed, and content is 60 percent new.

- *Case Applications.* 58 percent new.
- *New Management in the News in MyLab Management.* News articles are posted regularly, along with discussion questions that help students to understand management issues in current events.

Solving Teaching and Learning Challenges

Many students who take a principles of management course have difficulty understanding why they are taking the course in the first place. They presume that management is common sense, unambiguous, and dependent on intuition. They also need practice applying the concepts they are learning to real-world situations. Additionally, many students may not aim to be managers upon graduation, so they may struggle to see the parallels between this course and their career goals. We wrote *Fundamentals of Management* to address these challenges by developing a "management sense" grounded in theory for students while showing them how to apply concepts learned to real-world situations and enabling them to develop the necessary skills to be successful in any career.

Developing a "Management Sense"

Bust This Myth and Debunking Chapter Openers

Bust This Myth chapter openers include common myths that students may have about management. This feature debunks the common myths, helping students to better understand and develop their own management sense. Each one is accompanied by a Bust This Myth Video Exercise in *MyLab Management.*

The reality is that in 2017, more than 85 percent of the 176 countries in the International Monetary Fund *increased* their global exports.[1] While anti-globalization sentiment also has increased, **globalization is not disappearing any time soon!** It remains an important issue that organizational leaders must recognize and manage.

Globalization is a trend that's come and gone!

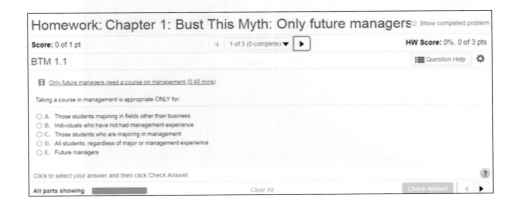

Homework: Chapter 1: Bust This Myth: Only future managers   Show completed problem

Score: 0 of 1 pt   1 of 3 (0 complete) ▼ ▶   HW Score: 0%, 0 of 3 pts

BTM 1.1   ☰ Question Help ⚙

▣ Only future managers need a course on management (0.46 mins)

Taking a course in management is appropriate ONLY for:

○ A. Those students majoring in fields other than business
○ B. Individuals who have not had management experience
○ C. Those students who are majoring in management
○ D. All students, regardless of major or management experience
○ E. Future managers

Click to select your answer and then click Check Answer   ?

All parts showing   Clear All   Check Answer ◀ ▶

The ***Think Like a Manager*** video series in *MyLab Management* shows students difficult business scenarios and asks them to respond through multiple choice question assignable activities.

Apply Concepts to the Real World

The **NEW *Entrepreneurship Module: Managing Entrepreneurial Ventures***, reflects the recent growth in entrepreneurial ventures, helping students to understand trends happening in the real world.

Murad Sezer/Reuters

Making Ethical Decisions in Today's Workplace

CVS Health Corporation announced in early 2018 that it would stop "materially" altering the beauty images used in its marketing materials that appear in its stores and on its websites and social media channels.[35] Although the change applies to the marketing materials it creates, the drugstore chain has also asked global brand partners—including Revlon, L'Oreal, and Johnson & Johnson—to join its effort. The company will use a watermark—the "CVS Beauty Mark"—on images that have not been altered. What does that mean? You're seeing real, not digitally modified, persons. The person featured in those images did not have their size, shape, skin or eye color, wrinkles, or other characteristics enhanced or changed. The company's goal is for all images in the beauty sections of CVS's stores to reflect the "transparency" commitment by 2020. Not surprisingly, there are pros and cons to this decision. And not surprisingly, there are ethical considerations associated with the decision.

Discussion Questions:

5 Striving for more realistic beauty/body image ideals: Who are potential stakeholders in this situation and what stake do they have in this decision?

6 From a generic viewpoint, how do ethical issues affect decision making? In this specific story, what potential ethical considerations do you see in the decision by CVS to stop altering beauty images and start using more realistic images?

This text **tackles tough issues** such as globalization/anti-globalization, having civil conversations, anti-bias, and ethical dilemmas—giving students an accurate depiction of the business environment today.

To help students apply management concepts to the real world, the cases ask students to assess a situation and answer questions about "how" and "why" and "what would you do?" These Case Applications cover a variety of companies, including Uber, Netflix, General Electric, Tesla, and more.

(Case Application for Chapter 14, Tesla)

CASE APPLICATION #3

Goals and Controls

Topic: Role of goals in controlling, control process, efficiency and effectiveness

Tesla. Elon Musk. You've probably heard of both. Tesla was founded in 2003 by a group of engineers who wanted to prove that buyers didn't need to compromise looks and performance to drive electric—that electric cars could be "better, quicker, and more fun to drive than gasoline cars."[60] Musk was not part of that original group but led the company's Series A investment (the name typically given to a company's first round of venture capital financing) and joined Tesla's board of directors as chairman. He soon took an active role in the company and oversaw the design of Tesla's first car, the Roadster, which was launched in 2008. Next came the Model S, introduced in 2012 as the world's first premium all-electric sedan. The next product line expansion was the Model X in 2015, a sport utility vehicle, which achieved a 5-star safety rating from the National Highway Safety Administration. The Model 3 was introduced in 2016 and production began in 2017. From the beginning, Musk has maintained that Tesla's long-term strategic goal was to create affordable mass-market

Experiential Exercise

Now, for a little fun! Organizations (work and educational) often use team-building exercises to help teams improve their performance. In your assigned group, *select two* of the characteristics of effective teams listed in Exhibit 10-6 and develop a team-building exercise for each characteristic. In developing your exercise, focus on helping a group improve that particular characteristic. Be creative! Write a group report describing your exercises, being sure to explain how your exercises will help a group improve or develop that characteristic. Be prepared to share your ideas with your class! OR, be prepared to demonstrate the team-building exercise!

Then, once you've concluded the assigned group work, you are to personally evaluate your "group" experience in working on this task. How did your group work together? What went "right?" What didn't go "right?" What could your group have done to improve its work performance and satisfaction with the group effort?

NEW! Experiential Exercises are all new. Each one is a hands-on activity in which students typically collaborate with other students to complete a task.

Developing Employability Skills

For students to succeed in a rapidly changing job market, they should be aware of their career options and how to go about developing a variety of skills. With *MyLab Management* and *Fundamentals of Management*, we focus on developing these skills in the following ways:

A new ***Employability Skills Matrix*** at the end of Chapter 1 provides students with a visual guide to features that support the development of skills employers are looking for in today's business graduates, helping students to see from the start of the semester the relevance of the course to their career goals.

EMPLOYABILITY SKILLS MATRIX					
	Critical Thinking	Communication	Collaboration	Knowledge Application and Analysis	Social Responsibility
Classic Concepts in Today's Workplace	✓	✓	✓	✓	
Making Ethical Decisions in Today's Workplace	✓	✓	✓	✓	✓
Managing Technology in Today's Workplace	✓	✓	✓	✓	✓
MyLab: Write It, Watch It, Try It	✓	✓		✓	
Management Skill Builder— Practicing the Skill		✓	✓	✓	
Experiential Exercise		✓	✓	✓	
Case Application 1	✓			✓	✓
Case Application 2	✓	✓		✓	
Case Application 3	✓		✓		

[Employability Skills Matrix from Chapter 1]

Boxed Features Highlight Opportunities to Develop Key Employability Skills.

Classic Concepts in Today's Workplace help students to understand a classic management concept. Hofstede's five dimensions of national culture, are still beneficial to managers in today's workplaces.

◀◀◀ Classic Concepts in Today's Workplace ▶▶▶

Hofstede's 5 Dimensions of National Culture

An illuminating study of the differences in cultural environments was conducted by Geert Hofstede in the 1970s and 1980s.[11] He surveyed more than 116,000 IBM employees in 40 countries about their work-related values and found that managers and employees vary on five dimensions of national culture:

- **Power distance.** The degree to which people in a country accept that power in institutions and organizations is distributed unequally. It ranges from relatively equal (low power distance) to extremely unequal (high power distance).

value relationships and show sensitivity and concern for the welfare of others.

- **Uncertainty avoidance.** This dimension assesses the degree to which people in a country prefer structured over unstructured situations and whether people are willing to take risks.
- **Long-term versus short-term orientation.** People in cultures with long-term orientations look to the future and value thrift and persistence. A short-term orientation values the past and present and emphasizes respect for tradition and fulfilling social obligations.

The following table shows a few highlights of four of Hofstede's cultural dimensions and how different countries rank on those dimensions.

Here's one way to UNDERSTAND CULTURAL DIFFERENCES!

Making Ethical Decisions in Today's Workplace

Walt Disney Company. *Star Wars*. Two powerful forces combined. But is that force for good or for not-so-good?[30] It's not surprising that the popularity of the *Star Wars* franchise has given Walt Disney Co. exceptional power over the nation's movie theaters. The theater owners want the *Star Wars* releases, and there's only one way to get them...through Disney. With the latest release, movie theaters had to agree to "top-secret" terms that many theater owners said were the most oppressive and demanding they had ever seen. Not only were they required to give Disney about 65 percent of ticket revenue, there were also requirements about when, where, and how the movie could be shown. You'd think that because Disney needs the theaters to show their movies they might be better off viewing them as "partners" rather than subordinates. What do you think?

Discussion Questions:

5 Is there an ethical issue here? Why or why not? What stakeholders might be affected and how might they be affected? How can identifying stakeholders help a manager decide the most responsible approach?

6 Working together in your "assigned" group, discuss Disney's actions. Do you agree with those actions? Look at the pros and cons, including how the various stakeholders are affected. Prepare a list of arguments both pro and con. (To be a good problem solver and critical thinker, you have to learn how to look at issues from all angles!)

Making Ethical Decisions in Today's Workplace presents students with an ethical dilemma and encourages them to practice their skills in ethical decision making and critical decision making.

Managing Technology in Today's Workplace
MONITORING EMPLOYEES

Technological advances have made the process of managing an organization much easier.[30] And technological advancements have also provided employers a means of sophisticated employee monitoring. Although most of this monitoring is designed to enhance worker productivity, it could, and has been, a source of concern over worker privacy. These advantages bring with them difficult questions regarding what managers have the right to know about employees and how far they can go in controlling employee behavior, both on and off the job. Consider the following:

- The mayor of Colorado Springs, Colorado, reads the e-mail messages that city council members send to each other from their homes. He defended his actions by saying he was making sure that e-mails to each other were not being used to circumvent the state's "open meeting" law that requires most council business to be conducted publicly.

Just how much control a company should have over the private lives of its employees also becomes an issue. Where should an employer's rules and controls end? Does the boss have the right to dictate what you do on your free time and in your own home? Could your boss keep you from engaging in riding a motorcycle, skydiving, smoking, drinking alcohol, or eating junk food? Again, the answers may surprise you. Today many organizations, in their quest to control safety and health insurance costs, are delving into their employees' private lives.

Although controlling employees' behaviors on and off the job may appear unjust or unfair, nothing in our legal system prevents employers from engaging in these practices. Rather, the law is based on the premise that if employees don't like the rules, they have the option of quitting. Managers, too, typically defend their actions in terms of ensuring quality, productivity

Managing Technology in Today's Workplace describes how managers are using technology to monitor employee performance, looking at ways to have a more efficient and effective workplace.

Personal Inventory Assessments is a collection of online exercises designed to promote self-reflection and engagement in students, helping them better understand management concepts. These assessments help develop professionalism and awareness of oneself and others, skills necessary for future career success.

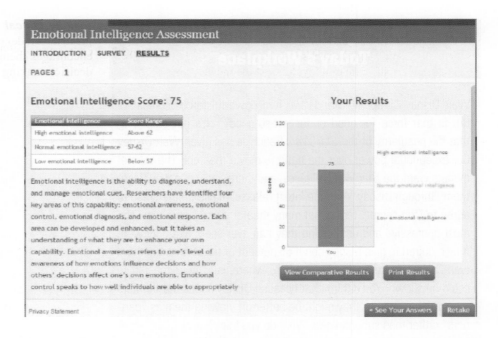

End-of-Chapter Management Skill Builder helps students move from merely knowing concepts to actually being able to use that knowledge.

The skill-building exercises included at the end of each chapter help you apply and use management concepts. We chose these skills because of their relevance to developing management competence and their linkage to one or more of the topic areas in this book.

> ### Management Skill Builder | UNDERSTANDING CULTURE
>
> An organization's culture is a system of shared meaning. When you understand your organization's culture, you know, for example, whether it encourages teamwork, rewards innovation, or stifles initiative. When interviewing for a job, the more accurate you are at assessing the culture, the more likely you are to find a good person–organization fit. And once inside an organization, understanding the culture allows you to know what behaviors are likely to be rewarded and which are likely to be punished.[48]

Expanded **Module on Professionalism and Employability**

In this newly expanded module, students are provided with very practical information in terms of being professional and employable. It's good to remind students that there is a future beyond getting their degree. But they must prepare themselves for it, with solid academic learning *and* practical advice.

Chapter by Chapter Changes

In addition to all these major changes, here is a chapter-by-chapter list of the topic additions and changes in the Eleventh Edition:

Chapter 1

- Rewrote box feature questions to focus on skills
- New Making Ethical Decisions box
- Added material on employability skills, including Employability Skills Matrix
- New Experiential Exercise
- Two new cases (Walmart's management training, Intel's "chip" problem)
- Updated one case (Zappo's holacracy)
- Added "Topic" to Case Apps
- Highlighted different employability skill in each case

History Module

- Added new section on Other Early Twentieth-Century Contributors: A Diversity Perspective

Chapter 2

- Rewrote box feature questions to focus on skills
- Added "revision bias" to section on Common Errors
- New Being Ethical box
- Added information on stumbling blocks to creativity
- New Experiential Exercise

- One new case (Panera Bread Company)
- Updated two cases (UPS, Baseball Data Analytics)
- Added "Topic" to Case Apps
- Highlighted different employability skills in each case

Quantitative Decision-Making Tools Module

Chapter 3

- New opening Myth/Debunked
- Rewrote box feature questions to focus on skills
- New Being Ethical box
- Added new information about anti-globalization
- New Experiential Exercise
- Two new cases (Chinese battery companies, NCAA basketball scandal)
- Updated one case (Keurig)
- Added "Topic" to Case Apps
- Highlighted different employability skill in each case

Chapter 4

- Rewrote box feature questions to focus on skills
- New Being Ethical box
- Added new section on Current Issues in Organizational Culture
- New Experiential Exercise
- Two new cases (Uber, full pay transparency)
- Updated one case (movie theatre industry)
- Added "Topic" to Case Apps
- Highlighted different employability skill in each case

Chapter 5

- Rewrote box feature questions to focus on skills
- Added new section on managing disruptive innovation
- New Being Ethical box
- New Experiential Exercise
- Updated one case (UnderArmour)
- Two new cases (Volkswagen, Swiss watch industry)
- Added "Topic" to Case Apps
- Highlighted different employability skills in each case

Managing Entrepreneurial Ventures Module

- New Module

Chapter 6

- Rewrote box feature questions to focus on skills
- Added new material on digital tools as strategic weapons
- Added new material on crisis planning
- New Managing Technology in Today's Workplace box (using social media for environmental scanning)
- New Experiential Exercise
- Updated one case (Zara)
- Two new cases (Ford Motor Company, Domino's Pizza)
- Added "Topic" to Case Apps
- Highlighted different employability skills in each case

Chapter 7

- Rewrote box feature questions to focus on skills
- New Being Ethical box
- Added new material on remote work
- New Experiential Exercise
- One new case (United Air)
- Updated two cases (NASA, PfizerWorks)
- Added "Topic" to Case Apps
- Highlighted different employability skills in each case

Chapter 8

- New opening Myth/Debunked
- New examples
- Rewrote box feature questions to focus on skills
- New Being Ethical box
- Added additional material on sexual harassment
- Moved diversity material to this chapter
- Added discussion on inclusion
- New Experiential Exercise
- One new case (Starbucks and racial-bias training)
- Updated two cases (résumé discrepancies, attracting tech talent)
- Added "Topic" to Case Apps
- Highlighted different employability skills in each case

Professionalism and Employability Module

- New material on professionalism and employability
- Revised material on careers

Chapter 9

- Rewrote box feature questions to focus on skills
- Added material on multicultural brokers
- New Experiential Exercise
- Two new cases (Microsoft and W. L. Gore)
- Updated case (health-care industry)
- Added "Topic" to Case Apps
- Highlighted different employability skills in each case

Chapter 10

- Rewrote box feature questions to focus on skills
- Expanded discussion of generational differences in the workplace
- New Experiential Exercise
- Two new cases (Virgin Group, Adobe Systems)
- Updated case (Google)
- Added "Topic" to Case Apps
- Highlighted different employability skills in each case

Chapter 11

- Rewrote box feature questions to focus on skills
- New Experiential Exercise
- One new case (unlimited vacation time)
- Two updated cases (Gravity Payments, Patagonia)

- Added "Topic" to Case Apps
- Highlighted different employability skills in each case

Chapter 12

- Rewrote box feature questions to focus on skills
- New Being Ethical box
- New material on toxic bosses
- New Experiential Exercise
- Two new cases (General Electric, L'Oreal)
- One updated case (developing Gen Y leaders)
- Added "Topic" to Case Apps
- Highlighted different employability skills in each case

Chapter 13

- Rewrote box feature questions to focus on skills
- New material added to discussion of emotions and communication
- Reworked visual spread
- Added discussion of alternate reality (AR)
- New material on having civil conversations in the workplace

- New material on workplace design
- New Experiential Exercise
- One new case (anytime feedback)
- Two updated cases (athletes and Twitter and eliminating e-mail)
- Added "Topic" to Case Apps
- Highlighted different employability skills in each case

Chapter 14

- Rewrote box feature questions to focus on skills
- New Being Ethical box
- New Experiential Exercise
- Two new cases (Chipotle, Tesla)
- One updated case (positive feedback)
- Added "Topic" to Case Apps
- Highlighted different employability skills in each case

Managing Operations Module

- New presentation of material as a module

Instructor Teaching Resources

This program comes with the following teaching resources.

Supplements available to instructors at www.pearsonglobaleditions.com	Features of the Supplement
Instructor's Resource Manual authored by Veronica Horton	• Chapter-by-chapter summaries • Chapter Outlines with teaching tips • Answers to Case Application discussion questions • Solutions to all questions and exercises in the book
Test Bank authored by Carol Heeter	Over 2,500 multiple-choice, true/false, and essay questions with answers and these annotations: • Learning Objective • AACSB learning standard (Written and Oral Communication; Ethical Understanding and Reasoning; Analytical Thinking; Information Technology; Interpersonal Relations and Teamwork; Diverse and Multicultural Work Environments; Reflective Thinking; Application of Knowledge) • Difficulty level (Easy, Moderate, Challenging) • Question Category (Critical Thinking, Concept, Application, Analytical, or Synthesis)
TestGen® Computerized Test Bank	TestGen allows instructors to: • Customize, save, and generate classroom tests • Edit, add, or delete questions from the Test Bank • Analyze test results • Organize a database of tests and student results
PowerPoint Presentation authored by Veronica Horton	Presents basic outlines and key points from each chapter. Slides meet accessibility standards for students with disabilities. Features include, but not limited to: • Keyboard and Screen Reader access • Alternative text for images • High-color contrast between background and foreground colors

Acknowledgments

Writing and publishing a textbook requires the talents of a number of people whose names never appear on the cover. We'd like to recognize and thank a phenomenal team of talented people who provided their skills and abilities in making this book a reality. This team includes Kris Ellis-Levy, our specialist portfolio manager; Claudia Fernandes, our senior content producer; Carlie Marvel, our senior product marketer, Nicole Price, our field marketing manager; Stephanie Wall, our director of portfolio management; Nancy Moudry, our highly talented and gifted photo researcher; Lauren Cook, our talented digital media whiz who co-created the "Bust The Myth" videos; and Kristin Jobe, associate managing editor, Integra-Chicago.

We also want to thank our reviewers—past and present—for the insights they have provided us:

David Adams, *Manhattanville College*
Lorraine P. Anderson, *Marshall University*
Maria Aria, *Camden Community College*
Marcia Marie Bear, *University of Tampa*
Barbara Ann Boyington, *Brookdale Community College*
Reginald Bruce, *University of Louisville*
Jon Bryan, *Bridgewater State University*
Elena Capella, *University of San Francisco*
James Carlson, *Manatee Community College*
Pam Carstens, *Coe College*
Casey Cegielski, *Auburn University*
Michael Cicero, *Highline Community College*
Evelyn Delanee, *Daytona Beach Community College*
Kathleen DeNisco, *Erie Community College, South Campus*
Jack Dilbeck, *Ivy Tech State College*
Fred J. Dorn, *University of Mississippi*
Michael Drafke, *College of DuPage*
Myra Ellen Edelstein, *Salve Regina University*
Deborah Gilliard, *Metropolitan State College, Denver*
Robert Girling, *Sonoma State University*
Patricia Green, *Nassau Community College*
Gary Greene, *Manatee Community College, Venice Campus*
Kenneth Gross, *The University of Oklahoma*
Jamey Halleck, *Marshall University*
Aaron Hines, *SUNY New Paltz*
Robyn Hulsart, *Austin Peavy State University*
Todd E. Jamison, *Chadron State College*

Edward A. Johnson, *University of North Florida*
Kayvan Miri Lavassani, *North Carolina Central*
Kim Lukaszewski, *SUNY New Paltz*
Brian Maruffi, *Fordham University*
Mantha Vlahos Mehallis, *Florida Atlantic University*
Christine Miller, *Tennessee Technological University*
Diane Minger, *Cedar Valley College*
Kimberly K. Montney, *Kellogg Community College*
James H. Moore, *Arizona State University*
Clara Munson, *Albertus Magnus College*
Jane Murtaugh, *College of DuPage*
Francine Newth, *Providence College*
Leroy Plumlee, *Western Washington University*
Pollis Robertson, *Kellogg Community College*
Cynthia Ruszkowski, *Illinois State University*
Thomas J. Shaughnessy, *Illinois Central College*
Andrea Smith-Hunter, *Siena College*
Martha Spears, *Winthrop University*
Jeff Stauffer, *Ventura College*
Kenneth R. Tillery, *Middle Tennessee State University*
Robert Trumble, *Virginia Commonwealth University*
Philip Varca, *University of Wyoming*
Margaret Viets, *University of Vermont*
Brad Ward, *Kellogg Community College*
Lucia Worthington, *University of Maryland University College*
Seokhwa Yun, *Montclair State University*

Thank You!

Steve, Mary, and Dave would like to thank you for considering and choosing our book for your management course. All of us have several years of teaching under our belt, and we know how challenging yet rewarding it can be. Our goal is to provide you with the best resources available to help you excel in the classroom!

For their contribution to the Global Edition, Pearson would like to thank Hussein Ismail, Lebanese American University; Stephanie Pougnet, University of Applied Sciences Western Switzerland; and Andrew Richardson, University of Leeds; and for their review of the new content, David Ahlstrom, Chinese University of Hong Kong; Elsa Chan, City University of Hong Kong; Tan Wei Lian, Taylor's University; Goh See Kwong, Taylor's University; and Yanfeng Zheng, The University of Hong Kong.

About the Authors

STEPHEN P. ROBBINS received his Ph.D. from the University of Arizona. He previously worked for the Shell Oil Company and Reynolds Metals Company and has taught at the University of Nebraska at Omaha, Concordia University in Montreal, the University of Baltimore, Southern Illinois University at Edwardsville, and San Diego State University. He is currently professor emeritus in management at San Diego State.

Dr. Robbins's research interests have focused on conflict, power, and politics in organizations, behavioral decision making, and the development of effective interpersonal skills. His articles on these and other topics have appeared in such journals as *Business Horizons*, the *California Management Review, Business and Economic Perspectives, International Management, Management Review, Canadian Personnel and Industrial Relations*, and the *Journal of Management Education*.

Dr. Robbins is the world's best-selling textbook author in the areas of management and organizational behavior. His books have sold more than 10 million copies and have been translated into 20 languages. His books are currently used at more than 1,500 U.S. colleges and universities, as well as hundreds of schools throughout Canada, Latin America, Australia, New Zealand, Asia, and Europe.

For more details, see stephenprobbins.com.

MARY COULTER (Ph.D., University of Arkansas) held different jobs, including high school teacher, legal assistant, and city government program planner, before completing her graduate work. She has taught at Drury University, the University of Arkansas, Trinity University, and Missouri State University. She is currently professor emeritus of management at Missouri State University. In addition to *Fundamentals of Management*, Dr. Coulter has published other books with Pearson including *Management* (with Stephen P. Robbins), *Strategic Management in Action*, and *Entrepreneurship in Action*.

When she's not busy writing, Dr. Coulter enjoys puttering around in her flower gardens; trying new recipes; reading all different types of books; and enjoying many different activities with husband Ron, daughters and sons-in-law Sarah and James and Katie and Matt, and most especially with her two grandkids, Brooklynn and Blake, who are the delights of her life!

DAVID A. DECENZO (Ph.D., West Virginia University) is president of Coastal Carolina University in Conway, South Carolina. He has been at Coastal since 2002 when he took over leadership of the E. Craig Wall Sr. College of Business. As president, Dr. DeCenzo has implemented a comprehensive strategic planning process, ensured fiscal accountability through policy and practice, and promoted assessment and transparency throughout the university. Before joining the Coastal faculty in 2002, he served as director of partnership development in the College of Business and Economics at Towson University in Maryland. He is an experienced industry consultant, corporate trainer, public speaker, and board member. Dr. DeCenzo is the author of numerous textbooks that are used widely at colleges and universities throughout the United States and the world. Dr. DeCenzo and his wife, Terri, have four children: Mark, Meredith, Gabriella, and Natalie, and reside in Pawleys Island, South Carolina.

Managing Today

1

Management Myth

Only those who want to be managers need to take a course in management.

Management Myth

DEBUNKED!

Anyone who works in an organization **—not just managers—** can gain insight into how organizations work and the behaviors of their boss and coworkers by taking a course in management.

ASSUME for a moment that it's your first day in an introductory physics class. Your instructor asks you to take out a piece of paper and "describe Newton's second law of motion." How would you react? We think that you, like most students, would respond with something like "How would I know? That's why I'm taking this course!"

Now let's change the situation to the first day in an introductory management class. Your instructor asks you to write an answer to the question: "What traits does one need to be an effective leader?" When we've done this on the first day, we find that students always have an answer. Everyone seems to think they know what makes a good leader.

This example illustrates a popular myth about the study of management: It's just common sense. Well, we can assure you… it's not! When it comes to managing, much of what passes for common sense is just plain misguided or even wrong. You might be surprised to know that the *academic* study of management is filled with insights, based on extensive research, which often run counter to what seems to be common sense. That's why we decided to tackle head-on this common-sense perception by opening each chapter with a particular "management myth" and then "debunking" this myth by explaining how it *is* just a common-sense myth.

Take a minute to re-look at this chapter's "management myth" and "management myth debunked." This "debunked" myth often surprises students majoring in subjects like accounting, finance, statistics, information technology, or advertising. Since they don't

Learning Outcomes

expect to be managers, they see spending a semester studying management as a waste of time and irrelevant to their career goals. Later in this chapter, we'll explain why the study of management is valuable to *every* student, no matter what you're majoring in or whether you are a manager or aspire to be a manager. ●

Although we'd like to think that all managers are good at what they do, you may have discovered through jobs you've had that managers can be good at what they do or maybe not so good, or even good one day and not so good the next! One thing you need to understand is that all managers—good or not so good—have important jobs to do. And this book is about the work managers do. In this chapter, we introduce you to managers and management: who they are, where they work, what management is, what they do, and why you should spend your time studying management, including how you can develop important employability skills. Finally, we'll wrap up the chapter by looking at some key factors reshaping and redefining organizations *and* the way managers manage.

Who Are Managers and Where Do They Work?

1-1 Tell who managers are and where they work.

There's no prototype or standard criteria as to who can be a manager. Managers today can be under age 18 or over age 80. They may be women as well as men, and they can be found in all industries and in all countries. They manage entrepreneurial businesses, large corporations, government agencies, hospitals, museums, schools, and not-for-profit enterprises. Some hold top-level management jobs while others are supervisors or team leaders. However, all managers share one common element: They work in an organizational setting. An **organization** is a deliberate collection of people brought together to accomplish some specific purpose. For instance, your college or university is an organization, as are the United Way, your neighborhood convenience store, the New Orleans Saints football team, fraternities and sororities, the Cleveland Clinic, and global companies such as Alibaba Group, Lego, and Starbucks. These and all organizations share three common characteristics. (See Exhibit 1–1.)

What Three Characteristics Do All Organizations Share?

The *first* characteristic of an organization is that it has a *distinct purpose*, which is typically expressed as a goal or set of goals. For example, Mark Zuckerberg, CEO of Facebook, facing increased public scrutiny over things his company was doing and not doing in relation to protecting its community of users and the global community at large, stated that his company's goal was to fix those important issues and to get back to its original purpose—providing meaningful interactions between family and friends.[1] The *second*

organization
A deliberate collection of people brought together to accomplish some specific purpose

Exhibit 1–1 Three Characteristics of Organizations

characteristic is that *people* in an organization work to achieve those goals. How? By making decisions and engaging in work activities to make the desired goal(s) a reality. For instance, at Facebook, many employees work to create the programming and algorithms that are crucial to the company's business. Others provide supporting services by monitoring content or addressing user problems. Finally, the *third* characteristic is that an organization is *structured* in some way that defines and limits the behavior of its members. Facebook, like most large organizations, has a structure with different businesses, departments, and functional areas. Within that structure, rules, regulations, and policies might guide what people can or cannot do; some members will supervise other members; work teams might be formed or disbanded; or job descriptions might be created or changed so organizational members know what they're supposed to do. That structure is the setting within which managers manage.

How Are Managers Different from Nonmanagerial Employees?

Although managers work in organizations, not everyone who works in an organization is a manager. For simplicity's sake, we'll divide organizational members into two categories: nonmanagerial employees and managers. **Nonmanagerial employees** are people who work directly on a job or task and have no responsibility for overseeing the work of others. The employees who ring up your sale at Home Depot, take your order at the Starbucks drive-through, or process your class registration forms are all nonmanagerial employees. These nonmanagerial employees may be called associates, team members, contributors, or even employee partners. **Managers**, on the other hand, are individuals in an organization who direct and oversee the activities of other people in the organization so organizational goals can be accomplished. A manager's job isn't about *personal* achievement—it's about helping *others* do their work. That may mean coordinating the work of a departmental group, leading an entire organization, or supervising a single person. It could involve coordinating the work activities of a team with people from different departments or even people outside the organization, such as contract employees or individuals who work for the organization's suppliers. This distinction doesn't mean, however, that managers don't ever work directly on tasks. Some managers do have work duties not directly related to overseeing the activities of others. For example, an insurance claims supervisor might process claims in addition to coordinating the work activities of other claims employees.

What Titles Do Managers Have?

Although they can have a variety of titles, identifying exactly who the managers are in an organization shouldn't be difficult. In a broad sense, managers can be classified as top, middle, first-line, or team leaders. (See Exhibit 1–2.) **Top managers** are those at or near the top of an organization. They're usually responsible for making decisions about the direction of the organization and defining policies and values that affect all organizational members. Top managers typically have titles such as vice president, president, chancellor, managing director, chief operating officer (COO), chief executive officer (CEO), or chairperson of the board. **Middle managers** are those managers found between the lowest and top levels of the organization. These individuals often manage other managers and maybe some nonmanagerial employees and are typically responsible for translating the goals set by top managers into specific details that lower-level managers will see get done. Middle managers may have such titles as department or agency head, project leader, unit chief, district manager, division manager, or store manager. **First-line managers** are those individuals responsible for directing the day-to-day activities of nonmanagerial employees and/or team leaders. First-line managers are often called supervisors,

Aditi Banga is an associate product manager at Pocket Gems, a firm in San Francisco that makes and publishes mobile games such as Pet Tap Hotel and Paradise Cove. Collaborating with multiple teams of engineers and designers, she manages games from initial concept through development to product launch.

Stephen Lam/Reuters

Exhibit 1–2 Management Levels

team leaders
Individuals who are responsible for leading and facilitating the activities of a work team

scientific management
The use of scientific methods to define the "one best way" for a job to be done

- Top Managers
- Middle Managers
- First-Line Managers
- Team Leaders

shift managers, office managers, department managers, or unit coordinators. We want to point out a special type of manager that has become more common as organizations use employee work teams. **Team leaders** are individuals who are responsible for leading and facilitating the activities of a work team.

◄◄◄ Classic Concepts in Today's Workplace ►►►

The terms *management* and *manager* are actually centuries old.[2] One source says that the word *manager* originated in 1588 to describe one who manages. The specific use of the word as a person who oversees a business or public organization is believed to have originated in the early part of the 18th century. However, used in the way we're defining it in terms of overseeing and directing organizational members, *management* and *manager* are more appropriate to the early-twentieth-century time period. The word *management* was first popularized by Frederick Winslow Taylor. Taylor is a "biggie" in management history, so let's look at his contributions to how management is practiced today.

- In 1911, Taylor's book, *Principles of Scientific Management*, took the business world by storm—his ideas spread in the United States and to other countries and inspired others.
- Why? His theory of **scientific management**: the use of scientific methods to define the *"one best way"* for a job to be done.
- Taylor, a mechanical engineer in Pennsylvania steel companies, observed workers and was continually shocked by how inefficient they were:
  — Employees used vastly different techniques to do the same job and often "took it easy" on the job.
  — Few, if any, work standards existed.
  — Workers were placed in jobs with little or no concern for matching their abilities and aptitudes with the tasks they were required to do.

> Management: Finding one best way to do a job?

- The result was worker output only about *one-third* of what was possible.
- Taylor's remedy? Apply scientific management to these manual shop-floor jobs.
- The result was phenomenal increases in worker output and efficiency—in the range of *200 percent or more*!
- Because of his work, Taylor is known as the "father" of scientific management.

Want to try your hand at using scientific management principles to be more efficient? Choose a task you do regularly such as laundry, grocery shopping, studying for exams, cooking dinner, etc. Analyze that task by writing down the steps involved in completing it. What activities could be combined or eliminated? Find the "one best way" to do this task. See if you can become more efficient—keeping in mind that changing habits isn't easy to do.

Discussion Questions:

1 Are Taylor's views still relevant to how management is practiced today? Why or why not?

2 You lead a team of shelf stockers at a local health foods store. You've been asked by your store manager to find a way to make your work team more efficient. Using Taylor's scientific management principles, write a list of possible ideas to share with your manager.

What Is Management?

1-2 Define *management*.

Simply speaking, management is what managers do. But that simple statement doesn't tell us much. A better explanation is that **management** is the process of getting things done, effectively and efficiently, with and through other people. We need to look closer at some key words in this definition.

A *process* refers to a set of ongoing and interrelated activities. In our definition of management, it refers to the primary activities or functions that managers perform—functions that we'll discuss in more detail in the next section.

Talk about an interesting way to be efficient!

ROWE—or results-only work environment—was a radical experiment tried at Best Buy headquarters. In this flexible work program, employees were judged only on tasks completed or results, not on how many hours they spent at work. Employees couldn't say whether they worked fewer hours because they stopped counting, BUT **employee productivity jumped 41 percent!**[3]

Do you order stuff from Amazon? A lot of people obviously do because Amazon ships out millions of packages every day. It's currently looking at innovative ways to send more items with less cardboard.[4] Why? To be more efficient and effective and to satisfy younger consumers who are passionate about minimizing environmental impact. Efficiency and effectiveness have to do with the work being done and how it's being done. **Efficiency** means doing a task correctly ("doing things right") and getting the most output from the least amount of inputs. Because managers deal with scarce inputs—including resources such as people, money, and equipment—they're concerned with the efficient use of those resources. Managers everywhere, much like those at Amazon, want to minimize resource usage and costs.

It's not enough, however, just to be efficient. Managers are also concerned with completing important work activities. In management terms, we call this **effectiveness**. Effectiveness means "doing the right things" by doing those work tasks that help the organization reach its goals. Whereas efficiency is concerned with the *means* of getting things done, effectiveness is concerned with the *ends*, or attainment of organizational goals. (See Exhibit 1–3.)

management
The process of getting things done, effectively and efficiently, through and with other people

efficiency
Doing things right, or getting the most output from the least amount of inputs

effectiveness
Doing the right things, or completing work activities so that organizational goals are attained

---

Exhibit 1–3 Efficiency and Effectiveness

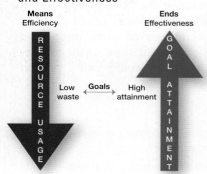

A quick overview of managers and **efficiency & effectiveness**

- The concepts are different, but related, because both are focused on how organizational work gets done.
- It's easier to be effective if you ignore efficiency.
- Poor managers often allow
  —both inefficiency and ineffectiveness OR effectiveness achieved without regard for efficiency.
- Good managers are concerned with
  —both attaining goals (effectiveness) and doing so as efficiently as possible.

3 Ways to Look at What Managers Do

1-3 Describe what managers do.

ORGANIZATIONS ARE NOT ALIKE, and neither are managers' jobs. But their jobs do share some common elements, as you'll see in these three approaches to describing what managers do.

1

4 Functions Approach

- Says that managers perform certain activities, tasks, or functions as they direct and oversee others' work.

- WHAT Fayol said managers do: First person to identify five common activities managers engage in: plan, organize, command, coordinate, and control (POCCC).[5]

- Today, the management functions have been condensed to four: **planning**, **organizing**, **leading**, and **controlling**.

- See Exhibit 1–4 for what managers do when they P-O-L-C.

Exhibit 1–4 Four Management Functions

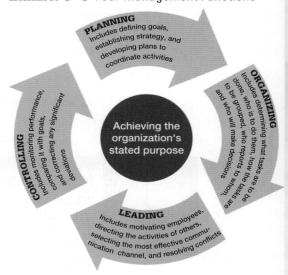

PLANNING Includes defining goals, establishing strategy, and developing plans to coordinate activities

ORGANIZING Includes determining what tasks are to be done, who is to do them, how the tasks are to be grouped, who reports to whom, and who will make decisions

LEADING Includes motivating employees, directing the activities of others, selecting the most effective communication channel, and resolving conflicts

CONTROLLING Includes monitoring performance, comparing it with goals, and correcting any significant deviations

Achieving the organization's stated purpose

THEN | P O C C C
plan   organize   command   coordinate   control

NOW | P O L C
planning   organizing   leading   controlling

Jacques Boyer/Roger-Violiet/The Image Works

Jacques Boyer/Roger-Violet/The Image Works

Who: Henri Fayol—an engineer/executive at a large French mining company
When: Early 1900s
How: Personal experience and observations

---

planning
Defining goals, establishing strategy, and developing plans to coordinate activities

organizing
Determining what needs to be done, how it will be done, and who is to do it

leading
Directing and coordinating the work activities of an organization's people

controlling
Monitoring activities to ensure that they are accomplished as planned

Management Roles Approach

- Says that managers engage in certain "roles" as they manage others.

- WHAT Mintzberg said managers do: He identified and defined **managerial roles**—specific categories of managerial actions or behaviors expected of a manager. (Not sure what a "role" is? Think of the different roles you play—such as student, employee, volunteer, bowling team member, boyfriend/girlfriend, sibling, and so forth—and the different things you're expected to do in those roles.)

- Exhibit 1–5 shows Mintzberg's 10 separate, but interrelated roles.

Exhibit 1–5 Mintzberg's Managerial Roles

Source: Based on Mintzberg, Henry, *The Nature of Managerial Work,* 1st edition, © 1973. Harper & Row.

Christinne Muschi/Toronto Star/ Getty Images

Who: Henry Mintzberg
When: late 1960s
How: Empirical study of five chief executives at work.[6]

Which Approach—Functions or Roles—Is Better at Defining What Managers Do?

— Both approaches appear to do a good job of describing what managers do.

— However, the *functions* approach stands out! It continues to be popular due to its clarity and simplicity.[7] But, don't disregard the roles approach; it offers another way to understand and appreciate what managers do.

---

managerial roles
Specific categories of managerial behavior; often grouped around interpersonal relationships, information transfer, and decision making

interpersonal roles
Involving people (subordinates and persons outside the organization) and other duties that are ceremonial and symbolic in nature

decisional roles
Entailing making decisions or choices

informational roles
Involving collecting, receiving, and disseminating information

3 Skills and Competencies

- Says that managers need certain skills and competencies as they manage others.
- WHAT these researchers say managers do: Identified four general management skills including:[8]

Analyze and diagnose

— **CONCEPTUAL SKILLS:** Analyzing and diagnosing complex situations to see how things fit together and to facilitate making good decisions.

— **INTERPERSONAL SKILLS:** Working well with other people both individually and in groups by communicating, motivating, mentoring, delegating, etc.

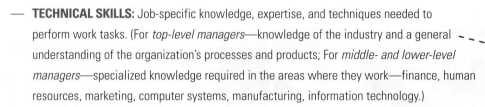

Working well with others

— **TECHNICAL SKILLS:** Job-specific knowledge, expertise, and techniques needed to perform work tasks. (For *top-level managers*—knowledge of the industry and a general understanding of the organization's processes and products; For *middle- and lower-level managers*—specialized knowledge required in the areas where they work—finance, human resources, marketing, computer systems, manufacturing, information technology.)

Possessing expert job knowledge

— **POLITICAL SKILLS:** Building a power base and establishing the right connections to get needed resources for their groups. *Want to learn more?* Assess and develop *your* political skill by completing the PIA and the Management Skill Builder found at the end of the chapter on p. 47.

Political adeptness

- Other important managerial competencies:[9] decision making, team building, decisiveness, assertiveness, politeness, personal responsibility, trustworthiness, loyalty, professionalism, tolerance, adaptability, creative thinking, resilience, listening, self-development.

Who: Robert Katz and others
When: 1970s to present
How: Studies by various researchers

Is the Manager's Job Universal?

So far, we've discussed the manager's job as if it were a generic activity. If management is truly a generic discipline, then what a manager does should be the same whether he or she is a top-level executive or a first-line supervisor; in a business firm or a government agency; in a large corporation or a small business; or located in Paris, Texas, or Paris, France. Is that the case? Let's take a closer look.

Is a manager **a manager no matter** where or what he or she manages?

LEVEL IN THE ORGANIZATION. Although a supervisor of the Genius Bar in an Apple Store may not do exactly the same things that Apple's CEO Tim Cook does, it doesn't mean that their jobs are inherently different. The differences are of degree and emphasis but not of activity.

As managers move up in an organization, they do more planning and less direct overseeing of others. (See Exhibit 1–6.) All managers, regardless of level, make decisions. They plan, organize, lead, and control, but the amount of time they spend on each activity is not

conceptual skills
A manager's ability to analyze and diagnose complex situations

interpersonal skills
A manager's ability to work with, understand, mentor, and motivate others, both individually and in groups

technical skills
Job-specific knowledge and techniques needed to perform work tasks

political skills
A manager's ability to build a power base and establish the right connections

Exhibit 1–6 Management Activities by Organizational Level

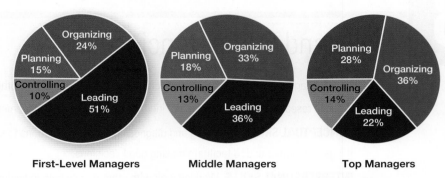

First-Level Managers

Organizing 24%
Planning 15%
Controlling 10%
Leading 51%

Middle Managers

Planning 18%
Organizing 33%
Controlling 13%
Leading 36%

Top Managers

Planning 28%
Organizing 36%
Controlling 14%
Leading 22%

Source: Based on T. A. Mahoney, T. H. Jerdee, and S. J. Carroll, "The Job(s) of Management," *Industrial Relations* 4, no. 2 (1965), p. 103.

Founder and owner of ReelSonar, Alex Lebedev and his employees design and develop digital fishing equipment. As a small business owner, Alex plans, organizes, leads, and controls. He performs basically the same functions as managers in large firms do although the activities differ in degree and emphasis.

Ted S. Warren/AP Images

necessarily constant. In addition, "what" they plan, organize, lead, and control changes with the manager's level. For example, as we'll demonstrate in Chapter 7, top managers are concerned with designing the overall organization's structure, whereas lower-level managers focus on designing the jobs of individuals and work groups.

PROFIT VERSUS NOT-FOR-PROFIT. Does a manager who works for the U.S. Postal Service, the Memorial Sloan-Kettering Cancer Center, or the Convoy of Hope do the same things that a manager at Amazon or Symantec does? That is, is the manager's job the same in both profit and not-for-profit organizations? The answer, for the most part, is yes. All managers make decisions, set goals, create workable organization structures, hire and motivate employees, secure legitimacy for their organization's existence, and develop internal political support in order to implement programs. Of course, the most important difference between the two is how performance is measured. Profit—the "bottom line"—is an unambiguous measure of a business organization's effectiveness. Not-for-profit organizations don't have such a universal measure, which makes performance measurement more difficult. But don't think this means that managers in those organizations can ignore finances. Even not-for-profit organizations need to make money to continue operating. However, in not-for-profit organizations, "making a profit" for the "owners" is not the primary focus.

SIZE OF ORGANIZATION. Would you expect the job of a manager in a local FedEx store that employs 12 people to be different from that of a manager who runs the FedEx World HUB in Memphis with over 12,000 employees? This question is best answered by looking at the jobs of managers in small businesses and comparing them with our previous discussion of managerial roles. First, however, let's define a small business.

No commonly agreed-upon definition of a small business is available because different criteria are used to define *small.* For example, an organization can be classified as a small business using such criteria as number of employees, annual sales, or total assets. For our purposes, we'll describe a **small business** as an independent business having fewer than 500 employees that doesn't necessarily engage in any new or innovative practices and has relatively little impact on its industry.[10] So, *is* the job of managing a small business different from that of managing a large one? Yes, some differences appear to exist. As Exhibit 1–7 shows, the small business manager's most important role is that of spokesperson. He or she spends a great deal of time performing outwardly directed actions such as meeting with customers,

small business
An independent business having fewer than 500 employees that doesn't necessarily engage in any new or innovative practices and has relatively little impact on its industry

Exhibit 1–7 Managerial Roles in Small and Large Businesses

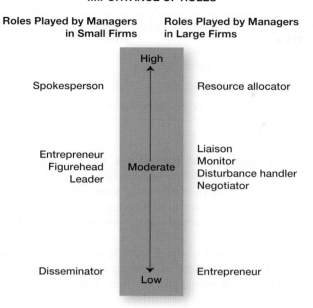

IMPORTANCE OF ROLES

Roles Played by Managers in Small Firms | Roles Played by Managers in Large Firms

High

Spokesperson — Resource allocator

Entrepreneur / Figurehead / Leader — Moderate — Liaison / Monitor / Disturbance handler / Negotiator

Disseminator — Low — Entrepreneur

Source: Based on J. G. P. Paolillo, "The Manager's Self-Assessments of Managerial Roles: Small vs. Large Firms," *American Journal of Small Business* (January–March 1984), pp. 61–62.

arranging financing with bankers, searching for new opportunities, and stimulating change. In contrast, the most important concerns of a manager in a large organization are directed internally—deciding which organizational units get what available resources and how much of them. Accordingly, the entrepreneurial role—looking for business opportunities and planning activities for performance improvement—appears to be least important to managers in large firms, especially among first-level and middle managers.

Compared with a manager in a large organization, a small business manager is more likely to be a generalist. His or her job will combine the activities of a large corporation's chief executive with many of the day-to-day activities undertaken by a first-line supervisor. Moreover, the structure and formality that characterize a manager's job in a large organization tend to give way to informality in small firms. Planning is less likely to be a carefully orchestrated ritual. The organization's design will be less complex and structured, and control in the small business will rely more on direct observation than on sophisticated, computerized monitoring systems. Again, as with organizational level, we see differences in degree and emphasis but not in the activities that managers do. Managers in both small and large organizations perform essentially the same activities, but how they go about those activities and the proportion of time they spend on each are different. (You can find more information on managing small, entrepreneurial organizations in Entrepreneurship Module.)

MANAGEMENT CONCEPTS AND NATIONAL BORDERS. The last generic issue concerns whether management concepts are transferable across national borders. If managerial concepts were completely generic, they would also apply universally in any country in the world, regardless of economic, social, political, or cultural differences. Studies that have compared managerial practices among countries have not generally supported the universality of management concepts. In Chapter 3, we'll examine some specific differences between countries and describe their effect on managing. At this point, it's important for you to understand that most of the concepts discussed in the rest of the book primarily apply to the United States, Canada, Great Britain, Australia, and other English-speaking countries. Managers likely will have to modify these concepts if they want to apply them in India, China, Chile, or other countries whose economic, political, social, or cultural environments differ from that of the so-called free-market democracies.

Why Study Management?

1-4 Explain why it's important to study management.

Good managers are important because:

- Organizations need their skills and abilities, especially in today's uncertain, complex, and chaotic environment.
- They're critical to getting things done.
- They play a crucial role in employee satisfaction and engagement.

Making Ethical Decisions in Today's Workplace

▶ **50%** of employees have left a job to get away from a manager.[11]

▶ **$319–$398 billion** is the estimated annual cost to the U.S. economy of disengaged managers. Managers' engagement with their jobs and organizations has a direct impact on whether employees are engaged with their jobs and organizations.[12]

▶ **32%** of employees rated their boss as "horrible" in a Monster.com survey.[13]

Discussion Questions:

3 Looking at these statistics, what is the potential ethical dilemma here? What stakeholders might be affected and how might they be affected? What personal, organizational, and environmental factors might be important? What are possible alternatives to addressing the potential ethical issue(s)? What alternative(s) would you choose and what would you need to do to act on it?

4 What could organizations do to help their managers be better at managing?

Well…we're finally at the point where we're going to address the chapter-opening myth! You may still be wondering *why* you need to take a management class. Especially if you're majoring in accounting or marketing or information technology, you may not see how studying management is going to help you in your career. Let's look at some reasons you may want to understand more about management.

First, all of us have a vested interest in improving the way organizations are managed. Why? Because we interact with them every day of our lives and an understanding of management offers insights into many organizational aspects. When you renew your driver's license or get your car tags, are you frustrated that a seemingly simple task takes so long? Are you surprised when well-known businesses you thought would never fail went bankrupt? Are you shocked when you see news stories (with accompanying cellphone videos) showing unfortunate instances of employees in customer-service settings mistreating customers? Are you annoyed when you use a drive-through and get ready to enjoy your food or drink and realize something is missing or that it's not what you ordered? Such problems are mostly the result of managers doing a poor job of managing.

Organizations that are well managed—such as Apple, Starbucks, Nike, Southwest Airlines, and Alphabet—develop a loyal following and find ways to prosper even when the economy stinks. Poorly managed organizations may find themselves with a declining customer base and reduced revenues and may have to file for bankruptcy protection even in a strong economy. For instance, Gimbel's, RadioShack, W. T. Grant, Hollywood Video, Dave & Barry's, Circuit City, Eastern Airlines, and Enron were once thriving corporations. They employed tens of thousands of people and provided goods and services on a daily basis to hundreds of thousands of customers. You may not recognize some of these names because these companies no longer exist. Poor management did them in. By taking a management course, you can begin to recognize poor management and know what good managers should be doing. Maybe you'll even aspire to being a manager!

Finally, another reason for studying management is the *reality that for most of you, once you graduate from college and begin your career, you will either manage or be managed.* For those who plan to be managers, an understanding of management forms the foundation on which to build your own management skills and abilities. For those of you who don't see yourself managing, you're still likely to have to work with managers. Also, assuming that you'll have to work for a living and recognizing that you're likely to work in an organization, you're likely to have some managerial responsibilities even if you're not a manager. Our experience tells us that you can gain a great deal of insight into the way your boss (and coworkers) behave and how organizations function by studying management. Our point is that you don't have to aspire to be a manager to gain valuable information from a course in management.

What Factors Are Reshaping and Redefining Management?

1-5 Describe the factors that are reshaping and redefining management.

Welcome to the **new world of management!**

Changing Workplaces + Changing Workforce

- Digitization, automation, and changing views of jobs/careers are disrupting the way we work.[14]
- "NextGen work"—the next generation of work, defined as part-time, freelance, contract, temporary, or independent contract work—is predicted to continue to rise. Individuals—and organizations—are looking for alternative ways to get work done. [15]
- Some 43 percent of U.S. employees work remotely all or some of the time.[16]
- Sexual harassment allegations and accusations of workplace misconduct have dominated the news and triggered much-needed calls for action.
- As mobile and social technologies continue to proliferate, more organizations are using apps and mobile-enhanced websites for managing their workforces and for other organizational work.
- Data breaches, large-scale and small, are raising new alarms about organizational information security lapses.

In today's world, managers are dealing with changing workplaces, a changing workforce, changing technology, and global uncertainties. For example, grocery stores continue to struggle to retain their customer base and to keep costs down. At Publix Super Markets, the large grocery chain in the southeastern United States, everyone, including managers, is looking for ways to better serve customers. The company's president, Todd Jones, who started his career bagging groceries at a Publix in New Smyrna Beach, Florida, is guiding the company through these challenges by keeping everyone's focus—from baggers to checkers to stockers—on exceptional customer service.[17] And with Amazon's purchase of Whole Foods, the whole grocery store industry now faces an entirely different challenge.[18] Or consider the management challenges faced by the *Seattle Post-Intelligencer* (P-I) when it, like many other newspapers,

Claire Hobean, operations manager for Re-Time Pty. Ltd., models the Australian firm's innovative Re-Timer glasses at a consumer electronics show. The medical device innovation uses bright light therapy to assist in the treatment of insomnia, jet lag, and Seasonal Affective Disorder by helping reset a person's natural body clock.

struggled to find a way to be successful in an industry that was losing readers and revenues at an alarming rate. Managers made the decision to go all-digital, and the P-I became an Internet-only news source. Difficult actions followed as the news staff was reduced from 165 to less than 20 people. In its new "life" as a digital news source, the organization faces other challenges—challenges for the manager who needs to plan, organize, lead, and control in this changed environment.[19] Managers everywhere are likely to have to manage in changing circumstances, and the fact is that *how* managers manage is changing. Throughout the rest of this book, we'll be discussing these changes and how they're affecting the way managers plan, organize, lead, and control. We want to highlight four specific areas that are important to organizations and managers everywhere: customers, innovation, social media, and sustainability.

Steve Marcus/Reuters

Why Are Customers Important to the Manager's Job?

When John Chambers was CEO of Cisco Systems, he wanted voicemails forwarded to him from dissatisfied customers because he thought it was important to hear firsthand the emotions and frustrations they were experiencing. He couldn't get that type of insight by reading an e-mail.[20] This manager understands the importance of customers. Chris McCarthy, president of MTV Networks also understands how important customers are. He is listening to his young audience and responding with what they want to see on MTV. Result? MTV's ratings are rising.[21] Organizations need customers. Without them, most organizations would cease to exist. Yet, focusing on the customer has long been thought by many managers to be the responsibility of the marketers. We're discovering, however, that employee attitudes and behaviors play a big role in customer satisfaction. Think of the times you've been treated poorly (or superbly) by an employee during a service encounter and how that affected the way you felt about the situation.

Managers are recognizing that delivering consistent high-quality customer service is essential for survival and success in today's competitive environment and that employees are an important part of that equation.[22] The implication is clear—they must create a customer-responsive organization where employees are friendly and courteous, accessible, knowledgeable, prompt in responding to customer needs, and willing to do what's necessary to please the customer.[23]

:::::: Managing Technology in Today's Workplace ::::::

IS IT STILL MANAGING WHEN WHAT YOU'RE MANAGING ARE ROBOTS?

The workplaces of tomorrow will include workers who are faster, smarter, more responsible—and who just happen to be robots.[24] Surprised? Although robots have been used in factory and industrial settings for a long time, it's becoming more common to find robots in the office and other work settings, and it's bringing about new ways of looking at how work is done and at what and how managers manage. So what *would* a manager's job be like managing robots? And even more intriguing is how these "workers" might affect how human coworkers interact with them.

As machines have become smarter and smarter, researchers have been exploring the human-machine interaction and how people interact with the smart devices that are now such an integral part of our professional and personal lives. One insight is that people find it easy to bond with a robot, even one that doesn't look or sound anything like a real person. In a workplace setting, if a robot moves around in a "purposeful way," people tend to view it, in some ways, as a coworker. People name their robots and can even describe the robot's moods and tendencies. As humanoid/telepresence robots become more common, the humanness becomes even more evident. For example, when Erwin Deininger, the electrical engineer at Reimers Electra Steam, a small company in Clear Brook, Virginia, moved to the Dominican Republic when his wife's job transferred

her there, he was able to still be "present" at the company via his VGo telepresence robot. Now "robot" Deininger moves easily around the office and shop floor, allowing the "real" Deininger to do his job just as if he were there in person. The company's president, satisfied with how the robot solution has worked out, has been surprised at how he acts around it, feeling at times that he's interacting with Deininger himself. As technology continues to advance and humanoid robots get better at walking, talking, and looking like humans, they're envisioned doing jobs such as companions for the elderly, teachers of schoolchildren, and retail or office assistants.[25]

There's no doubt that robotic technology will continue to be incorporated into organizational settings. The manager's job will become even more exciting and challenging as humans and machines work together to accomplish the organization's goals.

Discussion Questions:

5 What's your response to the title of this box: *Is* it still managing when what you're managing are robots? Discuss.

6 If you had to manage people and robots, how do you think your job as manager might be different than what the chapter describes? (Think in terms of functions, roles, and skills/competencies.)

Why Is Innovation Important to the Manager's Job?

Success in business today demands innovation. Innovation means doing things differently, exploring new territory, and taking risks. And innovation isn't just for high-tech or other technologically sophisticated organizations; innovative efforts are needed in all types, all levels, all areas, and all sizes of organizations. You'd expect companies like Amazon, Google, Uber, and Apple to be on a list of the world's most innovative companies.[26] But what about the likes of International Dairy Queen?[27] Although, the 78-year-old restaurant chain is not on a list of "most innovative," it's experimenting with different formats and approaches to appeal to an increasingly demanding market. Even non-tech businesses need to innovate to prosper. Or how about Kickstarter, which created the crowdfunding phenomenon? Now, it's looking at ways to better encourage creativity among potential projects and startups and is also expanding its business beyond fundraising into publishing and distribution. In today's challenging environment, innovation *is* critical and managers need to understand what, when, where, how, and why innovation can be fostered and encouraged throughout an organization. In a presentation a few years ago, a manager in charge of Walmart's global business explained his recipe for success (personal and organizational): continually look for new ways to do your job better; that is, be innovative. Managers not only need to be innovative personally, but also encourage their employees to be innovative. We'll share stories of innovative practices and approaches throughout the book.

Importance of Social Media to the Manager's Job

You probably can't imagine a time when employees did their work without e-mail or Internet access. Yet, some 20 years ago, as these communication tools were becoming more common in workplaces, managers struggled with the challenges of providing guidelines for using them. Today, it's all about **social media**, which are forms of electronic communication through which users create online communities to share ideas, information, personal messages, and other content. Social platforms such as Facebook, Twitter, LinkedIn, Tumblr, Instagram, and others are used by more than a billion people.[28] And employees don't just use these on their personal time, but also for work purposes. A recent survey of more than 4,000 companies showed that 72 percent used internal social media tools—such as Slack, Yammer, Chatter, or embedded applications such as Microsoft Teams—to facilitate employee communication.[29] That's why managers again are struggling with guidelines for employee use as they attempt to navigate the power and peril of social media. For example, at grocery chain SuperValu, managers realized that keeping 135,000-plus employees connected and engaged was imperative to continued success.[30] They decided to adopt an internal social media tool to foster cooperation and collaboration among its 10 distinct store brands operating in 48 states.

And they're not alone. More and more businesses are turning to social media not just as a way to connect with customers, but also as a way to manage their human resources and tap into their innovation and talent. That's the potential power of social media. But the potential peril is in how it's used. When the social media platform becomes a way for boastful employees to brag about their accomplishments, for managers to publish one-way messages to employees, or for employees to argue or gripe about something or someone they don't like at work, then it's lost its usefulness. To avoid this, managers need to remember that social media is a tool that needs to be managed to be beneficial. At SuperValu, store managers and assistant managers use the social media system. Although sources say it's too early to draw any conclusions, it appears that managers who actively make use of the system are having better store sales revenues than those who don't. In the

Managing in a sustainable way is so important to Dell Technologies that the company enlisted actor and environmental activist Adrian Grenier as a Social Good Advocate to communicate its sustainability initiatives to stakeholders. Dell is embedding sustainability into every aspect of its operations, from product design to zero-waste manufacturing and green packaging and shipping.

Jack Plunkett/AP Images

sustainability
A company's ability to achieve its business goals and increase long-term shareholder value by integrating economic, environmental, and social opportunities into its business strategies

remainder of the book, we'll look at how social media is affecting how managers manage, especially in the areas of human resource management, communication, teams, and strategy.

Importance of Sustainability to the Manager's Job

BMW is probably not a company that comes to mind in a section describing sustainability. Yet, BMW, the iconic German manufacturer of high-performance luxury autos, is making a huge bet on green, wired cars for those who reside in cities.[31] Its all-electric car is unlike anything that BMW—or any other car manufacturer—has made. The car's weight-saving, carbon-fiber body is layered with electronic services and smartphone apps ready to make life simpler and more efficient for the owner and better for the planet. Company executives recognized that it had to add products that would meet the challenges of a changing world. This corporate action by a well-known global company affirms that sustainability and green management have become mainstream issues for managers.

What's emerging in the twenty-first century is the concept of managing in a sustainable way, which has had the effect of widening corporate responsibility not only to managing in an efficient and effective way, but also to responding strategically to a wide range of environmental and societal challenges.[32] Although "sustainability" may mean different things to different people, the World Business Council for Sustainable Development describes a scenario where all earth's inhabitants can live well with adequate resources.[33] From a business perspective, **sustainability** has been defined as a company's ability to achieve its business goals and increase long-term shareholder value by integrating economic, environmental, and social opportunities into its business strategies.[34] Sustainability issues are now moving up the business agenda. Managers at BMW, McDonald's, Walmart, Levi Strauss, L'Oreal, and other global businesses are discovering that running an organization in a more sustainable way will mean making informed business decisions based on (1) communicating openly with various stakeholders and understanding their requirements and (2) factoring economic, environmental, and social aspects into how they pursue their business goals. Throughout the rest of the book, we'll explore sustainability as it relates to various aspects of managing. Just look for this ♲ for those conversations.

What Employability Skills Are Critical for Getting and Keeping a Job?

1-6 Describe the key employability skills gained from studying management that are applicable to your future career, regardless of your major.

What about getting and keeping a job? Is that your main concern? Well, studying management can help you with that!

We assume that you're pursuing a college degree because you'd like to get a good job or a better job than the ones you've had. Wouldn't you love to increase your odds of getting that job upon graduation and then succeeding at that job, crafting a long and flourishing career path? We want that for you, too! Studying management *can help you develop and improve your employability skills*. Entry-level employees and working professionals can benefit from having solid foundations in skills such as critical thinking, communication, problem solving, collaboration, and so forth. Throughout this text, you'll learn and practice many employability skills that hiring managers identify as important to success in a variety of business settings, including small and large firms, nonprofit organizations, and public service. Such skills will also be useful if you plan to start your own business. These skills include:

- *Critical thinking* involves purposeful and goal-directed thinking used to define and solve problems and to make decisions or form judgments related to a particular situation or set of circumstances. It involves cognitive, metacognitive, and dispositional components that may be applied differently in specific contexts. Thinking critically typically involves elaborating on information or an idea; describing important details and prioritizing them based on significance; identifying details that reveal bias; embellishing an idea, description, or an answer/response; making conclusions based on evidence that explain a collection of facts, data, or ideas; summarizing information in a concise and succinct manner; determining the order of events and defining cause and effect relationships; identifying influencing factors that cause events to occur; and so forth.

- *Communication* is defined as effective use of oral, written, and nonverbal communication skills for multiple purposes (e.g., to inform, instruct, motivate, persuade, and share ideas); effective listening; using technology to communicate; and being able to evaluate the effectiveness of communication efforts—all within diverse contexts.

- *Collaboration* is a skill in which individuals can actively work together on a task, constructing meaning and knowledge as a group through dialogue and negotiation that results in a final product reflective of their joint, interdependent actions.

- *Knowledge application and analysis* is defined as the ability to learn a concept and then apply that knowledge appropriately in another setting to achieve a higher level of understanding.

- *Social responsibility* includes skills related to both business ethics and corporate social responsibility. Business ethics includes sets of guiding principles that influence the way individuals and organizations behave within the society that they operate. Being ethical at your job involves the ability to identify potential ethical dilemma(s); the affected stakeholders; the important personal, organizational, and external factors; possible alternatives; and the ability to make an appropriate decision based on these things. Corporate social responsibility is a form of ethical behavior that requires that organizational decision makers understand, identify, and eliminate unethical economic, environmental, and social behaviors.

CRITICAL THINKING

- Using purposeful and goal-directed thinking
- Applying information differently in different contexts
- Elaborating on information or an idea
- Describing important details and prioritizing them according to significance
- Identifying details that reveal bias
- Embellishing an idea, description, or answer/response
- Making conclusions based on evidence
- Summarizing information
- Determining order of events
- Defining cause and effect relationships

COMMUNICATION

- Effectively using oral, written, and nonverbal communication for multiple purposes
- Effectively listening
- Using technology to communicate
- Critically analyzing messages
- Adapting one's communication in diverse cultural contexts
- Evaluating effectiveness of communication in diverse contexts

COLLABORATION

- Actively working together on a task or finding solutions to problem situations
- Constructing meaning and knowledge as a group
- Being able to dialogue and negotiate in a group
- Being able to work jointly and interdependently in a group
- Working with others to select, organize, and integrate information and ideas from a variety of sources and formats
- Being able to appropriately resolve conflict, making sure all voices are heard

KNOWLEDGE APPLICATION AND ANALYSIS

- Recalling previously learned material
- Describing concepts in your own words
- Demonstrating knowledge of facts and key concepts
- Learning a concept and applying that knowledge to real-life situations
- Thinking through solutions to specific problems and generalizing these processes to other situations
- Combining ideas into a new whole or proposing solutions
- Assessing the value of material for a given purpose

SOCIAL RESPONSIBILITY

- Identifying potential ethical dilemmas; affected stakeholders; important personal, organizational and external factors; and possible alternatives
- Making appropriate decisions based on the preceding factors
- Applying ethical reasoning and critical analysis to real-world scenarios

Each chapter is loaded with opportunities for you to use and work on the skills you'll need to be successful in the twenty-first century workplace. Skills that will help you get a job and pursue a fulfilling career path, wherever that might take you! The following Employability Skills Matrix links these five employability skills with special features found in each chapter. Our unique features include (1) three distinctive boxes—Classic Concepts in Today's Workplace (historical management concepts and how they're used today), Being Ethical: A 21st-Century Skill (a real-life, contemporary ethics dilemma), and Managing Technology in Today's Workplace (ways technology is changing the workplace); (2) MyLab assignments, particularly Write It, Watch It, and Try It; (3) Management Skill Builder, which highlights a specific management skill and provides an opportunity to "do" that skill; (4) Experiential Exercise, which is another learning-by-doing, hands-on assignment where you "do" something, usually within a group; and (5) Case Applications, real-life stories of people and organizations. Within these features, you'll have the opportunity to think critically and apply your knowledge as you consider special cases and concepts. You'll also have the opportunity to improve your collaboration and communication skills by learning what you might do or say in the described situations to adapt to the work world positively and effectively. And you'll be confronted with ethical dilemmas in which you'll consider the ethics of particular behaviors in the workplace. All five of these skills are critical to success whether you pursue a career in management or some other field since, as the previous section pointed out, the workplace and workforce are changing and will continue to change. These skills will help you successfully navigate those changes.

Wrapping It Up . . .

Managers Matter!

As you can see, being a manager is both challenging and exciting! One thing we know for sure is that *managers do matter* to organizations. The Gallup Organization, which has polled millions of employees and tens of thousands of managers, has found that *the single most important variable in employee productivity and loyalty isn't pay or benefits or workplace environment; it's the quality of the relationship between employees and their direct supervisors.* Gallup also found that employees' relationship with their manager is the largest factor in **employee engagement**—which is when employees are connected to, satisfied with, and enthusiastic about their jobs—accounting for at least 70 percent of an employee's level of engagement.[35] And Gallup found that when companies increase their number of talented managers and double the rate of engaged employees, their EPS (earnings per share) is 147 percent higher than their competitors.[36] That's significant! This same research also showed that talented managers contribute about 48 percent higher profit to their companies than do average managers.[37] Finally, a different study found that when a poor manager was replaced with a great one, employee productivity increased by 12 percent.[38] What can we conclude from such reports? That talented managers *do* matter and will continue to matter to organizations!

EMPLOYABILITY SKILLS MATRIX

	Critical Thinking	Communication	Collaboration	Knowledge Application and Analysis	Social Responsibility
Classic Concepts in Today's Workplace	✓	✓	✓	✓	
Making Ethical Decisions in Today's Workplace	✓	✓	✓	✓	✓
Managing Technology in Today's Workplace	✓	✓	✓	✓	✓
MyLab: Write It, Watch It, Try It	✓	✓		✓	
Management Skill Builder—Practicing the Skill		✓	✓	✓	
Experiential Exercise		✓	✓	✓	
Case Application 1	✓			✓	✓
Case Application 2	✓	✓		✓	
Case Application 3	✓		✓		

CHAPTER SUMMARY BY LEARNING OUTCOME

1-1 Tell who managers are and where they work.

Managers are individuals who work in an organization directing and overseeing the activities of other people. Managers are usually classified as top, middle, first-line, or team leader. Organizations, which are where managers work, have three characteristics: goals, people, and a deliberate structure.

1-2 Define *management*.

Management is the process of getting things done, effectively and efficiently, with and through other people. Efficiency means doing a task correctly ("doing things right") and getting the most output from the least amount of inputs. Effectiveness means "doing the right things" by doing those work tasks that help the organization reach its goals.

1-3 Describe what managers do.

What managers do can be described using three approaches: functions, roles, and skills/competencies. The functions approach says that managers perform four functions: planning, organizing, leading, and controlling. Mintzberg's roles approach says that what managers do is based on the 10 roles they use at work, which are grouped around interpersonal relationships, the transfer of information, and decision making. The skills/competencies approach looks at what managers do in terms of the skills and competencies they need and use. Four critical management skills are conceptual, interpersonal, technical, and political. Additional managerial competencies include aspects such as dependability, personal orientation, emotional control, communication, and so forth. All managers plan, organize, lead, and control, although how they do these activities and how often they do them may vary according to their level in the organization, whether the organization is profit or not-for-profit, the size of the organization, and the geographic location of the organization.

1-4 Explain why it's important to study management.

One reason it's important to study management is that all of us interact with organizations daily so we have a vested interest in seeing that organizations are well managed. Another reason is the reality that in your career, you will either manage or be managed. By studying management you can gain insights into the way your boss and fellow employees behave and how organizations function. Finally, taking a course in management will help you develop and improve your employability skills. These skills—which include critical thinking, communication, collaboration, knowledge application and analysis, and social responsibility—are essential to getting and keeping a job.

1-5 Describe the factors that are reshaping and redefining management.

In today's world, managers are dealing with changing workplaces, a changing workforce, global economic and political uncertainties, and changing technology. Four areas of critical importance to managers are delivering high-quality customer service, encouraging innovative efforts, using social media efficiently and effectively, and recognizing how sustainability contributes to an organization's effectiveness.

1-6 Describe the key employability skills gained from studying management that are applicable to your future career, regardless of your major.

The key employability skills gained from studying management include critical thinking, communication, collaboration, knowledge application and analysis, and social responsibility. These skills will help you be successful in a variety of business settings.

DISCUSSION QUESTIONS

1-1 What is an organization and what characteristics do organizations share?

1-2 "Roles define the manager." Do you agree or disagree with this statement? Discuss what you think managers do.

1-3 In today's environment, which is more important to organizations—efficiency or effectiveness? Explain your choice.

1-4 Are there any differences between the managerial functions in a for-profit organization and a not-for-profit organization? Explain.

1-5 Using any of the popular business periodicals (such as *Bloomberg Businessweek, Fortune, Wall Street Journal, Fast Company*), find examples of managers doing each of the four management functions. Write up a description and explain how these are examples of that function.

1-6 Consider your local greengrocer. Discuss how managers of such small businesses can adopt Mintzberg's ten managerial roles to run their business.

1-7 Business is changing over time and requires management methods to evolve. What are the factors that contribute to management changes?

1-8 Is there one best "style" of management? Why or why not?

1-9 In what ways can managers at each of the four levels of management contribute to efficiency and effectiveness?

Applying: Getting Ready for the Workplace

Management Skill Builder | BECOMING POLITICALLY ADEPT

Anyone who has had much work experience knows that organizational politics exists everywhere. That is, people try to influence the distribution of advantages and disadvantages within the organization in their favor. Those who understand organizational politics typically thrive. Those who don't, regardless of how good their actual job skills are, often suffer by receiving less positive performance reviews, fewer promotions, and smaller salary increases. If you want to succeed as a manager, it helps to be politically adept. Research has shown that people differ in their political skills.[39] Those who are politically skilled are more effective in their use of influence tactics. Political skill also appears to be more effective when the stakes are high. Finally, politically skilled individuals are able to exert their influence without others detecting it, which is important in being effective so that you're not labeled as playing politics. A person's political skill is determined by (1) his or her networking ability, (2) interpersonal influence, (3) social astuteness, and (4) apparent sincerity.

MyLab Management
PERSONAL INVENTORY ASSESSMENT

Go to **www.pearson.com/mylab/management** to complete the Personal Inventory Assessment related to this chapter.

PERSONAL INVENTORY ASSESSMENT

Skill Basics

Forget, for a moment, the ethics of politicking and any negative impressions you might have of people who engage in organizational politics. If you want to become more politically adept in your organization, follow these steps:

- *Develop your networking ability.* A good network can be a powerful tool. You can begin building a network by getting to know important people in your work area and the organization and then developing relationships with individuals in positions of power. Volunteer for committees or offer your help on projects that will be noticed by those in positions of power. Attend important organizational functions so that you can be seen as a team player and someone who's interested in the organization's success. Start a file list of individuals that you meet, even if for a brief moment. Then, when you need advice on work, use your connections and network with others throughout the organization.

- *Work on gaining interpersonal influence.* People will listen to you when they're comfortable and feel at ease around you. Work on your communication skills so that you can communicate easily and effectively with others. Work on developing a good rapport with people in all areas and at all levels of your organization. Be open, friendly, and willing to pitch in. The amount of interpersonal influence you have will be affected by how well people like you.

- *Develop your social astuteness.* Some people have an innate ability to understand people and sense what they're thinking. If you don't have that ability, you'll have to work at developing your social astuteness by doing things such as saying the right things at the right time, paying close attention to people's facial expressions, and trying to determine whether others have hidden agendas.

- *Be sincere.* Sincerity is important to getting people to want to associate with you. Be genuine in what you say and do. And show a genuine interest in others and their situations.

Practicing The Skill

Take each of the components of political skill and spend one week working on it as you navigate your school life and work life. Keep a journal (or brief set of notes) describing your experiences—good and bad. Were you able to begin developing a network of people you could rely on or connect with for school or work commitments? How did you try to become better at influencing those around you? Did you work at communicating better or at developing a good rapport with coworkers or class project team members? Did you work at developing your social astuteness, maybe by starting to recognize and interpret people's facial expressions and the meaning behind those expressions? Did you make a conscious effort to be more sincere in your relationships with others, especially those that are not close friends? What could you have done differently to be more politically skilled? Once you begin to recognize what's involved with political skills, you should find yourself becoming more connected and better able to influence others—that is, more politically adept.

Experiential Exercise

Welcome to our annual management R&R (retreat and retrospective)! We thought we'd have some fun this year playing a game we're calling "Good Boss, Bad Boss." What, you ask, is "Good Boss, Bad Boss?" It's an activity in which we're going to explore what "good" bosses are like and what they do and what "bad" bosses are like and what they do. We hope in completing this that (1) you'll have fun talking about this with your team, sharing stories and experiences, and (2) maybe, just maybe, you'll recognize your own characteristics and behaviors as a "boss." Are you more like a "good" boss or a "bad" boss? While we're doing this as a fun activity, we encourage you to stop and think about how we (all of us) "manage/lead" and its impact on our employees. And always remember, through our actions and behaviors, we DO affect our employees' work experiences and efforts!

Here are your instructions:

(1) In your "assigned" team, talk about good bosses. What do they do that makes them "good"? What characteristics do they have? How do they treat employees? How do they get their employees to be efficient and effective? Then, do the same thing for bad bosses. What do they do that makes them "bad"? What characteristics do they have? How do they treat employees? How do they discourage their employees from being efficient and effective? To help you get started, think about bosses you've had—or maybe even about successes/failures you've had as you've "bossed"!

(2) Make a master list of your ideas about "good" bosses and one for "bad" bosses.

(3) Create a chart summarizing this information that you can share with the rest of the groups. Although it's not required, if you can think of an appropriate meme or other visual, create and share that also.

(4) Finally, identify three "takeaways" that you think are most important from what your team discussed. What are the three traits of bosses that everyone wants to work for? Make a list of these and briefly explain why you think they're important. Focus on what we (all of the company managers) might do to be bosses who would be considered "good"! We plan to compile all of these and use them in our management training modules.

CASE APPLICATION #1

Training Better Managers...Now at Walmart
Topic: Management training

Walmart, the world's largest retailer, is a mega-business with more than 11,700 retail units in 28 countries and approximately 2.3 million associates around the world. That's a lot of employees to manage! Its most recent annual revenues were more than $485.3 billion with profits of more than $13.6 billion. Because of its position as the United States's largest private employer, Walmart often finds itself at the center of controversy over employee-related issues, from sick day policies[40] to wage concerns.[41] However, in 2016, the company created its Walmart Academy training program, a program intended to help those employees in lower-level management positions be more successful in their careers. Currently, there are some 100 of these academies across the United States. Since its inception, more than 150,000 store supervisors and department managers have gone through the weeks-long training.[42]

What does the training include? Topics cover advanced retail skills, including merchandising, ordering, and inventory control, plus managerial skills, including better communication and motivating employees. All management training is designed with the goal of helping transform the in-store shopping experience into a consistently positive one. As the industry faces increasing competitive pressures from Amazon and other online sellers, brick-and-mortar retailers are being forced to provide customers with something that makes the customer want to come to their store again and again. For Walmart, this means that if the company wants to create a more pleasant in-store shopping experience, it needs a well-trained and engaged workforce. That starts with the managers who, in turn, take that focus back to training their employees to be attentive to customers. Walmart thinks this effort is so vital that it has spent $2.7 billion (yes, that's billion!) on employee training and raising employee wages. That's a significant investment. However, there are companies that evidently don't focus on training managers as Walmart does. Here are some startling statistics[43]:

> ## Helping employees **take charge of their careers!**

- 26 percent of new managers feel they're unprepared to transition into management roles.
- 58 percent of new managers don't receive any training to help them make the transition.
- 48 percent of first-time managers fail in that transition.

Considering the important role that managers play in employee motivation and engagement, investing in training, like Walmart is doing, seems to be a good investment.

Discussion Questions

1-10 Why would a company want employees in lower-level management positions to be more successful in their careers? (*Hint:* Think efficiency/effectiveness and the four functions of management.)

1-11 What benefits and challenges do you see to a training program such as this?

1-12 What additional managerial topics might you suggest be covered in the Walmart Academy training program? Think in terms of the three ways to look at what managers do.

1-13 Many college graduates are reluctant to pursue a career in a retail organization...even at the world's largest. Discuss how a company like Walmart could attract talented graduates.

1-14 Does an organization have an ethical responsibility to assist new managers transition into their positions? Why or why not?

CASE APPLICATION #2

Managing without Managers
Topic: Spotify

"Spotify, a Swedish commercial music service, is widely credited with dramatically changing the way consumers access and use music on a day-to-day basis. It has succeeded in moving consumers away from buying music and them toward a model of renting the music they enjoy for a monthly fee. Launched in 2008, the music giant was turned into the business we know today by Swedish entrepreneur Daniel Ek, who wanted to create a service that would be easier and more convenient for customers to use than the now-illegal file-sharing websites that were popular at the time.[44]

Like many technology companies, Spotify has a flat organizational structure rather than complex hierarchies of management. For companies like Spotify, to get to the customer as quickly as possible, it is imperative that they work in a fast-moving way that allows changes in content. In order to work at the greatest efficiency, Spotify have adopted a management and organizational structure based upon squads, chapters, tribes, and guilds. Although there is little literature on organizational tribes or chapters, these do provide a useful way for Spotify to organize their staff and reporting structures in an industry where many are trying to remove managers entirely.[45]

Squads are the building blocks of the organizational structure at Spotify. These small teams work in a way that is similar to a small startup business. These squads sit together in one shared space to work as effectively as possible on one long-term mission, which is usually improving a specific area or part of the Spotify experience. Squads do not have a manager and instead work together to ensure that the overall problem is solved. Each squad does, however, have a "product owner" whose job is to ensure that work is prioritized across the whole squad. Within each squad you will find employees with different skills who can contribute toward the squad achieving their goal.[46]

Tribes are groups of squads that work in similar areas. This means that all the squads working on web-based services are part of the same tribe, and squads who work on the mobile Spotify application will be part of a different tribe. Each tribe, like the individual squads, can work autonomously, with very little traditional management. Within the Spotify offices, the multiple squads that make up each tribe sit close together to allow collaboration between squads as needed; however, the ethos of Spotify is to discourage squads and tribes being dependent on one another so that change can happen as quickly as possible, which is incredibly important in the ever-changing technology market.

To manage the staff and structure throughout the organization, Spotify utilizes what they call "chapters," which are collections of people who have similar skills but who work in various squads; for example, a chapter may include all of the programmers in the various squads within one tribe. It is within these chapters that we see more of a link to traditional management theory, with clearer lines of management and responsibility for staff members, their development, pay, and progression. The only time people may work outside their tribe is when taking part in "guild" activities. Guilds are cross-tribe groups of people who have similar interests but—again—do not have any formal management; they are autonomous and self-managed, working on projects or problems that interest them.

As a fast-moving technology company, it is of course essential for Spotify to be able to react, change, and adapt their online content quickly. By approaching management in a non-traditional manner, they allow individuals to be more creative while meeting the overall goals of the business. There are, however, potential difficulties in adopting this more relaxed attitude to management, as there is a lack of control overall and many opportunities for the freedom offered to staff to be misused.

The rise of technology companies such as Spotify is changing the landscape of management, for many are trying to avoid traditional management practices altogether. Spotify is somewhat unique in its field as they have recognized the need for management within the organization but attempted to find a unique way of balancing the need for freedom and creativity in the workforce while still undertaking basic management activities. As Spotify grows in size, they may need to reflect upon their approach to management.

Discussion Questions

1-15 Who undertakes management at Spotify?

1-16 How might Spotify manage poorly performing individuals or teams? Do you think this could be a problem at Spotify? Why or why not?

1-17 Are there any similarities to traditional management at Spotify?

1-18 Do you think that this approach to management would be effective at another company?

CASE APPLICATION #3

Destroying the World
Topic: Data Security and Data Breaches

You used to be able to tell who the bad guys were. But in our increasingly digital online world, those days are long gone. Now, the bad guys are faceless and anonymous. And they can and do inflict all kinds of damage on individuals, businesses, governments, and other organizations. Surveys show that data breach attacks are happening with alarming regularity. And while your home and school PCs are hopefully well protected from data theft and viruses, don't think that you're in the clear. Data thieves are also targeting smartphones and other mobile devices. And in early 2018, the potential for these thieves to steal your information on your personal devices or information stored on others' computing devices rose dramatically.

The news broke in early 2018 that independent researchers had discovered flaws in chip designs made by Intel Corporation that hackers could exploit to steal data thought to be secure.[47] Every PC, smartphone, and server was exposed and vulnerable. These flaws, code-named Meltdown and Spectre, are unprecedented in their potential information security vulnerabilities.

Intel has been the world's foremost chipmaker for well over 25 years. It makes about 90 percent of the world's computer processors and some 99k percent of the server chips that run the internet.[48] Intel is a big company with a solid reputation for reliability. However, this whole situation is likely to

> ## Managing talented people in a **work environment that's quickly shifting can be quite** challenging!

be viewed as a significantly critical error and misstep by Intel. How did it all come to light?

In June 2017, a security team at Google's Project Zero notified Intel that it had discovered the flaws in Intel's chips. Who or what is Project Zero? It's the name of team of security analysts employed by Google who are tasked with finding "zero-day vulnerabilities." The sole mission of this team of top security researchers is to identify and incapacitate the most serious security flaws in the world's software so there are zero days of vulnerability.[49] (If you're interested, a thorough technical description of what the team found can be read at https://googleprojectzero.blogspot.com/. Look for a blog post by Jann Horn posted on January 3, 2018.) After being notified of the potentially catastrophic flaw, Intel, behind the scenes, worked on fixes with Alphabet Inc.'s Google unit and other "key" computer makers and cloud computing companies.[50] Intel had planned to make the discovery public on January 9, 2018. However, on January 3, 2018, the U.K. website the *Register* broke the news about the flaws. Now, the cat was out of the bag, and the fallout was just beginning. Another issue that eventually came to light was the disclosure that Intel had told Chinese companies Lenovo and Alibaba of the security issues before it had alerted key national security agencies of the U.S. government.[51]

As Intel and other tech companies work on patches for the chip flaws, managers of data centers at companies around the world are working to protect their data and their customers. It's a challenge because quick fixes aren't perfect and long-term fixes won't be easy. And the hackers keep hacking. As data security breaches have become all too common, managing those individuals who work to identify and protect data in an environment that's quickly shifting can be quite challenging.

Discussion Questions

1-19 In addition to the challenges of "fixing" the flaws, what other issues are Intel's top managers going to have to address? (*Hint:* Think about who might be affected and how they might be affected...both inside and outside the company.)

1-20 Look at the timeline of how these flaws were discovered. Do you think Intel should have done anything differently? Explain.

1-21 Keeping professionals excited about work that is routine, standardized, *and* chaotic is a major challenge for managers at data security companies. How could they use technical, human, and conceptual skills to maintain an environment that encourages innovation and professionalism?

1-22 In your "assigned" team, discuss Intel's disclosure about the computer security flaws to Chinese companies before disclosure to U.S. government agencies and officials. What potential ethical issues do you see here? What advice would you have given to the top management team at Intel about their decisions and actions?

Endnotes

1. F. Janjoo, "The Difficulties with Facebook's News Feed Overhaul," *New York Times Online,* January 12, 2018; L. I. Alpert and B. Mullin, "Facebook Rethings Its News Feed," *Wall Street Journal,* January 12, 2018, pp. B1+; and D. Seetharaman, "Zuckerberg Vows to Work on Fixing Facebook," *Wall Street Journal,* January 5, 2018, pp. B1+.

2. From the Past to the Present box based on Dictionary. com Unabridged, based on the *Random House Dictionary,* © Random House, Inc. 2009, http:// dictionary.reference.com/browse/ manage; *Online Etymology Dictionary,* www.etymonline. com, June 5, 2009; P. F. Drucker, *Management: Revised Edition* (New York: HarperCollins Publishers, 2008); and F. W. Taylor, *Principles of Scientific Management* (New York: Harper, 1911), p. 44. For other information on Taylor, see S. Wagner-Tsukamoto, "An Institutional Economic Reconstruction of Scientific Management: On the Lost Theoretical Logic of Taylorism," *Academy of Management Review,* January 2007, pp. 105–17; R. Kanigel, *The One Best Way: Frederick Winslow Taylor and the Enigma of Efficiency* (New York: Viking, 1997); and M. Banta, *Taylored Lives: Narrative Productions in the Age of Taylor, Veblen, and Ford* (Chicago: University of Chicago Press, 1993).

3. S. Stevenson, "Don't Go to Work," http://www.slate.com/ articles/business/psychology_ of_management/2014/05/ best_buy_s_rowe_experiment_ can_results_only_work_

environments_actually_be.html, May 11, 2014; S. Miller, "Study: Flexible Schedules Reduce Conflict, Lower Turnover," www. shrm.org, April 13, 2011; K. M. Butler, "We Can ROWE Our Way to a Better Work Environment," EBN.BenefitNews.com, April 1, 2011, p. 8; P. Moen, E. L. Kelly, and R. Hill, "Does Enhancing Work-Time Control and Flexibility Reduce Turnover? A Naturally Occurring Experiment," *Social Problems,* February 2011, pp. 69–98; and R. J. Erickson, "Task, Not Time: Profile of a Gen Y Job," *Harvard Business Review,* February 2008, p. 19.

4. L. Stevens and E. E. Phillips, "More Amazon Orders, Fewer Boxes," *Wall Street Journal,* December 21, 2017, p. B3.

5. H. Fayol, *Industrial and General Administration* (Paris: Dunod, 1916).

6. H. Mintzberg, *The Nature of Managerial Work* (New York: Harper & Row, 1973).

7. S. J. Carroll and D. A. Gillen, "Are the Classical Management Functions Useful in Describing Managerial Work?" *Academy of Management Review,* January 1987, p. 48.

8. See, for example, J. G. Harris, D. W. DeLong, and A. Donnellon, "Do You Have What It Takes to Be an E-Manager?" *Strategy and Leadership,* August 2001, pp. 10–14; C. Fletcher and C. Baldry, "A Study of Individual Differences and Self-Awareness in the Context of Multi-Source Feedback," *Journal of Occupational and Organizational Psychology,* September 2000, pp. 303–19; and R. L. Katz, "Skills of an Effective Administrator," *Harvard Business*

Review, September–October 1974, pp. 90–102.

9. R. P. Tett, H. A. Guterman, A. Bleier, and P. J. Murphy, "Development and Content Validation of a 'Hyperdimensional' Taxonomy of Managerial Competence," *Human Performance* 13, no. 3 (2000), pp. 205–51.

10. "Frequently Asked Questions," U.S. Small Business Administration, www.sba.gov/advo, September 2008; T. L. Hatten, *Small Business: Entrepreneurship and Beyond* (Upper Saddle River, NJ: Prentice Hall, 1997), p. 5; L. W. Busenitz, "Research on Entrepreneurial Alertness," *Journal of Small Business Management,* October 1996, pp. 35–44; and J. W. Carland, F. Hoy, W. R. Boulton, and J. C. Carland, "Differentiating Entrepreneurs from Small Business Owners: A Conceptualization," *Academy of Management Review* 9, no. 2 (1984), pp. 354–59.

11. T. Nolan, "The No. 1 Employee Benefit That No One's Talking About," Gallup Inc., news.gallup. com, December 21, 2017.

12. State of the American Manager: Analytics and Advice for Leaders, Gallup Inc., http://www.gallup. com/services/182138/state-american-manager.aspx.

13. K. Tynan, "The Truth about Management," *TD,* June 2017, pp. 48–51.

14. J. Hess and S. Olsen, "What Will Work Look Like in 2030?" *Stratey+Business,* www.strategy-business.com, December 18, 2017.

15. "Why Is the Gig Economy So Appealing?" *TD,* January 2018, p. 13; and "#GigResponsibly: The Rise of NextGen Work," Manpower Group, 2017,

http://www.manpowergroup. co.uk/the-word-on-work/ gig-responsibly/.

16. J. Useem, "When Working from Home Doesn't Work," *Atlantic,* November 2017, pp. 26–28.

17. T. W. Martin, "May I Help You?" *Wall Street Journal,* April 23, 2009, p. R4.

18. H. Haddon, "Amazon's Grocery Sales Get a Lift," *Wall Street Journal,* January 17, 2018, p. B2.

19. "Contact the Staff of seattlepi. com," http://www.seattlepi.com/ pistaff/; and W. Yardley and R. Perez-Peña, "Seattle Paper Shifts Entirely to the Web," *New York Times Online,* March 17, 2009.

20. F. F. Reichheld, "Lead for Loyalty," *Harvard Business Review,* July–August 2001, p. 76.

21. J. Ringen, "MTV Strikes a Chord With Gen Z," *Fast Company,* November 2017, pp. 48–52.

22. See, for instance, H. Ernst, W. D. Hoyer, M. Krafft, and K. Krieger, "Customer Relationship Management and Company Performance—The Mediating Role of New Product Performance," *Journal of the Academy of Marketing Science,* April 2011, pp. 290–306; J. P. Dotson and G. M. Allenby, "Investigating the Strategic Influence of Customer and Employee Satisfaction on Firm Financial Performance," *Marketing Science,* September–October 2010, pp. 895–908; R. Grewal, M. Chandrashekaran, and A. V. Citrin, "Customer Satisfaction Heterogeneity and Shareholder Value," *Journal of Marketing Research,* August 2010, pp. 612–26; M. Riemann, O. Schilke, and J. S. Thomas,

"Customer Relationship Management and Firm Performance: The Mediating Role of Business Strategy," *Journal of the Academy of Marketing Science*, Summer 2010, pp. 326–46; and K. A. Eddleston, D. L. Kidder, and B. E. Litzky, "Who's the Boss? Contending with Competing Expectations from Customers and Management," *Academy of Management Executive*, November 2002, pp. 85–95.

23. See, for instance, S. Alguacil-Mallo, "A Customer-Centric State of Mind," *TD,* April 2018, pp. 38–42; C. B. Blocker, D. J. Flint, M. B. Myers, and S. F. Slater, "Proactive Customer Orientation and Its Role for Creating Customer Value in Global Markets," *Journal of the Academy of Marketing Science*, April 2011, pp. 216–33; G. A. Gorry and R. A. Westbrook, "Once More, with Feeling: Empathy and Technology in Customer Care," *Business Horizons*, March–April 2011, pp. 125–34; M. Dixon, K. Freeman, and N. Toman, "Stop Trying to Delight Your Customers," *Harvard Business Review*, July–August 2010, pp. 116–22; D. M. Mayer, M. G. Ehrhart, and B. Schneider, "Service Attribute Boundary Conditions of the Service Climate-Customer Satisfaction Link," *Academy of Management Journal*, October 2009, pp. 1034–50; B. A. Gutek, M. Groth, and B. Cherry, "Achieving Service Success through Relationships and Enhanced Encounters," *Academy of Management Executive*, November 2002, pp. 132–44; Eddleston, Kidder, and Litzky, "Who's the Boss? Contending with Competing Expectations from Customers and Management"; S. D. Pugh, J. Dietz, J. W. Wiley, and S. M. Brooks, "Driving Service Effectiveness through Employee-Customer Linkages," *Academy of Management Executive*, November 2002, pp. 73–84; S. D. Pugh, "Service with a Smile: Emotional Contagion in the Service Encounter," *Academy of Management Journal*, October 2001, pp. 1018–27; W. C. Tsai, "Determinants and Consequences of Employee Displayed Positive Emotions," *Journal of Management* 27, no. 4 (2001), pp. 497–512; E. Naumann and D. W. Jackson Jr., "One More Time: How Do You Satisfy Customers?", *Business Horizons,* May-June 1999, pp. 71-76; and M. D. Hartline and O. C. Ferrell, "The Management of Customer-Contact Service Employees: An Empirical Investigation," *Journal of Marketing*, October 1996, pp. 52–70.

24. Technology and the Manager's Job box based on D. Bennett, "I'll Have My Robots Talk to Your Robots," *Bloomberg Businessweek*, February 21–27, 2011, pp. 52–62; E. Spitznagel, "The Robot Revolution Is Coming," *Bloomberg Businessweek*, January 17–23, 2011, pp. 69–71; G. A. Fowler, "Holiday Hiring Call: People vs. Robots," *Wall Street Journal*, December 20, 2010, pp. B1+; A. Schwartz, "Bring Your Robot to Work Day," *Fast Company.com*, November 2010, pp. 72–74; and P. J. Hinds, T. L. Roberts, and H. Jones, "Whose Job Is It Anyway? A Study of Human-Robot Interaction in a Collaborative Task," *Human-Computer Interaction*, March 2004, pp. 151–81.

25. J. Bellini, "The Robot Revolution: Humanoid Potential—Moving Upstream," *Wall Street Journal Online*, https://www.wsj.com/articles/the-robot-revolution-humanoid-potential-moving-upstream-1517221862; and A. Martin, "SoftBank, Alibaba Team Up on Robot," *Wall Street Journal Online*, https://www.wsj.com/articles/pepper-softbanks-emotional-robot-goes-global-1434618111.

26. "The World's 50 Most Innovative Companies," *Fast Company,* March 2017.

27. N. Friedman, "Buffett's New Leaderat Dairy Queen," *Wall Street Journal,* February 3–4, 2018, p. B3.

28. "Top 15 Most Popular Social Networking Sites," http://www.ebizmba.com/articles/social-networking-websites, February 2015; and "Social Media Update 2014," Pew Research Center, http://www.pewinternet.org/2015/01/09/social-media-update-2014/, January 9, 2015.

29. P. Leonardi and T. Neeley, "What Managers Need to Know about Social Tools," *Harvard Business Review*, November–December 2017, pp. 118–26.

30. D. Ferris, "Social Studies: How to Use Social Media to Build a Better Organization," *Workforce Online*, February 12, 2012.

31. A. Taylor III, "BMW Gets Plugged In," *Fortune,* March 18, 2013, pp. 150–56.

32. KPMG Global Sustainability Services, *Sustainability Insights,* October 2007.

33. *Vision 2050* Report, Overview, www.wbcsd.org/vision2050.aspx.

34. *Symposium on Sustainability—Profiles in Leadership,* New York, October 2001.

35. J.Harter and A.Adkins,"Employees Want a Lot More from Their Managers," www.gallup.com/businessjournal, April 8, 2015.

36. R. Beck and J. Harter, "Why Great Managers Are So Rare," www.gallup.com/businessjournal, March 26, 2014.

37. Ibid.

38. S. Bailey, "No Manager Left Behind," *Chief Learning Officer*, February 2015, p. 30.

39. S. Y. Todd, K. J. Harris, R. B. Harris, and A. R. Wheeler, "Career Success Implications of Political Skill," *Journal of Social Psychology,* June 2009, pp. 179–204; G. R. Ferris, D. C. Treadway, P. L. Perrewé, R. L. Brouer, C. Douglas, and S. Lux, "Political Skill in Organizations," *Journal of Management,* June 2007, pp. 290–329; K. J. Harris, K. M. Kacmar, S. Zivnuska, and J. D. Shaw, "The Impact of Political Skill on Impression Management Effectiveness," *Journal of Applied Psychology,* January 2007, pp. 278–85; and G. R. Ferris, D. C. Treadway, R. W. Kolodinsky, W. A. Hochwarter, C. J. Kacmar, C. Douglas, and D. D. Frink, "Development and Validation of the Political Skill Inventory," *Journal of Management,* February 2005, pp. 126–52.

40. R. Abrams, "Walmart Is Accused of Punishing Workers for Sick Days," *New York Times Online,* June 1, 2017.

41. L. Thomas, "As Wal-Mart Blitzes Internet Retail, Debate Rages over Company's Impact on US Wages," *CNBC,* https://www.cnbc.com/2017/04/20/wal-mart-still-front-and-center-of-debate-over-minimum-wages.html.

42. M. Corkery, "At Walmart Academy, Training Better Managers. But with a Better Future?" *New York Times Online,* August 8, 2017.

43. M. S. Plakhotnik and T. S. Rocco, "A Succession Plan for First-Time Managers," *T&D,* December 2011, pp. 42–45; P. Brotherton, "New Managers Feeling Lost at Sea," *T&D,* June 2011, p. 25; and "How Do We Help a New Manager Manage?" *Workforce Management Online,* June 16, 2011.

44. H. Kniberg, "Spotify Engineering Culture (Part 1)," 2014, www.labs.spotify.com/2014/03/27/spotify-engineering-culture-part-1/, March 27, 2014.

45. H. Kniberg, "Spotify Engineering Culture (Part 2)," 2014, https://labs.spotify.com/2014/09/20/spotify-engineering-culture-part-2/ (last accessed October 21, 2015).

46. D. Lynskey, "Is Daniel Ek, Spotify Founder, Going to Save the Music Industry … or Destroy It?" November 10, 2013, http://www.theguardian.com/technology/2013/nov/10/daniel-ek-spotify-streaming-music (last accessed October 21, 2015).

47. M. Chafkin and I. King, "Dying Inside," *Bloomberg Businessweek,* January 22, 2018, pp. 53–55.

48. Ibid.

49. A. Greenberg, "Meet 'Project Zero," Google's Secret Team of Bug-Hunting Hackers," *Wired Online,* https://www.wired.com/2014/07/google-project-zero/, July 15, 2014.

50. R. McMillan and L. Lin, "Intel Told China of Flaw before U.S., *Wall Street Journal,* January 29, 2018, pp. A1+.

51. Ibid.

History Module
A BRIEF HISTORY OF MANAGEMENT'S ROOTS

Henry Ford once said, "History is more or less bunk." Well…Henry Ford was wrong! History is important because it can put current activities in perspective. We propose that you need to know management history because it can help you understand what today's managers do. In this module, you'll find an annotated timeline that discusses key milestones in management theory. *Check out each chapter's "Classic Concepts in Today's Workplace" box feature where we highlight a key person and his or her contributions or a key historical factor and its effect on contemporary management concepts.* We believe this approach will help you better understand the origins of many contemporary management concepts.

Early Management
Management has been practiced a long time. Organized endeavors directed by people responsible for planning, organizing, leading, and controlling activities have existed for thousands of years. Regardless of what these individuals were called, someone had to perform those functions.

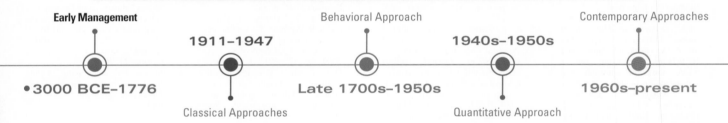

Early Management

1911–1947

Behavioral Approach

1940s–1950s

Contemporary Approaches

• 3000 BCE–1776

Classical Approaches

Late 1700s–1950s

Quantitative Approach

1960s–present

3000–2500 BCE

The Egyptian pyramids are proof that projects of tremendous scope, employing tens of thousands of people, were completed in ancient times.[1] It took more than 100,000 workers some 20 years to construct a single pyramid. Someone had to plan what was to be done, organize people and materials to do it, make sure those workers got the work done, and impose some controls to ensure that everything was done as planned. That someone was managers.

1400s

At the arsenal of Venice, warships were floated along the canals, and at each stop, materials and riggings were added to the ship.[2] Sounds a lot like a car "floating" along an assembly line, doesn't it? In addition, the Venetians used warehouse and inventory systems to keep track of materials, human resource management functions to manage the labor force (including wine breaks), and an accounting system to keep track of revenues and costs.

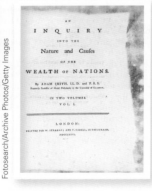

1776

Although this is an important date in U.S. history, it's also important because it's the year Adam Smith's *Wealth of Nations* was published. In it, he argued the economic advantages of the **division of labor (or job specialization)**—that is, breaking down jobs into narrow, repetitive tasks. Using division of labor, individual productivity could be increased dramatically. Job specialization continues to be a popular way to determine how work gets done in organizations. As you'll see in Chapter 5, it does have its drawbacks.

1780s–Mid-1800s

The Industrial Revolution may be the most important pre-twentieth-century influence on management. Why? Because with the industrial age came the birth of the corporation. With large, efficient factories pumping out products, someone needed to forecast demand, make sure adequate supplies of materials were available, assign tasks to workers, and so forth. Again, that someone was managers! It was indeed a historic event for two reasons: (1) because of all the organizational aspects (hierarchy, control, job specialization, and so forth) that became a part of the way work was done and (2) because management had become a necessary component to ensure the success of the enterprise.

Classical Approaches

Beginning around the turn of the twentieth century, the discipline of management began to evolve as a unified body of knowledge. Rules and principles were developed that could be taught and used in a variety of settings. These early management proponents were called classical theorists.

Early Management
3000 BCE–1776

• 1911–1947
Classical Approaches

Late 1700s–1950s

Behavioral Approach

1940s–1950s

Quantitative Approach

Contemporary Approaches
1960s–present

Bettmann/Getty Images

1911

That's the year Frederick W. Taylor's *Principles of Scientific Management* was published. His groundbreaking book described a theory of **scientific management**—the use of scientific methods to determine the "one best way" for a job to be done. His theories were widely accepted and used by managers around the world, and Taylor became known as the "father" of scientific management.[3] (Taylor's work is profiled in Chapter 1's "From the Past to the Present" box.) Other major contributors to scientific management were Frank and Lillian Gilbreth (early proponents of time-and-motion studies and parents of the large family described in the original book *Cheaper by the Dozen*) and Henry Gantt (whose work on scheduling charts was the foundation for today's project management).

Hulton Archive/Getty Images

1916–1947

Unlike Taylor, who focused on an individual production worker's job, Henri Fayol and Max Weber (depicted in the photo) looked at organizational practices by focusing on what managers do and what constituted good management. This approach is known as **general administrative theory**. Fayol was introduced in Chapter 1 as the person who first identified five management functions. He also identified 14 **principles of management**—fundamental rules of management that could be applied to all organizations.[4] (See Exhibit HM–1 for a list of these 14 principles.) Weber is known for his description and analysis of bureaucracy, which he believed was an ideal, rational form of organization structure, especially for large organizations. In Chapter 7, we elaborate on these two important management pioneers.

Exhibit HM–1 Fayol's 14 Principles of Management

1 **Division of Work.** This principle is the same as Adam Smith's "division of labor." Specialization increases output by making employees more efficient.

2 **Authority.** Managers must be able to give orders. Authority gives them this right. Along with authority, however, goes responsibility. Whenever authority is exercised, responsibility arises.

3 **Discipline.** Employees must obey and respect the rules that govern the organization. Good discipline is the result of effective leadership, a clear understanding between management and workers regarding the organization's rules, and the judicious use of penalties for infractions of the rules.

4 **Unity of Command.** Every employee should receive orders from only one superior.

5 **Unity of Direction.** Each group of organizational activities that have the same objective should be directed by one manager using one plan.

6 Subordination of Individual Interests to the General Interest. The interests of any one employee or group of employees should not take precedence over the interests of the organization as a whole.

7 Remuneration. Workers must be paid a fair wage for their services.

8 **Centralization.** Centralization refers to the degree to which subordinates are involved in decision making. Whether decision making is centralized (to management) or decentralized (to subordinates) is a question of proper proportion. The task is to find the optimum degree of centralization for each situation.

9 **Scalar Chain.** The line of authority from top management to the lowest ranks represents the scalar chain. Communications should follow this chain. However, if following the chain creates delays, cross-communications can be allowed if agreed to by all parties and if superiors are kept informed. Also called chain of command.

10 **Order.** People and materials should be in the right place at the right time.

11 **Equity.** Managers should be kind and fair to their subordinates.

12 **Stability of Tenure of Personnel.** High employee turnover is inefficient. Management should provide orderly personnel planning and ensure that replacements are available to fill vacancies.

13 **Initiative.** Employees who are allowed to originate and carry out plans will exert high levels of effort.

14 **Esprit de Corps.** Promoting team spirit will build harmony and unity within the organization.

Other Early Twentieth-Century Contributors: A Diversity Perspective

We don't want to leave you with the impression that the only individuals contributing to the early discipline of management were white males. Here are a few outstanding diverse individuals whose business acumen is noteworthy:

Michael Ochs Archives/Stringer/Getty Images

Handout/Toyota Motor Corporation/ Getty Images News/Getty Images

Madam C. J. Walker:
Personal necessity led Walker to invent a line of African American hair care products in 1905. Her entrepreneurial talents and insights led her to become one of the first American women to become a self-made millionaire.[5]

Kiichiro Toyoda:
The founder of Toyota Motor Company created a "flow-based [manufacturing] system" that was focused on keeping the production line running smoothly rather than operating at maximum speed. Toyoda's early recognition of the key to efficient and effective manufacturing led to the creation of the Toyota Production System with its host of practices including, for example, just-in-time manufacturing and continuous improvement.[7]

Charles Clinton Spaulding:
A prominent black business leader in the insurance industry in the early 1900s, Spaulding recognized the importance of effectively managing a business and the importance of practices such as transformational leadership, employee development, diversity, corporate social responsibility, and a strong positive organizational culture.[6]

Prudencio Unanue and Joseph A. Unanue:
This father-and-son team, using their management skills and foresight, turned a small, family-owned business, Goya Foods (which initially sold food to the Latino communities in New York), into the largest Latino-owned food distributor in the United States and eventually expanded into global distribution.[8]

Behavioral Approach

The behavioral approach to management focused on the actions of workers. How do you motivate and lead employees in order to get high levels of performance?

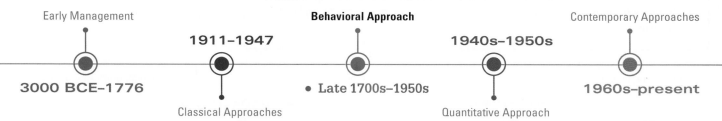

Early Management

Behavioral Approach

Contemporary Approaches

1911–1947

1940s–1950s

3000 BCE–1776

• **Late 1700s–1950s**

1960s–present

Classical Approaches

Quantitative Approach

Ken Welsh/Newscom

Late 1700s–Early 1900s

Managers get things done by working with people. Several early management writers recognized how important people are to an organization's success.[9] For instance, Robert Owen, who was concerned about deplorable working conditions, proposed an idealistic workplace. Hugo Munsterberg, a pioneer in the field of industrial psychology, suggested using psychological tests for employee selection, learning theory concepts for employee training, and studies of human behavior for employee motivation. Mary Parker Follett was one of the first to recognize that organizations could be viewed from both individual *and* group behavior. She thought that organizations should be based on a group ethic rather than on individualism.

Archive PL / Alamy Stock Photo

1924–Mid-1930s

The **Hawthorne studies**, a series of studies that provided new insights into individual and group behavior, were without question the most important contribution to the behavioral approach to management.[10] Conducted at the Hawthorne (Cicero, Illinois) Works of the Western Electric Company, the studies were initially designed as a scientific management experiment. Company engineers wanted to see the effect of various lighting levels on worker productivity. Using control and experimental groups of workers, they expected to find that individual output in the experimental group would be directly related to the intensity of the light. However, much to their surprise, they found that productivity in both groups varied with the level of lighting. Not able to explain it, the engineers called in Harvard professor Elton Mayo. Thus began a relationship that lasted until 1932 and encompassed numerous experiments in the behavior of people at work. What were some of their conclusions? Group pressures can significantly affect individual productivity, and people behave differently when they're being observed. Scholars generally agree that the Hawthorne studies had a dramatic impact on management beliefs about the role of people in organizations and led to a new emphasis on the human behavior factor in managing organizations.

1930s–1950s

The human relations movement is important to management history because its supporters never wavered from their commitment to making management practices more humane. Proponents of this movement uniformly believed in the importance of employee satisfaction—a satisfied worker was believed to be a productive worker.[11] So they offered suggestions like employee participation, praise, and being nice to people to increase employee satisfaction. For instance, Abraham Maslow, a humanistic psychologist, who's best known for his description of a hierarchy of five needs (a well-known theory of employee motivation), said that once a need was substantially satisfied, it no longer served to motivate behavior. Douglas McGregor developed Theory X and Theory Y assumptions, which related to a manager's beliefs about an employee's motivation to work. Even though both Maslow's and McGregor's theories were never fully supported by research, they're important because they represent the foundation from which contemporary motivation theories were developed. Both are described more fully in Chapter 11.

Shutterstock

1960s–Today

An organization's people continue to be an important focus of management research. The field of study that researches the actions (behaviors) of people at work is called **organizational behavior (OB)**. OB researchers do empirical research on human behavior in organizations. Much of what managers do today when managing people—motivating, leading, building trust, working with a team, managing conflict, and so forth—has come out of OB research. These topics are explored in depth in Chapters 9–13.

Quantitative Approach

The quantitative approach, which focuses on the application of statistics, optimization models, information models, computer simulations, and other quantitative techniques to management activities, provided tools for managers to make their jobs easier.

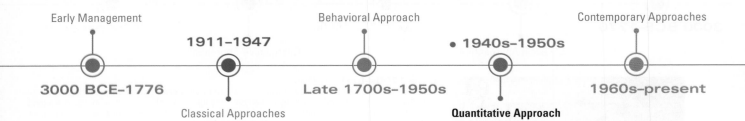

Early Management

1911–1947

Behavioral Approach

● **1940s–1950s**

Contemporary Approaches

3000 BCE–1776

Late 1700s–1950s

1960s–present

Classical Approaches

Quantitative Approach

1940s

The **quantitative approach** to management—which is the use of quantitative techniques to improve decision making—evolved from mathematical and statistical solutions developed for military problems during World War II. After the war was over, many of these techniques used for military problems were applied to businesses.[12] For instance, one group of military officers, dubbed the "Whiz Kids," joined Ford Motor Company in the mid-1940s and immediately began using statistical methods to improve decision making at Ford. You'll find more information on these quantitative applications in the Quantitative Decision-Making Aids module.

1950s

After World War II, Japanese organizations enthusiastically embraced the concepts espoused by a small group of quality experts, the most famous being W. Edwards Deming (show in photo) and Joseph M. Juran. As these Japanese manufacturers began beating U.S. competitors in quality comparisons, Western managers soon took a more serious look at Deming's and Juran's ideas.[13] Their ideas became the basis for **total quality management (TQM)**, which is a management philosophy devoted to continual improvement and responding to customer needs and expectations. We'll look more closely at Deming and his beliefs about TQM in the Managing Operations module.

Contemporary Approaches

Most of the early approaches to management focused on managers' concerns inside the organization. Starting in the 1960s, management researchers began to look at what was happening in the external environment outside the organization.

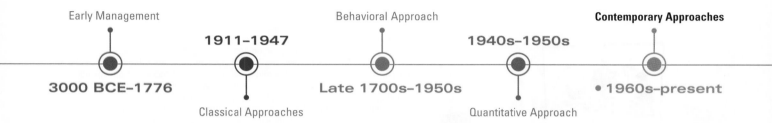

Early Management

1911–1947

Behavioral Approach

Contemporary Approaches

1940s–1950s

3000 BCE–1776

Late 1700s–1950s

Classical Approaches

Quantitative Approach

• 1960s–present

1960s

Although Chester Barnard, a telephone company executive, wrote in his 1938 book *The Functions of the Executive* that an organization functioned as a cooperative system, it wasn't until the 1960s that management researchers began to look more carefully at systems theory and how it related to organizations.[14] The idea of a system is a basic concept in the physical sciences. As related to organizations, the **systems approach** views systems as a set of interrelated and interdependent parts arranged in a manner that produces a unified whole. Organizations function as **open systems,** which means they are influenced by and interact with their environment. Exhibit HM–2 illustrates an organization as an open system. A manager has to efficiently and effectively manage all parts of the system in order to achieve established goals. See Chapter 4 for additional information on the external and internal factors that affect how organizations are managed.

Exhibit HM–2 Organization as an Open System

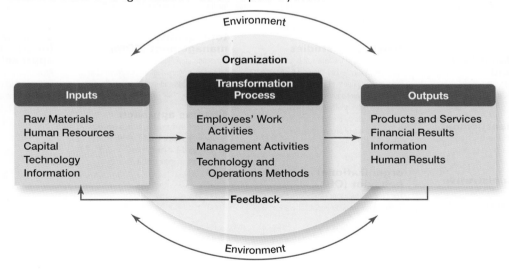

Contemporary Approaches

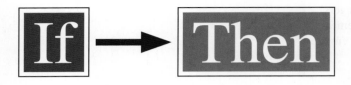

1960s

Early management theorists proposed management principles that they generally assumed to be universally applicable. Later research found exceptions to many of these principles. The **contingency approach (or situational approach)** says that organizations, employees, and situations are different and require different ways of managing. A good way to describe contingency is "if...then." *If* this is the way my situation is, *then* this is the best way for me to manage in this situation. One of the earliest contingency studies was done by Fred Fiedler and looked at what style of leadership was most effective in what situation.[15] Popular contingency variables have been found to include organization size, the routineness of task technology, environmental uncertainty, and individual differences.

1980s–Present

Although the dawn of the information age is said to have begun with Samuel Morse's telegraph in 1837, we've seen dramatic changes in information technology in the latter part of the twentieth century and continue to see advances that directly affect the manager's job.[16] Managers now may manage employees who are working from home or working halfway around the world. An organization's computing resources used to be mainframe computers locked away in temperature-controlled rooms and only accessed by the experts. Now, practically everyone in an organization is connected—wired or wireless—with devices no larger than the palm of the hand. Just like the impact of the Industrial Revolution in the 1700s on the emergence of management, the information age has brought dramatic changes that continue to influence the way organizations are managed. The impact of digitization and information technology on how managers do their work is so profound that we've included in each chapter a boxed feature on "Managing Technology in Today's Workplace."

Andriy Popov/Alamy Stock Photo

Industrial Revolution
The advent of machine power, mass production, and efficient transportation beginning in the late eighteenth century in Great Britain

division of labor (or job specialization)
The breakdown of jobs into narrow repetitive tasks

scientific management
The use of the scientific method to define the one best way for a job to be done

general administrative theory
Descriptions of what managers do and what constitutes good management practice

principles of management
Fayol's fundamental or universal principles of management practice

Hawthorne studies
Research done in the late 1920s and early 1930s devised by Western Electric industrial engineers to examine the effect of different work environment changes on worker productivity, which led to a new emphasis on the human factor in the functioning of organizations and the attainment of their goals

organizational behavior (OB)
The field of study that researches the actions (behaviors) of people at work

quantitative approach
The use of quantitative techniques to improve decision making

total quality management (TQM)
A managerial philosophy devoted to continual improvement and responding to customer needs and expectations

systems approach
An approach to management that views an organization as a system, which is a set of interrelated and interdependent parts arranged in a manner that produces a unified whole

open systems
Systems that dynamically interact with their environment

contingency approach (or situational approach)
An approach to management that says that individual organizations, employees, and situations are different and require different ways of managing

Endnotes

1. C. S. George Jr., *The History of Management Thought,* 2nd ed. (Upper Saddle River, NJ: Prentice Hall, 1972), p. 4.

2. Ibid., pp. 35–41.

3. F. W. Taylor, *Principles of Scientific Management* (New York: Harper, 1911), p. 44. For other information on Taylor, see S. Wagner-Tsukamoto, "An Institutional Economic Reconstruction of Scientific Management: On the Lost Theoretical Logic of Taylorism," *Academy of Management Review,* January 2007, pp. 105–17; R. Kanigel, *The One Best Way: Frederick Winslow Taylor and the Enigma of Efficiency* (New York: Viking, 1997); and M. Banta, *Taylored Lives: Narrative Productions in the Age of Taylor, Veblen, and Ford* (Chicago: University of Chicago Press, 1993).

4. H. Fayol, *Industrial and General Administration* (Paris: Dunod, 1916); M. Weber, *The Theory of Social and Economic Organizations,* ed. T. Parsons, trans. A. M. Henderson and T. Parsons (New York: Free Press, 1947); and M. Lounsbury and E. J. Carberry, "From King to Court Jester? Weber's Fall from Grace in Organizational Theory," *Organization Studies* 26, no. 4 (2005), pp. 501–25.

5. "Madame C. J. Walker Biography," https://www.biography.com/people/madam-cj-walker-9522174.

6. L. C. Prieto and S. T. A. Phipps, "Re-discovering Charles Clinton Spaulding's 'The Administration of Big Business': Insight into Early 20th Century African-American Management Thought," *Journal of Management History* 22, no. 1 (2016), pp. 73–90.

7. "Business Pioneers in Industry," https://www.ft.com/content/c18fd 2c6-cc99-11e4-b5a5-00144feab 7de.

8. Geraldo L. Cavada, "Entrepreneurs from the Beginning: Latino Business & Commerce since the 16th Century," https://www.nps.gov/heritageinitiatives/latino/latinothemestudy/businesscommerce.htm.

9. R. A. Owen, *A New View of Society* (New York: E. Bliss and White, 1825); H. Munsterberg, *Psychology and Industrial Efficiency* (Boston: Houghton Mifflin, 1913); and M. P. Follett, *The New State: Group Organization the Solution of Popular Government* (London: Longmans, Green, 1918).

10. E. Mayo, *The Human Problems of an Industrial Civilization* (New York: Macmillan, 1933); and F. J. Roethlisberger and W. J. Dickson, *Management and the Worker* (Cambridge, MA: Harvard University Press, 1939). Also see G. W. Yunker, "An Explanation of Positive and Negative Hawthorne Effects: Evidence from the Relay Assembly Test Room and Bank Wiring Observation Room Studies," paper presented, Academy of Management Annual Meeting, August 1993, Atlanta, Georgia; S. R. Jones, "Was There a Hawthorne Effect?" *American Sociological Review,* November 1992, pp. 451–68; S. R. G. Jones, "Worker Interdependence and Output: The Hawthorne Studies Reevaluated," *American Sociological Review,* April 1990, pp. 176–90; J. A. Sonnenfeld, "Shedding Light on the Hawthorne Studies," *Journal of Occupational Behavior,* April 1985, pp. 111–30; B. Rice, "The Hawthorne Defect: Persistence of a Flawed Theory," *Psychology Today,* February 1982, pp. 70–74; R. H. Franke and J. Kaul, "The Hawthorne Experiments: First Statistical Interpretations," *American Sociological Review,* October 1978, pp. 623–43; and A. Carey, "The Hawthorne Studies: A Radical Criticism," *American Sociological Review,* June 1967, pp. 403–16.

11. A. Maslow, "A Theory of Human Motivation," *Psychological Review,* July 1943, pp. 370–396; see also A. Maslow, *Motivation and Personality* (New York: Harper & Row, 1954); and D. McGregor, *The Human Side of Enterprise* (New York: McGraw-Hill, 1960).

12. P. Rosenzweig, "Robert S. McNamara and the Evolution of Management," *Harvard Business Review,* December 2010, pp. 86–93; and C. C. Holt, "Learning How to Plan Production, Inventories, and Work Force," *Operations Research,* January–February 2002, pp. 96–99.

13. T. A. Stewart, "A Conversation with Joseph Juran," *Fortune,* January 11, 1999, pp. 168–70; J. R. Hackman and R. Wageman, "Total Quality Management: Empirical, Conceptual, and Practical Issues," *Administrative Science Quarterly,* June 1995, pp. 309–42; B. Krone, "Total Quality Management: An American Odyssey," *The Bureaucrat,* Fall 1990, pp. 35–38; and A. Gabor, *The Man Who Discovered Quality* (New York: Random House, 1990).

14. C. I. Barnard, *The Functions of the Executive* (Cambridge, MA: Harvard University Press, 1938); and K. B. DeGreene, *Sociotechnical Systems: Factors in Analysis, Design, and Management* (Upper Saddle River, NJ: Prentice Hall, 1973), p. 13.

15. F. E. Fiedler, *A Theory of Leadership Effectiveness* (New York: McGraw-Hill, 1967).

16. "Information Age: People, Information & Technology—An Exhibition at the National Museum of American History," Smithsonian Institution, http://photo2.si.edu/infoage/infoage.html, June 11, 2009; and P. F. Drucker, *Management,* Revised Edition (New York: HarperCollins Publishers, 2008).

A good decision should be defined by its outcome.

Management Myth · Myth

Management
Myth
DEBUNKED!

A good decision should be judged by the process used, not the results achieved. In some cases, a good decision results in an undesirable outcome. As a decision maker, you can control the process. But in the real world, factors outside your control can adversely affect the outcome. Using the right process may not always result in a desirable outcome, but it increases the probability!

DECISION MAKERS

at Fox Sports, a unit of 21st Century Fox, paid $200 million for the U.S. English-language rights to broadcast the 2018 FIFA World Cup in Moscow. Over a four-and-a-half week span, this was to be, by far, the biggest production undertaken in Fox Sports history... more than 350 hours of programming across multiple networks and digital platforms.[1] Everything seemed to be proceeding as planned until the U.S. team lost to Trinidad and Tobago—a loss that meant the U.S. team would not participate in the sport's premier tournament. Without the U.S. team, the network faced possible lower viewership, meaning a tougher time selling advertising (the major source of revenue for the network) and not being able to meet the "guarantees" on audience exposure. For Fox Sports, significant revenue was at stake. Was this, then, a bad decision? Our debunked myth suggests that if the initial process used by the decision makers at Fox Sports was thorough and reasonable, then no, it was not a bad decision. A real-world factor—the unexpected U.S. team loss—outside the company's control affected the outcome. Despite this, decision makers at Fox Sports adapted to the new circumstances and decided to put greater effort into storytelling and marketing. After all, many World Cup advertisers were global companies that still wanted to get out the message about their brands to large global audiences.

Managers at all organizational levels and in all areas make a lot of decisions—routine and nonroutine; minor and major. The overall quality of those decisions goes a long way in determining an organization's success or failure. To be a successful

Learning Outcomes

manager—and to be a valued employee— you need to know about decision making. In this chapter, we'll look at types of decisions and how decisions should be made. But we'll also consider some common biases and errors that can undermine the quality of decisions and discuss contemporary issues facing managerial decision makers. •

How do Managers Make Decisions?

2-1 Describe the decision-making process.

How do businesses put new ideas into action? Through lots of decisions, that's how. When Bertucci's, a shopping-mall restaurant chain in New England and the mid-Atlantic region, wanted to create a spin-off chain with a more contemporary, "hipper" appeal, managers had lots of decisions to make over a nine-month period from concept to opening. Managers hope, of course, that those decisions prove to be good ones.[2]

How often do companies expect people to be strong decision makers? Forty hours a week...that is, pretty much all day, every work day![3]

Decision making is typically described as choosing among alternatives, but this view is overly simplistic. Why? Because decision making is a process, not a simple act of choosing among alternatives. Exhibit 2–1 illustrates the **decision-making process** as a set of eight steps that begins with identifying a problem; it moves through selecting an alternative that can alleviate the problem and concludes with evaluating the decision's effectiveness. This process is as applicable to your decision about what you're going to do on spring break as it is to the decisions UPS executives are making as they deal with issues that could affect the organization's future profitability (see Case Application #1 on p. 89). The process can also be used to describe both individual and group decisions. Let's take a closer look at the process in order to understand what each step entails by using a simple example most of us can relate to—the decision to buy a car.

What Defines a Decision Problem?

Step 1. The decision-making process begins with the identification of a **problem** or, more specifically, a discrepancy between an existing and a desired state of affairs.[4] Take the case of a sales manager for Pfizer. The manager is on the road a lot and spent nearly $6,000 on

decision-making process
A set of eight steps that includes identifying a problem, selecting a solution, and evaluating the effectiveness of the solution

problem
A discrepancy between an existing and a desired state of affairs

Exhibit 2–1 **The Decision-Making Process**

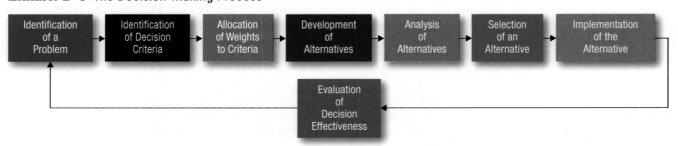

Branislav Nenin/Shutterstock

The steps involved in buying a vehicle provide a good example of the decision-making process. For this young woman, the process starts with the first step of identifying the problem of needing a car so she can drive to her new job and ends with the last step in the process of evaluating the results of her decision.

auto repairs over the past few years. Now her car has a blown engine, and cost estimates indicate it's not economical to repair. Furthermore, convenient public transportation is unavailable. So, we have a problem—a discrepancy between the manager's need to have a car that works and the fact that her current one doesn't.

Identifying problems is
IMPORTANT...
and CHALLENGING![5]

In our example, a blown engine is a clear signal to the manager that she needs a new car, but few problems are that obvious. In the real world, most problems don't come with neon signs identifying them as such. And problem identification is subjective. *A manager who mistakenly solves the wrong problem perfectly is just as likely to perform poorly as the manager who fails to identify the right problem and does nothing.* So, how do managers become aware they have a problem? They have to make a comparison between current reality and some standard, which can be (1) past performance, (2) previously set goals, or (3) the performance of some other unit within the organization or in other organizations. In our car-buying example, the standard is past performance—a car that runs.

What is Relevant in the Decision-Making Process?

Step 2. Once a manager has identified a problem that needs attention, the **decision criteria** that will be important in solving the problem must be identified. In our vehicle-buying example, the sales manager assesses the factors that are relevant in her decision, which might include criteria such as price, model (two-door or four-door), size (compact or intermediate), manufacturer (French, Japanese, South Korean, German, American), optional equipment (self-parking, navigation system, side-impact protection, leather interior), and repair records. These criteria reflect what she thinks is relevant in her decision. Every decision maker has criteria—whether explicitly stated or not—that guide his or her decision making. Note that in this step in the decision-making process, what's not identified can be as important as what is because it's still guiding the decision. For instance, although the sales manager didn't consider fuel economy to be a criterion and won't use it to influence her choice of car, she had to assess that criteria before choosing to include or not include it in her relevant criteria.

How Does the Decision Maker Weight the Criteria and Analyze Alternatives?

Steps 3, 4, and 5. In many decision-making situations, the criteria are not all equally important.[6] So, the decision maker has to allocate weights to the items listed in step 2 in order to give them their relative priority in the decision (step 3). A simple approach is to give the most important criterion a weight of 10 and then assign weights to the rest against that standard. Thus, in contrast to a criterion that you gave a 5, the highest-rated factor is twice as important. The idea is to use your personal preferences to assign priorities to the relevant criteria in your decision and indicate their degree of importance by assigning a weight to each. Exhibit 2–2 lists the criteria and weights that our manager developed for her vehicle replacement decision. What is the most important criterion in her decision? Price. What has low importance? Performance and handling.

Then the decision maker lists the alternatives that could successfully resolve the problem (step 4). No attempt is made in this step to evaluate these alternatives, only to list them.[7] This is the step where a decision maker may need to be creative, a topic we'll discuss later in the chapter. (Also, see the Management Skill Builder at the end of the chapter.) Let's assume in

decision criteria
Factors that are relevant in a decision

Exhibit 2–2 Important Criteria and Weights in a Car-Buying Decision

CRITERION	WEIGHT
Price	10
Interior comfort	8
Durability	5
Repair record	5
Performance	3
Handling	1

our example that our manager identifies 12 cars as viable choices: Jeep Compass, Ford Focus, Hyundai Elantra, Ford Fiesta SES, Volkswagen Golf GTI, Toyota Prius, Mazda 3 MT, Kia Soul, BMW i3, Nissan Cube, Toyota Camry, and Honda Fit Sport MT.

Once the alternatives have been identified, the decision maker critically analyzes each one (step 5). How? By evaluating it against the criteria. The strengths and weaknesses of each alternative become evident as they're compared with the criteria and weights established in steps 2 and 3. Exhibit 2–3 shows the assessed values that the manager assigned each of her 12 alternatives after she had test-driven each car. Keep in mind that the ratings shown in Exhibit 2–3 are based on the assessment made by the sales manager. Again, we're using a scale of 1 to 10. Some assessments can be achieved in a relatively objective fashion. For instance, the purchase price represents the best price the manager can get online or from local dealers, and consumer magazines report data from owners on frequency of repairs. Others, like how well the car handles, are clearly personal judgments.

Most decisions involve **judgments**.

Personal judgments by a decision maker are reflected in (1) the criteria chosen in step 2, (2) the weights given to the criteria, and (3) the evaluation of alternatives. The influence of personal judgment explains why two car buyers with the same amount of money may look at two totally distinct sets of alternatives or even look at the same alternatives and rate them differently.

Exhibit 2–3 Assessment of Possible Car Alternatives

ALTERNATIVES	INITIAL PRICE	INTERIOR COMFORT	DURABILITY	REPAIR RECORD	PERFORMANCE	HANDLING	TOTAL
Jeep Compass	2	10	8	7	5	5	37
Ford Focus	9	6	5	6	8	6	40
Hyundai Elantra	8	5	6	6	4	6	35
Ford Fiesta SES	9	5	6	7	6	5	38
Volkswagen Golf GTI	5	6	9	10	7	7	44
Toyota Prius	10	5	6	4	3	3	31
Mazda 3 MT	4	8	7	6	8	9	42
Kia Soul	7	6	8	6	5	6	38
BMW i3	9	7	6	4	4	7	37
Nissan Cube	5	8	5	4	10	10	42
Toyota Camry	6	5	10	10	6	6	43
Honda Fit Sport MT	8	6	6	5	7	8	40

Exhibit 2–4 Evaluation of Car Alternatives: Assessment Criteria × Criteria Weight

ALTERNATIVES	INITIAL PRICE [10]		INTERIOR COMFORT [8]		DURABILITY [5]		REPAIR RECORD [5]		PERFORMANCE [3]		HANDLING [1]		TOTAL
Jeep Compass	2	20	10	80	8	40	7	35	5	15	5	5	195
Ford Focus	9	90	6	48	5	25	6	30	8	24	6	6	223
Hyundai Elantra	8	80	5	40	6	30	6	30	4	12	6	6	198
Ford Fiesta SES	9	90	5	40	6	30	7	35	6	18	5	5	218
Volkswagen Golf GTI	5	50	6	48	9	45	10	50	7	21	7	7	221
Toyota Prius	10	100	5	40	6	30	4	20	3	9	3	3	202
Mazda 3 MT	4	40	8	64	7	35	6	30	8	24	9	9	202
Kia Soul	7	70	6	48	8	40	6	30	5	15	6	6	209
BMW i3	9	90	7	56	6	30	4	20	4	12	7	7	215
Nissan Cube	5	50	8	64	5	25	4	20	10	30	10	10	199
Toyota Camry	6	60	5	40	10	50	10	50	6	18	6	6	224
Honda Fit Sport MT	8	80	6	48	6	30	5	25	7	21	8	8	212

Exhibit 2–3 shows only an assessment of the 12 alternatives against the decision criteria; it does not reflect the weighting done in step 3. If one choice had scored 10 on every criterion, obviously you wouldn't need to consider the weights. Similarly, if all the weights were equal—that is, all the criteria were equally important to you—each alternative would be evaluated merely by summing up the appropriate lines in Exhibit 2–3. For instance, the Ford Fiesta SES would have a score of 38 and the Toyota Camry a score of 43. But if you multiply each alternative assessment against its weight, you get the figures in Exhibit 2–4. For instance, the Kia Soul scored a 40 on durability, which was determined by multiplying the weight given to durability [5] by the manager's appraisal of the car on this criterion [8]. The sum of these scores represents an evaluation of each alternative against the previously established criteria and weights. Notice that the weighting of the criteria has changed the ranking of alternatives in our example. The Volkswagen Golf GTI, for example, has gone from first to third. Looking at the analysis, both initial price and interior comfort worked against the Volkswagen.

What Determines the Best Choice?

Step 6. Now it's time to choose the best alternative from among those assessed. Because we determined all the pertinent factors in the decision, weighted them appropriately, and identified and assessed the viable alternatives, this step is fairly simple. Choose the alternative that generated the highest score in step 5. In our vehicle example (Exhibit 2–4), the manager would choose the Toyota Camry. On the basis of the criteria identified, the weights given to the criteria, and her assessment of each car on the criteria, the Toyota scored highest [224 points] and, thus, became the best alternative.

What Happens in Decision Implementation?

Step 7. Although the choice process is completed in the previous step, the decision may still fail if it's not implemented properly (step 7). Therefore, this step, **decision implementation**, involves putting the decision into action. If others will be affected by the decision, implementation also includes conveying the decision to those affected and getting their commitment to it.[8] *Want people to be committed to a decision?* Let them participate in the decision-making process. We'll discuss later in the chapter how groups can help a manager do this.

decision implementation
Putting a decision into action

Exhibit 2–5 Common Decision-Making Errors and Biases

What is the Last Step in the Decision Process?

Step 8. In the last step in the decision-making process, managers appraise the outcome of the decision to see *whether the problem was resolved*. Did the alternative chosen in step 6 and implemented in step 7 accomplish the desired result? For our sales manager, that means does she have a car that reliably works? Evaluating the results of a decision is part of the managerial control process, which we'll discuss in Chapter 14.

What Common Errors Are Committed in the Decision-Making Process?

When managers make decisions, they use their own particular style, and may use "rules of thumb," or **heuristics**, to simplify their decision making.[9] Rules of thumb can be useful because they help make sense of complex, uncertain, and ambiguous information. However, even though managers may use rules of thumb, that doesn't mean those rules are reliable. Why? Because they may lead to errors and biases in processing and evaluating information. Exhibit 2–5 identifies 13 common decision errors and biases that managers make. Let's look briefly at each.[10]

Which of these **are YOU guilty** of when making decisions?
Learn to recognize these biases so your decision making
won't be negatively affected!

- *Overconfidence bias* is when decision makers tend to think they know more than they do or hold unrealistically positive views of themselves and their performance.

- *Immediate gratification bias* describes decision makers who tend to want immediate rewards and to avoid immediate costs. For these individuals, decision choices that provide quick payoffs are more appealing than those in the future. The

- *Anchoring effect* describes when decision makers fixate on initial information as a starting point and then, once set, fail to adequately adjust for subsequent information. First impressions, ideas, prices, and estimates carry unwarranted weight relative to information received later.

- *Selective perception bias* is when decision makers selectively organize and interpret events based on their biased perceptions. This influences the information they pay attention to, the problems they identify, and the alternatives they develop.

heuristics
Judgmental shortcuts or "rules of thumb" used to simplify decision making

- *Confirmation bias* is exhibited when decision makers seek out information that reaffirms their past choices and discount information that contradicts past judgments. These people tend to accept at face value information that confirms their preconceived views and are critical and skeptical of information that challenges these views.

- *Framing bias* happens when decision makers select and highlight certain aspects of a situation while excluding others. By drawing attention to specific aspects of a situation and highlighting them, while at the same time downplaying or omitting other aspects, they distort what they see and create incorrect reference points.

- *Availability bias* occurs when decision makers tend to remember events that are the most recent and vivid in their memory. The result? It distorts their ability to recall events in an objective manner and results in distorted judgments and probability estimates.

- *Representation bias* is when decision makers assess the likelihood of an event based on how closely it resembles other events or sets of events. Managers exhibiting this bias draw analogies and see identical situations where they don't exist.

- *Randomness bias* describes when decision makers try to create meaning out of random events. They do this because most decision makers have difficulty dealing with chance even though random events happen to everyone and there's nothing that can be done to predict them.

- *Sunk costs error* takes place when decision makers forget that current choices can't correct the past. They incorrectly fixate on past expenditures of time, money, or effort in assessing choices rather than on future consequences. Instead of ignoring sunk costs, they can't forget them.

- *Self-serving bias* describes decision makers who are quick to take credit for their successes and to blame failure on outside factors.

- *Hindsight bias* is the tendency for decision makers to falsely believe that they would have accurately predicted the outcome of an event once that outcome is actually known.

- *Revision bias* is the tendency of decision makers to assume that when an object or idea has been changed (revised) in some way, it's actually been improved and is better than the original, regardless of whether it truly is better.

How can managers avoid the negative effects of these decision errors and biases? **1** Be aware of them and then don't use them! **2** Pay attention to "how" decisions are made, try to identify heuristics being used, and critically evaluate how appropriate those are. **3** Ask colleagues to help identify weaknesses in decision-making style and then work on improving those weaknesses.

What Are the 3 Approaches Managers Can Use to Make Decisions?

2-2 Explain the three approaches managers can use to make decisions.

Decision making is the essence of management.[11]

- Everyone in an organization makes decisions, _but_ it's particularly important to managers.
- Managers _make decisions_—mostly routine ones like which employee will work what shift, what information to include in a report, how to resolve a customer's complaint, etc.—as they **plan, organize, lead**, and **control**. See Exhibit 2–6.

Exhibit 2–6 Decisions Managers May Make

Planning
■ What are the organization's long-term objectives?
■ What strategies will best achieve those objectives?
■ What should the organization's short-term objectives be?
■ How difficult should individual goals be?

Leading
■ How do I handle unmotivated employees?
■ What is the most effective leadership style in a given situation?
■ How will a specific change affect worker productivity?
■ When is the right time to stimulate conflict?

Organizing
■ How many employees should I have report directly to me?
■ How much centralization should there be in an organization?
■ How should jobs be designed?
■ When should the organization implement a different structure?

Controlling
■ What activities in the organization need to be controlled?
■ How should those activities be controlled?
■ When is a performance deviation significant?
■ What type of management information system should the organization have?

Source: Robbins, Stephen P., Coulter, Mary, _Management_, 13th Ed., © 2016, p. 45. Reprinted and electronically reproduced by permission of Pearson Education, Inc., New York, NY.

McCarony/Fotolia

- Managers _want to be good decision makers_ and _exhibit good decision-making behaviors_ so they appear **competent** and **intelligent** to their boss, employees, and coworkers.

Here are the 3 approaches managers use to make decisions:

1 Rational Model

- This approach assumes: Decision makers ACT RATIONALLY.[12] How? By using **rational decision making**; that is, by making logical and consistent choices to maximize value.[13]

rational decision making
Describes choices that are consistent and value-maximizing within specified constraints

(Check out the two decision-making tools described in the Managing Technology in Today's Workplace box on p. 74.)

"Rational" decision makers and decisions:

Should Be:	Can Ever Be?
Fully objective and logical ·······►	Can we ever be fully objective and logical?
Problem is clear and unambiguous ·······►	Can problems ever be totally clear and unambiguous?
Clear and specific goal regarding decision ·······►	Can a goal ever be made that clear and specific?
All possible alternatives and consequences known ·······►	Can all possible alternatives and consequences ever be known?
Alternative selected maximizes likelihood of achieving goal ·······►	Can any alternative ever really do that?
Organization's best interests are considered ·······►	Managers should do this but may face factors beyond their control.

Bottom line: Although rationality is based on clarity, objectivity, logic, and complete knowledge, it's not a very realistic approach.

2

Bounded Rationality

iQoncept/Fotolia

- The **bounded rationality** approach assumes that managers make rational decisions but are limited (bounded) by their ability to process information.[14]

- Most decisions managers make don't fit the assumption of perfect rationality.

- No one can possibly analyze _all_ information on _all_ alternatives so they . . .

- **satisfice**—that is, accept solutions that are "good enough," rather than spend time and other resources trying to maximize. *(See Classic Concepts in Today's Workplace box on p. 73.)*

Example: As a newly graduated finance major, you look for a job as a financial planner—minimum salary of $55k, and within 100 miles of your hometown. After searching several different options, you accept a job as a business credit analyst at a bank 50 miles away at a starting salary of $53k. HOORAY! If, however, you'd *maximized*—that is, continued to search all possible alternatives—you'd have eventually found this financial planning job at a trust company 25 miles away with a starting salary of $59k. However, the first job offer was *satisfactory*—"good enough"—and you took it! Your decision making was still rational . . . but within the bounds of your abilities to process information!

bounded rationality
Making decisions that are rational within the limits of a manager's ability to process information

satisfice
Accepting solutions that are "good enough"

Who: Bounded rationality and satisficing are the work of Herbert A. Simon, who won a Nobel Prize in economics for his work on decision making.

What: His primary concern was how people use logic and psychology to make choices and proposed that individuals were limited in their ability to "grasp the present and anticipate the future." This bounded rationality made it difficult for them to "achieve the best possible decisions," but they made "good enough" or "satisficing" choices.[15]

How: Simon's important contributions to management thinking stemmed from his belief that understanding organizations

When faced with too many choices, we SATISFICE!

meant studying the complex network of decisional processes that were inherent.

Why: His work in bounded rationality helps us make sense of how managers can behave rationally and still make satisfactory decisions, even given the limits of their capacity to process information.

Discussion Questions:

1 Is satisficing settling for second best? What do you think? In your "assigned" group, discuss your opinions about this.

2 How does knowing about bounded rationality help managers be better decision makers?

- Most decisions don't fit the assumptions of perfect rationality, so managers satisfice. But decisions can also be influenced by (1) the organization's culture, (2) internal politics, (3) power considerations, and (4) a phenomenon called:

escalation of commitment An increased commitment to a previous decision despite evidence that it may have been wrong.[16]

- *Why* would anyone—especially managers—escalate commitment to a bad decision?

  — Hate to admit that initial decision may have been flawed.

  — Don't want to search for new alternatives.

    Bottom line: Bounded rationality is a more realistic approach as managers are rational within their abilities to process information about alternatives.

3 Intuition and Managerial Decision Making

When deciding yay or nay on new shoe styles, Diego Della Valle, chairman of Tod's luxury shoe empire, doesn't use common decision-making tools like focus groups or poll testing. Nope…he wears the shoes for a few days. If they're not to his liking, his verdict: No! **His intuitive decision-making approach has helped make Tod's a successful multinational company.**[17]

Smalik/Fotolia

- This approach assumes that managers make decisions on the basis of experience, feelings, and accumulated judgment.

  — Described as subconscious reasoning.[18]

  — Five different aspects of intuition: See Exhibit 2–7.[19]

Almost **half of managers rely on intuition** more often than formal analysis **to make decisions** about their companies.[20]

Exhibit 2–7 What Is Intuition?

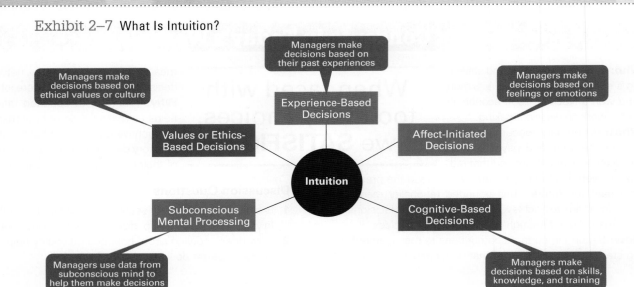

Sources: Based on J. Evans, "Intuition and Reasoning: A Dual-Process Perspective," *Psychological Inquiry*, October–December 2010, pp. 313–26; T. Betsch and A. Blockner, "Intuition in Judgment and Decision Making: Extensive Thinking Without Effort," *Psychological Inquiry*, October–December 2010, pp. 279–94; R. Lange and J. Houran, "A Transliminal View of Intuitions in the Workplace," *North American Journal of Psychology*, 12, no. 3 (2010), pp. 501–16; E. Dane and M. G. Pratt, "Exploring Intuition and Its Role in Managerial Decision Making," *Academy of Management Review*, January 2007, pp. 33–54; M. H. Bazerman and D. Chugh, "Decisions without Blinders," *Harvard Business Review*, January 2006, pp. 88–97; C. C. Miller and R. D. Ireland, "Intuition in Strategic Decision Making: Friend or Foe in the Fast-Paced 21st Century," *Academy of Management Executive*, February 2005, pp. 19–30; E. Sadler-Smith and E. Shefy, "The Intuitive Executive: Understanding and Applying 'Gut Feel' in Decision-Making," *Academy of Management Executive*, November 2004, pp. 76–91; and L. A. Burke and M. K. Miller, "Taking the Mystery Out of Intuitive Decision Making," *Academy of Management Executive*, October 1999, pp. 91–99.

- Bottom line: Intuitive decision making can be useful to managers, especially when following these suggestions:

  — Use it to complement, not replace, other decision-making approaches.[21]

  — Look to act quickly with limited information because of past experience with a similar problem.

  — Pay attention to the intense feelings and emotions experienced when making decisions. The payoff? Better decisions![22]

Managing Technology in Today's Workplace

MAKING BETTER DECISIONS WITH TECHNOLOGY

Information technology is providing managers with a wealth of decision-making support.[23] Two decision-making tools include *expert systems* and *neural networks*.

EXPERT SYSTEMS:

- Encode relevant expert experience using software programs.
- Act as that expert in analyzing and solving unstructured problems.
- Guide users through problems by asking sequential questions about the situation and drawing conclusions based on answers given.
- Make decisions easier for users through programmed rules modeled on actual reasoning processes of experts.
- Allow employees and lower-level managers to make high-quality decisions normally made only by upper-level managers.

NEURAL NETWORKS:

- Use computer software to imitate the structure of brain cells and connections among them.

- Can distinguish patterns and trends too subtle or complex for human beings.
- Can perceive correlations among hundreds of variables, unlike our limited human brain capacity, which can only easily assimilate no more than two or three variables at once.
- Can perform many operations simultaneously, recognizing patterns, making associations, generalizing about problems not exposed to before, and learning through experience.
- Example: banks using neural network systems to catch fraudulent credit card activities in a matter of hours, not days.

Discussion Questions:

3 Can a manager ever have too much data when making decisions? Explain.

4 How can technology help managers make better decisions?

What Types of Decisions and Decision-Making Conditions Do Managers Face?

2-3 Describe the types of decisions and decision-making conditions managers face.

Laura Ipsen is a senior vice president and general manager at Smart Grid, a business unit of Cisco Systems, which is working on helping utility companies find ways to build open, interconnected systems. She describes her job as "like having to put together a 1,000-piece puzzle, but with no box top with the picture of what it looks like and with some pieces missing."[24] Decision making in that type of environment is quite different from decision making done by a manager of a local Gap store.

The types of problems managers face in decision-making situations often determine how it's handled. In this section, we describe a categorization scheme for problems and types of decisions and then show how the type of decision making a manager uses should reflect the characteristics of the problem.

How Do Problems Differ?

Some problems are straightforward. The goal of the decision maker is clear, the problem familiar, and information about the problem easily defined and complete. Examples might include a supplier who is late with an important delivery, a customer who wants to return an Internet purchase, a TV news team that has to respond to an unexpected and fast-breaking event, or a university that must help a student who is applying for financial aid. Such situations are called **structured problems**.

Many situations faced by managers, however, are **unstructured problems**. They are new or unusual. Information about such problems is ambiguous or incomplete. Examples of unstructured problems include the decision to enter a new market segment, hire an architect to design a new office park, or merge two organizations. So, too, is the decision to invest in a new, unproven technology. For instance, when Takeshi Idezawa founded his mobile messaging app LINE, he faced a situation best described as an unstructured problem.[25]

How Does a Manager Make Programmed Decisions?

Decisions are also divided into two categories: programmed and nonprogrammed (described in the next section). **Programmed**, or routine, **decisions** are the most efficient way to handle structured problems.

An auto mechanic damages a customer's rim while changing a tire. What does the shop manager do? Because the company probably has a standardized method for handling this type of problem, it's considered a programmed decision. For example, the manager may replace the rim at the company's expense. *Decisions are programmed* to the extent that (1) they are repetitive and routine and (2) a specific approach has been worked out for handling them. Because the problem is well structured, the manager does not have to go to the trouble and expense of an involved decision process. Programmed decision making is relatively simple and tends to rely heavily on previous solutions. The develop-the-alternatives stage in the decision-making process is either nonexistent or given little attention. Why? Because once

structured problem
A straightforward, familiar, and easily defined problem

unstructured problem
A problem that is new or unusual for which information is ambiguous or incomplete

programmed decision
A repetitive decision that can be handled using a routine approach

procedure
A series of interrelated, sequential steps used to respond to a structured problem

rule
An explicit statement that tells employees what can or cannot be done

policy
A guideline for making decisions

nonprogrammed decision
A unique and nonrecurring decision that requires a custom-made solution

the structured problem is defined, its solution is usually self-evident or at least reduced to only a few alternatives that are familiar and that have proved successful in the past. In many cases, programmed decision making becomes decision making by precedent. Managers simply do what they and others have done previously in the same situation. The damaged rim does not require the manager to identify and weight decision criteria or develop a long list of possible solutions.

For structured problems, use: — Procedures
— Rules
— Policies

PROCEDURES. A **procedure** is a series of interrelated sequential steps that a manager can use when responding to a well-structured problem. The only real difficulty is identifying the problem. Once the problem is clear, so is the procedure. For instance, a purchasing manager receives a request from computing services for licensing arrangements to install 250 copies of Norton by Symantec antivirus software. The purchasing manager knows that a definite procedure is in place for handling this decision. Has the requisition been properly filled out and approved? If not, he can send the requisition back with a note explaining what is deficient. If the request is complete, the approximate costs are estimated. If the total exceeds $8,500, three bids must be obtained. If the total is $8,500 or less, only one vendor need be identified and the order placed. The decision-making process is merely executing a simple series of sequential steps.

RULES. A **rule** is an explicit statement that tells a manager what he or she must—or must not—do. Rules are frequently used by managers who confront a structured problem because they're simple to follow and ensure consistency. In the preceding example, the $8,500 cutoff rule simplifies the purchasing manager's decision about when to use multiple bids.

Catering managers for ballroom events use policies, procedures, and rules in making programmed decisions. These guidelines help the managers perform their day-today operations efficiently, ensure compliance with food safety and health regulations, and help provide consistent customer service.

POLICIES. A third guide for making programmed decisions is a **policy**. It provides guidelines to channel a manager's thinking in a specific direction. The statement that "we promote from within, whenever possible" is an example of a policy. In contrast to a rule, a policy establishes parameters for the decision maker rather than specifically stating what should or should not be done. Policies often leave interpretation up to the decision maker. It's in such instances that ethical standards/dilemmas may come into play.

How Do Nonprogrammed Decisions Differ from Programmed Decisions?

When problems are unstructured, managers must rely on **nonprogrammed decisions** in order to develop unique solutions. Examples of nonprogrammed decisions include deciding whether to acquire another organization, deciding which global markets offer the most potential, or deciding whether to sell off an unprofitable division. Such decisions are unique and nonrecurring. When a manager confronts an unstructured problem, no cut-and-dried solution is available. A custom-made, nonprogrammed response is required.

SeventyFour/Shutterstock

The creation of a new organizational strategy is a nonprogrammed decision. This decision is different from previous organizational decisions because the issue is new; a different set of environmental factors exists, and other conditions have changed. For example, Amazon's strategy to "get big fast" helped the company grow tremendously. But this strategy came at a cost—perennial financial losses. To turn a profit, CEO Jeff Bezos made decisions regarding how to organize orders, anticipate demand, ship more efficiently, establish foreign partnerships, and create a marketplace for other sellers to sell their books on Amazon. As a result, Amazon has moved toward profitability.

How Are Problems, Types of Decisions, and Organizational Level Integrated?

Exhibit 2–8 describes the relationship among types of problems, types of decisions, and level in the organization. Structured problems? Use programmed decision making. Unstructured problems? Use nonprogrammed decision making. Lower-level managers essentially confront familiar and repetitive problems so they most typically rely on programmed decisions such as standard operating procedures. However, as managers move up the organizational hierarchy, the problems they confront are likely to become less structured. Why? Because lower-level managers handle the routine decisions themselves and only pass upward decisions that they find unique or difficult. Similarly, managers pass down routine decisions to their employees so they can spend their time on more problematic issues.

MANAGERIAL DECISIONS: **Real World—Real Advice**

- Few managerial decisions are either fully programmed or fully nonprogrammed. Most fall somewhere in between.
- At the top level, most problems that managers face *are* unique—that is, nonprogrammed.
- Programmed routines may help even in situations requiring a nonprogrammed decision.
- Top-level managers often create policies, standard operating procedures, and rules—that is, programmed decision making—for lower-level managers in order to control costs and other variables.
- Programmed decision making can facilitate organizational efficiency—maybe that's why it's so popular!
- Programmed decisions minimize the need for managers to exercise discretion.
- Discretion—the ability to make sound judgments—costs money because it's an uncommon and valuable quality and managers who have it are paid more.
- Even in some programmed decisions, individual judgment may be needed.

Exhibit 2–8 Types of Problems, Types of Decisions, and Organizational Level

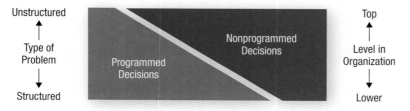

certainty
A situation in which a decision maker can make accurate decisions because all outcomes are known

risk
A situation in which a decision maker is able to estimate the likelihood of certain outcomes

uncertainty
A situation in which a decision maker has neither certainty nor reasonable probability estimates available

What Decision-Making Conditions Do Managers Face?

When making decisions, managers face three different conditions: certainty, risk, and uncertainty. Let's look at each.

The ideal situation for making decisions is one of **certainty**, which is a situation where a manager can make accurate decisions because the outcome of every alternative is known. For example, when South Dakota's state treasurer decides where to deposit excess state funds, he knows exactly the interest rate being offered by each financial institution and the amount that will be earned on the funds. He is certain about the outcomes of each alternative. As you might expect, most managerial decisions aren't like this.

Far more common is a situation of **risk**, conditions in which the decision maker is able to estimate the likelihood of certain outcomes. Under risk, managers have historical data from past personal experiences or secondary information that lets them assign probabilities to different alternatives.

What happens if you face a decision where you're not certain about the outcomes and can't even make reasonable probability estimates? We call this condition **uncertainty**. Managers do face decision-making situations of uncertainty. Under these conditions, the choice of alternative is influenced by the limited amount of available information and by the psychological orientation of the decision maker.

How Do Groups Make Decisions?

2-4 Discuss group decision making.

Work teams are common at Amazon. Jeff Bezos, founder and CEO, uses a **"two-pizza" philosophy**—that is, a team should be small enough that it can be fed with two pizzas.[26]

Do managers make a lot of decisions in groups? You bet they do! Many decisions in organizations, especially important decisions that have far-reaching effects on organizational activities and people, are typically made in groups. It's a rare organization that doesn't at some time use committees, task forces, review panels, work teams, or similar groups as vehicles for making decisions. Why? In many cases, these groups represent the people who will be most affected by the decisions being made. Because of their expertise, these people are often best qualified to make decisions that affect them.

Studies tell us that managers spend a significant portion of their time in meetings. Undoubtedly, a large portion of that time is involved with defining problems, arriving at solutions to those problems, and determining the means for implementing the solutions. It's possible, in fact, for groups to be assigned any of the eight steps in the decision-making process.

What Are the Advantages and Disadvantages of Group Decision Making?

Decisions can be made by individuals or by groups—each approach has its own set of strengths and neither is ideal for all situations.

Advantages of Group Decisions

- *More complete information.*[27]
- *Diversity of experiences and perspectives* brought to the decision process.[28]
- *More alternatives generated* due to greater quantity and diversity of information, especially when group members represent different specialties.
- *Increased acceptance of a solution* by having people who will be affected by a certain solution and who will help implement it participate in the decision.[29]
- *Increased legitimacy* because the group decision-making process is consistent with democratic ideals, and decisions made by groups may be perceived as more legitimate than those made by a single person, which can appear autocratic and arbitrary.

Disadvantages of Group Decisions

- *Time-consuming*—assembling the group, getting decisions made.
- *Minority domination* can unduly influence the final decision because group members are never perfectly equal—they differ in rank, experience, knowledge about the problem, influence on other members, verbal skills, assertiveness, etc.[30]
- *Ambiguous responsibility.* Group members share responsibility, BUT who is actually responsible for final outcome?[31] Individual decision—it's clear. Group decision—it's not.
- *Pressures to conform.* Have you ever been in a group where your views didn't match the group's consensus views and you remained silent? Maybe others felt the same way and also remained silent. This is what Irving Janis called **groupthink**, a form of conformity in which group members withhold deviant, minority, or unpopular views in order to give the *appearance of agreement.*[32]

The Tragedy of Groupthink

<u>What It Does</u>

Hinders decision making, possibly jeopardizing the quality of the decision by:

- Undermining critical thinking in the group.
- Affecting a group's ability to objectively appraise alternatives.
- Deterring individuals from critically appraising unusual, minority, or unpopular views.

<u>How Does It Occur?</u>

Here are some things to watch out for:

- Group members rationalize resistance to assumptions.
- Members directly pressure those who express doubts or question the majority's views and arguments.
- Members who have doubts or differing points of view avoid deviating from what appears to be group consensus.
- An illusion of unanimity prevails. Full agreement is *assumed* if no one speaks up.

<u>What Can Be Done to Minimize Groupthink?</u>

- Encourage cohesiveness.
- Foster open discussion.
- Have an impartial leader who seeks input from all members.[33]

When Are Groups Most Effective?

Well, that depends on the *criteria you use for defining effectiveness*, such as accuracy, speed, creativity, and acceptance. Group decisions tend to be more accurate. On average, groups tend to make better decisions than individuals, although groupthink may occur.[34] However, if decision

> **groupthink**
> When a group exerts extensive pressure on an individual to withhold his or her different views in order to appear to be in agreement

Making Ethical Decisions in Today's Workplace

CVS Health Corporation announced in early 2018 that it would stop "materially" altering the beauty images used in its marketing materials that appear in its stores and on its websites and social media channels.[35] Although the change applies to the marketing materials it creates, the drugstore chain has also asked global brand partners—including Revlon, L'Oreal, and Johnson & Johnson—to join its effort. The company will use a watermark—the "CVS Beauty Mark"—on images that have not been altered. What does that mean? You're seeing real, not digitally modified, persons. The person featured in those images did not have their size, shape, skin or eye color, wrinkles, or other characteristics enhanced or changed. The company's goal is for all images in the beauty sections of CVS's stores to reflect the "transparency" commitment by 2020. Not surprisingly, there are pros and cons to this decision. And not surprisingly, there are ethical considerations associated with the decision.

Discussion Questions:

5 Striving for more realistic beauty/body image ideals: Who are potential stakeholders in this situation and what stake do they have in this decision?

6 From a generic viewpoint, how do ethical issues affect decision making? In this specific story, what potential ethical considerations do you see in the decision by CVS to stop altering beauty images and start using more realistic images?

brainstorming
An idea-generating process that encourages alternatives while withholding criticism

nominal group technique
A decision-making technique in which group members are physically present but operate independently

electronic meeting
A type of nominal group technique in which participants are linked by computer

effectiveness is defined in terms of speed, individuals are superior. If creativity is important, groups tend to be more effective than individuals. And if effectiveness means the degree of acceptance the final solution achieves, the nod again goes to the group.

The *effectiveness* of group decision making is *also influenced by the size of the group*. The larger the group, the greater the opportunity for heterogeneous representation. On the other hand, a larger group requires more coordination and more time to allow all members to contribute. This means that groups probably shouldn't be too large: A minimum of five to a maximum of about fifteen members is best. Groups of five to seven individuals appear to be the most effective (remember Amazon's "two-pizza" rule!). Because five and seven are odd numbers, decision deadlocks are avoided. You can't consider effectiveness without also assessing efficiency. Groups almost always stack up as a poor second in efficiency to the individual decision maker. Yet, with few exceptions, group decision making consumes more work hours than does individual decision making.

Bottom Line on Using Groups or Individuals to Make Decisions: Do **increases in effectiveness offset losses in efficiency?**

How Can You Improve Group Decision Making?

Use these techniques to make group decisions more creative: (1) brainstorming, (2) the nominal group technique, and (3) electronic meetings.

WHAT IS BRAINSTORMING? **Brainstorming** is a relatively simple idea-generating process that specifically encourages any and all alternatives while withholding criticism of those alternatives.[36] In a typical brainstorming session, a half-dozen to a dozen people sit around a table. Of course, technology is changing where that "table" is. The group leader states the problem in a clear manner that is understood by all participants. Members then shout out, offer up, fire off, "freewheel" as many alternatives as they can in a given time. No criticism is allowed, and all the alternatives are recorded for later discussion and analysis.[37] And not surprisingly, when brainstorming, destructive group dynamics need to be avoided.[38] (We'll further explore group dynamics in Chapter 9.)

HOW DOES THE NOMINAL GROUP TECHNIQUE WORK? The **nominal group technique** helps groups arrive at a preferred solution by restricting discussion during the decision-making process.[39] Group members must be present, as in a traditional committee meeting, but they're required to operate independently. They secretly write a list of general problem areas or potential solutions to a problem. The chief advantage of this technique is that it permits the group to meet formally but does not restrict independent thinking or lead to groupthink, as can often happen in a traditional interacting group.[40]

HOW CAN ELECTRONIC MEETINGS ENHANCE GROUP DECISION MAKING? Another approach to group decision making blends the nominal group technique with information technology and is called the **electronic meeting**.

Once the technology is in place, the concept is simple. Numerous people sit around a table with laptops or tablets. Participants are presented issues and type their responses onto their computers. Individual comments, as well as aggregate votes, are displayed on a projection screen in the room.

The major advantages of electronic meetings are anonymity, honesty, and speed.[41] Participants can anonymously type any message they want, and it will flash on the screen for all to see with a keystroke. It allows people to be brutally honest with no penalty. And it's fast—chitchat is eliminated, discussions do not digress, and many participants can "talk" at once without interrupting the others.

Electronic meetings *are* significantly faster and much cheaper than traditional face-to-face meetings.[42] Nestlé, for instance, uses the approach for many of its meetings, especially globally focused meetings.[43] However, as with all other forms of group activities, electronic meetings have some drawbacks. Those who type quickly can outshine those who may be verbally eloquent but lousy typists; those with the best ideas don't get credit for them; and the process lacks the informational richness of face-to-face oral communication. However, group decision making is likely to include extensive usage of electronic meetings.[44]

A variation of the electronic meeting is the videoconference. Using technology to link different locations, people can have face-to-face meetings even when they're thousands of miles apart. This capability has enhanced feedback among the members, saved countless hours of business travel, and ultimately saved companies such as Nestlé and Logitech hundreds of thousands of dollars. As a result, they're more effective in their meetings and have increased the efficiency with which decisions are made.[45]

Brainstorming is an important way of improving group decision making at SAP AG, a provider of enterprise software. Employees working at SAP headquarters in Walldorf, Germany, use white boards during a brainstorming session to develop product and service innovations following the company's decision to target the growing online software market.

Krisztian Bocsi/Bloomberg/Getty Images

What Contemporary Decision-Making Issues Do Managers Face?

2-5 Discuss contemporary issues in managerial decision making.

Bad decisions can cost MILLIONS!

Today's business world revolves around making decisions, often risky ones, with incomplete or inadequate information, and under intense time pressure. Most managers make one decision after another; and as if that weren't challenging enough, more is at stake than ever before since bad decisions can cost millions. We're going to look at three important issues—❶ national culture, ❷ creativity and design thinking, and ❸ big data—that managers face in today's fast-moving and global world.

How Does National Culture Affect Managers' Decision Making?

Research shows that, to some extent, decision-making practices differ from country to country.[46] The way decisions are made—whether by group, by team members, participatively, or autocratically by an individual manager—and the degree of risk a decision maker is willing to take are just two examples of decision variables that reflect a country's cultural environment. For example, in India, power distance and uncertainty avoidance (see Chapter 3) are high. There, only very senior-level managers make decisions, and they're likely to make safe decisions. In contrast, in Sweden, power distance and uncertainty avoidance are low. Swedish managers are not afraid to make risky decisions. Senior managers in Sweden also push decisions down to lower levels. They encourage lower-level managers and employees to take part in decisions that affect them. In countries such as Egypt, where time pressures are low, managers make decisions at a slower and more deliberate pace than managers do in the United States. And in Italy, where history and traditions are valued, managers tend to rely on tried and proven alternatives to resolve problems.

Punit Paranjpe/AFP/Getty Images

Rajesh Gopinathan is the chief executive officer and managing director of Tata Consultancy Services (TCS), a leading global IT solutions and consulting firm based in Mumbai, India. In India, where power distance and uncertainty avoidance are high, Gopinathan takes a long-term perspective and has an immense influence in making corporate strategic decisions.

Decision making in Japan is much more group oriented than in the United States.[47] The Japanese value conformity and cooperation. Before making decisions, Japanese CEOs collect a large amount of information, which is then used in consensus-forming group decisions called **ringisei**. Because employees in Japanese organizations have high job security, managerial decisions take a long-term perspective rather than focusing on short-term profits, as is often the practice in the United States.

Senior managers in France and Germany also adapt their decision styles to their countries' cultures. In France, for instance, autocratic decision making is widely practiced, and managers avoid risks. Managerial styles in Germany reflect the German culture's concern for structure and order. Consequently, German organizations generally operate under extensive rules and regulations. Managers have well-defined responsibilities and accept that decisions must go through channels.

As managers deal with employees from diverse cultures, they need to recognize common and accepted behavior when asking them to make decisions. Some individuals may not be as comfortable as others with being closely involved in decision making, or they may not be willing to experiment with something radically different. *Managers who accommodate the diversity in decision-making philosophies and practices can expect a high payoff if they capture the perspectives and strengths that a diverse workforce offers.*

Why Are Creativity and Design Thinking Important in Decision Making?

How do most of you take and save photos today? It's highly unlikely that you've ever had to insert film into a camera, shoot the photos you wanted while hoping you "got the shot," remove the film from the camera, take the film to be processed, and then pick up your photos later. When Apple, Facebook, Snapchat, and Instagram wanted to make this process easier and better, someone making decisions about future products had to *be creative* and they had to *use design thinking*. Both are important to decision makers today.

UNDERSTANDING CREATIVITY. A decision maker needs **creativity**: the ability to produce novel and useful ideas. These ideas are different from what's been done before but are also appropriate to the problem or opportunity presented. Why is creativity important to decision making? It allows the decision maker to appraise and understand the problem more fully, including "seeing" problems others can't see. However, creativity's most obvious value is in helping the decision maker identify all viable alternatives.

Most people have creative potential that they can use when confronted with a decision-making problem. But to unleash that potential, they have to get out of the psychological ruts most of us get into and learn how to think about a problem in divergent ways.

How can you **unleash YOUR** creativity?

We can start with the obvious. People differ in their inherent creativity. Einstein, Edison, Dali, and Mozart were individuals of exceptional creativity. Not surprisingly, exceptional creativity is scarce.

A study of lifetime creativity of 461 men and women found that:

- Fewer than 1 percent were exceptionally creative.
- 10 percent were highly creative.
- About 60 percent were somewhat creative.

ringisei
Japanese consensus-forming group decisions

creativity
The ability to produce novel and useful ideas

These findings suggest that most of us have some creative potential, *if* we can learn to unleash it.

Given that most people have the capacity to be at least moderately creative, what can individuals and organizations do to stimulate employee creativity? The best answer to this question lies in a three-component model of creativity based on an extensive body of research.[48] This model proposes that individual creativity essentially requires ❶ expertise, ❷ creative-thinking skills, and ❸ intrinsic task motivation. Studies confirm that the higher the level of each of these three components, the higher the creativity.

Expertise is the foundation of all creative work. Dali's understanding of art and Einstein's knowledge of physics were necessary conditions for them to be able to make creative contributions to their fields. And you wouldn't expect someone with a minimal knowledge of programming to be highly creative as a software engineer. The potential for creativity is enhanced when individuals have abilities, knowledge, proficiencies, and similar expertise in their fields of endeavor.

The second component is *creative-thinking skills*. It encompasses personality characteristics associated with creativity, the ability to use analogies, as well as the talent to see the familiar in a different light. For instance, the following individual traits have been found to be associated with the development of creative ideas: intelligence, independence, self-confidence, risk taking, internal locus of control, tolerance for ambiguity, and perseverance in the face of frustration. The effective use of analogies allows decision makers to apply an idea from one context to another. One of the most famous examples in which analogy resulted in a creative breakthrough was Alexander Graham Bell's observation that it might be possible to take concepts that operate in the ear and apply them to his "talking box." He noticed that the bones in the ear are operated by a delicate, thin membrane. He wondered why, then, a thicker and stronger piece of membrane shouldn't be able to move a piece of steel. Out of that analogy the telephone was conceived. Of course, some people have developed their skill at being able to see problems in a new way. They're able to make the strange familiar and the familiar strange. For instance, most of us think of hens laying eggs. But how many of us have considered that a hen is only an egg's way of making another egg?

The final component is *intrinsic task motivation*—the desire to work on something because it's interesting, involving, exciting, satisfying, or personally challenging. This motivational component is what turns creative *potential* into *actual* creative ideas. It determines the extent to which individuals fully engage their expertise and creative skills. So creative people often love their work, to the point of seeming obsessed. Importantly, an individual's work environment and the organization's culture (which we discussed in Chapter 4) can have a significant effect on intrinsic motivation.

Knowing what can enhance creativity is important, but you also need to recognize what can block it. Recognizing these stumbling blocks to creativity can be the first step in removing them!

5 organizational factors that can block your creativity:

- expected evaluation—focusing on how your work is going to be evaluated
- surveillance—being watched while you're working
- external motivators—emphasizing external, tangible rewards
- competition—facing win–lose situations with your peers
- constrained choices—being given limits on how you can do your work.

Apple—a great example of how **design thinking benefits** an organization.

UNDERSTANDING DESIGN THINKING. The way managers approach decision making—using a rational and analytical mindset in identifying problems, coming up with alternatives, evaluating alternatives, and choosing one of those alternatives—may not be the best and certainly not the only choice in today's environment. That's where design thinking comes in. **Design thinking** has been described as "approaching management problems as designers approach design problems."[49] More organizations are beginning to recognize how design thinking can benefit them.[50] For instance, Apple has long been celebrated for its design thinking. The company's lead designer, Jonathan "Jony" Ive (who was behind some of Apple's most successful products including the iPod and iPhone) had this to say about Apple's design approach, "We try to develop products that seem somehow inevitable. That leave you with the sense that that's the only possible solution that makes sense."[51]

While many managers don't deal specifically with product or process design decisions, they still make decisions about work issues that arise, and design thinking can help them be better decision makers. What can the design thinking approach teach managers about making better decisions? Well, it begins with (1) the first step in the decision-making process of identifying problems. Design thinking says that managers should look at problem identification collaboratively and integratively with the goal of gaining a deep understanding of the situation. They should look not only at the rational aspects, but also at the emotional elements. Then invariably, of course, design thinking would (2) influence how managers identify and evaluate alternatives—steps 2 through 5 in the decision-making process. A traditional manager (educated in a business school, of course) would look at the alternatives, rationally evaluate them, and select the one with the highest payoff. However, using design thinking, a manager would say, "What is something completely new that would be lovely if it existed but doesn't now?"[52] Design thinking means opening up your perspective and gaining insights by using observation and inquiry skills, and not relying simply on rational analysis. We're not saying that rational analysis isn't needed; we are saying that there's more needed in making effective decisions, especially in today's world.

How is big data changing the way managers make decisions?

Big Data Today.

- Amazon.com, Earth's biggest online retailer, earns billions of dollars of revenue each year—estimated at one-third of sales—from its "personalization technologies" such as product recommendations and computer-generated e-mails.[53]
- At AutoZone, decision makers use software that gleans information from a variety of databases and allows its 5,000-plus local stores to target deals and hopefully reduce the chance that customers will walk away without making a purchase. AutoZone's chief information officer says, "We think this is the direction of the future."[54]
- It's not just businesses that are exploiting big data. A team of San Francisco researchers was able to predict the magnitude of a disease outbreak halfway around the world by analyzing phone patterns from mobile phone usage.[55]
- Follain, the natural beauty chain, is using big data to find customers the best combination of products for their specific needs and provide them with the most effective natural beauty brands on the market.[56]
- Restaurants are using big data to learn more about their customers. Much of that data comes from OpenTable, an online restaurant reservations booking company.[57]

Yes, there's a ton of information out there. And businesses—and other organizations—are finally figuring out how to use it. So what is **big data**? It's the vast amount of quantifiable

design thinking
Approaching management problems as designers approach design problems

big data
The vast amount of quantifiable information that can be analyzed by highly sophisticated data processing

information that can be analyzed by highly sophisticated data processing. One IT expert described big data with "3V's: high volume, high velocity, and/or high variety information assets."[58]

What does big data have to do with decision making? A lot, as you can imagine. With this type of data at hand, decision makers have very powerful tools to help them make decisions. However, experts caution that collecting and analyzing data for data's sake is wasted effort. Goals are needed when collecting and using this type of information. As one individual said, "Big data is a descendant of Taylor's 'scientific management' of more than a century ago."[59] While Taylor used a stopwatch to time and monitor a worker's every movement, big data uses math modeling, predictive algorithms, and artificial intelligence (AI) software to measure and monitor people and machines like never before.[60] (See Case Application #2 at the end of the chapter.) But managers need to really examine and evaluate how big data might contribute to their decision making before jumping in with both feet.

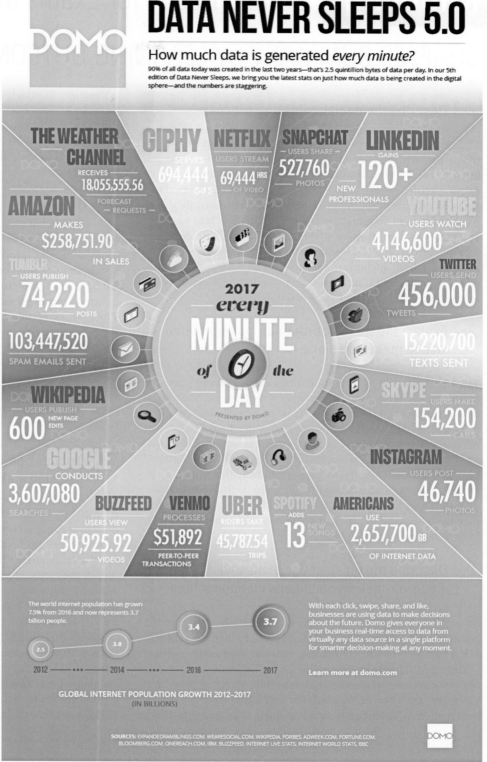

Data Never Sleeps 5.0. DOMO, Inc.

CHAPTER SUMMARY BY LEARNING OUTCOME

2-1 Describe the decision-making process.

The decision-making process consists of eight steps: (1) identify a problem, (2) identify decision criteria, (3) weight the criteria, (4) develop alternatives, (5) analyze alternatives, (6) select alternative, (7) implement alternative, and (8) evaluate decision effectiveness. As managers make decisions, they may use heuristics to simplify the process, which can lead to errors and biases in their decision making. The 13 common decision-making errors and biases include overconfidence, immediate gratification, anchoring, selective perception, confirmation, framing, availability, representation, randomness, sunk costs, self-serving bias, hindsight, and revision bias.

2-2 Explain the three approaches managers can use to make decisions.

The first approach is the rational model. The assumptions of rationality are as follows: The problem is clear and unambiguous; a single, well-defined goal is to be achieved; all alternatives and consequences are known; and the final choice will maximize the payoff. The second approach, bounded rationality, says that managers make rational decisions but are bounded (limited) by their ability to process information. In this approach, managers satisfice, which is when decision makers accept solutions that are good enough. Finally, intuitive decision making is making decisions on the basis of experience, feelings, and accumulated judgment.

2-3 Describe the types of decisions and decision-making conditions managers face.

Programmed decisions are repetitive decisions that can be handled by a routine approach and are used when the problem being resolved is straightforward, familiar, and easily defined (structured). Nonprogrammed decisions are unique decisions that require a custom-made solution and are used when the problems are new or unusual (unstructured) and for which information is ambiguous or incomplete. Certainty involves a situation in which a manager can make accurate decisions because all outcomes are known. With risk, a manager can estimate the likelihood of certain outcomes in a situation. Uncertainty is a situation in which a manager is not certain about the outcomes and can't even make reasonable probability estimates.

2-4 Discuss group decision making.

Groups offer certain advantages when making decisions—more complete information, more alternatives, increased acceptance of a solution, and greater legitimacy. On the other hand, groups are time-consuming, can be dominated by a minority, create pressures to conform, and cloud responsibility. Three ways of improving group decision making are brainstorming (utilizing an idea-generating process that specifically encourages any and all alternatives while withholding any criticism of those alternatives), the nominal group technique (a technique that restricts discussion during the decision-making process), and electronic meetings (the most recent approach to group decision making, which blends the nominal group technique with sophisticated computer technology).

2-5 Discuss contemporary issues in managerial decision making.

As managers deal with employees from diverse cultures, they need to recognize common and accepted behavior when asking them to make decisions. Some individuals may not be as comfortable as others with being closely involved in decision making, or they may not be willing to experiment with something radically different. Also, managers need to be creative in their decision making because creativity allows them to appraise and understand the problem more fully, including "seeing" problems that others can't see. Design thinking also influences the way that managers approach decision making, especially in terms of identifying problems and how they identify and evaluate alternatives. Finally, big data is changing what and how decisions are made, but managers need to evaluate how big data might contribute to their decision making.

DISCUSSION QUESTIONS

2-1 Why is decision making often described as the essence of a manager's job?

2-2 Provide an eight-step illustration of any decision-making process undertaken by you.

2-3 As decision making is personalized, do you think bias often plays an important role for a CEO or a first-line manager? Explain the potential daily bias that managers may encounter.

2-4 What is intuitive decision making? In your opinion, when is this method best used? What are the major drawbacks of this managerial decision-making style?

2-5 Herbert A. Simon started work on bounded rationality and satisficing because of his hypothesis that people had a limited ability to grasp the present and anticipate the future. Discuss the problems associated with making decisions using the rational model.

2-6 Describe a decision you've made that closely aligns with the assumptions of perfect rationality. Compare this decision with the process you used to select your college. Did you depart from the rational model in your college decisions? Explain.

2-7 Explain how a manager might deal with making decisions under conditions of uncertainty.

2-8 Why do companies invest in nurturing group decision making rather than individual decision making? Explain the advantages and disadvantages of both techniques.

2-9 Why does a decision maker need to be creative? In which steps of the decision-making process is creativity likely to be most important?

2-10 What is big data? How can managers effectively use big data to improve their decision making? Should managers be cautious in using big data?

Applying: Getting Ready for the Workplace

Management Skill Builder | BEING A CREATIVE DECISION MAKER

Many decisions that managers make are routine, so they can fall back on experience and "what's worked in the past." But other decisions—especially those made by upper-level managers—are unique and haven't been confronted before. The uniqueness and variety of problems that managers face demand creativity—the ability to produce novel and useful ideas. If managers are to successfully progress upward in an organization, they'll find an increasing need to develop creative decisions. Creativity is partly a frame of mind. You need to expand your mind's capabilities—that is, open yourself up to new ideas. Every individual has the ability to improve his or her creativity, but many people simply don't try to develop that ability.

MyLab Management
PERSONAL INVENTORY ASSESSMENT

Go to **www.pearson.com/mylab/management** to complete the Personal Inventory Assessment related to this chapter.

P I A PERSONAL INVENTORY ASSESSMENT

Skill Basics

Creativity is a skill you can develop. Here are some suggestions on how you can do this:

- *Think of yourself as creative.* Research shows that if you think you can't be creative, you won't be. Believing in your ability to be creative is the first step in becoming more creative.

- *Pay attention to your intuition.* Every individual has a subconscious mind that works well. Sometimes answers will come to you when you least expect them. Listen to that "inner voice." In fact, most creative people will keep a notepad near their bed and write down ideas when the thoughts come to them.

- *Move away from your comfort zone.* Every individual has a comfort zone in which certainty exists. But creativity and the known often do not mix. To be creative, you need to move away from the status quo and focus your mind on something new.

- *Determine what you want to do.* This includes such things as taking time to understand a problem before beginning to try to resolve it, getting all the facts in mind, and trying to identify the most important facts.

- *Think outside the box.* Use analogies whenever possible (for example, could you approach your problem like a fish out of water and look at what the fish does to cope? Or can you use the things you have to do to find your way when it's foggy to help you solve your problem?). Use different problem-solving strategies such as verbal, visual, mathematical, or theatrical. Look at your problem from a different perspective or ask yourself what someone else, like your grandmother, might do if faced with the same situation.

- *Look for ways to do things better.* This may involve trying consciously to be original, not worrying about looking foolish, keeping an open mind, being alert to odd or puzzling facts, thinking of unconventional ways to use objects and the environment, discarding usual or habitual ways of doing things, and striving for objectivity by being as critical of your own ideas as you would those of someone else.

- *Find several right answers.* Being creative means continuing to look for other solutions even when you think you have solved the problem. A better, more creative solution just might be found.

- *Believe in finding a workable solution.* Like believing in yourself, you also need to believe in your ideas. If you don't think you can find a solution, you probably won't.

- *Brainstorm with others.* Creativity is not an isolated activity. Bouncing ideas off of others creates a synergistic effect.

- *Turn creative ideas into action.* Coming up with creative ideas is only part of the process. Once the ideas are generated, they must be implemented. Keeping great ideas in your mind, or on papers that no one will read, does little to expand your creative abilities.

Based on J. V. Anderson, "Mind Mapping: A Tool for Creative Thinking," *Business Horizons,* January–February 1993, pp. 42–46; and T. Proctor, *Creative Problem Solving for Managers* (New York: Routledge, 2005).

Practicing the Skill

Read through this scenario and follow the directions at the end of it:

Every time the phone rings, your stomach clenches and your palms start to sweat. And it's no wonder! As sales manager for Brinkers, a machine tool parts manufacturer, you're besieged by calls from customers who are upset about late deliveries. Your boss, Carter Hererra, acts as both production manager and scheduler. Every time your sales representatives negotiate a sale, it's up to Carter to determine whether production can actually meet the delivery date the customer specifies. And Carter invariably says, "No problem." The good thing about this is that you make a lot of initial sales. The bad news is that production hardly ever meets the shipment dates that Carter authorizes. And he doesn't seem to be all that concerned about the aftermath of late deliveries. He says, "Our customers know they're getting outstanding quality at a great price. Just let them try to match that anywhere. It can't be done. So even if they have to wait a couple of extra days or weeks, they're still getting the best deal they can." Somehow the customers don't see it that way. And they let you know about their unhappiness. Then it's up to you to try to soothe the relationship. You know this problem has to be taken care of, but what possible solutions are there? After all, how are you going to keep from making your manager mad or making the customers mad?

Break into groups of three. Assume you're the sales manager. What creative solutions can your group come up with to deal with this problem?

Experiential Exercise

Even in today's digital workplace, procedures, rules, and policies are important tools as they can help managers and employees do their jobs more efficiently and effectively. Working together in your "assigned" group, write a procedure, a rule, and a policy for your instructor to use in your class as a "seated" class. Write another procedure, rule, and policy for your instructor to use in your class as an "online" class. For both sets, be sure to explain how it fits the characteristics of a procedure, a rule, or a policy. Refer back to p. 76 for information.

CASE APPLICATION #1

 Big Brown Numbers
Topic: Efficiency, sustainability

It's the world's largest package delivery company with the instantly recognizable trucks.[61] Every day, United Parcel Service (UPS) transports more than 20 million packages and documents throughout the United States and to more than 220 countries and territories, including every address in North America and Europe. (Total worldwide delivery volume was 5.1 billion packages and documents in 2017.) Delivering those packages efficiently and on time is what UPS gets paid to do, and that takes a massive effort in helping drivers to make decisions about the best routes to follow.

Efficiency and uniformity have always been important to UPS. The importance of work rules, procedures, and analytic tools are continually stressed to drivers through training and retraining. For instance, drivers are taught to hold their keys on a pinky finger so they don't waste time fumbling in their pockets for the keys. And for safety reasons, they're taught no-left turns and no backing up. Now, however, the company has been testing and rolling out a quantum leap in its long-used business model of uniformity and efficiency. It goes by the name ORION, which stands for On-Road Integrated Optimization and Navigation. What it boils down to is helping UPS drivers shave millions of miles off their delivery routes using decision algorithms built by a team of mathematicians. Consider that each UPS driver makes an average of 120 stops per day. The efficiency challenge is deciding the best order to make all those stops (6,689,502,913,449,135 + 183 zeroes of possible alternatives)—taking into consideration "variables such as special delivery times, road regulations, and the existence of private roads that don't appear on a map?"[62] Another description of the logistics decision challenge: There are more ways to deliver packages along an average driver's route "than there are nanoseconds that Earth has existed."[63] Any way you look at it, that's a lot of alternatives. The human mind can't even begin to figure it out. But the ORION algorithm, which has taken 10

> ## UPS has been described as an **EFFICIENCY FREAK**.

years and an estimated hundreds of millions of dollars to build, is the next best thing. IT experts have described ORION as the largest investment in operations research ever by any company.

So what does ORION do? Instead of searching for the one best answer, ORION is designed to refine itself over time, leading to a balance between an optimum result and consistency to help drivers make the best possible decisions about route delivery. And considering how many miles UPS drivers travel every day, saving a dollar or two here and there can add up quickly. When a driver "logs on" his delivery information acquisition device (DIAD) at the beginning of his shift each workday, what comes up are two possible ways to make the day's package deliveries: one that uses ORION and one that uses the "old" method. The driver can choose to use either one but if ORION is not chosen, the driver is asked to explain the decision. The roll-out of ORION hasn't been without challenges. Some drivers have been reluctant to give up autonomy; others have had trouble understanding ORION's logic—why deliver a package in one neighborhood in the morning and come back to the same neighborhood later in the day. But despite the challenges, the company is committed to ORION, saying that "a driver together with ORION is better than each alone."[64]

Discussion Questions

2-11 Why is efficiency and safety so important to UPS?

2-12 Would you characterize a driver's route decisions as structured or unstructured problems? Programmed or nonprogrammed decisions? Explain.

2-13 How would ORION technology help drivers make better decisions? (Think of the steps in the decision-making process.)

2-14 How is UPS being a sustainable corporation?

CASE APPLICATION #2

The Business of Baseball

Topic: Manchester City Football: Big Data Champions

In most football teams, the minutes before the match are spent in the locker room, where the coach provides last-minute tips and delivers a motivational speech to the players. However, Manchester City Football Club follows a different ritual: The players spend 15 minutes before each match with its performance analyst team,[65] discussing what they had done well or wrong in previous matches. For instance, the defense examines several factors: the number of crosses, effective or ineffective tackles, balls lost or recovered, the relationship with midfield, and maneuvers to protect their penalty area.

The day after the match, the analysis team, led by Gavin Fleig, Head of Performance Analysis at Manchester City Football Club, gives each player a detailed and personalized report of all their moves during the match, giving each player accurate feedback on the improvements required. In a 2012 interview with *Forbes*,[66] Fleig said that the goal of the performance analysis unit is both to help the club makes smarter decisions by relying on objective and more informative data and to enhance players' performance by helping them to become more reflective and aware of their unique features, actions, and moves on the pitch.

To illustrate how the performance analysis team helps improve performance, take Manchester City's performance and the set-piece goals scored in the 2010–2011 season. According to the analyst team, Manchester City was underperforming more than any other club in Premier League, with only one set-piece goal scored over 21 matches. More than 500 corner kicks were studied by the analyst team to understand what lead to the goal. The players were then presented with videos illustrating the best tactics and moves applied by other teams. This helped Manchester City to score 9 goals in the first 15 matches of the next season from corners, which represents a tremendous improvement in their performance.

Data analysis is a critical decision-making support tool for Manchester City's managers at all levels, including the youth teams. For example, future young players can learn their role and characteristics within the different formation plays and what aspects they need to focus on to develop their talent. Big data is thus a means to achieve Manchester City's strategic goals in youth team development, which is to integrate young, homegrown talents into the first team's formation. Since the performance analysts started helping the team, Manchester City has gotten the best defensive records for two consecutive years since 2012, and it won the title in the 2011–2012 and 2013–2014 seasons after more than four decades of no wins. Of course, big data is not the only factor behind these successes, but it was very important.

To continue being a leader in football big data, in 2016, Manchester City organized a global hackathon, with more than 400 applications received from all over the world,[67] during which data and football experts created algorithms and simulations using data from real players that had never before been made available to external actors. The challenge was to create algorithms that could help identify new moves, passes, running, and pressure to be more affective. The winning team, who received a cash prize of £7000 and the promise to collaborate with the performance analysis team, created a learning machine algorithm that tracks decision-making during games.

Discussion Questions

2-15 What types of decisions are made by football managers? Would you characterize these decisions as structured or unstructured problems? Explain.

2-16 Describe how football managers can use big data to make better decisions, referring to rationality, bounded rationality, intuition, and evidence-based management.

2-17 What type(s) of conditions are more likely to influence the performance analyst team's work: certainty, uncertainty, or risks? Explain.

2-18 Do you think it is appropriate for football managers to use only quantitative information to evaluate their players' performance during a season? Why or why not?

2-19 How can big data transform football decisions in the future?

CASE APPLICATION #3

Slicing the Line
Topic: Galloping to the Right Decision

Once considered the "sport of kings," horse racing today has evolved in to a multi-billion-dollar entertainment industry. Owners, jockeys, trainers, and horses travel the globe in search of a win. Crossing the finish line in one of the top three places can yield significant earnings from the modest racing circuits in small cities and extravagant payouts from the most prestigious venues. In the Hong Kong circuit alone, winning owners can earn up to 60 percent of prize money, ranging from $100,000 to over $3 million per weekly race over a season. A winning jockey and trainer can easily earn 10 percent each from an owner's winnings.

Fans from all walks of life share in the enthusiasm as they fill massive grandstands and hotel rooms. Hong Kong's world-class Happy Valley Racecourse can draw up to 55,000 spectators on any given night. The Dubai Cup, with the largest purse in all of horseracing at $10,000,000, attracts not only the top horses in the world but entices tourists to visit the United Arab Emirates and enjoy themselves at the spectacular Meydon Hotel, which overlooks the Dubai racecourse. And the Kentucky Derby continues to draw record-breaking crowds to the U.S. city of Louisville, where ticket prices for this spectacle can range from $43 for general admission tickets to $11,000 for an upper clubhouse seat.

As the business of horse racing continues to grow, risk and uncertainty in this high-stakes affair looms heavy for its decision makers. Each decision can mean the difference between winning and losing. Owners with large and small pocketbooks alike seek returns on their investment. And a jockey's livelihood for the month can be decided in a matter of seconds.

An owner must assess whether to invest in the potential of young colt or buy an experienced mare. Pedigree, age, and past performance are just a few factors alongside sentiment: tradition can decide whether a buyer seeks a thoroughbred from England's hallowed breeding grounds in Newmarket or the bloodline of an Arabian. Evaluating the return on investment must be weighed against the cost of ownership, including training and boarding fees.

Decisions do not rest only in ownership. A jockey makes split-second decisions during a race while galloping at speeds exceeding 35 mph. Not knowing a horse's tendencies or using the wrong race strategy could lead to life-threatening injury to horse or rider. A well-prepared jockey studies course dimensions and the patterns of competitors. Horse preparation relies on the daily decisions of the trainer, who must decide optimal diets and appropriate equipment, such as proper, fitting horseshoes. This extends to exercise routines monitored by data collected via smartphone apps and the tracking of graphical data.

Science permeates the sport. Race teams seek competitive advantage via genetic testing and aerobic measurements. Yet, at the end of the day, many decisions are still made by one's love and feel for the horse.

Discussion Questions

2-20 What are some examples of rational and intuitive decision making that you may see in horse racing?

2-21 A jockey from Melbourne, Australia, is convinced by a friend to race at the last minute in Happy Valley, Hong Kong, without a track preview. How would bounded rationality affect the jockey who normally races in Australia?

2-22 What decision-making approaches could an owner use to help decide what type of horse to buy?

Endnotes

1. J. Flint, Z. Vranica, and L. O-Reilly, "U.S. Soccer Trips Up Fox Sports," *Wall Street Journal*, October 12, 2017, pp. B1+.

2. J. Zucker, "Proof in the Eating," *Fast Company*, March 2013, pp. 34+.

3. A. Blackman, "Inside the Executive Brain," *Wall Street Journal*, April 28, 2014, p. R1.

4. See, for example, A. Nagurney, J. Dong, and P. L. Mokhtarian, "Multicriteria Network Equilibrium Modeling with Variable Weights for Decision-Making in the Information Age with Applications to the Telecommuting and Teleshopping," *Journal of Economic Dynamics and Control*, August 2002, pp. 1629–50.

5. J. Flinchbaugh, "Surfacing Problems Daily: Advice for Building a Problem-Solving Culture," *Industry Week*, April 2011, p. 12; "Business Analysis Training Helps Leaders Achieve an Enterprise-Wide Perspective," *Leader to Leader*, Fall 2010, pp. 63–65; D. Okes, "Common Problems with Basic Problem Solving," *Quality*, September 2010, pp. 36–40; and J. Sawyer, "Problem-Solving Success Tips," *Business and Economic Review*, April–June 2002, pp. 23–24.

6. See J. Figueira and B. Ray, "Determining the Weights of Criteria in the Electre Type of Methods with a Revised Simons' Procedure," *European Journal of Operational Research*, June 1, 2002, pp. 317–26.

7. For instance, see M. Elliott, "Breakthrough Thinking," *IIE Solution*, October 2001, pp. 22–25; and B. Fazlollahi and R. Vahidov, "A Method for Generation of Alternatives by Decision Support Systems," *Journal of Management Information Systems*, Fall 2001, pp. 229–50.

8. D. Miller, Q. Hope, R. Eisenstat, N. Foote, and J. Galbraith, "The Problem of Solutions: Balancing Clients and Capabilities," *Business Horizons*, March–April 2002, pp. 3–12.

9. E. Teach, "Avoiding Decision Traps," *CFO*, June 2004, pp. 97–99; and D. Kahneman and A. Tversky, "Judgment under Uncertainty: Heuristics and Biases," *Science* 185 (1974) pp. 1124–31.

10. Information for this section taken from S. P. Robbins, *Decide & Conquer* (Upper Saddle River, NJ: Financial Times/Prentice Hall, 2004).

11. T. A. Stewart, "Did You Ever Have to Make Up Your Mind?" *Harvard Business Review*, January 2006, p.12; and E. Pooley, "Editor's Desk," *Fortune*, June 27, 2005, p. 16.

12. J. G. March, "Decision-Making Perspective: Decisions in Organizations and Theories of Choice," in A. H. Van de Ven and W. F. Joyce, eds., *Perspectives on Organization Design and Behavior* (New York: Wiley-Interscience, 1981), pp. 232–33.

13. See T. Shavit and A. M. Adam, "A Preliminary Exploration of the Effects of Rational Factors and Behavioral Biases on the Managerial Choice to Invest in Corporate Responsibility," *Managerial and Decision Economics*, April 2011, pp. 205–13; A. Langley, "In Search of Rationality: The Purposes behind the Use of Formal Analysis in Organizations," *Administrative Science Quarterly*, December 1989, pp. 598–631; and H. A. Simon, "Rationality in Psychology and Economics," *Journal of Business*, October 1986, pp. 209–24.

14. See D. R. A. Skidd, "Revisiting Bounded Rationality," *Journal of Management Inquiry*, December 1992, pp. 343–47; B. E. Kaufman, "A New Theory of Satisficing," *Journal of Behavioral Economics*, Spring 1990, pp. 35–51; and N. McK. Agnew and J. L. Brown, "Bounded Rationality: Fallible Decisions in Unbounded Decision Space," *Behavioral Science*, July 1986, pp. 148–61.

15. Classic Concepts in Today's Workplace box based on M. Ibrahim, "Theory of Bounded Rationality," *Public Management*, June 2009, pp. 3–5; D. A. Wren, *The Evolution of Management Thought*, 4th ed. (New York: John Wiley & Sons, 1994), p. 291; and H. A. Simon, *Administrative Behavior* (New York: Macmillan Company, 1945).

16. See, for example, G. McNamara, H. Moon, and P. Bromiley, "Banking on Commitment: Intended and Unintended Consequences of an Organization's Attempt to Attenuate Escalation of Commitment," *Academy of Management Journal*, April 2002, pp. 443–52; V. S. Rao and A. Monk, "The Effects of Individual Differences and Anonymity on Commitment to Decisions," *Journal of Social Psychology*, August 1999, pp. 496–515; C. F. Camerer and R. A. Weber, "The Econometrics and Behavioral Economics of Escalation of Commitment: A Re-examination of Staw's Theory," *Journal of Economic Behavior and Organization*, May 1999, pp. 59–82; D. R. Bobocel and J. P. Meyer, "Escalating Commitment to a Failing Course of Action: Separating the Roles of Choice and Justification," *Journal of Applied Psychology*, June 1994, pp. 360–63; and B. M. Staw, "The Escalation of Commitment to a Course of Action," *Academy of Management Review*, October 1981, pp. 577–87.

17. L. Alderman, "A Shoemaker That Walks but Never Runs," *New York Times Online*, October 8, 2010.

18. C. Flora, "When to Go with Your Gut," *Women's Health*, June 2009, pp. 68–70.

19. See E. Bernstein, "When to Go with Your Gut," *Wall Street Journal*, October 10, 2017, p. A15; J. Evans, "Intuition and Reasoning: A Dual-Process Perspective," *Psychological Inquiry*, October–December 2010, pp. 313–26; T. Betsch and A. Blockner, "Intuition in Judgment and Decision Making: Extensive Thinking without Effort," *Psychological Inquiry*, October–December 2010, pp. 279–94; R. Lange and J. Houran, "A Transliminal View of Intuitions in the Workplace," *North American Journal of Psychology* 12, no. 3 (2010), pp. 501–16; E. Dane and M. G. Pratt, "Exploring Intuition and Its Role in Managerial Decision Making," *Academy of Management Review*, January 2007, pp. 33–54; M. H. Bazerman and D. Chugh, "Decisions without Blinders," *Harvard Business Review*, January 2006, pp. 88–97; C. C. Miller and R. D. Ireland, "Intuition in Strategic Decision Making: Friend or Foe in the Fast-Paced 21st Century," *Academy of Management Executive*, February 2005, pp. 19–30; E. Sadler-Smith and E. Shefy, "The Intuitive Executive: Understanding and Applying 'Gut Feel' in Decision-Making," *Academy of Management Executive*, November 2004, pp. 76–91; and L. A. Burke and M. K. Miller, "Taking the Mystery Out of Intuitive Decision Making," *Academy of Management Executive*, October 1999, pp. 91–99.

20. Miller and Ireland, "Intuition in Strategic Decision Making," p. 20.

21. E. Sadler-Smith and E. Shefy, "Developing Intuitive Awareness in Management Education," *Academy of Management Learning & Education*, June 2007, pp. 186–205.

22. M. G. Seo and L. Feldman Barrett, "Being Emotional during Decision Making—Good or Bad? An Empirical Investigation," *Academy of Management Journal*, August 2007, pp. 923–40.

23. Managing Technology in Today's Workplace box based on M. Xu, V. Ong, Y. Duan, and B. Mathews, "Intelligent Agent Systems for Executive Information Scanning, Filtering, and Interpretation: Perceptions and Challenges," *Information Processing & Management*, March 2011, pp. 186–201; J. P. Kallunki, E. K. Laitinen, and H. Silvola, "Impact of Enterprise Resource Planning Systems on Management Control Systems and Firm Performance," *International Journal of Accounting Information Systems*, March 2011, pp. 20–39; H. W. K. Chia, C. L. Tan, and S. Y. Sung, "Enhancing Knowledge Discovery via Association-Based Evolution of Neural Logic Networks," *IEEE Transactions on Knowledge and Data Engineering*, July 2006, pp. 889–901; F. Harvey, "A Key Role in Detecting Fraud Patterns: Neural Networks," *Financial Times*, January 23, 2002, p. 3; D. Mitchell and R. Pavur, "Using Modular Neural Networks for Business Decisions," *Management Decision*, January–February 2002, pp. 58–64; B. L. Killingsworth, M. B. Hayden, and R. Schellenberger, "A Network Expert System Management System of Multiple Domains," *Journal of Information Science*, March–April 2001, p. 81; and S. Balakrishnan, N. Popplewell, and M. Thomlinson, "Intelligent Robotic Assembly," *Computers & Industrial Engineering*, December 2000, p. 467.

24. "Next: Big Idea," *Fast Company*, December 2010–January 2011, pp. 39–40.

25. H. McCracken, "50 Most Innovative Companies: LINE," *Fast Company*, March 2015, pp. 84+.

26. A. Deutschman, "Inside the Mind of Jeff Bezos," *Fast Company*, August 2004, pp. 50–58.

27. See, for instance, S. Schulz-Hardt, A. Mojzisch, F. C. Brodbeck, R. Kerschreiter, and D. Frey, "Group Decision Making in Hidden Profile Situations: Dissent as a Facilitator for Decision Quality," *Journal of Personality and Social Psychology*, December 2006, pp. 1080–83; and C. K. W. DeDreu and M. A. West, "Minority Dissent and Team Innovation: The Importance of Participation in Decision Making," *Journal of Applied Psychology*, December 2001, pp. 1191–1201.

28. S. Mohammed, "Toward an Understanding of Cognitive Consensus in a Group Decision-Making Context," *Journal of Applied Behavioral Science*, December 2001, p. 408.

29. M. J. Fambrough and S. A. Comerford, "The Changing Epistemological Assumptions of Group Theory," *Journal of Applied Behavioral Science*, September 2006, pp. 330–49.

30. R. A. Meyers, D. E. Brashers, and J. Hanner, "Majority-Minority Influence: Identifying Argumentative Patterns and Predicting Argument-Outcome Links," *Journal of Communication*, Autumn 2000, pp. 3–30.

31. See, for instance, T. Horton, "Groupthink in the Boardroom," *Directors and Boards*, Winter 2002, p. 9.

32. I. L. Janis, *Groupthink* (Boston: Houghton Mifflin, 1982). See also J. Chapman, "Anxiety and Defective Decision Making: An Elaboration of the Groupthink Mode," *Management Decision*, October 2006, pp. 1391–1404.

33. See, for example, T. W. Costello and S. S. Zalkind, eds., *Psychology in Administration: A Research Orientation* (Upper Saddle River, NJ: Prentice Hall, 1963), pp. 429–30; R. A. Cooke and J. A. Kernaghan, "Estimating the Difference between Group versus Individual Performance on Problem Solving Tasks," *Group and Organization Studies*, September 1987, pp. 319–42; and L. K. Michaelsen, W. E. Watson, and R. H. Black, "A Realistic Test of Individual versus Group Consensus Decision Making," *Journal of Applied Psychology*, October 1989, pp. 834–39. See also J. Hollenbeck, D. R. Ilgen, J. A. Colquitt, and A. Ellis, "Gender Composition, Situational Strength, and Team Decision-Making Accuracy: A Criterion Decomposition Approach," *Organizational Behavior and Human Decision Processes*, May 2002, pp. 445–75.

34. See, for example, L. K. Michaelsen, W. E. Watson, and R. H. Black, "A Realistic Test of Individual versus Group Consensus Decision Making," *Journal of Applied Psychology*, October 1989, pp. 834–39; and P. W. Pease, M. Beiser, and M. E. Tubbs, "Framing Effects and Choice Shifts in Group Decision Making," *Organizational Behavior and Human Decision Processes*, October 1993, pp. 149–65.

35. M. Eltagouri, "'We Have A Responsibility': CVS Vows to Stop Altering Beauty Images in Its Ads and Stores," *Washington Post Online*, January 16, 2018; and A. Bruell and S. Terlep, "CVS Vows to Stop Altering Beauty Images in Its Marketing," *Wall Street Journal Online*, January 15, 2018.

36. J. Wagstaff, "Brainstorming Requires Drinks," *Far Eastern Economic Review*, May 2, 2002, p. 34.

37. T. Kelley, "Six Ways to Kill a Brainstormer," *Across the Board*, March–April 2002, p. 12.

38. H. Gregersen, "Better Brainstorming," *Harvard Business Review*, March–April 2018, pp. 64–71.

39. K. L. Dowling and R. D. St. Louis, "Asynchronous Implementation of the Nominal Group Technique: Is It Effective," *Decision Support Systems*, October 2000, pp. 229–48.

40. See also B. Andersen and T. Fagerhaug, "The Nominal Group Technique," *Quality Progress*, February 2000, p. 144.

41. J. Burdett, "Changing Channels: Using the Electronic Meeting System to Increase Equity in Decision Making," *Information Technology, Learning, and Performance Journal*, Fall 2000, pp. 3–12.

42. "Fear of Flying," *Business Europe*, October 3, 2001, p. 2.

43. "VC at Nestlé," *Business Europe*, October 3, 2001, p. 3.

44. M. Roberti, "Meet Me on the Web," *Fortune: Tech Supplement*, Winter 2002, p. 10.

45. See also, J. A. Hoxmeier and K. A. Kozar, "Electronic Meetings and Subsequent Meeting Behavior: Systems as Agents of Change," *Journal of Applied Management Studies*, December 2000, pp. 177–95.

46. See, for instance, P. Berthon, L. F. Pitt, and M. T. Ewing, "Corollaries of the Collective: The Influence of Organizational Culture and Memory Development on Perceived Decision-Making Context," *Academy of Marketing Science Journal*, Spring 2001, pp. 135–50.

47. J. de Haan, M. Yamamoto, and G. Lovink, "Production Planning in Japan: Rediscovering Lost Experiences or New Insights," *International Journal of Production Economics*, May 6, 2001, pp. 101–09.

48. T. M. Amabile, "Motivating Creativity in Organizations," *California Management Review*, Fall 1997, pp. 39–58.

49. D. Dunne and R. Martin, "Design Thinking and How It Will Change Management Education: An Interview and Discussion," *Academy of Management Learning & Education*, December 2006, p. 512.

50. M. Korn and R. E. Silverman, "Forget B-School, D-School Is Hot," *Wall Street Journal*, June 7, 2012, pp. B1+; R. Martin and J. Euchner, "Design Thinking," *Research Technology Management*, May/June 2012, pp. 10–14; T. Larsen and T. Fisher, "Design Thinking: A Solution to Fracture-Critical Systems," *DMI News & Views*, May 2012, p. 31; T. Berno, "Design Thinking versus Creative Intelligence," *DMI News & Views*,

May 2012, p. 28; J. Liedtka and Tim Ogilvie, "Helping Business Managers Discover Their Appetite for Design Thinking," *Design Management Review* 1 (2012), pp. 6–13; and T. Brown, "Strategy by Design," *Fast Company*, June 2005, pp. 52–54.

51. C. Guglielmo, "Apple Loop: The Week in Review," *Forbes.com*, May 25, 2012, p. 2.

52. Dunne and Martin, "Design Thinking and How It Will Change Management Education," p. 514.

53. K. Cukier and V. Mayer-Schönberger, "The Financial Bonanza of Big Data," *Wall Street Journal*, March 8, 2013, p. A15.

54. R. King and S. Rosenbush, "Big Data Broadens Its Range," *Wall Street Journal*, March 14, 2013, p. B5.

55. "Big Data, Big Impact: New Possibilities for International Development," *World Economic Forum*, weforum.org, 2012.

56. E. Segrano, "These Natural Beauty Brands Are Using Big Data to Give Skin Care a Makeover," *Fast Company Online*, April 18, 2017.

57. N. Ungerleider, "How Restaurants Use Big Data to Learn More about Their Customers," *Fast Company Online*, March 28, 2017.

58. D. Laney, "The Importance of 'Big Data': A Definition," www.gartner.com/it-glossary/big-data/, March 22, 2013.

59. S. Lohr, "Sure, Big Data Is Great. But So Is Intuition," *New York Times Online*, December 29, 2012.

60. S. Schechner, "Algorithms Move Into Management," *Wall Street Journal*, December 11, 2017, pp. B1+.

61. UPS Fact Sheet, https://pressroom.ups.com/assets/pdf/pressroom/fact%20sheet/UPS_Fact_Sheet.pdf, updated February 16, 2018; S. Rosenbush and L. Stevens, "At UPS, the Algrithm Is the Driver," *Wall Street Journal*, February 17, 2015, pp. B1+; D. Zax, "Brown Down: UPS Drivers vs. the UPS Algorithm," http://www.fastcompany.com/3004319/brown-down-ups-drivers-vs-ups-algorithm, January 3, 2013; T. Bingham and P. Galagan, "Delivering 'On-Time, Every Time' Knowledge and Skills to a World of Employees," *T&D*, July 2012, pp. 32–37; J. Levitz, "UPS Thinks Outside the Box on Driver Training," *Wall Street Journal*, April 6, 2010, pp. B1+; and K. Kingsbury, "Road to Recovery," *Time*, March 8, 2010, pp. Global 14–Global 16.

62. Hong Kong Jockey Club website; P. Catton and C. Herrings, "Do Horses Really Need Jockeys?" *The Wall Street Journal*, www.wsj.com, May 3, 2012; McKenzie, "Space-age Skyscrapers and Sheiks: Racing's New World Order," CNN website, http://edition.cnn.com/2013/03/29/sport/dubai-world-cup-horse-racing/,

March 29, 2013; C. Galofaro, "The Latest: Keep Black Cats Away from Baffert," *Associated Press*, http://bigstory.ap.org/article/7c6d91b3926346b9b8989426a666044e/latest-fans-stream-churchill-downs-derby-day, May 3, 2015; A. Waller, J. Daniels, N. Weaver, P. Robinson, 2000.

63. Zax, "Brown Down."

64. C. Chiappinelli, "Buzzwords, Hidden Dimensions, and Innovation: A UPS Story," https://www.esri.com/about/newsroom/publications/wherenext/buzzwords-hidden-dimensions-and-innovation-a-ups-story/, September 7, 2017; and Rosenbush and Stevens, "At UPS, the Algorithm Is the Driver."

65. Andy Hunter, "Manchester City to Open the Archive on Player Data and Statistics," *The Guardian*, August 16, 2012, https://www.theguardian.com/football/blog/2012/aug/16/manchester-city-player-statistics.

66. Zach Slaton, "The Analyst behind Manchester City's Rapid Rise (Part 1)," *Forbes*, August 16, 2012, http://www.forbes.com/sites/zach-slaton/2012/08/16/the-analyst-behind-manchester-citys-player-investments-part-1/#1fef1e401b21.

67. Taylor Bloom, "Manchester City's First Football Data Hackathon A Roaring Success," *SportTechie*, August 1, 2016, http://www.sporttechie.com/2016/08/01/sports-tech-wire/manchester-citys-first-football-data-hackathon-a-roaring-success/.

68. Hong Kong Jockey Club website; P. Catton and C. Herrings, "Do Horses Really Need Jockeys?" *The Wall Street Journal*, www.wsj.com, May 3, 2012; McKenzie, "Space-age Skyscrapers and Sheiks: Racing's New World Order," CNN website, http://edition.cnn.com/2013/03/29/sport/dubai-world-cup-horse-racing/, March 29, 2013; C. Galofaro, "The Latest: Keep Black Cats Away from Baffert," *Associated Press*, http://bigstory.ap.org/article/7c6d91b3926346b9b8989426a666044e/latest-fans-stream-churchill-downs-derby-day, May 3, 2015; A. Waller, J. Daniels, N. Weaver, P. Robinson, 2000. "Jockey Injuries in the United States," *Journal of the American Medical Association*, 283(10), 1326–28; J. Roach, "The Science of Horse Racing," www.nbcnews.com, 2013.

Quantitative Module
QUANTITATIVE DECISION-MAKING TOOLS

In this module, we'll look at several decision-making tools and techniques, as well as some popular tools for managing projects.[1] Specifically, we'll introduce you to payoff matrices, decision trees, break-even analysis, ratio analysis, linear programming, queuing theory, and economic order quantity. The purpose of each method is to provide managers with a tool to assist in the decision-making process and to provide more complete information to make better-informed decisions.

Payoff Matrices

In Chapter 2, we introduced you to the topic of uncertainty and how it can affect decision making. Although uncertainty plays a critical role by limiting the amount of information available to managers, another factor is their psychological orientation. For instance, the optimistic manager will typically follow a *maximax* choice (maximizing the maximum possible payoff), the pessimist will often pursue a *maximin* choice (maximizing the minimum possible payoff), and the manager who desires to minimize his "regret" will opt for a *minimax* choice. Let's briefly look at these different approaches using an example.

Consider the case of a marketing manager at Visa International in New York. He has determined four possible strategies (we'll label these S1, S2, S3, and S4) for promoting the Visa card throughout the northeastern United States. However, he is also aware that one of his major competitors, American Express, has three competitive strategies (CA1, CA2, and CA3) for promoting its own card in the same region. In this case, we'll assume that the Visa executive has no previous knowledge that would allow him to place probabilities on the success of any of his four strategies. With these facts, the Visa card manager formulates the matrix in Exhibit QM–1 to show the various Visa strategies and the resulting profit to Visa, depending on the competitive action chosen by American Express.

In this example, if our Visa manager is an optimist, he'll choose S4 because that could produce the largest possible gain ($28 million). Note that this choice maximizes the maximum possible gain (maximax choice). If our manager is a pessimist, he'll assume only the worst can occur. The worst outcome for each strategy is as follows: S1 = $11 million, S2 = $9 million, S3 = $15 million, and S4 = $14 million. Following the maximin choice, the pessimistic manager would maximize the minimum payoff—in other words, he'd select S3.

In the third approach, managers recognize that once a decision is made it will not necessarily result in the most profitable payoff. What could occur is a "regret" of profits forgone (given up)—regret referring to the amount of money that could have been made had a different strategy been

Exhibit QM–1 Payoff Matrix for Visa

VISA MARKETING STRATEGY	AMERICAN EXPRESS'S RESPONSE (IN $MILLIONS)		
	CA1	CA2	CA3
S1	13	14	11
S2	9	15	18
S3	24	21	15
S4	18	14	28

Exhibit QM–2 Regret Matrix for Visa

VISA MARKETING STRATEGY	AMERICAN EXPRESS'S RESPONSE (IN $MILLIONS)		
	CA1	CA2	CA3
S1	11	7	17
S2	15	6	10
S3	0	0	13
S4	6	7	0

used. Managers calculate regret by subtracting all possible payoffs in each category from the maximum possible payoff for each given—in this case, for each competitive action. For our Visa manager, the highest payoff, given that American Express engages in CA1, CA2, or CA3, is $24 million, $21 million, or $28 million, respectively (the highest number in each column). Subtracting the payoffs in Exhibit QM–1 from these figures produces the results in Exhibit QM–2.

The maximum regrets are S1 = $17 million, S2 = $15 million, S3 = $13 million, and S4 = $7 million. The minimax choice minimizes the maximum regret, so our Visa manager would choose S4. By making this choice, he'll never have a regret of profits forgone of more than $7 million. This result contrasts, for example, with a regret of $15 million had he chosen S2 and American Express had taken CA1.

Decision Trees

Decision trees are a useful way to analyze hiring, marketing, investment, equipment purchases, pricing, and similar decisions that involve a progression of decisions. They're called decision trees because, when diagrammed, they look a lot like a tree with branches. Typical decision trees encompass expected value analysis by assigning probabilities to each possible outcome and calculating payoffs for each decision path.

Exhibit QM–3 illustrates a decision facing Becky Harrington, the midwestern region site selection supervisor for Barry's Brews. Becky supervises a small group of specialists who analyze potential locations and make store site recommendations to the midwestern region's director. The lease on the company's store in Winter Park, Florida, is expiring, and the property owner has decided not to renew it. Becky and her group have to make a relocation recommendation to the regional director. Becky's group has identified an excellent site in a nearby shopping mall in Orlando. The mall owner has offered her two comparable locations: one with 12,000 square feet (the same as she has now) and the other a larger, 20,000-square-foot space. Becky's initial decision concerns whether to recommend renting the larger or smaller location. If she chooses the larger space and the economy is strong, she estimates the store will make a $320,000 profit. However, if the economy is poor, the high operating costs of the larger store will mean that the profit will be only $50,000. With the smaller store, she estimates the profit at $240,000 with a good economy and $130,000 with a poor one.

As you can see from Exhibit QM–3, the expected value for the larger store is $239,000 [(.70 × 320) + (.30 × 50)]. The expected value for the smaller store is $207,000 [(.70 × 240) + (.30 × 130)]. Given these projections, Becky is planning to recommend the rental of the larger store space. What if Becky wants to consider the implications of initially renting the smaller space and then expanding if the economy picks up? She can extend the decision tree to include this second decision point. She has calculated three options: no expansion, adding 4,000 square feet, and adding 8,000 square feet. Following the approach used for Decision Point 1, she could calculate the profit potential by extending the branches on the tree and calculating expected values for the various options.

decision trees
A diagram used to analyze a progression of decisions. When diagrammed, a decision tree looks like a tree with branches.

Exhibit QM–3

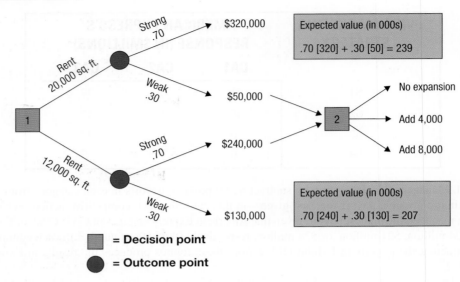

Break-Even Analysis

How many units of a product must an organization sell in order to break even—that is, to have neither profit nor loss? A manager might want to know the minimum number of units that must be sold to achieve his or her profit objective or whether a current product should continue to be sold or should be dropped from the organization's product line. **Break-even analysis** is a widely used technique for helping managers make profit projections.[2]

Break-even analysis is a simplistic formulation, yet it is valuable to managers because it points out the relationship among revenues, costs, and profits. To compute the break-even point (BE), the manager needs to know the unit price of the product being sold (P), the variable cost per unit (VC), and the total fixed costs (TFC).

An organization breaks even when its total revenue is just enough to equal its total costs. But total cost has two parts: a fixed component and a variable component. Fixed costs are expenses that do not change, regardless of volume, such as insurance premiums and property taxes. Fixed costs, of course, are fixed only in the short term because, in the long run, commitments terminate and are, thus, subject to variation. Variable costs change in proportion to output and include raw materials, labor costs, and energy costs.

The break-even point can be computed graphically or by using the following formula:

$$BE = [TFC/(P - VC)]$$

This formula tells us that (1) total revenue will equal total cost when we sell enough units at a price that covers all variable unit costs and (2) the difference between price and variable costs, when multiplied by the number of units sold, equals the fixed costs.

When is break-even analysis useful? To demonstrate, assume that, at Jose's Bakersfield Espresso, Jose charges $1.75 for an average cup of coffee. If his fixed costs (salary, insurance, etc.) are $47,000 a year and the variable costs for each cup of espresso are $0.40, Jose can compute his break-even point as follows: $47,000/(1.75 − .40) = 34,815 (about 670 cups of espresso sold each week), or when annual revenues are approximately $60,926. This same relationship is shown graphically in Exhibit QM–4.

How can break-even analysis serve as a planning and decision-making tool? As a planning tool, break-even analysis could help Jose set his sales objective. For example, he could establish the profit he wants and then work backward to determine what sales level is needed to reach that profit. As a decision-making tool, break-even analysis could also tell Jose how much volume has to increase in order to break even if he is currently operating at a loss, or how much volume he can afford to lose and still break even if he is currently operating profitably.

break-even analysis
A technique for identifying the point at which total revenue is just sufficient to cover total costs

Exhibit QM–4

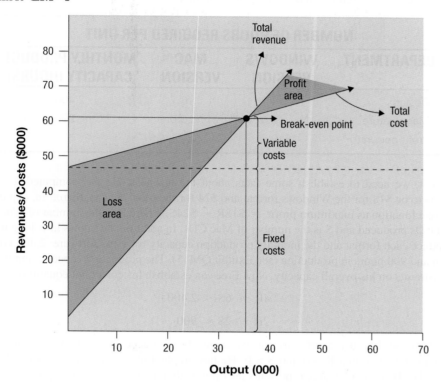

In some cases, such as the management of professional sports franchises, break-even analysis has shown the projected volume of ticket sales required to cover all costs to be so unrealistically high that management's best choice is to sell or close the business.

Linear Programming

Matt Free owns a software development company. One product line involves designing and producing software that detects and removes viruses. The software comes in two formats: Windows and Mac versions. He can sell all of these products that he can produce, which is his dilemma. The two formats go through the same production departments. How many of each type should he make to maximize his profits?

A close look at Free's operation tells us he can use a mathematical technique called **linear programming** to solve his resource allocation dilemma. As we will show, linear programming is applicable to his problem, but it cannot be applied to all resource allocation situations. Besides requiring limited resources and the objective of optimization, it requires that there be alternative ways of combining resources to produce a number of output mixes. A linear relationship between variables is also necessary, which means that a change in one variable will be accompanied by an exactly proportional change in the other. For Free's business, this condition would be met if it took exactly twice the time to produce two diskettes—irrespective of format—as it took to produce one.

Many different types of problems can be solved with linear programming. Selecting transportation routes that minimize shipping costs, allocating a limited advertising budget among various product brands, making the optimum assignment of personnel among projects, and determining how much of each product to make with a limited number of resources are just a few. To give you some idea of how linear programming is useful, let's return to Free's situation. Fortunately, his problem is relatively simple, so we can solve it rather quickly. For complex linear programming problems, computer software has been designed specifically to help develop solutions.

linear programming
A mathematical technique that solves resource allocation problems

Exhibit QM–5 Production Data for Virus Software

NUMBER OF HOURS REQUIRED PER UNIT			
DEPARTMENT	WINDOWS VERSION	MAC VERSION	MONTHLY PRODUCT CAPACITY (HOURS)
Design	4	6	2,400
Manufacture	2.0	2.0	900
Profit per unit	$18	$24	

First, we need to establish some facts about the business. He has computed the profit margins to be $18 for the Windows format and $24 for the Mac. He can, therefore, express his objective function as maximum profit = $18R + $24S, where R is the number of Windows-based CDs produced and S is the number of Mac CDs. In addition, he knows how long it takes to produce each format and the monthly production capacity for virus software: 2,400 hours in design and 900 hours in production (see Exhibit QM–5). The production capacity numbers act as constraints on his overall capacity. Now Free can establish his constraint equations:

$$4R + 6S < 2,400$$

$$2R + 2S < 900$$

Of course, because a software format cannot be produced in a volume less than zero, Matt can also state that R > 0 and S > 0. He has graphed his solution as shown in Exhibit QM–6. The beige shaded area represents the options that do not exceed the capacity of either department. What does the graph mean? We know that total design capacity is 2,400 hours. So if Matt decides to design only the Windows format, the maximum number he can produce is 600 (2,400 hours ÷ hours of design for each Windows version). If he decides to produce all Mac versions, the maximum he can produce is 400 (2,400 hours ÷ 6 hours of design for Mac). This design constraint is shown in Exhibit QM–6 as line BC. The other constraint Matt faces is that of production. The maximum of either format he can produce is 450 because each takes two hours to copy, verify, and package. This production constraint is shown in the exhibit as line DE.

Free's optimal resource allocation will be defined at one of the corners of this feasibility region (area ACFD). Point F provides the maximum profits within the constraints stated. At point A, profits would be zero because neither virus software version is being

Exhibit QM–6

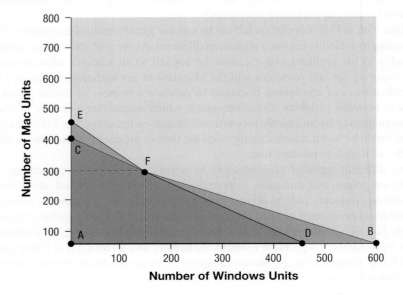

produced. At points C and D, profits would be \$9,600 (400 units @ \$24) and \$8,100 (450 units @ \$18), respectively. At point F, profits would be \$9,900 (150 Windows units @ \$18 + 300 Mac units @ \$24).[3]

Queuing Theory

You are a supervisor for a branch of Bank of America outside of Cleveland, Ohio. One of the decisions you have to make is how many of the six teller stations to keep open at any given time. **Queuing theory**, or what is frequently referred to as waiting line theory, could help you decide.

A decision that involves balancing the cost of having a waiting line against the cost of service to maintain that line can be made more easily with queuing theory. These types of common situations include determining how many gas pumps are needed at gas stations, tellers at bank windows, toll takers at toll booths, or check-in lines at airline ticket counters. In each situation, management wants to minimize cost by having as few stations open as possible yet not so few as to test the patience of customers. In our teller example, on certain days (such as the first of every month and Fridays), you could open all six windows and keep waiting time to a minimum, or you could open only one, minimize staffing costs, and risk a riot.

The mathematics underlying queuing theory is beyond the scope of this book, but you can see how the theory works in our simple example. You have six tellers working for you, but you want to know whether you can get by with only one window open during an average morning. You consider 12 minutes to be the longest you would expect any customer to wait patiently in line. If it takes 4 minutes, on average, to serve each customer, the line should not be permitted to get longer than three deep (12 minutes ÷ 4 minutes per customer = 3 customers). If you know from past experience that, during the morning, people arrive at the average rate of two per minute, you can calculate the probability (P) of customers waiting in line as follows:

$$P_n = \left[1 - \left(\frac{\text{Arrival rate}}{\text{Service rate}}\right)\right] \times \left[\frac{\text{Arrival rate}}{\text{Service rate}}\right]^n$$

where $n = 3$ customers, arrival rate = 2 per minute, and service rate = 4 minutes per customer.

Putting these numbers into the foregoing formula generates the following:

$$P_n = [1 - 2/4] \times [2/4]^3 = (1/2) \times (8/64) = (8/128) = .0625$$

What does a P of .0625 mean? It tells you that the likelihood of having more than three customers in line during the average morning is 1 chance in 16. Are you willing to live with four or more customers in line 6 percent of the time? If so, keeping one teller window open will be enough. If not, you will have to assign more tellers to staff more windows.

Economic Order Quantity Model

When you order checks from a bank, have you noticed that the reorder form is placed about two-thirds of the way through your supply of checks? This practice is a simple example of a **fixed-point reordering system**. At some preestablished point in the process, the system is designed to "flag" the fact that the inventory needs to be replenished. The objective is to minimize inventory carrying costs while at the same time limiting the probability of *stocking out* of the inventory item. In recent years, retail stores have increasingly been using their computers to perform this reordering activity. Their cash registers are connected to their computers, and each sale automatically adjusts the store's inventory record. When the inventory of an item hits the critical point, the computer tells management to reorder.

One of the best-known techniques for mathematically deriving the optimum quantity for a purchase order is the **economic order quantity (EOQ)** model (see Exhibit QM–7). The EOQ model seeks to balance four costs involved in ordering and carrying inventory: the purchase costs (purchase price plus delivery charges less discounts), the ordering costs (paperwork, follow-up, inspection when the item arrives, and other processing costs), carrying costs (money tied up in inventory, storage, insurance, taxes, etc.), and stock-out costs (profits forgone from orders lost.

queuing theory
Also known as waiting line theory, it is a way of balancing the cost of having a waiting line versus the cost of maintaining the line. Management wants to have as few stations open as possible to minimize costs without testing the patience of its customers.

fixed-point reordering system
A method for a system to "flag" the need to reorder inventory at some preestablished point in the process

economic order quantity (EOQ)
A model that seeks to balance the costs involved in ordering and carrying inventory, thus minimizing total costs associated with carrying and ordering costs

Exhibit QM–7

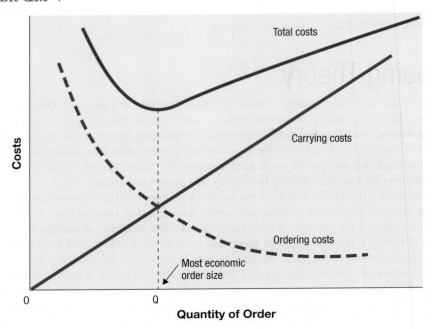

the cost of reestablishing goodwill, and additional expenses incurred to expedite late shipments). When these four costs are known, the model identifies the optimal order size for each purchase.

The objective of the economic order quantity (EOQ) model is to minimize the total costs associated with the carrying and ordering costs. As the amount ordered gets larger, average inventory increases and so do carrying costs. For example, if annual demand for an inventory item is 26,000 units, and a firm orders 500 each time, the firm will place 52 [26,000/500] orders per year. This order frequency gives the organization an average inventory of 250 [500/2] units. If the order quantity is increased to 2,000 units, fewer orders (13) [26,000/2,000] will be placed. However, average inventory on hand will increase to 1,000 [2,000/2] units. Thus, as holding costs go up, ordering costs go down, and vice versa. The optimum economic order quantity is reached at the lowest point on the total cost curve. That's the point at which ordering costs equal carrying costs—or the economic order quantity (see point Q in Exhibit QM–7).

To compute this optimal order quantity, you need the following data: forecasted demand for the item during the period (D); the cost of placing each order (OC); the value or purchase price of the item (V); and the carrying cost (expressed as a percentage) of maintaining the total inventory (CC). Given these data, the formula for EOQ is as follows:

$$EOQ = \sqrt{\frac{2 \times D \times OC}{V \times CC}}$$

Let's work an example of determining the EOQ. Take, for example, Barnes Electronics, a retailer of high-quality sound and video equipment. The owner, Sam Barnes, wishes to determine the company's economic order quantities of high-quality sound and video equipment. The item in question is a Sony compact voice recorder. Barnes forecasts sales of 4,000 units a year. He believes that the cost for the sound system should be $50. Estimated costs of placing an order for these systems are $35 per order and annual insurance, taxes, and other carrying costs at 20 percent of the recorder's value. Using the EOQ formula, and the preceding information, he can calculate the EOQ as follows:

$$EOQ = \sqrt{\frac{2 \times 4,000 \times 35}{50 \times .20}}$$

$$EOQ = \sqrt{28,000}$$

$$EOQ = 167.33 \quad \text{or} \quad 168 \text{ units}$$

The inventory model suggests that it's most economical to order in quantities or lots of approximately 168 recorders. Stated differently, Barnes should order about 24[4,000/168] times a year. However, what would happen if the supplier offers Barnes a 5 percent discount on purchases if he buys in minimum quantities of 250 units? Should he now purchase in quantities of 168 or 250? Without the discount, and ordering 168 each time, the annual costs for these recorders would be as follows:

With the 5 percent discount for ordering 250 units, the item cost [$50 × ($50 × .05)] would be $47.5.

Purchase cost:	$50 × $4,000 =	$200,000
Carrying cost (average number of inventory units times value of item times percentage):	168/2 × $50 × .2 =	840
Ordering costs (number of orders times cost to place order):	24 × $35 =	840
Total cost:	=	$201,680

The annual inventory costs would be as follows:

Purchase cost:	$47.50 × $4,000 =	$190,000.00
Carrying cost:	250/2 × $47.50 × .2 =	1,187.50
Ordering cost:	16 × $35 =	560.00
Total cost:	=	$191,747.50

These calculations suggest to Barnes that he should take advantage of the 5 percent discount. Even though he now has to stock larger quantities, the annual savings amounts to nearly $10,000. A word of caution, however, needs to be added. The EOQ model assumes that demand and lead times are known and constant. If these conditions can't be met, the model shouldn't be used. For example, it generally shouldn't be used for manufactured component inventory because the components are taken out of stock all at once, in lumps, or odd lots, rather than at a constant rate. Does this caveat mean that the EOQ model is useless when demand is variable? No. The model can still be of some use in demonstrating trade-offs in costs and the need to control lot sizes. However, more sophisticated lot sizing models are available for handling demand and special situations. The mathematics for EOQ, like the mathematics for queuing theory, go far beyond the scope of this text.

Endnotes

1. Readers are encouraged to see B. Render, R. M. Stair, and M. E. Hanna, *Quantitative Analysis for Management*, 9th ed. (Upper Saddle River, NJ: Prentice Hall, 2005).

2. J. Schmid, "Getting to Breakeven," *Catalog Age*, November 2001, pp. 89–90.

3. We want to acknowledge and thank Professor Jeff Storm of Virginia Western Community College for his assistance in this example.

Important Managerial Issues

3

Management **Myth** Myth

Globalization is a trend that's come and gone!

Management **DEBUNKED!** Myth

The reality is that in 2017, more than 85 percent of the 176 countries in the International Monetary Fund *increased* their global exports.[1] While anti-globalization sentiment also has increased, **globalization is not disappearing any time soon!** It remains an important issue that organizational leaders must recognize and manage.

THE current anti-globalization sentiment started over a decade ago during the global financial crisis, a crisis that illustrated and underscored how interconnected the world's economies actually were. The belief that "when the ship starts sinking, we're all going down" was a typical reaction felt around the world. However, current data on trade, financial flows, and other global economic measures show that globalization has stayed steady, with some measures showing slight increases.[2] Despite the intensifying political rhetoric, free trade—through free trade agreements such as the European Union, the North American Free Trade Agreement (NAFTA), Trans-Pacific Partnership (TPP), and others—has had the positive effect of improving the quality of life for people around the world. In developing countries, millions of people have been lifted out of desperate poverty. In developed countries, consumers have enjoyed cheaper goods and profitable investments. Even the oft-cited drawback of job losses as companies moved production overseas has been offset by lower consumer prices and an increase in the number of new, more efficient businesses. The implications for managers: Globalization is still an important issue that must be recognized and addressed. And political debate over issues such as immigration and nationalism will continue to be important parts of that conversation. Organizational leaders must make wise decisions about the type and extent of globalization pursued. That's what we'll be looking at in the first part of this chapter. In the remainder of the chapter, we'll thoroughly explore the issue of organizations behaving in a socially responsible manner and employees behaving ethically. Just listen to or read news reports from around the world every day and you'll see why we these are important to discuss! One other thing we need to point out. Not only are these "important" managerial issues, they're "integrative" managerial issues. Why? Because these issues are woven throughout everything a manager does, and are integrated throughout an organization—no matter the size, type, or location. So let's dig in! ●

Learning Outcomes

3-1 Explain globalization and its impact on organizations. p. 105

3-2 Describe what managers need to know about managing in a global organization. p. 109

3-3 Discuss how society's expectations are influencing managers and organizations. p. 112

3-4 Discuss the factors that lead to ethical and unethical behavior in organizations. p. 115

What Is Globalization and How Does It Affect Organizations?

3-1 Explain globalization and its impact on organizations.

Even if you don't ever anticipate working internationally, learn all you can about globalization so you can recognize opportunities and threats that have the potential to impact your career.

I (this is your co-author Mary "speaking" here). Love. Cashews. Chocolate-covered cashews, honey-roasted cashews, plain cashews, salted cashews, you name it. Little did I realize when I purchased a bag (or a dozen bags!) to enjoy, the vast array of complex global forces behind the cashew industry that brought those bags of yumminess to my doorstep in an Amazon Prime box delivered by my local UPS delivery driver. It's a fascinating story that shows how industries (and businesses) change as a result of globalization.[3] (It's highly likely that products that you love and use have a global "story" as well!) An important issue that managers must deal with is globalization. For years, India was the cashew capital of the world. Thousands of Indians (primarily women) were employed in the highly labor-intensive industry. Protecting those workers was important, so the Indian government enacted specific labor laws and regulations to do that. By the 1990s, India was the king of cashews as it accounted for a solid 80 percent of the global cashew market. However, almost 2,000 miles away, Vietnamese cashew processors were investing in automated equipment and becoming much more efficient than those labor-intensive Indian processors, thus creating a significant competitive threat to India's market domination. Those laws intended to protect the Indian workers most likely ended up harming them as cashew processing switched to the more efficient Vietnamese businesses. That's not the end of the story, however. Even in something as seemingly simple as cashew processing, the forces and impacts of globalization don't and won't stay the same. Although Vietnam may have the upper hand now, much of the cashew processing appears to be shifting to countries in Africa. And that's the reality—and challenge—of today's global environment where your product, your competition, and even your workforce can be found anywhere and at any time.

Recalling our discussion in Chapter 4 that identified global forces as one component of the external environment, we know that managers of organizations doing business globally face challenges such as changing laws and regulations, catastrophic natural disasters that immediately can disrupt time-sensitive supply chains, global economic meltdowns, continually changing domestic and global competitors, heated political discussions over topics such as immigration and protectionism, and even potential terrorist threats. Despite such challenges, we reemphasize our debunked myth that globalization isn't about to disappear. Nations and businesses have been trading with each other for centuries through all kinds of disasters, wars, and economic/political/cultural ups and downs. Over the last couple of decades, we've seen an explosion of companies—big *and* small—operating almost anywhere in the world. Geographic borders mean little when it comes to doing business. For instance, BMW, a German firm, builds cars in South Carolina. McDonald's sells hamburgers in China. Tata, an Indian company, purchased the Jaguar brand—which started as a British company—from Ford Motor Company, a U.S. company. Even IBM, a pioneer of American high-tech innovation, now has more employees in India than in the United States.[4]

global village
A boundaryless world where goods and services are produced and marketed worldwide

global sourcing
Purchasing materials or labor from around the world, wherever it is cheapest

exporting
Making products domestically and selling them abroad

importing
Acquiring products made abroad and selling them domestically

The world is still a **global village**—that is, a boundaryless world where goods and services are produced and marketed worldwide—but how managers do business in that global village is changing. To be effective in this boundaryless world, managers need to adapt to this changed environment, as well as to be more understanding of cultures, systems, and techniques that are different from their own.

What Does It Mean to Be "Global"?

There are three different ways for organizations to be considered "global." For instance, organizations are considered global if they exchange goods and services with consumers in other countries. Such ❶ *marketplace globalization* is the most common approach to being global. However, many organizations, especially high-tech organizations, are considered global because they ❷ *use managerial and technical employee talent from other countries.* One factor that affects *talent globalization* is immigration laws and regulations. Managers must be alert to changes in those laws. Finally, an organization can be considered global if it ❸ *uses financial sources and resources outside its home country, which is known as financial globalization.*[5] As might be expected, any time there's a global economic slowdown—like the one that started in 2008 and continued for about a decade—the availability of financial resources globally is affected. Now, however, as countries' economies have begun the slow process of recovery, global financial resources are following.

How Do Organizations Go Global?

As organizations go global, they often use different approaches. (See Exhibit 3–1.) At first, managers may want to get into a global market with minimal investment. At this stage, they may start with **global sourcing** (also called global outsourcing), which is purchasing materials or labor from around the world wherever it is cheapest. The goal: take advantage of lower costs in order to be more competitive. For instance, Massachusetts General Hospital uses radiologists in India to interpret CT scans.[6] Although global sourcing may be the first step to going international for many companies, they often continue using this approach because of the competitive advantages it offers. However, during the last economic crisis, many organizations reconsidered their decisions to source globally. For instance, Dell, Apple, and American Express were just a few U.S. companies that scaled back some of their offshore customer service operations. Others brought manufacturing back home. For instance, Apple decided to build some Mac computers in the United States for the first time in about a decade.

Exhibit 3–1 How Organizations Go Global

Source: Robbins, Stephen P., Coulter, Mary, *Management*, 13th Ed., © 2016, p. 106. Reprinted and electronically reproduced by permission of Pearson Education, Inc., New York, NY.

The company had faced political pressure to hire U.S. workers and to "reduce its reliance on foreign subcontractors whose treatment of workers" has been strongly criticized.[7] As companies think about the best places to do business, they face choices of *offshore* (in another global location), *onshore* (at home), or *nearshore* (in countries close to home).[8] Then, as a company takes that next step in going global, each successive stage beyond global sourcing requires more investment and thus entails more risk for the organization.

The next step in going global may involve **exporting** the organization's products to other countries—that is, making products domestically and selling them abroad. In addition, an organization might do **importing**, which involves acquiring products made abroad and selling them domestically. Both usually entail minimal investment and risk, which is why many small businesses often use these approaches to doing business globally.

Finally, managers might use **licensing** or **franchising**, which are similar approaches involving one organization giving another organization the right to use its brand name, technology, or product specifications in return for a lump-sum payment or a fee that is usually based on sales. The only difference is that licensing is primarily used by manufacturing organizations that make or sell another company's products, and franchising is primarily used by service organizations that want to use another company's name and operating methods. For example, New Delhi consumers can enjoy Subway sandwiches, Namibians can dine on KFC fried chicken, and Russians can consume Dunkin' Donuts—all because of *franchises* in these countries. On the other hand, Anheuser-Busch InBev *licensed* the right to brew and market its Budweiser beer to brewers such as Labatt in Canada, Modelo in Mexico, and Kirin in Japan.

Once an organization has been doing business internationally for a while and has gained experience in international markets, managers may decide to make more of a direct investment. One way to do this is through a **global strategic alliance**, which is a partnership between an organization and a foreign company partner or partners in which both share resources and knowledge in developing new products or building production facilities. For example, Honda Motor and General Electric teamed up to produce a new jet engine. A specific type of strategic alliance in which the partners form a separate, independent organization for some business purpose is called a **joint venture**. For example, Hewlett-Packard has had numerous joint ventures with various suppliers around the globe to develop different components for its computer equipment. These partnerships provide a relatively easy way for companies to compete globally.

Finally, managers may choose to directly invest in a foreign country by setting up a **foreign subsidiary** as a separate and independent facility or office. This subsidiary can be managed as a multidomestic organization (local control) or as a global organization (centralized control). As you can probably guess, this arrangement involves the greatest commitment of resources and poses the greatest amount of risk. For instance, United Plastics Group of Westmont, Illinois, built three injection-molding facilities in Suzhou, China. The company's executive vice president for business development says that level of investment was necessary because "it fulfilled our mission of being a global supplier to our global accounts."[9]

Ng Han Guan/AP Images

Greg Gilligan, managing director of PGA TOUR China's new series, and Hong Li, co-founder and chairwoman of Shankai Sports, shake hands during a ceremony announcing a global strategic alliance. In partnership with PGA Tour China, Beijing-based Shankai will manage the day-to-day operations of the new golf tournament series for a 20-year period starting in 2018.

licensing
An agreement in which an organization gives another the right, for a fee, to make or sell its products, using its technology or product specifications

franchising
An agreement in which an organization gives another organization the right, for a fee, to use its name and operating methods

global strategic alliance
A partnership between an organization and foreign company partner(s) in which both share resources and knowledge in developing new products or building production facilities

joint venture
A specific type of strategic alliance in which the partners agree to form a separate, independent organization for some business purpose

foreign subsidiary
A direct investment in a foreign country that involves setting up a separate and independent facility or office

MNC (multinational corporation)
Any type of international company that maintains operations in multiple countries

multidomestic corporation
An MNC that decentralizes management and other decisions to the local country where it's doing business

transnational (borderless) organization
An MNC where artificial geographic boundaries are eliminated

global corporation
An MNC that centralizes management and other decisions in the home country

What Are the Different Types of Global Organizations?

MNC
(multinational corporation):

"Which product is right for you?"

Multidomestic corporation:
An MNC in which management and other decisions are *decentralized* to the *local* country in which it is operating.

- Rely on local employees to manage the business.
- Tailor strategies to each country's unique characteristics.
- Used by many consumer product companies.

Lyroky/Alamy
Stock Photo

John Deere's green-and-yellow tractors are a familiar sight in farm country. Although John Deere once struggled selling its farm equipment overseas, its line of *highly customizable products* has made the company a ton of money.

"We don't want *people* to think we're based in any one place."

Transnational (borderless) organization:
An MNC where artificial *geographical boundaries are eliminated*.

- Country of origin or where business is conducted becomes irrelevant.
- Increases efficiency and effectiveness in a competitive global marketplace.

Ford's Focus RS is an example of a great global product. The company's "One Ford" engineering structure continues to work well. Please feel free to re-write the caption! It just needs to reflect the transnational/borderless approach.

VDWI Automotive/Alamy Stock Photo

"This decision we're making at headquarters has company-wide, world-wide implications."

Global corporation:
An MNC in which management and other decisions are *centralized* in the *home* country.

- World market is treated as an integrated whole.
- Focus is on control and global efficiency.

Mouse in the House/Alamy
Stock Photo

Sony Corporation's strengths in product innovation are legendary: the Walkman, the Handycam, the PlayStation. New products are developed and launched globally *under the guidance and oversight of corporate headquarters*.

What Do Managers Need to Know about Managing in a Global Organization?

3-2 Describe what managers need to know about managing in a global organization.

A global world brings new challenges for managers, especially in managing in a country with a different national culture.[10] A specific challenge comes from the need to recognize the differences that might exist and then find ways to make interactions effective.

U.S. managers once held (and some still hold) a rather parochial view of the world of business. **Parochialism** is a narrow focus in which managers see things only through their own eyes and from their own perspectives; they don't recognize that people from other countries have different ways of doing things or that they live differently from Americans. This view can't succeed in a global village—nor is it the dominant view held today. Changing such perceptions requires understanding that countries have different cultures and environments.

Watch your attitude! A person with a **parochial attitude** cannot succeed in today's world.

All countries have different values, morals, customs, political and economic systems, and laws, all of which can affect how a business is managed. For instance, in the United States, laws guard against employers taking action against employees solely on the basis of their age. Similar laws can't be found in all other countries. Thus, managers must be aware of a country's laws when doing business there. Also, managers need to be aware of current political views on issues such as immigration, free trade, and nationalism as they navigate the global environment. Why? Because these could affect an organization's business processes, people, and workplace environment.

The most important and challenging differences for managers to understand, however, are those related to a country's social context or culture. For example, status is perceived differently in different countries. In France, status is often the result of factors important to the organization, such as seniority, education, and the like. In the United States, status is more a function of what individuals have accomplished personally. Managers need to understand societal issues (such as status) that might affect business operations in another country and recognize that organizational success can come from a variety of managerial practices. Fortunately, managers have help in this regard by turning to the research that is being done on the differences in cultural environments.

HOFSTEDE'S FRAMEWORK. Geert Hofstede's framework is one of the most widely referenced approaches for analyzing cultural variations. His work has had a major impact on what we know about cultural differences among countries and is highlighted in our "Classic Concepts in Today's Workplace" box.

GLOBE FINDINGS. Although Hofstede's work has provided the basic framework for differentiating among national cultures, most of the data are over 30 years old. Another more recent research program, called **Global Leadership and Organizational Behavior Effectiveness (GLOBE)**, is an ongoing cross-cultural investigation of leadership and national culture. Using data from more than 17,000 managers in 62 societies around the world, the GLOBE research team (led by Robert House) has identified nine dimensions on which national cultures differ.[12] For each of these dimensions, we have indicated which countries rated high, which rated moderate, and which rated low.

parochialism
A narrow focus in which managers see things only through their own eyes and from their own perspective

GLOBE
The Global Leadership and Organizational Behavior Effectiveness research program, a program that studies cross-cultural leadership behaviors

◄◄◄ Classic Concepts in Today's Workplace ►►►

Hofstede's 5 Dimensions of National Culture

An illuminating study of the differences in cultural environments was conducted by Geert Hofstede in the 1970s and 1980s.[11] He surveyed more than 116,000 IBM employees in 40 countries about their work-related values and found that managers and employees vary on five dimensions of national culture:

- **Power distance.** The degree to which people in a country accept that power in institutions and organizations is distributed unequally. It ranges from relatively equal (low power distance) to extremely unequal (high power distance).

- **Individualism versus collectivism.** Individualism is the degree to which people in a country prefer to act as individuals rather than as members of groups. Collectivism is the equivalent of low individualism.

- **Achievement versus nurturing.** Quantity of life is the degree to which values such as assertiveness, the acquisition of money and material goods, and competition are important. Quality of life is the degree to which people

value relationships and show sensitivity and concern for the welfare of others.

- **Uncertainty avoidance.** This dimension assesses the degree to which people in a country prefer structured over unstructured situations and whether people are willing to take risks.

- **Long-term versus short-term orientation.** People in cultures with long-term orientations look to the future and value thrift and persistence. A short-term orientation values the past and present and emphasizes respect for tradition and fulfilling social obligations.

The following table shows a few highlights of four of Hofstede's cultural dimensions and how different countries rank on those dimensions.

> ## Here's one way to UNDERSTAND CULTURAL DIFFERENCES!

Discussion Questions:

1 Using Hofstede's data for Mexico and the United States, how do you think employees in each country (a) might react to a team-based rewards program; (b) would be likely to view their relationship with their boss; (c) might react to a change in work processes?

2 What does this example tell you about the importance of understanding cultural differences?

Country	Individualism/ Collectivism	Power Distance	Uncertainty Avoidance	Achievement/ Nurturing[a]
Australia	Individual	Small	Moderate	Strong
Canada	Individual	Moderate	Low	Moderate
England	Individual	Small	Moderate	Strong
France	Individual	Large	High	Weak
Greece	Collective	Large	High	Moderate
Italy	Individual	Moderate	High	Strong
Japan	Collective	Moderate	High	Strong
Mexico	Collective	Large	High	Strong
Singapore	Collective	Large	Low	Moderate
Sweden	Individual	Small	Low	Weak
United States	Individual	Small	Low	Strong
Venezuela	Collective	Large	High	Strong

[a]A weak achievement score is equivalent to high nurturing.

Source: Based on G. Hofstede, "Motivation, Leadership, and Organization: Do American Theories Apply Abroad?" *Organizational Dynamics*, Summer 1980: 42–63.

- *Assertiveness.* The extent to which a society encourages people to be tough, confrontational, assertive, and competitive versus modest and tender. (*High:* Spain, United States, and Greece. *Moderate:* Egypt, Ireland, and Philippines. *Low:* Sweden, New Zealand, and Switzerland.)

- *Future orientation.* The extent to which a society encourages and rewards future-oriented behavior such as planning, investing in the future, and delaying gratification. (*High:* Denmark, Canada, and Netherlands. *Moderate:* Slovenia, Egypt, and Ireland. *Low:* Russia, Argentina, and Poland.)

- *Gender differentiation.* The extent to which a society maximizes gender role differences. (*High:* South Korea, Egypt, and Morocco. *Moderate:* Italy, Brazil, and Argentina. *Low:* Sweden, Denmark, and Slovenia.)

- *Uncertainty avoidance.* As defined in Hofstede's landmark research, the GLOBE team defined this term as a society's reliance on social norms and procedures to alleviate the unpredictability of future events. (*High:* Austria, Denmark, and Germany. *Moderate:* Israel, United States, and Mexico. *Low:* Russia, Hungary, and Bolivia.)

- *Power distance.* As in the original research, the GLOBE team defined this as the degree to which members of a society expect power to be unequally shared. (*High:* Russia, Spain, and Thailand. *Moderate:* England, France, and Brazil. *Low:* Denmark, Netherlands, and South Africa.)

- *Individualism/collectivism.* Again, this term was defined similarly to the original research as the degree to which individuals are encouraged by societal institutions to be integrated into groups within organizations and society. A low score is synonymous with collectivism. (*High:* Greece, Hungary, and Germany. *Moderate:* Hong Kong, United States, and Egypt. *Low:* Denmark, Singapore, and Japan.)

- *In-group collectivism.* In contrast to focusing on societal institutions, this dimension encompasses the extent to which members of a society take pride in membership in small groups such as their family and circle of close friends and the organizations in which they are employed. (*High:* Egypt, China, and Morocco. *Moderate:* Japan, Israel, and Qatar. *Low:* Denmark, Sweden, and New Zealand.)

- *Performance orientation.* This dimension refers to the degree to which a society encourages and rewards group members for performance improvement and excellence. (*High:* United States, Taiwan, and New Zealand. *Moderate:* Sweden, Israel, and Spain. *Low:* Russia, Argentina, and Greece.)

- *Humane orientation.* This cultural aspect is the degree to which a society encourages and rewards individuals for being fair, altruistic, generous, caring, and kind to others. (*High:* Indonesia, Egypt, and Malaysia. *Moderate:* Hong Kong, Sweden, and Taiwan. *Low:* Germany, Spain, and France.)

The GLOBE studies confirm the validity of Hofstede's dimensions and extend his research rather than replace it. GLOBE's added dimensions provide an expanded and updated measure of countries' cultural differences. It's likely that cross-cultural studies of human behavior and organizational practices will increasingly use the GLOBE dimensions to assess differences between countries.

What Does Society Expect from Organizations and Managers?

3-3 Discuss how society's expectations are influencing managers and organizations.

social responsibility (corporate social responsibility, or CSR)
A business firm's intention, beyond its legal and economic obligations, to do the right things and act in ways that are good for society

social obligation
When a business firm engages in social actions because of its obligation to meet certain economic and legal responsibilities

social responsiveness
When a business firm engages in social actions in response to some popular social need

Jet Blue launched its social responsibility initiative Soar with Reading as a literacy program designed to inspire and encourage kids' imaginations "to take flight" through reading. One part of the program involves distributing free books for children in need through vending machines JetBlue installs in disadvantaged neighborhoods throughout the communities the airline serves.

It's an **incredibly simple, but totally world-changing,** idea.

What is *it*? The business model followed by TOMS shoes: For each pair of shoes sold, a pair is donated to a child in need. As a contestant on the CBS reality show *The Amazing Race,* Blake Mycoskie, founder of TOMS, visited Argentina and "saw lots of kids with no shoes who were suffering from injuries to their feet." He was so moved by the experience that he wanted to do something. That *something* is what TOMS Shoes does now by blending charity with commerce. Those shoe donations—now more than 70 million pairs—have been central to the success of the TOMS brand. In recent years, the company has used its "one for one" model to sell other products including eyewear, coffee, and bags.

What *does* society expect from organizations and managers? That may seem like a hard question to answer, but not for Blake Mycoskie. Even though he has stepped away from the CEO's job, he still believes that society expects organizations and managers to be responsible and ethical *and* to give something back. However, as we found out in now-well-known stories of notorious financial scandals at Wells Fargo, Enron, Bernard Madoff Investment Securities, HealthSouth, and others, some managers *don't* act responsibly or ethically.

How Can Organizations Demonstrate Socially Responsible Actions?

Few terms have been defined in as many different ways as *social responsibility*—profit maximization, going beyond profit making, voluntary activities, and concern for the broader social system are but a few.[13] These descriptions fall into two camps. On one side is the classical—or purely economic—view that management's only social responsibility is to maximize profits.[14] On the other side is the socioeconomic position, which holds that management's responsibility goes beyond making profits to include protecting and improving society's welfare.[15]

When *we* talk about **social responsibility** (also known as **corporate social responsibility, or CSR**), we mean a business firm's intention, beyond its legal and economic obligations, to do the right things and act in ways that are good for society. Note that this definition assumes that a business ❶ obeys the law and ❷ pursues economic interests. But also note that this definition ❸ views a business as a moral agent. *In its effort to do good for society, it must differentiate between right and wrong.*

We can understand social responsibility better if we compare it to two similar concepts. **Social obligations** are those activities a business firm engages in to meet certain economic and legal responsibilities. It does the minimum that the law requires and only pursues social goals to the extent that they contribute to its economic goals. **Social responsiveness**

Jesus Aranguren/AP Images

is characteristic of the business firm that engages in social actions in response to some popular social need. Managers in these companies are guided by social norms and values and make practical, market-oriented decisions about their actions.[16] A U.S. business that meets federal pollution standards or safe packaging regulations is meeting its social obligation because laws mandate these actions. However, when it provides on-site child-care facilities for employees or packages products using recycled paper, it's being socially responsive to working parents and environmentalists who have voiced these social concerns and demanded such actions. For many businesses, their social actions are probably better viewed as being socially responsive rather than socially responsible, at least according to our definitions. Although such actions are still good for society, social responsibility adds an *ethical imperative* to do those things that make society better and to not do those that could make it worse.

Should Organizations Be Socially Involved?

Would an organization's views on social responsibility be important to you in deciding whether to work there? It is for a lot of young adults!

The importance of corporate social responsibility surfaced in the 1960s when social activists questioned the singular economic objective of business. Even today, good arguments can be made for and against businesses being socially responsible. (See Exhibit 3–2.) Yet, arguments aside, times have changed. **Managers regularly confront decisions that have a dimension of social responsibility:** philanthropy, pricing, employee relations, resource conservation, product quality, and doing business in countries with oppressive governments are just a few. To address these issues, managers may reassess packaging design, recyclability of products, environmental safety practices, outsourcing decisions, foreign supplier practices, employee policies, and the like.

Another way to look at this issue is whether social involvement affects a company's economic performance, which numerous studies have done.[17] Although most found a small positive relationship between social involvement and economic performance, no generalizable conclusions can be made because these studies have shown that the relationship is affected by various contextual factors such as firm size, industry, economic conditions, and regulatory environment.[18] Other researchers have questioned causation. If a study showed that social involvement and economic performance were positively related, this didn't necessarily mean that social involvement *caused* higher economic performance. It could simply mean that high profits afforded companies the "luxury" of being socially involved.[19] Such concerns can't be taken lightly. In fact, one study found that if the flawed empirical analyses in these studies were "corrected," social responsibility had a neutral impact on a company's financial performance.[20] Another found that participating in social issues not related to the organization's primary stakeholders had a negative effect on shareholder value.[21] Despite all these concerns, after reanalyzing several studies, other researchers have concluded that *managers can afford to be (and should be) socially responsible.*[22]

Exhibit 3–2 Arguments For and Against Social Responsibility

FOR

Public expectations
Public opinion now supports businesses pursuing economic and social goals.

Long-run profits
Socially responsible companies tend to have more secure long-run profits.

Ethical obligation
Businesses should be socially responsible because responsible actions are the right thing to do.

Public image
Businesses can create a favorable public image by pursuing social goals.

Better environment
Business involvement can help solve difficult social problems.

Discouragement of further governmental regulation
By becoming socially responsible, businesses can expect less government regulation.

Balance of responsibility and power
Businesses have a lot of power and an equally large amount of responsibility is needed to balance against that power.

Stockholder interests
Social responsibility will improve a business's stock price in the long run.

Possession of resources
Businesses have the resources to support public and charitable projects that need assistance.

Superiority of prevention over cures
Businesses should address social problems before they become serious and costly to correct.

AGAINST

Violation of profit maximization
Business is being socially responsible only when it pursues its economic interests.

Dilution of purpose
Pursuing social goals dilutes business's primary purpose—economic productivity.

Costs
Many socially responsible actions do not cover their costs and someone must pay those costs.

Too much power
Businesses have a lot of power already; if they pursue social goals, they will have even more.

Lack of skills
Business leaders lack the necessary skills to address social issues.

Lack of accountability
There are no direct lines of accountability for social actions.

Source: Robbins, Stephen P., Coulter, Mary, *Management*, 13th Ed., © 2016, p. 154. Reprinted and electronically reproduced by permission of Pearson Education, Inc., New York, NY.

 ## What Is Sustainability and Why Is It Important?

Being **green** at the world's largest retailer

- $485.9 billion in revenues
- 2.3 million employees
- 11,700+ stores

Sustainability goal:
Enhance the sustainability of operations and value chains.

Sustainability achievements:
26 percent of locations globally use renewable energy. 77 percent of global waste diverted from landfills. $200 billion worth of goods sold evaluated for sustainability performance.

Yes, we're talking about Walmart. And considering its size, Walmart is probably the last company you'd think of for being highlighted in a section describing sustainability. However, Walmart has committed to improving its sustainability efforts. Walmart's corporate actions affirm that sustainability has definitely become a mainstream issue for managers.

We introduced you to sustainability in Chapter 1 as we discussed factors reshaping management in today's organizations. Just a refresher: We defined **sustainability** as a company's ability to achieve its business goals and increase long-term shareholder value by integrating economic, environmental, and social opportunities into its business strategies.[23] Organizations are widening their responsibility not just to managing in an efficient and effective way, but also to responding strategically to a wide range of environmental and societal challenges.[24] Like the managers at Walmart (and others committed to being sustainable) are discovering, running an organization in a more sustainable way means making informed business decisions based on thorough and ongoing communication with various stakeholders, understanding their requirements, and factoring economic, environmental, and social aspects into how they pursue their business goals.

Seventy-five percent of workplaces have at least one green technology practice.[25]

The idea of practicing sustainability affects many aspects of business, from the creation of products and services to their use and subsequent disposal by consumers. (Check out Case Application #2 on Keurig Green Mountain Inc. and the Experiential Exercise at the end of the chapter.) Following sustainability practices is one way in which organizations can show their commitment to being responsible. *In today's world, where many individuals have diminishing respect for businesses, few organizations can afford the bad press or potential economic ramifications of being seen as socially irresponsible.* Managers also want to be seen as ethical, which is the topic we're going to look at next.

Making Ethical Decisions in Today's Workplace

How important is building and maintaining the trust of a company's customers? Volkswagen set itself apart from the competition when it developed the so-called clean diesel engine, millions of which were placed in cars throughout Europe, the United States, and other countries. Marketing materials heralded the VW diesel engines as good for the environment because they emitted low levels of harmful nitrogen oxides. However, it was revealed that VW knowingly installed software that, when the car was being tested for emissions, cleared and cleaned these pollutants from the exhaust. Knowingly defeating emissions testing has all but destroyed VW's credibility and consumer trust in its products. How ironic that the Volkswagen Group's Audi brand coined the phrase *truth in engineering*. Since the news came to light, VW's CEO resigned and senior engineers' employment was terminated.[26]

Discussion Questions:

3 What is the ethical dilemma here? What stakeholders might be affected and how might they be affected? What personal, organizational, and environmental factors might be important? What ethical safeguards do you think need to be in place to prevent this from happening again?

4 Whose responsibility is it to ensure that ethical practices are in place and implemented? What can other organizations learn from this situation?

What Factors Determine Ethical and Unethical Behavior?

3-4 Discuss the factors that lead to ethical and unethical behavior in organizations.

- Employees at a law firm in Florida that handled foreclosures for Freddie Mac and Fannie Mae changed thousands of documents and hid them when company officials came to conduct audits.[27]
- A Paris court found Jérôme Kerviel, a former financial trader at French bank Société Générale, guilty of triggering a massive trading scandal that created severe financial problems for his employer. Mr. Kerviel claims that the company turned a blind eye to his questionable but hugely profitable methods.[28]
- The National Football League finally admitted in federal court documents that it "expects nearly a third of retired players to develop long-term cognitive problems" and that players may see the problems happening at noticeably younger ages.[29]

sustainability
A company's ability to achieve its business goals and increase long-term shareholder value by integrating economic, environmental, and social opportunities into its business strategies

You might be wondering about the connection among these three unrelated stories. When you read about these decisions, behaviors, and outcomes, you might be tempted to conclude that businesses just aren't ethical. Although that isn't the case, *managers do face ethical issues*, as the preceding examples show.

Ethics commonly refers to a set of rules or principles that defines right and wrong conduct.[30] Right or wrong behavior, though, may at times be difficult to determine. Most recognize that something illegal is also unethical. But what about questionable "legal" areas or strict organizational policies? For instance, what if you managed an employee who worked all weekend on a rush project and you told him to take off two days sometime later and mark it down as "sick days" because your company had a clear policy that overtime would not be compensated for any reason?[31] Would that be wrong? As a manager, how will you handle such situations? As an employee, how will you react when ethical dilemmas arise?

In What Ways Can Ethics Be Viewed?

To better understand what's involved with managerial ethics, we need to first look at three different perspectives on how managers make ethical decisions.[32] The **utilitarian view of ethics** says that ethical decisions are made solely on the basis of their outcomes or consequences. The goal of utilitarianism is to provide the greatest good for the greatest number. In the **rights view of ethics**, individuals are concerned with respecting and protecting individual liberties and privileges such as the right of free consent, the right to privacy, the right of free speech, and so forth. Making ethical decisions under this view is fairly simple because the goal is to avoid interfering with the rights of others who might be affected by the decision. Finally, under the **theory of justice view of ethics**, an individual imposes and enforces rules fairly and impartially. For instance, a manager would be using the theory of justice perspective by deciding to pay individuals who are similar in their levels of skills, performance, or responsibility the same and not base that decision on arbitrary differences such as gender, personality, or personal favorites. The goal of this approach is to be equitable, fair, and impartial in making decisions.

Whether a manager (or any employee, for that matter) acts **ethically or unethically depends** on several factors.

These factors include an individual's morality, values, personality, and experiences; the organization's culture; and the ethical issue being faced.[33] People who lack a strong moral sense are much less likely to do the wrong things if they are constrained by rules, policies, job descriptions, or strong cultural norms that discourage such behaviors. For example, suppose that someone in your class stole the final exam and is selling a copy for $50. You need to do well on the exam or risk failing the course. You suspect that some classmates have bought copies, which could affect any results because your professor grades on a curve. Do you buy a copy because you fear that without it you'll be disadvantaged, do you refuse to buy a copy and try your best, or do you report your knowledge to your instructor? This example of the stolen final exam illustrates how *ambiguity over what is ethical* can be a problem for managers and employees.

How Can Managers Encourage Ethical Behavior?

At a Senate hearing exploring the accusations that Wall Street firm Goldman Sachs deceived its clients during the housing-market meltdown, Arizona senator John McCain said, "I don't know if Goldman has done anything *illegal*, but there's no doubt their behavior was *unethical*."[34] You have to wonder what the firm's managers were thinking or doing while such ethically questionable decisions and actions were occurring. It's pretty obvious that they weren't encouraging ethical behaviors!

Managing Technology in Today's Workplace
THE ETHICS OF DATA ANALYTICS

Every time you click on anything in Facebook or do a search in Google or purchase anything on Amazon or post anything on Instagram, data are being collected about you. Technology has evolved to the point where companies can capture data about consumer habits any time they access a website, post on social media, do a search, or purchase something online. But it's not just on external websites that data are being collected and analyzed. A recent article in the *Wall Street Journal* discussed how certain companies have been analyzing a wide variety of data points on employees to try to pinpoint who is likely to leave the organization.[35] Since employee turnover costs money and time, companies want to try to get an early handle on it so managers can take action before an employee—and especially a good employee—decides to leave.

Statisticians and data scientists have expressed misgivings about the lack of ethical guidelines for big data research and analytics, especially online. Just because we have the technology to collect these vast amounts of quantifiable information that can be analyzed by highly sophisticated data processing, should we? *And* should

organizations (managers) be using it? When it was discovered that Facebook had manipulated news feeds either positively or negatively of more than half a million randomly selected users to see how emotions spread on social media, people were outraged. But Facebook isn't the only one that manipulates and analyzes user data. Google, Yahoo!, Amazon, and others also manipulate and analyze these data, all under the guise of "improving the user experience."[36] The technology of data analytics itself is ethics-free; it's neither good nor bad. But it's in *how* the technology is used that ethical concerns can arise.

Discussion Questions:
5 What does it mean that the technology of data analytics is ethics-free?

6 Is it even possible for managers to ethically use big data? Discuss this in your "assigned" group and come up with arguments for both sides: Yes, it is possible for managers to ethically use big data and No, it is not possible for managers to ethically use big data.

If managers are serious about **encouraging ethical behaviors**, there are a number of things they can do.

Like what? Hire employees with high ethical standards, establish codes of ethics, lead by example, link job goals and performance appraisal, provide ethics training, and implement protective mechanisms for employees who face ethical dilemmas. By themselves, such actions won't have much of an impact. But if an organization has a comprehensive ethics program in place, it can potentially improve an organization's ethical climate. The key variable, however, is *potentially*. A well-designed ethics program does not guarantee the desired outcome. Sometimes corporate ethics programs are mostly public relations gestures that do little to influence managers and employees. For instance, even Enron, often thought of as the "poster child" of corporate wrongdoing, outlined values in its final annual report that most would consider ethical—communication, respect, integrity, and excellence. Yet the way top managers behaved didn't reflect those values at all.[37] We want to look at three ways that managers can encourage ethical behavior and create a comprehensive ethics program.

CODES OF ETHICS. Codes of ethics are popular tools for attempting to reduce employee ambiguity about what's ethical and what's not.[38] A **code of ethics** is a formal document that states an organization's primary values and the ethical rules it expects managers and nonmanagerial employees to follow. Ideally, these codes should be specific enough to guide organizational members in what they're supposed to do yet loose enough to allow for freedom of judgment. Research shows that 97 percent of organizations with more than 10,000 employees have written codes of ethics. Even in smaller organizations, nearly 93 percent have them.[39] And codes of ethics are becoming more popular globally. Research by the Institute for Global Ethics says that shared values such as honesty, fairness, respect, responsibility, and caring are embraced worldwide.[40]

code of ethics
A formal document that states an organization's primary values and the ethical rules it expects managers and nonmanagerial employees to follow

The effectiveness of such codes depends heavily on whether management supports them and ingrains them into the corporate culture, and how individuals who break the codes are treated.[41] If management considers them to be important, regularly reaffirms their content, follows the rules itself, and publicly reprimands rule breakers, ethics codes can be a strong foundation for an effective corporate ethics program.[42]

ETHICAL LEADERSHIP. Tim Cook has been CEO of Apple Inc since 2011. Although it's an extremely successful company, Apple is viewed by some as the epitome of greedy capitalism with no concern for how its products are manufactured. Cook, who was named one of the 100 Most Influential People in Business Ethics by *Ethisphere*, has increased the company's focus on supply chain ethics and compliance issues. It was the first technology company to join the Fair Labor Association, which means that organization can now review the company's labor practices within the supply chain. In addition, at a recent annual stockholders' meeting with investors and journalists, Cook, who was challenged by a spokesperson from a conservative think tank to explain how the company's sustainability efforts were in the best interests of shareholders, bluntly and clearly said that Apple wasn't just about making a profit and that "We want to leave the world better than we found it."[43]

Doing business ethically requires a commitment from managers. Why? Because they're the ones who uphold the shared values and set the cultural tone. Managers must be good ethical role models both in words *and,* more importantly, in actions. For example, if managers take company resources for their personal use, inflate their expense accounts, or give favored treatment to friends, they imply that such behavior is acceptable for all employees.

What you DO is *far more important* than what you SAY in getting employees to act ethically!

Managers also set the tone through their reward and punishment practices. The choices of when to reward with pay increases and promotions send a strong signal to employees. As we said earlier, when an employee is rewarded for achieving impressive results in an ethically questionable manner, it indicates to others that those ways are acceptable. When an employee does something unethical, managers must punish the offender and publicize the fact by making the outcome visible to everyone in the organization. This practice sends a message that doing wrong has a price and it's not in employees' best interests to act unethically! (See Exhibit 3–3 for suggestions on being an ethical leader.)

Through his words and actions, L'Oreal's CEO and chairman Jean-Paul Agon is committed to doing business ethically. Leading by example, he expects all managers and employees to model ethical behavior and integrates ethical principles into all of L'Oreal's business practices that build relationships of trust with the company's customers.

Charles Platiau/Reuters

ETHICS TRAINING. Yahoo! used an off-the-shelf online ethics training package, but employees said that the scenarios used to demonstrate different concepts didn't resemble those that might come up at Yahoo! and were too middle-American and middle-aged for the global company with a youthful workforce. So the company changed its ethics training! The new ethics training package is more animated and interactive and has more realistic storylines for the industry. The 45-minute training module covers the company's code of conduct and resources available to help employees understand it.[44]

Like Yahoo!, more and more organizations are setting up seminars, workshops, and similar ethics training programs to encourage ethical behavior. Such training programs aren't without controversy; the primary concern is whether ethics can be taught.

Exhibit 3–3 **Being an Ethical Leader**

> - Be a good role model by being ethical and honest.
> - Tell the truth always.
> - Don't hide or manipulate information.
> - Be willing to admit your failures.
> - Share your personal values by regularly communicating them to employees.
> - Stress the organization's or team's important shared values.
> - Use the reward system to hold everyone accountable to the values.

Critics stress that the effort is pointless because people establish their individual value systems when they're young. Proponents note, however, that several studies have shown that values can be learned after early childhood. In addition, they cite evidence that shows that teaching ethical problem solving can make an actual difference in ethical behaviors;[45] that training has increased individuals' level of moral development;[46] and that, if nothing else, ethics training increases awareness of ethical issues in business.[47]

CHAPTER SUMMARY BY LEARNING OUTCOME

3-1 Explain globalization and its impact on organizations.

Organizations are considered global if they exchange goods and services with consumers in other countries, if they use managerial and technical employee talent from other countries, or if they use financial sources and resources outside their home country. Businesses going global are usually referred to as multinational corporations (MNCs). As an MNC, they may operate as a multidomestic corporation, a global corporation, or a transnational or borderless organization. When a business goes global, it may start with global sourcing, move to exporting or importing, use licensing or franchising, pursue a global strategic alliance, or set up a foreign subsidiary.

3-2 Describe what managers need to know about managing in a global organization.

In doing business globally, managers need to be aware of different laws, economic systems, as well as political views on issues such as immigration and free trade. But the biggest challenge is understanding the different country cultures. Two cross-cultural frameworks that managers can use are Hofstede's and GLOBE.

3-3 Discuss how society's expectations are influencing managers and organizations.

Society expects organizations and managers to be responsible and ethical. An organization's social involvement can be from the perspective of social obligation, social responsiveness, or social responsibility. After much analysis, researchers have concluded that managers can afford to be (and should be) socially responsible. Sustainability has become an important societal issue for managers and organizations.

3-4 Discuss the factors that lead to ethical and unethical behavior in organizations.

Ethics can be viewed from the utilitarian view, the rights view, or the theory of justice view. Whether a manager acts ethically or unethically depends on his or her morality, values, personality, and experiences; the organization's culture; and the ethical issue being faced. Managers can encourage ethical behavior by hiring employees with high ethical standards, establishing a code of ethics, leading by example, linking ethical behavior to job goals and performance appraisal, providing ethics training, and implementing protective mechanisms for employees who face ethical dilemmas.

DISCUSSION QUESTIONS

3-1 How does the concept of a global village affect organizations and managers?

3-2 Discuss how society's expectations are influencing managers and organizations.

3-3 Should managers be parochialistic? Why or why not?

3-4 What are the managerial implications of Hofstede's research on cultural environments? The GLOBE study?

3-5 How might the cultural differences in the GLOBE dimensions affect how managers (a) use work groups, (b) develop goals/plans, (c) reward outstanding employee performance, and (d) deal with employee conflict?

3-6 How are social responsibility, social obligation, and social responsiveness different? Similar?

3-7 Should organizations be socially involved?

3-8 Describe how a manager would approach ethical decisions according to each of the three views on ethics.

3-9 Discuss specific ways managers can encourage ethical behavior.

3-10 How can organizational leaders be good role models when it comes to ethical behavior?

Applying: Getting Ready for the Workplace

Management Skill Builder | **BUILDING HIGH ETHICAL STANDARDS**

Ethics encompasses the rules and principles we use to define right and wrong conduct. Many organizations have formally written ethical codes to guide managers and employees in their decisions and actions. But individuals need to establish their own personal ethical standards. If managers are to successfully lead others, they need to be seen as trustworthy and ethical.

MyLab Management
PERSONAL INVENTORY ASSESSMENT

Go to **www.pearson.com/mylab/management** to complete the Personal Inventory Assessment related to this chapter.

Skill Basics

To be more ethical in your leadership, focus on what *you* can do and what *your organization* can do. Here are some suggestions on how to do this:

What You Can Do:

- *Know your values.* What's important to you? Where do you draw the line?

- *Think before you act.* Will your actions injure someone? What are your ulterior motives? Will your actions jeopardize your reputation?

- *Consider all consequences.* If you make the wrong decision, what will happen? Every decision comes with consequences and you should be sure you've considered their implications.

- *Apply the "publicity test."* What would your family and friends think if your actions were described in detail on the front page of your local newspaper or on the local TV news?

- *Seek opinions from others. Ask advice from others you respect.* Use their experience and listen to their perspectives.

What Your Organization Can Do:

- *Create a formal ethics code.* Organizations should set down their ethical standards and policies in a formal ethical code. The code should be widely distributed to all employees.

- *Set an ethical culture.* Visibly reward employees who set a high ethical standard and visibly punish those who engage in unethical practices.

- *Ensure managers are role models.* Employees look to their immediate superior and upper management for cues as to what is or is not acceptable behavior. Managers need to be positive ethical role models.

- *Offer ethics workshops.* Employees should participate in regular ethics training to reinforce the importance of high ethical standards, to interpret the organization's ethical code, and to allow employees to clarify what they may see as "gray areas."

- *Appoint an ethics "advisor."* A senior executive should be available for employees to meet and confer with to confidentially discuss ethical concerns.

- *Protect employees who report unethical practices.* Mechanisms need to be put in place that protect employees from retributions or other negative consequences

should they reveal unethical practices that are a threat to others.

Based on L. Nash, "Ethics without the Sermon," *Harvard Business Review*, November–December 1981, pp. 78–92; W. D. Hall, *Making the Right Decision: Ethics for Managers* (New York: John Wiley, 1993); and L. K. Trevino and K. A. Nelson, *Managing Business Ethics: Straight Talk about How to Do It Right* (New York: John Wiley, 1995).

Practicing the Skill

We're taking a little different approach with this chapter's skill practice. Form into teams of four or five people. Using a copy of your college's code of conduct, answer the following questions: How many of the team members were aware of the code? How many had read it? Evaluate the code's provisions and policies. Are you uncomfortable with any of the code's provisions? Why? How effective do you think they have been in shaping student and faculty behavior? If they haven't been effective, what could be done to improve them?

Be prepared to present your team's findings to the class.

Experiential Exercise

We very much appreciate you, our employees, and we believe that we have a responsibility to you. Not just to provide a paycheck (although that's pretty important), but also to provide and sustain a safe, healthy, and functional workplace. We would like to see ourselves on the forefront of sustainable workplace and workforce practices.[48] To achieve sustainability, we're going to have to identify and put in place practical and efficient work processes that (1) help us reduce each employee's carbon footprint (to be more "green,") and (2) provide you with occupational wellness programs and stress-reducing strategies. By doing this, we can achieve a sustainable work environment and a sustainable and productive work force. . .YOU. However, we don't want to dictate what this is going to look like! We want you to be involved in creating this. Therefore, we're going to assign each of you to a team that will brainstorm and come up with some creative ways that we can proceed to have a healthy and sustainable environment both inside and outside our organization. Use the following template to guide your group's discussion.[49] We've given you one idea! Now, it's your turn! Provide at least 2 ideas for each workplace dimension. Show us what you got!! We know you can come up with some great ideas!

Steps to Sustainability

Workplace Dimension	Initial Steps	Where We Want to Be
FOOD	Provide indoor/outdoor dining options	Have an on-site kitchen facility for employee use
OFFICE DESIGN		
EMPLOYEE FITNESS		
FACILITY MAINTENANCE		

CASE APPLICATION #1

Global Control

Topic: Global organization, global ethics, and social responsibility

You're starting to see them everywhere...charging stations for electric vehicles (EVs). That's a sure sign that the global auto industry is going through a massive change. You shouldn't be surprised, therefore, that experts are predicting that electric vehicles (EVs) will be as cheap as gasoline models by 2025. Or that by the year 2040, one-third of the global auto fleet will be EVs.[50] The highest demand for EVs likely will be driven by the world's biggest economies: Europe, the United States, and China. Rather than fossil-fuel powered cars, which require millions of barrels a day of oil production, batteries are becoming "the" essential products. The decline in oil production—which will lead to serious consequences for oil-exporting countries—is being offset by rising production of lithium-ion batteries. That's where the next boom is coming!

The lithium-ion batteries that power EVs are the same type of batteries that power your laptops and smartphones. Producing those rechargeable batteries, requires cobalt, and the world's biggest producer of cobalt is Congo. Who do you think is the biggest consumer of cobalt from Congo? It's not who you might think. It's China.[51] Chinese companies betting big on battery production, are keenly aware of Congo's importance to controlling the battery market. And these Chinese companies now dominate the first steps in the lithium-ion battery production process and produce over three-fourths of all refined cobalt chemicals.

One Chinese company in particular, Contemporary Amperex Technology Ltd., or CATL, has quickly become the EV battery production leader.[52] Now, it's looking to expand abroad. It's gearing up by building a massive $1.3 billion battery production complex in Ningde, a city in eastern China. The complex will be second in size only to Tesla Inc.'s mammoth Gigafactory in Sparks, Nevada. However, with this huge expansion, CATL will surpass the capacity of all other suppliers combined. When the factory is up and running (planned for 2020), it will be the largest EV battery manufacturer in the world. As one consultant described, CATL's "intentions are very clear." It wants to be the biggest battery producer in the world, which means doing business beyond China. Right now, however, 99 percent of CATL's business comes from home contracts in China. Some of these have included foreign automakers that "have been forced to partner with local battery makers" if they want to sell EVs in China. Where is CATL looking to go next? Europe and of course, the United States. Can it succeed in the global market? Will it be able to compete without government support? Only time will tell. It's already acquired a contract manufacturer in Finland and has added offices in Paris and facilities in Germany. It's definitely making global moves.

The challenges of ADAPTING TO INDUSTRY CHANGE

Discussion Questions

3-11 How does this story illustrate a global village?

3-12 Using Exhibit 3-1, what approach is China's CATL using to go global? Explain your choice(s).

3-13 What kind of MNC do you think CATL is? Explain your choice.

3-14 How would Hofstede's dimensions of national culture and GLOBE findings be useful to CATL's management as it moves to Europe and eventually the United States?

3-15 As much as 14 percent of the cobalt output in Congo comes from mining done by *creuseurs* or freelancers.[53] U.S. and European companies are leery of doing business with cobalt suppliers who buy from these *creuseurs*, partly because some of the miners are children. These children rarely wear safety masks or other safety equipment and can suffer crippling injuries doing this dangerous job. (a) Does this response by these companies fall under the classical view of social responsibility or the socioeconomic view of social responsibility? Explain. (b) Look at the definition of social responsibility in the chapter and discuss the ethical factors in this scenario.

CASE APPLICATION #2

 Serious about Sustainability?
Topic: Protect the Bees!

Each year, 10 to 16 percent of global harvests is lost to plant pests, a loss that is estimated at around €175 billion, according to the latest report by the Food and Agriculture Organization.[54] Pests pose a threat to the global food supply and may lead to economic losses at the national level.[55] Moreover, they have a major impact on the profits of small farmers, many of whom depend on their harvests for subsistence. Pests are also mobile, and as food and beverage trade increases, infested food products in boxes and containers spread diseases and invasive organisms to other countries, infesting trees, and destroying forests.[56]

Pesticides have commonly been used to fight pests, and Bayer, a German multinational life science company, is one of many global companies that specialize in pesticide products. With more than 150 years of experience under its belt, in addition to its pharmaceutical line of products, Bayer is one of world's oldest multinational corporations specializing in pest control and crop sciences. The Bayer Group has 241 consolidated companies in 79 countries around the world, and its global headquarters is based in Leverkusen, Germany.

On its website, Bayer claims that their insecticides are developed to be safe and pose no threat to humans and the environment, provided they are used "responsibly and correctly."[57] Bayer claims a tradition of environmental safety over a period of several years, including rigorous testing of all its products and ensuring that they meet environmental safety standards and EU regulations. In addition, Bayer has focused heavily in recent years on data transparency by providing easy and fast public access to many of its products' test results.

However, environmentalists have criticized pesticide manufacturers on many fronts. According to the Pesticide Action Network UK, a non-profit organization for promotion of safe and sustainable practices, a very large percentage of the pesticides reach destinations other than its target pests, contaminating water, soil, plants, and living organisms in the process.[58] Bayer was one of three pesticide manufacturers who were heavily criticized recently for their use of substances known as neonicotinoids. Mass deaths of bees in recent years have shocked the scientific community.[59] Bees are considered one of the world's most important pollinator of food crops and a major player in maintaining our ecosystem. Scientists agree that there are several reasons for the increasing rates of bee deaths, one of which is the use of pesticides.[60] A recent study by the European Food Safety Authority confirmed the dangers of neonicotinoids to bees.[61] In 2018, after more reports surfaced about the harmful effects of neonicotinoids on bees, the European Union voted to ban three types of neonicotinoids, one of which is manufactured by Bayer.

However, the chemical giant has condemned the ban and touted the benefits of neonicotinoids for pest control and particularly for farmers. In a public statement, Bayer argued that the ban will not really help bees and other pollinators but will only lead to major agricultural consequences for farmers as there are no alternatives in the fight against the pests it targets. Bayer claimed that the substance is safe for bees—when used in accordance with the instructions on the label.[62] They said that alternative ways to support and protect bees need to be explored rather applying a total ban on the substance. Bayer will be appealing against the EU ruling.

For many environmentalists in Europe, however, the ban was good news. Their concern about the impact of pesticides on the environment sits comfortably with a recent study in the journal *Nature Plants*, which states that slashing the use of pesticides will not hurt the output of farms.[63]

Discussion Questions

3-16 Do you think the European Union's ban of one of Bayer's products in Europe will affect its use and reputation in other territories? Why or why not?

3-17 Do you think that the environmentalists have overstated the dangers of Bayer's products to bees?

3-18 Do you believe that Bayer is demonstrating socially responsible actions? Explain.

3-19 Do you agree with Bayer that the European Union's ban on some neonicotinoids is a "bad deal for Europe"? Discuss.

3-20 What lessons have you learned from this case about being socially responsible?

CASE APPLICATION #3

Flagrant Foul
Topic: 50 Years of Data Fraud

"In March 2018, Hiroya Kawasaki, the CEO of Kobe Steel, resigned over a big scandal. One of the largest steelmakers in Japan and a major supplier of metal parts to corporate giants like Mitsubishi, Panasonic, Ford, and Boeing, Kobe Steel admitted to having falsified its product specifications, misrepresenting the strength and durability of the parts sold to many of its clients.[64] The fake data affected more than 600 customers and sent shock waves through the supply-chain industry.

The news turned the company upside down, causing a series of resignations of many other key executives. A number of middle managers also faced pay cuts or similar measures. Kobe admitted that its executives and managers were aware of the fraud; some board members were also aware of this issue but did not report the problems in the board meetings. In a recent statement, Kobe blamed the overemphasis on productivity and profitability as having pushed Kobe's executives to act as they did.

Kobe Steel issued an apology statement on its website: as of December 20, 2018, users who visit the site are first greeted with a prominent statement saying, "We are extremely sorry for our misconduct." It goes on to announce that Kobe's employees are going back to the roots of "monozukuri," an old Japanese philosophy based on ethics and professional work in manufacturing. Amidst this scandal, Kawasaki stressed the need for a new way of management at Kobe Steel that would be "a fundamental transformation."[65] Yet Kobe Steel already had a 16-page-long code of ethics that was formulated as early as 2000, comprising ethical principles that included transparency and data accuracy.[66]

Kawasaki also admitted that that data fraud at the company was not something new and that it had been going on since the 1970s. The scandal was brought to light in October 2017 after a four-month-long internal investigation led to the discovery of the data fraud in its steel and machinery divisions. Kobe Steel has admitted that the scandal is very likely to decrease its profits sharply. Indeed, Kobe Steel's shares fell by more than 40 percent when the scandal first broke in late 2017. However, recent reports show that Kobe Steel is slowly recovering and has posted its first profit in three years despite the scandal, and it is predicting a profit of ¥45 billion in the year ending March 2019.[67] However, the company is still subject to an ongoing investigation by the U.S. Department of State, which could eventually penalize it and deal another financial blow.

Discussion Questions

3-21 Whom do you hold most responsible for the latest data fraud scandal at Kobe Steel?

3-22 How do you explain the statement by Kobe Steel that an overemphasis on productivity and profits led to the acts of fraud?

3-23 What kind of cultural transformation do you think is needed at Kobe Steel?

3-24 Do you believe that Kobe Steel will fully recover from the scandal? Can you think of any companies that recovered from similar scandals?

3-25 Kobe Steel's code of ethics appeared to have had little effect on the managers of the company. Briefly list the actions that you would recommend to ensure that Kobe Steel's employees actually abide by the ethical code.

Endnotes

1. J. Zumbrun, "Nations Are in Rare Economic Harmony," *Wall Street Journal*, January 23, 2018, p. R8.
2. P. Ghemawat, "Globalization in the Age of Trump," *Harvard Business Review*, July–August 2017, pp. 112–23.
3. B. Spindle and V. Agarwal, "Cashews: The Snack Built by Globalization," *Wall Street Journal*, December 2/3, 2017, pp. A1+.
4. V. Goel, "IBM Now Has More Employees in India Than in the U.S.," *New York Times Online*, September 28, 2017.
5. E. Beinhocker, I. Davis, and L. Mendonca, "The 10 Trends You Have to Watch," *Harvard Business Review*, July–August 2009, pp. 55–60.
6. B. Davis, "Migration of Skilled Jobs Abroad Unsettles Global-Economy Fans," *Wall Street Journal*, January 26, 2004, p. A1.
7. E. Frauenheim, "Bringing the Jobs Back Home: How 'Reshoring' Is Coming to America," www.workforce.com, February 7, 2013; J. E. Lessin and J. R. Hagerty, "A Mac That's 'Made in U.S.A.,'" *Wall Street Journal*, December 7, 2012, B1+; and V. Shannon, "Apple to Resume U.S. Manufacturing," *New York Times Online*, December 6, 2012.
8. A. Pande, "How to Make Onshoring Work," *Harvard Business Review*, March 2011, p. 30; P. Davidson, "Some Manufacturing Heads Back to USA," *USA Today*, August 6, 2010, pp. 1B+; and V. Couto, A. Divakaran, and M. Mani, "Is Backshoring the New Offshoring?" *Strategy & Business*, October 21, 2008, pp. 1–3.
9. J. Teresko, "United Plastics Picks China's Silicon Valley," *Industry Week*, January 2003, p. 58.
10. "Global Business: Getting the Frameworks Right," *Organization for Economic Cooperation and Development*, April 2000, p. 20.
11. Classic Concepts in Today's Workplace box based on D. Holtbrügge and A. T. Mohr, "Cultural Determinants of Learning Style Preferences," *Academy of Management Learning & Education*, December 2010, pp. 622–37; G. Hofstede, "The GLOBE Debate: Back to Relevance," *Journal of*

International Business Studies, November 2010, pp. 1339–46; G. A. Gelade, P. Dobson, and K. Auer, "Individualism, Masculinity, and the Sources of Organizational Commitment," *Journal of Cross-Cultural Psychology*, September 2008, pp. 599–617; G. Hofstede, "The Cultural Relativity of Organizational Practices and Theories," *Journal of International Business Studies*, Fall 1983, pp. 75–89; and G. Hofstede, *Culture Consequences: International Differences in Work-Related Values* (Beverly Hills, CA: Sage Publications, 1980), pp. 25–26. For an interesting discussion of collectivism and teams, see C. Gomez, B. L. Kirkman, and D. Shapiro, "The Impact of Collectivism and In-Group Membership on the Evaluation Generosity of Team Members," *Academy of Management Journal*, December 2000, pp. 1097–106. Hofstede's term for what we've called quantity of life and quality of life was actually "masculinity versus femininity," but we've changed his terms because of their strong sexist connotation.
12. R. J. House, N. R. Quigley, and M. S. deLuque, "Insights from Project GLOBE: Extending Advertising Research Through a Contemporary Framework," *International Journal of Advertising* 29, no. 1 (2010), pp. 111–39; R. R. McRae, A. Terracciano, A. Realo, and J. Allik, "Interpreting GLOBE Societal Practices Scale," *Journal of Cross-Cultural Psychology*, November 2008, pp. 805–10; J. S. Chhokar, F. C. Brodbeck, and R. J. House, *Culture and Leadership across the World: The GLOBE Book of In-Depth Studies of 25 Societies* (Philadelphia: Lawrence Erlbaum Associates, 2007); and R. J. House, P. J. Hanges, M. Javidan, P. W. Dorfman, and V. Gupta, *Culture, Leadership, and Organizations: The GLOBE Study of 62 Societies* (Thousand Oaks, CA: Sage Publications, 2004).
13. D. Dearlove and S. Crainer, "Enterprise Goes Social," *Chief Executive*, March 2002, p. 18; and "Bronze Winner: Ben & Jerry's Citizen Cool," *Brandweek*, March 18, 2002, p. R-24.
14. M. Friedman, *Capitalism and Freedom* (Chicago: University

of Chicago Press, 1962); and M. Friedman, "The Social Responsibility of Business Is to Increase Profits," *New York Times Magazine*, September 13, 1970, p. 33.
15. See, for instance, N. A. Ibrahim, J. P. Angelidis, and D. P. Howell, "The Corporate Social Responsiveness Orientation of Hospital Directors: Does Occupational Background Make a Difference?" *Health Care Management Review*, Spring 2000, pp. 85–92.
16. See, for example, D. J. Wood, "Corporate Social Performance Revisited," *Academy of Management Review*, October 1991, pp. 703–08; and S. L. Wartick and P. L. Cochran, "The Evolution of the Corporate Social Performance Model," *Academy of Management Review*, October 1985, p. 763.
17. See, for instance, R. Lacy and P. A. Kennett-Hensel, "Longitudinal Effects of Corporate Social Responsibility on Customer Relationships," *Journal of Business Ethics*, December 2010, pp. 581–97; S. Arendt and M. Brettel, "Understanding the Influence of Corporate Social Responsibility on Corporate Identity, Image, and Firm Performance," *Management Decision* 48, no. 10 (2010), pp. 1469–92; J. Peloza, "The Challenge of Measuring Financial Impacts from Investments in Corporate Social Performance," *Journal of Management*, December 2009, pp. 1518–41; J. D. Margolis and H. Anger Elfenbein, "Do Well by Doing Good? Don't Count on It," *Harvard Business Review*, January 2008, pp. 19–20; M. L. Barnett, "Stakeholder Influence Capacity and the Variability of Financial Returns to Corporate Social Responsibility," *Academy of Management Review* 32, no. 3 (2007), pp. 794–816. A. D. O. Neubaum and S. A. Zahra, "Institutional Ownership and Corporate Social Performance: The Moderating Effects of Investment Horizon, Activism, and Coordination," *Journal of Management*, February 2006, pp. 108–31; B. A. Waddock and S. B. Graves, "The Corporate Social Performance—Financial

Performance Link," *Strategic Management Journal*, April 1997, pp. 303–19; J. B. McGuire, A. Sundgren, and T. Schneeweis, "Corporate Social Responsibility and Firm Financial Performance," *Academy of Management Journal*, December 1988, pp. 854–72; K. Aupperle, A. B. Carroll, and J. D. Hatfield, "An Empirical Examination of the Relationship between Corporate Social Responsibility and Profitability," *Academy of Management Journal*, June 1985, pp. 446–63; and P. Cochran and R. A. Wood, "Corporate Social Responsibility and Financial Performance," *Academy of Management Journal*, March 1984, pp. 42–56.
18. "The Challenge of Measuring Financial Impacts from Investments in Corporate Social Performance."
19. B. Seifert, S. A. Morris, and B. R. Bartkus, "Having, Giving, and Getting: Slack Resources, Corporate Philanthropy, and Firm Financial Performance," *Business & Society*, June 2004, 135–61; and McGuire, Sundgren, and Schneeweis, "Corporate Social Responsibility and Firm Financial Performance."
20. A. McWilliams and D. Siegel, "Corporate Social Responsibility and Financial Performance: Correlation or Misspecification?" *Strategic Management Journal*, June 2000, pp. 603–09.
21. A. J. Hillman and G. D. Keim, "Shareholder Value, Stakeholder Management, and Social Issues: What's the Bottom Line?" *Strategic Management Journal* 22 (2001), pp. 125–39.
22. M. Orlitzky, F. L. Schmidt, and S. L. Rynes, "Corporate Social and Financial Performance," *Organization Studies* 24, no. 3 (2003), pp. 403–41.
23. Symposium on Sustainability: Profiles in Leadership, New York, October 2001.
24. G. Unruh and R. Ettenson, "Growing Green," *Harvard Business Review*, June 2010, pp. 94–100; G. Zoppo, "Corporate Sustainability," *DiversityInc*, May 2010, pp. 76–80; and KPMG Global Sustainability Services, *Sustainability Insights*, October 2007.

25. J. Yang and P. Trap, "Applying Green Tech at Work," *USA Today*, May 13, 2013, p. 1B.

26. W. Quigley, "VW Case Shows Need for Ethics in Cost-Benefit Toolkit," *Albuquerque Journal online*, www.abqjournal.com, October 15, 2015; J. Ewing, "Volkswagen Engine-Rigging Scheme Said to Have Begun in 2008," *New York Times Online*, October 5, 2015; "After a Year of Stonewalling, Volkswagen Finally Came Clean," www.cnbc.com, September 24, 2015; and J. Plungis and D. Hull, "VW's Emissions Cheating Found by Curious Clean-Air Group," *Bloomberg Businessweek Online*, September 19, 2015.

27. S. Armour and T. Frank, "Ex-Worker: Law Firm Ran 'Foreclosure Mill,'" *USA Today*, October 19, 2010, p. 3B.

28. N. Clark, "Rogue Trader at Societe Generale Gets Jail Term," *New York Times Online*, October 5, 2010.

29. K. Belson, "Brain Trauma to Affect One in Three Players, NFL Agrees," *New York Times Online*, September 12, 2014.

30. S. A. DiPiazza, "Ethics in Action," *Executive Excellence*, January 2002, pp. 15–16.

31. This example is based on J. F. Viega, T. D. Golden, and K. Dechant, "Why Managers Bend Company Rules," *Academy of Management Executive*, May 2004, pp. 84–90.

32. G. F. Cavanaugh, D. J. Moberg, and M. Valasquez, "The Ethics of Organizational Politics," *Academy of Management Journal*, June 1981, pp. 363–74.

33. J. Liedtka, "Ethics and the New Economy," *Business and Society Review*, Spring 2002, p. 1.

34. R. M. Kidder, "Can Disobedience Save Wall Street?" *Ethics Newsline*, www.globalethics.org, May 3, 2010.

35. R. E. Silverman and N. Waller, "Thinking of Quitting? The Boss Knows," *Wall Street Journal*, March 14, 2015, pp. A1+.

36. V. Goel, "Facebook Tinkers with Users' Emotions in News Feed Experiment, Stirring Outcry," *New York Times Online*, June 29, 2014.

37. P. M. Lencioni, "Make Your Values Mean Something," *Harvard Business Review*, July 2002, p. 113.

38. D. H. Schepers, "Setting Global Standards: Guidelines for Creating Codes of Conduct in Multinational Corporations," *Business and Society*, December 2003, p. 496; and B. R. Gaummitz and J. C. Lere, "Contents of Codes of Ethics of Professional Business Organizations in the United States," *Journal of Business Ethics*, January 2002, pp. 35–49.

39. M. Weinstein, "Survey Says: Ethics Training Works," *Training*, (November 2005): 15.

40. J. E. Fleming, "Codes of Ethics for Global Corporations," *Academy of Management News*, June 2005, p. 4.

41. T. F. Shea, "Employees' Report Card on Supervisors' Ethics: No Improvement," *HR Magazine*, April 2002, p. 29.

42. See also A. G. Peace, J. Weber, K. S. Hartzel, and J. Nightingale, "Ethical Issues in eBusiness: A Proposal for Creating the eBusiness Principles," *Business and Society Review*, Spring 2002, pp. 41–60.

43. L-M. Eleftheriou-Smith, "Apple's Tim Cook: 'Business Isn't Just about Making Profit'"; and P. Elmer-Dewitt, "Apple's Tim Cook Picks a Fight with Climate Change Deniers," tech.fortune.com, March 1, 2014.

44. E. Finkel, "Yahoo Takes New 'Road' on Ethics Training," *Workforce Management Online*, July 2010.

45. T. A. Gavin, "Ethics Education," *Internal Auditor*, April 1989, pp. 54–57.

46. L. Myyry and K. Helkama, "The Role of Value Priorities and Professional Ethics Training in Moral Sensitivity," *Journal of Moral Education* 31, no. 1 (2002), pp. 35–50; and W. Penn and B. D. Collier, "Current Research in Moral Development as a Decision Support System," *Journal of Business Ethics*, January 1985, pp. 131–36.

47. J. A. Byrne, "After Enron: The Ideal Corporation," *BusinessWeek*, August 19, 2002, pp. 68–71; D. Rice and C. Dreilinger, "Rights and Wrongs of Ethics Training,"

Training & Development Journal, May 1990, pp. 103–09; and J. Weber, "Measuring the Impact of Teaching Ethics to Future Managers: A Review, Assessment, and Recommendations," *Journal of Business Ethics*, April 1990, pp. 182–90.

48. "General Sustainability: What Are Sustainable Workplace Practices, and How Can They Benefit the Company's Bottom Line," https://www.shrm.org/resourcesandtools/tools-and-samples/hr-qa/pages/sustainableworkplacepracticesandhowtheybenefitthebottomline.aspx, December 17, 2012.

49. M. Padgett Powers, "In the Green," *HR Magazine*, October 2017, pp. 26–34.

50. J. Shankelman, "The Electric Car Revolution Is Accelerating," https://www.bloomberg.com/news/articles/2017-07-06/the-electric-car-revolution-is-accelerating, July 7, 2017.

51. S. Patterson and R. Gold, "There's a Global Race to Control Batteries—and China Is Winning," *Wall Street Journal*, February 12, 2018, pp. A1+.

52. J. Ma, D. Stringer, Z. Zhang, and S. Kim, "Electric Battery Makers Should Fear This Factory," *Bloomberg Businessweek*, February 12, 2018, pp. 19–20.

53. Ibid.

54. FAO, "Global Body Adopts New Measures to Stop the Spread of Plant Pests," April 18, 2018, http://www.fao.org/news/story/en/item/1118322/icode/.

55. D. Roiz, A. Fournier, C. J. A. Bradshaw, B. Leroy, M. Barbet-Massin, and J. Salles, "Massive yet Grossly Underestimated Global Costs of Invasive Insects," 2016, *Nature Communications*.

56. FAO, "Global Body Adopts New Measures to Stop the Spread of Plant Pests."

57. Bayer, "Why Insecticides Matter to Us," Crop Science, https://www.cropscience.bayer.co.za/en/Products/Insecticides.aspx.

58. Pesticide Action Network UK, "Pesticides in Our Environment," http://www.pan-uk.org/our-environment/.

59. Susan Milius, "The Mystery of Vanishing Honeybees Is Still Not Definitively Solved," *Science News*, January 17, 2018, https://www.sciencenews.org/article/mystery-vanishing-honeybees-still-not-definitively-solved.

60. "Matt McGrath, "Pesticides Linked to Bee Deaths Found in Most Honey Samples," *BBC News*, October 5, 2017, https://www.bbc.com/news/science-environment-41512791.

61. European Food Safety Authority, "Neonicotinoids: Risks to Bees Confirmed," https://www.efsa.europa.eu/en/press/news/180228.

62. "Neonicotinoid Ban: A Sad Day for Farmers and a Bad Deal for Europe," *Bayer News*, April 27, 2018, https://media.bayer.com/baynews/baynews.nsf/id/Neonicotinoid-ban-a-sad-day-for-farmers-and-a-bad-deal-for-Europe.

63. Martin Lechenet, Fabrice Dessaint, Guillaume Py, David Makowski, and Nicolas Munier-Jolain, "Reducing Pesticide Use While Preserving Crop Productivity and Profitability on Arable Farms," *Nature Plants* 3 (17008), March 1, 2017, https://www.nature.com/articles/nplants20178.

64. "Factbox: Kobe Steel's Affected Customers—From Computer Chips to Space Ships," *Reuters*, November 5, 2017, https://www.reuters.com/article/us-kobe-steel-scandal-customers-factbox/factbox-kobe-steels-affected-customers-from-computer-chips-to-space-ships-idUSKBN1D5019.

65. Tomomi Kikuchi, "Kobe Steel CEO Announces Resignation over Quality Scandal," March 6, 2018, https://asia.nikkei.com/Business/Kobe-Steel-CEO-announces-resignation-over-quality-scandal.

66. Kobelco, "Kobe Steel, Ltd. Corporate Code of Ethics," http://www.kobelco.co.jp/english/about_kobelco/kobesteel/cce/1_cce_en2.pdf.

67. "UPDATE 2-Kobe Steel Posts First Profit in Three Years Despite Data Fraud Scandal," *Reuters*, April 27, 2018, https://af.reuters.com/article/metalsNews/idAFL3N1S43HP.

4

Management Myth

It doesn't matter what an organization's culture is like. I can be happy working anywhere.

Management Myth DEBUNKED?

Anyone who thinks they can be happy working in any type of organizational setting might be in for a big surprise! Even working at a company rated as "a best company to work for" won't be for everyone. **To be happy, don't just "settle" for a job...find a workplace and a culture that "fit" you!**

WOULDN'T

it be nice to one day find a job you enjoy in an organization you're excited to go to every day (or at least most days!)? Although other factors influence job choice, an organization's culture can be an important indicator of "fit"—will I like working here and does this seem like a place where I can fit in and contribute? Organizational cultures differ and so do people. In the second part of this chapter, we'll look at what organizational culture is and what elements make up an organization's culture. Before that, however, we need to look at the external environment organizations face.

"Dynamic forces are sweeping across the globe, reshaping our lives and creating a wave of opportunities...."[1] No successful organization, or its managers, can operate without understanding the dynamic external environment that surrounds it. To better understand this external environment, we need to look at the important forces that are affecting the way organizations are managed today. ●

Learning Outcomes

What Is the External Environment and Why Is It Important?

4-1 Explain what the external environment is and why it's important.

One of the biggest mistakes managers make today is **failing to adapt** to the changing world. That's also one of the biggest mistakes you can make as an employee!

external environment
Factors, forces, situations, and events outside the organization that affect its performance

When the Eyjafjallajökull volcano erupted in Iceland, who would have thought that it would lead to a shutdown at the BMW plant in Spartanburg, South Carolina, or the Nissan Motor auto assembly facility in Japan?[2] Yet, in our globalized and interconnected world, such an occurrence shouldn't be surprising at all. As volcanic ash grounded planes across Europe, supplies of tire-pressure sensors from a company in Ireland couldn't be delivered on time to the BMW plant or to the Nissan plant. Because we live in a "connected" world, managers need to be aware of the impact of the external environment on their organization.

The term **external environment** refers to factors, forces, situations, and events outside the organization that affect its performance. As shown in Exhibit 4–1, it includes several different components. The economic component encompasses factors such as interest rates, inflation, employment/unemployment rates, disposable income levels, stock market fluctuations, and business cycle stages. The demographic component is concerned with trends in population characteristics such as age, race, gender, education level, geographic location, and family composition. The technological component is concerned with scientific or industrial innovations. The sociocultural component is concerned with societal and cultural factors such as values, attitudes, trends, traditions, lifestyles, beliefs, tastes, and patterns of behavior. The political/legal component looks at federal, state, and local laws, as well as laws of other countries and global laws. It also includes a country's political conditions and stability. And the global component encompasses those issues (like a volcano eruption, political instability, terrorist attack, etc.) associated with globalization and a world economy. Although *all* these components potentially constrain managers' decisions and actions, we're going to take a more in-depth look at just two—economic and demographic.

What Is the Economy Like Today?

Snapshots of the **economic context**:

- Digital currencies (also called virtual currencies or cryptocurrencies) are growing explosively. In Sweden, for instance, the use of cash has fallen rapidly.[3]
- After years of minimal inflation, U.S. manufacturers and food companies are facing rising material and ingredient costs as robust global economic growth stimulates demand.[4]
- Europe's economic recovery is being stifled by "zombie companies"—companies that are being kept afloat by cash/credit infusions from banks and shareholders despite the fact that they have not turned a profit in years. The result: thriving businesses cannot get needed capital to grow.[5]
- Climate change is reshaping supply networks, manufacturing processes, resource availability, and even workspace design.
- Entry-level jobs now are more "thinking" oriented and include more sophisticated responsibilities, reinforcing our emphasis on employability skills such as critical thinking, creative problem solving, and knowledge application and analysis.

Exhibit 4–1 Components of the External Environment

Source: Robbins, Stephen P., Coulter, Mary, *Management*, 13th Ed., © 2016, p. 73. Reprinted and electronically reproduced by permission of Pearson Education, Inc., New York, NY.

After several years in crisis mode, the U.S. economy and other global economies seem to have turned the corner. However, it's not now, nor will it ever be, smooth sailing in the economic arena for managers. After all, when you're dealing with important factors such as jobs, incomes, prices of natural resources and consumer goods, stock market valuations, and business cycle stages, managers have to pay attention to those that could constrain organizational decisions and actions. Here's a quick overview of some of the more interesting characteristics of today's economy that have the potential to influence a manager's planning, organizing, leading, and controlling:

- The slowdown in productivity has moderated globally although it continues to lag in the United States. Productivity (how much a worker produces in a hour) is an important measure of how well an economy is doing. Factors that affect productivity include types and pace of innovation, changes in work practices, technology, levels of workforce education/training/skill, etc.[6]
- Global trade grew strongly from the late 1970s through 2008, when it collapsed during the last global recession. However, recent indicators show global trade inching up, with the strongest growth in Europe and Asia.[7]
- Total U.S. employment is up. The 4.1 percent unemployment rate has held steady and is at the lowest level in years.[8] Workers are benefiting from broad-based gains in income and employment for over a decade.[9]
- Many U.S. workers, while employed in a steady job, may not have a reliable income. Why? By using flexible work schedules, businesses are exerting more control over employees' work hours, leading to more volatile paychecks.[10]
- Many businesses in low-wage industries (restaurants, retail, warehousing, and other services) are using part-time workers to soften the impact of health-care law mandates.[11]
- According to a Pew Research Center poll, only 17 percent of Americans believe the American dream—work hard and you can achieve success and riches—is out of reach. By race/ethnicity, the number who say it's out of reach is 15 percent of whites, 19 percent of blacks, and 17 percent of Hispanics.[12]

Despite these numbers, the World Economic Forum has identified a significant risk facing business leaders and policy makers over the next decade: "severe income disparity."[13] Let's briefly look at this issue to show that managers are constrained not just by the actual economic numbers, but also by societal attitudes about the economy.

ECONOMIC INEQUALITY AND THE ECONOMIC CONTEXT. A Harris Interactive Poll found that only 10 percent of adults think that economic inequality is "*not* a problem at all." Most survey respondents believed that it is either a major problem (57 percent) or a minor problem (23 percent).[14] Why has this issue become so sensitive? After all, individuals who worked hard, took risks, and were rewarded because of their hard work or creativity have long been admired. And yes, an income gap has always existed. In the United States, that gap between the rich and the rest has been much wider than in other developed nations for decades and was accepted as part of our country's values and way of doing things. However, our acceptance of an ever-increasing income gap may be diminishing.[15] As economic growth languished and sputtered, and as people's belief that anyone could grab hold of an opportunity and have a decent shot at prosperity wavered, social discontent over growing income gaps increased. The bottom line is that business leaders need to recognize how societal attitudes in the economic context also may create constraints as they make decisions and manage their businesses.

Lastly, in this section on the economy, we want to take a look at an interesting phenomenon taking place in the United States and around the globe—the sharing economy.

THE SHARING ECONOMY. Have you heard of Airbnb, Uber, Mobike, DogVacay, TaskRabbit, or Zipcar? These are just a few of the companies—maybe you've used one—that are part of what is called the "sharing economy." What is the **sharing economy**? It's an economic environment in which asset owners share with other individuals through a peer-to-peer service, for a fee, their underutilized physical assets (such as a home, car, clothing, tools, or other physical assets). Some analysts have included the sharing of knowledge, expertise, skills, or time, as well.[16] The concept behind the sharing economy is putting underutilized assets to good use. Asset owners "rent out" assets they're not using to consumers who need those assets but who don't want to, or who can't afford to, purchase them. As the sharing economy has grown, other terms—such as collaborative economy, on-demand economy, gig economy, freelance economy, peer economy, access economy, crowd economy, digital economy, and platform economy—have been used to better describe the various iterations of sharing that take place.[17] Even some economics experts have said that these arrangements aren't really "sharing" but are better described as market-mediated since there's a service or company that mediates the exchange between consumers. They suggest that the arrangement is more like an "access economy" because what consumers are looking for is convenient access to assets they need but don't have, and they're not concerned with developing a business or social relationship with the asset owner.[18] Whatever form or definition it takes, these new-economy platforms are likely to remain an important part of our global economic system.

The other external component we want to specifically look at is demographics. Why? Changes and trends in this component tend to be closely linked to the workplace and managing.

omnipotent view of management
The view that managers are directly responsible for an organization's success or failure

symbolic view of management
The view that much of an organization's success or failure is due to external forces outside managers' control

sharing economy
An economic environment in which asset owners share with other individuals through a peer-to-peer service, for a set fee, their underutilized physical assets or their knowledge, expertise, skills, or time

---

◄◄◄ Classic Concepts in Today's Workplace ►►►

Just how much **difference does a manager** make in how an organization performs?

Management theory proposes two perspectives in answering this question: the omnipotent view and the symbolic view.

Omnipotent view of management:
- Managers are directly responsible for an organization's success or failure.
- Differences in performance are due to decisions and actions of managers.
- Good managers: anticipate change, exploit opportunities, correct poor performance, lead their organizations.
- Profits ↑. Managers get the credit and rewards.
- Profits ↓. Managers often get fired.
- Someone—*the manager*—is held accountable for poor performance.
- This view helps explain turnover among college and professional sports coaches.

Managers: All-powerful or helpless?

Symbolic view of management:
- Manager's ability to affect performance outcomes is constrained by external factors.
- Managers don't have a significant effect on organization's performance.
- Performance is influenced by factors over which managers have little control (economy, customers, governmental policies, competitors' actions, etc.).
- Managers *symbolize* control and influence by developing plans, making decisions, and engaging in other managerial activities to make sense out of random, confusing, and ambiguous situations.
- Manager's part in organizational success or failure is limited.

In reality, managers are neither all-powerful nor helpless. But their decisions and actions are constrained. *External* constraints come from the organization's external environment and *internal* constraints come from the organization's culture.

Discussion Questions:

1 Why do you think these two perspectives on management are important? How might these concepts help you succeed in your role as an employee of an organization? Explain.

2 How are these views similar? Different?

Imagine China/Newscom

Jack Ma, chairman of Chinese e-commerce firm Alibaba, is training young Africans about entrepreneurship, the Internet, and the value of continual learning. With a large percentage of young people in Africa's fast-growing population, age is an important demographic for domestic and global managers as they educate and develop skills young Africans need to succeed in the workplace.

What Role Do Demographics Play?

Demography is destiny. Have you ever heard this phrase? What it means is that the size and characteristics of a country's population can have a significant effect on what it's able to achieve. For instance, experts say that by 2050, "emerging economies led by India and China will collectively be larger than the developed economies. Small European nations with low birthrates such as Austria, Belgium, Denmark, Norway, and Sweden will drop off the list of the 30 biggest economies."[19] **Demographics**—the characteristics of a population used for purposes of social studies—can and do have a significant impact on how managers manage. Those population characteristics include things such as age, income, sex, race, education level, ethnic makeup, employment status, geographic location, and so forth—pretty much the types of information collected on governmental census surveys.

Age is a **particularly important demographic** for managers.

Why? Because the workplace often has different age groups all working together. (See Chapter 10, p. 378–381, for a more detailed look at the challenges of generational differences in the workplace.) *Baby Boomers. Gen X. Gen Y. Gen Z.* Ever heard or seen these terms? They're names given by population researchers to four age groups found in the U.S. population.

- *Baby Boomers* are those individuals born between 1946 and 1964. You've heard so much about "boomers" because there are so many of them. The sheer number of people in that cohort has meant they've had a significant impact on every aspect of the external environment (from the educational system and entertainment/lifestyle choices to the Social Security system, health-care choices, and so forth) as they've gone through various life-cycle stages.

- *Gen X* is used to describe those individuals born between 1965 and 1977. This age group has been called the baby bust generation because it followed the baby boom and is one of the smaller age cohorts.

- *Gen Y* (or the "Millennials") is an age group typically considered to encompass those individuals born between 1978 and 1994. As the children of the Baby Boomers, this age group is also large in number and making its imprint on external environmental conditions as well. From technology to clothing styles to work attitudes, Gen Y, now the majority age group in the workforce, is helping shape today's workplaces.[20]

- *Gen Z* is the youngest identified age group. Although demographers don't agree on the exact range of birth years for Gen Z, most group them as being born between 1995 and 2010. Gen Z is huge; those under age 20 represent 25.9 percent of the U.S. population.[21] One thing that characterizes Gen Z is that it is the most diverse and multicultural of any generation in the United States.[22] Another thing that characterizes this group is that their primary means of social interaction is online, where they freely express their opinions and attitudes. It's the first group whose only reality revolves around the "Internet, mobile devices, and social networking."[23]

Demographic age cohorts are important because large numbers of people at certain stages in the life cycle can constrain decisions and actions taken by managers of businesses, governments, educational institutions, and other organizations. Studying demographics involves looking not only at current statistics, but also at future trends. What *are* some future trends?

- Recent analysis of birth rates shows that more than 80 percent of babies being born worldwide are from Africa and Asia.[24]
- Two-thirds of India's 1.2 billion people are below 35 years of age.[25]
- By 2050, it's predicted that China will have more people age 65 and older than the rest of the world combined.[26]

demographics
The characteristics of a population used for purposes of social studies

- For most of human history, individuals over the age of 65 have never exceeded 3 or 4 percent of a country's population. By 2050, however, this number could potentially reach 25 percent, on average.[27]
- By 2060, the population of older Americans is expected to more than double.[28]

Just imagine how these population trends are likely to impact global organizations and the way managers manage.

technology	

technology
Any equipment, tools, or operating methods that are designed to make work more efficient

How Does the External Environment Affect Managers?

4-2 Discuss how the external environment affects managers.

Knowing *what* the various components of the external environment are and examining certain aspects of that environment are important for managers. However, understanding *how* the environment affects managers is equally as important. We're going to look at three ways the external environment constrains and challenges managers: (1) through its impact on jobs and employment, (2) through the environmental uncertainty that is present, and (3) through the various stakeholder relationships that exist between an organization and its external constituencies.

JOBS AND EMPLOYMENT. As any or all of the external environmental conditions change, one of the most powerful constraints managers face is the impact of such changes on jobs and employment—both in poor conditions and in good conditions. The power of

---

:::::::: Managing Technology in Today's Workplace ::::::::
CAN TECHNOLOGY IMPROVE THE WAY MANAGERS MANAGE?

Continuing advancements in technology offer many exciting possibilities for how workers work and managers manage. **Technology** includes any equipment, tools, or operating methods that are designed to make work more efficient. One area where technology has had an impact is in the process where inputs (labor, raw materials, and the like) are transformed into outputs (goods and services to be sold). In years past, this transformation was usually performed by human labor. With technology, however, human labor has been replaced with electronic and computer equipment. From robots in offices to online banking systems to social networks where employees interact with customers, technology has made the work of creating and delivering goods and services more efficient and effective.

Another area where technology has had a major impact is in information. Information technology (IT) has created the ability to circumvent the physical confines of working only in a specified

> Eighty billion. That's the number of "things" (smartphones, smartwatches, climate-control system sensors, kitchen refrigerators, cars, etc.) IDC predicts will be connected **to the Internet by 2025**. This **Internet of Things (IoT)** is transforming businesses and disrupting industries and societies around the world.[29]

organizational location. With notebook and desktop computers, tablets, smartphones, organizational intranets, and other IT tools, organizational members who work mainly with information can do that work from any place at any time.

Finally, technology is also changing the way managers manage, especially in terms of how they interact with employees who may be working anywhere and anytime. Effectively communicating with telecommuting individuals who may simply be working from home or who may be working halfway around the world and ensuring that work goals are being met are challenges that managers must address. Throughout the rest of the book, we'll look at how managers are meeting those challenges in the ways they plan, organize, lead, and control.

Discussion Questions:

3 Is management easier or harder with all the available technology? Explain your position.

4 What benefits does technology provide and what problems does technology pose for (a) employees and (b) managers?

this constraint was painfully obvious during the past global recession as millions of jobs were eliminated and unemployment rates rose to levels not seen in many years. Although such readjustments aren't bad in and of themselves, they do create challenges for managers who must balance work demands and having enough people with the right skills to do an organization's work.

Flexible Work Arrangements:

As companies embrace new forms of flexibility in the workplace to adapt to changing market needs, have you thought about what YOU want "work" to look like? What type of work model appeals to you? Traditional? Flexible? Something in between?

Not only do changes in external conditions affect the types of jobs that are available, they affect how those jobs are created, designed, and managed. For instance, many employers are using flexible work arrangements with tasks done by freelancers hired on an as-needed basis, or by temporary workers who work full-time but are not permanent employees, or by individuals who share jobs. Keep in mind that these approaches are used because of the constraints from the external environment. As a manager, you'll need to recognize how such work arrangements affect the way you plan, organize, lead, and control. Flexible work arrangements have become so prevalent and such an important management approach today that we'll discuss them in other chapters as well. Be sure to pay attention to these discussions as it will help you as you envision and plan for your career.

ASSESSING ENVIRONMENTAL UNCERTAINTY.   Another constraint posed by external environments is the amount of uncertainty found in that environment, which can affect organizational outcomes. **Environmental uncertainty** refers to the degree of change, predictability of change, and complexity in an organization's environment. The matrix in Exhibit 4–2 shows these two aspects.

The first dimension of uncertainty is the degree of unpredictable change. If the components in an organization's environment change frequently and the change is unpredictable, it's a *dynamic* environment. If change is minimal and is predictable, it's a *stable* one. A stable environment might be one in which there are no new competitors, few technological breakthroughs by current competitors, little activity by pressure groups to influence

Exhibit 4–2 Environmental Uncertainty Matrix

Degree of Change	
Stable	**Dynamic**
Cell 1	**Cell 2**
Stable and predictable environment	Dynamic and unpredictable environment
Few components in environment	Few components in environment
Components are somewhat similar and remain basically the same	Components are somewhat similar but are continually changing
Minimal need for sophisticated knowledge of components	Minimal need for sophisticated knowledge of components
Cell 3	**Cell 4**
Stable and predictable environment	Dynamic and unpredictable environment
Many components in environment	Many components in environment
Components are not similar to one another and remain basically the same	Components are not similar to one another and are continually changing
High need for sophisticated knowledge of components	High need for sophisticated knowledge of components

(Degree of Complexity — Simple / Complex)

the organization, and so forth. For instance, Almarai, based in Saudi Arabia, faces a relatively stable environment for its food products. One external concern is ongoing competition from local and regional competitors. Another concern is changes in government policies that are leading to higher costs for electricity and water. Almarai is therefore focusing on improving efficiencies to boost profitability and arranging long-term supply sources through its international subsidiaries.[30] In contrast, the recorded music industry faces a dynamic (highly uncertain and unpredictable) environment. Digital formats, apps, music-streaming sites, and artists releasing selected songs on their personal social media accounts turned the industry upside down and brought high levels of uncertainty.

Manjunath Kiran/AFP/GettyImages

Software developers and designers from communities throughout the world are valuable stakeholders for Yahoo!. The company builds relationships with these computer experts by staging hacking events, like the one shown here in Bangalore, India, that may result in technological innovations.

The other dimension of uncertainty describes the degree of **environmental complexity**, which looks at the number of components in an organization's environment, how similar the components are, and the extent of the knowledge that the organization has about those components. An organization that has few competitors, customers, suppliers, or government agencies to deal with, or that needs little information about its environment, has a less complex and thus less uncertain environment.

How does the concept of environmental uncertainty influence managers? Looking again at Exhibit 4–2, each of the four cells represents different combinations of degree of complexity and degree of change. Cell 1 (stable-simple environment) represents the lowest level of environmental uncertainty and cell 4 (dynamic and complex environment) the highest. Not surprisingly, managers have the greatest influence on organizational outcomes in cell 1 and the least in cell 4. Because uncertainty is a threat to an organization's effectiveness, managers try to minimize it. Given a choice, managers would prefer to operate in the least uncertain environments, but they rarely control that choice. In addition, the nature of the external environment today is that most industries are facing more dynamic change, making their environments more uncertain.

MANAGING STAKEHOLDER RELATIONSHIPS. How does Amazon continue to enter and dominate ever-widening markets? One reason is that it understands the importance of building relationships with its various stakeholders: customers, advertisers, shippers, suppliers. The nature of stakeholder relationships is another way in which the environment influences managers. The more obvious and secure these relationships, the more influence managers will have over organizational outcomes.

Stakeholders are any constituencies in an organization's environment that are affected by that organization's decisions and actions. These groups have a stake in or are significantly influenced by what the organization does. In turn, these groups can influence the organization. For example, think of the groups that might be affected by the decisions and actions of Starbucks—coffee bean farmers, employees, specialty coffee competitors, local communities, and so forth. Some of these stakeholders, in turn, may impact the decisions and actions of Starbucks' managers. The idea that organizations have stakeholders is now widely accepted by both management academics and practicing managers.[32]

Making Ethical Decisions in Today's Workplace

Walt Disney Company. Star Wars. Two powerful forces combined. But is that force for good or for not-so-good?[31] It's not surprising that the popularity of the Star Wars franchise has given Walt Disney Co. exceptional power over the nation's movie theaters. The theater owners want the Star Wars releases, and there's only one way to get them...through Disney. With the latest release, movie theaters had to agree to "top-secret" terms that many theater owners said were the most oppressive and demanding they had ever seen. Not only were they required to give Disney about 65 percent of ticket revenue, there were also requirements about when, where, and how the movie could be shown. You'd think that because Disney needs the theaters to show their movies they might be better off viewing them as "partners" rather than subordinates. What do you think?

Discussion Questions:

5 Is there an ethical issue here? Why or why not? What stakeholders might be affected and how might they be affected? How can identifying stakeholders help a manager decide the most responsible approach?

6 Working together in your "assigned" group, discuss Disney's actions. Do you agree with those actions? Look at the pros and cons, including how the various stakeholders are affected. Prepare a list of arguments both pro and con. (To be a good problem solver and critical thinker, you have to learn how to look at issues from all angles!)

Exhibit 4–3 identifies the most common stakeholders an organization might have to deal with. Note that these stakeholders include internal and external groups. Why? Because both can affect what an organization does and how it operates.

Why should managers even care about managing stakeholder relationships? For one thing, it can lead to desirable organizational outcomes such as improved predictability of environmental changes, more successful innovations, greater degree of trust among stakeholders, and greater organizational flexibility to reduce the impact of change. For instance, social media company Facebook is spending more on lobbying and meeting with government officials as lawmakers and regulators look at sweeping changes to online privacy laws. The company is "working to shape its image on Capitol Hill and avert measures potentially damaging to its information-sharing business."[33]

Can stakeholder management affect organizational performance? The answer is yes! Management researchers who have looked at this issue are finding that managers of high-performing companies tend to consider the interests of all major stakeholder groups as they make decisions.[34]

Another reason for managing external stakeholder relationships is that it's the "right" thing to do. Because an organization depends on these external groups as sources of inputs (resources) and as outlets for outputs (goods and services), managers should consider the interests of stakeholders as they make decisions. We'll address this issue in more detail in the next chapter when we look at corporate social responsibility and business ethics.

As we've tried to make clear throughout this section, it's not going to be "business as usual" for organizations or for managers. Managers will always have hard decisions to make about how they do business and about their people. It's important that you understand how changes in the external environment will affect your organizational and management experiences. Now, we need to switch gears and look at the internal aspects of the organization—specifically, its culture.

Exhibit 4–3 Organizational Stakeholders

What Is Organizational Culture?

EACH OF US HAS A UNIQUE PERSONALITY that influences the way we act and interact. An organization has a personality, too—we call it **CULTURE**. Here's what **YOU** need to know about **organizational culture**!

4-3 Define *organizational culture* and explain why it's important.

1 **Culture is perceived.** It's not something that can be physically touched or seen, but employees perceive it on the basis of what they experience within the organization.

2 **Culture is descriptive.** It's concerned with how members perceive or describe the culture, not with whether they like it.

3 **Culture is shared.** Even though individuals may have different backgrounds or work at different organizational levels, they tend to describe the organization's culture in similar terms.

Smith Collection/Gado Images/Alamy Stock Photo

Jerome Brunet/ZUMA Press, Inc./ Alamy Stock Photo

Google has created a creative and innovative culture at their headquarters in California with an android googleplex, bikes, and bringing your dog to work.

Kristoffer Tripplaar/Alamy Stock Photo

organizational culture
The shared values, principles, traditions, and ways of doing things that influence the way organizational members act

Dimensions of Organizational Culture

Exhibit 4–4

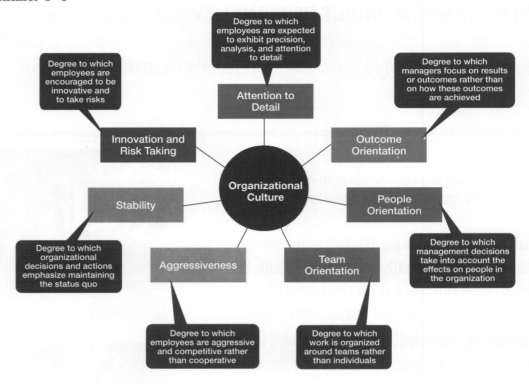

How Can Culture Be Described?

The seven dimensions (shown in Exhibit 4–4):[35]

- Range from *low* (not typical of the culture) to *high* (especially typical of the culture).

- Provide a composite picture of the organization's culture.

  An organization's culture may be shaped by one particular cultural dimension more than the others, thus influencing the organization's personality and the way organizational members work. For example:

  — *Apple's* focus is product innovation (innovation and risk taking). The company "lives and breathes" new-product development, and employees' work behaviors support that goal.

  — *Southwest Airlines* has made its employees a central part of its culture (people orientation) and shows this through the way it treats them.

Where Does Culture Come From?	How Do Employees Learn the Culture?
Usually reflects the vision or **mission** of founders.	Organizational stories: narrative tales of significant events or people.
Founders project an image of *what the organization should be and what its values are.*	**Corporate rituals:** repetitive sequences of activities that express and reinforce important organizational values and goals.
Founders can "impose" their vision on employees because of new organization's small size.	**Material symbols or artifacts:** layout of facilities, how employees dress, size of offices, material perks provided to executives, furnishings, and so forth.
Organizational members *create a shared history* that binds them into a community and reminds them of "who we are."	**Language:** special acronyms; unique terms to describe equipment, key personnel, customers, suppliers, processes, products.

How Does Organizational Culture Affect Managers?

4-4 Describe how organizational culture affects managers.

Ambrosia Humphrey, vice president of talent at Hootsuite, understands the power of organizational culture and how it affects her as a manager. Nurturing and nourishing the company's culture is one of her top priorities. And she does this by continually creating employee experiences that reflect an important company value—transparency. For instance, she's organized all-staff "Ask Me Anything" discussions with the company's CEO. Another tactic she's used is employee "hackathons" in which staff members get together to tackle problems. And, of course, she embraces social media as part of her commitment to transparency to employees, customers, and the community. Employees are encouraged to tweet about their perspectives on what it's like to work at Hootsuite. Those postings have ranged from pictures taken at rooftop meetings to employees complimenting other employees for their hard work to links to media reports about the company as a great place to work.[36]

The two main ways that an organization's culture affects managers are (1) its effect on what employees do and how they behave and (2) its effect on what managers do.

How Does Culture Affect What Employees Do?

"I think of culture as guardrails . . . what you stand for, essentially the ground rules so that people know how to operate."[37]

Remember what we said as we debunked the chapter-opening myth. You want to look for a culture where you will fit in and thrive. An organization's culture has an effect on what employees do, depending on how strong, or weak, the culture is. **Strong cultures**—those in which the key values are deeply held and widely shared—have a greater influence on employees than do weaker cultures. The more employees accept the organization's key values and the greater their commitment to those values, the stronger the culture is. Most organizations have moderate to strong cultures; that is, there is relatively high agreement on what's important, what defines "good" employee behavior, what it takes to get ahead, and so forth. The stronger a culture becomes, the more it affects what employees do and the way managers plan, organize, lead, and control.[38]

Also, in organizations with a strong culture, that culture can substitute for the rules and regulations that formally guide employees. In essence, strong cultures can create predictability, orderliness, and consistency without the need for written documentation. Therefore, the stronger an organization's culture, the less managers need to be concerned with developing formal rules and regulations. Instead, those guides will be internalized in employees when they accept the organization's culture. If, on the other hand, an organization's culture is weak—if no dominant shared values are present—its effect on employee behavior is less clear.

Southwest Airlines' strong culture of customer service, hard work, respect, caring, and fun affects what its employees do and how they behave. After Hurricane Harvey, pilots and aircrew assisted in the Operations Pets Alive rescue effort by transporting orphaned animals from shelters in Houston to a pet center in San Diego where they became available for adoption.

CPEN1/ZOB/Southwest Airlines/Cover Images/Newscom

How Does Culture Affect What Managers Do?

Say What? Ten percent of executives say they *have not* identified or communicated an organizational culture.[39]

Houston-based Apache Corp. has become one of the best performers in the independent oil drilling business because it has fashioned a culture that values risk taking and quick decision making. Potential hires are judged on how much initiative they've shown in getting projects done at other companies. And company employees are handsomely rewarded if they meet profit and production goals.[40] Because an organization's culture constrains what they can and cannot do and how they manage, it's particularly relevant to managers. Such constraints are rarely explicit. They're not written down. It's unlikely they'll even be spoken. But they're there, and all managers quickly learn *what to do* and *not do* in their organization. For instance, you won't find the following values written down, but each comes from a real organization:

- Look busy even if you're not.
- If you take risks and fail around here, you'll pay dearly for it.
- Before you make a decision, run it by your boss so that he or she is never surprised.
- We make our product only as good as the competition forces us to.
- What made us successful in the past will make us successful in the future.
- If you want to get to the top here, you have to be a team player.

The link between values such as these and managerial behavior is fairly straightforward. Take, for example, a so-called ready-aim-fire culture. In such an organization, managers will study and analyze proposed projects endlessly before committing to them. However, in a ready-fire-aim culture, managers take action and then analyze what has been done. Or, say an organization's culture supports the belief that profits can be increased by cost cutting and that the company's best interests are served by achieving slow but steady increases in quarterly earnings. In that culture, managers are unlikely to pursue programs that are innovative, risky, long term, or expansionary. In an organization whose culture conveys a basic distrust of employees, managers are more likely to use an authoritarian leadership style than a democratic one. Why? The culture establishes for managers appropriate and expected behavior. You can see this in action at Winegardner & Hammons, a hotel management firm, where company leaders have built a "Winning Workplace Culture" with four characteristics: a positive work environment in which managers are encouraged to make employees feel cared for and valued; an employee selection process that encourages managers to focus on selecting the "right" employees; an employee engagement program that's based on training managers so they have the right skills, knowledge, and experience to nurture an engaging work environment; and a strengths-based workplace in which managers continually reinforce employees' strengths. What has this cultural focus led to? *Thirty-four percent lower employee turnover* and *11 percent higher profitability*.[41] That's the kind of outcomes that can be achieved *if* you pay attention to your organizational culture and *if* managers recognize appropriate and expected behavior in that culture.

As shown in Exhibit 4–5, a manager's decisions are influenced by the culture in which he or she operates. An organization's culture, especially a strong one, influences and constrains the way managers plan, organize, lead, and control.

Exhibit 4–5 Managerial Decisions Affected by Culture

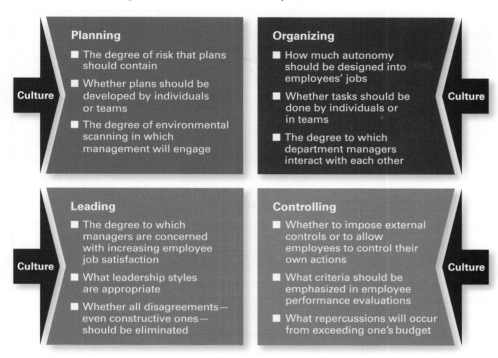

Planning
- The degree of risk that plans should contain
- Whether plans should be developed by individuals or teams
- The degree of environmental scanning in which management will engage

Culture

Organizing
- How much autonomy should be designed into employees' jobs
- Whether tasks should be done by individuals or in teams
- The degree to which department managers interact with each other

Culture

Leading
- The degree to which managers are concerned with increasing employee job satisfaction
- What leadership styles are appropriate
- Whether all disagreements— even constructive ones— should be eliminated

Culture

Controlling
- Whether to impose external controls or to allow employees to control their own actions
- What criteria should be emphasized in employee performance evaluations
- What repercussions will occur from exceeding one's budget

Culture

Source: Robbins, Stephen P., Coulter, Mary, *Management*, 13th Ed., © 2016, p. 86. Reprinted and electronically reproduced by permission of Pearson Education, Inc., New York, NY.

What Are Current Issues in Organizational Culture?

4-5 Describe current issues in organizational culture.

Corporate leaders increasingly are recognizing that organizational culture is a critical business issue, particularly since an organization's culture can be a "driver" of employee productivity, engagement, and retention. What current cultural issues are managers focusing on? We've identified five that we think are important. Let's take a look.

Creating a Customer-Responsive Culture

In Chapter 1, we discussed why customers are so important to organizations and managers. A customer-responsive culture can lead to more satisfied employees and customers, which in turn can affect performance results. What does a customer-responsive culture look like? Exhibit 4-6 describes five characteristics of customer-responsive cultures and offers suggestions as to what managers can do to create that type of culture.[42]

Creating an Innovative Culture

Innovation was also introduced in Chapter 1 as an important issue for organizations and managers. How important is culture to innovation? More than half of senior executives surveyed said that the most important driver of innovation for companies was a supportive culture.[43] But not every company has established a culture that fosters innovation. In fact, in a survey of employees, about half expressed that a culture of management support is very important to generating innovative ideas, but only 20 percent believed that management actually provides such support.[44]

Exhibit 4–6 Creating a Customer-Responsive Culture

Characteristics of Customer-Responsive Culture	Suggestions for managers
Type of employee	Hire people with personalities and attitudes consistent with customer service: friendly, attentive, enthusiastic, patient, good listening skills
Type of job environment	Design jobs so employees have as much control as possible to satisfy customer, without rigid rules and procedures
Empowerment	Give service-contact employees the discretion to make day-to-day decision on job-related activites
Role clarity	Reduce uncertainty about what service-contact employees can and cannot do by continual training on product knowledge, listening, and other behavioral skills
Consistent desire to satisfy and delight customer	Clarify organization's commitment to doing whatever it takes, even if it's outside an employee's normal job requirements

Source: Robbins, Stephen P., Coulter, Mary A., *Management* (Subscription). 14th Ed., © 2018. Reprinted and electronically reproduced by permission of Pearson Education, Inc., New York, NY.

What does an innovative culture look like? Here's one perspective offered by Swedish researcher Goran Ekvall:[45]

- *Challenge and involvement:* Are employees involved in, motivated by, and committed to the long-term goals and success of the organization?
- *Freedom:* Can employees independently define their work, exercise discretion, and take initiative in their day-to-day activities?
- *Trust and openness:* Are employees supportive and respectful of each other?
- *Idea time:* Do individuals have time to elaborate on new ideas before taking action?
- *Playfulness/humor:* Is the workplace spontaneous and fun?
- *Conflict resolution:* Do individuals make decisions and resolve issues based on the good of the organization versus personal interests?
- *Debates:* Are employees allowed to express opinions and suggest ideas to be considered and reviewed?
- *Risk taking:* Do managers tolerate uncertainty and ambiguity, and are employees rewarded for taking risks?

Creating a Sustainability Culture

Sustainability was another important management issue introduced in Chapter 1. For many companies, sustainability is incorporated into the organization's overall culture. For example, Johnson & Johnson's Senior Director of Environment said, "Sustainability is embedded in our culture. It's been a part of who we are for more than 65 years, long before the notion of sustainability became trendy."[46] What can companies do to create a sustainability culture?

Get everyone involved in defining what sustainability means to the organization. When people employees aren't "on board" with it, it's going to be hard to improve or measure sustainability efforts.

Get employees—individuals or teams—involved in finding ways to be more sustainable.

Create rituals to reinforce the importance of sustainability. For instance, a day/week devoted to different sustainability practices or beginning every corporate meeting with a sustainability topic.

Use rewards. Tie employee bonuses to meeting sustainability goals. Or, give prizes when an employee does something that supports or exemplifies the sustainability culture.

When managers and organizations embed sustainability practices in the culture, the culture reinforces those practices. If sustainability is an important cultural value, it needs to be nurtured to grow and become a defining trait.

Creating an Ethical Culture

An **ethical culture** is one in which the shared concept of right and wrong behavior in the workplace reflects the core values of an organization and influences the ethical decision making of employees. Ethical cultures champion clear ethical standards. In addition, organizational leaders model ethical behavior and demand employees also be committed to behaving ethically. In an ethical culture, employees and managers are open to discussing ethical issues and are reinforced for their ethical behavior.[47] We'll explore business ethics more fully in the next chapter. Stay tuned!

Creating a Learning Culture

As the first part of this chapter clearly showed us, today's quick-changing business environment requires adaptability by managers and employees alike. That means "having employees who are able to think, relate, learn, and adapt continuously."[48] Work cultures geared to constant learning will be of critical importance.

What about YOU?

Will you be one of those employees who learns continuously? Do you want to stand out as a top candidate and a star employee? Develop your employability skills now and watch it happen!

Creating a learning culture starts with buy-in at the top. Organizational leaders must absolutely understand what it takes for a learning culture to work and be absolutely committed to it. In a learning culture, everyone agrees on a shared vision and everyone recognizes the inherent inter-relationships among the organization's processes, activities, functions, and external environment. It also fosters a strong sense of community, caring for each other, and trust. A learning culture encourages employees to freely communicate openly, share, experiment, and learn without fear of criticism or punishment.

ethical culture
A culture in which the shared concept of right and wrong behavior in the workplace reflects the organization's core values and influences employees' ethical decision making

CHAPTER SUMMARY BY LEARNING OUTCOME

4-1 Explain what the external environment is and why it's important.

The external environment refers to factors, forces, situations, and events outside the organization that affect its performance. It includes economic, demographic, political/legal, sociocultural, technological, and global components. The external environment is important because it poses constraints and challenges to managers.

4-2 Discuss how the external environment affects managers.

There are three ways that the external environment affects managers: its impact on jobs and employment, the amount of environmental uncertainty, and the nature of stakeholder relationships.

4-3 Define *organizational culture* and explain why it's important.

Organizational culture is the shared values, principles, traditions, and ways of doing things that influence the way organizational members act. It's important because of the impact it has on decisions, behaviors, and actions of organizational employees.

4-4 Describe how organizational culture affects managers.

Organizational culture affects managers in two ways: through its effect on what employees do and how they behave, and through its effect on what managers do as they plan, organize, lead, and control.

4-5 Describe current issues in organizational culture.

Current issues in organizational culture include creating a customer-responsive culture, an innovative culture, a sustainability culture, an ethical culture, and a learning culture. These cultural issues are particularly relevant in today's business environment as managers focus on ways that an organization's culture can drive employee productivity, engagement, and retention.

DISCUSSION QUESTIONS

4-1 How much impact do managers actually have on an organization's success or failure?

4-2 Why do managers need an understanding of what happens outside their organizations? Give examples of how changes in the external environment can affect their job.

4-3 How has the changed economy affected what managers do? Find two or three examples in current business periodicals of activities and practices that organizations are using. Discuss them in light of the changed environment.

4-4 Why is it important for managers to pay attention to demographic trends and shifts?

4-5 Businesses operate in the external environment. Discuss whether managers experience environmental stability in their business operations. In this context, provide local examples of environmental stability and environmental uncertainty.

4-6 "Businesses are built on relationships." What do you think this statement means? What are the implications for managing the external environment?

4-7 Discuss why organizational culture plays a major role in business operations and employee behaviors. Explain its impact on CEOs, managers, and employees.

4-8 What steps can encourage organizational culture to evolve over time?

4-9 Discuss the impact of a strong culture on organizations and managers.

4-10 Pick one of the five current issues in organizational culture and tell in which dimension(s) of organizational culture (Exhibit 4-4) you think it would most likely be found. Explain your thinking. Also, explain your opinion as to why that particular issue is important to today's organizations.

Applying: Getting Ready for the Workplace

Management Skill Builder | UNDERSTANDING CULTURE

An organization's culture is a system of shared meaning. When you understand your organization's culture, you know, for example, whether it encourages teamwork, rewards innovation, or stifles initiative. When interviewing for a job, the more accurate you are at assessing the culture, the more likely you are to find a good person–organization fit. And once inside an organization, understanding the culture allows you to know what behaviors are likely to be rewarded and which are likely to be punished.[49]

MyLab Management

PERSONAL INVENTORY ASSESSMENT

Go to **www.pearson.com/mylab/management** to complete the Personal Inventory Assessment related to this chapter.

Skill Basics

Organizational cultures differ. So do individuals. The better you're able to match your personal preferences to an organization's culture, the more likely you are to find satisfaction in your work, the less likely you are to leave, and the greater the probability that you'll receive positive performance evaluations.

The ability to read an organization's culture can be a valuable skill. For instance, if you're looking for a job, you'll want to choose an employer whose culture is compatible with your values and in which you'll feel comfortable. If you can accurately assess a potential employer's culture before you make your job decision, you may be able to save yourself a lot of grief and reduce the likelihood of making a poor choice. Similarly, you'll undoubtedly have business transactions with numerous organizations during your professional career, such as selling a product or service, negotiating a contract, arranging a joint work project, or merely seeking

out who controls certain decisions in an organization. The ability to assess another organization's culture can be a definite plus in successfully performing those pursuits.

For the sake of simplicity, we're going to look at this skill from the perspective of a job applicant. We'll assume you're interviewing for a job, although these skills are generalizable to many situations. Here's a list of things you can do to help learn about an organization's culture:

- *Do background work.* Get the names of former employees from friends or acquaintances, and talk with them. Also talk with members of professional trade associations to which the organization's employees belong and executive recruiters who deal with the organization. Look for clues in stories told in annual reports and other organizational literature, and check out the organization's websites for evidence of high turnover or recent management shake-ups.

- *Observe the physical surroundings.* Pay attention to signs, posters, pictures, photos, style of dress, length of hair, degree of openness between offices, and office furnishings and arrangements.

- *Make notes about those individuals you met.* Whom did you meet? How did they expect to be addressed?

- *How would you characterize the style of the people you met?* Are they formal? Casual? Serious? Jovial? Open? Reticent about providing information?

- *Look at the organization's human resources manual.* Are there formal rules and regulations printed there? If so, how detailed are they? What do they cover?

- *Ask questions of the people you meet.* The most valid and reliable information tends to come from asking the same questions of many people (to see how closely their responses align). Questions that will give you insights into organizational processes and practices might include: What's the background of the founders? What's the background of current senior managers? What are these managers' functional specialties, and were they promoted from within or hired from outside? How does the organization integrate new employees? Is there a formal orientation program? Are there formal employee training programs and, if so, how are they structured? How does your boss define his or her job success? How would you define fairness in terms of reward allocations? Can you identify some people here who are on the "fast track"? What do you think has put them on the fast track? Can you identify someone in the organization who seems to be considered a deviant, and how has the organization responded to this person? Can you describe a decision that someone made that was well received? Can you describe a decision that didn't work out well, and what were the consequences for that decision maker? Could you describe a crisis or critical event that has occurred recently in the organization, and how did top management respond?

Practicing the Skill

After spending your first three years after college graduation as a freelance graphic designer, you're looking at pursuing a job as an account executive at a graphic design firm. You feel that the scope of assignments and potential for technical training far exceed what you'd be able to do on your own, and you're looking to expand your skills and meet a brand-new set of challenges. However, you want to make sure you "fit" into the organization where you're going to be spending more than eight hours every workday. Write a brief paper describing how you would find a place where you'll be happy and where your style and personality will be appreciated.

Experiential Exercise

Organizational culture is a management topic that a lot of people find very interesting! So you're going to explore organizational culture using a series of questions we've come up with.

- Is work supposed to be fun? Is a "good" organizational culture dependent on whether employees have fun at work?
- Lousy cultures have miserable managers. Which came first? The lousy culture or the miserable managers? How would you go about "fixing" this?
- An organization's culture should never change. Agree or disagree?
- Organizational culture can "make or break" an organization.
- The right culture with the right values will always produce the best organizational performance. Agree or disagree?
- Management experts say it's important to "invest" in your organization's culture. What do you think that means?
- How could you tell if you aren't (or one of your employees isn't) a good fit for the organization's culture?
- You can "shape" the culture of your work environment. Agree or disagree? (*Hint:* You might want to look at the current issues in organizational culture as you talk about this.)

Pick two—only two—of these questions to discuss in your "assigned" group. From your discussion, write down your group's most important insights about organizational culture. Also, what did you learn from your group's discussion that will help you as you prepare to launch or pursue your career goals?

CASE APPLICATION #1

Bad Ride. Bumpy Ride.

Topic: Organizational culture, organizational values, leader's influence on culture

You could say the beginning of the end for Uber founder and CEO Travis Kalanick was the February 2017 blog post by former Uber engineer Susan Fowler that outlined a toxic work culture hostile to women and filled with managers (from top down) willing to turn a blind eye to abuses of employees, competitors, customers, laws, law enforcement officials...you name it.

According to the company's website, Uber started (like many entrepreneurial businesses) because of an annoying problem.[50] Travis Kalanick and a friend were having trouble hailing a cab on a snowy Paris evening in 2008. Their solution (although it didn't help them with their immediate problem): Wouldn't it be great to just tap a button and get a ride. Thus, the Uber app was conceived. And it totally disrupted an industry! Today, Uber is the world's biggest ride-hailing company, a global service with more than 14,000 employees in more than 600 cities. And it became the most highly valued startup in history (to the tune of some $70 billion).[51] But the founder's aggressive style and approach to doing business was fraught with danger, especially as seen in the values that shaped Uber's culture.

Kalanick, a tech entrepreneur who had already sold one startup for almost $19 million, shaped Uber's mission around certain foundational beliefs: pursue hypergrowth at all costs; win at all costs; be confrontational, but be "principled"; and mottos such as "Always Be Hustlin'" and "Toe-Stepping."[52] And quite interestingly, nowhere was there any indication that collaboration and teamwork were valued. After the Fowler blog post, others came forward to describe a "baller" work environment where achievements were celebrated by chest bumps and where males would engage in push-up contests. Although that type of atmosphere is not criminal, it likely alienated female employees and other employees who didn't want to get caught up in that type of behavior.[53]

As if these corporate values and culture weren't enough, there were the decisions and actions by Kalanick and other managers. Here are just a few examples:

- A dashcam video went viral of Kalanick heatedly arguing over fares with an Uber driver.
- A *New York Times* report was released on a secret Uber technology, called Greyball, that the company developed to identify and deny service to riders who had violated Uber's contractual terms.
- After a horrific rape of a 26-year-old passenger by a Uber driver in India, the company's president for the Asia-Pacific region somehow obtained and shared the confidential medical record. Executives proposed an outrageous theory that the rape might have been a setup by an Indian rival. [54]
- The company, which had a reputation for ignoring local labor laws and taxi rules, had become a favorite target for law enforcement officials. So, the company routinely used a remote system to lock down office equipment to shield files from police raids.[55]
- Key executives, drivers, and employees at rival ride-hailing companies were secretly spied upon for the express purpose of acquiring trade secrets.[56]
- A data breach was hidden for over a year.[57]
- Unsafe cars were knowlingly leased to drivers in Singapore.[58]

After months of trying to cope with all of the issues and not getting anywhere, some of the firm's biggest investors eventually forced out Kalanick. It was felt that a change in leadership would provide Uber with the opportunity to refocus and recreate a new culture.[59] The board's new choice for a CEO was Dara Khosrowshahi, Expedia's CEO. Khosrowshahi faces a host of challenges, including replenishing Uber's depleted executive ranks and implementing changes mandated by the board to address allegations of ignored complaints of sexism and sexual harassment. Khosrowshahi also needs to focus on Uber's finances. Internal sources say that the new CEO is 180 degrees different from Kalanick: "humble, a good listener, and a diplomat."[60] Maybe the ride will be smoother now!

Discussion Questions

4-11 What role does a CEO play in an organization's culture? What role do other leaders/managers play and what role should they play?

4-12 Using Exhibit 4-4, describe Uber's culture under its founder.

4-13 Which view of management do you see played out here? The omnipotent or the symbolic? Explain.

4-14 What advice about organizational culture would you give the new CEO?

4-15 From an ethics perspective, what part of this situation disturbs you the most? What career advice, as far as ethical behavior, could you take away from this story?

CASE APPLICATION #2

Not Sold Out
Topic: The Power of Presence

How do you successfully manage a growing international company? CEO Christian Chabot of Seattle-based Tableau believes that being there physically is an important piece in the often-complex puzzle of international management.

International growth is nothing new for Tableau. As a leading provider of analytics and business intelligence software solutions, the company, which was founded in 2004, has more than 35,000 clients in over a dozen countries. Tableau provides software tools and interactive dashboards that allow users to generate useful business insights through the analysis and visualization of data. The company is on the cutting edge of data-imaging solutions for end-users with products such as Elastic, which allows users to create graphics from spreadsheets.

Despite tough competition in the market for business intelligence from software giants such as Microsoft, Tableau has continued to maintain its share of the marketplace, and the company's value continues to grow, with a 64 percent increase in revenue over last year. Much of the company's growth is attributed to the company's international expansion, with an 86 percent increase in revenue last year from international markets, which now account for a quarter of the company's total revenues.

While more than half of their current 2,800 employees work in the company's Seattle headquarters, Tableau has 14 locations around the world in places such as Shanghai, Singapore, Sydney, and London. About 400 of the new employees will be hired beyond their Seattle headquarters, and Tableau's expansion will include opening new international offices.

International growth creates many challenges for companies, particularly when they open and staff branch locations in different countries. Cultural differences, time differences, and just the geographic distance can make it difficult to sustain the same management practices at home and abroad. How has Chabot managed the quick growth of this international company? One strategy was to spend almost a year abroad working in the company's London office. His time at that location helped grow regional sales but also provided the CEO with valuable insights to support further international expansion.

Chabot reported that the time he spent in London highlighted the importance of managing culture and people. Prior to the trip, he did not have a true understanding of the challenges of international employees working for a U.S.-based company. For instance, he found that many working in international branch offices did not feel like they were taken seriously by those at the home office. Geographically remote workers can feel disconnected from a global company, particularly when they report to management they have never met in person at their headquarters.

Chabot's time working in London was valuable for employees in all of the company's locations, as his actions sent the message that he felt that employees outside the headquarters were important. Although he spent time only in London, the fact that he spent a year away from the home office emphasized his belief that locations beyond Seattle are important for the company's success. Chabot's experience is having such a profound impact on the company's success that Tableau is now encouraging other executives to spend time at international offices.[61]

Discussion Questions

4-16 Tableau staffs its international offices primarily with host country nationals. What are the advantages and disadvantages of this staffing strategy?

4-17 Do you agree with Chabot that the company will benefit if more executives spend time in international offices? Why or why not?

4-18 As Tableau executives get ready to spend time in the company's international offices, how can they prepare for the cultural differences they will encounter?

4-19 What are some of the challenges Tableau will face as it hires 1,000 new employees in one year?

CASE APPLICATION #3

Extreme Openness
Topic: Organizational culture, openness, pay transparency

Social media is altering the way employee salaries are negotiated and changed. It used to be that how much you were paid at your job was something you never talked about, especially with others outside your family and maybe your friends. However, a number of websites now allow employees to anonymously post their annual pay and provide an overview of salary ranges for various jobs at a given organization. Other websites collect pay data from market surveys and publish it online.[62] This "social media-driven salary information" has shifted the balance of power in pay discussions.[63] Although employers often may ask for salary histories of job applicants and desired salary, now job applicants and even current employees can be prepared with at least some salary information. Even if the data may not be totally accurate, individuals feel empowered to talk about what their expectations are about fair pay.

Recent surveys show that Millennials aren't as apprehensive about sharing information about their pay with their coworkers as older workers are. Nearly half say that they would or do discuss pay with friends. Yet only 36 percent of Americans overall feel comfortable talking about their compensation with others.[64] This attitude shift is forcing some employers to take a close look at their overall compensation and promotion system.

Although proponents of full pay transparency point out the benefits of sharing this information with employees, others say there are drawbacks.[65] For instance, how does an organization reward individuals whose performance is exemplary, even though the performance contributions may not be visible to everyone? This situation is quite common in organizations where work is highly collaborative and coworkers' contributions may not be apparent to each other. That makes it difficult for everyone to agree on how those contributions should be valued. Another problem is how employees respond when they feel their pay isn't "fair." Often, resentment sets in, and dissatisfied/upset employees respond by decreasing their work contributions or by leaving. So, the goal of hoping to motivate and retain employees by sharing pay information might have the opposite effect.

> ## Full pay transparency ... the Good, the Bad, and the Reality

Discussion Questions

4-20 Is salary transparency a good thing? Explain your position.

4-21 Using Exhibit 4–4, in which dimension(s) of organizational culture do you believe pay transparency would fall? Explain.

4-22 Will this trend toward salary openness affect how managers manage? If so, how? If not, why not?

4-23 Has social media's role in pay transparency been a good thing or a negative thing? Discuss.

4-24 In your "assigned" team, discuss your opinions about sharing salary information. Work together to identify additional potential drawbacks of full pay transparency. Be prepared to share these with classmates.

Endnotes

1. "A Transforming World," Report by Merrill Lynch Wealth Management, http://www.ml.com/publish/content/application/pdf/GWMOL/AR9D50CF-MLWM.pdf, May 2014.

2. C. Matlack, "The Growing Peril of a Connected World," *Bloomberg Businessweek*, December 6–12, 2010, pp. 63–64.

3. S. Russolillo, "Countries Urged to Weigh Issuing Digital Currencies," *Wall Street Journal*, September 19, 2017, p. B6.

4. A. Tangel, H. Torry, and H. Haddon, "Inflation Creeps Into U.S. Supply Chain," *Wall Street Journal*, February 10-11, 2018, pp. B1–B2.

5. E. Sylvers and T. Fairless, "Zombie Companies Haunt Europe's Economic Recovery," *Wall Street Journal*, November 16, 2017, pp. A1+.

6. G. Ip, "Sluggish Productivity Hampers Wage Gains," *Wall Street Journal*, March 7–8, 2015, pp. A1+; R. Miller, "How Productive Is the U.S.?" *Bloomberg Businessweek*, March 2, 2015, pp. 16–17; and "Global Productivity Slowdown Moderated in 2013—2014 May See Better Performance," The Conference Board, https://www.conference-board.org/pdf_free/economics/TED3.pdf, 2014.

7. Latest Quarterly Trade Trends, World Trade Organization, https://www.wto.org/english/res_e/statis_e/daily_update_e/latest_trade_trends_e.pdf, January 25, 2018.

8. "The Employment Situation—January 2018, https://www.bls.gov/news.release/pdf/empsit.pdf.

9. B. Casselman, "After 7 Years of Job Growth, Room for More, or Danger Ahead?" *New York Times Online*, December 8, 2017.

10. P. Cohen, "Steady Jobs, but With Pay and Hours That Are Anything But," *New York Times Online*, May 31, 2017.

11. P. Davidson, "Firms Go with Part-Timers to Get around Health Law," *USA Today*, December 31, 2014, p. 3B.

12. S. Smith, "Most Think the 'American Dream' Is within Reach for Them," Pew Research Center, http://www.pewresearch.org/fact-tank/2017/10/31/most-think-the-american-dream-is-within-reach-for-them/, October 31, 2017.

13. E. Pfanner, "Economic Troubles Cited as the Top Risks in 2012," *New York Times Online*, January 11, 2012; and E. Pfanner, "Divining the Business and Political Risks of 2012," *New York Times Online*, January 11, 2012.

14. C. Hausman, "Americans See Inequality as a Major Problem," *Ethics Newsline*, www.globalethics.org/news-line, April 9, 2012.

15. E. Porter, "Inequality Undermines Democracy," *New York Times Online*, March 20, 2012.

16. T. Meelen and K. Frenken, "Stop Saying Uber Is Part of the Sharing Economy," http://www.fastcoexist.com/3040863/stop-saying-uber-is-part-of-the-sharing-economy, January 14, 2015; and "The Rise of the Sharing Economy," *The Economist*, http://www.economist.com/news/leaders/21573104-internet-everything-hire-rise-sharing-economy, March 9, 2013.

17. A. Rinne, "What Exactly Is the Sharing Economy?" World Economic Forum, https://www.weforum.org/agenda/2017/12/when-is-sharing-not-really-sharing/, December 13, 2017.

18. G. M. Eckhardt and F. Bardhi, "The Sharing Economy Isn't about Sharing at All," *Harvard Business Review*, https://hbr.org/2015/01/the-sharing-economy-isnt-about-sharing-at-all, January 28, 2015.

19. P. Coy, "If Demography Is Destiny, Then India Has the Edge," *Bloomberg Businessweek*, January 17–23, 2011, pp. 9–10.

20. S. Brownstone, "Millennials Will Become the Majority in the Workforce in 2015. Is Your Company Ready?" http://www.fastcoexist.com/3037823/millennials-will-become-the-majority-in-the-workforce-in-2015-is-your-company-ready, November 4, 2014.

21. J. Villa, "How Hispanic Gen Z Will Change Everything," www.media.post, March 4, 2015.

22. R. Bernstein, "Move over Millennials—Here Comes Gen Z," *Ad Age*, http://adage.com/article/cmo-strategy/move-millennials-gen-z/296577/, January 21, 2015.

23. R. Friedrich, M. Peterson, and A. Koster, "The Rise of Generation C," *Strategy+Business*, Spring 2011, pp. 1–8.

24. S. Cardwell, "Where Do Babies Come From?" *Newsweek*, October 19, 2009, p. 56.

25. N. Mandhana, "India Confronts Demographic Bulge," *Wall Street Journal*, January 23, 2018, p. R10.

26. Y. Hori, J-P. Lehmann, T. Ma Kam Wah, and V. Wang, "Facing up to the Demographic Dilemma," *Strategy+Business Online*, Spring 2010; and E. E. Gordon, "Job Meltdown or Talent Crunch?" *Training*, January 2010, p. 10.

27. M. Chand and R. L. Tung, "The Aging of the World's Population and Its Effects on Global Business," *Academy of Management Perspectives*, November 2014, pp. 409–29.

28. Catalyst. *Catalyst Quick Take: Generations in the Workplace* (New York: Catalyst, July 20, 2017).

29. M. Kanellos, "152,000 Smart Devices Every Minute In 2025: IDC Outlines the Future of Smart Things," *Forbes Online*, https://www.forbes.com/sites/michaelkanellos/2016/03/03/152000-smart-devices-every-minute-in-2025-idc-outlines-the-future-of-smart-things/#42c729144b63, March 3, 2016.

30. Eliot Beer, "Almarai Profits Up 14%, But Costs Set to Soar," Food Navigator.com, January 28, 2016, http://www.foodnavigator.com/Regions/Middle-East/Almarai-profits-up-14-but-costs-set-to-soar (accessed December 12, 2016); Dean Best, "Almarai Reports Bakery Boost as Poultry Sales Nosedive," *Just Food*, October 10, 2016, http://www.just-food.com/news/almarai-reports-bakery-boost-as-poultry-sales-nosedive_id134636.aspx (accessed December 12, 2016).

31. J. Queenan, "The Disney Empire Plans to Strike Back," Wall Street Journal, November 11-12, 2017, p. C11; and E. Schwartzel, "Disney's Force Awakens against Local Movie Theaters," Wall Street Journal, November 2, 2017, p. A1, A4.

32. J. S. Harrison and C. H. St. John, "Managing and Partnering with External Stakeholders," *Academy of Management Executive*, May 1996, pp. 46–60.

33. J. Swartz, "Facebook Changes Its Status in Washington," *USA Today*, January 13, 2011, pp. 1B+.

34. S. L. Berman, R. A. Phillips, and A. C. Wicks, "Resource Dependence, Managerial Discretion, and Stakeholder Performance," Academy of Management Proceedings Best Conference Paper, August 2005; A. J. Hillman and G. D. Keim, "Shareholder Value, Stakeholder Management, and Social Issues: What's the Bottom Line?" *Strategic Management Journal*, March 2001, pp. 125–39; J. S. Harrison and R. E. Freeman, "Stakeholders, Social Responsibility, and Performance: Empirical Evidence and Theoretical Perspectives," *Academy of Management Journal*, July 1999, pp. 479–87; and J. Kotter and J. Heskett, *Corporate Culture and Performance* (New York: The Free Press, 1992).

35. J. A. Chatman and K. A. Jehn, "Assessing the Relationship between Industry Characteristics and Organizational Culture: How Different Can You Be?" *Academy of Management Journal*, June 1994, pp. 522–53; and C. A. O'Reilly III, J. Chatman, and D. F. Caldwell, "People and Organizational Culture: A Profile Comparison Approach to Assessing Person-Organization Fit," *Academy of Management Journal*, September 1991, pp. 487–516.

36. T. Lytle, "Social Work," *HR Magazine*, August 2014, pp. 40–42.

37. A. Bryant, "On a Busy Road, a Company Needs Guardrails, an interview with Christopher J. Nassetta, president and chief executive of Hilton Worldwide," *New York Times Online*, October 13, 2012.

38. E. H. Schein, *Organizational Culture and Leadership* (San Francisco: Jossey-Bass, 1985), pp. 314–15.

39. "Executive Views on Organizational Culture," *T&D*, November 2014, p. 19.

40. C. Palmeri, "The Fastest Drill in the West," *BusinessWeek*, October 24, 2005, pp. 86–88.

41. C. Kenkel and S. Sorenson, "How Winegardner & Hammons Built a Winning Culture," Gallup Business Journal, http://www.gallup.com/businessjournal/175394/winegardner-hammons-built-winning-workplace-culture.aspx, September 18, 2014.

42. Based on J. McGregor, "Customer Service Champs," *BusinessWeek*, March 3, 2008, pp. 37–57; B. Schneider, M. G. Ehrhart, D. M. Mayer, J. L. Saltz, and K. Niles-Jolly, "Understanding Organization-Customer Links in Service Settings," *Academy of Management Journal*, December 2006, pp. 1017–32; B. A. Gutek, M. Groth, and B. Cherry, "Achieving Service Success through Relationships and Enhanced Encounters," *Academy of Management Executive*, November 2002, pp. 132–44; K. A. Eddleston, D. L. Kidder, and B. E. Litzky, "Who's the Boss? Contending with Competing Expectations from Customers and Management," *Academy of Management Executive*, November 2002, pp. 85–95; S. D. Pugh, J. Dietz, J. W. Wiley, and S. M. Brooks, "Driving Service Effectiveness through Employee-Customer Linkages," *Academy of Management Executive*, November 2002, pp. 73–84; L. A. Bettencourt, K. P. Gwinner, and M. L. Mueter, "A Comparison of Attitude, Personality, and Knowledge Predictors of Service-Oriented Organizational Citizenship Behaviors," *Journal of Applied Psychology*, February 2001, pp. 29–41; M. D. Hartline, J. G. Maxham III, and D. O. McKee, "Corridors of Influence in the Dissemination of Customer-Oriented Strategy to Customer Contact Service Employees," *Journal of Marketing*, April 2000, pp. 35–50; L. Lengnick-Hall and

C. A. Lengnick-Hall, "Expanding Customer Orientation in the HR Function," *Human Resource Management*, Fall 1999, pp. 201–14; M. D. Hartline and O. C. Ferrell, "The Management of Customer-Contact Service Employees: An Empirical Investigation," *Journal of Marketing*, October 1996, pp. 52–70; and M. J. Bitner, B. H. Booms, and L. A. Mohr, "Critical Service Encounters: The Employee's Viewpoint," *Journal of Marketing*, October 1994, pp. 95–106.

43. J. Yang and R. W. Ahrens, "Culture Spurs Innovation," *USA Today*, February 25, 2008, p. 1B.

44. Accenture, "Corporate Innovation Is within Reach: Nurturing and Enabling an Entrepreneurial Culture," www.accenture.com, 2013.

45. J. Cable, "Building An Innovative Culture," *Industry Week*, March 2010, pp.32-37; M. Hawkins, "Create a Climate of Creativity," *Training*, January 2010, p. 12; and L. Simpson, "Fostering Creativity," *Training*, December 2001, p. 56.

46. M. Laff, "Triple Bottom Line," *T&D* 63 (February 2009), pp. 34–39.

47. M. Kaptein, "Developing and Testing a Measure for the Ethical Culture of Organizations: The Corporate Ethical Virtues Model," *Journal of Business Ethics* 29 (2008), pp. 923–47.

48. M. Feffer, "8 Tips for Creating a Learning Culture," *HR Magazine*, August 2017, p. 51.

49. Based on A. L. Wilkins, "The Culture Audit: A Tool for Understanding Organizations," *Organizational Dynamics*, Autumn 1983, pp. 24–38; H. M. Trice and J. M. Beyer, *The Culture of Work Organizations* (Upper Saddle River, NJ: Prentice Hall, 1993), pp. 358–62; and D. M. Cable, L. Aiman-Smith, P. W. Mulvey, and J. R. Edwards, "The Sources and Accuracy of Job Applicants' Beliefs about Organizational Culture," *Academy of Management Journal*, December 2000, pp. 1076–85.

50. "Our Trip History," https://www.uber.com/our-story/.

51. A. Carr, "Uber's Driving Lessons," *Fast Company*, September 2017, pp. 25–27.

52. Ibid.

53. M. della Cava, J. Guynn, and J. Swartz, "Uber in Crisis Over 'Baller' Culture," *USA Today/Springfield News-Leader*, February 27, 2017, p. 4B.

54. E. Newcomer and B. Stone, "The Fall of Travis Kalanick," *Bloomberg Businessweek*, January 22, 2015, pp. 46–51.

55. J. Muskus, Technology Section, *BloombergBusinesweek*, January 15, 2018, pp. 22–24.

56. M. Isaac, "Uber Engaged in 'Illegal' Spying on Rivals, Ex-Employee Says," *New York Times Online*, December 15, 2017.

57. G. Bensinger and R. McMillan, "Security Shake-Up at Uber," *Wall Street Journal*, December 4, 2017, p. B4.

58. D. MacMillan and N. Purnell, "Uber Knowingly Leased Unsafe Cars to Drivers," *Wall Street Journal*, August 4, 2017, pp. A1+.

59. G. Bensinger and M. Farrell, "Uber's Backers Force Out Leader," June 22, 2017, pp. A1+.

60. Newcomer and Stone, "The Fall of Travis Kalanick," p. 51.

61. T. Soper, "Tableau Software Set to Hire Another 1,000 Employees in 2016; CEO Says Business 'Flourishing,'" www.geekwire.com, December 14, 2015; N. Ungerleider, "What Tinder Did for Dating, Tableau Wants to Do for Spreadsheets." *Fast Company* online, www.fastcompany.com, February 24, 2015; "Tableau's Q3 Earnings: International Expansion & New Products Drive Top-Line Growth," *Forbes* online, www.forbes.com, November 11, 2015; "Tableau's Entry into China a Good Move as Company Targets International Growth," *Forbes* online, www.forbes.com, August 21, 2015; T. Soper, "How to Lead a Global Company: What Tableau's CEO Learned during His Year in London," www.geekwire.com, December 25, 2015.

62. J. Sammer, "The 'Yelping' of Pay: Managing Expectations in the Era of Online Salary Data," SHRM, https://www.shrm.org/resourcesandtools/hr-topics/compensation/pages/yelping-of-pay.aspx, May 1, 2017.

63. Ibid.

64. K. Gee, "Pay Is Less Secretive in Millennial Workforce," *Wall Street Journal*, October 26, 2017, pp. B1, B6.

65. T. Zenger, "The Downside of Full Pay Transparency," *Wall Street Journal*, August 14, 2017, p. R6.

Managing Change and Innovation

There's nothing managers can do to reduce the stress inherent in today's jobs.

Shutterstock

Management

DEBUNKED?

Myth

It's an unusual employee today who isn't dealing with stress. Cutbacks, increased workloads, open workspace designs, work/life conflicts, and 24/7 communication access are just a few of the things that have increased job stress. However, organizations are not ignoring this problem. **Smart managers are redesigning jobs, realigning schedules, and introducing employee assistance programs** to help employees cope with the increasing stresses in their work and in balancing their work and personal lives.

STRESS

can be an unfortunate consequence of change and anxiety, both at work and personally. However, change is a constant for organizations and thus for managers and for employees. Large companies, small businesses, entrepreneurial startups, universities, hospitals, and even the military are changing the way they do things. For instance, Japanese convenience stores, which are found everywhere in Japan, are experimenting with labor-saving technologies to offset rising labor costs. As owners and franchisees adapt to and implement the changes, consumers must adapt, as well.[1] Although change has always been part of a manager's job, it's become even more so in recent years. And because change can't be (and shouldn't be) eliminated, managers must learn how to manage it successfully. In this chapter, we're going to look at organizational change efforts and how to manage those, the ways that managers can deal with the stress that exists in organizations, and how managers can stimulate innovation in their organizations. Finally, we'll look at the impact of disruptive innovation. ●

Learning Outcomes

5-1 Define *organizational change* and compare and contrast views on the change process. p. 157

5-2 Explain how to manage resistance to change. p. 162

5-3 Describe what managers need to know about employee stress. p. 164

5-4 Discuss techniques for stimulating innovation. p. 168

5-5 Explain what disruptive innovation is and why managing it is important. p. 173

What Is Change and How Do Managers Deal with It?

5-1 Define *organizational change* and compare and contrast views on the change process.

If it weren't for change, a **manager's job** would be relatively easy.

Print publications—magazines, newspapers, textbooks, etc.—have struggled to find a profitable way to compete in a digital world. When Ross Levinsohn took over as CEO of the *L.A. Times*, he faced wary (and weary) employees.[2] After all, the staff had already been through a decade's worth of different leaders promising positive changes. But Levinsohn proceeded with his strategy of refocusing the newspaper on digital subscriptions and licensing content. In addition, he planned to invest more in coverage of entertainment and culture, which seems strategically appropriate given the *Times*' geographic location. This organization's managers are doing what managers everywhere must do—implement change!

Change makes a manager's job more challenging. Without it, managing would be relatively easy. Planning would be easier because tomorrow would be no different from today. The issue of organization design would be solved because the environment would be free from uncertainty and there would be no need to adapt. Similarly, decision making would be dramatically simplified because the outcome of each alternative could be predicted with near pinpoint accuracy. It would also simplify the manager's job if competitors never introduced new products or services, if customers didn't make new demands, if government regulations were never modified, if technology never advanced, or if employees' needs always remained the same. But that's not the way it is.

Change is an organizational reality. Most managers, at one point or another, will have to change some things in their workplace. We call these changes **organizational change**, which is any alteration or adaptation of an organization's structure, technology, or people. (See Exhibit 5–1.) Let's look more closely at each.

1. **Changing *structure*:** Includes any change in authority relationships, coordination mechanisms, degree of centralization, job design, or similar organization structure variables. Examples might be restructuring work units, empowering employees, decentralizing, widening spans of control, reducing work specialization, or creating work teams. All of these may involve some type of structural change.
2. **Changing *technology*:** Encompasses modifications in the way work is done or the methods and equipment used. Examples might be computerizing work processes and procedures, adding robotics to work areas, installing energy usage monitors, equipping employees with mobile communication tools, implementing social media tools, or installing a new computer operating system.
3. **Changing *people*:** Refers to changes in employee attitudes, expectations, perceptions, or behaviors. Examples might be changing employee attitudes and behaviors to better support a new customer service strategy, using team building efforts to make a team more innovative, or training employees to adopt a "safety-first" focus.

> **organizational change**
> Any alteration of an organization's people, structure, or technology

Exhibit 5–1 Categories of Organizational Change

Structure	Technology	People
Authority relationships	Work processes	Attitudes
Coordinating mechanisms	Work methods	Expectations
Job redesign	Equipment	Perceptions
Spans of control		Behavior

Why Do Organizations Need to Change?

In Chapter 4, we pointed out that both external and internal forces constrain managers. These same forces also bring about the need for change. Let's briefly review these factors.

WHAT EXTERNAL FORCES CREATE A NEED TO CHANGE?   The Mayo Clinic is well known for success in treating complex medical cases. Now it's going through a tricky turn-around by rethinking most aspects of its system. Why change what seems to be working and working well? Because external forces were a looming threat to the clinic.[3] The external forces that create the need for organizational change come from various sources. In recent years, the *marketplace* has affected firms such as AT&T and Lowe's because of new competition. AT&T, for example, faces competition from local cable companies and from Internet services such as Hulu and Skype. Lowe's, too, must now contend with a host of aggressive competitors such as Home Depot and Menard's. *Government laws and regulations* are also an impetus for change. For example, when the Patient Protection and Affordable Care Act was signed into law, thousands of businesses were faced with decisions on how best to offer employees health insurance, revamp benefit reporting, and educate employees on the new provisions. Even today, organizations continue to deal with the requirements of improving health insurance accessibility.

Technology also creates the need for organizational change. The Internet has changed pretty much everything—the way we get information, how we buy products, and how we get our work done. Technological advancements have created significant economies of scale for many organizations. For instance, technology allows Scottrade to offer its clients the opportunity to make online trades without a broker. The assembly line in many industries has also undergone dramatic change as employers replace human labor with technologically advanced mechanical robots. Also, the fluctuation in *labor markets* forces managers to initiate changes. For example, the shortage of registered nurses in the United States has led many hospital administrators to redesign nursing jobs and to alter their rewards and benefits packages for nurses, as well as join forces with local universities to address the nursing shortage.

As the news headlines remind us, *economic* changes affect almost all organizations. For instance, prior to the mortgage market meltdown, low interest rates led to significant growth in the housing market. This growth meant more jobs, more employees hired, and significant increases in sales in other businesses that supported the building industry. However, as the economy soured, it had the opposite effect on the housing industry and other industries as credit markets dried up and businesses found it difficult to get the capital they needed to operate.

Internal forces created the need for change at Reebok. To increase its focus on fitness and innovation, Reebok moved its headquarters from a suburban location, where employees worked from their own offices, to Boston, where they work in open spaces that foster communication and collaboration and encourage them to think and act like they are part of a new start-up.

Getty Images

WHAT INTERNAL FORCES CREATE A NEED TO CHANGE?   It's hard to believe, but until recently, Southwest Airlines was a company that still sent faxes. And while most other airlines' employees used tablets to do their jobs, Southwest's didn't. To say Southwest has been slow in migrating to digital solutions would be an understatement. However, a major digital transformation has been approved by organizational leaders. Its reason for waiting so long was because it competes on the basis of low costs and managers were hesitant to overspend on work operations. However, they finally realized that to stay competitive, they were going to have to change. Thus, the decision to spend $800 million on a technological overhaul . . . $300 million for new operations technology and $500 million for a new reservation system. It's a lot of money, but Southwest expects to see significant earnings boosts from workflow improvements in efficiency and effectiveness.[4] As you can see from this example, internal forces can also create the need for organizational change. These internal forces tend to originate primarily from the internal operations of the organization or from the impact of external changes. (It's also important to recognize that such changes are a normal part of the organizational life cycle.)[5]

When managers redefine or modify an organization's *strategy*, that action often introduces a host of changes. For example, Southwest Airlines bringing in new digital technology is an internal force for change. Because of this action, employees may face job redesign, undergo training to operate the new equipment, or be required to establish new interaction patterns within their work groups. Another internal force for change is that the *composition of an organization's workforce* changes in terms of age, education, gender, nationality, and so forth. A stable organization in which managers have been in their positions for years might need to restructure jobs in order to retain more ambitious employees by affording them some upward mobility. The compensation and benefits systems might also need to be reworked to reflect the needs of a diverse workforce and market forces in which certain skills are in short supply. *Employee attitudes*, such as job dissatisfaction, may lead to increased absenteeism, resignations, and even strikes. Such events will, in turn, often lead to changes in organizational policies and practices.

Who Initiates Organizational Change?

Organizational changes need a **catalyst.**

People who act as catalysts and assume the responsibility for managing the change process are called **change agents**.[6] WHO can be a change agent?

- Any *manager* can. We assume organizational change is initiated and carried out by a manager within the organization.
- OR any *nonmanager*—for example, an *internal staff specialist* or an *outside consultant* whose expertise is in change implementation—can.

For major systemwide changes, an organization will often hire outside consultants for advice and assistance. Because these consultants come from the outside, they offer an objective perspective that insiders usually lack. However, the problem is that outside consultants may not understand the organization's history, culture, operating procedures, and personnel. They're also prone to initiating more drastic changes than insiders—which can be either a benefit or a disadvantage—because they don't have to live with the repercussions after the change is implemented. In contrast, internal managers who act as change agents may be more thoughtful (and possibly more cautious) because they must live with the consequences of their actions.

How Does Organizational Change Happen?

We often use two metaphors in describing the change process.[7] These two metaphors represent distinctly different approaches to understanding and responding to change. Let's take a closer look at each one.

1 WHAT IS THE "CALM WATERS" METAPHOR? The **"calm waters" metaphor** envisions the organization as a large ship crossing a calm sea. The ship's captain and crew know exactly where they're going because they've made the trip many times before. Change appears as the occasional storm, a brief distraction in an otherwise calm and predictable trip. Until recently, the "calm waters" metaphor dominated the thinking of practicing managers and academics. The prevailing model for handling change in such circumstances is best illustrated in Kurt Lewin's three-step description of the change process.[8] (See Exhibit 5–2.)

"calm waters" metaphor
A description of organizational change that likens that change to a large ship making a predictable trip across a calm sea and experiencing an occasional storm

change agents
People who act as change catalysts and assume the responsibility for managing the change process

Exhibit 5–2 The Three-Step Change Process

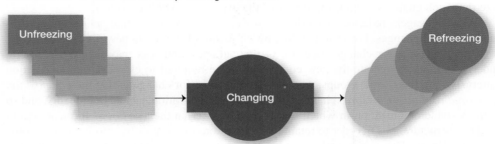

According to Lewin, successful change requires unfreezing the status quo, changing to a new state, and freezing the new change to make it permanent. The status quo can be considered an equilibrium state. Unfreezing is necessary to move from this equilibrium. It can be achieved in one of three ways:

- Increase the driving forces, which direct behavior away from the status quo.
- Decrease the restraining forces, which hinder movement from the existing equilibrium.
- Do both.

Once the situation has been "unfrozen," the change itself can be implemented. However, just introducing change doesn't mean it's going to take hold. The new situation needs to be "frozen" so that it can be sustained over time. Unless this last step is done, the change is likely to be short-lived, with employees reverting to the previous equilibrium state. The objective, then, is to freeze at the new equilibrium state and stabilize the new situation by balancing the driving and restraining forces. (Read more about Lewin and his organizational research in the Classic Concepts in Today's Workplace box.)

◄◄◄ Classic Concepts in Today's Workplace ▶▶▶

Who Is Kurt Lewin?

- German-American psychologist, known for his research on group dynamics
- Often called the father of modern social psychology (an academic field of study that uses scientific methods to "understand and explain how the thought, feeling, and behavior of individuals are influenced by the actual, imagined, or implied presence of other human beings")[10]

What Did He Do?

- Described group behavior as an intricate set of symbolic interactions and forces that affect group structure and also modify individual behavior.
- One particular study that looked at modifying family food habits during World War II provided new and important insights into how best to introduce change.

Major Lessons from His Work:

- Change is more easily introduced *through group decision making* than through lectures and individual appeals.

> Lewin's ideas have helped us better understand **ORGANIZATIONAL CHANGE.**

- Change is more readily accepted *when people feel they have an opportunity to be involved in the change* rather than being simply asked or told to change.

- Use force field analysis to *look at the factors (forces) that influence* a change situation
- Forces either *drive* or *block* movement toward a goal.
- Make change work and overcome resistance by *increasing the driving forces, decreasing the blocking forces,* or *doing both.*

Discussion Questions:

1 Explain force field analysis and how it can be used in organizational change.

2 What advice do you see from Lewin's ideas that could help you as you deal with change? Be specific in describing. What about managers? What might they use?

Note how Lewin's three-step process treats change as a break in the organization's equilibrium state.[9] The status quo has been disturbed, and change is necessary to establish a new equilibrium state. Although this view might have been appropriate to the relatively calm environment faced by most organizations during the twentieth century, it's increasingly obsolete as a description of the kinds of "seas" that current managers have to navigate.

2 WHAT IS THE "WHITE-WATER RAPIDS" METAPHOR? As former chair of Nielsen Media Research (the company best known for its TV ratings, which are frequently used to determine how much advertisers pay for TV commercials), Susan Whiting had to tackle significant industry changes. Video-on-demand services, streaming technologies, smartphones, tablet computers, and other changing technologies have made data collection much more challenging for the media research business. Here's what she had to say about the business environment: "If you look at a typical week I have, it's a combination of trying to *lead a company in change in an industry in change*."[11] That's a pretty accurate description of what change is like in our second change metaphor—white-water rapids. It's also consistent with a world that's increasingly dominated by information, ideas, and knowledge.[12]

In the **"white-water rapids" metaphor**, the organization is seen as a small raft navigating a raging river with uninterrupted white-water rapids. Aboard the raft are half a dozen people who have never worked together before, who are totally unfamiliar with the river, who are unsure of their eventual destination, and who, as if things weren't bad enough, are traveling at night. In the white-water rapids metaphor, change is the status quo and managing change is a continual process.

To get a feeling of what managing change might be like in a white-water rapids environment, consider attending a college that had the following rules: Courses vary in length. When you sign up, you don't know how long a course will run; it might go for 2 weeks or 30 weeks. Furthermore, the instructor can end a course at any time with no prior warning. If that isn't challenging enough, the length of the class changes each time it meets: Sometimes the class lasts 20 minutes; other times it runs for three hours. And the time of the next class meeting is set by the instructor during this class. There's one more thing. All exams are unannounced, so you have to be ready for a test at any time. To succeed in this type of environment, you'd have to respond quickly to changing conditions. Students who were overly structured or uncomfortable with change wouldn't succeed.

DOES EVERY MANAGER FACE A WORLD OF CONSTANT AND CHAOTIC CHANGE? Well, maybe not *every* manager, but it *is* becoming more the norm. The stability and predictability of the calm waters metaphor don't exist. Disruptions in the status quo are not occasional and temporary, and they're not followed by a return to calm waters. Many managers never get out of the rapids. Like Susan Whiting, just described, they face constant forces in the environment (external *and* internal) that bring about the need for planned organizational change.

> Most organizational **changes don't happen** by chance.

HOW DO ORGANIZATIONS IMPLEMENT PLANNED CHANGES? At the Wyndham Peachtree Conference Center in Georgia, businesses bring groups of employees to try their hand at the ancient Chinese water sport of dragon boat racing. Although the physical exercise is an added benefit, it's the team-building exercise in which participants learn about communication, collaboration, and commitment that's meant to be the longest-lasting benefit.[13]

As president and CEO of DeNA Company, a Japanese Internet firm, Isao Moriyasu manages in a white-water rapids environment where change is the status quo and managing change is a continual process. Moriyasu is rapidly acquiring firms and developing new services as DeNA expands from its base in Japan to countries worldwide.

Kiyoshi Ota/Bloomberg/Getty Images

organization development (OD)
Efforts that assist organizational members with a planned change by focusing on their attitudes and values

survey feedback
A method of assessing employees' attitudes toward and perceptions of a change

process consultation
Using outside consultants to assess organizational processes such as workflow, informal intra-unit relationships, and formal communication channels

team-building
Using activities to help work groups set goals, develop positive interpersonal relationships, and clarify the roles and responsibilities of each team member

intergroup development
Activities that attempt to make several work groups more cohesive

Most organizational changes don't happen by chance. Often managers make a concerted effort to alter some aspect of the organization. Whatever happens—especially in terms of structure or technology—ultimately affects the organization's people. Efforts to assist organizational members with a planned change are referred to as **organization development (OD)**.

In facilitating long-term, organization-wide changes, managers use OD to constructively change the attitudes and values of organization members so they can more readily adapt to and be more effective in achieving the new directions of the organization.[14] When OD efforts are planned, organization leaders are, in essence, attempting to change the organization's culture.[15] However, a fundamental issue of OD is its reliance on employee participation to foster an environment in which open communication and trust exist.[16] Persons involved in OD efforts acknowledge that change can create stress for employees. Therefore, OD attempts to involve organizational members in changes that will affect their jobs and seeks their input about how the change is affecting them (just as Lewin suggested).

Any organizational activity that assists with implementing planned change can be viewed as an OD technique. The more popular OD efforts in organizations rely heavily on group interactions and cooperation and include:

1. **Survey feedback**. Employees are asked about their attitudes and perceptions of the change they're encountering. Employees are generally asked to respond to a set of specific questions regarding how they view such organizational aspects as decision making, leadership, communication effectiveness, and satisfaction with their jobs, coworkers, and management.[17] The data that a change agent obtains are used to clarify problems that employees may be facing. As a result of this information, the change agent takes some action to remedy the problems.

2. **Process consultation**. Outside consultants help managers perceive, understand, and act on organizational processes they're facing.[18] These elements might include, for example, workflow, informal relationships among unit members, and formal communications channels. Consultants give managers insight into what is going on. It's important to recognize that consultants are not there to solve these problems. Rather, they act as coaches to help managers diagnose the interpersonal processes that need improvement. If managers, with the consultants' help, cannot solve the problem, the consultants will often help managers find experts who can.

3. **Team-building**. In organizations made up of individuals working together to achieve goals, OD helps them become a team. How? By helping them set goals, develop positive interpersonal relationships, and clarify the roles and responsibilities of each team member. It's not always necessary to address each area because the group may be in agreement and understand what's expected. The *primary* focus of team-building is to increase members' trust and openness toward one another.[19]

4. **Intergroup development**. Different groups focus on becoming more cohesive. That is, intergroup development attempts to change attitudes, stereotypes, and perceptions that one group may have toward another group. The goal? Better coordination among the various groups.

How Do Managers Manage Resistance to Change?

5-2 Explain how to manage resistance to change.

We know that it's better for us to eat healthy and to be physically active, yet few of us actually follow that advice consistently and continually. We resist making lifestyle changes. Volkswagen Sweden and ad agency DDB Stockholm did an experiment to see if they could get people to change their behavior and take the healthier option of using the stairs instead of riding an escalator.[20] How? They put a working piano keyboard on stairs in a Stockholm subway station to see if commuters would use it. The experiment was a resounding success as stair traffic rose 66 percent. The lesson: People *can change* if you make the change appealing!

Managers should be motivated to initiate change because they're concerned with improving their organization's effectiveness. But change isn't easy in any organization. It can be disruptive and scary. And people and organizations can build up inertia and not want to change.

People resist change even if **it might be beneficial!** How about YOU? How do you **respond to change**?

Let's look at why people in organizations resist change and what can be done to lessen that resistance.

Why Do People Resist Organizational Change?

It's often said that most people hate any change that doesn't jingle in their pockets. Resistance to change is well documented.[21] Why *do* people resist organizational change? The main reasons include:[22]

1. UNCERTAINTY. *Change replaces the known with uncertainty and we don't like uncertainty.* No matter how much you may dislike attending college (or certain classes), at least you know what's expected of you. When you leave college for the world of full-time employment, you'll trade the known for the unknown. Employees in organizations are faced with similar uncertainty. For example, when quality control methods based on statistical models are introduced into manufacturing plants, many quality control inspectors have to learn the new methods. Some may fear that they'll be unable to do so and may develop a negative attitude toward the change or behave poorly if required to use them.

2. HABIT. *We do things out of habit.* Every day when you go to school or work you probably get there the same way, if you're like most people. We're creatures of habit. Life is complex enough—we don't want to have to consider the full range of options for the hundreds of decisions we make every day. To cope with this complexity, we rely on habits or programmed responses. But when confronted with change, our tendency to respond in our accustomed ways becomes a source of resistance.

3. CONCERN OVER PERSONAL LOSS. *We fear losing something already possessed.* Change threatens the investment you've already made in the status quo. The more that people have invested in the current system, the more they resist change. Why? They fear losing status, money, authority, friendships, personal convenience, or other economic benefits that they value. This helps explain why older workers tend to resist change more than younger workers, since they generally have more invested in the current system and more to lose by changing.

4. CHANGE IS NOT IN ORGANIZATION'S BEST INTERESTS. *We believe that the change is incompatible with the goals and interests of the organization.* For instance, an employee who believes that a proposed new job procedure will reduce product quality can be expected to resist the change. Actually, this type of resistance can be beneficial to the organization if expressed in a positive way.

What Are Some Techniques for Reducing Resistance to Organizational Change?

At an annual 401(k) enrollment meeting, the CEO of North American Tool, frustrated at his employees' disinterest in maxing out their investments, brought in a big bag, unzipped it, and upended it over a table.[23] Cash poured out—$9,832 to be exact—the amount employees had failed to claim the prior year. He gestured at the money and said, "This is your money. It should be in your pocket. Next year, do you want it on the table or in your pocket?" When the 401(k) enrollment forms were distributed, several individuals signed up. Sometimes to get people to change, *you first have to get their attention.*

(continued on p. 168)

What Reaction Do Employees Have to Organizational Change?

Yuri Arcurs/Alamy

5-3 Describe what managers need to know about employee stress.

Change often creates stress for employees!

Employee Stress Levels in Six Major Economies[24]	
United Kingdom	**35%** of employees
Brazil	**34%** of employees
Germany	**33%** of employees
United States	**32%** of employees
GLOBAL AVERAGE	**29%** of employees
China	**17%** of employees
India	**17%** of employees

What Is **Stress?**

- **Stress**—response to anxiety over intense demands, constraints, or opportunities.[25, 26]
- Not always bad; can be positive, especially when there's potential gain.
  — *Functional stress*—allows a person to perform at his or her highest level at crucial times.
- Often associated with **constraints** *(an obstacle that prevents you from doing what you desire)*, **demands** *(the loss of something desired)*, and **opportunities** *(the possibility of something new, something never done)*.
  Examples: Taking a test or having your annual work performance review.

  > **stress**
  > Response to anxiety over intense demands, constraints, or opportunities

- Even if conditions may be right for stress to surface, that doesn't mean it will.

For **potential stress** to become **actual stress**: • there is uncertainty over the outcome and • the outcome is important.

- How do you know when you're stressed? See the symptoms listed in Exhibit 5-3.

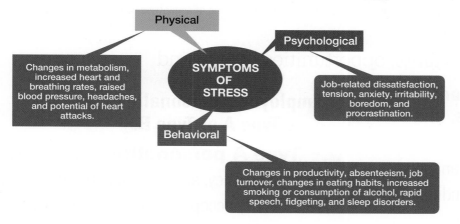

Exhibit 5–3 Symptoms of Stress

Too much stress can also have tragic consequences. In Japan, there's a stress phenomenon called **karoshi** (pronounced kah-roe-she), which is translated as death from overwork. To combat this problem, companies in Japan are trying creative ways to encourage their employees from working too many hours.[27]

karoshi
A Japanese term that refers to a sudden death caused by overworking

2

What Causes Stress? **Stressors**
Job-related factors:

- Examples: Pressures to avoid errors or complete tasks in a limited time period; changes in the way reports are filed; a demanding supervisor; unpleasant coworkers

  1 **Task demands:** Stress due to an employee's job—job design (autonomy, task variety, degree of automation); working conditions (temperature, noise, etc.); physical work layout (overcrowded or in visible location with constant interruptions); work quotas, especially when excessive;[29] high level of task interdependence with others.

  2 **Role demands:** Stress due to employee's particular role.

   ■ **Role conflicts**: expectations that may be hard to reconcile or satisfy.

   ■ **Role overload**: created when employee is expected to do more than time permits.

   ■ **Role ambiguity**: created when role expectations are not clearly understood—employee not sure what he or she is to do.

Two-thirds
of Millennials are stressed at work more or all the time.[28]

stressors
Factors that cause stress

role conflicts
Work expectations that are hard to satisfy

role overload
Having more work to accomplish than time permits

role ambiguity
When role expectations are not clearly understood

3 **Interpersonal demands:** Stress due to other employees—little or no social support from colleagues; poor interpersonal relationships.

4 **Organization structure:** Stress due to excessive rules; no opportunity to participate in decisions that affect an employee.

5 **Organizational leadership:** Stress due to managers' supervisory style in a culture of tension, fear, anxiety, unrealistic pressures to perform in the short run, excessively tight controls, and routine firing of employees who don't measure up.

Personal factors:
Life demands, constraints, opportunities of any kind

1

Family issues, personal economic problems, and so forth.

- Can't just ignore! Managers need to be understanding of these personal factors.[30]

2

Employees' personalities —Type A or Type B.

- **Type A personality**—chronic sense of time urgency, excessive competitive drive, and difficulty accepting and enjoying leisure time; more likely to shows symptoms of stress.

- **Type B personality**—little to no sense of time urgency or impatience.

- Stress comes from the hostility and anger associated with Type A behavior. Surprisingly, though, Type Bs are just as susceptible.

Type A personality
People who have a chronic sense of urgency and an excessive competitive drive

Type B personality
People who are relaxed and easygoing and accept change easily

Beyond Fotomedia GmbH/Alamy

How Can Stress Be Managed?

1bestofphoto/Alamy

1 General guidelines:

- Stress can never be totally eliminated!

- Not all stress is dysfunctional.

- Reduce dysfunctional stress by controlling job-related factors and offering help for personal stress.

2 Job-related factors:

- **Employee selection**—provide a realistic job preview and make sure an employee's abilities match the job requirements.

- **On-the-job**—improve organizational communications to minimize ambiguity; use a performance planning program such as MBO to clarify job responsibilities, provide clear performance goals, and reduce ambiguity through feedback; redesign job, if possible, especially if stress can be traced to boredom (increase challenge) or to work overload (reduce the workload); allow employees to participate in decisions and to gain social support, which also lessen stress.[31]

3 Personal factors:

- Not easy for manager to control directly

- Ethical considerations

Does a manager have the **right to intrude** —even subtly—
in an employee's personal life?

- If the manager believes it's ethical and the employee is receptive, consider employee assistance and wellness programs,[32] which are designed to assist employees in areas where they might be having difficulties (financial planning, legal matters, health, fitness, or stress).[33]

  ■ **Employee assistance programs (EAPs)**[34]— the goal is to get a productive employee back on the job as quickly as possible.

  ■ **Wellness programs**—the goal is to keep employees healthy and well, in all life areas.

Samantha Craddock/Alamy

---

employee assistance programs (EAPs)	**wellness programs**
Programs offered by organizations to help employees overcome personal and health-related problems	Programs offered by organizations to help employees prevent health problems

Exhibit 5–4 Techniques for Reducing Resistance to Change

TECHNIQUE	WHEN USED	ADVANTAGE	DISADVANTAGE
Education and communication	When resistance is due to misinformation	Clear up misunderstandings	May not work when mutual trust and credibility are lacking
Participation	When resisters have the expertise to make a contribution	Increase involvement and acceptance	Time-consuming; has potential for a poor solution
Facilitation and support	When resisters are fearful and anxiety-ridden	Can facilitate needed adjustments	Expensive; no guarantee of success
Negotiation	When resistance comes from a powerful group	Can "buy" commitment	Potentially high cost; opens doors for others to apply pressure too
Manipulation and co-optation	When a powerful group's endorsement is needed	Inexpensive, easy way to gain support	Can backfire, causing change agent to lose credibility
Coercion	When a powerful group's endorsement is needed	Inexpensive, easy way to gain support	May be illegal; may undermine change agent's credibility

When managers see resistance to change as dysfunctional, what can they do? Several strategies have been suggested in dealing with resistance to change. These approaches include education and communication, participation, facilitation and support, negotiation, manipulation and co-optation, and coercion. These tactics are summarized here and described in Exhibit 5–4. Managers should view these techniques as tools and use the most appropriate one depending on the type and source of the resistance.

- *Education and communication* can help reduce resistance to change by helping employees see the logic of the change effort. This technique, of course, assumes that much of the resistance lies in misinformation or poor communication.
- *Participation* involves bringing those individuals directly affected by the proposed change into the decision-making process. Their participation allows these individuals to express their feelings, increase the quality of the process, and increase employee commitment to the final decision.
- *Facilitation and support* involve helping employees deal with the fear and anxiety associated with the change effort. This help may include employee counseling, therapy, new skills training, or a short paid leave of absence.
- *Negotiation* involves exchanging something of value for an agreement to lessen the resistance to the change effort. This resistance technique may be quite useful when the resistance comes from a powerful source.
- *Manipulation and co-optation* refer to covert attempts to influence others about the change. They may involve twisting or distorting facts to make the change appear more attractive.
- *Coercion* involves the use of direct threats or force against those resisting the change.

How Can Managers Encourage Innovation in an Organization?

5-4 Discuss techniques for stimulating innovation.

"Innovation is the **key to continued** success."

"We innovate today to **secure the future**."

These two quotes (the first by Ajay Banga, the CEO of MasterCard, and the second by Sophie Vandebroek, former chief technology officer of Xerox Innovation Group) reflect how important innovation is to organizations.[35] **SUCCESS IN BUSINESS TODAY DEMANDS INNOVATION.** In the dynamic, chaotic world of global competition, organizations must create new products and services and adopt state-of-the-art technology if they're going to compete successfully.[36]

What companies come to mind when you think of successful innovators? Maybe Apple with all its cool work and entertainment gadgets. Maybe Tesla with its cars, rockets, and Hyperloop. Maybe Amazon for innovatively expanding its reach into different industry sectors. Or even maybe Square, for its mobile payments and products that serve households that are "unbanked" or "underbanked." What's the secret to the success of these innovator champions?[37] What can other managers do to make their organizations more innovative? In the following pages, we'll try to answer those questions as we discuss the factors behind innovation.

> **creativity**
> The ability to produce novel and useful ideas
>
> **innovation**
> The process of taking a creative idea and turning it into a useful product, service, or method of operation

How Are Creativity and Innovation Related?

- **Creativity** refers to the ability to combine ideas in a unique way or to make unusual associations between ideas.[38] A creative organization develops unique ways of working or novel solutions to problems. For instance, at Mattel, company officials introduced "Project Platypus," a special group that brings people from all disciplines—engineering, marketing, design, and sales—and tries to get them to "think outside the box" in order to "understand the sociology and psychology behind children's play patterns." To help make this kind of thinking happen, team members embarked on such activities as imagination exercises, group crying, and stuffed-bunny throwing. What does throwing stuffed bunnies have to do with creativity? It's part of a juggling lesson where team members tried to learn to juggle two balls and a stuffed bunny. Most people can easily learn to juggle two balls but can't let go of that third object. Creativity, like juggling, is learning to let go—that is, to "throw the bunny."[39] Creativity by itself isn't enough, though.
- The outcomes of the creative process need to be turned into useful products or work methods, which is defined as **innovation**. Thus, the *innovative organization is characterized by its ability to channel creativity into useful outcomes*. When managers talk about changing an organization to make it more creative, they usually mean they want to stimulate and nurture innovation.

What's Involved in Innovation?

Some people believe that creativity is inborn; others believe that with training, anyone can be creative. The latter group views creativity as a fourfold process.[40]

1. *Perception* involves the way you see things. Being creative means seeing things from a unique perspective. One person may see solutions to a problem that others cannot or will not see at all. The movement from perception to reality, however, doesn't occur instantaneously.
2. Instead, ideas go through a process of *incubation*. Sometimes employees need to sit on their ideas, which doesn't mean sitting and doing nothing. Rather, during this incubation period, employees should collect massive amounts of data that are stored, retrieved, studied, reshaped, and finally molded into something new. During this period, it's common for years to pass. Think for a moment about a time you struggled for an answer on a test. Although you tried hard to jog your memory, nothing worked. Then suddenly, like a flash of light, the answer popped into your head. You found it!
3. *Inspiration* in the creative process is similar. Inspiration is the moment when all your efforts successfully come together. Although inspiration leads to euphoria, the creative work isn't complete. It requires an innovative effort.
4. *Innovation* involves taking that inspiration and turning it into a useful product, service, or way of doing things. Thomas Edison is often credited with saying that "Creativity is 1 percent inspiration and 99 percent perspiration." That 99 percent, or the innovation, involves testing, evaluating, and retesting what the inspiration found. It's usually at this stage that an individual involves others more in what he or she has been working on. Such involvement is critical because even the greatest invention may be delayed, or lost, if an individual cannot effectively deal with others in communicating and achieving what the creative idea is supposed to do.

Taco Bell is an innovative organization that channels employee creativity into new products such as the Naked Egg Taco, a breakfast item made with a shell sculpted from a fried egg and filled with potatoes, cheese, and meat. Before launching the new taco at its stores, Taco Bell hosted several "Bell and Breakfast" tasting events, such as the one shown here in New York City, to give guests the chance to try the Naked Egg.

Dia Dipasupil/Getty Images Entertainment/Getty Images

Managing Technology in Today's Workplace
HELPING INNOVATION FLOURISH

When employees are busy doing their regular job tasks, how can innovation ever flourish? When job performance is evaluated by what you get done, how you get it done, and when you get it done, how can innovation ever happen? This has been a real challenge facing organizations wanting to be more innovative. One solution has been to give employees mandated time to experiment with their own ideas on company-related projects.[41] For instance, Google has its "20% Time" initiative, which encourages employees to spend 20 percent of their time at work on projects not related to their job descriptions. Other companies—Facebook, Apple, LinkedIn, 3M, Hewlett-Packard, among others—have similar initiatives. Hmmm...so having essentially one day a week to work on company-related ideas you have almost seems too good to be true. But, more importantly, does it really spark innovation? Well, it can. At Google, it led to the autocomplete system, Google News, Gmail, and Adsense. However, such "company" initiatives do face tremendous obstacles, despite how good they sound on paper. These challenges include:

- Strict employee monitoring in terms of time and resources leading to a reluctance to use this time since most employees have enough to do just keeping up with their regular tasks.

- When bonuses/incentives are based on goals achieved, employees soon figure out what to spend their time on.
- What happens to the ideas that employees do have?
- Unsupportive managers and coworkers who may view this as a "goof-around-for-free-day."
- Obstacles in the corporate bureaucracy.

So, how can companies make it work? Suggestions include: top managers need to support the initiatives/projects and make that support known; managers need to support employees who have that personal passion and drive, that creative spark—clear a path for them to pursue their ideas; perhaps allow employees more of an incentive to innovate (rights to design, etc.); and last, but not least, don't institutionalize it. Creativity and innovation, by their very nature, involve risk and reward. Give creative individuals the space to try and to fail and to try and to fail as needed.

Discussion Questions:

3 What benefits do you see with such mandated experiment time for (a) organizations? (b) individuals?

4 What obstacles do these initiatives face and how can managers overcome those obstacles?

How Can a Manager Foster Innovation?

The systems model (inputs → transformation process → outputs) can help us understand how organizations become more innovative.[42] If an organization wants innovative products and work methods (*outputs*), it has to take its *inputs* and *transform* them into those outputs. Those *inputs* include creative people and groups within the organization. But as we said earlier, having creative people isn't enough. The *transformation process* requires having the right environment to turn those inputs into innovative products or work methods. This "right" environment—that is, an environment that stimulates innovation—includes three variables: the organization's structure, culture, and human resource practices. (See Exhibit 5–5.)

HOW DO STRUCTURAL VARIABLES AFFECT INNOVATION?　Research into the effect of structural variables on innovation shows five things.[43]

1. An organic-type structure positively influences innovation. Because this structure is highly adaptive and flexible, it facilitates the collaboration and sharing of ideas that are critical to innovation. (We'll look in more detail at organic organizations as a form of organizational structure in Chapter 7.)

Exhibit 5–5 Innovation Variables

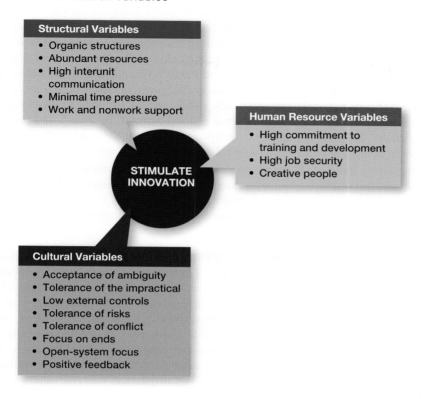

2. The availability of plentiful resources provides a key building block for innovation. With an abundance of resources, managers can afford to purchase innovations, can afford the cost of instituting innovations, and can absorb failures.

3. Frequent communication between organizational units helps break down barriers to innovation.[44] Cross-functional teams, task forces, and other such organizational designs facilitate interaction across departmental lines and are widely used in innovative organizations.

4. Extreme time pressures on creative activities are minimized despite the demands of white-water-rapids-type environments. Although time pressures may spur people to work harder and may make them feel more creative, studies show that it actually causes them to be less creative.[45]

5. When an organization's structure explicitly supports creativity, employees' creative performance can be enhanced. Beneficial kinds of support include encouragement, open communication, readiness to listen, and useful feedback.[46]

HOW DOES AN ORGANIZATION'S CULTURE AFFECT INNOVATION? Innovative organizations tend to have similar cultures.[47] They encourage experimentation; reward both successes and failures; and celebrate mistakes. An innovative organization is likely to have the following characteristics.

• *Accepts ambiguity.* Too much emphasis on objectivity and specificity constrains creativity.

• *Tolerates the impractical.* Individuals who offer impractical, even foolish, answers to what-if questions are not stifled. What at first seems impractical might lead to innovative solutions.

• *Keeps external controls minimal.* Rules, regulations, policies, and similar organizational controls are kept to a minimum.

• *Tolerates risk.* Employees are encouraged to experiment without fear of consequences should they fail. Mistakes are treated as learning opportunities.

• *Tolerates conflict.* Diversity of opinions is encouraged. Harmony and agreement between individuals or units are *not* assumed to be evidence of high performance.

idea champions
Individuals who actively and enthusiastically support new ideas, build support for, overcome resistance to, and ensure that innovations are implemented

- *Focuses on ends rather than means.* Goals are made clear, and individuals are encouraged to consider alternative routes toward meeting the goals. Focusing on ends suggests that there might be several right answers to any given problem.

- *Uses an open-system focus.* Managers closely monitor the environment and respond to changes as they occur. For example, at Starbucks, product development depends on "inspiration field trips to view customers and trends." When Michelle Gass (now Kohl's Corporation's chief merchandise and customer officer) was in charge of Starbucks marketing, she had her team travel to several trendy global cities to visit local Starbucks and other dining establishments to "get a better sense of local cultures, behaviors, and fashions."[48] Her rationale? Seeing and experiencing firsthand different ideas and different ways to think about things can be so much more valuable than reading about them.

- *Provides positive feedback.* Managers provide positive feedback, encouragement, and support so employees feel that their creative ideas receive attention. For instance, Mike Lazaridis, co-founder of BlackBerry maker Research in Motion, said "I think we have a culture of innovation here, and [engineers] have absolute access to me. I live a life that tries to promote innovation."[49]

WHAT HUMAN RESOURCE VARIABLES AFFECT INNOVATION? In this category, we find that innovative organizations (1) actively promote the training and development of their members so their knowledge remains current, (2) offer their employees high job security to reduce the fear of getting fired for making mistakes, and (3) encourage individuals to become **idea champions**, actively and enthusiastically supporting new ideas, building support, overcoming resistance, and ensuring that innovations are implemented. Research finds that idea champions have common personality characteristics: extremely high self-confidence, persistence, energy, and a tendency toward risk taking. They also display characteristics associated with dynamic leadership. They inspire and energize others with their vision of the potential of an innovation and through their strong personal conviction in their mission. They're also good at gaining the commitment of others to support their mission. In addition, idea champions have jobs that provide considerable decision-making discretion. This autonomy helps them introduce and implement innovations in organizations.[50]

How Does Design Thinking Influence Innovation?

We introduced you to the concept of design thinking in a previous chapter. Well, undoubtedly, there's a strong connection between design thinking and innovation. "Design thinking can do for innovation what TQM did for quality."[51] Just as TQM provides a process for improving quality throughout an organization, design thinking can provide a process for coming up with things that don't exist. When a business approaches innovation with a design thinking mentality, the emphasis is on getting a deeper understanding of what customers need and want. It entails knowing customers as real people with real problems—not just as sales targets or demographic statistics. But it also entails being able to convert those customer insights into real and usable products. For instance, at Intuit, the company behind TurboTax software, founder Scott Cook felt the company was "lagging behind in innovation."[52] So he decided to apply design thinking. He called the initiative "Design for Delight," and it involved customer field research to understand their "pain points"—that is, what most frustrated them as they worked in the office and at home. Then, Intuit staffers brainstormed (they nicknamed it "painstorm") a wide array of possible ideas to address customer problems, which they would then try out with customers to find ones that worked best. For example, one pain point uncovered by an Intuit team was how customers could take pictures of

Airbnb co-founders Brian Chesky and Joe Gebbia applied design thinking that focused on travelers' interests, behaviors, needs, and wants in creating an innovative approach to lodging. Their online marketplace connects people wanting to rent their home with people looking for a place to stay. Chesky is shown here visiting the owner of a bed and breakfast in Cape Town, South Africa.

Mike Hutchings/Reuters

tax forms to reduce typing errors. Some younger customers, used to taking photos with their smartphones, were frustrated that they couldn't just complete their taxes on their mobiles. To address this, Intuit developed a mobile app called SnapTax, which was downloaded more than a million times by customers. That's how design thinking works in innovation.

What Is Disruptive Innovation and Why Is Managing It So Important?

5-5 Explain what disruptive innovation is and why managing it is important.

Twenty-five years ago, every Main Street in the United States had a bookstore. Chains like Barnes & Noble and Borders had hundreds of locations. In addition, there were literally thousands of small, family-owned bookstores scattered across America. Then, along came **Amazon.com**. Amazon offered book buyers a million-plus titles at super-low prices, all accessible without leaving the comfort of home. Amazon single-handedly disrupted the brick-and-mortar bookstore. And it continues to disrupt retail, health care, trucking, and even possibly banking.

What Is Disruptive Innovation?

Disruptive innovation describes innovations in products, services, or processes that radically change an industry's rules of the game.[54] Oftentimes, a smaller company with fewer resources successfully challenges established companies.[55] Those smaller companies prove themselves to be disruptive by serving overlooked segments of possible consumers with products or services at relatively low prices. Although the term "disruptive innovation" is relatively new, the concept isn't. For instance, economist Joseph Shumpeter used the term "creative destruction" almost 80 years ago to describe how capitalism builds on processes that destroy old technologies but replaces them with new and better ones.[56] That, in essence is disruptive innovation. In practice, disruptive innovation has been around for centuries. Vanderbilt's railroads disrupted the sailing-ship business. Alexander Bell's telephone rang the death-knell for Western Union's telegraphy. Ford and other automobile builders destroyed horse-drawn buggy manufacturers. As Exhibit 5–6 shows, there is no shortage of businesses that have suffered at the expense of disruptive innovation.

It's helpful to distinguish disruptive innovation from sustaining innovation. When most of us think of innovations, we think of things like the HDTV, backup cameras on cars, fingerprint technology on smartphones, or even Double-Stuf Oreos. These are examples of **sustaining innovation** because they sustain the status quo. These sustaining innovations

---

Making Ethical Decisions in Today's Workplace

The New York Yankees/Boston Red Sox rivalry is a long-standing tradition. And so is the practice of a baseball team spying on another team and trying to steal the signs used by the catcher and pitcher to indicate what type of pitch will come next. Nothing new there … until Boston added a bit of high-tech—an Apple Watch worn by an assistant athletic trainer—to gain an advantage over the Yankees and other teams.[53] When the Yankees general manager filed a detailed complaint with Major League Baseball's (MLB) commissioner, it didn't take long for the commissioner to investigate. The Boston team was fined an undisclosed amount, and all 30 MLB teams were "strongly" reminded that the use of electronic devices to steal signs during games is prohibited. But face it, how long until the next high-tech product is used the same way?

Discussion Questions:

5 Do you think this bit of high-tech spying is unethical? Explain your answer and be prepared to defend it! Does the fact that the individual wearing the "offending" piece of high-tech was an assistant athletic trainer change your opinion? Discuss.

6 What challenges do managers face when monitoring the use of high-tech products in work situations, including products as seemingly harmless as a smart watch or a fitness tracker? In your assigned group, brainstorm possible ethical considerations and how organizations might address the use of these.

Disruptive innovation
Innovations in products, services, or processes that radically change an industry's rules of the game

sustaining innovation
Innovations that represent small and incremental changes in established products rather than dramatic breakthroughs

Exhibit 5–6 Examples of Past Disruptive Innovators

Established Business	Disruptor
Compact disc	Apple iTunes
Carbon paper	Xerox copy machine
Canvas tennis shoes	Nike athletic shoes
Portable radio	Sony Walkman
Sony Walkman	Apple iPod
Typewriters	IBM PC
Weekly news magazines	CNN
TV networks	Cable and Netflix
Local travel agencies	Expedia
Stockbrokers	eTrade
Traveler's checks	ATMs and Visa
Encyclopedias	Wikipedia
Newspaper classified ads	Craig's List
AM/FM radio stations	Sirius XM
Tax preparation services	Intuit's Turbo Tax
Yellow Pages	Google
Paper maps	Garmin's GPS
Paperback books	Kindle
Lawyers	Legal Zoom
Taxis	Uber

Source: Robbins, Stephen P., Coulter, Mary, *Management* (Subscription), 14th Ed., © 2018. Reprinted and electronically reproduced by permission of Pearson Education, Inc., New York, NY.

represent small and incremental changes in established products rather than dramatic break-throughs. Original television sets disrupted the radio industry. HDTV just improved the quality of the TV picture.

Why Is Disruptive Innovation Important?

It's often said that "success breeds success." But success can also breed failure. How? By establishing a power structure within a company that is threatened by disruptive ideas. With entrenched organizational cultures and values that, on one hand, are important to guiding employees, but on the other hand, act as constraints on change. The fact is that disruptive innovations are a threat to many established businesses, and responding with sustaining innovations simply isn't enough. However, we need to recognize that not all "disruptive" innovations succeed. For example, the Segway "personal transporter" was introduced with much hype as a replacement to the automobile for short trips. It didn't happen.

What Are the Implications of Disruptive Innovation?

Disruptive innovation has the potential to upend entrepreneurs, corporate managers, and even your own career plans. Let's take a look at what the future might hold for each.

FOR ENTREPRENEURS. Think opportunity! Entrepreneurs thrive on change and innovation. Major disruptions open the door for new products and services to replace established and mature businesses. If you're looking to create a new business with a large potential, look for established businesses that can be disrupted with a cheaper, simpler, smaller, or more convenient substitute. We'll look more closely at the entrepreneurial process in the next chapter.

FOR CORPORATE MANAGERS. For managers in large, successful businesses, the challenge to disruptive innovation is to create an appropriate response. Contrary to popular belief, managers in these organizations are not powerless. They can become disruptive innovators themselves. But the evidence is overwhelming that their disruptive response must be carried out by a separate group that is physically and structurally disconnected from the business's main operations. How? By either creating a new business from the ground up or by acquiring a small company and keeping it separate from the corporate constraints.

> **skunk works**
> A small group within a large organization, given a high degree of autonomy and unhampered by corporate bureaucracy, whose mission is to develop a project primarily for the purpose of radical innovation

---

47 percent of business leaders say that finding and keeping employees to **counteract disruptive change** is a significant obstacle.[57]

These separate groups are sometimes referred to as **skunk works**—defined as a small group within a large organization, given a high degree of autonomy and unhampered by corporate bureaucracy, whose mission is to develop a project primarily for the purpose of radical innovation. These skunk works, in effect, are entrepreneurial operations running inside a large company. Their small size allows employees to be enthusiastic about their mission and to see the impact of their efforts. To be successful, though, they can't be hampered by the cultural values or cost structure of the parent organization. They need enough autonomy so that they don't have to compete for resources with projects in the primary organization.

FOR PERSONAL CAREER PLANNING. What career advice can we offer you in a disruptive world? Here are some suggestions:

- *Never get comfortable with a single employer.* You can't build your hopes on working in one organization for your entire career. Your first loyalty should be to yourself and making (and keeping) yourself marketable.

- *Keep your skills current.* Disruptive technologies will continue to make established jobs and professions obsolete. Learning no longer ends when you finish school. You need to make a continual commitment to learning new things.

- *Remember that YOU are responsible for your future.* Don't assume your employer is going to be looking out for your long-term interests. Your personal skill development (*Hint:* All those employability skills we're having you work on throughout this book), career progression, and retirement plans (yup ... not too early to start thinking about that, too) are all decisions that you need to make. Don't delegate your future to someone else. You need to actively manage your career.

- *Finally, take risks while you're young.* Few people have achieved great results without taking a risk. They quit a secure job, or went back to school, or moved to a new city, or started a new business. While risks don't always pay off, setbacks or failures are much easier when you're 25 than when you are 55.

CHAPTER SUMMARY BY LEARNING OUTCOME

5-1 Define *organizational change* and compare and contrast views on the change process.

Organizational change is any alteration of an organization's people, structure, or technology. The "calm waters" metaphor of change suggests that change is an occasional disruption in the normal flow of events and can be planned and managed as it happens, using Lewin's three-step change process (unfreezing, changing, and freezing). The "white-water rapids" view of change suggests that change is ongoing, and managing it is a continual process.

5-2 Explain how to manage resistance to change.

People resist change because of uncertainty, habit, concern about personal loss, and the belief that a change is not in the organization's best interests. Techniques for managing resistance to change include education and communication (educating employees about and communicating to them the need for the change), participation (allowing employees to participate in the change process), facilitation and support (giving employees the support they need to implement the change), negotiation (exchanging something of value to reduce resistance), manipulation and co-optation (using negative actions to influence), selecting people who are open to and accept change, and coercion (using direct threats or force).

5-3 Describe what managers need to know about employee stress.

Stress is the adverse reaction people have to excessive pressure placed on them from extraordinary demands, constraints, or opportunities. The symptoms of stress can be physical, psychological, or behavioral. Stress can be caused by personal factors and by job-related factors. To help employees deal with stress, managers can address job-related factors by making sure an employee's abilities match the job requirements, improving organizational communications, using a performance planning program, or redesigning jobs. Addressing personal stress factors is trickier, but managers could offer employee counseling, time management programs, and wellness programs.

5-4 Discuss techniques for stimulating innovation.

Creativity is the ability to combine ideas in a unique way or to make unusual associations between ideas. Innovation is turning the outcomes of the creative process into useful products or work methods. An innovative environment encompasses structural, cultural, and human resource variables.

Important structural variables include an organic-type structure, abundant resources, frequent communication between organizational units, minimal time pressure, and support. Important cultural variables include accepting ambiguity, tolerating the impractical, keeping external controls minimal, tolerating risk, tolerating conflict, focusing on ends not means, using an open-system focus, and providing positive feedback. Important human resource variables include high commitment to training and development, high job security, and encouraging individuals to be idea champions.

Design thinking can also play a role in innovation. It provides a process for coming up with products that don't exist.

5-5 Explain what disruptive innovation is and why managing it is important.

Disruptive innovation describes innovations in products, services, or processes that radically change an industry's rules of the game. It's important because it can catch established organizations by surprise if they're not aware of the drawbacks of entrenched organizational cultures and values and their potential to act as constraints on change. Disruptive innovation has the potential to surprise and upend entrepreneurs, corporate managers, and personal career plans.

DISCUSSION QUESTIONS

5-1 Why is managing change an integral part of every manager's job?

5-2 Contrast the calm waters and white-water rapids metaphors of change. Which of these would you use to describe your current life? Why is that one your choice?

5-3 Describe Lewin's three-step change process. How is it different from the change process needed in the white-water rapids metaphor of change?

5-4 How are opportunities, constraints, and demands related to stress? Give an example of each.

5-5 Organizations typically have limits to how much change they can absorb. As a manager, what signs would you look for that might suggest your organization has exceeded its capacity to change?

5-6 Every manager deals with change. Provide an example to illustrate this point. In this context, how do middle managers plan organizational development?

5-7 What can influence innovation in organizations?

5-8 Research information on how to be a more creative person. Write down suggestions in a bulleted list format and be prepared to present your information in class.

5-9 How does an innovative culture make an organization more effective? Could an innovative culture ever make an organization less effective? Why or why not?

5-10 How can organizations and individuals benefit from disruptive innovation? How can they not become victims of disruptive innovation?

Applying: Getting Ready for the Workplace

Management Skill Builder | STRESS MANAGEMENT

It's no secret that employees, in general, are more stressed out today than previous generations. Heavier workloads, longer hours, continual reorganizations, technology that breaks down traditional barriers between work and personal life, and reduced job security are among factors that have increased employee stress. This stress can lead to lower productivity, increased absenteeism, reduced job satisfaction, and higher quit rates. When stress is excessive, managers need to know how to reduce it.

MyLab Management
PERSONAL INVENTORY ASSESSMENT

 PERSONAL INVENTORY ASSESSMENT

Go to **www.pearson.com/mylab/management** to complete the Personal Inventory Assessment related to this chapter.

Controlling Workplace Stress

As our debunked Management Myth pointed out, workplace stress is a reality *and* managers can do something about it. In this PIA, you'll assess how you control workplace stress.

Skill Basics

Eliminating all stress at work isn't going to happen and it shouldn't. Stress is an unavoidable consequence of life. It also has a positive side—when it focuses concentration and creativity. But when it brings about anger, frustration, fear, sleeplessness, and the like, it needs to be addressed.

Many organizations have introduced stress-reduction interventions for employees. These include improved employee selection and placement, helping employees set realistic goals, training in time management, redesign of jobs, increased involvement of employees in decisions that affect them, expanded social support networks, improved organizational communications, and organizationally supported wellness programs. But what can *you* do, on your own, to reduce stress if your employer doesn't provide such programs or if you need to take additional action? The following individual interventions have been suggested:

• *Implement time-management techniques.* Every person can improve his or her use of time. Time is a unique resource in that, if it's wasted, it can *never* be replaced. While people talk about *saving time*, it can never actually be saved. And if it's lost, it can't be retrieved. The good news is that it's a resource we all have in equal amounts. Everyone gets the same 24 hours a day, 7 days a week to use. When tasks seem to exceed the hours you have available, stress often results. But effective management of time can reduce stress. Time-management training can, for example, teach you how to prioritize tasks by importance and urgency, schedule activities according to those priorities, avoid confusing actions with accomplishments, and understand your productivity cycle so you can handle the most demanding tasks during the high part of your cycle when you are most alert and productive.

- *Create personal goals.* Goal setting is designed to help you better prioritize your activities and better manage how you direct your efforts. Goals become, in effect, a personal planning tool. For instance, setting long-term goals provides general direction; while short-term goals—such as weekly or daily "to do" lists—reduce the likelihood that important activities will be overlooked and help you to maximize the use of your time.

- *Use physical exercise.* A large body of evidence indicates that noncompetitive physical exercise can help you to release tension that builds up in stressful situations. These activities include aerobics, walking, jogging, swimming, and riding a bicycle. Physical exercise increases heart capacity, lowers the at-rest heart rate, provides a mental diversion from work pressures, and offers a means to "let off steam."

- *Practice relaxation training.* You can teach yourself to reduce tension through meditation, deep-breathing exercises, and guided imaging. They work by taking your mind off the sources of stress, achieving a state of deep relaxation, and releasing body tension.

- *Expand your social support network.* Having friends, family, or work colleagues to talk to provides an outlet when stress levels become excessive. Expanding your social support network, therefore, can be a means for tension reduction. It provides you with someone to hear your

problems and to offer a more objective perspective on the situation.[58]

Practicing the Skill

Read through this scenario and follow the directions at the end of it:

Dana had become frustrated in her job at Taylor Books—a chain of 22 bookstores in Georgia and Florida. After nearly 13 years as director of marketing, she felt she needed new challenges. When she was offered the job as senior account supervisor for Dancer Advertising in Tampa, she jumped at the opportunity. Now, after four months on the job, she's not so certain she made the right move.

At Taylor, she worked a basic 8-to-5 day. She was easily able to balance her work responsibilities with her personal responsibilities as a wife and mother of two children—ages 4 and 7. But her new job is very different. Clients call any time— day, night, and weekends—with demands. People in Dancer's creative department are constantly asking for her input on projects. And Dana's boss expects her not only to keep her current clients happy, but also to help secure new clients by preparing and participating in presentations and working up budgets. Last month alone, Dana calculated that she spent 67 hours in the office plus another 12 at home working on Dancer projects. Short on sleep, frazzled by the hectic pace, having no time for her family or chores, she's lost five pounds and broken out in hives. Her doctor told her the hives were stress-induced and she needed to sort out her life.

Dana really likes her job as an account executive but feels the demands and pulls of the job are overwhelming. Yesterday she called her old boss at Taylor Books and inquired about coming back. His reply, "Dana, we'd love to have you back here but we filled your slot. We could find something for you in marketing but you wouldn't be director and the pay would be at least a third less."

If you were Dana, what would you do? Be specific.

Experiential Exercise

Creativity is highly prized in Western society cultures and in most organizational settings. However, most people don't consider themselves to be creative. What about you? Would you describe yourself as creative? Like intelligence, it's a trait that everyone possesses in some capacity. In this Experiential Exercise, you're going to "exercise" your creativity. But we won't force you to work on your own! You'll be working with your assigned group. Here's your assignment:

- Choose one of the two familiar consumer products shown here.
- Identify at least five different uses for these products other than the original use and write them down. Be as descriptive as you can.
- Choose your Top 3 uses and be prepared to share with your class.
- BE CREATIVE! (That should go without saying!) So, how about having fun with this!
- Write a paragraph describing your experience with your group doing this. Was it a struggle or fairly easy? How did you feel . . . stressed or comfortable? What did you learn about your comfort with being creative? What might you do to change your approach to being creative?

world of vector/Shutterstock

EAR BUD CORDS   MASON JAR LIDS

CASE APPLICATION #1

Defeating the System
Topic: Changing culture

In one of the worst business ethics scandals in history, the world learned in 2015 that Volkswagen (VW) intentionally circumvented government exhaust emission tests for years by installing so-called defeat devices on its clean diesel vehicles.[59] This revelation was a shock to many given the company's long-standing success in the auto industry. Volkswagen, one of the world's most recognized brands, was founded in 1937. The company, headquartered in Germany, employs more than half a million people around the world. Worldwide, the Volkswagen Group has a long history of dramatic innovations. At its Electronics Research Laboratory based in Silicon Valley, the company blends German engineering with American ingenuity.[60]

Researchers at West Virginia University (WVU) first discovered the violation when they started studying clean diesel engines. When they tested the performance of Volkswagen vehicles, they were surprised to find that on-the-road emissions exceeded government allowances by almost 40 times. Further investigation by the U.S. Environmental Protection Agency (EPA) found that the vehicles were actually equipped with software that could essentially "trick" emission testing systems. The diesel engines would detect when they were being tested for emissions and change the vehicle's performance to improve testing results. Once on the road, the vehicle would switch out of the test mode, emitting excessive nitrogen oxide pollutants, as the WVU researchers discovered.

The EPA's finding covered about 500,000 cars sold in the United States only. But Volkswagen later admitted that about 11 million cars worldwide were fitted with this software. It will be a long time before Volkswagen realizes all the damage from this ethical blunder.

How could such a blatant ethical violation occur? It may take years to sort out who is to blame. CEO Martin Winterkorn, who resigned in response to the scandal, initially claimed not to know about the devices. While many high-ranking executives were suspended, no one is sure who knew about or authorized the software. In fact, some believe that the driven, performance-based culture may be more to blame than any individual.

Winterkorn, who reinforced the unique culture, was described as a hard-charging perfectionist who was committed to secure the top spot among global car manufacturers. He was known to criticize employees publicly, and this generated both fear among employees and the commitment to do whatever necessary to ensure the company's success. The company's culture has been described as "confident, cutthroat, and insular."[61] It is possible that arrogance led VW managers to assume that U.S. government or other officials wouldn't discover the misleading emissions tests.

What's more unsettling was VW's response to the scandal. At first, the company suggested a technical problem with the cars, but it finally admitted the software devices were designed to cheat the system. And initially, the company reported that only a limited number of cars were affected; however, as more details were uncovered, the company admitted that more cars were outfitted with the device and that these actions occurred over a longer period of time than originally reported.

Current CEO Matthias Müller says he is trying to accelerate change at the automaker. He's urging employees to prepare for rapid shifts in the auto industry, including, for example, autonomous driving, electric vehicles, "smart" engines, and picture navigation. Considering the fact that since 2015, when he was named CEO, he has spent as much time managing this ethics crisis as managing the business, change **is** what is needed.[62] And not only leading change into the world of modern automotive technologies, but changing the culture of a company. With a clear vision for the future direction that VW must go, Müller is making necessary, but difficult, decisions that are meeting resistance from managers and employees. However, that has not deterred him from doing what he believes is best to make VW a winner again.[63]

Note: In March 2017, VW pleaded guilty as a corporation to criminal charges stemming from the deception and a top Volkswagen official in the United States was handed a seven-year prison sentence. To this point, the scandal has cost the carmaker more than $20 billion in fines and settlements and tarnished its reputation.[64] In addition, Chief Executive Matthias Müller has been replaced by Herbert Diess, a former BMW executive who runs the VW brand.[65] Diess says he is committed to 'evolution' but at a faster pace.[66]

> ## Unethical practices **force change.**

Discussion Questions

5-11 What external or internal forces—or both—for change do you see described in this case? Would you describe VW's environment as more calm waters or white-water rapids? Explain.

5-12 Change needs to happen at VW. In the chapter, we defined change as any alteration of an organization's people, structure, or technology. Which of these needs changing at Volkswagen? Discuss.

5-13 What organizational development (OD) efforts might work at VW? Explain your choice(s). What challenges will managers face in making these changes?

5-14 Look at the reasons people resist change. Which do you think are happening at VW? What approach(es) would you

recommend for overcoming this resistance to change? Give your rationale for each approach you choose.

5-15 Is an innovative culture always going to be at odds with an ethical culture? Or is an innovative *and* ethical culture possible? Gather your thoughts on this and then in your assigned group, come up with an answer. Support your conclusions.

CASE APPLICATION #2

The Next Big Thing
Topic: Organizational change, innovative culture

It all started with a simple plan to make a superior T-shirt. As special teams captain during the mid-1990s for the University of Maryland football team, Kevin Plank hated having to repeatedly change the cotton T-shirt he wore under his jersey as it became wet and heavy during the course of a game.[67] He knew there had to be a better alternative and set out to make it. After a year of fabric and product testing, Plank introduced the first Under Armour compression product—a synthetic shirt worn like a second skin under a uniform or jersey. And it was an immediate hit! The silky fabric was light and made athletes feel faster and fresher, giving them, according to Plank, an important psychological edge. Today, Under Armour continues to passionately strive to make all athletes better by relentlessly pursuing innovation and design. A telling sign of the company's philosophy is found over the door of its product design studios: "We have not yet built our defining product."

Today, Baltimore-based Under Armour (UA) is a $5 billion company. In 22 years, it has grown from a college startup to a "formidable competitor of the Beaverton, Oregon, behemoth" (better known as Nike, a $34.4 billion company). In the fragmented U.S. sports apparel market, UA sells products from shirts, shorts, and footwear to underwear, wearable fitness technology, and hats. In addition, more than 100 universities wear UA uniforms. The company's logo—an interlocking U and A—is becoming almost as recognizable as the Nike swoosh.

Starting out, Plank sold his shirts using the only advantage he had—his athletic connections. Drawing on his own personal team experiences, "he knew at least 40 NFL players well enough to call and offer them the shirt." He was soon joined by another Maryland player, Kip Fulks, who played lacrosse. Fulks used the same

Protecting Our House
THROUGH INNOVATION

relationship-based "six-degrees strategy" in the lacrosse world. Believe it or not, the strategy worked. UA sales quickly gained momentum. However, selling products to teams and schools would take a business only so far. That's when Plank began to look at the mass market. In 2000, he made his first deal with a big-box store, Galyan's (which was eventually bought by Dick's Sporting Goods). Today, more than 66 percent of UA's sales come from wholesaling to retailers such as Dick's. But UA hasn't forgotten where it started, either. The company has all-school deals with a number of Division 1 schools. Although that doesn't seem like a lot of revenue, such deals do give the company brand identity.

Despite its marketing successes, innovation continues to be the name of the game at UA. How important is innovation to the company's heart and soul? Consider what you have to do to enter its new products lab. "Place your hands inside a state-of-the-art scanner that reads—and calculates—the exact pattern of the veins on the back. If it recognizes the pattern—which it does for only 20 employees—you're in. If it doesn't, the vault-like door won't budge." In the unmarked lab at the company's headquarters campus in Baltimore, products being developed include a shirt that can monitor an athlete's heart rate, a running shoe designed like your spine, and a sweatshirt that repels water almost as well as a duck. There's also work being done on a shirt that may help air condition your body by reading your vital signs.

Despite its innovation push, Under Armour has suffered recent revenue declines. The year 2017 was a rough one for the company. CEO Kevin Plank said that the company would step up restructuring efforts. Three top executives were let go as was roughly 2 percent of its workforce.[68] Also, the company was looking at ways to connect better with its female customers.[69]

Finally, the company admitted that it had suffered "operational challenges" when trying to implement an ERP (enterprise resource planning) system. The implementation problems were so severe that the company's financial outlook was affected.[70]

So what's next for Under Armour? With a motto that refers to protecting this house, innovation will continue to be important. Building a business beyond what it's known for—that is, what athletes wear next to their skin—is going to be challenging. However, Plank is completely devoted to Under Armour's focus on finding ways to use technology in all the company's products to make athletes better. He says, "There's not a product we can't build."

Discussion Questions

5-16 What do you think of UA's approach to innovation? Would you expect to see this type of innovation in an athletic wear company? Explain.

5-17 What do you think UA's culture might be like in regards to innovation? (*Hint:* Refer to the list on pp. 171–172).

5-18 How might design thinking help UA improve its innovation efforts?

5-19 What's your interpretation of the company's philosophy posted prominently over the door of its design studio? What does it say about innovation? Make a list of lessons that managers could learn from UA's innovation approach that you could share with real managers.

CASE APPLICATION #3

Time to Change?
High-Tech and High-Touch Hospitality?

It was Swiss hotelier César Ritz, founder of the Parisian Hôtel Ritz back in 1898, who coined the familiar phrase "the customer is always right." For the modern hospitality manager who must constantly deal with online guest reviews, the statement holds as true today as it did 120 years ago.

A frustrated attempt to plan a family vacation led Stephen Kaufer to co-found TripAdvisor in 2000 and help people make better travel decisions. In the hospitality industry, platforms like TripAdvisor have strengthened the bargaining power of customers. Now more than ever, hospitality managers are continuously challenged to offer memorable experiences for good reviews and more bookings. Some have invested in new technology; others have hired designated teams to respond to online reviews with personalized messages, for the human touch remains a competitive advantage in the hospitality industry, even in a high-tech world.[72]

On the supply side, digital tech has led to fiercer competition. Back in 2007, when they could not afford the rent of their apartment in San-Francisco, Brian Chesky and Joe Gebbia put an air mattress in their living room and turned it into a bed and breakfast. Then, with Nathan Blecharczyk, they created Airbedandbreakfast.com, a website offering short-term living accommodations. In 2009, the name was shortened to Airbnb.com, and the offer was extended to a variety of properties, including castles, boats, tipis, igloos, and even private islands. Together, the world's largest hotel companies add up to more than 3.8 million rooms nowadays, according to *STR*. Yet this is less than what Airbnb offers—more than 4 million listings worldwide, bookable in one click.

Hotel and restaurant guidebooks, local travel agencies, vacation rentals, and hotels were established businesses once, but sites like Airbnb and TripAdvisor have turned that on its head. Today, the latter has become an online travel agency like its former parent company Expedia and has acquired a number of vacation rental portals like HouseTrip.

TripAdvisor might be Airbnb biggest competitor, but hotels' next competitors may be something altogether different. Arnaud Bertrand, co-founder of *HouseTrip*,[73] thinks the next big threat is self-driving cars, for people may be freed from driving to spend that traveling time working, sleeping, and entertaining themselves—all things we normally do in a hotel room!

Discussion Questions

5-20 What forces are driving disruptive innovations in the hospitality industry?

5-21 Which innovations are disruptive ones, and which are sustaining ones? Which of them are product, service, process, organizational, or marketing innovations? Discuss.

5-22 What role have entrepreneurs like Airbnb and TripAdvisor's founders played in terms of disruptive innovations?

5-23 In your assigned group, suppose you have been asked to write a report on the implications of disruptive innovations in the hospitality industry for corporate managers of established hotel and restaurant businesses. Come up with recommendations to help these managers transform disruptive innovations into business opportunities.

Endnotes

1. L. Du and Y. Takeo, "Automation's Bleeding Edge," *Bloomberg Businessweek,* March 12, 2018, pp. 3–33.

2. B. Mullin, "L.A. Times Chief Plots Change," *Wall Street Journal,* October 25, 2017, p. B5.

3. R. Winslow, "Mayo's Tricky Task: Revamp What Works," *Wall Street Journal,* June 3–4, 2017, pp. A1+.

4. S. Carey, "Southwest Pushes System Upgrade," *Wall Street Journal,* May 10, 2017, p. B3; and N. Ungerleider, "Southwest Airlines' Digital Transformation Takes Off," *Fast Company Online,* March 27, 2017.

5. K. Grzbowska, "The Social Aspect of Introducing Changes into the Organization," *International Journals of Human Resources Development and Management,* February 2, 2007, p. 67; and I. M. Jawahar and G. L. McLaughlin, "Toward a Descriptive Stakeholder Theory: An Organizational Life Cycle Approach," *Academy of Management Review,* July 2001, pp. 397–415.

6. E. Shannon, "Agent of Change," *Time,* March 4, 2002, p. 17; B. Kenney, "SLA Head Shaffer Resigns Abruptly: Did 'Change Agent' Move Too Fast in Aggressive Restructuring?" *Library Journal,* March 15, 2002, pp. 17–19; and T. Mudd, "Rescue Mission," *Industry Week,* May 1, 2000, pp. 30–37.

7. The idea for these metaphors came from P. Vaill, *Managing as a Performing Art: New Ideas for a World of Chaotic Change* (San Francisco: Jossey Bass, 1989).

8. K. Lewin, *Field Theory in Social Science* (New York: Harper & Row, 1951).

9. R. E. Levasseur, "People Skills: Change Management Tools—Lewin's Change Model," *Interfaces,* August 2001, pp. 71–74.

10. L. S. Lüscher and M. W. Lewis, "Organizational Change and Managerial Sensemaking: Working through Paradox," *Academy of Management Journal,* April 2008, pp. 221–40; F. Buckley and K. Monks, "Responding to Managers' Learning Needs in an Edge-of-Chaos Environment: Insights from Ireland," *Journal of Management,* April 2008, pp. 146–63; and G. Hamel, "Take It Higher," *Fortune,* February 5, 2001, pp. 169–70.

11. D. Lieberman, "Nielsen Media Has Cool Head at the Top," *USA Today,* March 27, 2006, p. 3B.

12. Classic Concepts in Today's Workplace box based on D. A. Wren and A. G. Bedeian, *The Evolution of Management Thought,* 6th ed. (Hoboken, NJ: John Wiley & Sons, 2009); "Biography and Quotes of Kurt Lewin," *About.com, psychology.about.com* (July 15, 2009); and K. T. Lewin, "The Dynamics of Group Action," *Educational Leadership,* January 1944, pp. 195–200.

13. L. Freifeld, "Paddle to Collaborate," *Training,* November–December 2010, p. 6.

14. S. Hicks, "What Is Organization Development?" *Training and Development,* August 2000, p. 65; and H. Hornstein, "Organizational Development and Change Management: Don't Throw the Baby Out with the Bath Water," *Journal of Applied Behavioral Science,* June 2001, pp. 223–27.

15. J. Wolfram and S. Minahan, "A New Metaphor for Organization Development," *Journal of Applied Behavioral Science,* June 2006, pp. 227–43.

16. See, for instance, H. B. Jones, "Magic, Meaning, and Leadership: Weber's Model and the Empirical Literature," *Human Relations,* June 2001, p. 753.

17. G. Akin and I. Palmer, "Putting Metaphors to Work for a Change in Organizations," *Organizational Dynamics,* Winter 2000, 67–79.

18. J. Grieves, "Skills, Values or Impression Management: Organizational Change and the Social Processes of Leadership, Change Agent Practice, and Process Consultation," *Journal of Management Development,* May 2000, p. 407.

19. M. McMaster, "Team Building Tips," *Sales & Marketing Management,* January 2002, 140; and "How To: Executive Team Building," *Training and Development,* January 2002, p. 16.

20. S. Shinn, "Stairway to Reinvention," *BizEd,* January–February 2010, p. 6; M. Scott, "A Stairway to Marketing Heaven," *BusinessWeek,* November 2, 2009, p. 17; and The Fun Theory, http://thefuntheory.com, November 10, 2009.

21. See, for example, J. Robison and D. Jones, "Overcoming the Fear of Change," *Gallup Management Journal Online,* January 7, 2011; J. D. Ford, L. W. Ford, and A. D'Amelio, "Resistance to Change: The Rest of the Story," *Academy of Management Review,* April 2008, pp. 362–77; A. Deutschman, "Making Change: Why Is It So Hard to Change Our Ways?" *Fast Company,* May 2005, pp. 52–62; S. B. Silverman, C. E. Pogson, and A. B. Cober, "When Employees at Work Don't Get It: A Model for Enhancing Individual Employee Change in Response to Performance Feedback," *Academy of Management Executive,* May 2005, pp. 135–47; C. E. Cunningham, C.

A. Woodward, H. S. Shannon, J. MacIntosh, B. Lendrum, D. Rosenbloom, and J. Brown, "Readiness for Organizational Change: A Longitudinal Study of Workplace, Psychological and Behavioral Correlates," *Journal of Occupational and Organizational Psychology,* December 2002, pp. 377–92; M. A. Korsgaard, H. J. Sapienza, and D. M. Schweiger, "Beaten before Begun: The Role of Procedural Justice in Planning Change," *Journal of Management* 28, no. 4 (2002), pp. 497–516; R. Kegan and L. L. Lahey, "The Real Reason People Won't Change," *Harvard Business Review,* November 2001, pp. 85–92; S. K. Piderit, "Rethinking Resistance and Recognizing Ambivalence: A Multidimensional View of Attitudes Toward an Organizational Change," *Academy of Management Review,* October 2000, pp. 783–94; C. R. Wanberg and J. T. Banas, "Predictors and Outcomes of Openness to Changes in a Reorganizing Workplace," *Journal of Applied Psychology,* February 2000, pp. 132–42; A. A. Armenakis and A. G. Bedeian, "Organizational Change: A Review of Theory and Research in the 1990s," *Journal of Management* 25, no. 3 (1999), pp. 293–315; and B. M. Staw, "Counterforces to Change," in P.S. Goodman and Associates (eds.), *Change in Organizations* (San Francisco: Jossey-Bass, 1982), pp. 87–121.

22. A. Reichers, J. P. Wanous, and J. T. Austin, "Understanding and Managing Cynicism about Organizational Change," *Academy of Management Executive,* February 1997, pp. 48–57; P. Strebel, "Why Do Employees Resist Change?" *Harvard Business Review,* May–June 1996, pp. 86–92; and J. P. Kotter and L. A. Schlesinger, "Choosing Strategies for Change," *Harvard Business Review,* March–April 1979, pp. 107–09.

23. D. Heath and C. Heath, "Passion Provokes Action," *Fast Company,* February 2011, pp. 28–30.

24. S. D'Mello, "Stress: The Global Economic Downturn Has Taken Its Toll on Employees. What's the Impact for Organizations?" A 2011/2012 Kenexa® High Performance Institute Worktrends™ Report, http://khpi.com/documents/KHPI-WorkTrends-Report-Stress, 2011/2012; and "Stress: By the Numbers," *AARP The Magazine,* September/October 2011, p. 30.

25. Adapted from the UK National Work-Stress Network, www.workstress.net.

26. R. S. Schuler, "Definition and Conceptualization of Stress in Organizations," *Organizational Behavior and Human Performance,* April 1980, p. 191.

27. G. Nishiyama and J. Fujikawa, "Japan, Home of Overwork, Wants Employees to Stop," *Wall Street Journal,* November 3, 2017, pp. A1+.

28. C. Coppel, "Learning, for When the Stress Ball Fails," *TD,* September 2017, p. 18.

29. See, for example, "Stressed Out: Extreme Job Stress: Survivors' Tales," *Wall Street Journal,* January 17, 2001, p. B1.

30. See, for instance, S. Bates, "Expert: Don't Overlook Employee Burnout," *HR Magazine,* August 2003, p. 14.

31. H. Benson, "Are You Working Too Hard?" *Harvard Business Review,* November 2005, pp. 53–58; B. Cryer, R. McCraty, and D. Childre, "Pull the Plug on Stress," *Harvard Business Review,* July 2003, pp. 102–07; C. Daniels, "The Last Taboo"; C. L. Cooper and S. Cartwright, "Healthy Mind, Healthy Organization—A Proactive Approach to Occupational Stress," *Human Relations,* April 1994, pp. 455–71; C. A. Heaney et al., "Industrial Relations, Worksite Stress Reduction and Employee Well-Being: A Participatory Action Research Investigation," *Journal of Organizational Behavior,* September 1993, pp. 495–510; C. D. Fisher, "Boredom at Work: A Neglected Concept," *Human Relations,* March 1993, pp. 395–417; and S. E. Jackson, "Participation in Decision Making as a Strategy for Reducing Job-Related Strain," *Journal of Applied Psychology,* February 1983, pp. 3–19. *Fortune,* October 28, 2002, pp. 137–144.

32. T. Barton, "Brave Face," *Employee Benefits,* January 2011, p. 41; and "Employee Assistance Programs," *HR Magazine,* May 2003, p. 143.

33. S. Barrett, "Employee Assistance Programs," *Employee Benefits,* January 2011, pp. 49–52; "EAPs with the Most," *Managing Benefits Plans,* March 2003, p. 8; and K. Tyler, "Helping Employees Cope with Grief," *HR Magazine,* September 2003, pp. 55–58.

34. N. Faba, "The EAP Problem," *Benefits Canada,* March 2011, p. 7; D. A. Masi, "Redefining the EAP Field," *Journal of Workplace Behavioral Health,* January–March 2011, pp. 1–9; R. M. Weiss, "Brinksmanship Redux: Employee Assistance Programs' Precursors and Prospects," *Employee Responsibilities & Rights Journal,* December 2010, pp. 325–43;

and F. Hansen, "Employee Assistance Programs (EAPs) Grow and Expand Their Reach," *Compensation and Benefits Review*, March–April 2000, p. 13.

35. A. Saha-Bubna and M. Jarzemsky, "MasterCard President Is Named CEO," *Wall Street Journal*, April 13, 2010, p. C3; and S. Vandebook, "Quotable," *IndustryWeek*, April 2010, p. 18.

36. R. M. Kanter, "Think Outside the Building," *Harvard Business Review*, March 2010, p. 34; T. Brown, "Change By Design," *BusinessWeek*, October 5, 2009, pp. 54–56; J. E. Perry-Smith and C. E. Shalley, "The Social Side of Creativity: A Static and Dynamic Social Network Perspective," *Academy of Management Review*, January 2003, pp. 89–106; and P. K. Jagersma, "Innovate or Die: It's Not Easy, but It Is Possible to Enhance Your Organization's Ability to Innovate," *Journal of Business Strategy*, January–February 2003, pp. 25–28.

37. "The World's 50 Most Innovative Companies, 2018," *Fast Company*, March/April 2018, pp. 20+.

38. These definitions are based on T. M. Amabile, *Creativity in Context* (Boulder, CO: Westview Press, 1996).

39. C. Salter, "Mattel Learns to 'Throw the Bunny,'" *Fast Company*, November 2002, p. 22; and L. Bannon, "Think Tank in Toyland," *Wall Street Journal*, June 6, 2002, pp. B1, B3.

40. C. Vogel and J. Cagan, *Creating Breakthrough Products: Innovation from Product Planning to Program Approval* (Upper Saddle River, NJ: Prentice Hall, 2002).

41. R. Tate, "Google Couldn't Kill 20 Percent Time Even If It Wanted To," wired.com, August 21, 2013; C. Mims, "Google Engineers Insist 20% Time Is Not Dead—It's Just Turned into 120% Time," qz.com, August 16, 2013; R. Neimi, "Inside the Moonshot Factory," *Bloomberg Businessweek*, May 22, 2013, 5 pp. 6–61; and A. Foege, "The Trouble with Tinkering Time," *Wall Street Journal*, January 19/20, 2013, p. C3.

42. R. W. Woodman, J. E. Sawyer, and R. W. Griffin, "Toward a Theory of Organizational Creativity," *Academy of Management Review*, April 1993, pp. 293–321.

43. T. M. Egan, "Factors Influencing Individual Creativity in the Workplace: An Examination of Quantitative Empirical Research," *Advances in Developing Human Resources*, May 2005, pp. 160–81; N. Madjar, G. R. Oldham, and M. G. Pratt, "There's No Place Like Home? The Contributions of Work and Nonwork Creativity Support to Employees' Creative Performance," *Academy of Management Journal*, August 2002, pp. 757–67; T. M. Amabile, C. N. Hadley, and S. J. Kramer, "Creativity Under the Gun," *Harvard Business Review*, August 2002, pp. 52–61; J. B.

Sorensen and T. E. Stuart, "Aging, Obsolescence, and Organizational Innovation," *Administrative Science Quarterly*, March 2000, pp. 81–112; G. R. Oldham and A. Cummings, "Employee Creativity: Personal and Contextual Factors at Work," *Academy of Management Journal*, June 1996, pp. 607–34; and F. Damanpour, "Organizational Innovation: A Meta-Analysis of Effects of Determinants and Moderators," *Academy of Management Journal*, September 1991, pp. 555–90.

44. P. R. Monge, M. D. Cozzens, and N. S. Contractor, "Communication and Motivational Predictors of the Dynamics of Organizational Innovations," *Organization Science*, May 1992, pp. 250–74.

45. Amabile, Hadley, and Kramer, "Creativity Under the Gun."

46. Madjar, Oldham, and Pratt, "There's No Place Like Home? The Contributions of Work and Nonwork Creativity Support to Employees' Creative Performance."

47. See, for instance, J. E. Perry-Smith, "Social Yet Creative: The Role of Social Relationships in Facilitating Individual Creativity," *Academy of Management Journal*, February 2006, pp. 85–101; C. E. Shalley, J. Zhou, and G. R. Oldham, "The Effects of Personal and Contextual Characteristics on Creativity: Where Should We Go from Here?" *Journal of Management* 30, no. 6 (2004), pp. 933–58; Perry-Smith and Shalley, "The Social Side of Creativity: A Static and Dynamic Social Network Perspective"; J. M. George and J. Zhou, "When Openness to Experience and Conscientiousness Are Related to Creative Behavior: An Interactional Approach," *Journal of Applied Psychology*, June 2001, pp. 513–24; J. Zhou, "Feedback Valence, Feedback Style, Task Autonomy, and Achievement Orientation: Interactive Effects on Creative Behavior," *Journal of Applied Psychology* 83 (1998), pp. 261–76; T. M. Amabile, R. Conti, H. Coon, J. Lazenby, and M. Herron, "Assessing the Work Environment for Creativity," *Academy of Management Journal*, October 1996, pp. 1154–84; S. G. Scott and R. A. Bruce, "Determinants of Innovative People: A Path Model of Individual Innovation in the Workplace," *Academy of Management Journal*, June 1994, pp. 580–607; R. Moss Kanter, "When a Thousand Flowers Bloom: Structural, Collective, and Social Conditions for Innovation in Organization," in B. M. Staw and L. L. Cummings (eds.), *Research in Organizational Behavior*, vol. 10 (Greenwich, CT: JAI Press, 1988), pp. 169–211; and Amabile, *Creativity in Context*.

48. J. McGregor, "The World's Most Innovative Companies," *BusinessWeek*, April 24, 2006, p. 70.

49. Ibid.

50. J. Ramos, "Producing Change That Lasts," *Across the Board*, March 1994, pp. 29–33; T. Stjernberg and A. Philips, "Organizational Innovations in a Long-Term Perspective: Legitimacy and Souls-of-Fire as Critical Factors of Change and Viability," *Human Relations*, October 1993, pp. 1193–2023; and J. M. Howell and C. A. Higgins, "Champions of Change," *Business Quarterly*, Spring 1990, pp. 31–32.

51. J. Liedtka and T. Ogilvie, *Designing for Growth: A Design Thinking Tool Kit for Managers* (New York: Columbia Business School Press, 2011).

52. R. E. Silverman, "Companies Change Their Way of Thinking," *Wall Street Journal*, June 7, 2012, p. B8; and R. L. Martin, "The Innovation Catalysts," *Harvard Business Review*, June 2011, pp. 82–87.

53. B. Witz, "Manfred Fines Red Sox Over Stealing Signs and Issues Warning to All 30 Teams," *New York Times Online*, September 15, 2017; J. Ward, S. Pecanha and S. Manchester, "How Red Sox Used Tech, Step by Step to Steal Signs From Yankees," *New York Times Online,* Septemper 6, 2017; M. S. Schmidt, "Boston Red Sox Used Apple Watches to Steal Signs Against Yankees," *New York Times Online*, September 5, 2017; and T. Kepner, "The Ancient Yankees-Red Sox Rivalry Gets a High-Tech Boost," *New York Times Online*, September 5, 2017.

54. See C. M. Christensen, *The Innovator's Dilemma: When New Technologies Cause Great Firms to Fail* (Boston: Harvard Business Review Press, 1997); and "What Disruptive Innovation Means: The Economist Explains," *The Economist Online*, www.economist.com, January 25, 2015.

55. C. M. Christensen, M. Raynor, and R. McDonald, "What Is Disruptive Innovation?," *Harvard Business Review*, December 2015, pp. 44–53.

56. J. Schumpeter, *Capitalism, Socialism, and Democracy* (New York: Harper & Row), 1942.

57. "Keeping Pace with Change," *TD*, October 2017, p. 17.

58. Based on J. E. Newman and T. A. Beehr, "Personal and Organizational Strategies for Handling Job Stress," *Personnel Psychology*, Spring 1979, pp. 1–38; M. T. Matteson and J. M. Ivancevich, "Individual Stress Management Interventions: Evaluation of Techniques," *Journal of Management Psychology*, January 1987, pp. 24–30; and K. M. Richardson and H. R. Rothstein, "Effects of Occupational Stress Management Intervention Programs: A Meta-Analysis," *Journal of Occupational Health Psychology*, January 2008, pp. 69–93.

59. J. Ewing, "Engineering a Deception: What Led to Volkswagen's Diesel Scandal," *New York Times Online*, March 16, 2017.

60. "Innovation," http://update.vw.com/innovation/index.htm.

61. J. Ewing and G. Bowley, "The Engineering of Volkswagen's Aggressive Ambition," *New York Times Online*, December 13, 2015.

62. W. Boston, "VW Chief Contends With Scandal," *Wall Street Journal*, September 13, 2017, p. B9.

63. W. Boston, "VW's CEO Knows the Future Is Electric: His Company Isn't So Sure," *Wall Street Journal Online*, August 1, 2017.

64. M. Spector and M. Colias, "VW Manager Sentenced in Fraud," *Wall Street Journal*, December 7, 2017, p. B2.

65. W. Boston, "Volkswagen Prepares to Replace CEO," *Wall Street Journal*, April 11, 2018, pp. B1+.

66. W. Boston, "Volkswagen CEO Sets His Course," *Wall Street Journal*, April 14-15, 2018, p. B4.

67. S. Ember, "Under Armour Is Swinging for the Stars," *New York Times Online*, June 14, 2015; 2014 Annual Report, "Letter to the Shareholders," http://files.shareholder.com/downloads/UARM/165448209x0x816471/3BEBC664-8584-4F22-AC0B-844CB2949814/UA_2014_Annual_Report.PDF, January 31, 2015; B. Horovitz, "In Search of Next Big Thing," *USA Today*, July 9, 2012, pp. 1B+; Press Release, "Under Armour Reports Fourth Quarter Net Revenues Growth of 34% and Fourth Quarter EPS Growth of 40%," investor.underarmour.com, January 26, 2012; D. Roberts, "Under Armour Gets Serious," *Fortune*, November 7, 2011, pp. 153–62; E. Olson, "Under Armour Applies Its Muscle to Shoes," *New York Times Online*, August 8, 2011; M. Townsend, "Under Armour's Daring Half-Court Shot," *Bloomberg Businessweek*, November 1–7, 2010, pp. 24–25; and E. Olson, "Under Armour Wants to Dress Athletic Young Women," *New York Times Online*, August 31, 2010.

68. A. Prang, "Under Armour Steps Up Restructuring," *Wall Street Journal*, February 14, 2018, p. B3; and C. Jones, "Under Armour to Cut Job in Bid to Regain Footing," *USA Today*, August 2, 2017, p. 5B.

69. N. Bomey, "Under Armour Not Connecting with Female Customers," *USA Today-Springfield News-Leader*, November 1, 2017, p. 3B.

70. Ibid.

71. M. Dalton, "Time Runs Out for Swiss Watch Industry," *Wall Street Journal*, March 13, 2018, p. A8.

72. C. Martin-Rios and T. Ciobanu, "Hospitality Innovation Strategies: An Analysis of Success Factors and Challenges," *Tourism Management*, 70 (2018): 218–29, https://doi.org/10.1016/j.tourman.2018.08.018.

73. "Disruptive Innovation? What Disruptive Innovation?" *Hospitality Insights*, June 27, 2017 https://hospitalityinsights.ehl.edu/what-is-disruptive-innovation-hospitality.

Entrepreneurship Module
MANAGING ENTREPRENEURIAL VENTURES

What Is the Context of Entrepreneurship and Why Is It Important?

When you think of software start-ups, you, like most people, probably think of software focused on knowledge workers—employees who use spreadsheets, presentation software, communication tools, etc. But the newest surge in programs for mobile devices focuses on the blue-collar workforce.[1] And believe it or not, that's a pretty big market! Some 113 million workers who, until recently, relied on desktop programs or paper and pencil are now able to be more productive with technology. New mobile-based software start-ups are targeting people in occupations such as plumbing, contracting, garage-door installation, and other field-services. Mobile software for the blue-collar worker is a market ripe for entrepreneurship!

What Is Entrepreneurship?

Nick Gilson is an entrepreneur. Growing up in Rhode Island, he often sailed with his father and even once helped him build a catamaran, which are faster than traditional yachts because of their twin-hulled design. Nick wondered if a similar design could be applied to snowboards. So, as a teen, Nick decided he was going to design a snowboard based on the double-hulled catamaran design. In 2013, he co-founded Gilson Boards. The snowboards feature two runners along the bottom, which gives a rider more versatility and control in different snow conditions. By 2016, the company had sold more than 1,000 boards with a revenue approaching $1 million. Now, with 11 full-time employees, company sales have grown 200 percent every year. And it's branched out with its unique design into a line of skis.[2] Nick Gilson is engaged in **entrepreneurship**, the process of capitalizing on opportunities by starting new businesses for the purposes of changing, revolutionizing, transforming, or introducing new products or services. An entrepreneur sees an opportunity or an unmet need and won't stop searching and searching until finding a way to meet that need.

Many people think that entrepreneurial ventures and small businesses are the same, but they're not. Entrepreneurs create **entrepreneurial ventures (EVs)**—organizations that pursue opportunities, are characterized by innovative practices, and have growth and profitability as their main goals. On the other hand, a **small business** is an independent business having fewer than 500 employees that doesn't necessarily engage in any new or innovative practices and that has relatively little impact on its industry. A small business isn't necessarily entrepreneurial because it's small. To be entrepreneurial means that the business is innovative and seeks out new opportunities. Even though entrepreneurial ventures may start small, they pursue growth. Some new small firms may grow, but many remain small businesses, by choice or by default.

As we continue our exploration of what entrepreneurship is, it may help to clarify the concept by explaining what it *isn't*. Although entrepreneurial activities have been studied for well over three centuries, there are some common misconceptions about it.[3]

1. *Successful entrepreneurship needs only a great idea.* Having a great idea is only part of the equation for successful entrepreneurship. Understanding the demands of the different phases of the entrepreneurial process, taking an organized approach to developing the EV, and coping with the challenges of managing the EV are also key ingredients to successful entrepreneurship.

2. *Entrepreneurship is easy.* You may think that because you're pursuing your passion and have an intense desire to succeed, it's going to be easy. Be forewarned, however!

---

entrepreneurship
The process of capitalizing on opportunities by starting new businesses for the purposes of changing, revolutionizing, transforming, or introducing new products or services

entrepreneurial ventures (EVs)
Organizations that pursue opportunities, are characterized by innovative practices, and have growth and profitability as their main goals

small business
An independent business having fewer than 500 employees that doesn't necessarily engage in any new or innovative practices and that has relatively little impact on its industry

Entrepreneurship is not easy! It takes commitment, determination, and hard work. And even if you have those qualities, it still isn't effortless. Entrepreneurs often encounter difficulties and setbacks, but the successful entrepreneurs are those who push on in spite of the difficulties.

3. *Entrepreneurship is a risky gamble.* Typically, because entrepreneurship involves pursuing new and untested approaches and ideas, it must be a gamble, right? Not really. Although entrepreneurs aren't afraid to take risks, entrepreneurship involves calculated risks, not unnecessary ones. In fact, there are times when successful entrepreneurship means avoiding or minimizing risks.

4. *Entrepreneurship is found only in small-sized businesses.* Many people have the mistaken idea that entrepreneurship is associated only with small-sized organizations. The truth is that entrepreneurship can be found in any size organization. On the other hand, just because an organization is small doesn't automatically make it entrepreneurial.

5. *Entrepreneurial ventures and small businesses are the same thing.* This is a widespread misconception that we addressed earlier.

Is Entrepreneurship Different from Self-Employment?

Many people confuse entrepreneurship with self-employment. Are they the same? The answer is: sometimes. Let's start by defining self-employment.

Self-employment refers to individuals who work for profit or fees in their own business, profession, trade, or farm.[4] This arrangement focuses on established professions such as electricians, bookkeepers, or insurance agents. Recall our definition of entrepreneurship as a process of capitalizing on opportunities by starting new businesses for the purposes of changing, revolutionizing, transforming, or introducing new products or services. Now let's look at three points of comparison of the two.

First, both entrepreneurs and self-employed individuals understand market needs. For instance, Hector recognizes a demand for house-cleaning services, and he decides to start a business cleaning houses for a fee. There is nothing revolutionary about cleaning houses (though it is a worthy endeavor). Hector is *self-employed.* In contrast, Valentin Stalf, CEO of German financial services startup N26, is an entrepreneur. He created a service that combines all an individual's financial life—with accounts and cards from numerous companies—into a single, simplified financial services platform using cross-service partnerships and alliances.[5] He saw an opportunity to make financial services more efficient and useful for customers. Serving market needs provides both Hector and Valentin the opportunity to provide services or products at a profit.

Second, entrepreneurs may be self-employed or they become employees of the company they have started. For instance, Alfred co-founders, CEO Marcela Sapone and COO Jessica Beck, turned their idea for an app-based, on-demand personal concierge service into a thriving business, where they're now employees...the highest level employees![6] Self-employed individuals always work for themselves. They are not paid employees of another company, and they rely on their own initiative to ensure they're generating income. Also, self-employed individuals make all the decisions about how the work gets done. Finally, self-employment does not preclude having one or more employees. For example, Hector's cleaning business took off and he realized he couldn't handle everything himself. So he hired two individuals to help him better meet clients' needs.

Third, tax requirements and certain laws require that both entrepreneurs and self-employed individuals create a legally recognized organization. There are several types, which we'll discuss later in this chapter. Hector may set up a sole proprietorship, while Valentin's company may be registered as a corporation.

Tech entrepreneur **Demet Mutlu** is the founder and CEO of Trendyol Group. After discovering the potential of online retailing in Turkey, she used $300,000 of her own funds to launch her fashion portal in 2009 and then raised more than $50 million from venture capitalists to grow her firm into the largest fashion e-commerce firm in Turkey with 13 million customers and an annual growth rate of 90 percent.

Murad Sezer/Reuters

◄◄◄ Classic Concepts in Today's Workplace ►►►

Entrepreneurship is not a twentieth- or twenty-first century phenomenon, although the current popularity of startups, new venture teams, and entrepreneurial exploits would tend to make you think that it was. Early in the eighteenth century, the French term *entrepreneur* was used to describe a "go-between" or a "between-taker." Richard Cantillon, a noted economist and author in the 1700s, is regarded by many as the originator of the term *entrepreneur*.[7] He used the term to refer to a person who took an active risk-bearing role in pursuing opportunities. This individual—the entrepreneur—served as the bridge between someone who had the capital (money) but who chose not to personally pursue those opportunities. Instead, the individual (or group of individuals) financed the pursuit of opportunities and the entrepreneur served as the go-between—the actively involved risk taker. Exhibit EM–1

shows other important historical developments in the development of entrepreneurship theory.

Although this is only a small portion of entrepreneurship's long and colorful past, keep in mind that the history of entrepreneurship continues to unfold. Its history is still being written today. Throughout the rest of this chapter, we'll highlight much of what we know about entrepreneurship today.

Discussion Questions:

1 How does looking at the history of entrepreneurship help you in your understanding of entrepreneurship today?

2 Do the historical descriptions of entrepreneurship shown in Exhibit EM–1 still make sense today? Take each one and write how you would explain it to one of your friends who's not a business major.

Exhibit EM–1 Historical Developments in the Development of Entrepreneurship Theory

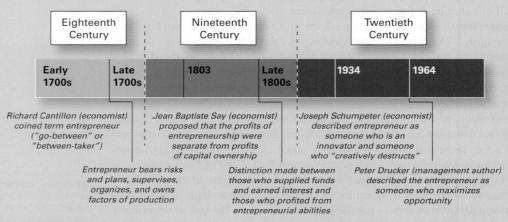

Source: Robbins, Stephen P., Coulter, Mary, *Entrepreneurship in Action*, 1st Ed., © 2001. Reprinted and electronically reproduced by permission of Pearson Education, Inc., New York, NY.

Who's Starting Entrepreneurial Ventures?

What about YOU? Do you want to be an entrepreneur?

Describing *who* entrepreneurs are has been (and continues to be) a favorite pursuit of researchers and business journalists. We're defining an **entrepreneur** as someone who initiates and actively operates an EV.[8] Inherent in this definition is the idea that the entrepreneur is not just the person who identifies the opportunity(ies) that are the basis for pursuing and initiating the EV, but is also that person who operates the EV. The entrepreneur "does" the venture as well as "dreams" it up.

Are there ways to describe different types of entrepreneurs? Yes! Based on our earlier definition of entrepreneurship, we've already described **opportunity-based entrepreneurs**, who are individuals who start an EV to pursue an opportunity. But those are not the only individuals who start EVs. Others are **necessity entrepreneurs** . . . also called accidental entrepreneurs, unintended entrepreneurs, or forced entrepreneurs. These individuals start an EV out of necessity—usually job loss. For instance, when the unemployment rate hovered at double digits and corporate downsizings were happening frequently, many corporate "refugees" became

entrepreneur
Someone who initiates and actively operates an entrepreneurial venture (EV)

opportunity-based entrepreneurs
Individuals who start an EV to pursue an opportunity

necessity entrepreneurs
Individuals who start an EV out of necessity

entrepreneurs. These individuals looked to entrepreneurship, not because they sensed some great opportunity, but because there were no jobs. Another type of entrepreneur is a **serial entrepreneur**, an individual who has sold or closed an original business, founded another business, sold or closed that business, and continues this cycle of entrepreneurial behavior. Finally, a **portfolio entrepreneur** is an individual who retains an original business and builds a portfolio of additional businesses through inheriting, establishing or purchasing them.

serial entrepreneur
An individual who has sold or closed an original business, founded another business, sold or closed that business, and continues this cycle of entrepreneurial behavior

portfolio entrepreneur
An individual who retains an original business and builds a portfolio of additional businesses through inheriting, establishing, or purchasing them

Why Is Entrepreneurship Important?

Using any number of sources, you can find statistics about how many small businesses there are, how many workers they employ, and how much of the gross national economic output they're responsible for. These statistics, as collected by various research firms and government agencies, reflect the economic activity of *all* small businesses, not just those of entrepreneurial ventures. Because we've made a point of distinguishing between small businesses and EVs, these statistics don't tell the whole story. Let's try to look at what entrepreneurship contributes. Then the questions become: How can we measure the importance of entrepreneurship? Does entrepreneurship contribute to economic vitality? And how does it do so?

Entrepreneurship is, and continues to be, important to every industry sector in the United States and around the world. Its importance can be shown in three areas: innovation, number of new startups, and job creation and employment.

INNOVATION. As we discussed in the last chapter, innovation is a process of creating, changing, experimenting, transforming, and revolutionizing. And as we know from our earlier definition, innovation is one of the key distinguishing characteristics of entrepreneurial activity. The "creative destruction" process of innovating leads to technological changes and employment growth.[9] Entrepreneurial firms act as agents of change by providing an essential source of new and unique ideas that might otherwise go untapped.

The passionate drive and hunger of entrepreneurs to forge new directions in products and processes and to take risks set in motion a series of decisions that lead to the innovations that are important for economic vitality. Without these new ideas, economic, technological, and social progress would be slow indeed.

NUMBER OF NEW STARTUPS. All businesses—whether they fit the definition of entrepreneurial or not—at one point were start-ups. The most convenient measure we have of the role that entrepreneurship plays in this economic statistic is to look at the number of new firms over a period of time. The Index of Entrepreneurial Activity by the Kauffman Foundation tracks the rate at which new businesses are formed. That measure bottomed out in 2013. However, by 2017 (the latest data available), startup activity was up, although the rate in the top 40 largest U.S. metropolitan areas continued to decline.[10] Another study of startups showed that from 1996 to 2007, the ratio of new firms to the total number of firms varied between 9.6 and 11.2. The rate in mid 2017 had dropped to 7.8.[11] Why is the creation of new firms important? It's important because these new firms contribute to economic development through benefits such as product-process innovations, increased tax revenues, social betterment, and job creation.

Entrepreneurship is important because it leads to innovations such as the new Choose Water eco-friendly and completely biodegradable water bottle developed by James Longcroft. The plastic-free, single-use bottle is made of recycled and natural materials that decompose within three weeks. Longcroft hopes that his innovation will replace single-use plastic bottles and help stop the rise of plastic waste pollution of the world's oceans.

JOB CREATION. We know that job creation is important to the overall long-term economic health of communities, regions, and nations. A recent research report suggested that business startups play an important role in job creation, but have a more limited effect on net job creation over time because fewer than half of all startups are still in business after five years. Also, the report noted that the influence of small business startups on net job creation varies by firm size. Startups with fewer than 20 employees tend to have a negligible effect on net job creation over

John Stillwell/PA Wire/AP Images

time, while startups with 20–499 employees tend to have a positive employment effect.[12] So, we can say that yes, EVs are important to job creation.

GLOBAL ENTREPRENEURSHIP. What about entrepreneurial activity outside the United States? What kind of impact has it had? An annual assessment of global entrepreneurship called the Global Entrepreneurship Monitor (GEM) studies the impact of entrepreneurial activity on economic growth in various countries. The GEM 2017/18 report covered 54 world economies that were divided into three clusters identified by phase of economic development: factor-driven economies, efficiency-driven economies, and innovation-driven economies. What did researchers find?[13]

- North America had the highest level of total entrepreneurial activity (TEA) for the 25- to 34-year-old age group at 23.4 percent.
- Latin America and Caribbean economies had the highest level of TEA for the 18- to 24-year-old age group at 16.5 percent, for the 35- to 44-year-old age group at 20.6 percent, and for the 45- to 54-year-old age group at 17.9 percent.
- Europe had the lowest TEA of all regions in all age groups.

What Do Entrepreneurs Do?

Describing what entrepreneurs do isn't an easy or simple task! No two entrepreneurs' work activities are exactly alike. In a general sense, entrepreneurs create something new, something different. They search for change, respond to it, and exploit it.

ASSESSING POTENTIAL AND STARTING UP. Initially, an entrepreneur is engaged in *assessing the potential for the entrepreneurial venture and then dealing with startup issues*. In exploring the entrepreneurial context, entrepreneurs gather information, identify potential opportunities, and pinpoint possible competitive advantage(s). Then, armed with this information, an entrepreneur researches the venture's feasibility—uncovering business ideas, looking at competitors, and exploring financing options.

After looking at the potential of the proposed venture and assessing the likelihood of pursuing it successfully, an entrepreneur proceeds to *plan the venture*. This process includes such activities as developing a viable organizational mission, exploring organizational culture issues, and creating a well-thought-out business plan. Once these planning issues have been resolved, the entrepreneur must look at *organizing the venture*, which involves choosing a legal form of business organization, addressing other legal issues such as patent or copyright searches, and coming up with an appropriate organizational design for structuring how work is going to be done.

LAUNCHING THE VENTURE. Only after these startup activities have been completed is the entrepreneur ready to actually launch the venture. A launch involves setting goals and strategies, and establishing the technology operations methods, marketing plans, information systems, financial accounting systems, and cash flow management systems.

MANAGING THE VENTURE. Once the entrepreneurial venture is up and running, the entrepreneur's attention switches to managing it. What's involved with actually managing the entrepreneurial venture? An important activity is *managing the various processes* that are part of every business: making decisions, establishing action plans, analyzing external and internal environments, measuring and evaluating performance, and making needed changes. Also, the entrepreneur must perform activities associated with *managing people*, including selecting and hiring, appraising and training, motivating, managing conflict, delegating tasks, and being an effective leader. Finally, the entrepreneur must *manage the venture's growth*, including such activities as developing and designing growth strategies, dealing with crises, exploring various avenues for financing growth, placing a value on the venture, and perhaps even eventually exiting the venture.

What Happens in the Entrepreneurial Process?

Starting and managing an EV involves four key steps:

1

Exploring the Entrepreneurial Context

The context includes: current economic, political/legal, social, and work environments.

Why is each of these important to look at? Because they help an entrepreneur:

- Determine the "rules" of the game and which decisions and actions are likely to lead to success.

- Recognize and confront the next critically important step in clarifying the EV. . . STEP 2!

Viacheslav Iakobchuk/Alamy Stock Photo

2

Identifying Opportunities and Possible Competitive Advantages

MORE on this . . . . coming soon . . . see the Planning section in this chapter!

3 Starting the Venture

Bringing the idea(s) to life! Includes:

- Researching the feasibility of the venture
- Planning the venture
- Organizing the venture
- Launching the venture

4 Managing the Venture   HOW?

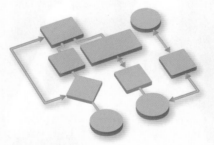

Managing Processes.

Managing People.

Managing Growth.

What Social Responsibility and Ethics Issues Face Entrepreneurs?

As entrepreneurs launch and manage their ventures, they're faced with the often-difficult issues of social responsibility and ethics.

social entrepreneur
An individual or organization that seeks out opportunities to improve society by using practical, innovative, and sustainable approaches

> 95 percent of small businesses believe that developing a positive reputation and relationship in communities where they do business is important for achieving business goals.[14]

Despite the importance they place on corporate citizenship, more than half of those small firms lacked formal programs for connecting with their communities. In fact, some 70 percent admitted that they failed to consider community goals in their business plans. We discussed in an earlier chapter why organizations need to be socially involved, and it is just as important for entrepreneurs to think long and hard about when, where, and how to be socially responsible.

SOCIAL RESPONSIBILITY AND SOCIAL ENTREPRENEURS. Some entrepreneurs do take their social responsibilities seriously. The world's social problems are many, and viable solutions are few. But numerous people and organizations are trying to do something. We use the term "social entrepreneur" to describe these individuals. A **social entrepreneur** is an individual or organization that seeks out opportunities to improve society by using practical, innovative, and sustainable approaches. For example, Deane Kirchner, George Wang, and Kiah Williams co-founded SIRIUM, which stands for Supporting Initiatives to Redistribute Unused Medicine. The group recognized that unexpired medications worth billions of dollars are discarded while underfunded medical clinics do not have the means to purchase medication for low-income patients. Kirchner and her team use a digital platform for hospitals and clinics to find matches, and SIRIUM then ships medication to where it's needed most. "Our goal is to save lives by saving unused medications," says Kirchner. "We thought we could use technology to bridge this gap between surplus and need."[15]

♻ Other entrepreneurs have pursued opportunities with products and services that protect the global environment. For example, PurposeEnergy of Woburn, Massachusetts, developed a technology that removes waste by-products from the beer brewing industry and changes them to renewable natural gas, treated water, and organic fertilizer. Another company, Botl of Toronto, Canada, sells a biodegradable portable water filter. Founder Emily Wilkinson sought to protect the environment by reducing the amount of plastic waste going into landfills. Rather than using and disposing one plastic container of filtered bottled water after another, consumers can quickly filter tap water in any container by dropping the filter in and then shaking it.

What can we learn from social entrepreneurs? Although many businesses have committed to doing business ethically and responsibly, perhaps there is more they can do, as these social entrepreneurs show. Maybe it's simply a matter of collaborating with public groups or nonprofit organizations to address a social issue. Or maybe it's providing services and products where they're needed but not available. Or it may involve nurturing individuals who passionately and unwaveringly believe they have an idea that could make the world a better place and simply need the organizational support to pursue it.

ENTREPRENEURIAL ETHICS. Ethical considerations also play a role in the decisions and actions of entrepreneurs. Entrepreneurs do need to be aware of the ethical consequences of what they do.

Social entrepreneur Keller Rinaudo is co-founder and CEO of Zipline, a California-based robotics firm that makes drones, called "zips," and uses them to deliver vaccines, medicines, and blood transfusions to hospitals and health centers in Rwanda. Zipline's mission is "to bring life-saving medicine to the most difficult to reach places on the planet." To achieve its mission, Zipline plans to expand its service globally.

James Akena/Reuters

The example they set—particularly for other employees—can be profoundly significant in influencing behavior.

If ethics are important, how do entrepreneurs stack up? Unfortunately, not well! In a survey of employees from different sizes of businesses who were asked if they thought their organization was highly ethical, 20 percent of employees at companies with 99 or fewer employees disagreed.[16] Entrepreneurs, like organizational managers, need to be aware of the importance of doing business ethically and providing an ethically strong environment to encourage ethical decisions and actions.

What's Involved in Planning New Ventures?

Although pouring a bowl of cereal may seem like a simple task, even the most awake and alert morning person has probably ended up with cereal on the floor. (Have you ever done that?!) Philippe Meert, a product designer based in Erpe-Mere, Belgium, came up with a better way. Meert sensed an opportunity to correct the innate design flaw of cereal boxes and developed the Cerealtop, a plastic cover that snaps onto a cereal box and channels the cereal into a bowl.[17]

The first thing that entrepreneurs like Philippie Meert must do is to identify opportunities and possible competitive advantages. Once they've identified the opportunities, they're ready to start the venture by researching its feasibility and then planning for its launch.

What Initial Efforts Must Entrepreneurs Make?

When Jeff Bezos first saw that Internet usage was increasing by 2,300 percent a month, he knew that something dramatic was happening. With such unbelievably rapid growth, Bezos was determined to be a part of it. He quit his successful career as a stock market researcher and hedge fund manager on Wall Street and pursued his vision for online retailing, now Amazon.com.[18]

What would you have done if you had seen that type of number somewhere? Ignored it? Written it off as a fluke? This is a prime example of identifying environmental opportunities. (Remember our definition of opportunities in Chapter 6 as positive trends in the external environment.) These trends provide unique and distinct possibilities for innovating and creating value. Entrepreneurs need to be able to pinpoint these pockets of opportunity that a changing context provides. After all, "organizations do not see opportunities, individuals do."[19] And they need to do so quickly, especially in dynamic environments, before those opportunities disappear or are exploited by others.[20]

Recent research also has shown that small trends—microtrends—can be just as important as huge social and economic changes in pinpointing opportunities to satisfy new needs in the marketplace.[21]

The late Peter Drucker, a well-known management author, identified seven potential sources of opportunity that entrepreneurs might look for in the external context.[22] Let's take a quick look.

1. *The unexpected.* When situations and events are unanticipated, opportunities can be found. The event may be an unexpected success (positive news) or unexpected failure (bad news). Either way, it may present opportunities for entrepreneurs to pursue.

2. *The incongruous.* When something is incongruous, it exhibits inconsistencies and incompatibilities in the way it appears. Things "ought to be" a certain way, but aren't. When conventional wisdom about the way things should be no longer holds true, for whatever reason, opportunities are present. Entrepreneurs who are willing to "think outside the box"—that is, think beyond the traditional and conventional approaches—may find pockets of potential profitability.

3. *The process need.* What happens when technology doesn't immediately come up with the "big discovery" that's going to fundamentally change the nature of some product or service? What happens is the emergence of pockets of entrepreneurial opportunity in the various stages of the process as researchers, scientists, and technicians continue to work for the monumental breakthrough. Because the full leap hasn't been possible, opportunities abound in the tiny steps.

4. *Industry and market structures.* When changes in technology change the structure of an industry and market, existing firms can become obsolete if they're not attuned to the changes or are unwilling to change. (Remember our discussion of disruptive innovation in the last chapter.) Even changes in social values and consumer tastes can shift the structures of industries and markets. These markets and industries become open targets for nimble and smart entrepreneurs.

5. *Demographics.* The characteristics of the world population are changing. These changes influence industries and markets by altering the types and quantities of products and services desired and customers' buying power. Although many of these changes are fairly predictable if you stay alert to demographic trends (think of the aging of the U.S. population and what products/services are desired), others aren't as obvious. Either way, significant entrepreneurial opportunities can be realized by anticipating and meeting the changing needs of the population.

6. *Changes in perception.* Perception is one's view of reality. When changes in perception take place, the facts do not vary, but their meanings do. Changes in perception get at the heart of people's psychographic profiles—what they value, what they believe in, and what they care about. Changes in attitudes and values create potential market opportunities for alert entrepreneurs.

7. *New knowledge.* New knowledge is a significant source of entrepreneurial opportunity. Although not all knowledge-based innovations are significant, new knowledge ranks pretty high on the list of sources of entrepreneurial opportunity! It takes more than just having new knowledge, though. Entrepreneurs must be able to do something with that knowledge and to protect important proprietary information from competitors.

Being alert to opportunities is only part of an entrepreneur's initial efforts. He or she must also understand competitive advantage. As we discuss in Chapter 6, when an organization has a competitive advantage, it has something that other competitors don't have, does something better than other organizations, or does something that others can't. Competitive advantage is a necessary ingredient for an EV's long-term success and survival. Getting and keeping a competitive advantage is tough. However, it is something that entrepreneurs must consider as they begin researching the venture's feasibility.

How Should Entrepreneurs Research the Venture's Feasibility?

It's important for entrepreneurs to research a venture's feasibility by generating and evaluating business ideas. EVs thrive on ideas. Generating ideas is an innovative, creative process. It's also one that will take time—not only in the beginning stages of the EV, but throughout the life of the business. Where do ideas come from?

Where do entrepreneurs say their idea for a business came from?[23]

- 34.3 percent said sudden insight/chance
- 23.5 percent said following a passion
- 11.8 percent said a suggestion or collaboration
- 10.8 percent said market research
- 7.8 percent said "other"

---

feasibility study
An analysis of the various aspects of a proposed entrepreneurial venture designed to determine its feasibility

GENERATING IDEAS. Entrepreneurs cite unique and varied sources for their ideas. In another survey, 60 percent of the respondents said that "working in the same industry" was the major source of an idea for an EV. Other respondents cited personal interests or hobbies, looking at familiar and unfamiliar products and services, and opportunities in external environmental sectors.[24]

Here's what entrepreneurs should look for as they explore idea sources: limitations of what's currently available, new and different approaches, advances and breakthroughs, unfilled niches, or trends and changes.

EVALUATING IDEAS. Evaluating entrepreneurial ideas revolves around personal and marketplace considerations. Each of these assessments will provide an entrepreneur with key information about the idea's potential. Exhibit EM–2 describes some questions that entrepreneurs might ask as they evaluate potential ideas.

A more structured evaluation approach that an entrepreneur might want to use is a **feasibility study**, which is an analysis of the various aspects of a proposed entrepreneurial venture designed to determine its feasibility. Not only is a well-prepared feasibility study an effective evaluation tool to determine whether an entrepreneurial idea is a potentially successful one, it also can serve as a basis for the all-important business plan. Exhibit EM–3 provides an outline of a possible approach to a feasibility study. Yes, it covers a lot of territory and takes a significant amount of time, energy, and effort to prepare it. But, an entrepreneur's potential future success is worth that investment.

"GETTING THE DIRT" ON COMPETITORS. Part of researching an EV's feasibility is looking at potential competitors. Here are some questions that might help entrepreneurs get information:

- What types of products or services are competitors offering?
- What are the major characteristics of these products or services?
- What are their products' strengths and weaknesses?
- How do they handle marketing, pricing, and distribution?
- What do they attempt to do differently from other competitors?
- Do they appear to be successful at it? Why or why not?
- What are they good at?
- What competitive advantage(s) do they appear to have?
- What are they not so good at?
- What competitive disadvantage(s) do they appear to have?
- How large and profitable are these competitors?

Exhibit EM–2 Evaluating Potential Ideas

Personal Considerations	Marketplace Considerations
• Do you have the capabilities to do what you've selected?	• Who are the potential customers for your idea: who, where, how many?
• Are you ready to be an entrepreneur?	• What similar or unique product features does your proposed idea have compared to what's currently on the market?
• Are you prepared emotionally to deal with the stresses and challenges of being an entrepreneur?	• How and where will potential customers purchase your product?
• Are you prepared to deal with rejection and failure?	
• Are you ready to work hard?	• Have you considered pricing issues and whether the price you'll be able to charge will allow your venture to survive and prosper?
• Do you have a realistic picture of the venture's potential?	
• Have you educated yourself about financing issues?	• Have you considered how you will need to promote and advertise your proposed entrepreneurial venture?
• Are you willing and prepared to do continual financial and other types of analyses?	

Exhibit EM–3 Feasibility Study

A. Introduction, historical background, description of product or service
1. Brief description of proposed entrepreneurial venture
2. Brief history of the industry
3. Information about the economy and important trends
4. Current status of the product or service
5. How you intend to produce the product or service
6. Complete list of goods or services to be provided
7. Strengths and weaknesses of the business
8. Ease of entry into the industry, including competitor analysis

B. Accounting considerations
1. Pro forma balance sheet
2. Pro forma profit and loss statement
3. Projected cash flow analysis

C. Management considerations
1. Personal expertise–strenths and weaknesses
2. Proposed organizational design
3. Potential staffing requirements
4. Inventory management methods
5. Production and operations management issues
6. Equipment needs

D. Marketing considerations
1. Detailed product description
2. Identify target market (who, where, how many)
3. Describe place product will be distributed (location, traffic, size, channels,etc.)
4. Price determination (competition, price lists, etc.)
5. Promotion plans (role of personal selling, advertising, sales promotion,etc.)

E. Financial considerations
1. Start-up costs
2. Working capital requirements
3. Equity requirements
4. Loans–amounts, type, conditions
5. Breakeven analysis
6. Collateral
7. Credit references
8. Equipment and building financing–costs and methods

F. Legal considerations
1. Proposed business structure (type; conditions, terms, liability, responsibility; insurance needs; buyout and succession issues)
2. Contracts, licenses, and other legal documents

G. Tax considerations: sales/property/employee; federal, state, and local

H. Appendix: charts/graphs, diagrams, layouts, résumés, etc.

Source: Robbins, Stephen P., Coulter, Mary, *Management* (Subscription), 14th Ed., © 2018. Reprinted and electronically reproduced by permission of Pearson Education, Inc., New York, NY.

Once an entrepreneur has this information, he or she should assess how the proposed EV is going to "fit" into this competitive arena. Will the EV be able to compete successfully? This type of competitor analysis becomes an important part of the feasibility study and the business plan. If, after all this analysis, the situation looks promising, the final part of researching the venture's feasibility is to look at the various financing options. This step isn't the final determination of how much funding the venture will need or where this funding will come from but is simply gathering information about various financing alternatives.

Exhibit EM–4 Possible Funding Sources

- Entrepreneur's personal resources (personal savings, home equity, personal loans, credit cards, etc.)
- Financial institutions (banks, savings and loan institutions, government-guaranteed loan, credit unions, etc.)
- **Venture capitalists**—external equity financing provided by professionally managed pools of investor money
- **Angel investors**—a private investor (or group of private investors) who offers financial backing to an entrepreneurial venture in return for equity in the venture
- **Initial public offering (IPO)**—the first public registration and sale of a company's stock
- National, state, and local governmental business development programs
- Other sources including television shows, judged competitions, crowdfunding, business accelerator programs, etc.

Source: Robbins, Stephen P., Coulter, Mary, *Management* (Subscription), 14th Ed., © 2018. Reprinted and electronically reproduced by permission of Pearson Education, Inc., New York, NY.

SHOW ME THE MONEY. Getting financing isn't easy, unless you have a rich relative who's opened his or her pockets. Because funds likely will be needed to start the venture, an entrepreneur must research the various financing options. Possible financial options available to entrepreneurs are shown in Exhibit EM–4.

What Planning Do Entrepreneurs Need to Do?

16%... how much more likely entrepreneurs who write formal plans are to achieve viability.[25]

Yes, planning is important to entrepreneurial ventures because it can increase the odds of success. Once a venture's feasibility has been thoroughly researched, an entrepreneur then must look at planning the venture. The most important thing that an entrepreneur does in planning the venture is developing a **business plan**—a written document that summarizes a business opportunity and defines and articulates how the identified opportunity is to be seized and exploited.

For many would-be entrepreneurs, developing and writing a business plan seems like a daunting task. However, a good business plan is valuable. It pulls together all of the elements of the entrepreneur's vision into a single coherent document. The business plan requires careful planning and creative thinking. But if done well, it can be a convincing document that serves many functions. It serves as a blueprint and road map for operating the business. And the business plan is a "living" document, guiding organizational decisions and actions throughout the life of the business, not just in the startup stage.

A written business plan can range from basic to thorough. The most basic type of business plan would simply include an *executive summary*, sort of a mini-business plan that's no longer than two pages. A *full business plan* is the traditional business plan, which we describe fully next.

If an entrepreneur has completed a feasibility study, much of the information included in it becomes the basis for the business plan. A good business plan covers six major areas: executive summary, analysis of opportunity, analysis of the context, description of the business, financial data and projections, and supporting documentation.

business plan
A written document that summarizes a business opportunity and defines and articulates how the identified opportunity is to be seized and exploited

Executive summary. The executive summary summarizes the key points that the entrepreneur wants to make about the proposed entrepreneurial venture. These might include a brief mission statement; primary goals; brief history of the entrepreneurial venture, maybe in the form of a timeline; key people involved in the venture; nature of the business; concise product or service descriptions; brief explanations of market niche, competitors, and competitive advantage; proposed strategies; and selected key financial information.

Analysis of opportunity. In this section of the business plan, an entrepreneur presents the details of the perceived opportunity, which essentially includes (1) sizing up the market by describing the demographics of the target market, (2) describing and evaluating industry trends, and (3) identifying and evaluating competitors.

Analysis of the context. Whereas the opportunity analysis focuses on the opportunity in a specific industry and market, the context analysis takes a much broader perspective. Here, the entrepreneur describes the broad external changes and trends taking place in the economic, political-legal, technological, and global environments.

Description of the business. In this section, an entrepreneur describes how the entrepreneurial venture is going to be organized, launched, and managed. It includes a thorough description of the mission statement; a description of the desired organizational culture; marketing plans, including overall marketing strategy, pricing, sales tactics, service/warranty policies, and advertising and promotion tactics; product development plans such as an explanation of development status, tasks, difficulties and risks, and anticipated costs; operational plans, including a description of proposed geographic location, facilities and needed improvements, equipment, and work flow; human resource plans, including a description of key management persons, composition of board of directors and their background experience and skills, current and future staffing needs, compensation and benefits, and training needs; and an overall schedule and timetable of events.

Financial data and projections. Every effective business plan contains financial data and projections. Although the calculations and interpretation may be difficult, they are absolutely critical. No business plan is complete without financial information. Financial plans should cover at least three years and contain projected income statements, pro forma cash flow analysis (monthly for the first year and quarterly for the next two), pro forma balance sheets, breakeven analysis, and cost controls. If major equipment or other capital purchases are expected, the items, costs, and available collateral should be listed. All financial projections and analyses should include explanatory notes, especially where the data seem contradictory or questionable.

Supporting documentation. This *is* an important component of an effective business plan. The entrepreneur should back up his or her descriptions with charts, graphs, tables, photographs, or other visual tools. In addition, it might be important to include information (personal and work-related) about the key participants in the entrepreneurial venture.

Just as the idea for an entrepreneurial venture takes time to germinate, so does the writing of a good business plan. It's important for an entrepreneur to put serious thought and consideration into the plan. It's not an easy thing to do. However, the resulting document should be valuable in current and future planning efforts.

What Additional Planning Considerations Do Entrepreneurs Need to Address?

Before launching a new EV, an entrepreneur should give serious thought to the organizational values, vision and mission, and the organizational culture he or she desires for the new venture. Why? Because these will define and shape what and how decisions are made and what and how the EV's work is done. Let's take a quick look at each.

ORGANIZATIONAL VALUES, VISION, AND MISSION. An **organizational vision** is a broad comprehensive picture of what an entrepreneur wants his or her organization to become. The vision provides a vibrant and compelling picture of the future and presents a view of what the EV can be. The vision is the statement of the entrepreneur's dream.

organizational vision
A broad comprehensive picture of what an entrepreneur wants his or her organization to become

The culture that Yvon Chouinard, the founder of Patagonia, established for his outdoor clothing company is reflected in the title of his book, *Let My People Go Surfing*. Patagonia's employees are passionate about their work, the quality products they make, caring for the environment, and their flexible workplace that allows them to pick up boards and wetsuits at their office and enjoy surfing during their lunch hour.

When an organizational leader—in this case, an entrepreneur—articulates a distinct vision, all current and future decisions and actions will be guided by this vision. By articulating the vision, the entrepreneur maps out an overall picture of where he or she would like the EV to be in the future. This vision is based on the entrepreneur's values. What beliefs does the business owner have about doing business and dealing with customers, employees, quality, ethics, growth, integrity, innovation, flexibility, and so forth? What's valued by an entrepreneur will not only be the basis for the organizational vision, but also for how employees do their jobs. For instance, if employees know that outstanding customer service is valued, then this will be reflected in how they make decisions and encourage them to act in ways that champion customer service.

While an organization's *vision* provides an overall picture of what the EV is about, the mission is a more specific definition of what the EV is in business to do. We introduce the concept of mission in Chapter 6 and define it as a statement of an organization's purpose. The mission statement serves as a guide to all employees and prevents them from "wandering aimlessly" with no sense of what they're in business to do and the reason for their jobs.

ORGANIZATIONAL CULTURE. When you walk into a particular business, do you get a certain impression about what is important and about the way work is done there? Do you get the feeling that employees are excited and motivated by what they do or that employees are there just because it provides a paycheck? Does it seem that customers are important and valued or that customers are seen as intrusions on getting work done? Do you get the feeling that this organization is warm, relaxed, and open or that this organization is formal, structured, and set in its ways? Just as individuals have personalities, so do organizations. This personality is called *culture*, and we introduced you to organizational culture back in Chapter 4. We bring it up again here because the source of an organization's culture—those shared values, beliefs, and behavioral norms—reflect the beliefs, values, and vision of the founder(s). Because the founder (entrepreneur) has the original idea, he or she also may have certain beliefs and biases about how best to pursue the idea. This person establishes the early culture of the organization by projecting an image of what the organization should be. The small size of a startup also helps the founder(s) instill the values and vision in organizational members as they come on board. These people either "buy into" the culture or they don't join the organization. The culture is learned through stories, rituals, material symbols, and language, which give the culture life. These are the ways in which employees see, experience, and learn about an organization's culture. Even the physical work space plays a role in reflecting and reinforcing the culture. For instance, if collaboration among employees is important and valued, then the work space should be arranged to support and facilitate open discussion. Or, if innovativeness is an important company value, the work space should support people in experimenting and being creative.

What's Involved in Organizing an Entrepreneurial Venture?

Roy Ng, chief operating officer of Twilio in San Francisco, redesigned his organization's structure by transforming it into an employee-empowered company. He wanted to drive authority down through the organization so employees were responsible for their own efforts. One way he did this was by creating employee teams to handle specific projects. These small teams can work rapidly and independently, and provide a means for employees to have the same level of passion, resourcefulness, and productivity that characterized the startup in its earliest days.[26]

Once the startup and planning issues for the entrepreneurial venture have been addressed, the entrepreneur is ready to begin organizing the entrepreneurial venture. The main organizing issues an entrepreneur must address include the legal forms of organization, organizational design and structure, and human resource management.

What Are the Legal Forms of Organization for Entrepreneurial Ventures?

The first organizing decision that an entrepreneur must make is a critical one. It's the form of legal ownership for the venture. The two primary factors affecting this decision are taxes and legal liability. An entrepreneur wants to minimize the impact of both of these factors. The right choice can protect the entrepreneur from legal liability as well as save tax dollars, in both the short run and the long run.

The three basic ways to organize an entrepreneurial venture are sole proprietorship, partnership, and corporation. However, when you include the variations of these basic organizational alternatives, you end up with six possible choices, each with its own tax consequences, liability issues, and pros and cons. These six choices are sole proprietorship, general partnership, limited liability partnership (LLP), C corporation, S corporation, and limited liability company (LLC). Exhibit EM–5 summarizes the basic information about each organizational alternative.

The decision regarding the legal form of organization is important because it has significant tax and liability consequences. Although the legal form of organization can be changed, it's not easy to do. An entrepreneur needs to think carefully about what's important—especially in the areas of flexibility, taxes, and amount of personal liability—in choosing the best form of organization.

What Type of Organizational Structure Should Entrepreneurial Ventures Use?

The choice of an appropriate organizational structure is also an important decision when organizing an entrepreneurial venture. At some point, successful entrepreneurs find that they can't do everything. They need people. The entrepreneur must then decide on the most appropriate structural arrangement for effectively and efficiently carrying out the organization's activities. Without a suitable type of organizational structure, an entrepreneurial venture may soon find itself in a chaotic situation.

In many small firms, the organizational structure tends to evolve with very little intentional and deliberate planning by the entrepreneur. For the most part, the structure may be very simple—one person does whatever is needed. As an entrepreneurial venture grows and the entrepreneur finds it increasingly difficult to go it alone, employees are brought on board to perform certain functions or duties that the entrepreneur can't handle. As the company continues to grow, these individuals tend to perform those same functions. Soon, each functional area may require managers and employees.

Letting go...can be difficult for an entrepreneur.

As the venture evolves to a more deliberate structure, an entrepreneur faces a whole new set of challenges. All of a sudden, he or she must share decision-making and operating responsibilities, which are typically the most difficult things for an entrepreneur to do—letting

Exhibit EM–5 Legal Forms of Business Organization

Structure	Ownership Requirements	Tax Treatment	Liability	Advantages	Drawbacks
Sole proprietorship	One owner	Income and lossess "pass through" to owner and are taxed at personal rate	Unlimited personal liability	Low start-up costs Freedom from most regulations Owner has direct control All profits go to owner Easy to exit business	Unlimited personal liability Personal finances at risk Miss out on many business tax deductions Total responsibility May be more difficult to raise financing
General partnership	Two or more owners	Income and lossess "pass through" to partners and are taxed at personal rate; flexibility in profit-loss allocations to partners	Unlimited personal liability	Ease of formation Pooled talent Pooled resources Somewhat easier access to financing Some tax benefits	Unlimited personal liability Divided authority and decisions Potential for conflict Continuity of transfer of ownership
Limited liability partnership (LLP)	Two or more owners	Income and lossess "pass through" to partners and are taxed at personal rate; flexibility in profit-loss allocations to partners	Limited although one partner must retain unlimited liability	Good way to acquire capital from limited partners	Cost and complexity of forming can be high Limited partners cannot participate in management of business without losing liability protection
C corporation	Unlimited number of shareholders; no limits on types of stocks or voting arrangements	Dividend income is taxed at corporate and personal shareholder levels; losses and deductions are corporate	Limited	Limited liability Transferable ownership Continuous existence Easier access to resources	Expensive to set up Closely regulated Double taxation Extensive record keeping Charter restrictions
S corporation	Up to 75 shareholders; no limits on types of stock or voting arrangements	Income and lossess "pass through" to partners and are taxed at personal rate; flexibility in profit-loss allocations to partners	Limited	Easy to set up Enjoy limited liability protection and tax benefits of partnership Can have a tax-exempt entity as a shareholder	Must meet certain requirements May limit future financing options
limited liability company (LLC)	Unlimited number of "members"; flexible membership arrangements for voting rights and income	Income and lossess "pass through" to partners and are taxed at personal rate; flexibility in profit-loss allocations to partners	Limited	Greater flexibility Not constrained by regulations on C and S corporations Taxed as partnership, not as corporation	Cost of switching from one form to this can be high Need legal and financial advice in forming operating agreement

Source: Robbins, Stephen P., Coulter, Mary, *Management* (Subscription), 14th Ed., © 2018. Reprinted and electronically reproduced by permission of Pearson Education, Inc., New York, NY.

go and allowing someone else to make decisions. *After all*, he or she reasons, *how can anyone know this business as well as I do?* Also, what might have been a fairly informal, loose, and flexible atmosphere that worked well when the organization was small may no longer be effective. Many entrepreneurs are greatly concerned about keeping that "small company" atmosphere alive even as the venture grows and evolves into a more structured arrangement. But having a structured organization doesn't necessarily mean giving up flexibility, adaptability, and freedom. In fact, the structural design may be as fluid as the entrepreneur feels comfortable with and yet still have the rigidity it needs to operate efficiently.

Organizational design decisions in entrepreneurial ventures also revolve around the six elements of organizational structure that we'll be discussing in Chapter 7: work specialization, departmentalization, chain of command, span of control, amount of centralization-decentralization, and amount of formalization. Decisions about these six elements will determine whether an entrepreneur has a more traditional or a more flexible design.

What Human Resource Management Issues Do Entrepreneurs Face?

As an entrepreneurial venture grows, additional employees must be hired to perform the increased workload. As employees are brought on board, two human resource management (HRM) issues of particular importance are employee recruitment and employee retention.

EMPLOYEE RECRUITMENT.   An entrepreneur wants to ensure that the venture has the people to do the required work. Recruiting new employees is one of the biggest challenges that entrepreneurs face. In fact, the ability of small firms to successfully recruit appropriate employees is consistently rated as one of the most important factors influencing organizational success.

Managing Technology in Today's Workplace

STARTUP IDEAS: CASHING IN ON TECHNOLOGY

We're going to do something a little different in this chapter's Managing Technology box. We thought it might be fun to look at some of the interesting and intriguing startup ideas found in recent news stories:

- Spoiler Alert was launched to address the $57 billion of food waste from restaurants, grocery stores, and commercial kitchens in the United States. The startup helps food manufacturers and wholesale distributors manage their unsold inventory and increase donations to food banks and other community programs.[27]

- When Washington, DC's popular Mediterranean restaurant Cava Mezze decided to expand its Cava Grill restaurant chain, it used a secret ingredient lovingly called "Raspberry Pi." Raspberry Pi is the technology behind a system of sensors that Cava uses to monitor everything from back-of-house operations and sound levels to customer wait times and food safety practices.[28]

- Ever had some autumn fun going through a corn maze? Maize Quest is a Pennsylvania business that uses high-tech digital technology to create elaborate, themed corn maze designs and then programs GPS-guided tractors to quickly carve those designs into cornfields.[29]

- Hari Mari is making flip-flops smarter. Like any brand that sells through other retailers, Hari Mari found it difficult to gather data about its customers. The company turned to former NFL pro Emmitt Smith, whose company designed a chip that could be embedded into products and electronically track the origins. With the chip-enabled flip-flops, customers will be able to download an app, giving them access to discounts and the ability to communicate directly with the company.[30]

- Antoine Hubert, co-founder and CEO of Ÿnsect (pronounced "IN-sect), is pursuing mealworm beetle larvae as a solution for a global food crisis. The "bugs" are turned into a super-high-protein product that can be fed to cows, chickens, fish, and pigs.[31]

- StepNpull is a simple device that allows bathroom users to open a door without touching their freshly washed hands to a dirty door handle. The product was introduced in 2007, and customers range from NASA and IKEA to the U.S. Navy and Buffalo Wild Wings.[32]

- Diamond Foundry is disrupting the diamond industry. The San Francisco–based company, founded by R. Martin Roscheisen, Jeremy Scholz, and Kyle Gazay, uses plasma reactors to turn tiny bits of diamond into gemstones. These diamonds look amazing and tend to sell for less than mined varieties.[33]

Discussion Questions:

3 Which one of these sounds like something you'd invest in? Why?

4 Write a list of questions you'd want to ask the founder(s) about the business.

Entrepreneurs, particularly, look for high-potential people who can perform multiple roles during various stages of venture growth. They look for individuals who "buy into" the venture's entrepreneurial culture—individuals who have a passion for the business. Unlike their corporate counterparts who often focus on filling a job by matching a person to the job requirements, entrepreneurs look to fill in critical skills gaps. They're looking for people who are exceptionally capable and self-motivated, flexible, and multiskilled and who can help grow the entrepreneurial venture. While corporate managers tend to focus on using traditional HRM practices and techniques, entrepreneurs are more concerned with matching characteristics of the person to the values and culture of the organization; that is, they focus on matching the person to the organization.

EMPLOYEE RETENTION. Getting competent and qualified people into the venture is just the first step in effectively managing the human resources. An entrepreneur wants to keep the people he or she has hired and trained. Scott Signore, founder and CEO of Matter Communications, a public relations agency based in Newburyport, Massachusetts, understands the importance of having good people on board and embracing a healthy, energetic, fun culture that sets it apart from others. The company's fun culture has helped land it on the *Boston Globe*'s Top Places to Work for three years in a row.[34]

A unique and important employee retention issue entrepreneurs must deal with is compensation. Whereas traditional organizations are more likely to view compensation from the perspective of monetary rewards (base pay, benefits, and incentives), smaller entrepreneurial firms are more likely to view compensation from a total rewards perspective. For these firms, compensation encompasses psychological rewards, learning opportunities, and recognition in addition to monetary rewards (base pay and incentives).

What's Involved in Leading an Entrepreneurial Venture?

The employees at software firm ClearCompany have to be flexible. Everyone is expected to contribute ideas. CEO and co-founder Andre Levoie said, "One way to give employees more [creative] freedom over how they work is to shift the focus from to-do lists and deadlines to goals and objectives—quantity to quality." In return, Levoie is a supportive leader who gives his employees considerable latitude.[35]

Taking on the role of a LEADER . . .

Leading is an important function of entrepreneurs. As an entrepreneurial venture grows and people are brought on board, an entrepreneur takes on a new role—that of a leader. In this section, we want to look at what's involved with that. First, we're going to look at the unique personality characteristics of entrepreneurs. Then we're going to discuss the important role entrepreneurs play in motivating employees through empowerment and leading the venture and employee teams.

What Type of Personality Characteristics Do Entrepreneurs Have?

Think of someone you know who is an entrepreneur. Maybe it's someone you personally know or maybe it's someone you've read about, like Elon Musk of Tesla and SpaceX or Bill Gates of Microsoft. How would you describe this person's personality? One of the most researched areas of entrepreneurship has been the search

Swedish entrepreneur Daniel Ek, co-founder and chief executive of Spotify, is proactive, self-confident, persistent, highly motivated, self-directed, resourceful, patient, and passionate about his work. These traits have contributed to Ek's success in launching the company, convincing investors that his music business was a good investment, and leading Spotify's rapid growth to become the biggest music-streaming service in the world.

Toru Yamanaka/AFP/Getty Images

to determine what—if any—psychological characteristics entrepreneurs have in common, what types of personality traits entrepreneurs have that might distinguish them from non-entrepreneurs, and what traits entrepreneurs have that might predict who will be a successful entrepreneur.

Is there a classic "entrepreneurial personality"? Trying to pinpoint specific personality characteristics that *all* entrepreneurs share is a problem. However, this hasn't stopped entrepreneurship researchers from listing common traits. For instance, one list of personality characteristics included the following: high level of motivation, abundance of self-confidence, ability to be involved for the long term, high energy level, persistent problem solver, high degree of initiative, ability to set goals, and moderate risk-taker. Another list of characteristics of "successful" entrepreneurs included high energy level, great persistence, resourcefulness, the desire and ability to be self-directed, and relatively high need for autonomy.

Another development in defining entrepreneurial personality characteristics was the proactive personality scale to predict an individual's likelihood of pursuing entrepreneurial ventures. The **proactive personality** is a personality trait describing those individuals who are more prone to take actions to influence their environment—that is, they're more proactive. Obviously, an entrepreneur is likely to exhibit proactivity as he or she searches for opportunities and acts to take advantage of those opportunities. Various items on the proactive personality scale were found to be good indicators of a person's likelihood of becoming an entrepreneur, including gender, education, having an entrepreneurial parent, and possessing a proactive personality. In addition, studies have shown that entrepreneurs have greater risk propensity than do managers. However, this propensity is moderated by the entrepreneur's primary goal. Risk propensity is greater for entrepreneurs whose primary goal is growth versus those whose focus is on producing family income.

proactive personality
A personality trait describing those individuals who are more prone to take actions to influence their environment

employee empowerment
Giving employees the power to make decisions and take actions on their own

How Can Entrepreneurs Motivate Employees?

At Sapient Corporation, a technology marketing and consulting company, co-founders Jerry Greenberg and J. Stuart Moore recognized that employee motivation was vitally important to their company's success.[36] They designed their organization so individual employees are part of an industry-specific team that works on an entire project rather than on one small piece of it. Their rationale was that people often feel frustrated when they're doing a small part of a job and never get to see the whole job from start to finish. They figured employees would be more motivated—and productive—if they got the opportunity to participate in all phases of a project.

When you're motivated to do something, don't you find yourself energized and willing to work hard at doing whatever it is you're excited about? Wouldn't it be great if all of a venture's employees were energized, excited, and willing to work hard at their jobs? Having motivated employees is an important goal for any entrepreneur, and employee empowerment is an important motivational tool entrepreneurs can use.

Although it's not easy for entrepreneurs to do, **employee empowerment**—giving employees the power to make decisions and take actions on their own—is an important motivational approach. Why? Because successful entrepreneurial ventures must be quick and nimble, ready to pursue opportunities and go off in new directions. Empowered employees can provide that flexibility and speed. When employees are empowered, they often display stronger work motivation, better work quality, higher job satisfaction, and lower turnover.

What about YOU? Do you find it easy to let others do
things that you normally have control over?

Empowerment is a philosophical concept that entrepreneurs have to "buy into." It doesn't come easily. In fact, it's hard for many entrepreneurs to do. Their life is tied

When entrepreneurs go bad. Mozido Inc. probably isn't a startup you've ever heard of. But its founder, Michael Liberty, was accused by the Securities and Exchange Commission of using millions stolen from Mozido to fund his lavish lifestyle. (Think...chartered flights, a dairy cow farm, and a movie production project by his former girlfriend.) Mozido, a fintech (financial technology) company, was established to provide mobile wallets and other payment products to almost 2 billion people globally who have no bank accounts. Sounds like a perfectly great idea, huh? However, Mr. Liberty and his associates were "tricking investors into believing they were funding fast-growing startup companies. They were not."[37]

When entrepreneurs go bad. Theranos Inc. was a company that set out to revolutionize the blood-testing industry. CEO Elizabeth Holmes, who dropped out of Stanford University as a 19-year-old sophomore, was widely lauded as Silicon Valley's first female billionaire startup founder. However, she was charged with fraud for raising more than $700 million from investors while deceiving them about what her company's technology was actually capable of. Holmes agreed to a settlement with federal regulators that took away her voting control of the company, banned her from being an officer or director of any public company for 10 years, and required that she pay a $500,000 penalty.[38]

These certainly aren't the only instances of entrepreneurs acting unethically or illegally. Just two of the most recent. When entrepreneurs go bad, their decisions and behaviors have a profound impact on the companies they founded, as well as the people who backed the companies and the individuals employed by the companies.

Discussion Questions:

5 A founder (entrepreneur) is expected to be the leader—the figurehead—of a startup. Could these circumstances have been prevented? Or are people who are going to make unethical/illegal choices just an unfortunate reality? Discuss.

6 What advice would you give a potential entrepreneur about being an ethical leader? In your "assigned" group, come up with a list of suggestions.

up in the business. They've built it from the ground up. But continuing to grow the entrepreneurial venture is eventually going to require handing over more responsibilities to employees. How can entrepreneurs empower employees? For many entrepreneurs, it's a gradual process.

Entrepreneurs can begin by ❶ using participative decision making, in which employees provide input into decisions. Although getting employees to participate in decisions isn't quite taking the full plunge into employee empowerment, at least it's a way to begin tapping into the collective array of employees' talents, skills, knowledge, and abilities.

Another way to empower employees is through ❷ delegation—the process of assigning certain decisions or specific job duties to employees. By delegating decisions and duties, the entrepreneur is turning over the responsibility for carrying them out.

When an entrepreneur is finally comfortable with the idea of employee empowerment, fully empowering employees means ❸ redesigning their jobs so they have discretion over the way they do their work. It's allowing employees to do their work effectively and efficiently by using their creativity, imagination, knowledge, and skills.

If an entrepreneur implements employee empowerment properly—that is, with complete and total commitment to the program and with appropriate employee training—results can be impressive for the entrepreneurial venture and for the empowered employees. The business can enjoy significant productivity gains, quality improvements, more satisfied customers, increased employee motivation, and improved morale. Employees can enjoy the opportunities to do a greater variety of work that is more interesting and challenging.

How Can Entrepreneurs Be Leaders?

The last topic we want to discuss in this section is the role of an entrepreneur as a leader. In this role, the entrepreneur has certain leadership responsibilities in leading the venture and in leading employee work teams.

Today's successful entrepreneur must be like the leader of a jazz ensemble known for its improvisation, innovation, and creativity. Max DePree, former head of Herman Miller Inc., a leading office furniture manufacturer known for its innovative leadership approaches, said it best in his book, *Leadership Jazz*, "Jazz band leaders must choose the music, find the right musicians, and perform—in public. But the effect of the performance depends on so many things—the environment, the volunteers playing the band, the need for everybody to perform as individuals and as a group, the absolute dependence of the leader on the members of the band, the need for the followers to play well. . . . The leader of the jazz band has the beautiful opportunity to draw the best out of the other musicians. We have much to learn from jazz band leaders, for jazz, like leadership, combines the unpredictability of the future with the gifts of individuals."

The way an entrepreneur leads the venture should be much like the jazz leader—drawing the best out of other individuals, even given the unpredictability of the situation. One way an entrepreneur does this is through the vision he or she creates for the organization. In fact, the driving force through the early stages of the entrepreneurial venture is often the visionary leadership of the entrepreneur. The entrepreneur's ability to articulate a coherent, inspiring, and attractive vision of the future is a key test of his or her leadership. But if an entrepreneur can do this, the results can be worthwhile. A study contrasting visionary and nonvisionary companies showed that visionary companies outperformed the nonvisionary ones by six times on standard financial criteria, and their stocks outperformed the general market by 15 times.

Many organizations—entrepreneurial and otherwise—are using employee work teams to perform organizational tasks, create new ideas, and resolve problems. The three most common types of employee work teams in entrepreneurial ventures are empowered teams (teams that have the authority to plan and implement process improvements), self-directed teams (teams that are nearly autonomous and responsible for many managerial activities), and cross-functional teams (work teams composed of individuals from various specialties who work together on various tasks).

Developing and using teams is necessary because technology and market demands are forcing entrepreneurial ventures to make products faster, cheaper, and better. Tapping into the collective wisdom of a venture's employees and empowering them to make decisions just may be one of the best ways to adapt to change. In addition, a team culture can improve the overall workplace environment and morale. For team efforts to work, however, entrepreneurs must shift from the traditional command-and-control style to a coach-and-collaboration style.

Media entrepreneur Robert Johnson cofounded Black Entertainment Television (BET), the first U.S. network targeting the African-American market. One of Johnson's major challenges in managing the growth of BET was getting advertisers and investors to support the expansion of the network's airtime from 2 hours a day to 24 hours a day. Securing financial backing helped BET grow to become one of the richest franchises in the cable industry

What's Involved in Controlling an Entrepreneurial Venture?

Philip McCaleb still gets a kick out of riding the scooters his Chicago-based company, Genuine Scooter Company, makes. However, in building his business, McCaleb has had to acknowledge his own limitations. As a self-described "idea guy," he knew that he would need someone else to come in and ensure that the end product was *what* it was supposed to be, was *where* it was supposed to be, and was there *when* it was supposed to be.[39]

Entrepreneurs must look at controlling their venture's operations in order to survive and prosper in both the short run and long run. The unique control issues that face entrepreneurs include managing growth, managing downturns, exiting the venture, and managing personal life choices and challenges.

How Is Growth Managed?

Growth is a natural and desirable outcome for entrepreneurial ventures. Growth is what distinguishes an entrepreneurial venture. Entrepreneurial ventures pursue growth. Growing slowly can be successful but so can rapid growth.

Growing successfully doesn't occur randomly or by luck. Successfully pursuing growth typically requires an entrepreneur to manage all the challenges associated with growing, which entails planning, organizing, and controlling for growth.

How Are Downturns Managed?

Although organizational growth is a desirable and important goal for entrepreneurial ventures, what happens when things don't go as planned—when the growth strategies don't result in the intended outcomes and, in fact, result in a decline in performance? There are challenges, as well, in managing the downturns.

Nobody likes to fail, especially entrepreneurs. However, when an entrepreneurial venture faces times of trouble, what can be done? How can downturns be managed successfully? The first step is recognizing that a crisis is brewing. An entrepreneur should be alert to the warning signs of a business in trouble. Some signals of potential performance decline include inadequate or negative cash flow, excess number of employees, unnecessary and cumbersome administrative procedures, fear of conflict and taking risks, tolerance of work incompetence, lack of a clear mission or goals, and ineffective or poor communication within the organization.

Although an entrepreneur hopes to never have to deal with organizational downturns, declines, or crises, these situations do occur. After all, nobody likes to think about things going bad or taking a turn for the worse. But that's exactly what the entrepreneur should do—think about it *before* it happens (we'll discuss feedforward control in Chapter 14). It's important to have an up-to-date plan for covering crises. It's like mapping exit routes from your home in case of a fire. An entrepreneur wants to be prepared before an emergency hits. This plan should focus on providing specific details for controlling the most fundamental and critical aspects of running the venture—cash flow, accounts receivable, costs, and debt. Beyond having a plan for controlling the venture's critical inflows and outflows, other actions would involve identifying specific strategies for cutting costs and restructuring the venture.

What's Involved with Exiting the Venture?

Getting out of an entrepreneurial venture may seem to be a strange thing for entrepreneurs to do. However, the entrepreneur may come to a point at which he or she decides it's time to move on. That decision may be based on the fact that the entrepreneur hopes to capitalize financially on the investment in the venture—called **harvesting**—or that the entrepreneur is facing serious organizational performance problems and wants to get out, or even on the entrepreneur's desire to focus on other pursuits (personal or business). The issues involved with exiting the venture include choosing a proper business valuation method and knowing what's involved in the process of selling a business.

Although the hardest part of preparing to exit a venture may involve valuing it, other factors are also important. These include being prepared, deciding who will sell the business, considering the tax implications, screening potential buyers, and deciding whether to tell employees before or after the sale. The process of exiting the entrepreneurial venture should be approached as carefully as the process of launching it. If the entrepreneur is selling the venture on a positive note, he or she wants to realize the value built up in the business. If the venture is being exited because of declining performance, the entrepreneur wants to maximize the potential return.

Why Is It Important to Think about Managing Personal Challenges as an Entrepreneur?

Being an entrepreneur is extremely exciting and fulfilling, yet extremely demanding. It involves long hours, difficult demands, and high stress. Yet, many rewards can come with being an entrepreneur as well. In this section, we want to look at how entrepreneurs can make it work—that is, how can they be successful and effectively balance the demands of their work and personal lives?

Entrepreneurs are a special group. They're focused, persistent, hardworking, and intelligent. Because they put so much of themselves into launching and growing their entrepreneurial ventures, many may neglect their personal lives. Entrepreneurs often have to make sacrifices to pursue their entrepreneurial dreams. However, they can make it work. They can balance their work and personal lives. But how?

One of the most important things an entrepreneur can do is *become a good time manager*. Prioritize what needs to be done. Use a planner (daily, weekly, monthly) to help schedule

harvesting
Exiting a venture when an entrepreneur hopes to capitalize financially on the investment in the venture

priorities. Some entrepreneurs don't like taking the time to plan or prioritize, or they think it's a ridiculous waste of time. Yet identifying the important duties and distinguishing them from those that aren't so important actually makes an entrepreneur more efficient and effective. In addition, part of being a good time manager is delegating those decisions and actions the entrepreneur doesn't have to be personally involved in to trusted employees. Although it may be hard to let go of some of the things they've always done, entrepreneurs who delegate effectively will see their personal productivity levels rise.

Another suggestion for finding that balance is to *seek professional advice* in those areas of business where it's needed. Although entrepreneurs may be reluctant to spend scarce cash, the time and energy saved and potential problems avoided in the long run are well worth the investment. Competent professional advisors can provide entrepreneurs with information to make more intelligent decisions. Also, it's important to *deal with conflicts* as they arise—both workplace and family conflicts. If an entrepreneur doesn't deal with conflicts, negative feelings are likely to crop up and lead to communication breakdowns. When communication falls apart, vital information may get lost, and people (employees *and* family members) may start to assume the worst. It can turn into a nightmare situation that feeds on itself. The best strategy is to deal with conflicts as they come up. Talk, discuss, argue (if you must), but an entrepreneur shouldn't avoid the conflict or pretend it doesn't exist.

Another suggestion for achieving that balance between work and personal life is to *develop a network of trusted friends and peers*. Having a group of people to talk with is a good way for an entrepreneur to think through problems and issues. The support and encouragement offered by these people can be an invaluable source of strength for an entrepreneur.

Finally, *recognize when your stress levels are too high*. Entrepreneurs *are* achievers. They like to make things happen. They thrive on working hard. Yet, too much stress can lead to significant physical and emotional problems (as we discuss in Chapter 5). Entrepreneurs have to learn when stress is overwhelming them and to do something about it. After all, what's the point of growing and building a thriving entrepreneurial venture if you're not around to enjoy it?

Skill Basics

Grit can be developed. The following steps will help you in practicing this skill.

- *Practice your resilience.* Resilience is the ability to bounce back. As you are faced with an obstacle . . . in school or even at work, if you're employed . . . notice your reaction to the challenge. Are you ready to quit? If so, it is time to build your resilience. Learn from your mistake and make yourself give it another try instead of giving up.

- *Pursue your passion.* Figure out what you are passionate about in life and pursue it. Our passions inspire us and give us the internal drive to keep moving forward. Identifying and pursuing your passion can help develop your perseverance.

- *Practice positive self-talk.* Grit means you have a strong belief in yourself. By engaging in positive self-talk, you can develop the internal motivation to keep moving forward even as you face obstacles. Remind yourself of your abilities and be your own biggest cheerleader. With every challenge you face, make sure you encourage yourself to keep moving forward with a positive attitude.

- *Build in practice time.* Understand that anything significant you are going to accomplish in life is going to take time and effort. When working toward a goal, you must consider how you can practice whatever it is you are trying to accomplish. For example, if you have the dream to open a restaurant, spend some time working in other restaurants to really understand the business before jumping in on your own.

- *Put together a support team.* Identify some trusted friends and let them know you are working on developing grit. Share with them your future goals and what you want to work toward. Ask them to encourage you when you're doubting yourself. Make sure you call them for support when you're feeling like you might want to give up.

Practicing The Skill

Identify a challenging goal you would like to attain. You can start small, but make sure it is something that will test your abilities. Remember you're trying to develop grit . . . perseverance and passion! For example, have you ever considered running a 5k race? Getting an A in your next statistics course? What is something significant you would like to accomplish?

Once you set your goal, use the steps above as you work toward your goal. Once you accomplish your goal, move on to a new one. As you overcome the challenges along the way, you'll find yourself developing grit. And then, you can accomplish anything!

Experiential Exercise

Entrepreneurship is highly regarded in many parts of the world. But, what if pursuing an entrepreneurial venture just isn't for you? Have you just wasted your time reading and studying this chapter? We hope not! Thinking entrepreneurially, even in a non-EV setting can give you a career edge. There are things that we've talked about in this chapter that you could use in your career to "become more entrepreneurial!" So, in this Experiential Exercise, you'll be working with your assigned group to come up with 7 Career Lessons for Being Entrepreneurial. Come up with seven things from this chapter that you think could help you think entrepreneurially and be useful to you in your career. Write them down, discuss why you think they're important, and explain how they could be applied in your career.

Endnotes

1. D. Gage, "Software for the Blue-Collar Workforce," *Wall Street Journal Online,* March 9, 2018.

2. K. Angel, "The Soft Edge That's Landing Solid Sales," *Bloomberg Businessweek,* August 28, 2017, pp. 39–40.

3. J. Chun, "To Tell the Truth," *Entrepreneur,* April 1998, pp. 106–113; and D. Kansas, "Don't Believe It," *Wall Street Journal,* October 15, 1993, p. R8.

4. U.S. Bureau of Labor Statistics, "Glossary," www.bls.gov, accessed March 26, 2018.

5. S. Narayanan, "How Can a Fintech Company Win 20 Million Customers?" *Stratey+Business Online,* March 14, 2018.

6. "The World's 50 Most Innovative Companies," *Fast Company,* March 2018, p. 86.

7. R. D. Hisrich and M. P. Peters, *Entrepreneurship* (Boston, MA: Irwin McGraw-Hill, 1998), p. 7.

8. J. Cunningham and J. Lescheron, "Defining Entrepreneurship," *Journal of Small Business Management,* January 1991, pp. 45–61.

9. "The Third Millennium: Small Business and Entrepreneurship in the Twenty-First Century," Office of Advocacy, U.S. Small Business Administration, www.sba.gov.

10. 2017 The Kauffman Index of Startup Activity, Kauffman Foundation, www.kauffman.org/kauffman-index.

11. M. J. Kravis, "The Great Productivity Slowdown," *Wall Street Journal,* May 5, 2017, p. A15.

12. R. J. Dilger, "Small Business Administration and Job Creation," Congressional Research Service, fas.org, February 2, 2018.

13. Global Report, 2017/18, Global Entrepreneurship Research Association, www.gemconsortium.org/report, 2018.

14. W. Royal, "Real Expectations," *Industry Week,* September 4, 2000, pp. 31–34.

15. D. Bornstein, "Recycling Unused Medicines to Save Money and Lives," *New York Times Online,* March 20, 2015.

16. C. Sundlund, "Trust Is a Must," *Entrepreneur,* October 2002, pp. 70–75.

17. B. I. Koerner, "Cereal in the Bowl, Not on the Floor," *New York Times* online, June 18, 2006.

18. G. B. Knight, "How Wall Street Whiz Found a Niche Selling Books on the Internet," *Wall Street Journal,* May 15, 1996, pp. A1+.

19. N. F. Krueger Jr., "The Cognitive Infrastructure of Opportunity Emergence," *Entrepreneurship Theory and Practice,* Spring 2000, p. 6.

20. D. P. Forbes, "Managerial Determinants of Decision Speed in New Ventures," *Strategic Management Journal,* April 2005, pp. 355–366.

21. M. Penn, "Small Trends Can Be Big," *Wall Street Journal,* March 17–18, 2018, p. C4.

22. P. Drucker, *Innovation and Entrepreneurship* (New York: Harper & Row, 1985).

23. P. Reikofski, "Where 'Aha' Comes From," *Wall Street Journal,* April 29, 2013, p. R2.

24. S. Greco, "The Start-Up Years," *Inc.500,* October 21, 1997, p. 57.

25. F. J. Greene and C. Hopp, "Are Formal Planners More Likely to Achieve New Venture Viability? A Counterfactual Model and Analysis," *Strategic Entrepreneurship Journal,* 2017, cited in *Harvard Business Review,* November–December 2017, p. 26.

26. C. Forrest, "How to Structure Your Startup as the Company Grows," *Tech Republic Online,* www.techrepublic.com, September 22, 2015.

27. H. Haddon, "Startups Serve Leftover Food to Market," *Wall Street Journal,* November 10, 2017, p. B4.

28. B. Paynter, "Made to Order," *FastCompany.com,* April 2017, p. 42.

29. S. Melendez, "Inside the Surprisingly High-Tech World of Corn Mazes," *FastCompany online,* December 1, 2017.

30. E. Segrano, "It Only Took 5,000 Years, But the Flip-Flop Is Finally Getting Smarter," *FastCompany online,* March 28, 2017.

31. V. Walt, "A Very Grubby Business," *Fortune,* April 1, 2018, pp. 27–29.

32. A. Zhu, "Springfield's StepNpull's Newest Customer is NASA," *Springfield, Missouri News-Leader,* April 1, 2018, p. 4A.

33. S. Mariker, "Disrupting DeBeers," *Fortune,* April 1, 2018, pp. 15–16.

34. "The Boston Globe Names PR Agency Matter Communications A Top Place to Work for 2015," *BusinessWire Online,* www.businesswire.com, November 16, 2015.

35. A. Levoie, "The Top Thing Employees Want from Their Bosses, and It's Not a Promotion," *Entrepreneur Online,* March 31, 2015.

36. S. Herrera, "People Power," *Forbes,* November 2, 1998, p. 212.

37. P. Rudegeair and R. Copeland, "Startup's Founder Is Accused of Fraud," *Wall Street Journal,* April 3, 2018, p. B10.

38. J. Carreyrou, "Theranos and CEO Punished in Fraud," *Wall Street Journal,* March 15, 2018, pp. A1+.

39. T. Siegel Bernard, "Scooter's Popularity Offers a Chance for Growth," *Wall Street Journal,* September 20, 2005, p. B3.

Planning and Goal Setting

6

Management Myth **Myth** Myth

Planning is a waste of time because no one can predict the future.

ESB Professional/Shutterstock

Management Myth DEBUNKED?

People say that the future is unpredictable. **No matter how well you plan, there's always the unexpected.** For managers, it might be a sudden recession, a new and innovative product from a competitor, the loss of a key customer, the loss of a key employee, or the breakdown of a long-established business model. This logic has led many to conclude that planning is a waste of time. Well, it's not. Flexible planning that includes multiple scenarios can prepare managers for a variety of situations, eliminating some of the unpredictability.

AS we learned in Chapter 1, organizations have a purpose, people, and a structure that supports and enables those people in carrying out that purpose. And in those organizations, managers develop goals, plans, and strategies for how best to achieve that purpose. For instance, Toyota Motor Corporation's president recently said that hybrid and electric vehicles would make up half of the company's global sales by 2030.[1] To achieve that goal, managers will establish plans and strategies. And, after evaluating the outcomes of those plans and strategies, managers might have to change direction as conditions change. But it all starts with planning! This chapter presents the basics of planning. You'll learn what planning is, how managers use strategic management, and how they set goals and establish plans. Finally, we'll look at some contemporary planning issues managers face. ●

Learning Outcomes

6-1 Discuss the nature and purposes of planning. p. 213

6-2 Explain what managers do in the strategic management process. p. 215

6-3 Compare and contrast approaches to goal setting and planning. p. 224

6-4 Discuss contemporary issues in planning. p. 230

What Is Planning and Why Do Managers Need to Plan?

6-1 Discuss the nature and purposes of planning.

All **managers plan**. Even if you're not a manager, you're likely to have to **plan when, where, and how to get your work assignments done**.

Planning is often called the primary management function because it establishes the basis for all the other things managers do as they organize, lead, and control. What is meant by the term *planning*? As we said in Chapter 1, planning involves defining the organization's objectives or goals, establishing an overall strategy for achieving those goals, and developing a comprehensive hierarchy of plans to integrate and coordinate activities. It's concerned with ends (*what* is to be done) as well as with means (*how* it's to be done).

Planning can be further defined in terms of whether it's *formal* or *informal*. All managers plan, even if it's only informally. In informal planning, very little, if anything, is written down. What is to be accomplished is in the heads of one or a few people. Furthermore, the organization's goals are rarely verbalized. Informal planning generally describes the planning that takes place in many smaller businesses. The owner-manager has an idea of where he or she wants to go and how he or she expects to get there. The planning may be general and lack continuity. Of course, you'll see informal planning in some large organizations, while some small businesses will have sophisticated formal plans. (See the Entrepreneurship Module for more in-depth information on planning in small and entrepreneurial organizations.)

When we use the term *planning* in this text, we're referring to formal planning. Formal planning means (1) defining specific goals covering a specific time period, (2) writing down these goals and making them available to organization members, and (3) using these goals to develop specific plans that clearly define the path the organization will take to get from where it is to where it wants to be.

Why Should Managers Formally Plan?

How does Wal-Mart Stores Inc.—the world's largest retailer with more than 11,700 stores worldwide—hope to compete against online giant Amazon? Walmart, like the other big-box retailers, didn't immediately recognize the online revolution. Most have struggled to come up with a plan to compete, if not beat, Amazon. After several years of futile attempts to capture online shoppers, Walmart has a new plan to win at e-commerce. Despite the challenges of taking on the industry behemoth (Amazon), Walmart.com now is the second-biggest e-commerce destination in the United States.[2] And Walmart's managers—from corporate to individual stores—know that planning is and will continue to be vital to the company's continued success excelling at brick-and-mortar *and* online shopping.[3]

Managers should plan for at least four reasons. (See Exhibit 6–1.) First, planning *establishes coordinated effort*. It gives direction to managers and nonmanagerial employees. When all organizational members understand where the organization is going and what they must contribute to reach the goals, they can begin to coordinate their activities, thus fostering teamwork and cooperation. On the other hand, not planning can cause organizational members or work units to work against one another and keep the organization from moving efficiently toward its goals.

Second, planning *reduces uncertainty* by forcing managers to look ahead, anticipate change, consider the impact of change, and develop appropriate responses. It also clarifies the consequences of the actions managers might take in response to change. Planning, then, is precisely what managers need in a changing environment.

Third, planning *reduces overlapping and wasteful activities*. Coordinating efforts and responsibilities before the fact is likely to uncover waste and redundancy. Furthermore, when means and ends are clear, inefficiencies become obvious.

Exhibit 6–1 Reasons for Planning

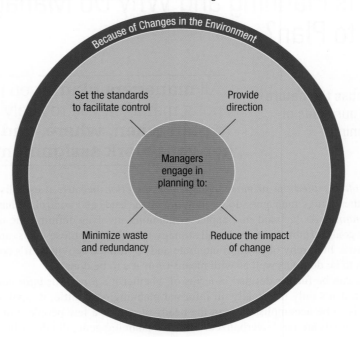

Finally, planning *establishes the goals or standards* that facilitate control. If organizational members aren't sure what they're working toward, how can they assess whether they've achieved it? When managers plan, they develop goals and plans. When they control, they see whether the plans have been carried out and the goals met. (We'll discuss controlling in depth in Chapter 14.) If significant deviations are identified, corrective action can be taken. Without planning, there are no goals against which to measure or evaluate work efforts.

What Are Some Criticisms of Formal Planning and How Should Managers Respond?

It makes sense for an organization to establish goals and direction, but critics have challenged some of the basic assumptions of planning.[4]

Criticism: *Planning may create rigidity.* Formal planning efforts can lock an organization into specific goals to be achieved within specific timetables. Such goals may have been set under the assumption that the environment wouldn't change. Forcing a course of action when the environment is random and unpredictable can be a recipe for disaster.

> **Manager's Response:** Managers need to remain flexible and not be tied to a course of action simply because it's the plan.

Criticism: *Formal plans can't replace intuition and creativity.* Successful organizations are typically the result of someone's vision, but these visions have a tendency to become formalized as they evolve. If formal planning efforts reduce the vision to a programmed routine, that too can lead to disaster.

> **Manager's Response:** Planning should enhance and support intuition and creativity, not replace it.

Criticism: *Planning focuses managers' attention on today's competition, not on tomorrow's survival.* Formal planning, especially strategic planning (which we'll discuss shortly), has a tendency to focus on how to best capitalize on existing business opportunities within the industry. Managers may not look at ways to re-create or reinvent the industry.

> **Manager's Response:** When managers plan, they should be open to forging into uncharted waters if there are untapped opportunities.

Criticism: *Formal planning reinforces success, which may lead to failure.* The American tradition has been that success breeds success. After all, if it's not broken, don't fix it. Right? Well maybe not! Success may, in fact, breed failure in an uncertain environment. It's hard to change or discard successful plans—to leave the comfort of what works for the uncertainty (and anxiety) of the unknown.

> **Manager's Response:** Managers may need to face that unknown and be open to doing things in new ways to be even more successful.

Does Formal Planning Improve Organizational Performance?

DOES it **PAY to PLAN**?

Does it pay to plan? Or have the critics of planning won the debate? Let's look at the evidence.

Contrary to what the critics of planning say, the evidence generally *supports* the position that organizations should have formal plans. Although most studies that have looked at the relationship between planning and performance have shown generally positive relationships, we can't say that organizations that formally plan always outperform those that don't.[5] But what can we conclude?

- *Formal planning* generally means higher profits, higher return on assets, and other positive financial results.
- The *quality of the planning process* and the *appropriate implementation of the plan* probably contribute more to high performance than does the extent of planning.
- In those organizations where formal planning did not lead to higher performance, the *environment*—for instance, governmental regulations, unforeseen economic challenges, and so forth—was often to blame. Why? Because managers may have fewer viable alternatives because of constraints in the environment.

One important aspect of an organization's formal planning is strategic planning, which managers do as part of the strategic management process.

What Do Managers Need to Know about Strategic Management?

6-2 Explain what managers do in the strategic management process.

- In order to satisfy customers' demands for less processed food, McDonald's has started using fresh beef in its Quarter Pounder burger. This move will complicate supply chain operations at its some 14,000 U.S. restaurants.[6]
- IBM reached a deal with The Weather Company to exploit opportunities for providing and distributing weather data. This type of data partnership is part of IBM's long-term strategy.[7]

- Because Japan is a fiercely competitive market for Coca-Cola, it introduces more than 100 new products a year there. The newest will have a splash of alcohol in it, Coca-Cola's first product in the alcohol category, known as chu-hi in Japan.[8]
- LEGO, the Danish maker of the familiar plastic bricks, continues to struggle as it and other toy companies attempt to compete for kids' attention amid the lure of videogames and other devices.[9]
- Apple's stockpile of cash topped $250 billion. The company was considering strategies for how best to use this strategic resource.[10]
- American Express's CEO is looking at strategies to competitively position itself with Millennials *and* to keep its current card users.[11]
- Target's CEO declares that the company's "strategy is working." After a dismal year, the company's multimillion plan to improve its stores and digital capabilities appears to be paying off.[12]

Zhang Xin, co-founder and CEO of SOHO China, poses in front of skyscrapers the firm built in Beijing. Xin and her husband started SOHO with a narrowly focused and highly successful strategy of developing commercial real estate in prime locations in Beijing and Shanghai that features architecture reflecting the spirit of a changing modern China.

Ton Koene/Newscom

- Managers at Papa John's are trying to figure out strategies to stand out in a crowded pizza market.[13]
- Amazon announced that it's expanding its discounted Prime program, a move aimed directly at Walmart's target market.[14]

These are just a few stories about company strategies you'll usually find in the business news weekly, if not daily. As you can see, strategic management is very much an important part of what managers do.

What Is Strategic Management?

Strategic management is what managers do to develop an organization's strategies. What are an organization's **strategies**? They're the plans for how the organization will do what it's in business to do, how it will compete successfully, and how it will attract and satisfy its customers in order to achieve its goals.

Why Is Strategic Management Important?

Like other big-box retailers, Best Buy struggled to find its footing in a retail environment totally disrupted by Amazon. And like many of those retailers, Best Buy had to find a way to not just defend itself against Amazon, but to thrive. The company's CEO, Hubert Joly, a positive and cheerful Frenchman, said the company's turnaround strategy involved reshaping nearly every piece of the company's business. From top to bottom, all aspects of the company's business model were restructured. And the company's revenues have beaten Wall Street's expectations in six of the last seven quarters.[15] This company's team of managers obviously understood why strategic management is important!

Why *is* strategic management so important? *One reason is that it can make a difference in how well an organization performs.* Why do some businesses succeed and others fail, even when faced with the same environmental conditions? Research has found a generally positive relationship between strategic planning and performance.[16] Those companies that strategically plan appear to have better financial results than those organizations that don't.

Another reason it's important has to do with the fact that *managers in organizations of all types and sizes face continually changing situations* (recall our discussion in Chapter 4). They cope with this uncertainty by using the strategic management process to examine relevant factors in planning future actions.

Finally, strategic management is important because *organizations are complex and diverse and each part needs to work together to achieve the organization's goals.* Strategic management helps do this. For example, with more than 2.3 million employees worldwide working in various departments, functional areas, and stores, Walmart uses strategic management to help coordinate and focus employees' efforts on what's important.

It's important to note that *strategic management isn't just for business organizations.* Even organizations such as government agencies, hospitals, educational institutions, nonprofit arts organizations, and social agencies need it. For example, the skyrocketing costs of a college education, competition from for-profit companies offering alternative educational environments, state budgets being slashed because of declining revenues, and cutbacks in federal aid for students and research have led many university administrators to assess their colleges' aspirations and identify a market niche in which they can survive and prosper.

strategic management
What managers do to develop an organization's strategies

strategies
Plans for how the organization will do what it's in business to do, how it will compete successfully, and how it will attract its customers in order to achieve its goals

What Are the Steps in the Strategic Management Process?

The **strategic management process** (see Exhibit 6–2) is a six-step process that encompasses strategy planning, implementation, and evaluation. The first four steps describe the planning that must take place, but implementation and evaluation are just as important! Even the best strategies can fail if managers don't implement or evaluate them properly.

STEP 1: *Identifying the organization's current mission, goals, and strategies.* Every organization needs a **mission**—a statement of its purpose. Defining the mission forces managers to identify what it's in business to do. For instance, the mission of Avon is "To be the company that best understands and satisfies the product, service, and self-fulfillment needs of women on a global level."[17] The mission of the National Heart Foundation of Australia is to "reduce suffering and death from heart, stroke, and blood vessel disease in Australia." These statements provide clues to what these organizations see as their purpose. What should a mission statement include? Exhibit 6–3 describes some typical components.

It's also important for managers to identify current goals and strategies. Why? So managers have a basis for assessing whether they need to be changed.

STEP 2: *Doing an external analysis.* We discussed the external environment in Chapter 4. Analyzing that environment is a critical step in the strategic management process. Managers do an external analysis so they know, for instance, what the competition is doing, what pending legislation might affect the organization, or what the labor supply is like in locations where it operates. In an external analysis, managers should examine all components of the environment (economic, demographic, political/legal, sociocultural, technological, and global) to see the trends and changes.

Once they've analyzed the environment, managers need to pinpoint opportunities that the organization can exploit and threats that it must counteract or buffer against. **Opportunities** are positive trends in the external environment; **threats** are negative trends.

STEP 3: *Doing an internal analysis.* Now we move to the internal analysis, which provides important information about an organization's specific resources and capabilities. An organization's **resources** are its assets—financial, physical, human, and intangible—that it uses to develop, manufacture, and deliver products to its customers. They're "what" the organization has. On the other hand, its **capabilities** are the skills and abilities needed to do the work activities in its business—"how" it does its work. The major value-creating capabilities of the organization are known as its **core competencies**.[18] Both resources and core competencies determine the organization's competitive weapons.

---

strategic management process
A six-step process that encompasses strategy planning, implementation, and evaluation

mission
A statement of an organization's purpose

opportunities
Positive trends in the external environment

threats
Negative trends in the external environment

resources
An organization's assets that it uses to develop, manufacture, and deliver products to its customers

capabilities
An organization's skills and abilities in doing the work activities needed in its business

core competencies
The major value-creating capabilities of an organization

Exhibit 6–2 The Strategic Management Process

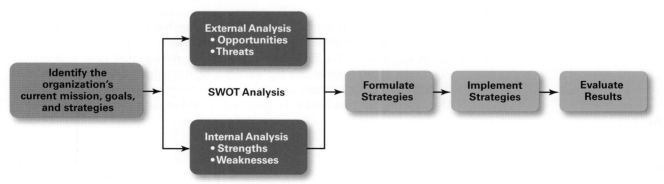

Exhibit 6–3 Components of a Mission Statement

Customers:	Who are the firm's customers?
Markets:	Where does the firm compete geographically?
Concern for survival, growth, and profitability:	Is the firm committed to growth and financial stability?
Philosophy:	What are the firm's basic beliefs, values, and ethical priorities?
Concern for public image:	How responsive is the firm to societal and environmental concerns?
Products or services:	What are the firm's major products or services?
Technology:	Is the firm technologically current?
Self-concept:	What are the firm's major competitive advantage and core competencies?
Concern for employees:	Are employees a valuable asset of the firm?

Source: Robbins, Stephen P., Coulter, Mary, *Management*, 13th Ed., © 2016, p. 238. Reprinted and electronically reproduced by permission of Pearson Education, Inc., New York, NY.

After completing an internal analysis, managers should be able to identify organizational strengths and weaknesses. Any activities the organization does well or any unique resources that it has are called **strengths**. **Weaknesses** are activities the organization doesn't do well or resources it needs but doesn't possess.

The combined external and internal analyses are called the **SWOT analysis** because it's an analysis of the organization's *s*trengths, *w*eaknesses, *o*pportunities, and *t*hreats. After completing the SWOT analysis, managers are ready to formulate appropriate strategies—that is, strategies that (1) exploit an organization's strengths and external opportunities, (2) buffer or protect the organization from external threats, or (3) correct critical weaknesses.

SWOT

STEP 4: *Formulating strategies.* As managers formulate strategies, they should consider the realities of the external environment and their available resources and capabilities and design strategies that will help an organization achieve its goals. Managers typically formulate three main types of strategies: corporate, business, and functional. We'll describe each shortly.

STEP 5: *Implementing strategies.* Once strategies are formulated, they must be implemented. No matter how effectively an organization has planned its strategies, performance will suffer if the strategies aren't implemented properly.

STEP 6: *Evaluating results.* The final step in the strategic management process is evaluating results. How effective have the strategies been at helping the organization reach its goals? What adjustments are necessary: Do assets need to be acquired or sold? Does the organization need to be reorganized? and so forth.

strengths
Any activities the organization does well or any unique resources that it has

weaknesses
Activities the organization doesn't do well or resources it needs but doesn't possess

SWOT analysis
The combined external and internal analyses

What Strategies Do Managers Use?

Exhibit 6–4 Organizational Strategies

Corporate		Multibusiness Corporation			
Competitive		Strategic Business Unit 1	Strategic Business Unit 2	Strategic Business Unit 3	
Functional	Research and Development	Manufacturing	Marketing	Human Resources	Finance

---

 1 **Corporate** Strategy `Multibusiness Corporation`

Specifies *what businesses* to be in and *what to do with those businesses.*

▶▶▶ Three main corporate strategies

❶ Growth Strategy. Organization expands the number of markets served or products offered, either through its current business(es) or through new business(es).

WAYS to grow:

- **Concentration:** Growing by focusing on primary line of business and increasing the number of products offered or markets served in this primary business.

- **Vertical integration:** Growing by gaining control of inputs or outputs or both.
  - Backward vertical integration—organization gains control of inputs by becoming its own supplier.
  - Forward vertical integration—organization gains control of outputs by becoming its own distributor.

- **Horizontal integration:** Growing by combining with competitors.

- **Diversification:** Growing by moving into a different industry.
  - Related diversification—different, but related, industries. "Strategic fit."
  - Unrelated diversification—different and unrelated industries. "No strategic fit."

Jojje11/Fotolia

❷ Stability Strategy. Organization continues—often during periods of uncertainty—to do what it is currently doing; to maintain things as they are.

- **Examples:** continuing to serve the same clients by offering the same product or service, maintaining market share, and sustaining current business operations.

The organization **doesn't grow**, but **doesn't fall** behind, either.

③ Renewal Strategy. Organization is in trouble and needs to address declining performance.

- **Retrenchment strategy:** Minor performance problems—need to stabilize operations, revitalize organizational resources and capabilities, and prepare organization to compete once again.

- **Turnaround strategy:** More serious performance problems requiring more drastic action.

In both renewal strategies, managers can (**1**) **cut costs** and (**2**) **restructure organizational operations**, but actions are more extensive in turnaround strategy.

2 Competitive Strategy

| Strategic Business Unit 1 | Strategic Business Unit 2 | Strategic Business Unit 3 |

How an organization will compete in its business(es).

- A small organization in only one line of business OR a large organization that has not diversified: Competitive strategy describes how it will compete in its primary or main market.

- Organizations in multiple businesses:

Each business will have its own competitive strategy.

- Those single businesses that are independent and formulate their own competitive strategies are often called **strategic bts units (SBUs)**.

▶ **Important Role of Competitive Advantage:**

Developing an effective competitive strategy requires understanding **competitive advantage**, which is what sets an organization apart; that is, its distinctive edge, which comes from:

- The *organization's core competencies*—doing something that others cannot do or doing it better than others can do it.
- The *company's resources*—having something that its competitors do not.

▼ **Types of Competitive Strategies:**

Porter's **competitive strategies** framework:[19]

① Cost leadership strategy	② Differentiation strategy	③ Focus strategy	④ Stuck in the middle
Having the lowest costs in its industry and aimed at broad market. • Highly efficient. • Overhead kept to a minimum. • Does everything it can to cut costs. • Product must be perceived as comparable in quality to that offered by rivals or at least acceptable to buyers.	Offering unique products that are widely valued by customers and aimed at broad market. • Product differences: exceptionally high quality, extraordinary service, innovative design, technological capability, or an unusually positive brand image.	A cost advantage (cost focus) or a differentiation advantage (differentiation focus) in a narrow segment or niche (which can be based on product variety, customer type, distribution channel, or geographical location).  Artursfoto/Fotolia	What happens if an organization can't develop a cost or differentiation advantage—bad place to be.

⟩⟩ Use **strategic management** to get a **sustainable competitive advantage.**

3 Functional Strategy

| Research and Development | Manufacturing | Marketing | Human Resources | Finance |

Those **strategies used by an organization's various functional departments** (marketing, operations, finance/accounting, human resources, and so forth) to support the competitive strategy.

What Strategic Weapons Do Managers Have?

If it's the Christmas/holiday season and you're a female between the ages of 25 to 54, you know where to turn for feel-good holiday movies. Yes, one of the Hallmark Channels. In 2018, between October–January, the company that owns the Hallmark-branded channels (Crown Media Family Network) premiered 34 new and original holiday movies. Each year's original (and rerun) movies have a sure-fire formula for success: "a quaint small town, flirtatious tree decorating, and snow." And the strategy works! The ratings among adult viewers under the age of 50 continue to grow. Company executives obviously understand how to successfully manage its various strategies in today's entertainment environment.[20]

In today's intensely competitive and chaotic marketplace, organizations are looking for whatever "weapons" they can use to do what they're in business to do and to achieve their goals. We think *six strategic "weapons" are important in today's environment*: ❶ customer service, ❷ employee skills and loyalty, ❸ innovation, ❹ quality, ❺ social media, and ❻ big data/digital tools. We've covered customer service in previous chapters and will discuss employee-related matters in Chapters 8 through 13. We've covered innovation in earlier chapters and will take a closer look, especially at disruptive innovation, in Chapter 5. That leaves the last three—quality, social media, and big data/digital tools—for us to look at now.

QUALITY AS A STRATEGIC WEAPON.   When W. K. Kellogg started manufacturing cornflake cereal in 1906, his goal was to provide customers with a high-quality, nutritious product that was enjoyable to eat. That *emphasis on quality is still important* today. Every Kellogg employee is responsible for maintaining the high quality of its products.

Many organizations use quality practices to build competitive advantage and attract and hold a loyal customer base. If implemented properly, *quality can be a way for an organization to create a sustainable competitive advantage.*[21] And if a business is able to continuously improve the quality and reliability of its products, it may have a competitive advantage that can't be taken away.[22] Incremental improvement is something that becomes an integrated part of an organization's operations and can develop into a considerable advantage.

Benchmark the best!

Managers in such diverse industries as health care, education, and financial services are discovering what manufacturers have long recognized—the benefits of **benchmarking**, which is the search for the best practices among competitors or noncompetitors that lead to their superior performance. The basic idea of benchmarking is that managers can improve quality by analyzing and then copying the methods of the leaders in various fields.

Backstory on BENCHMARKING

- *What:* First known benchmarking effort by an American company
- *When:* 1979
- *Who:* Xerox
- *How:* Japanese copier competitors had been traveling around, watching what others were doing and then using that knowledge to aggressively replicate their

---

corporate strategy
An organizational strategy that specifies what businesses a company is in or wants to be in and what it wants to do with those businesses

growth strategy
A corporate strategy in which an organization expands the number of markets served or products offered either through its current business(es) or through new business(es)

stability strategy
A corporate strategy in which an organization continues to do what it is currently doing

renewal strategy
A corporate strategy that addresses declining organizational performance

competitive strategy
An organizational strategy for how an organization will compete in its business(es)

strategic business units (SBUs)
An organization's single businesses that are independent and formulate their own competitive strategies

competitive advantage
What sets an organization apart; its distinctive edge

cost leadership strategy
When an organization competes on the basis of having the lowest costs in its industry

differentiation strategy
When an organization competes on the basis of having unique products that are widely valued by customers

focus strategy
When an organization competes in a narrow segment or niche with either a cost focus or a differentiation focus

functional strategy
Strategy used in an organization's various functional departments to support the competitive strategy

benchmarking
The search for the best practices among competitors or noncompetitors that lead to their superior performance

successes. Xerox's managers couldn't figure out how Japanese manufacturers could sell copiers in the United States for considerably less than Xerox's production costs.

- Xerox's head of manufacturing took a team to Japan to do a detailed study of its competitors' costs and processes. SPOILER ALERT! The team found their Japanese rivals light years ahead of Xerox in efficiency.
- Xerox benchmarked those efficiencies and began its strategic turnaround in the copier market.
- And there you have it, the history behind benchmarking!

Today, many organizations use benchmarking practices. For instance, the American Medical Association developed more than 100 standard performance measures to improve medical care. Nissan benchmarked Walmart's operations in purchasing, transportation, and logistics. And Southwest Airlines studied Indy 500 pit crews, who can change a race car's tire in under 15 seconds, to see how their gate crews could make their gate turnaround times even faster.[23]

SOCIAL MEDIA AS A STRATEGIC WEAPON. When Red Robin Gourmet Burgers launched its Tavern Double burger line, everything about the introduction needed to be absolutely on target. So what did company executives do? They utilized social media.[24] Using an internal social network resembling Facebook, managers in the 500+ locations in the restaurant chain were taught everything from the recipes to tips on efficiently making the burgers. That same internal network has been a great feedback tool. Company chefs have used tips and suggestions from customer feedback and from store managers to tweak the recipe.

Successful social media strategies should (1) help people—inside and outside the organization—connect and (2) reduce costs or increase revenue possibilities or both. As managers look at how to strategically use social media, it's important to have goals and a plan.

52 percent of **managers say social media are important**/somewhat important to their business.

It's not just for the social connections that organizations are employing social media strategies. Many are finding that social media tools can boost productivity.[25] For example, many physicians are tapping into online postings and sharing technologies as part of their daily routines. Collaborating with colleagues and experts allows them to improve the speed and efficiency of patient care. At TrunkClub, an online men's clothes shopping service that sends trunks with new clothing items to clients who've requested them, the CEO uses a software tool called Chatter to let the company's personal shoppers know about hot new shipments of shoes or clothes. He says that when he "chats" that information out to the team, he immediately sees the personal shoppers putting the items into customers' "trunks."[26] We'll look more closely at how managers can use social media for environmental scanning in this chapter's Managing Technology in Today's Workplace box on p. 232. When used strategically, social media can be a powerful weapon, as can big data and other digital tools!

Managers at American Airlines are using big data and digital tools as strategic weapons in making decisions about improving customer sales and contact experiences with its service agents and flight attendants. As critical strategic weapons, they help American meet its goal of providing passengers with the safest, most dependable, and friendliest service in the airline industry.

Mark Elias/Bloomberg/Getty Images

BIG DATA AND DIGITAL TOOLS AS STRATEGIC WEAPONS. Big data can be an effective counterpart to the information exchange generated through social media. All the enormous amounts of data collected about customers, partners, employees, markets, and other quantifiables can be used to respond to the needs of these same stakeholders. With big data, managers can measure and know more about their businesses and "translate that knowledge into improved decision making and performance."[27] Case in point: When Walmart began looking at its enormous database, it noticed that when a hurricane was forecasted, not only did sales of flashlights and batteries increase, but so did sales of Pop-Tarts. Now, when a hurricane is threatening, stores stock Pop-Tarts with other emergency storm supplies at the front entrance. This helps them better serve customers *and* drive sales.[28] By helping a business do what it's in business to do, compete successfully, and attract and satisfy its customers in order to achieve its goals, big data is a critical strategic weapon.

How do managers make sense of vast amounts of data? They can use **digital tools**—technology, systems, or software that allow the user to collect, visualize, understand, or analyze data. Specific examples of digital tools include software such as Microsoft Excel, online services such as Google Analytic, or networks that connect computers and people, such as we discussed in the previous section on social media.

Increasingly, digital tools enable managers to make decisions on a variety of quantitative information (big data). It's important to remember, though, that managers also make plans using their understanding of qualitative information, including internal (SWs) and external (OTs) factors. While digital tools are increasingly important, they should complement current planning approaches rather than replace them. Let's briefly look at three of the more prevalent digital tools available today.

DATA VISUALIZATION TOOLS. What do pie charts, bar charts, and trend lines have in common? They're methods to organize and summarize data for visual display. For example, managers can use bar charts or trend lines to display profits for several products or businesses or industries across multiple years.

CLOUD COMPUTING. Cloud computing refers to storing and accessing data on the Internet rather than on a computer's hard drive or a company's network. The cloud is just a metaphor for the Internet. Using cloud computing, managers can efficiently and effectively access vast amounts of data without having to invest in expensive hardware to do so.

INTERNET OF THINGS. We introduced this concept in Chapter 4. The IoT allows everyday "things" to generate and store data about their own performance and share that information across the Internet.

As a strategic weapon, these various types of digital tools enable managers to make sense of all the data that are generated. But, these tools are just that...tools. They complement planning approaches rather than replace them. So, once managers have the organization's strategies in place, it's time to set goals and develop plans to pursue those strategies.

Making Ethical Decisions in Today's Workplace

Do you shop? Well, you might be saying to yourself, that's kind of a ridiculous question...of course I shop. Well, here's another question: Do you realize the extent to which retail stores are spying on you as you shop?[29] Although most of us "accept" the fact that when we shop online, we're "allowing" the online retailer to install its cookies and to track our every move and click. Now, however, technology is being used more frequently in the physical retail environment. And it's more than cameras watching us. Many retailers are using cell phone tracking technology, personalized advertising, and super spy cams. Why? To track your behavior and to get you (and all those other shoppers) to buy more. Results from a recent survey showed that 80 percent of consumers do not want stores to track their movements via smartphone. And 44 percent said that a tracking program would make them less likely to shop with that store.

Discussion Questions:

1 What potential ethical dilemmas might there be in using a strategy of retail consumer tracking? (Think in terms of the various stakeholders who might be affected by this decision.)

2 What factors might influence a business's decision to use this strategy? Are possible ethical considerations more important than these factors? How does a decision maker weigh these things? Discuss these issues in your "assigned" group.

---

digital tools
Technology, systems, or software that allow the user to collect, visualize, understand, or analyze data

cloud computing
Storing and accessing data on the Internet rather than on a computer's hard drive or a company's network

How Do Managers Set Goals and Develop Plans?

6-3 Compare and contrast approaches to goal setting and planning.

goals (objectives)
Desired outcomes or targets

plans
Documents that outline how goals are going to be met

stated goals
Official statements of what an organization says, and wants its stakeholders to believe, its goals are

real goals
Those goals an organization actually pursues as shown by what the organization's members are doing

Planning = Goals + Plans

Planning involves two important aspects: goals and plans. **Goals (objectives)** are desired outcomes or targets. They guide managers' decisions and form the criteria against which work results are measured. **Plans** are documents that outline how goals are going to be met. They usually include resource allocations, budgets, schedules, and other necessary actions to accomplish the goals. As managers plan, they develop both goals and plans.

What Types of Goals Do Organizations Have and How Do They Set Those Goals?

Although it might seem that organizations have a single goal—for businesses, to make a profit, and for not-for-profit organizations, to meet the needs of some constituent group(s)—an organization's success can't be determined by a single goal. In reality, *all organizations have multiple goals*. For instance, businesses may want to increase market share, keep employees motivated, or work toward more environmentally sustainable practices. And a church provides a place for religious practices, but it also assists economically disadvantaged individuals in its community and acts as a social gathering place for church members.

TYPES OF GOALS. Most company goals can be classified as either strategic or financial. Financial goals are related to the financial performance of the organization, while strategic goals are related to all other areas of an organization's performance. For instance, McDonald's financial targets include 3 to 5 percent average annual sales and revenue growth, 6 to 7 percent average annual operating income growth, and returns on invested capital in the high teens.[30] An example of a strategic goal: Nissan's CEO's request for the company's GT-R super sports car: match or beat the performance of Porsche's 911 Turbo.[31] These goals are **stated goals**—official statements of what an organization says, and what it wants its stakeholders to believe, its goals are. However, stated goals—which can be found in an organization's charter, annual report, public relations announcements, or in public statements made by managers—are often conflicting and influenced by what various stakeholders think organizations should do. Such statements can be vague and probably better represent management's public relations skills instead of being meaningful guides to what the organization is actually trying to accomplish. It shouldn't be surprising then to find that an organization's stated goals are often irrelevant to what's actually done.[32]

Pierre-Andre Senizergues, founder and CEO of Sole Technology, set a goal for his company to be the first action sports firm to go carbon neutral by 2020. Shown here planting a tree in honor of his employees, he devised a six-point plan—from reducing water usage to using green production materials—to achieve his goal.

Amber Miller/Newscom

Stated vs. **Real Goals**

If you want to know an organization's **real goals**—those goals an organization actually pursues—observe what organizational members are doing. *Actions define priorities.* Knowing that real and stated goals may differ is important for recognizing what you might otherwise think are inconsistencies.

SETTING GOALS. As we said earlier, goals provide the direction for all management decisions and actions and form the criterion against which

Exhibit 6–5 Traditional Goal Setting

actual accomplishments are measured. Everything organizational members do should be oriented toward achieving goals. These goals can be set either through a process of traditional goal setting or by using management by objectives.

Traditional Goal Setting. In **traditional goal setting**, goals set by top managers flow down through the organization and become subgoals for each organizational area. (See Exhibit 6–5.) This traditional perspective assumes that top managers know what's best because they see the "big picture." And the goals passed down to each succeeding level guide individual employees as they work to achieve those assigned goals. Take a manufacturing business, for example. The president tells the vice president of production what he expects manufacturing costs to be for the coming year and tells the marketing vice president what level he expects sales to reach for the year. These goals are passed to the next organizational level and written to reflect the responsibilities of that level, passed to the next level, and so forth. Then, at some later time, performance is evaluated to determine whether the assigned goals have been achieved. Or that's the way it's supposed to happen. But in reality, it doesn't always do so. Turning broad strategic goals into departmental, team, and individual goals can be a difficult and frustrating process.

Another problem with traditional goal setting is that when top managers define the organization's goals in broad terms—such as achieving "sufficient" profits or increasing "market leadership"—these ambiguous goals have to be made more specific as they flow down through the organization. Managers at each level define the goals and apply their own interpretations and biases as they make them more specific. Clarity is often lost as the goals make their way down from the top of the organization to lower levels. But it doesn't have to be that way. For example, at Tijuana-based dj Orthopedics de Mexico, employee teams see the impact of their daily work output on company goals. The company's human resource manager says, "When people get a close connection with the result of their work, when they know every day what they are supposed to do and how they achieved the goals, that makes a strong connection with the company and their job."[33]

When the hierarchy of organizational goals *is* clearly defined, as it is at dj Orthopedics, it forms an integrated network of goals, or a **means-ends chain**. Higher-level goals (or ends) are linked to lower-level goals, which serve as the means for their accomplishment. In other words, the goals achieved at lower levels become the means to reach the goals (ends) at the next level. And the accomplishment of goals at that level becomes the means to achieve the goals (ends) at the next level and on up through the different organizational levels. That's how traditional goal setting is supposed to work.

Management by Objectives. Instead of using traditional goal setting, many organizations use **management by objectives (MBO)**, a process of setting mutually agreed-upon goals and using those goals to evaluate employee performance. If a manager were to use this approach, he or she would sit down with each member of his or her team and set goals and periodically review whether progress was being made toward achieving those goals. MBO

traditional goal setting
Goals set by top managers flow down through the organization and become subgoals for each organizational area

means-ends chain
An integrated network of goals in which higher-level goals are linked to lower-level goals, which serve as the means for their accomplishment

management by objectives (MBO)
A process of setting mutually agreed-upon goals and using those goals to evaluate employee performance

programs have four elements: ❶ goal specificity, ❷ participative decision making, ❸ an explicit time period, and ❹ performance feedback.[34] Instead of using goals to make sure employees are doing what they're supposed to be doing, MBO uses goals to motivate them as well. The appeal is that *it focuses on employees working to accomplish goals they've had a hand in setting.* (See the Classic Concepts in Today's Workplace box for more information on MBO.)

Studies of actual MBO programs have shown that it can increase employee performance and organizational productivity. For example, one review of MBO programs found productivity gains in almost all of them.[36] But is MBO relevant for today's organizations? Yes, if it's viewed as a way of setting goals, because research shows that *goal setting can be an effective tool in motivating employees,* as we'll discuss further in Chapter 11.[37]

Characteristics of Well-Written Goals. No matter which approach is used, goals have to be written, and some goals more clearly indicate what the desired outcomes are. Managers should develop well-written goals. Exhibit 6–6 lists the characteristics.[38] With these characteristics in mind, managers are now ready to actually set goals.

Steps in Setting Goals. Managers should follow six steps when setting goals.

1. *Review the organization's mission and employees' key job tasks.* The mission statement provides an overall guide to what's important, and goals should reflect that mission. In addition, it's important to define what you want employees to accomplish as they do their tasks.
2. *Evaluate available resources.* Don't set goals that are impossible to achieve given your available resources. Goals should be challenging, but realistic. After all, if the resources

◄◄◄ Classic Concepts in Today's Workplace ►►►

All you need to know about MBO!

Management by objectives (MBO) isn't new—it was a popular management approach in the 1960s and 1970s. The concept can be traced back to Peter Drucker, who first popularized the term in his 1954 book *The Practice of Management*.[35] Its appeal lies in its emphasis on converting overall objectives into specific objectives for organizational units and individual members.

How Is MBO Used?

- MBO makes goals practical and operational as they "cascade" down through the organization.
- Overall broad objectives are translated into specific objectives for each succeeding organizational level—division, departmental, and individual.
- Result: a hierarchy that links objectives at one level to those at the next level.
- For each individual employee, MBO provides specific personal performance objectives.
- If all individuals achieve their goals, then the unit's goals will be attained. If all units attain their goals, then the divisional goals will be met until…BOOM…the organization's overall goals are achieved!

Does MBO Work?

- Assessing MBO effectiveness is *not* easy!
- Research on goal-setting gives us some answers:
  - + Specific, difficult-to-achieve goals—an important part of MBO—produce a higher level of output than do no goals or generalized goals such as "do your best."
  - + Feedback—also an important part of MBO—favorably affects performance because it lets a person know whether his or her level of effort is sufficient or needs to be increased.
  - – Participation—also strongly advocated by MBO—has *not* shown any consistent relationship to performance.

ABSOLUTELY CRITICAL TO SUCCESS of MBO program:

Top management commitment to the process. When top managers have a high commitment to MBO and are personally involved in its implementation, productivity gains are higher than without that commitment.

Discussion Questions:

3 Why do you think management commitment is so important to the success of MBO programs?

4 Could you use MBO for your personal goals? Explain. If so, why? If not, why not?

Exhibit 6–6 Well-Written Goals

- Written in terms of outcomes rather than actions
- Measurable and quantifiable
- Clear as to a time frame
- Challenging yet attainable
- Written down
- Communicated to all necessary organizational members

Source: Robbins, Stephen P., Coulter, Mary, *Management*, 13th Ed., © 2016, p. 222. Reprinted and electronically reproduced by permission of Pearson Education, Inc., New York, NY.

strategic plans
Plans that apply to the entire organization and encompass the organization's overall goals

tactical plans
Plans that specify the details of how the overall goals are to be achieved

you have to work with won't allow you to achieve a goal no matter how hard you try or how much effort is exerted, you shouldn't set that goal.

3. *Determine the goals individually or with input from others.* Goals reflect desired outcomes and should be congruent with the organizational mission and goals in other organizational areas. These goals should be measurable, specific, and include a time frame for accomplishment.

4. *Make sure goals are well-written and then communicate them to all who need to know.* Writing down and communicating goals forces people to think them through. Written goals become visible evidence of the importance of working toward something.

5. *Build in feedback mechanisms to assess goal progress.* If goals aren't being met, change them as needed.

6. *Link rewards to goal attainment.* Employees want to know "What's in it for me?" Linking rewards to goal achievement will help answer that question.

Once the goals have been established, written down, and communicated, managers are ready to develop plans for pursuing the goals.

What Types of Plans Do Managers Use and How Do They Develop Those Plans?

Managers need plans to help them clarify and specify how goals will be met. Let's look first at the types of plans managers use.

TYPES OF PLANS. The most popular ways to describe plans are in terms of their *breadth* (strategic versus tactical), *time frame* (long term versus short), *specificity* (directional versus specific), and *frequency of use* (single-use versus standing). As Exhibit 6–7 shows, these types of plans aren't independent. That is, strategic plans are usually long term, directional, and single-use. Let's look at each type of plan.

Breadth. **Strategic plans** are those that apply to an entire organization and encompass the organization's overall goals. **Tactical plans** (sometimes referred to as operational plans) specify the details of how the overall goals are to be achieved. When McDonald's invested in the Redbox kiosk business, it was the result of strategic planning. Deciding when, where, and how to actually operate the business was the result of tactical plans in marketing, logistics, finance, and so forth.

Steve Smith, L.L. Bean's chief executive, plans to broaden the company's customer base by expanding beyond catalog and online selling and focusing more on opening new retail stores and by tripling its advertising spending to support in-store purchases. These tactical plans support L.L. Bean's strategic plan of improving the company's performance and ensuring its profitable growth.

Robert F. Bukaty/AP Images

Exhibit 6–7 Types of Plans

BREADTH OF USE	TIME FRAME	SPECIFICITY	FREQUENCY OF USE
Strategic	Long term	Directional	Single use
Tactical	Short term	Specific	Standing

Time Frame. The number of years used to define short-term and long-term plans has declined considerably due to environmental uncertainty. *Long term* used to mean anything over seven years. Try to imagine what you're likely to be doing in seven years. It seems pretty distant, doesn't it? Now, you can begin to understand how difficult it is for managers to plan that far in the future. Thus, **long-term plans** are now defined as plans with a time frame beyond three years. **Short-term plans** cover one year or less.

Specificity. Intuitively, it would seem that specific plans would be preferable to directional, or loosely guided, plans. **Specific plans** are plans that are clearly defined and leave no room for interpretation. For example, a manager who wants to increase his work unit's output by 8 percent over the next 12 months might establish specific procedures, budget allocations, and work schedules to reach that goal. However, when uncertainty is high and managers must be flexible in order to respond to unexpected changes, they'd likely use **directional plans**, flexible plans that set general guidelines. For example, Sylvia Rhone, president of Motown Records, had a simple goal—to "sign great artists."[39] She could create a specific plan to produce and market 10 albums from new artists this year. Or she might formulate a directional plan to use a network of people around the world to alert her to new and promising talent so she can increase the number of artists she has under contract. Sylvia, and any manager who engages in planning, must keep in mind that you have to weigh the flexibility of directional plans against the clarity you can get from specific plans.

Flexibility ↔ Clarity

Frequency of Use. Some plans that managers develop are ongoing, while others are used only once. A **single-use plan** is a one-time plan specifically designed to meet the needs of a unique situation. For instance, when Dell began developing a pocket-sized device for getting on the Internet, managers used a single-use plan to guide their decisions. In contrast, **standing plans** are ongoing plans that provide guidance for activities performed repeatedly. For example, when you register for classes for the upcoming semester, you're using a standardized registration plan at your college or university. The dates change, but the process works the same way semester after semester.

DEVELOPING PLANS. The process of developing plans is influenced by three contingency factors and by the planning approach followed.

Contingency Factors in Planning. Three contingency factors affect the choice of plans: (1) organizational level, (2) degree of environmental uncertainty, and (3) length of future commitments.[40]

Exhibit 6–8 shows the *relationship between a manager's level in the organization and the type of planning done.* For the most part, lower-level managers do operational (or tactical) planning while upper-level managers do strategic planning.

---

long-term plans
Plans with a time frame beyond three years

short-term plans
Plans with a time frame of one year or less

specific plans
Plans that are clearly defined and leave no room for interpretation

directional plans
Plans that are flexible and set general guidelines

single-use plan
A one-time plan specifically designed to meet the needs of a unique situation

standing plans
Plans that are ongoing and provide guidance for activities performed repeatedly

Exhibit 6–8 Planning and Organizational Level

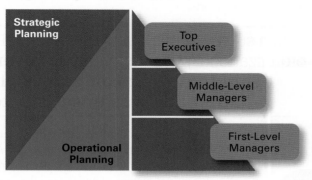

The second contingency factor is *environmental uncertainty*. When uncertainty is high, plans should be specific, but flexible. Managers must be prepared to change or amend plans as they're implemented. For example, at Continental Airlines (now part of United Airlines), the former CEO and his management team established a specific goal of focusing on what customers wanted most—on-time flights—to help the company become more competitive in the highly uncertain airline industry. Because of that uncertainty, the management team identified a "destination, but not a flight plan," and changed plans as necessary to achieve its goal of on-time service.

The last contingency factor also is related to the *time frame of plans*. The **commitment concept** says that plans should extend far enough to meet those commitments made when the plans were developed. Planning for too long or too short a time period is inefficient and ineffective. We can see the importance of the commitment concept, for example, with the plans that organizations make to increase their computing capabilities. At the data centers where companies' computers are housed, many have found their "power-hungry computers" generate so much heat that their electric bills have skyrocketed because of the increased need for air conditioning.[41] How does this illustrate the commitment concept? As organizations expand their computing technology, they're "committed" to whatever future expenses are generated by that plan. They have to live with the plan and its consequences.

---

38 percent of leaders say planning for next year is a challenge.[42] What about you? Do you find planning for next year to be a challenge? How can you be better at planning?

Approaches to Planning. Swisscom works closely with key suppliers, including Huawei, to jointly plan new technology for improving telecommunications services. At the UK retailer John Lewis, which is employee-owned, top managers discuss major plans and policies with the 15-member Partnership Board of employees. Executives at Inditex, the Spanish parent company of Zara and other thriving retail chains, seek input from small groups of employees and listen closely to store managers during the planning process, especially when preparing for the design and introduction of new products. In each of these situations, planning is done a little differently.[43]

In the traditional approach, planning is done entirely by top-level managers who often are assisted by a **formal planning department**, a group of planning specialists whose sole responsibility is to help write the various organizational plans. Under this approach, plans developed by top-level managers flow down through other organizational levels, much like the traditional approach to goal setting. As they flow down through the organization, the plans are tailored to the particular needs of each level. Although this approach makes managerial planning thorough, systematic, and coordinated, all too often the focus is on developing "the plan," a thick binder (or binders) full of meaningless

commitment concept
The idea that plans should extend far enough to meet those commitments made when the plans were developed

formal planning department
A group of planning specialists whose sole responsibility is to help write the various organizational plans

information that's stuck away on a shelf and never used by anyone for guiding or coordinating work efforts.

In a survey of managers about formal top-down organizational planning processes, **over 75 percent said that their company's planning approach was unsatisfactory**.[44]

A common complaint was that "plans are documents that you prepare for the corporate planning staff and later forget."[45] Although this traditional top-down approach to planning is used by many organizations, it's effective only if managers understand the importance of creating documents that organizational members actually use, not documents that look impressive but are never used.

Another approach to planning is to involve more organizational members in the process. In this approach, plans aren't handed down from one level to the next, but instead are developed by organizational members at the various levels and in the various work units to meet their specific needs. For instance, at Dell, employees from production, supply management, and channel management meet weekly to make plans based on current product demand and supply. In addition, work teams set their own daily schedules and track their progress against those schedules. If a team falls behind, team members develop "recovery" plans to try to get back on schedule.[46] When organizational members are more actively involved in planning, they see that the plans are more than just something written down on paper. They can actually see that the plans are used in directing and coordinating work.

Richard Lautens/Newscom

Virginia Poly, founder and CEO of Poly Placements, a Canadian recruiting firm, manages in a dynamic environment where clients continue to use more contingent workers. To succeed, she plans to keep her employees focused on building long-term relationships with customers and serving as consultants rather than transactional salespeople.

6-4 Discuss contemporary issues in planning.

What Contemporary Planning Issues Do Managers Face?

The second floor of the 21-story Hyundai Motor headquarters buzzes with data 24 hours a day. That's where you'd find the company's Global Command and Control Center (GCCC), which is modeled after the CNN newsroom with numerous "computer screens relaying video and data keeping watch on Hyundai operations around the world." Managers get information on parts shipments from suppliers to factories. Cameras watch assembly lines and closely monitor the company's massive Ulsan, Korea, factory looking for competitors' spies and any hints of labor unrest. The GCCC also keeps tabs on the company's R&D activities in Europe, Japan, and North America. Hyundai can identify problems in an instant and react quickly. The company is all about aggressiveness and speed and is representative of how a successful twenty-first-century company approaches planning.[47]

We conclude this chapter by addressing two contemporary issues in planning. Specifically, we're going to look at ❶ planning effectively in dynamic environments and crisis situations and then ❷ at how managers can use environmental scanning, especially competitive intelligence.

How Can Managers Plan Effectively in Dynamic Environments and in Crisis Situations?

Dynamic Environments and
Crisis Situations **= Planning** Challenges

As we saw in Chapter 4, the external environment is continually changing. How can managers effectively plan when the external environment is continually changing? We already discussed uncertain environments as one of the contingency factors that affect the types of plans managers develop. Because dynamic environments are more the norm than the exception, let's look at how they can effectively plan in such environments. We also want to take a quick look at how managers can help their organizations prepare for responding to a crisis.

DYNAMIC ENVIRONMENTS. In an uncertain environment, *managers should develop plans that are specific, but flexible.* Although this may seem contradictory, it's not. To be useful, plans need some specificity, but the plans should not be set in stone. Managers need to *recognize that planning is an ongoing process.* The plans serve as a road map although the destination may change due to dynamic market conditions. They should be ready to change directions if environmental conditions warrant. This flexibility is particularly important as plans are implemented. Managers need to *stay alert to environmental changes that may impact implementation and respond as needed.* Keep in mind, also, that even when the environment is highly uncertain, it's important to *continue formal planning in order to see any effect on organizational performance.* It's the persistence in planning that contributes to significant performance improvement. Why? It seems that, as with most activities, managers "learn to plan" and the quality of their planning improves when they continue to do it.[48] Finally, *make the organizational hierarchy flatter to effectively plan in dynamic environments.* A flatter hierarchy means lower organizational levels can set goals and develop plans because organizations have little time for goals and plans to flow down from the top. Managers should teach their employees how to set goals and to plan and then trust them to do it. And you need look no further than Bangalore, India, to find a company that effectively understands this. Just a decade ago, Wipro Limited was "an anonymous conglomerate selling cooking oil and personal computers, mostly in India." Today, it's a $8.5 billion-a-year global company with most of its business coming from information-technology services.[49] Accenture, EDS, IBM, and the big U.S. accounting firms know all too well the competitive threat Wipro represents. Not only are Wipro's employees economical, they're knowledgeable and skilled. And they play an important role in the company's planning. Since the information services industry is continually changing, employees are taught to analyze situations and to define the scale and scope of a client's problems in order to offer the best solutions. These employees are the ones on the front line with the clients and it's their responsibility to establish what to do and how to do it. It's an approach that positions Wipro for success no matter how the industry changes.

CRISIS SITUATIONS. On February 27, 2010, the fifth strongest earthquake ever recorded struck Chile. It was so strong that NASA estimated it tilted the Earth's axis by three inches.[50] (Mind boggling, isn't it!) The 2017–2018 flu season, which proved to be worse than expected, required many hospitals to make adjustments to facilities, processes, and procedures to handle the massive numbers of sick individuals.[51] Hurricane Harvey struck Houston with a fury in late August 2017 and left behind devastating flooding.[52] Cyber-attacks on major corporations, government agencies, and other institutions are happening more and more frequently. All of these are examples of crisis situations, which require managers to be prepared above-and-beyond the normal, everyday planning challenges associated with dynamic environments. How? Well, the first thing to remember in planning for a crisis is you can't wait until a crisis happens! A comprehensive crisis response plan needs to be prepared and in place. Experts suggest that it cover three critical dimensions:

environmental scanning
An analysis of the external environment, which involves screening large amounts of information to detect emerging trends

competitive intelligence
A type of environmental scanning that gives managers accurate information about competitors

people, preparedness, and testing.[53] When a crisis hits, an organization's *people* need to know what their response is to be. And they know this through *being prepared* (preparedness) and through *rehearsing simulated crises* (testing). All of this requires intense and deliberate planning. Worth it? You bet!

How Can Managers Use Environmental Scanning?

A manager's analysis of the external environment may be improved by **environmental scanning**, which involves screening large amounts of information to detect emerging trends. One of the fastest-growing forms of environmental scanning is **competitive intelligence**, which is accurate information about competitors that allows managers to anticipate competitors' actions rather than merely react to them.[54] It seeks basic information about competitors: Who are they? What are they doing? How will what they're doing affect us?

Many who study competitive intelligence suggest that much of the competitor-related information managers need to make crucial strategic decisions is available and accessible to the public.[56] In other words, competitive intelligence isn't organizational espionage. Advertisements, promotional materials, press releases, reports filed with government agencies, annual reports, want ads, newspaper reports, information on the Internet, and industry studies are readily accessible sources of information. Specific information on an industry and associated organizations is increasingly available through electronic databases. Managers can literally tap into this wealth of competitive information by purchasing access to databases. Attending trade shows and debriefing your own sales staff also can be good sources

::::: Managing Technology in Today's Workplace :::::
USING SOCIAL MEDIA FOR ENVIRONMENTAL SCANNING

While most companies have a strategy to use social media for marketing purposes, many companies have expanded their use of social media to support organizational planning.[55] A growing number of social media sites provide businesses with real-time information to support environmental scanning efforts.

Social media is particularly valuable in collecting competitor intelligence. Businesses can identify emerging trends by monitoring online conversations and other information transmitted via social media. For example, through LinkedIn, you might learn that a competitor is expanding a certain division as more people update their profiles indicating they are joining an organization. Or you could identify a competitor's strategic promotions or hires that might reflect a shift in their business.

It may seem like a daunting task to monitor social media; however, businesses can use new software tools and analytic techniques to learn about competitors, suppliers, and customers. For

How important is social media to a company's environmental scanning?

example, software can be used to calculate "buzz volume," which isolates relevant messages about a specific company's brand online.

To effectively gather business intelligence from social media, organizations should take a strategic approach, otherwise it's easy to get buried in the overwhelming amount of information that exists. This unprecedented access to immediate and endless information could shift how businesses do organizational planning. Managers must be able to shift plans quickly in response to trends or other intelligence identified via social media scanning efforts.

Discussion Questions:

5 With so much information available through social media, how can businesses focus their efforts to scan for relevant information?

6 How could managers determine if information gathered from social media is reliable and not fake? In your "assigned" group, discuss ideas.

of information on competitors. In addition, many organizations even regularly buy competitors' products and ask their own employees to evaluate them to learn about new technical innovations.[57]

In a changing global business environment, environmental scanning and obtaining competitive intelligence can be quite complex, especially when information must be gathered from around the world. However, managers could subscribe to news services that review newspapers and magazines from around the globe and provide summaries to client companies.

Managers do need to be careful about the way information, especially competitive intelligence, is gathered to prevent any concerns about whether it's legal or ethical. For instance, Starwood Hotels sued Hilton Hotels, alleging that two former employees stole trade secrets and helped Hilton develop a new line of luxury, trendy hotels designed to appeal to a young demographic.[58] The court filing said, "This is the clearest imaginable case of corporate espionage, theft of trade secrets, unfair competition, and computer fraud." Competitive intelligence becomes illegal corporate spying when it involves the theft of proprietary materials or trade secrets by any means. The Economic Espionage Act makes it a crime in the United States to engage in economic espionage or to steal a trade secret.[59] Difficult decisions about competitive intelligence arise because often there's a fine line between what's considered *legal and ethical* and what's considered *legal but unethical.* Although the top manager at one competitive intelligence firm contends that 99.9 percent of intelligence gathering is legal, there's no question that some people or companies will go to any lengths—some unethical—to get information about competitors.[60]

CHAPTER SUMMARY BY LEARNING OUTCOME

6-1 Discuss the nature and purposes of planning.

As the primary management function, planning establishes the basis for all the other things that managers do. The planning we're concerned with is formal planning; that is, specific goals covering a specific time period are defined and written down and specific plans are developed to make sure those goals are met. There are four reasons managers should plan: (1) it establishes coordinated efforts, (2) it reduces uncertainty, (3) it reduces overlapping and wasteful activities, and (4) it establishes the goals or standards that are used in controlling work. Although criticisms have been directed at planning, the evidence generally supports the position that organizations benefit from formal planning.

6-2 Explain what managers do in the strategic management process.

Managers develop the organization's strategies in the strategic management process, which is a six-step process encompassing strategy planning, implementation, and evaluation. The six steps are as follows: (1) Identify the organization's current mission, goals, and strategies; (2) do an external analysis; (3) do an internal analysis—steps 2 and 3 together are called SWOT analysis; (4) formulate strategies; (5) implement strategies; and (6) evaluate results. The end result of this process is a set of corporate, competitive, and functional strategies that allow the organization to do what it's in business to do and to achieve its goals. Six strategic weapons are important in today's environment: customer service, employee skills and loyalty, innovation, quality, social media, and big data.

6-3 Compare and contrast approaches to goal setting and planning.

The goals of most companies are classified as either strategic or financial. We can also look at goals as either stated or real. In traditional goal setting, goals set by top managers flow down through the organization and become subgoals for each organizational area. Organizations could also use management by objectives, which is a process of setting mutually agreed-upon goals and using those goals to evaluate employee performance. Plans can be described in terms of their breadth, time frame, specificity, and frequency of use. Plans can be developed by a formal planning department or by involving more organizational members in the process.

6-4 Discuss contemporary issues in planning.

One contemporary planning issue is planning in dynamic environments, which usually means developing plans that are specific but flexible. Also, it's important to continue planning even when the environment is highly uncertain. Finally, because there's little time in a dynamic environment for goals and plans to flow down from the top, lower organizational levels should be allowed to set goals and develop plans. Crisis planning should be done before a crisis occurs and should cover people, preparedness, and testing. Another contemporary planning issue is using environmental scanning to help do a better analysis of the external environment. One form of environmental scanning, competitive intelligence, can be especially helpful in finding out what competitors are doing, either by traditional methods or by using technology such as social media.

DISCUSSION QUESTIONS

6-1 Why are formal plans generated?

6-2 Discuss why planning is beneficial.

6-3 Describe in detail the six-step strategic management process.

6-4 How would SWOT analysis strengthen the strategic management process externally and internally?

6-5 "Organizations that fail to plan are planning to fail." Agree or disagree? Explain your position.

6-6 Managers can't empower all employees. How can MBO help in this circumstance?

6-7 Describe how managers can plan in today's dynamic environment.

6-8 What types of planning do you do in your personal life? Describe these plans in terms of being (a) strategic or operational, (b) short term or long term, (c) specific or directional, and (d) single-use or standing.

6-9 Do a personal SWOT analysis. Assess your personal strengths and weaknesses (skills, talents). What are you good at? What are you not so good at? What do you enjoy doing? Not enjoy doing? Then, identify career opportunities and threats by researching job prospects in the industry you're interested in. Look at trends and projections. You might want to check out the information the Bureau of Labor Statistics provides on job prospects. Once you have all this information, write a specific career action plan. Outline five-year career goals and what you need to do to achieve those goals.

6-10 What role does, and should, technology play in planning?

Applying: Getting Ready for the Workplace

Management Skill Builder | BEING A GOOD GOAL SETTER

It's been said that if you don't know where you're going, any road will get you there. It has also been said that the shortest distance between two points is a straight line. These two "adages" emphasize the importance of goals. Managers are typically judged on their ability to achieve goals. If individuals or units in the organization lack goals, there can be no direction or unity of effort. So successful managers are good at setting their own goals and helping others set goals.

MyLab Management
PERSONAL INVENTORY ASSESSMENT

 **PERSONAL INVENTORY ASSESSMENT**

Go to **www.pearson.com/mylab/management** to complete the Personal Inventory Assessment related to this chapter.

Skill Basics

In addition to your own focus on goals, employees should also have a clear understanding of what they're attempting to accomplish. Managers have the responsibility to help employees with this understanding as they set work goals. You can be more effective at helping employees set goals if you use the following eight suggestions:

- *Identify an employee's key job tasks.* Goal setting begins by defining what it is that you want your employees to accomplish. The best source for this information is each employee's job description.

- *Establish measurable, specific, and challenging goals for each key task.* Identify the level of performance expected of each employee. Specify the target toward which the employee is working.

- *Specify the deadlines for each goal.* Putting deadlines on each goal reduces ambiguity. Deadlines, however, should not be set arbitrarily. Rather, they need to be realistic given the tasks to be completed.

- *Allow the employee to participate actively.* When employees participate in goal setting, they're more likely to accept the goals. However, it must be sincere participation. That is, employees must perceive that you are truly seeking their input, not just going through the motions.

- *Prioritize goals.* When you give someone more than one goal, it's important to rank the goals in order of importance. The purpose of prioritizing is to encourage the employee to take action and expend effort on each goal in proportion to its importance.

- *Rate goals for difficulty and importance.* Goal setting should not encourage people to choose easy goals. Instead, goals should be rated for their difficulty and importance. When goals are rated, individuals can be given credit for trying difficult goals, even if they don't fully achieve them.

- *Build in feedback mechanisms to assess goal progress.* Feedback lets employees know whether their level of effort is sufficient to attain the goal. Feedback should be both self-generated and supervisor-generated. Feedback should also be frequent and recurring.

- *Link rewards to goal attainment.* It's natural for employees to ask, "What's in it for me?" Linking rewards to the achievement of goals will help answer that question.

Based on E. A. Locke and G. P. Latham, *Goal-Setting: A Motivational Technique That Works!* (Upper Saddle River, NJ: Prentice Hall, 1984); and E. A. Locke and G. P. Latham, "Building a Practically Useful Theory of Goal Setting and Task Motivation," *American Psychologist*, September 2002, pp. 705–17.

Practicing the Skill

Read through this scenario and follow the directions at the end of it:

You worked your way through college while holding down a part-time job bagging groceries at the Food Town supermarket chain. You liked working in the food industry, and when you graduated, you accepted a position with Food Town as a management trainee. Three years have passed, and you've gained experience in the grocery store industry and in operating a large supermarket. Several months ago, you received a promotion to store manager at one of the chain's locations. One of the things you've liked about Food Town is that it gives store managers a great deal of autonomy in running their stores. The company provides very general guidelines to its managers. Top management is concerned with the bottom line; for the most part, how you get there is up to you. Now that you're finally a store manager, you want to establish an MBO-type program in your store. You like the idea that everyone should have clear goals to work toward and then be evaluated against those goals.

Your store employs 70 people, although except for the managers, most work only 20 to 30 hours per week. You have six people reporting to you: an assistant manager; a weekend manager; and grocery, produce, meat, and bakery managers. The only highly skilled jobs belong to the butchers, who have strict training and regulatory guidelines. Other less-skilled jobs include cashier, shelf stocker, maintenance worker, and grocery bagger.

Specifically describe how you would go about setting goals in your new position. Include examples of goals for the jobs of butcher, cashier, and bakery manager.

Experiential Exercise

Organizations of all types and sizes have (or should have) mission statements. Your college/university likely has a mission or vision statement, as each department of your college/university probably does. Mission statements are important because they compel managers and decision makers to identify their reason for being in existence. Why does this organization exist? What is its purpose? As we said in the chapter, knowing the mission is important to planning efforts.

What about personal mission statements? Would having a personal mission statement be useful? Experts say YES![61] A personal mission statement can be an important component of both your personal and leadership development as you prepare for your future career. So, you're going to write one. Although this may sound simple to do, it's not going to be simple or easy. Our hope is that it will be something you'll want to keep, use, and revise when necessary and that it will help you be the person you'd like to be and live the life you'd like to live.

We recommend starting by doing some research on personal mission statements. Your personal mission statement may be one sentence or ten sentences, but it should identify your core values, your goals, and what is important to you. There are some wonderful Web resources that can guide you. Good luck! Your instructor will tell you what to do with your personal mission statement once you've completed it.

CASE APPLICATION #1

Fast Fashion

Topics: Primark Takes on Burberry and Alexander McQueen

The clothing retailer Primark, which offers a value range of products, competes directly with designer labels such as Burberry and Alexander McQueen. Primark began as Penneys in Dublin, the Republic of Ireland, in 1969, where it still operates under the same name, and by late 1971, there were 11 stores across the country. Primark's base increased rapidly when it entered Great Britain in 1973, and by the end of the following year the total number of stores had risen to 22. By 2000, with continued expansion and acquisition, Primark had a store count of 108. The clothing retailer's presence extended to Spain in 2006; the Netherlands in 2008; Portugal, Germany, and Belgium in 2009; Austria in 2012; France in 2013; and the United States in 2015. Primark is still one of the fastest-growing chains in Europe. The company has 287 stores with nearly 11 million square feet of retail space and employs more than 54,000 people in its stores throughout the world.

This growth was made possible thanks to Primark's extensive planning and goal setting. It was built on the fast-fashion trend that had hit the fashion industry and prided itself on encouraging its employees to set their own personal goals and to make use of the training programs offered.

Primark is one of the most sought-after retail employers. It has consistently had more applicants for jobs than available positions. Like other organizations, Primark has a purpose and a structure to support and enable its people in carrying out that purpose. The business, which prides itself on customer satisfaction, offers one of the best salary structures in retail but demands the very best, and it gets the best by hiring the brightest individuals interested in retail careers.

Goal-setting by employees is coupled with recognition of strong organizational skills by management. Primark's Management Trainee Program is aimed at graduates, with key training on buying because the company sources its products from around the world. Interestingly, Primark is one of the few retailers that do not have an online presence; the company believes that it does not need an e-commerce site (though it does deal with online retailers such as eBay, Amazon, and ASOS). In terms of planning and decision-making, the choice to not set up an e-commerce site makes perfect sense. Given that many of its fast-fashion clothing products begin as low as $4, it would take an enormous number of sales to offset the setup costs.

Primark does not advertise either. Instead, it relies on public relations, word of mouth, and the strategic positioning of key stores. Planning is focused on the ability to offer fast-fashion products at the lowest possible price. At the same time, it attempts to ensure that it operates within an ethical framework. Primark is a member of the Ethical Trading Initiative, and it supports local charitable organizations and community projects. It is also going through the process of replacing plastic carrier bags with paper bags.

Following criticism in the early 2000s for its use of Asian factories as the primary source of its products, Primark decided to acquire ethical trading status. Since 2014, Primark has continued to improve labor standards across its supply chain in China. Goals included increasing wages, delivering productivity benefits, and creating long-term and lasting improvements. In order to meet these goals, Primark has simply hired. Progress has been encouraging, and realistic solutions to basic problems have begun to yield major successes.

Primark's planning approach has clearly been working. According to research, 75 percent of a consumer's decisions are made in three seconds at the point of sale. Primark focuses on this and pays particular attention to instantly hooking consumers with its shop fittings, layout, and visual merchandising. Primark's planning for the future is well underway.[62]

Discussion Questions

6-11 Discuss Primark's decision to bypass e-commerce.

6-12 Differentiate Primark's marketing from that of other retailers.

6-13 Provide examples of fast-fashion chains in your country. How would they cope with competition from an expanding retailer like Primark?

6-14 What types of planning and goal-setting are described in this case? How would it help Primark's future operations and expansion?

CASE APPLICATION #2

Mapping a New Direction
Topic: From a Grocery Stall to an Empire

With nearly 500,000 employees and annual revenues exceeding £55 billion in 2017,[63] Tesco is one of the largest British multinational grocery retailers. The company has over 3,400 stores in many parts of the United Kingdom and operates in 11 other countries around the world. Tesco was founded in 1919 by Jack Cohen, who started out selling groceries from a stall in East End of London. He opened his first successful Tesco store in 1929 in Edgware in North London and, in just a few years tine, expanded to several other areas in the city.

To this day, Tesco has always looked for the best sites for its store locations and has continued to buy out its competition over the years,[64] including a mammoth purchase of T&S's 850 convenience stores in 2002.[65] Today, thanks to an aggressive yet well-planned expansion in the United Kingdom, Tesco has been able to become its number one grocery store, with a market share nearing 30 percent of the grocery sector. Tesco's expansion strategy helped in establishing a strong and powerful presence on the ground and, importantly, created a greater reach to its customers across many parts of the United Kingdom.

Underpinning Tesco's goals of aggressive expansion is a rigorous intelligence system that allows the retailer to use data to select the best sites and to accurately understand its customer base and their needs.[66] Armed with strong business intelligence capability,[67] Tesco is better able to customize its product offerings and prices to meet different kinds of customers under the same roof, ranging from "value" products, launched in 1993 for the price-sensitive customer, to "finest," launched in 1998 for the upper-class customer. In fact, the old strategy that had served the store in its early years was beginning to hurt the retailer, as customers became more selective in their choices and continual low prices were putting pressure on the company's profits just as it had to expand. Therefore, Tesco revitalized its brand with more emphasis on customer service and quality while keeping its original value-for-money tradition.

Creativity was also another factor contributing to Tesco's success. The retail giant is widely considered the most innovative in its industry. Tesco's product offerings have grown from a store selling groceries to a superstore where customers can virtually find anything, from electronics, to homeware, to clothing, to beauty products, to mobile phones. It also launched its first petrol station back in 1973 and ventured into various other types of businesses over the years, including coffeeshops, banking, and electronics. In addition to its varied product offerings, Tesco also leads the way in its online presence thanks to its e-commerce website, which first opened in year 2000 and currently serves more than 500,000 customers each week.[68] Finally, Tesco is also an innovator in its store concepts, opening different types of stores (such as Tesco Express) based on the different market needs.

However, things have not always been rosy for the giant retailer. In 2014, Tesco reported the biggest loss in its history: £6.4 billion, pre-tax.[69] Analysts primarily blamed over-ambitious international expansion plans that put great pressure on costs and diverted the company's attention away from its local market. Further, Tesco is facing strong local competition from low-cost chains such as Aldi and Lidl.[70] In response, Tesco embarked on a sweeping set of low-cost measures, including massive lay-offs and sales of its low-performing businesses locally and internationally. It also improved its customer service experience in many of its stores and reexamined its prices. The efforts paid off. In 2018, Tesco posted its highest growth in seven years and reported a pre-tax profit of £1.3 billion. Moreover, as part of its new plans, Tesco just completed its takeover of Booker Group, which is the largest food wholesaler in the United Kingdom,[71] potentially giving the retailer even more access to new customers and increasing its market share.

Discussion Questions

6-15 Based on what you have read in the case, does it pay to plan? Which parts of the strategic management process were mainly illustrated in this case?

6-16 Based on what you have read in the chapter, which strategic weapons is Tesco relying on here?

6-17 Do you believe gathering information is important for Tesco to win markets? Why or why not?

6-18 How do you describe Tesco's renewal strategy? Would you change anything about it?

CASE APPLICATION #3

 ## Using Tech to Sell Pizza
Topic: Revamping for the Future

Who hasn't heard of the Swedish furniture giant, IKEA? Established in 1943 by 17-year-old carpenter Ingvar Kamprad, who sold furniture via mail catalog, the company has grown to become one of the world's biggest furniture brands, with more than 424 stores in 52 markets and reaching €38.8 billion in sales in 2018.[72] IKEA's vision is to improve their customers' everyday lives, and the company follows through by offering a wide range of well-designed, functional home furniture at very reasonable prices. In line with its vision and aims, the company has been very successful in attracting millions of people to its stores with its unique product designs and low prices, making it the world's largest retail furniture company.[73] The store relies on several cost-cutting tactics to deliver lower prices to customers, including ready-to-assemble packages that lower shipping costs for the company.

IKEA achieved a record profit of €4.2 billion in the year 2016.[74] However, in 2017, the company's profits started to dwindle sharply, and in 2018, by the end of August, its profits almost halved.[75] The company, however, says that this is expected as it has been aggressively investing in online technologies and business transformation,[76] which has increased its costs for the time being; it expects profits to rebound by 2022.[77]

IKEA has been very slow in adapting to the online revolution. In fact, until recently, IKEA did not have an online presence in a number of its markets,[78] including Australia in 2017.[79] The store relied for decades on its old business model, which is to attract customers to its massive stores displaying unique low-priced furniture. As IKEA continued to face intense competition from competing online stores while at the same time itself missing out on potential growth opportunities from online sales, the world's biggest furniture store had to embark on a massive technological transformation. Adding to this urgency is IKEA's recent figures, which showed that its sales only grew by 2 percent in 2017, well below the 7 percent average of the previous five years.[80]

An enormous change of strategy has been undertaken. The company invested €2.8 billion in its business transformation, the majority of which was used to fund 14 new distribution centers for its online business.[81] IKEA is reportedly implementing a new strategy to have online solutions in all its markets in three years.[82]

Moreover, IKEA is also investing to improve its online shopping and delivery experience to reduce item delivery time to 24 hours.[83] Online shoppers may soon have the option of product-assembling services as well,[84] a stark contrast to its old strategy of relying on customer assembly. IKEA recently acquired tech company TaskRabbit, an online platform that allows customers to connect with individuals who will assemble the product for them.

IKEA is also investing in various other revolutionary technologies that will transform the company into a furniture retailer of the future.[85] The IKEA Place App offers an augmented reality shopping experience that allows customers to "try" their products in their home before buying. The company is also developing and offering smart products for the future that can be controlled remotely using an app.

Discussion Questions

6-19 In your opinion, how challenging is the environment that IKEA faces? How does planning help IKEA overcome the challenges?

6-20 For expanding into the tech domain, which company should IKEA benchmark? Explain.

6-21 Do you recall seeing an IKEA-sponsored ad, survey, or news item on social media recently? How can IKEA use social media as a strategic weapon for implementing its new plans successfully?

6-22 Working in a group, discuss the following: Do you think IKEA's investment in revamping its online shopping initiatives comes a little too late? What opportunities and challenges do you see?

Endnotes

1. C. Tsuneaoka, "Toyota Sees Half of Sales Coming from Hybrids, EVs," *Wall Street Journal Online,* December 13, 2017.

2. M. Jenks, "Amazon Won't Know What Hit 'Em!" *Bloomberg Businessweek,* May 5–14, 2017, pp. 42–47.

3. M. Wilson, "How Walmart Could Make You Ditch Amazon: Hearsay or Just Good Design?" *Fast Company Online,* September 25, 2017.

4. M. C. Mankins and R. Steele, "Stop Making Plans—Start Making Decisions," *Harvard Business Review,* January 2006, pp. 76–84; L. Bossidy and R. Charan, *Execution: The Discipline of Getting Things Done* (New York: Crown/Random House, 2002); P. Roberts, "The Art of Getting Things Done," *Fast Company,* June 2000, p. 162; H. Mintzberg, *The Rise and Fall of Strategic Planning* (New York: Free Press, 1994); G. Hamel and C. K. Prahalad, *Competing for the Future* (Boston: Harvard Business School Press, 1994); and D. Miller, "The Architecture of Simplicity," *Academy of Management Review,* January 1993, pp. 116–38.

5. See, for example, F. Delmar and S. Shane, "Does Business Planning Facilitate the Development of New Ventures?" *Strategic Management Journal,* December 2003, pp. 1165–85; R. M. Grant, "Strategic Planning in a Turbulent Environment: Evidence from the Oil Majors," *Strategic Management Journal,* June 2003, pp. 491–517; P. J. Brews and M. R. Hunt, "Learning to Plan and Planning to Learn: Resolving the Planning School/Learning School Debate," *Strategic Management Journal,* December 1999, pp. 889–913; C. C. Miller and L. B. Cardinal, "Strategic Planning and Firm Performance: A Synthesis of More Than Two Decades of Research," *Academy of Management Journal,* March 1994, pp. 1649–85; N. Capon, J. U. Farley, and J. M. Hulbert, "Strategic Planning and Financial Performance: More Evidence," *Journal of Management Studies,* January 1994, pp. 22–38; D. K. Sinha, "The Contribution of Formal Planning to Decisions," *Strategic Management Journal,* October 1990, pp. 479–92; J. A. Pearce II, E. B. Freeman, and R. B. Robinson Jr., "The Tenuous Link between Formal Strategic Planning and Financial Performance," *Academy of Management Review,* October 1987, pp. 658–75; L. C. Rhyne, "Contrasting Planning Systems in High, Medium, and Low

Performance Companies," *Journal of Management Studies,* July 1987, pp. 363–85; and J. A. Pearce II, K. K. Robbins, and R. B. Robinson Jr., "The Impact of Grand Strategy and Planning Formality on Financial Performance," *Strategic Management Journal,* March–April 1987, pp. 125–34.

6. P. McGroarty, "McDonald's Freshens Burgers," *Wall Street Journal Online,* wsj.com. March 7, 2018, pp. B1+.

7. S. Lohr, "IBM Scores Weather Data Deal and Starts Internet of Things Unit," *New York Times Online,* March 31, 2015.

8. T. Hsu and H. Ueno, "Coca-Cola's Move to Juice Up Sales in Japan: Add a Splash of Booze," *New York Times Online,* March 7, 2018.

9. D. Chopping and S. Chaudhuri, "Lego Struggles to Pick Itself Up," *Wall Street Journal,* March 7, 2018, p. B10.

10. T. Mickle, "Apple's Mountain of Cash Is Set to Top $250 Billion," *Wall Street Journal,* May 1, 2017, pp. A1+.

11. A. Andriotis, "AmEx Chief's Mission: Get Millennials, Keep the Rich," *Wall Street Journal Online,* October 20, 2017.

12. K. Safdar, "Target CEO: 'Strategy Is Working,'"*Wall Street Journal,* March 7, 2018, p. B3.

13. J. Jargon, "Papa John's Seeks New Marketing Recipe," *Wall Street Journal,* March 8, 2018, p. B6.

14. L. Stevens, "Amazon Targets Walmart's Market," *Wall Street Journal,* March 8, 2018, p. B2.

15. K. Roose, "Best Buy's Secrets for Thriving in the Age of Amazon," *New York Times Online,* September 18, 2017.

16. M. Gruber, F. Heinemann, M. Brettel, and S. Hungeling, "Configurations of Resources and Capabilities and Their Performance Implications: An Exploratory Study on Technology Ventures," *Strategic Management Journal,* December 2010, pp. 1337–56; T. H. Poister, "The Future of Strategic Planning in the Public Sector: Linking Strategic Management and Performance," *Public Administration Review,* December 2010, pp. S246–S254; J. González-Benito and Isabel Suárez-González, "A Study of the Role Played by Manufacturing Strategic Objectives and Capabilities in Understanding the Relationship between Porter's Generic Strategies and Business Performance," *British Journal of Management* 21 (2010), pp. 1027–43; J. A. Parnell and E. B. Dent, "The Role of Luck in the Strategy-Performance Relationship," *Management Decision* 47, no. 6 (2009), pp. 1000–21; H. J. Cho and V. Pucik, "Relationship

between Innovativeness, Quality, Growth, Profitability, and Market Value," *Strategic Management Journal,* June 2005, pp. 555–75; W. F. Joyce, "What Really Works," *Organizational Dynamics,* May 2005, pp. 118–129; M. A. Roberto, "Strategic Decision-Making Processes," *Group & Organization Management,* December 2004, pp. 625–58; A. Carmeli and A. Tischler, "The Relationships between Intangible Organizational Elements and Organizational Performance," *Strategic Management Journal,* December 2004, 1257–78; D. J. Ketchen, C. C. Snow, and V. L. Street, "Improving Firm Performance by Matching Strategic Decision-Making Processes to Competitive Dynamics," *Academy of Management Executive,* November 2004, pp. 29–43; E. H. Bowman and C. E. Helfat, "Does Corporate Strategy Matter?" *Strategic Management Journal* 22 (2001), pp. 1–23; P. J. Brews and M. R. Hunt, "Learning to Plan and Planning to Learn: Resolving the Planning School-Learning School Debate," *Strategic Management Journal* 20 (1999), pp. 889–913; D. J. Ketchen Jr., J. B. Thomas, and R. R. McDaniel Jr., "Process, Content and Context; Synergistic Effects on Performance," *Journal of Management* 22, no. 2 (1996), pp. 231–57; C. C. Miller and L. B. Cardinal, "Strategic Planning and Firm Performance: A Synthesis of More Than Two Decades of Research," *Academy of Management Journal,* December 1994, pp. 1649–65; and N. Capon, J. U. Farley, and J. M. Hulbert, "Strategic Planning and Financial Performance: More Evidence," *Journal of Management Studies,* January 1994, pp. 105–10.

17. From vision statement of Avon Products Inc. Copyright © by Avon Products Inc. Reprinted by permission.

18. C. K. Prahalad and G. Hamel, "The Core Competence of the Corporation," *Harvard Business Review,* May–June 1990, pp. 79–91.

19. C. H. Green, "Competitive Theory and Business Legitimacy," *BusinessWeek Online,* June 23, 2010; S. Parthasarathy, "Business Strategy" *Financial Management,* June 2010, pp. 32–33; M. E. Porter, *On Competition, Updated and Expanded Edition* (Boston: Harvard Business School, 2008); O. Ormanidhi and O. Stringa, "Porter's Model of Generic Competitive Strategies," *Business Economics,* July 2008, pp. 55–64; M. E. Porter, "The Five Competitive Forces That Shape Strategy," *Harvard Business*

Review, January 2008, pp. 78–93; N. Argyres and A. M. McGahan, "Introduction: Michael Porter's Competitive Strategy," *Academy of Management Executive,* May 2002, pp. 41–42; and N. Argyres and A. M. McGahan, "An Interview with Michael Porter," *Academy of Management Executive,* May 2002, pp. 43–52.

20. D. Snierson, "Hallmark to Debut 34 New Christmas Movies in 2018," ew.com. March 21, 2018; and J. Jurgensen, "On Hallmark, It's Always Christmas," *Wall Street Journal,* November 9, 2017, p. A11.

21. Managing Technology in Today's Workplace box based on D. McGinn, "From Harvard to Las Vegas," *Newsweek,* April 18, 2005, pp. E8–E14; G. Lindsay, "Prada's High-Tech Misstep," *Business 2.0,* March 2004, pp. 72–75; G. Loveman, "Diamonds in the Data Mine," *Harvard Business Review,* May 2003, pp. 109–13; and L. Gary, "Simplify and Execute: Words to Live by in Times of Turbulence," *Harvard Management Update,* January 2003, p. 12.

22. N. A. Shepherd, "Competitive Advantage: Mapping Change and the Role of the Quality Manager of the Future," *Annual Quality Congress,* May 1998, pp. 53–60; T. C. Powell, "Total Quality Management as Competitive Advantage: A Review and Empirical Study," *Strategic Management Journal,* May 1995, pp. 15–37; and R. D. Spitzer, "TQM: The Only Source of Sustainable Competitive Advantage," *Quality Progress,* June 1993, pp. 59–64.

23. R. Pear, "A.M.A. to Develop Measure of Quality of Medical Care," *New York Times Online,* February 21, 2006; and A. Taylor III, "Double Duty," *Fortune,* March 7, 2005, pp. 104–10.

24. T. Mullaney, "'Social Business' Launched This Burger," *USA Today,* May 17, 2012, pp. 1A+.

25. B. Acohido, "Social-Media Tools Boost Productivity," *USA Today,* August 13, 2012, pp. 1B+.

26. Ibid.

27. A. McAfee and E. Brynjolfsson, "Big Data: The Management Revolution," *Harvard Business Review,* October 2012, p. 62.

28. K. Cukier and V. Mayer-Schönberger, "The Financial Bonanza of Big Data," *Wall Street Journal,* March 8, 2013, p. A15.

29. K. Safdar, "Retailers Crack Down on Serial Returners," *Wall Street Journal,* March 14, 2018, pp. A1+; K. Draper, "Madison Square Garden Has Used Face-Scanning Technology on Customers," *New York Times Online,* March 13, 2018; "In-Store Cell Phone

Tracking Pits Consumers against Retailers: Transparency Is Vital if Retailers Want to Build Trust with Customers," adage.com, April 17, 2014; "New Study: Consumers Overwhelmingly Reject In-Store Tracking by Retailers," www.prweb.com, March 27, 2014; A. Farnham, "Retailers Snooping on Holiday Shoppers Raises Privacy Concerns," abcnews.go.com/Business/, December 10, 2013; V. Kopytoff, "Stores Sniff out Smartphones to Follow Shoppers," *MIT Technology Review*, www.technologyreview.com, November 12, 2013; "How Stores Spy on You," www.consumerreports.org, March 2013; J. O'Donnell and S. Meehan, "Retailers Want to Read Your Mind," *USA Today*, March 2, 2012, 1B+; and C. Duhigg, "How Companies Learn Your Secrets," *New York Times Online*, February 16, 2012.

30. McDonald's Annual Report 2007, www.mcdonalds.com (April 21, 2008).

31. S. Zesiger Callaway, "Mr. Ghosn Builds His Dream Car," *Fortune*, February 4, 2008, 56–58.

32. See, for instance, J. Pfeffer, *Organizational Design* (Arlington Heights, IL: AHM Publishing, 1978), pp. 5–12; and C. K. Warriner, "The Problem of Organizational Purpose," *Sociolo-gical Quarterly*, Spring 1965, pp. 139–46.

33. D. Drickhamer, "Braced for the Future," *Industry Week*, October 2004, pp. 51–52.

34. P. N. Romani, "MBO by Any Other Name Is Still MBO," *Supervision*, December 1997, pp. 6–8; and A. W. Schrader and G. T. Seward, "MBO Makes Dollar Sense," *Personnel Journal*, July 1989, pp. 32–37.

35. ClassicConceptsinToday'sWorkplace box based on P. F. Drucker, *The Practice of Management* (New York: Harper & Row, 1954); J. F. Castellano and H. A. Roehm, "The Problem with Managing by Objectives and Results," *Quality Progress*, March 2001, pp. 39–46; J. Loehr and T. Schwartz, "The Making of a Corporate Athlete," *Harvard Business Review*, January 2001, pp. 120–28; A. J. Vogl, "Drucker, of Course," *Across the Board*, November–December 2000, p. 1. For information on goals and goal setting, see, for example, E. A. Locke, "Toward a Theory of Task Motivation and Incentives," *Organizational Behavior and Human Performance*, May 1968, pp. 157–89; E. A. Locke, K. N. Shaw, L. M. Saari, and G. P. Latham, "Goal Setting and Task Performance: 1969–1980," *Psychological Bulletin*, July 1981, pp. 12–52; E. A. Locke and G. P. Latham, *A Theory of Goal Setting and Task Performance* (Upper Saddle River, NJ: Prentice Hall, 1990); P. Ward and M. Carnes, "Effects of Posting Self-Set Goals on Collegiate Football Players' Skill Execution During Practice

and Games," *Journal of Applied Behavioral Analysis*, Spring 2002, pp. 1–12; D. W. Ray, "Productivity and Profitability," *Executive Excellence*, October 2001, p. 14; D. Archer, "Evaluating Your Managed System," *CMA Management*, January 2000, pp. 12–14; and C. Antoni, "Management by Objectives: An Effective Tool for Teamwork," *International Journal of Human Resource Management*, February 2005, pp. 174–84. For information on participation in goal setting, see, for example, T. D. Ludwig and E. S. Geller, "Intervening to Improve the Safety of Delivery Drivers: A Systematic Behavioral Approach," *Journal of Organizational Behavior Management*, April 4, 2000, pp. 11–24; P. Latham and L. M. Saari, "The Effects of Holding Goal Difficulty Constant on Assigned and Participatively Set Goals," *Academy of Management Journal*, March 1979, pp. 163–68; M. Erez, P. C. Earley, and C. L. Hulin, "The Impact of Participation on Goal Acceptance and Performance: A Two Step Model," *Academy of Management Journal*, March 1985, pp. 50–66; and G. P. Latham, M. Erez, and E. A. Locke, "Resolving Scientific Disputes by the Joint Design of Crucial Experiments by the Antagonists: Application to the Erez Latham Dispute Regarding Participation in Goal Setting," *Journal of Applied Psychology*, November 1988, pp. 753–72. For information on effectiveness of MBO, see, for example, F. Dahlsten, A. Styhre, and M. Williander, "The Unintended Consequences of Management by Objectives: The Volume Growth Target at Volvo Cars," *Leadership & Organization Development Journal*, July 2005, pp. 529–41; J. R. Crow, "Crashing with the Nose Up: Building a Cooperative Work Environment," *Journal for Quality and Participation*, Spring 2002, pp. 45–50; and E. C. Hollensbe and J. P. Guthrie, "Group Pay-for-Performance Plans: The Role of Spontaneous Goal Setting," *Academy of Management Review*, October 2000, pp. 864–72.

36. R. Rodgers and J. E. Hunter, "Impact of Management by Objectives on Organizational Productivity," *Journal of Applied Psychology*, April 1991, pp. 322–36.

37. G. P. Latham, "The Motivational Benefits of Goal-Setting," *Academy of Management Executive*, November 2004, pp. 126–29.

38. For additional information on goals, see, for instance, P. Drucker, *The Executive in Action* (New York: HarperCollins Books, 1996), pp. 207–14; and E. A. Locke and G. P. Latham, *A Theory of Goal Setting and Task Performance* (Upper Saddle River, NJ: Prentice Hall, 1990).

39. J. L. Roberts, "Signed, Sealed, Delivered?" *Newsweek*, June 20, 2005, pp. 44–46.

40. Several of these factors were suggested by R. K. Bresser and R. C. Bishop, "Dysfunctional Effects of Formal Planning: Two Theoretical Explanations," *Academy of Management Review*, October 1983, pp. 588–99; and J. S. Armstrong, "The Value of Formal Planning for Strategic Decisions: Review of Empirical Research," *Strategic Management Journal*, July–September 1982, pp. 197–211.

41. K. Garber, "Powering the Information Age," *U.S. News & World Report*, April 2009, pp. 46–48; and S. Hamm, "It's Too Darn Hot," *BusinessWeek*, March 31, 2008, pp. 60–63.

42. "As Q4 Approaches, Which of the Following Is Most Challenging for You as a Leader?" SmartBrief on Leadership, smartbrief.com/leadership, October 15, 2013.

43. Nye Longman, "Swisscom: How to Transform a Telco," *Business Review Europe*, December 22, 2016, http://www.businessrevieweurope.eu/Swisscom-Ltd/profiles/227/Swisscom:-how-to-transform-a-telco (accessed December 22, 2016); Michael Skapinker and Andrea Felsted, "John Lewis: Trouble in Store," *Financial Times*, October 16, 2015, https://www.ft.com/content/92c95704-6c6d-11e5-8171-ba1968cf791a (accessed December 22, 2016); "The Management Style of Amancio Ortega," *The Economist*, December 17, 2016, http://www.economist.com/news/business/21711948-founder-inditex-has-become-worlds-second-richest-man-management-style-amancio (accessed December 22, 2016); Patricia Kowsmann, "Fast-Fashion Leader Inditex Charts Own Path," *Wall Street Journal*, December 6, 2016, http://www.wsj.com/articles/fast-fashion-leader-inditex-charts-own-path-1481020202 (accessed December 22, 2016).

44. A. Campbell, "Tailored, Not Benchmarked: A Fresh Look at Corporate Planning," *Harvard Business Review Online*, https://hbr.org/1999/03/tailored-not-benchmarked-a-fresh-look-at-corporate-planning, April 1999.

45. Ibid.

46. J. H. Sheridan, "Focused on Flow," *IW*, October 18, 1999, pp. 46–51.

47. A. Taylor III, "Hyundai Smokes the Competition," *Fortune*, January 18, 2010, pp. 62–71.

48. Brews and Hunt, "Learning to Plan and Planning to Learn: Resolving the Planning School/Learning School Debate."

49. R. J. Newman, "Coming and Going," *U.S. News and World Report*, January 23, 2006, pp. 50–52; T. Atlas, "Bangalore's Big Dreams," *U.S. News and World Report*, May 2, 2005, pp. 50–52; and K. H. Hammonds, "Smart, Determined, Ambitious, Cheap: The New Face of Global Competition," *Fast Company*, February 2003, pp. 90–97.

50. M. Useem and H. Singh, "The Best Management Is Less Management," *Strategy+Business Online*, January 3, 2018.

51. S. Toy, "Bad Flu Season Reshapes Hospitals," *Wall Street Journal*, February 2, 2018, p. A3.

52. S. Norton and A. Loten, "Technology Aids the Houston Relief Effort," *Wall Street Journal*, September 1, 2017, p. B4.

53. M. Butler, S. Menkes, and M. Michel, "Being Ready for a Crisis," *Strategy+BusinessOnline*, May 18, 2017.

54. See, for example, P. Tarraf and R. Molz, "Competitive Intelligence," *SAM Advanced Management Journal*, Autumn 2006, pp. 24–34; W. M. Fitzpatrick, "Uncovering Trade Secrets: The Legal and Ethical Conundrum of Creative Competitive Intelligence," *SAM Advanced Management Journal*, Summer 2003, pp. 4–12; L. Lavelle, "The Case of the Corporate Spy," *BusinessWeek*, November 26, 2001, pp. 56–58; C. Britton, "Deconstructing Advertising: What Your Competitor's Advertising Can Tell You about Their Strategy," *Competitive Intelligence*, January/February 2002, pp. 15–19; and L. Smith, "Business Intelligence Progress in Jeopardy," *InformationWeek*, March 4, 2002, p. 74.

55. J. Song, S. Shin, L. Jia, C. Cegielski, and R. Rainer, "The Effect of Social Media on Supply Chain Sensing Capability: An Environmental Scanning Perspective," 21st Americas Conference on Information Systems, August 2015, Puerto Rico, pp. 1–13; "Competitive Intelligence Becomes Even More Important," *Trends E-Magazine*, March 2015, pp. 1–5; M. Harrysson, E. Metayer, and H. Sarrazin, "How 'Social Intelligence' Can Guide Decisions," *McKinsey Quarterly*, 2012, no. 4, pp. 81–89; and M. Ojala, "Minding Your Own Business: Social Media Invades Business Research," *Online*, July/August 2012, pp. 51–53.

56. S. Greenbard, "New Heights in Business Intelligence," *Business Finance*, March 2002, pp. 41–46; K. A. Zimmermann, "The Democratization of Business Intelligence," *KN World*, May 2002, pp. 20–21; and C. Britton, "Deconstructing Advertising: What Your Competitor's Advertising Can Tell You about Their Strategy," *Competitive Intelligence*, January–February 2002, pp. 15–19.

57. C. Hausman, "Business-Ethics News Featured in World-Press Reports," *Ethics Newsline*, March 14, 2011; and L. Weathersby, "Take This Job and ***** It," *Fortune*, January 7, 2002, p. 122.

58. P. Lattiman, "Hilton and Starwood Settle Dispute," *New York Times Online*, December 22, 2010; "Starwood vs. Hilton," *Hotels' Investment Outlook*,

June 2009, 14; R. Kidder, "Hotel Industry Roiled by Corporate Espionage Claim," *Ethics Newsline*, www.globalethicslorg/news-line; Reuters, "Hilton Hotels Is Subpoenaed in Espionage Case," *New York Times Online*, April 22, 2009; T. Audi, "U.S. Probes Hilton over Theft Claims," *Wall Street Journal*, April 22, 2009, p. B1; and T. Audi, "Hilton Is Sued over Luxury Chain," *Wall Street Journal*, April 17, 2009, p. B1.

59. B. Rosner, "HR Should Get a Clue: Corporate Spying Is Real," *Workforce*, April 2001, pp. 72–75.

60. K. Western, "Ethical Spying," *Business Ethics*, September–October 1995, pp. 22–23.

61. C. Bjork, "Zara Builds Its Business around RFID," *Wall Street Journal*, September 17, 2014, pp. B1+; D. Roman and W. Kemble-Diaz, "Owner of Fast-Fashion Retailer Zara Keeps up Emerging-Markets Push," *Wall Street Journal*, June 14, 2012, p. B3; Press Releases, "Inditex Achieves Net Sales of 9,709 Million Euros, an Increase of 10 percent," www.inditex.com, February 22, 2012; C. Bjork, "'Cheap Chic' Apparel Sellers Heat up U.S. Rivalry on Web," *Wall Street Journal*, September 6, 2011, pp. B1+; A. Kenna, "Zara Plays Catch-up with Online Shoppers," *Bloomberg BusinessWeek*, August 29–September 4, 2011, pp. 24–25; K. Girotra and S. Netessine, "How to Build Risk into Your Business Model," *Harvard Business Review*, May 2011, pp. 100–05; M. Dart and R. Lewis, "Break the Rules the Way Zappos and Amazon Do," *Bloomberg BusinessWeek Online*, April 29, 2011; K. Cappell, "Zara Thrives by Breaking All the Rules," *BusinessWeek*, October 20, 2008, p. 66; and C. Rohwedder and K. Johnson, "Pace-Setting Zara Seeks More Speed to Fight Its Rising Cheap-Chic Rivals," *Wall Street Journal*, February 20, 2008, pp. B1+.

62. Associated British Foods Plc, www.abf.co.uk; Primark, www.primark.co.uk; R. Baker, "Primark Boldly Does Not Go Online," *Marketing Week*, August 25, 2011, www.marketingweek.co.uk; and M. Sheridan, C. Moore, and K. Nobbs, "Fast Fashion Requires Fast Marketing: The Role of Category Management in Fast Fashion Positioning," *Journal of Fashion Marketing and Management*, 10, 2006.

63. Tesco PLC, "Preliminary Results 2017/18," news release, https://www.tescoplc.com/news/news-releases/2018/preliminary-results-201718/.

64. Tim Clark and Szu Ping Chan, "A History of Tesco: The Rise of Britain's Biggest Supermarket," *The Telegraph*, October 4, 2014, https://www.telegraph.co.uk/finance/markets/2788089/A-history-of-Tesco-The-rise-of-Britains-biggest-supermarket.html.

65. Hannah Liptrot, "Tesco: Supermarket Superpower," *BBC News*, June 3, 2005 http://news.bbc.co.uk/2/hi/business/4605115.stm.

66. David Pollitt, "Retail Insights: Autumn 1998," *International Journal of Retail & Distribution Management* 26(7), 1998, pp. 1–17.

67. "Customer Intelligence: The Secret of Tesco's Success," *MoneyWeek*, May 9, 2007, https://moneyweek.com/31267/how-tesco-became-britains-top-supermarket/.

68. Tesco PLC, "History: About Us," https://www.tescoplc.com/about-us/history/.

69. Lauren Davidson and Graham Ruddick, "Tesco Reveals £6.4bn Loss: As It Happened," *The Telegraph*, April 22, 2015, https://www.telegraph.co.uk/finance/newsbysector/retailandconsumer/11553126/Tesco-reveals-6.4bn-loss.html.

70. Daniel Thomas, "Tesco Profits Rebound as Turnaround Continues," *BBC News*, April 11, 2018, https://www.bbc.com/news/business-43722494.

71. Sharon Marris, "Shareholders Back Tesco's £3.7bn Takeover of Booker," February 28, 2018, https://news.sky.com/story/shareholders-back-tescos-37bn-takeover-of-booker-11270932.

72. "IKEA Facts and Figures 2018," IKEA, https://highlights.ikea.com/2018/facts-and-figures/home/.

73. Harry Wallop, "Ikea: 25 Facts," *The Telegraph*, https://www.telegraph.co.uk/finance/newsbysector/retailandconsumer/9643122/Ikea-25-facts.html.

74. "IKEA's FY16 Profit Rises by 20%," *The Economist*, December 8, 2016, http://www.eiu.com/industry/article/354898619/ikeas-fy16-profit-rises-by-20/2016-12-08.

75. See https://www.ft.com/content/6ad34964-f2fa-11e8-ae55-df4bf40f9d0d

76. See https://www.ft.com/content/1a66c838-3cc1-11e8-b7e0-52972418fec4

77. Ben Stevens, "Ikea Says 40% Profit Drop Is All Part of the Plan," *Retail Gazette*, https://www.retailgazette.co.uk/blog/2018/11/ikea-says-40-profit-drop-part-plan/.

78. "IKEA Posts Record Profit, Sees Consumer Recovery Worldwide," *The Star Online*, https://www.thestar.com.my/business/business-news/2014/01/28/ikea-posts-record-profit/.

79. Sue Mitchell, "Ikea Australia to Test Online Store—Finally," *The Sydney Morning Herald*, June 8, 2016, https://www.smh.com.au/business/companies/ikea-australia-to-test-online-store--finally-20160606-gpcvqh.html.

80. Angela Monaghan, "Ikea to Cut 350 UK Jobs as It Refocuses on Small Outlets and Online," *The Guardian*, November 21, 2018, https://www.theguardian.com/business/2018/nov/21/ikea-to-cut-350-uk-jobs-as-it-refocuses-on-small-outlets-and-online.

81. Sarah Butler, "Ikea Profits Plunge as Revamp Takes Toll," *The Guardian*, November 28, 2018, https://www.theguardian.com/business/2018/nov/28/ikea-profits-revamp-takes-toll.

82. See https://www.ft.com/content/1a66c838-3cc1-11e8-b7e0-52972418fec4.

83. Angela Monaghan, "Ikea to Cut 350 UK Jobs as It Refocuses on Small Outlets and Online," *The Guardian*, November 21, 2018, https://www.theguardian.com/business/2018/nov/21/ikea-to-cut-350-uk-jobs-as-it-refocuses-on-small-outlets-and-online.

84. "IKEA Group Profit Falls as Invests in Online and City-Center Stores," *Reuters*, November 28, 2018, https://www.reuters.com/article/us-ikea-group-results/ikea-group-profit-falls-as-invests-in-online-and-city-center-stores-idUSKCN1NX0P5.

85. Bernard Marr, "The Digital Transformation to Keep IKEA Relevant: Virtual Reality, Apps and Self-Driving Cars," *Forbes*, October 19, 2018, https://www.forbes.com/sites/bernardmarr/2018/10/19/the-amazing-digital-transformation-of-ikea-virtual-reality-apps-self-driving-cars/#ba630d176bed.

Structuring and Designing Organizations

7

Management Myth
Myth
Myth

Bureaucracies are inefficient.

Rawpixel.com/
Shutterstock

Management **DEBUNKED!** Myth

People commonly assume that bureaucracies are inefficient. Critics claim these organizations are slow, rule-bound, and have too much "red tape." The media makes you think bureaucracies are extinct—replaced by empowered teams and loosely structured and adaptive organizations. Although many organizations today *do* look like that, **the truth is that bureaucracies are still alive and well.** Most medium-sized and large organizations are structured as a bureaucracy because its traits—specialization, formal rules and regulations, clear chain of command, and departmentalization—help efficiently structure people and tasks.

WELCOME to the fascinating world of organization structure and design in the twenty-first century! At the *Wall Street Journal*, a broad editorial reorganization created a new leadership structure with the goal of transforming the newspaper into a mobile-first news operation.[1] ♻ Many of the big fashion houses are hiring environmental experts and strengthening the role of their sustainability departments in response to socially conscious young consumers.[2]

These are examples of organizing in action. In this chapter, we present the basics of the organizing function of management. We define the concepts and their key components and how managers use these to create a structured environment in which organizational members can do their work efficiently and effectively. Once the organization's goals, plans, and strategies are in place, managers must develop a structure that facilitates the attainment of those goals and provides a way for people to work best. ●

Learning Outcomes

7-1 Describe six key elements in organizational design. p. 247

7-2 Identify the contingency factors that favor either the mechanistic model or the organic model of organizational design. p. 256

7-3 Compare and contrast traditional and contemporary organizational designs. p. 260

7-4 Discuss the design challenges faced by today's organizations. p. 265

What Are the Six Key Elements in Organizational Design?

7-1 Describe six key elements in organizational design.

A short distance south of McAlester, Oklahoma, employees in a vast factory complex make products that must be perfect. These people "are so good at what they do and have been doing it for so long that they have a 100 percent market share."[3] They make bombs for the U.S. military, and doing so requires a work environment that's an interesting mix of the mundane, structured, and disciplined, coupled with high levels of risk and emotion. The work gets done efficiently and effectively here. Work also gets done efficiently and effectively at San Diego–based videogame maker Psyonix Inc., although not in such a structured and formal way. Like many videogame makers, staffers at Psyonix do the most critical jobs and manage a network of independent contractors scattered around the globe.[4] At Psyonix, almost 40 percent of the people who work on the development of video games are contractors, not employees. Both of these organizations get needed work done, although each does so using a different structure.

Getting work done **efficiently & effectively.**

Organizing is all about that! Recall from Chapter 1 that we defined **organizing** as the function of management that determines what needs to be done, how it will be done, and who is to do it; in other words, the function that creates the organization's structure. When managers develop or change the organization's structure, they're engaging in **organization design**. This process involves making decisions about how specialized jobs should be, the rules to guide employees' behaviors, and at what level decisions are to be made. Although organization design decisions are typically made by top-level managers, it's important for everyone involved to understand the process. Why? Because each of us works in some type of organization structure, and we need to know how and why things get done. In addition, given the changing environment and the need for organizations to adapt, you should begin understanding what tomorrow's structures may look like—those will be the settings you'll be working in.

Few topics in management have undergone as much change in the past few years as that of organizing and organizational structure. Managers are reevaluating traditional approaches and exploring new structural designs that best support and facilitate employees doing the organization's work—designs that can achieve efficiency but are also flexible.

The basic concepts of organization design formulated by management writers such as Henri Fayol and Max Weber offered structural principles for managers to follow. (Look back at the History Module, p. 55.) Over 95 years have passed since many of those principles were originally proposed. Given that length of time and all the changes that have taken place, you'd think that those principles would be mostly worthless today. Surprisingly, they're not. They still provide valuable insights into designing effective and efficient organizations. Of course, we've also gained a great deal of knowledge over the years as to their limitations. In the following sections, we discuss the *six basic elements of organizational structure*: work specialization, departmentalization, authority and responsibility, span of control, centralization versus decentralization, and formalization.

1 What Is Work Specialization?

TRADITIONAL VIEW. At the Wilson Sporting Goods factory in Ada, Ohio, workers make every football used in the National Football League and most of those used in college and high school football games. To meet daily output goals, the workers specialize in job tasks such as molding, stitching and sewing, lacing, and so forth.[5] This is an example of **work specialization**, which is dividing work activities into separate job tasks. (That's why it's also known as division of labor.) Individual employees "specialize" in doing part of an activity rather than the entire activity in order to increase work output.

organizing
The function of management in which the organization's structure is created

organization design
When managers develop or change the organization's structure

work specialization
Dividing work activities into separate job tasks; also called division of labor

Exhibit 7–1 Economies and Diseconomies of Work

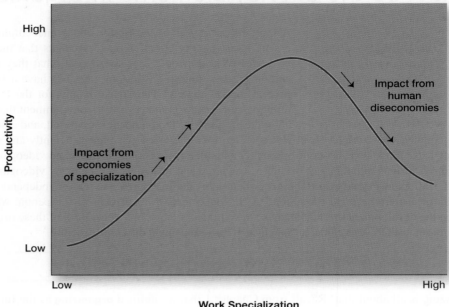

Work Specialization

Work specialization allows organizations to efficiently use the diversity of skills that workers have. In most organizations, some tasks require highly developed skills; others can be performed by employees with lower skill levels. If all workers were engaged in all the steps of, say, a manufacturing process, all would need the skills necessary to perform both the most demanding and the least demanding jobs. Thus, except when performing the most highly skilled or highly sophisticated tasks, employees would be working below their skill levels. In addition, skilled workers are paid more than unskilled workers, and because wages tend to reflect the highest level of skill, all workers would be paid at highly skilled rates to do easy tasks—an inefficient use of resources. This concept explains why you rarely find a cardiac surgeon closing up a patient after surgery. Instead, surgical residents learning the skill usually stitch and staple the patient after the surgeon has finished the surgery.

Early proponents of work specialization believed that it could lead to great increases in productivity. At the beginning of the twentieth century, that generalization was reasonable. Because specialization was not widely practiced, its introduction almost always generated higher productivity. But a good thing can be carried too far. At some point, the human diseconomies—boredom, fatigue, stress, low productivity, poor quality, increased absenteeism, and high turnover—outweigh the economic advantages (see Exhibit 7–1).[6]

TODAY'S VIEW.   Most managers today see work specialization as an important organizing mechanism because it helps employees be more efficient. For example, McDonald's uses high specialization to get its products made and delivered to customers efficiently. However, managers also have to recognize its limitations. That's why companies such as Avery-Dennison, Ford Australia, Hallmark, and American Express use minimal work specialization and instead give employees a broad range of tasks to do. Think about this when you're looking for a job. Are you going to be happiest in a highly specialized job or do you prefer a variety of work tasks?

2 What Is Departmentalization?

TRADITIONAL VIEW.   Early management writers argued that after deciding what job tasks will be done by whom, common work activities needed to be grouped back together so work was done in a coordinated and integrated way. How jobs are grouped together is called **departmentalization**. There are five common forms (see Exhibit 7–2), although an

departmentalization
How jobs are grouped together

organization may use its own unique classification. No single method of departmentalization was advocated by the early writers. The method or methods used would reflect the grouping that best contributed to the attainment of the goals of the organization and the individual units.

How are **activities** grouped?

1. One of the most popular ways to group activities is by functions performed, or **functional departmentalization**. A manager might organize the workplace by separating engineering, accounting, information systems, human resources, and purchasing specialists into departments. Functional departmentalization can be used in all types of organizations. Only the functions change to reflect the organization's objectives and activities. The major advantage to functional departmentalization is the achievement of economies of scale by placing people with common skills and specializations into common units.

Lacing is one of 13 separate tasks involved in hand-crafting a Wilson Sporting Goods football. The company uses work specialization in dividing job activities as an organizing mechanism that helps employees boost their productivity and makes efficient use of workers' diverse skills.

2. **Product departmentalization** focuses attention on major product areas in the corporation. Each product is under the authority of a senior manager who is a specialist in, and is responsible for, everything having to do with his or her product line. One company that uses product departmentalization is Nike. Its structure is based on its varied product lines, which include athletic and dress/casual footwear, sports apparel and accessories, and performance equipment. If an organization's activities were service related rather than product related, each service would be autonomously grouped. The advantage of product grouping is that it increases accountability for product performance because all activities related to a specific product are under the direction of a single manager.

3. The particular type of customer an organization seeks to reach can also dictate employee grouping. The sales activities in an office supply firm, for instance, can be divided into three departments that serve retail, wholesale, and government customers. A large law office can segment its staff on the basis of whether it serves corporate or individual clients. The assumption underlying **customer departmentalization** is that customers in each department have a common set of problems and needs that can best be met by specialists.

> **functional departmentalization**
> Grouping activities by functions performed
>
> **product departmentalization**
> Grouping activities by major product areas
>
> **customer departmentalization**
> Grouping activities by customer

Exhibit 7–2 Types of Departmentalization

• **Functional**	Groups employees based on work performed (e.g., engineering, accounting, information systems, human resources)
• **Product**	Groups employees based on major product areas in the corporation (e.g., women's footwear, men's footwear, and apparel and accessories)
• **Customer**	Groups employees based on customers' problems and needs (e.g., wholesale, retail, government)
• **Geographic**	Groups employees based on location served (e.g., North, South, Midwest, East)
• **Process**	Groups employees based on the basis of work or customer flow (e.g., testing, payment)

geographic departmentalization
Grouping activities on the basis of geography or territory

process departmentalization
Grouping activities on the basis of work or customer flow

cross-functional teams
Teams made up of individuals from various departments and that cross traditional departmental lines

chain of command
The line of authority extending from upper organizational levels to lower levels, which clarifies who reports to whom

authority
The rights inherent in a managerial position to give orders and expect the orders to be obeyed

4. Another way to departmentalize is on the basis of geography or territory—**geographic departmentalization**. The sales function might have western, southern, Midwestern, and eastern regions. If an organization's customers are scattered over a large geographic area, this form of departmentalization can be valuable. For instance, the organization structure of Coca-Cola reflects the company's operations in two broad geographic areas—the North American sector and the international sector (which includes the Pacific Rim, the European Community, Northeast Europe and Africa, and Latin America).

5. The final form of departmentalization is called **process departmentalization**, which groups activities on the basis of work or customer flow—like that found in many government offices or in health care clinics. Units are organized around common skills needed to complete a certain process. If you've ever been to a state office to get a driver's license, you've probably experienced process departmentalization. With separate departments to handle applications, testing, information and photo processing, and payment collection, customers "flow" through the various departments in sequence to get their licenses.

TODAY'S VIEW. Most large organizations continue to use most or all of the departmental groups suggested by the early management writers. Black & Decker, for instance, organizes its divisions along functional lines, its manufacturing units around processes, its sales around geographic regions, and its sales regions around customer groupings. However, many organizations use **cross-functional teams**, which are teams made up of individuals from various departments and that cross traditional departmental lines. These teams have been useful especially as tasks have become more complex and diverse skills are needed to accomplish those tasks.[7]

Also, today's competitive environment has refocused the attention of management on its customers. To better monitor the needs of customers and to be able to respond to changes in those needs, many organizations are giving greater emphasis to customer departmentalization.

3 What Are Authority and Responsibility?

TRADITIONAL VIEW. To understand authority and responsibility, you also have to be familiar with the **chain of command**, the line of authority extending from upper organizational levels to lower levels, which clarifies who reports to whom. Managers need to consider it when organizing work because it helps employees with questions such as "Who do I report to?" or "Who do I go to if I have a problem?" So, what *are* authority and responsibility?

Harley-Davidson uses cross-functional teams from the conception and design of its motorcycles to their production and product launch. Harley's teams of buyers, suppliers, marketers, operations personnel, engineers, and employees from other departments work together to provide customers with quality products.

H. Mark Weidman Photography/Alamy Stock Photo

Authority comes from **the position, not the person.**

Authority refers to the rights inherent in a managerial position to give orders and expect the orders to be obeyed. Authority was a major concept discussed by the early management writers as they viewed it as the glue that held an organization together.[8] It was delegated downward to lower-level managers, giving them certain rights while prescribing certain limits within which to operate. Each management position had specific inherent rights that incumbents acquired from the position's rank or title. Authority, therefore, is related to one's position within an organization and has nothing to do with the personal

Exhibit 7–3 Chain of Command and Line Authority

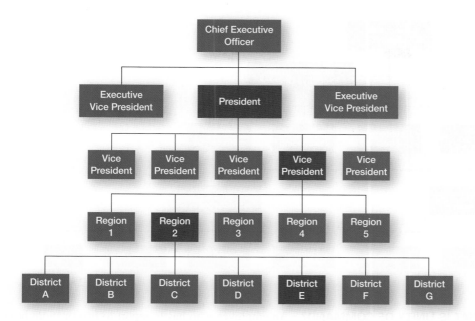

characteristics of an individual manager. When a position of authority is vacated, the person who has left the position no longer has any authority. The authority remains with the position and its new incumbent.

When managers delegate authority, they must allocate commensurate **responsibility**. That is, when employees are given rights, they also assume a corresponding obligation to perform. And they'll be held accountable for their performance! Allocating authority without responsibility and accountability creates opportunities for abuse. Likewise, no one should be held responsible or accountable for something over which he or she has no authority.

WHAT ARE THE DIFFERENT TYPES OF AUTHORITY RELATIONSHIPS?   The early management writers distinguished between two forms of authority: line authority and staff authority. **Line authority** entitles a manager to direct the work of an employee. It is the employer–employee authority relationship that extends from the top of the organization to the lowest echelon, according to the chain of command, as shown in Exhibit 7–3. As a link in the chain of command, a manager with line authority has the right to direct the work of employees and to make certain decisions without consulting anyone. Of course, in the chain of command, every manager is also subject to the direction of his or her superior.

Keep in mind that sometimes the term *line* is used to differentiate line managers from staff managers. In this context, *line* refers to managers whose organizational function contributes directly to the achievement of organizational objectives. In a manufacturing firm, line managers are typically in the production and sales functions, whereas managers in human resources and payroll are considered staff managers with staff authority. Whether a manager's function is classified as line or staff depends on the organization's objectives. For example, at Staff Builders, a supplier of temporary employees, interviewers have a line function. Similarly, at the payroll firm of ADP, payroll is a line function.

As organizations get larger and more complex, line managers may find that they don't have the time, expertise, or resources to get their jobs done effectively. In response, they create **staff authority** functions to support, assist, advise, and generally reduce some of their informational burdens. The hospital administrator who cannot effectively handle the purchasing of all the supplies the hospital needs creates a purchasing department, a staff department. Of course, the head of the purchasing department has line authority over the purchasing agents who work for him. The hospital administrator might also find that she is overburdened and needs an assistant. In creating the position of her assistant, she has created a staff position. Exhibit 7–4 illustrates line and staff authority.

responsibility
An obligation to perform assigned duties

line authority
Authority that entitles a manager to direct the work of an employee

staff authority
Positions with some authority that have been created to support, assist, and advise those holding line authority

Exhibit 7–4 Line versus Staff Authority

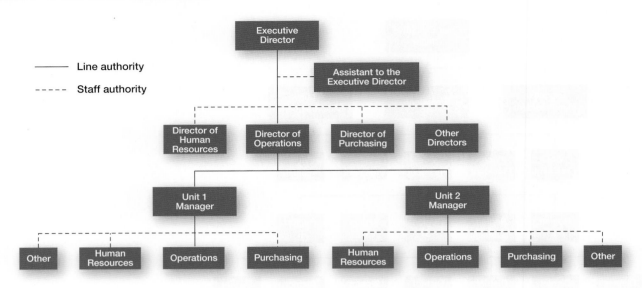

WHAT IS UNITY OF COMMAND? An employee who has to report to two or more bosses might have to cope with conflicting demands or priorities.[9] Accordingly, the early writers believed that each employee should report to only one manager, a term called **unity of command**. In those rare instances when the unity of command had to be violated, a clear separation of activities and a supervisor responsible for each was always explicitly designated.

One boss or more?

Unity of command was logical when organizations were relatively simple. Under some circumstances it is still sound advice and organizations continue to adhere to it. But advances in technology, for instance, allow access to organizational information that was once accessible only to top managers. And employees can interact with anyone else in the organization without going through the formal chain of command. Thus, in some instances, strict adherence to unity of command creates a degree of inflexibility that hinders an organization's performance and ability to respond to changing circumstances.

TODAY'S VIEW. The early management writers loved the idea of authority. They assumed that the rights inherent in one's formal position in an organization were the sole source of influence, and they believed that managers were all-powerful. This assumption might have been true 60—even 30—years ago. Organizations were simpler. Staff was less important. Managers were only minimally dependent on technical specialists. Under such conditions, influence is the same as authority. And the higher a manager's position in the organization, the more influence he or she had. However, *those conditions no longer exist.* Researchers and practitioners of management now recognize that you don't have to be a manager to have power and that power is not perfectly correlated with one's level in the organization.

Authority is an important concept in organizations, but an exclusive focus on authority produces a narrow, unrealistic view of influence. Today, we recognize that *authority is but one element in the larger concept of power.*

HOW DO AUTHORITY AND POWER DIFFER? Authority and power are often considered the same thing, but they're not. Authority is a right. Its legitimacy is based on an authority figure's position in the organization. Authority goes with the job. **Power**, on the other hand, refers to an individual's capacity to influence decisions. Authority is part of the larger concept of power. That is, the formal rights that come with an individual's position in the organization are just one means by which an individual can affect the decision process.

unity of command
Structure in which each employee reports to only one manager

power
An individual's capacity to influence decisions

Exhibit 7–5 Authority versus Power

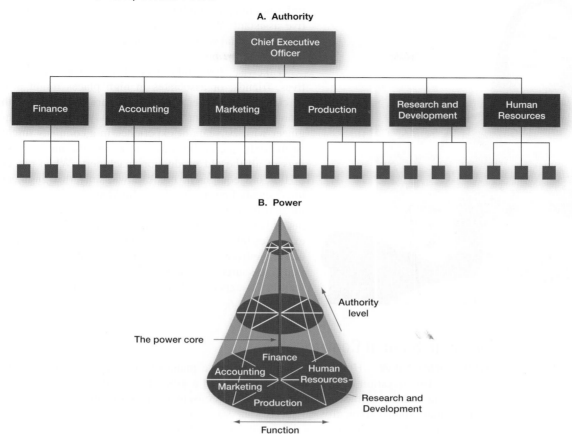

A. Authority

B. Power

Exhibit 7–5 visually depicts the difference between authority and power. The two-dimensional arrangement of boxes in part A portrays authority. The area in which the authority applies is defined by the horizontal dimension. Each horizontal grouping represents a functional area. The influence one holds in the organization is defined by the vertical dimension in the structure. The higher one is in the organization, the greater one's authority.

Power, on the other hand, is a three-dimensional concept (the cone in part B of Exhibit 7–5). It includes not only the functional and hierarchical dimensions, but also a third dimension called centrality. Although authority is defined by one's vertical position in the hierarchy, power is made up of both one's vertical position and one's distance from the organization's power core or center.

Think of the cone in Exhibit 7–5 as an organization. The center of the cone is the power core. The closer you are to the power core, the more influence you have on decisions. The existence of a power core is, in fact, the only difference between A and B in Exhibit 7–5. The vertical hierarchy dimension in A is merely one's level on the outer edge of the cone. The top of the cone corresponds to the top of the hierarchy, the middle of the cone to the middle of the hierarchy, and so on. Similarly, the functional groups in A become wedges in the cone. Each wedge represents a functional area.

The cone analogy explicitly acknowledges two facts: (1) The higher one moves in an organization (an increase in authority), the closer one moves to the power core; and (2) it is not necessary to have authority in order to wield power because one can move horizontally inward toward the power core without moving up. For instance, assistants often are powerful in a company even though they have little authority. As gatekeepers for their bosses, these assistants have considerable influence over whom their bosses see and when they see them. Furthermore, because they're regularly relied upon to pass information on to their bosses, they have some control over what their bosses hear. It's not unusual for a

Melissa Brenner, senior vice president of marketing for the National Basketball Association, has expert power. Her expertise in using Facebook, Instagram, and other social media in innovative ways is helping the NBA achieve its goal of enhancing fans' engagement and enjoyment of the game throughout the world.

$105,000-a-year middle manager to tread carefully in order not to upset the boss's $45,000-a-year administrative assistant. Why? Because the assistant has power. This individual may be low in the authority hierarchy but close to the power core.

Likewise, low-ranking employees who have relatives, friends, or associates in high places might also be close to the power core. So, too, are employees with scarce and important skills. The lowly production engineer with 20 years of experience in a company might be the only one in the firm who knows the inner workings of all the old production machinery. When pieces of this old equipment break down, only this engineer understands how to fix them. Suddenly, the engineer's influence is much greater than it would appear from his or her level in the vertical hierarchy. What do these examples tell us about power? They indicate that power can come from different areas. French and Raven identified five sources, or bases, of power: coercive, reward, legitimate, expert, and referent.[10] We summarize them in Exhibit 7–6.

4 What Is Span of Control?

TRADITIONAL VIEW. How many employees can a manager efficiently and effectively supervise? This question of **span of control** received a great deal of attention from early management writers. Although they came to no consensus on a specific number, most favored small spans—typically no more than six workers—in order to maintain close control.[11] However, several writers did acknowledge level in the organization as a contingency variable. They argued that as a manager rises in an organization, he or she has to deal with a greater number of unstructured problems, so top managers need a smaller span than do middle managers, and middle managers require a smaller span than do supervisors. Over the last decade, however, we've seen some change in theories about effective spans of control.[12]

span of control
The number of employees a manager can efficiently and effectively supervise

TODAY'S VIEW. Many organizations are increasing their spans of control. The span for managers at such companies as General Electric and Kaiser Aluminum has expanded significantly in the past decade. It has also expanded in the federal government, where efforts to increase the span of control are being implemented to save time in making decisions.[13] The most effective and efficient span of control is increasingly being determined by looking at contingency variables.

Exhibit 7–6 Types of Power

Coercive power	Power based on fear.
Reward power	Power based on the ability to distribute something that others value.
Legitimate power	Power based on one's position in the formal hierarchy.
Expert power	Power based on one's expertise, special skill, or knowledge.
Referent power	Power based on identification with a person who has desirable resources or personal traits.

Jennifer S. Altman/Bloomberg/Getty Images

How Many People **Can I** Effectively and Efficiently Manage?

Most effective and efficient span depends on:

- Employee managerial experience and training (more you have, larger span).
- Similarity of employee tasks (more similarity, larger span).
- Complexity of those tasks (more complex, smaller span).
- Physical proximity of employees (closer proximity, larger span).
- Amount and type of standardized procedures (more standardized, larger span).
- Sophistication of the organization's management information system (more sophisticated, larger span).
- Strength of the organization's value system (stronger the value system, larger span).
- Preferred managing style of the manager[14] (personal preference of more or fewer employees to manage).

5 How Do Centralization and Decentralization Differ?

TRADITIONAL VIEW.   One of the questions that needs to be answered when organizing is "At what level are decisions made?" **Centralization** is the degree to which decision making takes place at upper levels of the organization. **Decentralization** is the degree to which lower-level managers provide input or actually make decisions. Centralization-decentralization is not an either-or concept. Rather, it's a matter of degree. What we mean is that no organization is completely centralized or completely decentralized. Few, if any, organizations could effectively function if all their decisions were made by a select few people (centralization) or if all decisions were pushed down to the level closest to the problems (decentralization). Let's look, then, at how the early management writers viewed centralization as well as at how it exists today.

Early management writers proposed that centralization in an organization depended on the situation.[15] Their goal was the optimum and efficient use of employees. Traditional organizations were structured in a pyramid, with power and authority concentrated near the top of the organization. Given this structure, historically centralized decisions were the most prominent, but organizations today have become more complex and responsive to dynamic changes in their environments. As such, many managers believe that decisions need to be made by those individuals closest to the problems, regardless of their organizational level. In fact, the trend over the past several decades—at least in U.S. and Canadian organizations—has been a movement toward more decentralization in organizations.[16]

TODAY'S VIEW.   Today, managers often choose the amount of centralization or decentralization that will allow them to best implement their decisions and achieve organizational goals.[17] What works in one organization, however, won't necessarily work in another, so managers must determine the amount of decentralization for each organization and work units within it. When managers empower employees and delegate to them the authority to make decisions on those things that affect their work and to change the way that they think about work, that's decentralization. Notice, however, that it doesn't imply that top-level managers no longer make decisions.

6 What Is Formalization?

TRADITIONAL VIEW.   **Formalization** refers to how standardized an organization's jobs are and the extent to which employee behavior is guided by rules and procedures. Highly formalized organizations have explicit job descriptions, numerous organizational rules, and clearly defined procedures covering work processes. Employees have little discretion over what's done, when it's done, and how it's done. However, where formalization is low, employees have more discretion in how they do their work. Early management writers expected organizations to be fairly formalized, as formalization went hand-in-hand with bureaucratic-style organizations.

centralization
The degree to which decision making takes place at upper levels of the organization

decentralization
The degree to which lower-level managers provide input or actually make decisions

formalization
How standardized an organization's jobs are and the extent to which employee behavior is guided by rules and procedures

What Contingency Variables Affect Structural Choice?

7-2 Identify the contingency factors that favor either the mechanistic model or the organic model of organizational design.

Top managers typically think long and hard about **what structure will work best.**

Adamkaz/E+/getty images

IF these are the contingency factors,
THEN this is the most appropriate structure.

The **"THEN"**: Appropriate Organizational Structure (See Exhibit 7–7)

Exhibit 7–7 Mechanistic versus Organic Organizations

MECHANISTIC

☐ Rigid hierarchical relationships
☐ Fixed duties
☐ Many rules
☐ Formalized communication channels
☐ Centralized decision authority
☐ Taller structures

ORGANIC

☐ Collaboration (both vertical and horizontal)
☐ Adaptable duties
☐ Few rules
☐ Informal communication
☐ Decentralized decision authority
☐ Flatter structures

mechanistic organization
A bureaucratic organization; a structure that's high in specialization, formalization, and centralization

organic organization
A structure that's low in specialization, formalization, and centralization

Mechanistic OR Organic[18]

Mechanistic organization (or bureaucracy)

- Rigid and tightly controlled structure
- Combines traditional aspects of all six elements of organization structure

  - High specialization
  - Rigid departmentalization
  - Clear chain of command

- Narrow spans of control leading to taller structure
- Centralization
- High formalization

Organic organization

- Highly adaptive and flexible structure

- Collaboration (both vertical and horizontal)
- Adaptable duties
- Few rules
- Loose structure allows for rapid adjustment to change[19]

- Informal communication
- Decentralized decision authority
- Wider spans of control leading to flatter structures

The "IF": 4 Contingency Variables

❶ Strategy ⟶ Structure

- Based on work of Alfred Chandler[20]
- Goals are important part of organization's strategies; structure should facilitate goal achievement
- Simple strategy → simple structure
- Elaborate strategy → more complex structure
- Certain structural designs work best with different organizational strategies[21]
  — Passionate pursuit of innovation → organic
  — Passionate pursuit of cost control → mechanistic

Coloures-pic/Fotolia

❷ Size ⟶ Structure

- Considerable evidence that size (number of employees) affects structure[22]
- Magic number seems to be 2,000 employees
- **LARGE** organizations (> 2,000 employees)—mechanistic
- When an organization reaches this number, size is *less influential;* adding more employees has little impact as structure is already fairly mechanistic

A smaller organization with a more organic structure becomes more mechanistic if a significant number of new employees are added to it.

ORGANIC

fewer than 2,000 employees can be organic

MECHANISTIC

more than 2,000 employees forces organizations to become more mechanicstic

❸ Technology ⟶ Structure

- Technology is used—by every organization—to convert inputs into outputs

(See Exhibit 7–8 in the Classic Concepts in Today's Workplace on p. 259.)

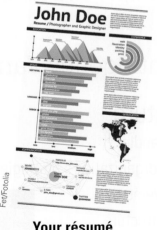

Your smartphone or tablet
standardized assembly line

Your résumé
custom design and print

Your bottle of ibuprofen
continuous-flow production process

❹ Environment ⟶ Structure

- Environment is a constraint on managerial discretion
- Environment also has a major effect on an organization's structure
  — Stable environment: Mechanistic structure
  — Dynamic/uncertain environment: Organic structure
- Helps explain why so many managers today have restructured their organizations to be lean, fast, and flexible.[23]

TODAY'S VIEW.   Although some formalization is necessary for consistency and control, many organizations today rely less on strict rules and standardization to guide and regulate employee behavior. For instance, consider the following situation:

> A customer comes into a branch of a large national package delivery chain and drops off a package for same-day shipping 37 minutes after the store's cut-off time. Although the counter clerk knows he's supposed to follow the rules, he also knows he could get the package processed and shipped out with no problem and wants to accommodate the customer. So he accepts the package and hopes that his manager won't find out.[24] Did this employee do something wrong? He did "break" the rule. But by "breaking" the rule, he actually brought in revenue and provided good customer service.

Considering there are numerous situations where rules may be too restrictive, many organizations have allowed employees some latitude, giving them sufficient autonomy to make those decisions that they feel are best under the circumstances. It doesn't mean throwing out all organizational rules because there always *will* be rules that are important for employees to follow—and these rules should be explained so employees understand why it's important to adhere to them. But for other rules, employees may be given some leeway.[25]

---

unit production
The production of items in units or small batches

mass production
Large-batch manufacturing

process production
Continuous flow or process production

 ◀◀◀ Classic Concepts in Today's Workplace ▶▶▶

- Initial research on Technology → Structure done by Joan Woodward.[26]

- Woodward, a British management scholar, studied small manufacturing firms in southern England to determine the extent to which structural design elements were related to organizational success.[27]

- No consistent pattern found UNTIL firms divided into three distinct technologies that had increasing levels of complexity and sophistication.

  - Least complex and sophisticvated: **Unit production**—the production of items in units or small batches

  - **Mass production**—large-batch manufacturing

  - Most complex and sophisticated: **process production**—continuous-process production

- One of the earliest *contingency* studies.

- Her answer to the "it depends on" question: Appropriate organizational design depends on what the organization's technology is. These design decisions can influence an organization's sustainability efforts.

- More recent studies also have shown that organizations adapt their structures to their technology depending on *how routine their technology is* for transforming inputs into outputs.

  - More routine technology, more likely to have mechanistic structure
  - More nonroutine technology, more likely to have organic structure

> ## How does technology affect organization design?

Discussion Questions:

1 Why is (a) mechanistic structure more appropriate for an organization with routine technology and (b) organic structure more appropriate for an organization with nonroutine technology?

2 Does Woodward's framework still apply to today's organizations? Why or why not?

Exhibit 7–8 Woodward's Findings on Technology and Structure

	UNIT PRODUCTION	MASS PRODUCTION	PROCESS PRODUCTION
Structural characteristics:	Low vertical differentiation	Moderate vertical differentiation	High vertical differentiation
	Low horizontal differentiation	High horizontal differentiation	Low horizontal differentiation
	Low formalization	High formalization	Low formalization
Most effective structure:	Organic	Mechanistic	Organic

What Are Some Common Organizational Designs?

7-3 Compare and contrast traditional and contemporary organizational designs.

In making structural decisions, managers have some common designs from which to choose: traditional and more contemporary. Let's look at some.

What Traditional Organizational Designs Can Managers Use?

When designing a structure, managers may choose one of the traditional organizational designs. These structures—simple, functional, and divisional—tend to be more mechanistic in nature. (See Exhibit 7–9 for a summary of the strengths and weaknesses of each.)

WHAT IS THE SIMPLE STRUCTURE? Most companies start as entrepreneurial ventures using a **simple structure**, which is an organizational design with low departmentalization, wide spans of control, authority centralized in a single person, and little formalization.[28] The simple structure is most widely used in smaller businesses, and its strengths should be obvious. It's fast, flexible, and inexpensive to maintain, and accountability is clear. However, it becomes increasingly inadequate as an organization grows because its few policies or rules to guide operations and its high centralization result in information overload at the top. As size increases, decision making becomes slower and can eventually come to a standstill as the single executive tries to continue making all the decisions. If the structure is not changed and adapted to its size, the firm can lose momentum and is likely to eventually fail. The simple structure's other weakness is that it's risky: Everything depends on one person. If anything happens to the owner-manager, the organization's information and

simple structure
An organizational design with low departmentalization, wide spans of control, authority centralized in a single person, and little formalization

Exhibit 7–9 Traditional Organization Designs

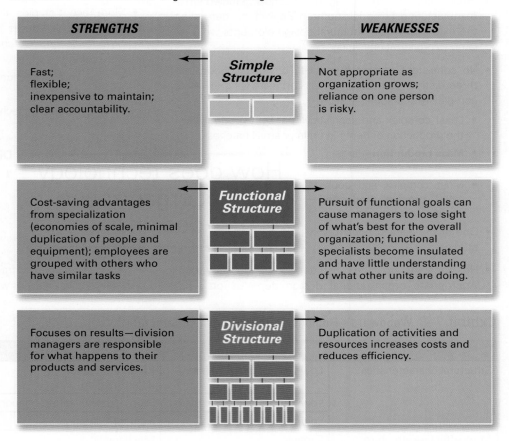

	STRENGTHS		WEAKNESSES	

| **Simple Structure** | Fast; flexible; inexpensive to maintain; clear accountability. | Not appropriate as organization grows; reliance on one person is risky. |

| **Functional Structure** | Cost-saving advantages from specialization (economies of scale, minimal duplication of people and equipment); employees are grouped with others who have similar tasks | Pursuit of functional goals can cause managers to lose sight of what's best for the overall organization; functional specialists become insulated and have little understanding of what other units are doing. |

| **Divisional Structure** | Focuses on results—division managers are responsible for what happens to their products and services. | Duplication of activities and resources increases costs and reduces efficiency. |

Source: Robbins, Stephen P., Coulter, Mary, *Management*, 13th Ed., © 2016, p. 304. Reprinted and electronically reproduced by permission of Pearson Education, Inc., New York, NY.

decision-making center is lost. As employees are added, however, most small businesses don't remain as simple structures. The structure tends to become more specialized and formalized. Rules and regulations are introduced, work becomes specialized, departments are created, levels of management are added, and the organization becomes increasingly bureaucratic. Two of the most popular bureaucratic design options grew out of functional and product departmentalizations and are called the functional and divisional structures.

> **functional structure**
> An organizational design that groups similar or related occupational specialties together
>
> **divisional structure**
> An organizational structure made up of separate business units or divisions

WHAT IS THE FUNCTIONAL STRUCTURE? A **functional structure** is an organizational design that groups similar or related occupational specialties together. You can think of this structure as functional departmentalization applied to the entire organization. For example, Revlon Inc. is organized around the functions of operations, finance, human resources, and product research and development.

The strength of the functional structure lies in the advantages that accrue from work specialization. Putting like specialties together results in economies of scale, minimizes duplication of personnel and equipment, and makes employees comfortable and satisfied because it gives them the opportunity to talk the same language as their peers. The most obvious weakness of the functional structure, however, is that the organization frequently loses sight of its best interests in the pursuit of functional goals. No one function is totally responsible for results, so members within individual functions become insulated and have little understanding of what people in other functions are doing.

WHAT IS THE DIVISIONAL STRUCTURE? The **divisional structure** is an organizational structure made up of separate business units or divisions.[29] In this structure, each division has limited autonomy, with a division manager who has authority over his or her unit and is responsible for performance. In divisional structures, however, the parent corporation typically acts as an external overseer to coordinate and control the various divisions, and often provides support services such as financial and legal. Health care giant Johnson & Johnson, for example, has three divisions: pharmaceuticals, medical devices and diagnostics, and consumer products. In addition, it has several subsidiaries that also manufacture and market diverse health care products.

The chief advantage of the divisional structure is that it focuses on results. Division managers have full responsibility for a product or service. The divisional structure also frees the headquarters staff from being concerned with day-to-day operating details so that they can pay attention to long-term and strategic planning. The major disadvantage of the divisional structure is duplication of activities and resources. Each division, for instance, may have a marketing research department. If there weren't any divisions, all of an organization's marketing research might be centralized and done for a fraction of the cost that divisionalization requires. Thus, the divisional form's duplication of functions increases the organization's costs and reduces efficiency.

What Contemporary Organizational Designs Can Managers Use?

Lean. Flexible. Innovative.

Managers are finding that the traditional designs often aren't appropriate for today's increasingly dynamic and complex environment. Instead, organizations need to be lean, flexible, and innovative—that is, more organic. So managers

A team-based structure at Whole Foods Market is key to its successful growth in becoming the world's leading retailer in natural and organic foods. Each store is organized in teams grouped from departments such as produce, meat, checkout, and prepared foods, shown in this photo. The entire company is structured around teams, including store leaders, regional presidents, and corporate executives.

Patrick T. Fallon/Bloomberg/Getty Images

are finding creative ways to structure and organize work by using designs such as team-based structures, matrix and project structures, and boundaryless structures.[30] (See Exhibit 7–10 for a summary of these designs.)

WHAT ARE TEAM STRUCTURES?   Larry Page and Sergey Brin, co-founders of Google, created a corporate structure that "tackles most big projects in small, tightly focused teams."[31] A **team structure** is one in which the entire organization is made up of work teams that do the organization's work.[32] In this structure, employee empowerment is crucial because there is no line of managerial authority from top to bottom. Rather, employee

Exhibit 7–10 Contemporary Organization Designs

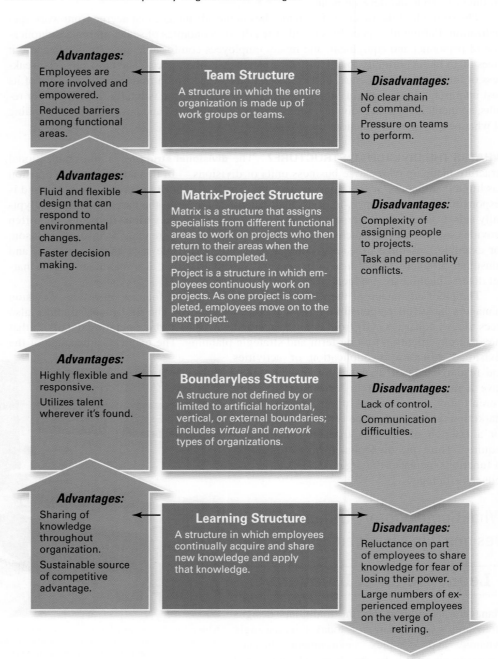

Source: Robbins, Stephen P., Coulter, Mary, *Management*, 13th Ed., © 2016, p. 315. Reprinted and electronically reproduced by permission of Pearson Education, Inc., New York, NY.

teams design and do work in the way they think is best, but are also held responsible for all work performance results in their respective areas. In large organizations, the team structure complements what is typically a functional or divisional structure. This allows the organization to have the efficiency of a bureaucracy while providing the flexibility of teams. For instance, companies such as Amazon, Boeing, Hewlett-Packard, Louis Vuitton, Motorola, and Xerox extensively use employee teams to improve productivity.

Although team structures have been positive, simply arranging employees into teams is not enough. Employees must be trained to work on teams, receive cross-functional skills training, and be compensated accordingly. Without a properly implemented team-based pay plan, many of the benefits of a team structure may be lost.[33] We'll cover teams more thoroughly in Chapter 9.

WHAT ARE MATRIX AND PROJECT STRUCTURES?   In addition to team-based structures, other popular contemporary designs are the matrix and project structures. The **matrix structure** assigns specialists from different functional departments to work on projects led by a project manager. When employees finish work on an assigned project, they go back to their functional departments. One unique aspect of this design is that it creates a *dual chain of command* because employees in a matrix organization have two managers, their functional area manager and their product or project manager, who share authority. (See Exhibit 7–11.) The project manager has authority over the functional members who are part of his or her project team in areas related to the project's goals. However, any decisions about promotions, salary recommendations, and annual reviews typically remain the functional manager's responsibility. To work effectively, both managers have to communicate regularly, coordinate work demands on employees, and resolve conflicts together.

> **matrix structure**
> A structure in which specialists from different functional departments are assigned to work on projects led by a project manager

Some 84 percent of American workers work in a matrix-type organization.[34]

Exhibit 7–11 Sample Matrix Structure

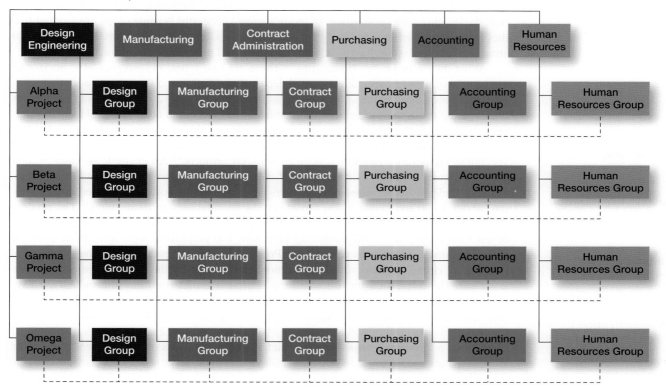

The primary strength of the matrix is that it can facilitate coordination of a multiple set of complex and interdependent projects while still retaining the economies that result from keeping functional specialists grouped together. The major disadvantages of the matrix are the confusion it creates and its propensity to foster power struggles. When you dispense with the chain of command and unity of command principles, you significantly increase ambiguity. Confusion can arise over who reports to whom. The confusion and ambiguity, in turn, are what trigger the power struggles.

Instead of a matrix structure, many organizations are using a **project structure**, in which employees continuously work on projects. Unlike the matrix structure, a project structure has no formal departments where employees return at the completion of a project. Instead, employees take their specific skills, abilities, and experiences to other projects. Also, all work in project structures is performed by teams of employees. For instance, at design firm IDEO, project teams form, disband, and form again as the work requires. Employees "join" project teams because they bring needed skills and abilities to that project. Once a project is completed, however, they move on to the next one.[35]

Project structures tend to be more flexible organizational designs.

- Advantages:
  - Employees can be deployed rapidly to respond to environmental changes.
  - No departmentalization or rigid organizational hierarchy to slow down decisions or actions.
  - Managers serve as facilitators, mentors, and coaches and work to eliminate or minimize organizational obstacles and ensure that teams have the resources they need to effectively and efficiently complete their work.
- Disadvantages:
  - Complexity of assigning people to projects.
  - Inevitable task and personality conflicts that arise.

WHAT IS A BOUNDARYLESS ORGANIZATION?   Another contemporary organizational design is the **boundaryless organization**, which is an organization whose design is not defined by, or limited to, the horizontal, vertical, or external boundaries imposed by a predefined structure.[36] Former GE chairman Jack Welch coined the term because he wanted to eliminate vertical and horizontal boundaries within GE and break down external barriers between the company and its customers and suppliers. Although the idea of eliminating boundaries may seem odd, many of today's most successful organizations are finding that they can operate most effectively by remaining flexible and *un*structured: that the ideal structure for them is *not* having a rigid, bounded, and predefined structure.[37]

What do we mean by "boundaries"? There are two types: (1) *internal*—the horizontal ones imposed by work specialization and departmentalization and the vertical ones that separate employees into organizational levels and hierarchies, and (2) *external*—the boundaries that separate the organization from its customers, suppliers, and other stakeholders. To minimize or eliminate these boundaries, managers might use virtual or network structural designs.

A **virtual organization** consists of a small core of full-time employees and outside specialists temporarily hired as needed to work on projects.[38] An example is when Second Life, a company creating a virtual world of colorful online avatars, was building its software. Founder Philip Rosedale hired programmers from around the world and divided up the work into about 1,600 individual tasks, "from setting up databases to fixing bugs." The process worked so well, the company used it for all sorts of work.[39] Another example is Nashville-based Emma Inc., an e-mail marketing firm with 100 employees who work from home or offices in Austin, Denver, New York, and Portland.[40] The biggest challenge they've faced is creating a "virtual" culture, a task made more challenging by the fact that the organization is virtual. The inspiration for this structural approach comes from the film industry. There, people are essentially "free agents" who move from project to project applying their skills—directing, talent casting, costuming, makeup, set design, and so forth—as needed.

Another structural option for managers wanting to minimize or eliminate organizational boundaries is a **network organization**, which is one that uses its own employees to do some work activities and networks of outside suppliers to provide other needed product components or work processes.[41] This organizational form is sometimes called a modular organization by

project structure
A structure in which employees continuously work on projects

boundaryless organization
An organization whose design is not defined by, or limited to, boundaries imposed by a predefined structure

virtual organization
An organization that consists of a small core of full-time employees and outside specialists temporarily hired as needed to work on projects

network organization
An organization that uses its own employees to do some work activities and networks of outside suppliers to provide other needed product components or work processes

manufacturing firms.[42] This structural approach allows organizations to concentrate on what they do best by contracting out other activities to companies that do those activities best. Many companies are using such an approach for certain organizational work activities. For instance, the head of development for Boeing's 787 airplane manages thousands of employees and some 100 suppliers at more than 100 sites in different countries.[43] Sweden's Ericsson contracts its manufacturing and even some of its research and development to more cost-effective contractors in New Delhi, Singapore, California, and other global locations.[44] And at Penske Truck Leasing, dozens of business processes such as securing permits and titles, entering data from drivers' logs, and processing data for tax filings and accounting have been outsourced to Mexico and India.[45]

What Are Today's Organizational Design Challenges?

7-4 Discuss the design challenges faced by today's organizations.

Changing the **Way Work** Is Done

As managers look for organizational designs that will best support and facilitate *employees doing their work efficiently and effectively*, there are certain challenges they must contend with. These include keeping employees connected, managing global structural issues, building a learning organization, and designing flexible work arrangements.

How Do You Keep Employees Connected?

Many organizational design concepts were developed during the twentieth century when work tasks were fairly predictable and constant, most jobs were full-time and continued indefinitely, and work was done at an employer's place of business under a manager's supervision.[47] That's not what it's like in many organizations today, as you saw in our preceding discussion of virtual and network organizations. A major structural design challenge for managers is finding a way to keep widely dispersed and mobile employees connected to the organization. The Managing Technology in Today's Workplace box describes ways that information technology can help.

How Do Global Differences Affect Organizational Structure?

Are there global differences in organizational structures? Are Australian organizations structured like those in the United States? Are German organizations structured like those in France or Mexico? Given the global nature of today's business environment, this is an issue with which managers need to be familiar. Researchers have concluded that the structures and strategies of organizations worldwide are similar, "while the behavior within them is maintaining its cultural uniqueness."[48] What does this mean for designing effective and efficient structures?

Making Ethical Decisions in Today's Workplace

The business press headlines consistently make it clear that employees shouldn't count on long-term employment with one employer. Career counselors and coaches (even textbook authors!) tell job seekers that they need to be responsible for their own careers and to prepare for the likelihood that they'll be changing jobs frequently. Employment trends also confirm that highly routine, well-defined, and stable jobs are disappearing.[46] Job security and stability seem to be relics of the past.

Discussion Questions:

3 Do you think that stability is good or bad for employees? How about you? Is stability important to you? Explain your answers.

4 Do employers have an ethical responsibility to provide security for employees or just a warning about a lack of security? Working in your assigned group, discuss and come up with an answer. Be prepared to defend your position.

VCG/Getty images

Zhang Ruimin is the chairman and CEO of Haier Group, a Chinese maker of home appliances. After taking over a failing refrigerator plant, Ruimin reorganized the company into project teams comprised of members from different divisions that focused on producing quality products based on customer needs. The new structure helped Haier return to profitability, compete globally, and become the world leader of major appliances by sales volume.

When designing or changing structure, managers may need to think about the cultural implications of certain design elements. For instance, one study showed that formalization—rules and bureaucratic mechanisms—may be more important in less economically developed countries and less important in more economically developed countries where employees may have higher levels of professional education and skills.[49] Other structural design elements may be affected by cultural differences as well.

How Do You Build a Learning Organization?

Doing business in an intensely competitive global environment, British retailer Tesco realized how important it was for its stores to run well behind the scenes. And it does so using a proven "tool" called Tesco in a Box, which promotes consistency in operations as well as being a way to share innovations. Tesco is an example of a **learning organization**, an organization that has developed the capacity to continuously learn, adapt, and change.[50] The concept of a learning organization doesn't involve a specific organizational design per se, but instead describes an organizational mind-set or philosophy that has significant design implications. In a learning organization, employees are practicing knowledge management by continually acquiring and sharing new knowledge and are willing to apply that knowledge in making decisions or performing their work. Some organizational design theorists even go so far as to say that an organization's ability to learn and to apply that learning as they perform the organization's work may be the only sustainable source of competitive advantage.

What would a learning organization look like? As you can see in Exhibit 7–12, the important characteristics of a learning organization revolve around (1) organizational design, (2) information sharing, (3) leadership, and (4) culture.

1. What types of organizational design elements would be necessary for learning to take place? In a learning organization, it's critical for members to share information and collaborate on work activities throughout the entire organization—across different functional specialties and even at different organizational levels—through minimizing or eliminating the existing structural and physical boundaries. In this type of boundaryless environment, employees are free to work together and collaborate in doing the organization's work the best way they can, and to learn from each other. Because of this need to collaborate, teams also tend to be an important feature of a learning organization's structural design. Employees work in teams on whatever activities need to be done, and these employee teams are empowered to make decisions about doing their work or resolving issues. Empowered employees and teams have little need for "bosses" who direct and control. Instead, managers serve as facilitators, supporters, and advocates for employee teams.

2. Learning can't take place without information. For a learning organization to "learn," information must be shared among members; that is, organizational employees must engage in knowledge management by sharing information openly, in a timely manner, and as accurately as possible. Because few structural and physical barriers exist in a learning

learning organization
An organization that has developed the capacity to continuously learn, adapt, and change

Exhibit 7–12 Characteristics of a Learning Organization

Sources: Based on P. M. Senge, *The Fifth Discipline: The Art and Practice of Learning Organizations* (New York: Doubleday, 1990); and R. M. Hodgetts, F. Luthans, and S. M. Lee, "New Paradigm Organizations: From Total Quality to Learning to World Class," *Organizational Dynamics*, Winter 1994, pp. 4–19.

organization, the environment is conducive to open communication and extensive information sharing.

3. Leadership plays an important role as an organization moves toward becoming a learning organization. What should leaders do in a learning organization? One of their most important functions is facilitating the creation of a shared vision for the organization's future and then keeping organizational members working toward that vision. In addition, leaders should support and encourage the collaborative environment that's critical to learning. Without strong and committed leadership throughout the organization, it would be extremely difficult to be a learning organization.

4. The organization's culture is important to being a learning organization. In a learning culture, everyone agrees on a shared vision and everyone recognizes the inherent interrelationships among the organization's processes, activities, functions, and external environment. It also fosters a strong sense of community, caring for each other, and trust. In a learning organization, employees feel free to communicate openly, share, experiment, and learn without fear of criticism or punishment.

How Can Managers Design Efficient and Effective Flexible Work Arrangements?

Accenture consultant Keyur Patel's job arrangement is becoming the norm, rather than the exception.[51] During a recent consulting assignment, he had three clocks on his desk: one set to Manila time (where his software programmers were), one to Bangalore (where another programming support team worked), and the third for San Francisco, where he was spending four days a week helping a major retailer implement IT systems to track and improve sales. And his cell phone kept track of the time in Atlanta, his home, where he headed on Thursday evenings.

For this new breed of professionals, life is a blend of home and office, work and leisure. Thanks to technology, work can now be done anywhere, anytime. As organizations adapt their structural designs to these new realities, we see more of them adopting flexible working arrangements. Such arrangements not only exploit the power of technology, but also give organizations the flexibility to deploy employees when and where needed. In this section, we're going to take a look at some different types of flexible work arrangements, including telecommuting; compressed workweeks, flextime, and job sharing; and contingent workforce. Where work is done most efficiently and effectively—office, home,

remote work
Doing work via virtual devices from any remote location

telecommuting
A work arrangement in which employees work at home and are linked to the workplace by virtual devices

combination—is an important workplace issue. The three main managerial concerns are productivity, innovation, and collaboration. Do flexible arrangements lead to greater productivity or inhibit innovation and collaboration? Another concern is that employees, especially younger ones, expect to be able to work remotely. Yes, the trend has been toward greater workplace flexibility, but does that flexibility lead to a bloated, lazy, and unproductive remote workforce? These are the challenges of designing work structures. As with the other structural options we've looked at, managers must evaluate these in light of the implications for decision making, communication, authority relationships, work task accomplishment, and so forth. For instance, IBM Corp. recently reevaluated its remote work strategy and decided that it was in the company's best interest to make a change. Thousands of its remote workers in the United States were given a choice: Either abandon working from home or leave the company.[52] But many other businesses still maintain a viable remote workforce.

WHAT'S INVOLVED IN REMOTE WORK OR TELECOMMUTING? Information technology has made remote work and telecommuting *possible* and external environmental changes have made it *necessary* for many organizations. **Remote work** is doing work via virtual devices from any remote location, either work done on the road or work done from home. **Telecommuting** specifically is a remote work arrangement in which employees work at home and are linked to the workplace by virtual devices. Needless to say, not every job is a candidate for remote work or telecommuting. But many are.

Working from home used to be considered a "cushy perk" for a few lucky employees, and such an arrangement wasn't allowed very often. Now, many businesses view telecommuting as a business necessity. For instance, at SCAN Health Plan, the company's chief financial officer said that getting more employees to telecommute provided the company a way to grow without having to incur any additional fixed costs such as office buildings, equipment, or parking lots.[53] In addition, some companies view the arrangement as a way to combat high gas prices and to attract talented employees who want more freedom and control over their work.

Despite its apparent appeal, many managers are reluctant to have their employees become "laptop hobos."[54] They argue that employees might waste time surfing the Internet or playing online games instead of working, ignore clients, and desperately miss the camaraderie and social exchanges of the workplace. In addition, managers worry about how they'll "manage" these employees. How do you interact with an employee and gain his or her trust when they're not physically present? And what if their work performance isn't up to par? How do you make suggestions for improvement? Another significant challenge is making sure that company information is kept safe and secure when employees are working from home.

Todd Horton is the founder and CEO of KangoGift, a human resources software firm that helps companies send performance awards to employees. KangoGift has four staffers who work together in Boston and six remote employees who work from their home offices in Europe and India. Horton is shown here with intern Minjee Kim at a co-work space where he holds staff meetings via Skype.

Employees often express the same concerns about working remotely, especially when it comes to the isolation of not being "at work." At Accenture, where employees are scattered around the world, the chief human resources officer says that it isn't easy to maintain that esprit de corps.[55] However, the company put in place a number of programs and processes to create that sense of belonging for its workforce including web conferencing tools, assigning each employee to a career counselor, and holding quarterly community events at its offices. In addition, the telecommuter employee may find that the line between work and home becomes even more blurred, which can be stressful.[56] These are important organizing issues and ones that managers and organizations must address when moving toward having employees telecommute.

Michael Dwyer/AP Images

Managing Technology in Today's Workplace
⊕THE CHANGING WORLD OF WORK

It's fair to say that the world of work will never be like it was 10 years ago.[57] IT has opened up new possibilities for employees to do their work in locations as remote as Patagonia or in the middle of downtown Seattle. Although organizations have always had employees who traveled to distant corporate locations to take care of business, these employees no longer have to find the nearest pay phone or wait to get back to "the office" to see what problems have cropped up. Instead, mobile computing and communication have given organizations and employees ways to stay connected, be more productive, and be more environmentally friendly. Let's look at some of the technologies that are changing the way work is done.

- Handheld devices with e-mail, calendars, and contacts can be used anywhere there's a wireless network. And these devices can be used to log into corporate databases and company intranets.
- Employees can videoconference using broadband networks and web cams.
- Many companies are giving employees key fobs with constantly changing encryption codes that allow them to log onto the corporate network to access e-mail and company data from any computer hooked up to the Internet.

- Cell phones switch seamlessly between cellular networks and corporate Wi-Fi connections.

The biggest issue in doing work anywhere, anytime is security. Companies must protect their important and sensitive information. However, software and other disabling devices have minimized security issues considerably. Even insurance providers are more comfortable giving their mobile employees access to information. For instance, Health Net Inc. gave BlackBerrys to many of its managers so they can tap into customer records from anywhere. One tech company CEO said that all types of organizations should start thinking about identifying and creating innovative apps that their workers could use in doing their jobs more efficiently and effectively and get those to them.

Discussion Questions:

5 (a) What benefits do you see with being able to do work anywhere, anytime? (Think in terms of benefits for an organization and for its human resources.) (b) How do you personally feel about being able to do work anywhere, anytime?

6 What other issues, besides security, do you see with being able to do work anywhere, anytime? (Again, think about this for an organization and for its employees.)

HOW CAN ORGANIZATIONS USE COMPRESSED WORKWEEKS, FLEXTIME, AND JOB SHARING? Although retail organizations recognize that erratic work schedules can take a toll on the well-being of service employees, they continued to use them because having stable employee work hours was believed to be just too costly. (Some of you may know this firsthand, having worked or possibly still working in retail.) Gap decided to see what impact steady hours—that is, more consistent start and stop times—would have.[58] In the recently completed study conducted at more than two dozen Gap retail stores, the researchers uncovered some surprising results. The study showed that more predictable and consistent hours for employees not only helped workers, but also had a positive effect on store profit. Here's another example of how an organization adapted its organizational structure in a changing environment. During the most recent economic crisis in the United Kingdom, accounting firm KPMG needed to reduce costs and decided to use flexible work options as a way of doing so.[59] The company's program, called Flexible Futures, offered employees four options to choose from: a four-day workweek with a 20 percent salary reduction; a 2- to 12-week sabbatical at 30 percent of pay; both options; or continue with their regular schedule. Some 85 percent of the UK employees agreed to the reduced-work-week plan. "Since so many people agreed to the flexible work plans, KPMG was able to cap the salary cut at about 10 percent for the year in most cases." The best thing, though, was that as a result of the plan, KPMG didn't have to do large-scale employee layoffs.

As this example shows, organizations sometimes find they need to restructure work using other forms of flexible work arrangements. (1) One approach is a **compressed workweek** in which employees work longer hours per day but fewer days per week. The most common arrangement is four 10-hour days (a 4–40 program). (2) Another alternative is **flextime** (also known as **flexible work hours**), which is a scheduling system in

compressed workweek
A workweek where employees work longer hours per day but fewer days per week

flextime (also known as flexible work hours)
A work scheduling system in which employees are required to work a specific number of hours per week but can vary when they work those hours within certain limits

job sharing
When two or more people split a full-time job

contingent workers
Temporary, freelance, or contract workers whose employment is *contingent* upon demand for their services

which employees are required to work a specific number of hours a week but are free to vary those hours within certain limits. In a flextime schedule, most companies designate certain common core hours when all employees are required to be on the job, but starting, ending, and lunch-hour times are flexible. (3) Another type of job scheduling is called **job sharing**—the practice of having two or more people split a full-time job. Organizations might offer job sharing to professionals who want to work but don't want the demands and hassles of a full-time position. For instance, at Ernst & Young, employees in many of the company's locations can choose from a variety of flexible work arrangements including job sharing. Many companies use job sharing during economic downturns to avoid employee layoffs.[60]

WHAT IS A CONTINGENT WORKFORCE? "When Julia Lee first heard of Tongal, she thought it was a scam. Tongal pays people—anyone with a good idea, really—to create online videos for companies such as Mattel, Allstate, and Popchips."[61] Tongal divides projects into stages and pays cash for the top-five ideas. On Lee's first submission—which only took three hours of work—she got $1,000. On another, she earned $4,000. In a year's time, she's earned some $6,000 for about 100 hours of work. Tongal isn't the only business doing this. The idea of breaking up a job into small pieces and using the Internet to find workers to do those tasks was pioneered by LiveOps and followed by **Amazon.com**'s Mechanical Turk and many others.

Switch on. Switch off.

"Companies want a workforce they can switch on and off as needed."[62] Although this quote may shock you, the truth is that the labor force already has begun shifting away from traditional full-time jobs toward **contingent workers**—temporary, freelance, or contract workers whose employment is *contingent* upon demand for their services. In today's economy, many organizations have responded by converting full-time permanent jobs into contingent jobs. It's predicted that by the end of the next decade, the number of contingent employees will have grown to about 40 percent of the workforce. (It's at 30 percent today.)[63] In fact, one compensation and benefits expert says that "a growing number of workers will need to structure their careers around this model."[64] That's likely to include you!

What are the implications for managers and organizations? Because contingent employees are not "employees" in the traditional sense of the word, managing them has its own set of challenges and expectations. Managers must recognize that because contingent workers lack the stability and security of permanent employees, they may not identify with the organization or be as committed or motivated. Managers may need to treat contingent workers differently in terms of practices and policies. However, with good communication and leadership, an organization's contingent employees can be just as valuable a resource to an organization as permanent employees are. Today's managers must recognize that it will be their responsibility to motivate their entire workforce, full-time and contingent, and to build their commitment to doing good work![65]

No matter what structural design managers choose for their organizations, the design should help employees do their work in the best, most efficient and effective way they can. The structure needs to help, not hinder, organizational members as they carry out the organization's work. After all, the structure is simply a means to an end.

Knowing: Getting Ready for Exams and Quizzes

CHAPTER SUMMARY BY LEARNING OUTCOME

7-1 Describe six key elements in organizational design.

The first element, *work specialization*, refers to dividing work activities into separate job tasks. The second, *departmentalization*, is how jobs are grouped together, which can be one of five types: functional, product, customer, geographic, or process. The third—*authority, responsibility*, and *power*—has to do with getting work done in an organization. Authority refers to the rights inherent in a managerial position to give orders and expect those orders to be obeyed. Responsibility refers to the obligation to perform when authority has been delegated. Power is the capacity of an individual to influence decisions and is not the same as authority. The fourth, *span of control*, refers to the number of employees a manager can efficiently and effectively manage. The fifth, *centralization and decentralization*, deals with where the majority of decisions are made—at upper organizational levels or pushed down to lower-level managers. The sixth, *formalization*, describes how standardized an organization's jobs are and the extent to which employees' behavior is guided by rules and procedures.

7-2 Identify the contingency factors that favor either the mechanistic model or the organic model of organizational design.

A *mechanistic* organization design is quite bureaucratic whereas an *organic* organization design is more fluid and flexible. The *strategy*-determines-structure factor says that as organizational strategies move from single product to product diversification, the structure will move from organic to mechanistic. As an organization's *size* increases, so does the need for a more mechanistic structure. The more nonroutine the *technology*, the more organic a structure should be. Finally, stable *environments* are better matched with mechanistic structures, but dynamic ones fit better with organic structures.

7-3 Compare and contrast traditional and contemporary organizational designs.

Traditional structural designs include simple, functional, and divisional. A *simple structure* is one with low departmentalization, wide spans of control, authority centralized in a single person, and little formalization. A *functional structure* is one that groups similar or related occupational specialties together. A *divisional structure* is one made up of separate business units or divisions. Contemporary structural designs include *team-based structures* (the entire organization is made up of work teams), *matrix and project structures* (where employees work on projects for short periods of time or continuously), and *boundaryless organizations* (where the structural design is free of imposed boundaries). A boundaryless organization can either be a virtual or a network organization.

7-4 Discuss the design challenges faced by today's organizations.

One design challenge lies in keeping employees connected, which can be accomplished through using information technology. Another challenge is understanding the global differences that affect organizational structure. Although structures and strategies of organizations worldwide are similar, the behavior within them differs, which can influence certain design elements. Another challenge is designing a structure around the mind-set of being a learning organization. Finally, managers are looking for organizational designs with efficient and effective flexible work arrangements. They're using options such as remote work, telecommuting, compressed workweeks, flextime, job sharing, and contingent workers.

DISCUSSION QUESTIONS

7-1 Discuss the six key concepts defining organization design.

7-2 What are the concepts of traditional and contemporary organizational design? Will these designs be influenced differently by management and the environment?

7-3 Compared to the strengths and weaknesses of a functional structure, what are the strengths and weaknesses of a simple structure?

7-4 Contrast the design of a boundaryless organization and a structureless organization. Explain the points of contrast with examples.

7-5 Contrast mechanistic and organic organizations.

7-6 Explain the contingency factors that affect organizational design.

7-7 With the availability of information technology that allows employees to work anywhere, anytime, is organizing still an important managerial function? Why or why not?

7-8 Researchers are now saying that efforts to simplify work tasks actually have negative results for both companies and their employees. Do you agree? Why or why not?

7-9 "The boundaryless organization has the potential to create a major shift in the way we work." Do you agree or disagree with this statement? Explain.

7-10 Draw an organization chart of an organization with which you're familiar (where you work, a student organization to which you belong, your college or university, etc.). Be very careful in showing the departments (or groups) and especially be careful to get the chain of command correct. Be prepared to share your chart with the class. When interviewing for a job, what information might an organization chart give you?

Applying: Getting Ready for the Workplace

Management Skill Builder | INCREASING YOUR POWER

Managerial jobs come with the power of authority. But sometimes that authority isn't enough to get things done. And other times you may not want to use your formal authority as a means of getting people to do what you want. You may, for instance, want to rely more on your persuasive skills than the power of your title. So effective managers increase their power by developing multiple sources of influence.

MyLab Management
PERSONAL INVENTORY ASSESSMENT

Go to **www.pearson.com/mylab/management** to complete the Personal Inventory Assessment related to this chapter.

Skill Basics

You can increase the likelihood that you'll survive and thrive in your organization if you learn how to develop a power base. Remember, because you have power doesn't mean you have to use it. But it's nice to be able to call upon it when you do need it. Four sources of power can be derived from your job. Another three sources are based on your personal unique characteristics.

• All management jobs come with the power to coerce, reward, and impose authority. *Coercive power* is based on fear. If you can dismiss, suspend, demote, assign unpleasant work tasks, or write a negative performance review on someone, you hold coercive power over that person. Conversely, if you can give someone something of positive value or remove something of negative value—like control pay rates, raises, bonuses, promotions, or work assignments—you have *reward power*. And all managerial positions provide some degree—though within specific limitations—to exert authority over subordinates. If you can tell someone to do something and they see this request to be within your formal job description, you have *authority power* over them.

- In addition to coercive, reward, and authoritative power, many managerial positions also possess *information power* that comes from access to and control over information. If you have data or knowledge that others need, and which only you have access to, it gives you power. Of course, you don't have to be a manager to have information power. Many employees are quite skilled at operating in secrecy, hiding technical short-cuts, or avoiding showing others exactly what they do—all with the intention of keeping important knowledge from getting into others' hands.

- You don't have to be a manager or control information to have power in an organization. You can also exert influence based on your expertise, admiration that others might have for you, and through charismatic qualities. If you have a special skill or unique knowledge that others in the organization depend on, you hold *expert power*. In our current age of specialization, this source of power is increasingly potent. If others identify with you and look up to you to the extent that they want to please you, you have *referent power*. It develops out of admiration and the desire to be like someone else. The final source of influence is *charismatic power*, which is an extension of referent power. If others will follow you because they admire your heroic qualities, you have charismatic power over them.

- Based on these sources of power, we can say that you can increase your power in organizations by (1) taking on managerial responsibilities, (2) gaining access to important

information, (3) developing an expertise that the organization needs, or (4) displaying personal characteristics that others admire.

Based on J. R. P. French Jr. and B. Raven, "The Bases of Social Power," in D. Cartwright (ed.), *Studies in Social Power* (Ann Arbor: University of Michigan Institute of Social Research, 1959), pp. 150–67; B. H. Raven, "The Bases of Power: Origin and Recent Developments," *Journal of Social Issues* 49 (1993), pp. 227–51; E. A. Ward, "Social Power Bases of Managers: Emergence of a New Factor," *Journal of Social Psychology*, February 2001, pp. 144–47; and B. H. Raven, "The Bases of Power and the Power/Interaction Model of Interpersonal Influence," *Analyses of Social Issues and Public Policy*, December 2008, pp. 1–22.

Practicing the Skill

Read through this scenario and follow the directions at the end of it:

Margaret is a supervisor in the online sales division of a large clothing retailer. She has let it be known that she is devoted to the firm and plans to build her career there. Margaret is hardworking and reliable, has volunteered for extra projects, has taken in-house development courses, and joined a committee dedicated to improving employee safety on the job. She undertook an assignment to research ergonomic office furniture for the head of the department and gave up several lunch hours to consult with the head of human resources about her report. Margaret filed the report late, but she explained the delay by saying that her assistant lost several pages that she had to redraft over the weekend. The report was well received, and several of Margaret's colleagues think she should be promoted when the next opening arises.

Evaluate Margaret's skill in building a power base. What actions has she taken that are helpful to her in reaching her goal? Is there anything she should have done differently?

Experiential Exercise

You want to convince your boss to let you work remotely from home. First, make a list of the pros and cons for your employer and for yourself. Then, consider how you can demonstrate your commitment to being an effective and efficient employee in this new work arrangement. How will you show your manager that you'll still be the eager and hardworking employee you are at the office?

First, come up with your own ideas. Be specific. Then, in your assigned group, discuss each person's ideas and come up with a master list of five suggestions for how you can *best demonstrate* your commitment to doing your work as efficiently and effectively while working from home as you do in the office. Be prepared to convince your instructor and other class members.

CASE APPLICATION #1

Turbulence at United Air

Topic: Organizational structure, employee behavior

2017 was a public relations nightmare for United Airlines. Several incidents involving United Air employees enforcing a variety of rules, regulations, and protocols in interactions with customers caused international outcry. First, in March, two teenagers wearing leggings for their flight from Minneapolis to Denver were stopped by the gate agent and not allowed to board for violating the United Airlines travel perk program. With travel perk passes, individuals fly free or for heavily discounted fares and are thus subject to a stricter dress code than regular passengers. The longstanding policy requires that those who enjoy the perks of airline employment, which includes free travel passes for family and guests, present themselves in a way that represents the airline well. So, the intent of a stricter dress code—a written code that all employees are aware of—is that the airline wants to present itself in a positive, favorable light. United defended its decision via Twitter, "Leggings are not inappropriate attire except in the case of someone traveling as a pass rider."[66]

How much employee flexibility is needed?

A second, more serious incident occurred when David Dao, a doctor, who needed to see his patients the following morning, was aboard a Louisville-bound flight from Chicago in April.[67] The flight was full, but four United employees needed to get to Louisville at the last minute to staff a flight, and it was announced that four people would need to give up their seats or else the flight would be canceled. When no one volunteered, gate agents invoked the airline's involuntary denial-of-boarding process. That means that customers who had paid the lowest fares, were not connecting to other flights, and had checked in last were at the top of the list to be removed. Customers' frequent-flyer status also was another consideration. United officials say that this is the procedure they followed in selecting Dr. Dao, his wife, and another couple for removal. After Dr. Dao declined to leave, United Air officials called Chicago Department of Aviation police officers to try to persuade him to go. However, Dr. Dao tried to keep the officers from pulling him out of his seat before being dragged out of it and forcibly removing him from the plane. Several cell phone videos captured the incident and soon went viral. Dao suffered a broken nose and concussion after his head was smashed into an armrest. United policy allowed for the involuntary removal of passengers from flights, although this time United was not as defensive. Dao later filed a lawsuit for its actions.[68] The suit was settled in late April. In addition, two of the Chicago airport security officers were fired for their role in the episode.[69]

Then, in late April, a third incident, in Houston, involved a soon-to-be-wed couple.[70] Michael and Amber were headed to Costa Rica for their wedding. When they boarded, they noticed a man sleeping in the row where their seats were assigned. Instead of disturbing him, they found some seats three rows away and sat there instead. A flight attendant asked them to return to their seats, which they did. However, a U.S. marshall approached them soon after and ejected them from the plane. According to United statements, the couple "repeatedly" tried to sit in upgraded seats and would not follow the crew's instructions, and, as such, they were within their power to eject the customers.

Then, in March 2018, a passenger's dog in a pet carrier died in an overhead compartment.[71] The passenger had been instructed by a flight attendant to put the dog there shortly after she boarded. The passenger was very adamant that she did not want to do that, but the flight attendant kept requesting that she comply because the pet carrier was a safety hazard. Eventually, the pet owner complied. When the flight arrived at its destination, the owner discovered that it had died. United responded that it is not the policy to put animals in the overhead compartment. The company said it was investigating who had put the dog in the overhead compartment and why.

These incidents suggest that employees do not have much latitude or flexibility when dealing with day-to-day policy issues. With airlines trying to minimize costs and boost efficiency, perhaps the organization structure was more focused on following rules rather than serving the customer. Many attribute this inflexibility to the strict rule-following bureaucracy created by United's managers.[72] In such an environment, employees may be reluctant to deviate from the rules, especially since employees are aware of the precedent that suggests that anyone who breaks the rules faces termination.

Discussion Questions

7-11 Evaluate how United Airlines handled each of these incidents. Do you think that United Airlines was within its power to respond the way its employees did? Why or why not?

7-12 How would you describe United Airlines' view of formalization? Do you think it's appropriate? Explain.

7-13 Using information from the chapter about the contingency factors that favor either the mechanistic or the organic model of organizational design, what do you think United Airlines' organizational structure should resemble? Be sure to think about this in terms of efficiency and effectiveness.

7-14 What do you think United Airlines should do in the future? What suggestions or enhancements might you have for its organizational structure?

7-15 How do employees' actions reflect an organization's stance as far as being responsible and ethical? How might United's managers encourage employees to be more responsible and ethical, even when rules must be followed?

CASE APPLICATION #2

Lift Off

Topic: Learning organization, knowledge resources

Over the years, NASA (National Aeronautics and Space Administration) has provided us with some spectacular moments—from Neil Armstrong's first steps on the moon to the Hubble Telescope's mesmerizing photos of distant stars and galaxies. As stated in NASA's Strategic Plan, its vision is: "We reach for new heights and reveal the unknown for the benefit of humankind." And its mission is: "Drive advances in science, technology, aeronautics, and space exploration to enhance knowledge, education, innovation, economic vitality, and stewardship of Earth."[73] These have guided (and continue to guide) its management team as decisions are made about projects, missions, and programs. When the space shuttle program—NASA's main project mission—ended in 2011, the organization struggled for a time with its purpose and identity. In fact, one agency program manager at that time described NASA's future as nothing but uncertainty. However, despite the ambiguity, NASA's leaders have been charting a new trajectory. Possible new goals include getting to an asteroid by 2025 and putting astronauts on Mars by 2030. (Here's a bit of trivia for you: Mars is 225,300,000 kilometers—140,000,000 miles—from earth.) And critical to achieving these goals is the necessity to guide this complex, technical organization and figure out how to best manage the vast array of knowledge resources that are so crucial to its future.

NASA, established by the National Aeronautics and Space Act on July 29, 1958, has led U.S. efforts in space exploration, including the Apollo lunar landing missions, the Skylab space station, and the reusable manned spacecraft—which we know better as the Space Shuttle. It's a unique organization where equipment costs millions of dollars and where people's lives can be at stake. Over the years, NASA has had many successful endeavors (and some tragic failures). Getting men on the moon, not once, but six times, reflects outstanding technological prowess, far superior to any other country. Being able to put a rocket into space with a shuttle that then comes back to earth and lands on its own is a reflection of the incredibly talented and knowledgeable employees that NASA has. Now, NASA is taking the first steps to develop new technologies and capabilities to send astronauts further into space than ever before. It achieved a major milestone in early December 2014 with the successful test flight of Orion, a spacecraft designed for ultra-long-distance journeys. Accomplishments such as these are possible only because of the people in NASA who bring their knowledge, talents, skills, and creativity to that organization. And "managing" those people requires an "organization" structure that allows, enhances, and encourages the sharing of knowledge. It's not an easy thing to design and do.

Managing the knowledge resources of **NASA**

One word that aptly describes NASA's organization environment is *complexity*. Not only is there technical complexity (yes, we are talking rocket science, here!), but also numerous projects are going on, change is an ongoing reality, and demands arise from numerous stakeholders both inside and outside the organization. And within this complexity, the challenge is finding a way to share the incredible wealth of knowledge within project teams and across the entire organization. How is NASA doing this?

Knowing how important it is to manage the organization's vast knowledge resources, NASA has identified knowledge-sharing activities currently being used and others that are needed. Some of these include: online tools such as collaboration and sharing sites, video libraries, portals, etc.; a search engine that allows tagging and classifications (taxonomy); a library of searchable case studies and publications; an index of defined processes or "lessons learned"; knowledge networks of location "experts," collaboration activities, collaborative workspaces, etc.; and forums, workshops and other social exchanges that bring people together. Through its knowledge management efforts, NASA administrators are showing that they understand how important it is for the organization's structure to contribute to efficiently and effectively managing its knowledge resources.

Discussion Questions

7-16 Would you call NASA a learning organization? Why or why not?

7-17 In what ways is NASA's environment complex?

7-18 How does complexity affect structural choice?

7-19 Using Exhibit 7–12, what suggestions would you make to managers at NASA about being a learning organization? Write these in a bulleted list format that you could distribute as a handout.

CASE APPLICATION #3

A New Kind of Structure

Topic: Virtual assistants

Admit it. Sometimes the projects you're working on (school, work, or both) can get pretty boring and monotonous. Wouldn't it be great to have a magic button you could push to get someone else to do that boring, time-consuming stuff? At Pfizer, that "magic button" is a reality for a large number of employees.

As a global pharmaceutical company, Pfizer is continually looking for ways to help employees be more efficient and effective. The company's senior director of organizational effectiveness found that the "Harvard MBA staff we hired to develop strategies and innovate were instead Googling and making PowerPoints." Indeed, internal studies conducted to find out just how much time its valuable talent was spending on menial tasks was startling. The average Pfizer employee was spending 20 percent to 40 percent of his or her time on support work (creating documents, typing notes, doing research, manipulating data, scheduling meetings) and only 60 percent to 80 percent on knowledge work (strategy, innovation, networking, collaborating, critical thinking). And the problem wasn't just at lower levels. Even the highest-level employees were affected. Take, for instance, Chaz, an executive director for global engineering. He enjoys his job—assessing environmental real estate risks, managing facilities, and controlling a multimillion-dollar budget. But he didn't so much enjoy having to go through spreadsheets and put together PowerPoints. Now, however, with Pfizer's "magic button," those tasks are passed off to individuals outside the organization.

Just what is this "magic button"? Originally called the Office of the Future (OOF), the renamed PfizerWorks allows employees to shift tedious and time-consuming tasks with the click of a single button on their computer desktop. They describe what they need on an online form, which is then sent to one of two Indian service-outsourcing firms. When a request is received, a team member in India calls the Pfizer employee to clarify what's needed and by when. The team member then e-mails back a cost specification for the requested work. If the Pfizer employee decides to proceed, the costs involved are charged to the employee's department. About this unique arrangement, Cain said that he relishes working with what he prefers to call his "personal consulting organization."

The number 66,500 illustrates just how beneficial PfizerWorks has been for the company. That's the number

> Wouldn't you like a **MAGIC BUTTON** ⬭ you could push to get someone else to do all your tedious and boring work?[74]

of work hours estimated to have been saved by employees who've used PfizerWorks. Other outcomes include: a reduction in project-related costs, employee productivity increased, turnaround time for projects reduced, and wide acceptance by Pfizer employees. What about Chaz's experiences? When he gave the virtual assistant company team a complex project researching strategic actions that worked when consolidating company facilities, the team put the report together in a month, something that would have taken him six months to do alone. He says, "Pfizer pays me not to work tactically, but to work strategically."

Discussion Questions

7-20 Describe and evaluate what Pfizer is doing with its PfizerWorks.

7-21 What structural implications—good and bad—does this approach have? (Think in terms of the six organizational design elements.)

7-22 Do you think this arrangement would work for other types of organizations? Why or why not? What types of organizations might it also work for?

7-23 What role do you think organizational structure plays in an organization's efficiency and effectiveness? Working together with your assigned group, discuss this.

Endnotes

1. L. I. Albert, "The Wall Street Journal Reorganizes Newsroom, Creates Senior Roles," *Wall Street Journal online,* July 13, 2017.
2. R. A. Smith, "The Most Creative New Job in Fashion," *Wall Street Journal,* March 14, 2018, pp. A11+.
3. B. Fenwick, "Oklahoma Factory Turns Out US Bombs Used in Iraq," *Planet Ark* www.-planetark.com, November 4, 2003; A. Meyer, "Peeking inside the Nation's Bomb Factory," *KFOR TV,* www.kfor.com, February 27, 2003; G. Tuchman, "Inside America's Bomb Factory," *CNN,* cnn.usnews.com, December 5, 2002; and C. Fishman, "Boomtown, U.S.A.," *Fast Company,* June 2002, pp. 106–14.
4. L. Weber, "For Videogame Makers, Hiring Is a Last Resort," *Wall Street Journal,* April 11, 2017, pp. A1+.
5. M. Boyle, "Super Bucks," *Fortune,* February 4, 2008, pp. 8–9; and M. Hiestand, "Making a Stamp on Football," *USA Today,* January 25, 2005, pp. 1C+.
6. S. E. Humphrey, J. D. Nahrgang, and F. P. Morgeson, "Integrating Motivational, Social, and Contextual Work Design Features: A Meta-Analytic Summary and Theoretical Expansion of the Work Design Literature," *Journal of Applied Psychology,* September 2007, pp. 1332–56.
7. E. Kelly, "Keys to Effective Virtual Global Teams," *Academy of Management Executive,* May 2001, pp. 132–33; and D. Ancona, H. Bresman, and K. Kaeufer, "The Comparative Advantage of X-Team," *MIT Sloan Management Review,* Spring 2002, pp. 33–39.
8. R. S. Benchley, "Following Orders," *Chief Executive,* March 2002, p. 6.
9. R. Preston, "Inside Out," *Management Today,* September 2001, p. 37; and R. D. Clarke, "Over Their Heads," *Black Enterprise,* December 2000, p. 79.
10. See J. R. P. French and B. Raven, "The Bases of Social Power," in D. Cartwright and A. F. Zander (eds.), *Group Dynamics: Research and Theory* (New York: Harper & Row, 1960), pp. 607–23.
11. L. Urwick, *The Elements of Administration* (New York: Harper & Row, 1944), pp. 52–53. See also, J. H. Gittel, "Supervisory Span, Relational Coordination, and Flight Departure Performance: A Reassessment of Post-Bureaucracy Theory," *Organizational Science,* July–August 2001, pp. 468–83.
12. S. Harrison, "Is There a Right Span of Control? Simon Harrison Assesses the Relevance of the Concept of Span of Control to Modern Businesses," *Business Review,* February 2004, pp. 10–13.
13. P. C. Light, "From Pentagon to Pyramids: Whacking at Bloat," *Government Executive,* July 2001, p. 100.
14. See, for instance, D. Van Fleet, "Span of Management Research and Issues," *Academy of Management Journal,* September 1983, pp. 546–52; and S. H. Cady and P. M. Fandt, "Managing Impressions with Information: A Field Study of Organizational Realities," *Journal of Applied Behavioral Science,* June 2001, pp. 180–204.
15. Henri Fayol, *General and Industrial Management,* trans. C. Storrs (London: Pitman Publishing, 1949), pp. 19–42.
16. J. Zabojnik, "Centralized and Decentralized Decision Making in Organizations," *Journal of Labor Economics,* January 2002, pp. 1–22.
17. See P. Kenis and D. Knoke, "How Organizational Field Networks Shape Interorganizational Tie-Formation Rates," *Academy of Management Review,* April 2002, pp. 275–93.
18. T. Burns and G. M. Stalker, *The Management of Innovation* (London: Tavistock, 1961).
19. D. Dougherty, "Re-imagining the Differentiation and Integration of Work for Sustained Product Innovation," *Organization Science,* September–October 2001, pp. 612–31.
20. A. D. Chandler Jr., *Strategy and Structure: Chapters in the History of the Industrial Enterprise* (Cambridge, MA: MIT Press, 1962).
21. See, for instance, L. L. Bryan and C. I. Joyce, "Better Strategy through Organizational Design," *McKinsey Quarterly* no. 2 (2007), pp. 21–29; D. Jennings and S. Seaman, "High and Low Levels of Organizational Adaptation: An Empirical Analysis of Strategy, Structure, and Performance," *Strategic Management Journal,* July 1994, pp. 459–75; D. C. Galunic and K. M. Eisenhardt, "Renewing the Strategy-Structure-Performance Paradigm," in B. M. Staw and L. L. Cummings (eds.), *Research in Organizational Behavior,* vol. 16 (Greenwich, CT: JAI Press, 1994), pp. 215–55; R. Parthasarthy and S. P. Sethi, "Relating Strategy and Structure to Flexible Automation: A Test of Fit and Performance Implications," *Strategic Management Journal* 14, no. 6 (1993), pp. 529–49; H. A. Simon, "Strategy and Organizational Evolution," *Strategic Management Journal,* January 1993, pp. 131–42; H. L. Boschken, "Strategy and Structure: Re-conceiving the Relationship," *Journal of Management,* March 1990, pp. 135–50; D. Miller, "The Structural and Environmental Correlates of Business Strategy," *Strategic Management Journal,* January–February 1987, pp. 55–76; and R. E. Miles and C. C. Snow, *Organizational Strategy, Structure, and Process* (New York: McGraw-Hill, 1978).
22. See, for instance, P. M. Blau and R. A. Schoenherr, *The Structure of Organizations* (New York: Basic Books, 1971); D. S. Pugh, "The Aston Program of Research: Retrospect and Prospect," in A. H. Van de Ven and W. F. Joyce (eds.), *Perspectives on Organization Design and Behavior* (New York: John Wiley, 1981), pp. 135–66; and R. Z. Gooding and J. A. Wagner III, "A Meta-Analytic Review of the Relationship between Size and Performance: The Productivity and Efficiency of Organizations and Their Subunits," *Administrative Science Quarterly,* December 1985, pp. 462–81.
23. See, for example, H. M. O'Neill, "Restructuring, Reengineering and Rightsizing: Do the Metaphors Make Sense?" *Academy of Management Executive* 8, no. 4 (1994), pp. 9–30; R. K. Reger, J. V. Mullane, L. T. Gustafson, and S. M. Demarie, "Creating Earthquakes to Change Organizational Mindsets," *Academy of Management Executive* 8, no. 4 (1994), pp. 31–41; and J. Tan, "Impact of Ownership Type on Environment–Strategy Linkage and Performance: Evidence from a Transitional Company," *Journal of Management Studies,* May 2002, pp. 333–54.
24. E. W. Morrison, "Doing the Job Well: An Investigation of Pro-Social Rule Breaking," *Journal of Management,* February 2006, pp. 5–28.
25. *Ibid.*

26. J. Woodward, *Industrial Organization: Theory and Practice* (London: Oxford University Press, 1965).

27. From the Classic Concepts in Today's Workplace box based on J. Woodward, *Industrial Organization: Theory and Practice*. Also, see, for instance, C. Perrow, "A Framework for the Comparative Analysis of Organizations," *American Sociological Review*, April 1967, pp. 194–208; J. D. Thompson, *Organizations in Action* (New York: McGraw-Hill, 1967); J. Hage and M. Aiken, "Routine Technology, Social Structure, and Organizational Goals," *Administrative Science Quarterly*, September 1969, pp. 366–77; C. C. Miller, W. H. Glick, Y. D. Wang, and G. Huber, "Understanding Technology-Structure Relationships: Theory Development and Meta-Analytic Theory Testing," *Academy of Management Journal*, June 1991, pp. 370–99; D. M. Rousseau and R. A. Cooke, "Technology and Structure: The Concrete, Abstract, and Activity Systems of Organizations," *Journal of Management*, Fall–Winter 1984, pp. 345–61; and D. Gerwin, "Relationships between Structure and Technology," in P.C. Nystrom and W. H. Starbuck (eds.), *Handbook of Organizational Design*, vol. 2 (New York: Oxford University Press, 1981), pp. 3–38.

28. H. Mintzberg, *Structure in Fives: Designing Effective Organizations* (Upper Saddle River, NJ: Prentice Hall, 1983), p. 157.

29. D. A. Garvin and L. C. Levesque, "The Multiunit Enterprise," *Harvard Business Review*, June 2008, pp. 106–17; and R. J. Williams, J. J. Hoffman, and B. T. Lamont, "The Influence of Top Management Team Characteristics on M-Form Implementation Time," *Journal of Managerial Issues*, Winter 1995, pp. 466–80.

30. See, for example, R. Greenwood and D. Miller, "Tackling Design Anew: Getting Back to the Heart of Organization Theory," *Academy of Management Perspectives*, November 2010, pp. 78–88; G. J. Castrogiovanni, "Organization Task Environments: Have They Changed Fundamentally Over Time?" *Journal of Management* vol. 28, no. 2 (2002), pp. 129–50; D. F. Twomey, "Leadership, Organizational Design, and Competitiveness for the 21st Century," *Global Competitiveness*, Annual 2002, pp. S31–S40; M. Hammer, "Processed Change: Michael Hammer Sees Process as 'the Clark Kent of Business Ideas'—A Concept That Has the Power to Change a Company's Organizational Design," *Journal of Business Strategy*, November–December 2001,

pp. 11–15; T. Clancy, "Radical Surgery: A View from the Operating Theater," *Academy of Management Executive*, February 1994, pp. 73–78; I. I. Mitroff, R. O. Mason, and C. M. Pearson, "Radical Surgery: What Will Tomorrow's Organizations Look Like?" *Academy of Management Executive*, February 1994, pp. 11–21; and R. E. Hoskisson, C. W. L. Hill, and H. Kim, "The Multidivisional Structure: Organizational Fossil or Source of Value?" *Journal of Management* 19, no. 2 (1993), pp. 269–98.

31. Q. Hardy, "Google Thinks Small," *Forbes*, November 14, 2005, pp. 198–202.

32. See, for example, D. R. Denison, S. L. Hart, and J. A. Kahn, "From Chimneys to Cross-Functional Teams: Developing and Validating a Diagnostic Model," *Academy of Management Journal*, December 1996, pp. 1005–23; D. Ray and H. Bronstein, *Teaming Up: Making the Transition to a Self-Directed Team-Based Organization* (New York: McGraw Hill, 1995); J. R. Katzenbach and D. K. Smith, *The Wisdom of Teams* (Boston: Harvard Business School Press, 1993); J. A. Byrne, "The Horizontal Corporation," *BusinessWeek*, December 20, 1993, pp. 76–81; B. Dumaine, "Payoff from the New Management," *Fortune*, December 13, 1993, pp. 103–10; and H. Rothman, "The Power of Empowerment," *Nation's Business*, June 1993, pp. 49–52.

33. C. Garvey, "Steer Teams with the Right Pay," *HR Magazine*, May 2002, pp. 70–78.

34. A. Moore, "Managing the Matrix," *TD*, May 2017, p. 16.

35. P. Kaihla, "Best-Kept Secrets of the World's Best Companies," *Business 2.0*, April 2006, p. 83; C. Taylor, "School of Bright Ideas," *Time Inside Business*, April 2005, pp. A8–A12; and B. Nussbaum, "The Power of Design," *BusinessWeek*, May 17, 2004, pp. 86–94.

36. See, for example, G. G. Dess, A. M. A. Rasheed, K. J. McLaughlin, and R. L. Priem, "The New Corporate Architecture," *Academy of Management Executive*, August 1995, pp. 7–20.

37. For additional readings on boundaryless organizations, see S. Rausch and J. Birkinshaw, "Organizational Ambidexterity: Antecedents, Outcomes, and Moderators," *Journal of Management*, June 2008, pp. 375–409; M. F. R. Kets de Vries, "Leadership Group Coaching in Action: The Zen of Creating High Performance Teams," *Academy of Management Executive*, February 2005, pp. 61–76; J. Child and R. G. McGrath, "Organizations Unfettered: Organizational Form in an Information-Intensive Economy," *Academy of*

Management Journal, December 2001, pp. 1135–48; M. Hammer and S. Stanton, "How Process Enterprises Really Work," *Harvard Business Review*, November–December 1999, pp. 108–18; T. Zenger and W. Hesterly, "The Disaggregation of Corporations: Selective Intervention, High-Powered Incentives, and Modular Units," *Organization Science* 8 (1997), pp. 209–22; R. Ashkenas, D. Ulrich, T. Jick, and S. Kerr, *The Boundaryless Organization: Breaking the Chains of Organizational Structure* (San Francisco: Jossey-Bass, 1997); R. M. Hodgetts, "A Conversation with Steve Kerr," *Organizational Dynamics*, Spring 1996, pp. 68–79; and J. Gebhardt, "The Boundaryless Organization," *Sloan Management Review*, Winter 1996, pp. 117–19. For another view of boundaryless organizations, see B. Victor, "The Dark Side of the New Organizational Forms: An Editorial Essay," *Organization Science*, November 1994, pp. 479–82.

38. See, for instance, Y. Shin, "A Person-Environment Fit Model for Virtual Organizations," *Journal of Management*, December 2004, pp. 725–43; D. Lyons, "Smart and Smarter," *Forbes*, March 18, 2002, pp. 40–41; W. F. Cascio, "Managing a Virtual Workplace," *Academy of Management Executive*, August 2000, pp. 81–90; Dess, Rasheed, McLaughlin, and Priem, "The New Corporate Architecture"; H. Chesbrough and D. Teece, "When Is Virtual Virtuous: Organizing for Innovation," *Harvard Business Review*, January–February 1996, pp. 65–73; and W. H. Davidow and M. S. Malone, *The Virtual Corporation* (New York: Harper Collins, 1992).

39. Q. Hardy, "Bit by Bit, Work Exchange Site Aims to Get Jobs Done," *New York Times Online*, November 6, 2011.

40. M. V. Rafter, "Cultivating a Virtual Culture," *Workforce Management Online*, April 5, 2012.

41. R. E. Miles, C. C. Snow, J. A. Matthews, G. Miles, and H. J. Coleman Jr., "Organizing in the Knowledge Age: Anticipating the Cellular Form," *Academy of Management Executive*, November 1997, pp. 7–24; C. Jones, W. Hesterly, and S. Borgatti, "A General Theory of Network Governance: Exchange Conditions and Social Mechanisms," *Academy of Management Review*, October 1997, pp. 911–45; R. E. Miles and C. C. Snow, "The New Network Firm: A Spherical Structure Built on Human Investment Philosophy," *Organizational Dynamics*, Spring 1995, pp. 5–18; and R. E. Miles and C. C. Snow,

"Causes of Failures in Network Organizations," *California Management Review* vol. 34, no. 4 (1992), pp. 53–72.

42. G. Hoetker, "Do Modular Products Lead to Modular Organizations?" *Strategic Management Journal*, June 2006, pp. 501–18; C. H. Fine, "Are You Modular or Integral?" *Strategy & Business*, Summer 2005, pp. 44–51; D. A. Ketchen Jr. and G. T. M. Hult, "To Be Modular or Not to Be? Some Answers to the Question," *Academy of Management Executive*, May 2002, pp. 166–67; M. A. Schilling, "The Use of Modular Organizational Forms: An Industry-Level Analysis," *Academy of Management Journal*, December 2001, pp. 1149–68; D. Lei, M. A. Hitt, and J. D. Goldhar, "Advanced Manufacturing Technology: Organizational Design and Strategic Flexibility," *Organization Studies* 17 (1996), pp. 501–23; R. Sanchez and J. Mahoney, "Modularity Flexibility and Knowledge Management in Product and Organization Design," *Strategic Management Journal* 17 (1996), pp. 63–76; and R. Sanchez, "Strategic Flexibility in Product Competition," *Strategic Management Journal* 16 (1995), pp. 135–59.

43. C. Hymowitz, "Have Advice, Will Travel," *Wall Street Journal*, June 5, 2006, pp. B1+.

44. S. Reed, A. Reinhardt, and A. Sains, "Saving Ericsson," *BusinessWeek*, November 11, 2002, pp. 64–68.

45. P. Engardio, "The Future of Outsourcing," *BusinessWeek*, January 30, 2006, pp. 50–58.

46. J. Zumbrun, "Is Your Job Routine? If So, It's Probably Disappearing," *Wall Street Journal Online*, April 8, 2015.

47. C. E. Connelly and D. G. Gallagher, "Emerging Trends in Contingent Work Research," *Journal of Management*, November 2004, pp. 959–83.

48. N. M. Adler, *International Dimensions of Organizational Behavior*, 5th ed. (Cincinnati, OH: South-Western, 2008), p. 62.

49. Managing Technology in Today's Workplace box based on R. Cheng, "So You Want to Use Your iPhone for Work? How the Smartest Companies Are Letting Employees Use Their Personal Gadgets to Do Their Jobs," *Wall Street Journal*, April 25, 2011, pp. R1+; B. Roberts, "Mobile Workforce Management," *HR Magazine*, March 2011, pp. 67–70; D. Darlin, "Software That Monitors Your Work, Wherever You Are," *New York Times Online* www. nytimesonline.com (April 12, 2009); D. Pauleen and B. Harmer, "Away from the Desk … Always," *Wall Street Journal*, December 15, 2008, p. R8; J. Marquez, "Connecting a Virtual Workforce," *Workforce Management Online*

www.workforce.com (September 22, 2008); R. Yu, "Work Away from Work Gets Easier with Technology," *USA Today*, November 28, 2006, p. 8B; M. Weinstein, "Going Mobile," *Training*, September 2006, pp. 24–29; C. Cobbs, "Technology Helps Boost Multitasking," *Springfield, Missouri News-Leader*, June 15, 2006, p. 5B; C. Edwards, "Wherever You Go, You're on the Job," *BusinessWeek*, June 20, 2005, pp. 87–90; and S. E. Ante, "The World Wide Work Space," *BusinessWeek*, June 6, 2005, pp. 106–08.

50. P. Olson, "Tesco's Landing," *Forbes,* June 4, 2007, pp. 116–18; and P. M. Senge, *The Fifth Discipline: The Art and Practice of Learning Organizations* (New York: Doubleday, 1990).

51. J. Marquez, "Connecting a Virtual Workforce," *Workforce Management Online*, February 3, 2009.

52. J. Simons, "IBM Says No to Home Work," *Wall Street Journal*, May 19, 2017, pp. A1+.

53. M. Conlin, "Home Offices: The New Math," *BusinessWeek*, March 9, 2009, pp. 66–68.

54. Ibid.

55. Marquez, "Connecting a Virtual Workforce."

56. S. Jayson, "Working at Home: Family-Friendly," *USA Today*, April 15, 2010, pp. 1A+; T. D. Hecht and N. J. Allen, "A Longitudinal Examination of the Work-Nonwork Boundary Strength Construct," *Journal of Organizational Behavior*, October 2009, pp. 839–62; and G. E. Kreiner, E. C. Hollensbe, and M. L. Sheep, "Balancing Borders and Bridges: Negotiating the Work-Home Interface via Boundary Work Tactics," *Academy of Management Journal*, August 2009, pp. 704–30.

57. P. B. Smith and M. F. Peterson, "Demographic Effects on the Use of Vertical Sources of Guidance by Managers in Widely Differing Cultural Contexts," *International Journal of Cross Cultural Management*, April 2005, pp. 5–26.

58. N. Scheiber, "A Find at Gap: Steady Hours Can Help Workers, and Profits," *New York Times online*, March 28, 2018; and R. Abrams, "Gap Says It Will Phase Out On-Call Scheduling of Employees," *New York Times Online*, August 26, 2015.

59. J. T. Marquez, "The Future of Flex," *Workforce Management Online*, January 2010.

60. S. Greenhouse, "Work-Sharing May Help Companies Avoid Layoffs," *New York Times Online*, June 16, 2009.

61. R. King, "Meet the Microworkers," *Bloomberg BusinessWeek Online*, February 1, 2011; and R. King, "Mechanical Serfdom Is Just That," *Bloomberg BusinessWeek Online*, February 1, 2011.

62. K. Bennhold, "Working (Part-Time) in the 21st Century," *New York Times Online*, December 29, 2010; and J. Revell, C. Bigda, and D. Rosato, "The Rise of Freelance Nation," *CNNMoney*, cnnmoney.com, June 12, 2009.

63. Revell, Bigda, and Rosato, "The Rise of Freelance Nation."

64. Ibid.

65. H. G. Jackson, "Flexible Workplaces: The Next Imperative," *HR Magazine*, March 2011, p. 8; E. Frauenheim, "Companies Focus Their Attention on Flexibility," *Workforce Management Online*, February 2011; P. Davidson, "Companies Do More with Fewer Workers," *USA Today*, February 23, 2011, pp. 1B+; M. Rich, "Weighing Costs, Companies Favor Temporary Help," *New York Times Online*, December 19, 2010; and P. Davidson, "Temporary Workers Reshape Companies, Jobs," *USA Today*, October 13, 2010, pp. 1B+.

66. Twitter.com, United Airlines, @united, March 26, 2017.

67. D. Victor and M. Stevens, "United Airlines Passenger Is Dragged from an Overbooked Flight," *New York Times Online*, April 10, 2017.

68. C. Drew, "United Takes Added Steps to Win Back Customers and Avoid More Ugly Events," *New York Times Online*, April 27, 2017.

69. M. Salam, "Security Officers Fired for United Airlines Dragging Episode," *New York Times Online*, October 17, 2017.

70. H. Baskas, "A Couple Headed to Their Wedding Says United Kicked Them Off the Plane," www.nbcnews.com, April 17, 2017.

71. L. Stack, "United Airlines Apologizes after Dog Dies in Overhead Compartment," *New York Times Online,* March 13, 2018.

72. A. Hartung, "Why United Airlines Abuses Customers: The Risks of Operational Excellence," *Forbes Online,* April 10, 2017.

73. M. Locker, "Making America Great Again in Space Won't Just Be a Job for NASA," *Fast Company Online,* January 3, 2018; and NASA Strategic Plan 2014, https://www.nasa.gov/sites/default/files/files/FY2014_NASA_SP_508c.pdf.

74. S. Silbermann, "How Culture and Regulation Demand New Ways to Sell," *Harvard Business Review,* July/August 2012, pp. 104–05; P. Miller and T. Wedell-Wedellsborg, "How to Make an Offer That Managers Can't Refuse?" *IESE Insight,* second quarter, no. 9 (2011), pp. 66–67; S. Hernández, "Prove Its Worth," *IESE Insight,* second quarter, no. 9 (2011), p. 68; T. Koulopoulos, "Know Thyself," *IESE Insight,* second quarter, no. 9 (2011), p. 69; M. Weinstein, "Retrain and Restructure Your Organization," *Training,* May 2009, p. 36; J. McGregor, "The Chore Goes Offshore," *BusinessWeek,* March 23 & 30, 2009, pp. 50–51; "Pfizer: Making It 'Leaner, Meaner, More Efficient,'" *BusinessWeek Online,* March 2, 2009; and A. Cohen, "Scuttling Scut Work," *Fast Company,* February 2008, pp. 42–43.

Managing Human Resources and Diversity

Management Myth

Myth

Myth

The single most important factor employers seek in a new college graduate is good grades.

Management Myth

DEBUNKED?

Yes, landing a good job after graduation can seem daunting. But new research suggests the formula is not all that difficult. Get excellent grades AND complete as many internships as possible.[1] So, yes, we hate to dash your dreams of no longer having to do homework or study for exams because good grades are important, but *not* the only factor employers seek in a new college graduate. What *should* you do? Be proactive in seeking out internship opportunities to give you a leg up on other job candidates AND pay attention to that GPA!

WHAT other qualities *will* recruiters be looking for?[2] They'll look for evidence of: problem-solving skills, the ability to work on a team, written communication skills, leadership, strong work ethic, analytical/quantitative skills, verbal communication skills, initiative, detail-oriented, flexibility/adaptability, technical skills, and interpersonal skills . . . all skills we're trying to emphasize. Organizations need people—talented people—to be successful in doing what they're in business to do. Once an organization's structure is in place, managers have to find people to fill the jobs that have been created or to remove people from jobs if business circumstances require it. That's where human resource management (HRM) comes in. It's an important task that involves having the *right number* of the *right people* in the *right place* at the *right time*. In this chapter, we'll look at the process managers use to do just that—a process that includes finding, interviewing, and assessing job applicants; helping new employees assimilate; recommending training; and assessing employee performance. In addition, we'll look at some contemporary HRM issues facing managers, as well as ways diversity and inclusion affect the HRM process. ●

Learning Outcomes

8-1 Describe the key components of the human resource management process and the important influences on that process. p. 283

8-2 Discuss the tasks associated with identifying and selecting competent employees. p. 287

8-3 Explain how employees are provided with needed skills and knowledge. p. 294

8-4 Describe strategies for retaining competent, high-performing employees. p. 298

8-5 Discuss contemporary issues in managing human resources. p. 303

8-6 Explain what workforce diversity and inclusion are and how they affect the HRM process. p. 307

What Is the Human Resource Management Process and What Influences It?

8-1 Describe the key components of the human resource management process and the important influences on that process.

As grocery chains face increasing competition from Amazon.com (and its purchase of Whole Foods Market), they're searching for ways to remain competitive. Kroger Co., for example, is hiring 11,000 workers to improve customer service and efficiency at its 2,800 supermarkets.[3] Its strategy? Invest in people and be positioned to better compete with Amazon.

The quality of an organization *is* to a large degree determined by the quality of the people it employs. Success for most organizations depends on finding the employees with the skills to successfully perform the tasks required to attain the company's strategic goals. Staffing and HRM decisions and actions are critical to ensuring that the organization hires and keeps the right people.

Getting that done is what **human resource management (HRM)** is all about. The eight important HRM activities (the green boxes) are shown in Exhibit 8–1.

human resource management (HRM)
The management function concerned with getting, training, motivating, and keeping competent employees

Exhibit 8–1 The Human Resource Management Process

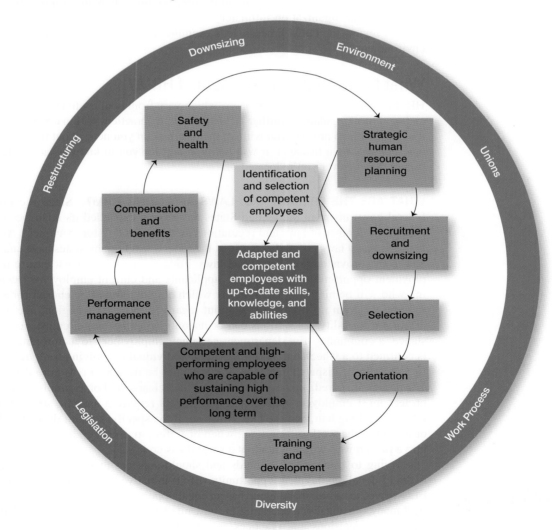

After an organization's strategy has been established and the organization structure designed, it's time to add the people—to acquire the talent! That's one of the most critical roles for HRM and one that has increased the importance of HR managers to the organization. The first three activities in the HRM process represent employment planning: the addition of staff through recruitment, the reduction in staff through downsizing, and selection. When executed properly, these steps lead to the identification and selection of competent, talented employees who can assist an organization in achieving its strategic goals.

Once you select the people you want, you need to help them adapt to the organization and ensure that their job skills and knowledge are kept current. These next two activities in the HRM process are accomplished through orientation and training. The last steps in the HRM process are designed to identify performance goals, correct performance problems if necessary, and help employees sustain a high level of performance over their entire work life. The activities involved include performance appraisal, and compensation and benefits. (HRM also includes safety and health issues, but we're not covering those topics in this book.) All these activities, if properly executed, will staff an organization with competent, high-performing employees who are capable of sustaining their performance levels over the long run.

HRM = Right People, Right Place, Right Time

Notice in Exhibit 8–1 that the entire process is influenced by the external environment. Many of the factors we discussed in Chapter 4 directly affect all management practices, but their effect is keenly felt in managing the organization's human resources because whatever happens to an organization ultimately influences what happens to its employees. So, before we review the HRM process, let's examine one external force that affects it—the legal environment.

What Is the Legal Environment of HRM?

HRM practices are governed by laws, which vary from country to country. State (or provincial) and local regulations further influence specific practices within countries. Consequently, it's impossible to provide you with all the information you need about the relevant regulatory environment. As a manager, it will be important for you to know what you legally can and cannot do wherever you're located.

WHAT ARE THE PRIMARY U.S. LAWS AFFECTING HRM? Since the mid-1960s, the federal government in the United States has greatly expanded its influence over HRM by enacting a number of laws and regulations (see Exhibit 8–2 for examples). Although we've not seen many laws enacted recently at the federal level, many states have enacted laws that add to the provisions of the federal laws. Today's employers must ensure that equal employment opportunities exist for job applicants and current employees. Decisions regarding who will be hired, for example, or which employees will be chosen for a management training program must be made without regard to race, sex, religion, age, color, national origin, or disability. Exceptions can occur only when special circumstances exist. For instance, a community fire department can deny employment to a firefighter applicant who is confined to a wheelchair, but if that same individual is applying for a desk job, such as a fire department dispatcher, the disability cannot be used as a reason to deny employment. The issues involved, however, are rarely that clear-cut. For example, employment laws protect most employees whose religious beliefs require a specific style of dress—robes, long shirts, long hair, and the like. However, if the specific style of dress may be hazardous or unsafe in the work setting (e.g., when operating machinery), a company could refuse to hire a person who would not adopt a safer dress code.

Trying to balance the "shoulds and should-nots" of these laws often falls within the realm of equal employment opportunity (EEO) initiatives and **affirmative action programs**. EEO strives to ensure that anyone has an equal opportunity based on his or her qualifications. And many organizations operating in the United States have affirmative action programs to ensure that decisions and practices enhance the employment, upgrading, and retention of members from protected groups such as minorities and females.

affirmative action programs
Programs that ensure that decisions and practices enhance the employment, upgrading, and retention of members of protected groups

Exhibit 8–2 Major HRM Laws

LAW OR RULING	YEAR	DESCRIPTION
Equal Employment Opportunity and Discrimination		
■ **Equal Pay Act**	1963	Prohibits pay differences for equal work based on gender
■ **Civil Rights Act, Title VII**	1964 (amended in 1972)	Prohibits discrimination based on race, color, religion, national origin, or gender
■ **Age Discrimination in Employment Act**	1967 (amended in 1978)	Prohibits discrimination against employees 40 years and older
■ **Vocational Rehabilitation Act**	1973	Prohibits discrimination on the basis of physical or mental disabilities
■ **Americans with Disabilities Act**	1990	Prohibits discrimination against individuals who have disabilities or chronic illnesses; also requires reasonable accommodations for these individuals
Compensation/Benefits		
■ **Worker Adjustment and Retraining Notification Act**	1990	Requires employers with more than 100 employees to provide 60 days' notice before a mass layoff or facility closing
■ **Family and Medical Leave Act**	1993	Gives employees in organizations with 50 or more employees up to 12 weeks of unpaid leave each year for family or medical reasons
■ **Health Insurance Portability and Accountability Act**	1996	Permits portability of employees' insurance from one employer to another
■ **Lilly Ledbetter Fair Pay Act**	2009	Changes the statute of limitations on pay discrimination to 180 days from each paycheck
■ **Patient Protection and Affordable Care Act**	2010	Health care legislation that puts in place comprehensive health insurance reforms
Health/Safety		
■ **Occupational Safety and Health Act (OSHA)**	1970	Establishes mandatory safety and health standards in organizations
■ **Privacy Act**	1974	Gives employees the legal right to examine personnel files and letters of reference
■ **Consolidated Omnibus Reconciliation Act (COBRA)**	1985	Requires continued health coverage following termination (paid by employee)

Source: Robbins, Stephen P., Coulter, Mary, *Management*, 13th Ed., © 2016, p. 341. Reprinted and electronically reproduced by permission of Pearson Education, Inc., New York, NY.

Operating within legal constraints, U.S. managers are not completely free to choose whom they hire, promote, or fire. Although laws and regulations have significantly helped to reduce employment discrimination and unfair employment practices and improve employee safety, they have, at the same time, reduced management's discretion over HR decisions.

ARE HRM LAWS THE SAME GLOBALLY? No. As a global manager, you'll need to know applicable laws and regulations. Further, managers of multinationals must understand the variety of laws that apply to employees in every country their firms operate in. Ireland-based Ryanair, for instance, generally hires pilots and cabin crew under Irish labor contracts, regardless of where they live and work for the airline. As a result, Ryanair's managers must navigate a complex set of obligations across national borders. In 2014, the airline lost a court appeal and paid a hefty fine to France over government-mandated social security and pension payments for workers based in France who had Irish labor contracts. Ryanair made all social payments as required in Ireland, but it became caught up in the legal battle because those amounts are lower than the social payments required under French law.

Not only do Federal laws differ widely, but these laws are also updated or changed from time to time. In Sweden, the amount of paid parental leave for fathers has been increased over the years to encourage men to use this benefit. Today, new parents receive 480 days of paid leave that can be divided between the parents as they choose. Another recent change increases

◄◄◄ Classic Concepts in Today's Workplace ►►►

Hugo Munsterberg, a pioneer in the field of industrial psychology, is "generally credited with creating the field."[4] As an admirer of Frederick W. Taylor and the scientific management movement, Munsterberg stated that "Taylor had introduced most valuable suggestions which the industrial world cannot ignore." Drawing on Taylor's works, Munsterberg stressed "the importance of efficiently using workers to achieve economic production." His research and work in showing organizations ways to improve the performance and well-being of workers was fundamental to the emerging field of management in the early 1900s.

Today, industrial-organizational psychology is defined as the scientific study of the workplace. Industrial-organizational (I/O) psychologists use scientific principles and research-based designs to generate knowledge about workplace issues. (Check out the Society for Industrial and Organizational

Scientifically studying the WORKPLACE

Psychology at www.siop.org.) They study organizational topics such as job performance, job analysis, performance appraisal, compensation, work/life balance, work sample tests, employee training, employment law, personnel recruitment and selection, and so forth. Their research has contributed much to the field that we call human resource management. And all of this is due to the early work done by Hugo Munsterberg.

Discussion Questions:

1 Why is it important to scientifically study the workplace? What can you learn from such studies that will be useful to you as you navigate the world of work?

2 Do you think it's easier today to scientifically study the workplace than it was back in Munsterberg's days? Why or why not?

protections for whistle-blowing employees who report serious violations so that firms are not allowed to retaliate against these employees. In addition, employers must now establish internal systems to enable employees to report violations internally. Managers of businesses that operate in Sweden need to be aware of these changes so they can take immediate steps to comply.

In Singapore, the Ministry of Manpower oversees regulation of HRM practices governed by laws such as the Employment Act and the Retirement and Re-employment Act. These laws determine minimum age for workers, terms of employment, detailed pay itemization, parental leave, retirement age, and pay for older workers. Laws have been changed in Singapore to increase the age of mandatory retirement, reflecting the ability and interest of employees to continue working as they age—and a corresponding need for employers to tap the knowledge, experience, and skills of these workers.

General Electric is a multinational employer committed to observing all the different labor laws of the 130 countries in which it operates. Shown here are employees of GE's wind turbine factory in Vietnam, a country whose Labour Code of Vietnam was first passed in 1994 and provides strong protections for employees.

Australia's labor and industrial relations laws were overhauled two decades ago to increase productivity and reduce union power. The Workplace Relations Bill gives employers greater flexibility to negotiate directly with employees on pay, hours, and benefits. It also simplifies federal regulation of labor–management relations. In 2015, the Fair Work Amendment Act extended family leave protection. The act provides that a request for extended unpaid parental leave cannot be refused unless the employer has given the employee a reasonable opportunity to discuss the request.[5]

AFP/Newscom

Here's a challenging HR issue for managers: the use of medical marijuana by employees. Although pot is still illegal at the federal level, 30 states plus the District of Columbia have now passed comprehensive medical marijuana laws, and almost one-third of those have legalized recreational use of the drug for adults 21 and older.[6] Federal prosecutors have been directed not to bring criminal charges against marijuana users who follow their states' laws. However, that puts employers in a difficult position as they try to accommodate state laws on medical marijuana use while having to enforce federal rules or company drug-use policies based on federal laws. Although courts have generally ruled that companies do not have to accommodate medical marijuana users, legal guidance is still not all that clear. Legal experts have warned employers to not run afoul of disability and privacy laws. In addition to the legal questions, employers are concerned about the challenge of maintaining a safe workplace. Employers should take a close look at their drug and alcohol policies to ensure that they are up to date by addressing issues such as marijuana and opioid use (another major issue facing HR managers) in the workplace.[7]

Discussion Questions:

3 What ethical issue(s) do you see here? What other stakeholders might be impacted by this and how might they be impacted? What ethical responsibilities do organizations have in light of this changed environment?

4 In your "assigned" group, discuss how this issue might affect HR processes such as recruitment, selection, performance management, compensation and benefits, and safety and health.

How Do Managers Identify and Select Competent Employees?

8-2 Discuss the tasks associated with identifying and selecting competent employees.

Woodward Inc., an engine and equipment components manufacturing facility, went after younger workers by holding a "Parents' Night" to inform parents of the employment opportunities for those kids who might not be pursuing the college alternative. Like many manufacturing businesses, Woodward Inc. is scrambling to fill open jobs.[8]

Every organization needs people to do whatever work is necessary for doing what the organization is in business to do. How do organizations get those people? And more importantly, what can they do to ensure they get competent, talented people? This first phase of the HRM process involves three tasks: **1** employment planning, **2** recruitment and downsizing, and **3** selection.

1 What Is Employment Planning?

Supply and Demand aren't just for economics—they're also important to HRM!

- Talent wars have come to Silicon Valley as Internet startups struggle to compete for scarce talent even as more-established companies such as Facebook, Uber, Twitter, and Google look to add employees as their businesses continue to grow.
- During the last economic downturn, Boeing cut more than 3,000 jobs, mostly from its commercial airplanes unit. During the same time, it added 106 employees to its defense unit and was looking for several hundred more.[9]

Juggling the supply of human resources to meet demand is a challenge for many companies.

work councils
Groups of nominated or elected employees who must be consulted when management makes decisions involving personnel

board representatives
Employees who sit on a company's board of directors and represent the interest of employees

Employment planning is the process by which managers ensure that they have the right number and kinds of people in the right places at the right times, people who are capable of effectively and efficiently completing those tasks that will help the organization achieve its goals. Employment planning, then, translates the organization's mission and goals into an HR plan that will allow the organization to achieve those goals. The process can be condensed into two steps: (1) assessing current human resources and future human resource needs and (2) developing a plan to meet those needs.

(1) HOW DOES AN ORGANIZATION DO A CURRENT HR ASSESSMENT? Managers begin by reviewing the current human resource status. This review is typically done by generating a **human resource inventory**. It's not difficult to generate an inventory in most organizations since the information for it is derived from forms completed by employees. Such inventories might list the name, education, training, prior employment, languages spoken, capabilities, and specialized skills of each employee in the organization. This inventory allows managers to assess what talents and skills are currently available in the organization.

Another part of the current assessment is **job analysis**. Whereas the human resources inventory is concerned with telling management what individual employees can do, job analysis is more fundamental. It's typically a lengthy process, one in which workflows are analyzed and skills and behaviors that are necessary to perform jobs are identified. For instance, what does an international reporter who works for the *Wall Street Journal* do? What minimal knowledge, skills, and abilities are necessary for the adequate performance of this job? How do the job requirements for an international reporter compare with those for a domestic reporter or for a newspaper editor? Job analysis can answer these questions. Ultimately, the purpose of job analysis is to determine the kinds of skills, knowledge, and attitudes needed to successfully perform each job. This information is then used to develop or revise job descriptions and job specifications.

Why IS **JOB ANALYSIS** so important?

Job analysis results in: Job description → describes the job
&
Job specification → describes the person

A **job description** is a written statement that describes the job—what a job holder does, how it's done, and why it's done. It typically portrays job content, environment, and conditions of employment. The **job specification** states the minimum qualifications that a person must possess to perform a given job successfully. It focuses on the person and identifies the knowledge, skills, and attitudes needed to do the job effectively. The job description and job specification are important documents when managers begin recruiting and selecting. For instance, the job description can be used to describe the job to potential candidates. The job specification keeps the manager's attention on the list of qualifications necessary for an incumbent to perform a job and assists in determining whether candidates are qualified. Furthermore, hiring individuals on the basis of the information contained in these two documents helps ensure that the hiring process does not discriminate.

(2) HOW ARE FUTURE EMPLOYEE NEEDS DETERMINED? Future human resource needs are determined by the organization's strategic goals and direction. Demand for human resources (employees) is a result of demand for the organization's products or services. On the basis of an estimate of total revenue, managers can attempt to establish the number and mix of people needed to reach that revenue. In some cases, however, the situation may be reversed. When particular skills are necessary and in scarce supply, the availability of needed human resources determines revenues. For example, managers of an upscale chain of assisted-living retirement facilities who find themselves with abundant business opportunities are limited in their ability to grow revenues by whether they can hire a qualified

employment planning
The process by which managers ensure they have the right numbers and kinds of people in the right places at the right time

human resource inventory
A report listing important information about employees such as name, education, training, skills, languages spoken, and so forth

job analysis
An assessment that defines jobs and the behaviors necessary to perform them

job description
A written statement that describes a job

job specification
A written statement of the minimum qualifications that a person must possess to perform a given job successfully

nursing staff to fully meet the needs of the residents. In most cases, however, the overall organizational goals and the resulting revenue forecast provide the major input in determining the organization's HR requirements.

After assessing both current capabilities and future needs, managers can estimate talent shortages—both in number and in kind—and highlight areas in which the organization is overstaffed. They can then develop a plan that matches these estimates with forecasts of future labor supply. Employment planning not only guides current staffing needs but also projects future employee needs and availability.

recruitment
Locating, identifying, and attracting capable applicants

2A How Do Organizations Recruit Employees?

Once managers know their current staffing levels—understaffed or overstaffed—they can begin to do something about it. If vacancies exist, they can use the information gathered through job analysis to guide them in **recruitment**—that is, the process of locating, identifying, and attracting capable applicants. On the other hand, if employment planning indicates a surplus, managers may want to reduce the labor supply within the organization and initiate downsizing or restructuring activities.

Needed! **Outstanding Job Applicants!**
Now...how do we get those?

WHERE DOES A MANAGER RECRUIT APPLICANTS?   The Internet has become a popular approach for recruiting job applicants, although there are other sources to find them. Exhibit 8–3 offers some guidance. The source that's used should reflect the local labor market, the type or level of position, and the size of the organization.

Which recruiting sources tend to produce superior applicants? Most studies have found that employee referrals generally produce the best applicants.[10] Why? First, applicants referred by current employees are prescreened by those employees. Because the recommenders know both the job and the person being recommended, they tend to refer well-qualified applicants.[11] Second, because current employees often feel that their reputation in the organization is at stake with a

Exhibit 8–3 Recruiting Sources

SOURCE	ADVANTAGES	DISADVANTAGES
Internet/social media	Reaches large numbers of people; can get immediate feedback	Generates many unqualified candidates
	92 percent of recruiters use social media when looking for potential candidates[12]	
Employee referrals	Knowledge about the organization provided by current employee; can generate strong candidates because a good referral reflects on the recommender	May not increase the diversity and mix of employees
Company Web site	Wide distribution; can be targeted to specific groups	Generates many unqualified candidates
College recruiting/job fairs	Large centralized body of candidates	Limited to entry-level positions
Professional recruiting organizations	Good knowledge of industry challenges and requirements	Little commitment to specific organization

Source: Robbins, Stephen P., Coulter, Mary, *Management*, 13th Ed., © 2016, p. 346. Reprinted and electronically reproduced by permission of Pearson Education, Inc., New York, NY.

referral, they tend to make referrals only when they are reasonably confident that the referral won't make them look bad. However, managers shouldn't always opt for the employee-referred applicant; such referrals may not increase the diversity and mix of employees.

2B How Does a Manager Handle Layoffs?

Coca-Cola laid off 1,600 to 1,800 of its corporate U.S. and international employees.[13] American Express cut costs by eliminating 4,000 jobs after failing to meet long-term revenue growth targets.[14] eBay cut 2,400 jobs (7 percent of its workforce) to adapt to changing conditions.[15]

In the past decade, and especially during the last few years, most global organizations, as well as many government agencies and small businesses, have been forced to shrink the size of their workforce or restructure their skill composition. Downsizing has become a relevant strategy for meeting the demands of a dynamic environment.

WHAT ARE DOWNSIZING OPTIONS? Obviously, people can be fired, but other restructuring choices may be more beneficial to the organization. Exhibit 8–4 summarizes a manager's major downsizing options. Keep in mind that, regardless of the method chosen, employees suffer. We discuss downsizing more fully—for both victims and survivors—later in this chapter.

3 How Do Managers Select Job Applicants?

Once the recruiting effort has developed a pool of applicants, the next step in the HRM process is to determine who is best qualified for the job. In essence, then, the **selection process** is a prediction exercise: It seeks to predict which applicants will be "successful" if hired; that is, who will perform well on the criteria the organization uses to evaluate its employees. In filling a network administrator position, for example, the selection process should be able to predict which applicants will be capable of properly installing, debugging, managing, and updating the organization's computer network. For a position as a sales representative, it should predict which applicants will be successful at generating high sales volumes. Consider, for a moment, that any selection decision can result in four possible outcomes. As shown in Exhibit 8–5, two outcomes would indicate correct decisions, and two would indicate errors.

selection process
Screening job applicants to ensure that the most appropriate candidates are hired

Exhibit 8–4 Downsizing Options

OPTION	DESCRIPTION
Firing	Permanent involuntary termination
Layoffs	Temporary involuntary termination; may last only a few days or extend to years
Attrition	Not filling openings created by voluntary resignations or normal retirements
Transfers	Moving employees either laterally or downward; usually does not reduce costs but can reduce intraorganizational supply–demand imbalances
Reduced workweeks	Having employees work fewer hours per week, share jobs, or through furloughs perform their jobs on a part-time basis
Early retirements	Providing incentives to older and more-senior employees for retiring before their normal retirement date
Job sharing	Having employees, typically two part-timers, share one full-time position

Exhibit 8–5 Selection Decision Outcomes

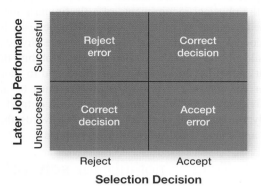

A decision is correct when (1) the applicant who was predicted to be successful (was accepted) later proved to be successful on the job or (2) the applicant who was predicted to be unsuccessful (was rejected) would not have been able to do the job if hired. In the former case, we have successfully accepted; in the latter case, we have successfully rejected. Problems occur, however, when we reject applicants who, if hired, would have performed successfully on the job (called *reject errors*) or accept those who subsequently perform poorly (*accept errors*). These problems are, unfortunately, far from insignificant. A generation ago, reject errors only meant increased selection costs because more applicants would have to be screened. Today, selection techniques that result in reject errors can open the organization to charges of employment discrimination, especially if applicants from protected groups are disproportionately rejected. Accept errors, on the other hand, have obvious costs to the organization, including the cost of training the employee, the costs generated or profits forgone because of the employee's incompetence, and the cost of severance and the subsequent costs of additional recruiting and selection screening. The *major intent of any selection activity is to reduce the probability of making reject errors or accept errors while increasing the probability of making correct decisions.* How? By using selection procedures that are both reliable and valid.

WHAT IS RELIABILITY?   **Reliability** addresses whether a selection device measures the same characteristic consistently. For example, if a test is reliable, any individual's score should remain fairly stable over time, assuming that the characteristics it's measuring are also stable. The importance of reliability should be self-evident. No selection device can be effective if it's low in reliability. Using such a device would be the equivalent of weighing yourself every day on an erratic scale. If the scale is unreliable—randomly fluctuating, say, 10 to 15 pounds every time you step on it—the results will not mean much. To be effective predictors, selection devices must possess an acceptable level of consistency.

WHAT IS VALIDITY?   Any selection device that a manager uses—such as application forms, tests, interviews, or physical examinations—must also demonstrate **validity**. Validity

reliability
The degree to which a selection device measures the same thing consistently

validity
The proven relationship between a selection device and some relevant criterion

In addition to using its online portal, Germany's Lufthansa Airline staged "casting" events to recruit candidates for 2,800 new flight attendant positions. In this photo, a veteran flight attendant places a Lufthansa head piece on an applicant at a casting session. The events generated an enthusiastic response from some 4,000 candidates, and the airline offered jobs to almost 1 in every 3 applicants.

Andreas Arnold/AP Images

is based on a proven relationship between the selection device used and some relevant measure. For example, we mentioned earlier a firefighter applicant who was wheelchair bound. Because of the physical requirements of a firefighter's job, someone confined to a wheelchair would be unable to pass the physical endurance tests. In that case, denying employment could be considered valid, but requiring the same physical endurance tests for the dispatching job would not be job related. Federal law prohibits managers from using any selection device that cannot be shown to be directly related to successful job performance. That constraint goes for entrance tests, too; managers must be able to demonstrate that, once on the job, individuals with high scores on such a test outperform individuals with low scores. Consequently, the burden is on the organization to verify that any selection device it uses to differentiate applicants is related to job performance.

Tests…not just **for school!**

HOW EFFECTIVE ARE TESTS AND INTERVIEWS AS SELECTION DEVICES?   Managers can use a number of selection devices to reduce accept and reject errors. The best-known devices include written and performance-simulation tests and interviews. Let's briefly review each device, giving particular attention to its validity in predicting job performance.

Typical *written tests* include tests of intelligence, aptitude, ability, and interest. Such tests have long been used as selection devices, although their popularity has run in cycles. Written tests were widely used after World War II, but beginning in the late 1960s, fell out of favor. They were frequently characterized as discriminatory, and many organizations could not validate that their written tests were job related. Today, written tests have made a comeback, although most of them are now Internet based.[16] Experts estimate that online personality tests are used by employers to assess personality, skills, cognitive abilities, and other traits of some 60 to 70 percent of prospective employees.[17] Managers are increasingly aware that poor hiring decisions are costly and that properly designed tests can reduce the likelihood of making such decisions. In addition, the cost of developing and validating a set of written tests for a specific job has declined significantly.

Research shows that tests of intellectual ability, spatial and mechanical ability, perceptual accuracy, and motor ability are moderately valid predictors for many semiskilled and unskilled operative jobs in an industrial organization.[18] However, an enduring criticism of written tests is that intelligence and other tested characteristics can be somewhat removed from the actual performance of the job itself.[19] For example, a high score on an intelligence test is not necessarily a good indicator that the applicant will perform well as a computer programmer. This criticism has led to an increased use of performance-simulation tests.

What better way to find out whether an applicant for a technical writing position at Apple can write technical manuals than to ask him or her to do it? That's why there's an increasing interest in **performance-simulation tests**. Undoubtedly, the enthusiasm for these tests lies in the fact that they're based on job analysis data and, therefore, should more easily meet the requirement of job relatedness than do written tests. Performance-simulation tests are made up of actual job behaviors rather than substitutes. The best-known performance-simulation tests are work sampling (a miniature replica of the job) and assessment centers (simulating real problems one may face on the job). The former is suited to persons applying for routine jobs, the latter to managerial personnel.

The advantage of performance simulation over traditional testing methods should be obvious. Because its content is essentially identical to job content, performance simulation should be a better predictor of short-term job performance and should minimize potential employment discrimination allegations. Additionally, because of the nature of their content and the methods used to determine content, well-constructed performance-simulation tests are valid predictors.

The *interview*, along with the application form, is an almost universal selection device. Few of us have ever gotten a job without undergoing one or more interviews. The irony of this is that the value of an interview as a selection device has been the subject of considerable debate.[20]

performance-simulation tests
Selection devices based on actual job behaviors

Interviews can be reliable and valid selection tools, but too often they're not. To be effective predictors, interviews need to be:

- structured,
- well organized, and have
- interviewers asking relevant questions.[21]

But those conditions don't characterize many interviews. The typical interview in which applicants are asked a varying set of essentially random questions in an informal setting often provides little in the way of valuable information. All kinds of potential biases can creep into interviews if they're not well structured and standardized.

What does research tell us about interviewing?

- Prior knowledge about the applicant biases the interviewer's evaluation.
- The interviewer tends to hold a stereotype of what represents a good applicant.
- The interviewer tends to favor applicants who share his or her own attitudes.
- The order in which applicants are interviewed will influence evaluations.
- The order in which information is elicited during the interview will influence evaluations.
- Negative information is given unduly high weight.
- The interviewer may make a decision concerning the applicant's suitability within the first four or five minutes of the interview.
- The interviewer may forget much of the interview's content within minutes after its conclusion.
- The interview is most valid in determining an applicant's intelligence, level of motivation, and interpersonal skills.
- Structured and well-organized interviews are more reliable than unstructured and unorganized ones.[22]

How Can I Be a **Good Interviewer?**

TIPS FOR MANAGERS: Make interviews more valid and reliable!

1. Review the job description and job specification to help in assessing the applicant.
2. Prepare a structured set of questions to ask all applicants for the job.
3. Review an applicant's résumé before meeting him or her.
4. Ask questions and listen carefully to the applicant's answer.
5. Write your evaluation of the applicant while the interview is still fresh in your mind.

One last popular modification to interviews has been the behavioral or situation interview.[23] In this type of interview, applicants are observed not only for what they say, but also how they behave. Applicants are presented with situations—often complex problems involving role playing—and are asked to "deal" with the situation. This type of interview provides an opportunity for interviewers to see how a potential employee will behave and how he or she will react under stress. Proponents of behavioral interviewing indicate such a process is much more indicative of an applicant's performance than simply having the individual tell the interviewer what he or she has done. In fact, research in this area indicates that behavioral interviews are nearly eight times more effective for predicting successful job performance.[24]

HOW CAN YOU "CLOSE THE DEAL"?   Interviewers who treat the recruiting and hiring of employees as if the applicants must be sold on the job and exposed only to an organization's positive characteristics are likely to have a workforce that is dissatisfied and prone to high turnover.[25]

Closing the **Deal!**

During the hiring process, every job applicant develops a set of expectations about the company and about the job for which he or she is interviewing. When the information an

realistic job preview (RJP)
A preview of a job that provides both positive and negative information about the job and the company

applicant receives is excessively inflated, a number of things happen that have potentially negative effects on the company: (1) Mismatched applicants are less likely to withdraw from the search process. (2) Inflated information builds unrealistic expectations so new employees are likely to become quickly dissatisfied and to resign prematurely. (3) New hires are prone to become disillusioned and less committed to the organization when they face the unexpected harsh realities of the job. (4) In many cases, these individuals feel that they were misled during the hiring process and may become problem employees.

To increase job satisfaction among employees and reduce turnover, managers should consider a **realistic job preview (RJP)**.[26] An RJP includes both positive and negative information about the job and the company. For example, in addition to the positive comments typically expressed in the interview, the applicant is told of the less attractive aspects of the job. For instance, he or she might be told that there are limited opportunities to talk to coworkers during work hours, that chances of being promoted are slim, or that work hours fluctuate so erratically that employees may be required to work during what are usually off hours (nights and weekends). Research indicates that applicants who have been given a realistic job preview hold lower and more realistic job expectations for the jobs they will be performing and are better able to cope with the frustrating elements of the job than are applicants who have been given only inflated information. The result is fewer unexpected resignations by new employees. For managers, realistic job previews offer a major insight into the HRM process.

Presenting only positive job aspects to an applicant may initially entice him or her to join the organization, but it may be a decision that both parties quickly regret.

It's just as important to *retain* **good people** as it is to *hire* them in the first place.

How Are Employees Provided with Needed Skills and Knowledge?

8-3 Explain how employees are provided with needed skills and knowledge.

If we've done our recruiting and selecting properly, we've hired competent individuals who can perform successfully on the job. But *successful performance requires more than possessing certain skills!* New hires must be acclimated to the organization's culture and be trained and given the knowledge to do the job in a manner consistent with the organization's goals. To achieve this, HRM uses orientation and training.

How Are New Hires Introduced to the Organization?

Once a job candidate has been selected, he or she needs to be introduced to the job and organization. This introduction is called **orientation**.[27] The major goals of orientation are to

- reduce the initial anxiety all new employees feel as they begin a new job;
- familiarize new employees with the job, the work unit, and the organization as a whole; and
- facilitate the outsider–insider transition.

Job orientation: (1) expands on the information the employee obtained during the recruitment and selection stages, (2) clarifies the new employee's specific duties and responsibilities as well as how his or her performance will be evaluated, and (3) corrects any unrealistic expectations new employees might hold about the job.

Work unit orientation: (1) Familiarizes an employee with the goals of the work unit, (2) clarifies how his or her job contributes to the unit's goals, and (3) provides an introduction to his or her coworkers.

Organization orientation: (1) Informs the new employee about the organization's goals, history, philosophy, procedures, and rules; (2) clarifies relevant HR policies such as work

orientation
Introducing a new employee to the job and the organization

Managing Technology in Today's Workplace

SOCIAL AND DIGITAL HR

HR has gone social and digital.[29] Mobile devices are increasingly being used to provide training in bite-sized lessons using videos and games. For instance, the 75,000-plus associates of realty company Keller Williams use their smartphones and tablets to view two- to three-minute video lessons on sales and customer service. Then, there are the few tech-forward marketing firms that are using tweets rather than the conventional résumé/job interview process. These "Twitterviews" are used in talent selection. One individual said, "The Web is your résumé. Social networks are your mass references." Many other firms are using social media platforms to expand their recruiting reach. Not only are social media tools being used by corporations to recruit applicants, they're being used to allow employees to collaborate by sharing files, images, documents, videos, and other documents.

On the digital side, HR departments using software that automates many basic HR processes associated with recruiting, selecting, orienting, training, appraising performance, and storing and retrieving employee information have cut costs and optimized service. One HR area where IT has contributed is in pre-employment assessments. For instance, at KeyBank, a Cleveland-based financial services organization, virtual "job tryout simulations" have been used in order to reduce 90-day turnover rates and create more consistency in staffing decisions. These simulations create an interactive multimedia experience and mimic key job tasks for competencies such as providing client service, adapting to change, supporting team members, following procedures, and working efficiently. Before using these virtual assessments, the bank was losing 13 percent of new tellers and call center associates in their first 90 days. After implementing the virtual assessments, that number dropped to 4 percent.

Another area where IT has had a significant impact is in training. In a survey by the American Society for Training and Development, 95 percent of the responding companies reported using some form of e-learning. Using technology to deliver needed knowledge, skills, and attitudes has had many benefits. As one researcher pointed out, e-learning can reduce the cost of training, but more importantly, can improve the way an organization functions. And in many instances, it seems to do that! For example, when Hewlett-Packard looked at how its customer service was affected by a blend of e-learning and other instructional methods, rather than just classroom training, it found that its sales representatives could answer customer questions more quickly and accurately. And Unilever found that after e-learning training for sales employees, sales increased by several million dollars.

Discussion Questions:

5 Does the use of all this technology make HR—which is supposed to be a "people-oriented" profession—less so? Why or why not?

6 You want a job after graduating from college. Knowing that you're likely to encounter online recruitment and selection procedures, how can you best prepare for making yourself stand out in the process? Prepare some ideas on your own and then, in your "assigned" group, share ideas. Come up with a *Top 3* and be prepared to share those with the class.

hours, pay procedures, overtime requirements, and benefits; and (3) may include a tour of the organization's physical facilities.

Managers have an obligation to make the integration of a new employee into the organization as smooth and anxiety-free as possible. Successful orientation, whether formal or informal:

- Results in an outsider–insider transition that makes the new member feel comfortable and fairly well-adjusted.
- Lowers the likelihood of poor work performance.
- Reduces the probability of a surprise resignation by the new employee only a week or two into the job.[28]

What Is Employee Training?

On the whole, planes don't cause airline accidents, people do. Most collisions, crashes, and other airline mishaps—nearly three-quarters of them—result from errors by the pilot or air traffic controller or from inadequate maintenance. Weather and structural failures typically account for the remaining accidents.[30] We cite these statistics to illustrate the

Employees at Villa Venture senior living community participate in a perception exercise during the Virtual Dementia Tour, a training tool that helps them understand Alzheimer's disease and other forms of dementia. The tour is a learning experience designed to improve employees' ability to care for victims of dementia.

importance of training in the airline industry. Such maintenance and human errors could be prevented or significantly reduced by better employee training, as shown by the unbelievably amazing "landing" of US Airways Flight 1549 in the Hudson River more than 10 years ago with no loss of life. Pilot Captain Chesley Sullenberger attributed the positive outcome to the extensive and intensive training that all pilots and flight crews undergo.[31]

Employee training is a learning experience that seeks a relatively permanent change in employees by improving their ability to perform on the job. Thus, training involves changing skills, knowledge, attitudes, or behavior.[32] This change may involve what employees know, how they work, or their attitudes toward their jobs, coworkers, managers, and the organization. It's been estimated, for instance, that U.S. business firms spend billions each year on formal courses and training programs to develop workers' skills.[33] Managers, of course, are responsible for deciding when employees are in need of training and what form that training should take.

Determining training needs typically involves answering several questions. If some of these questions sound familiar, you've been paying close attention. It's precisely the type of analysis that takes place when managers develop an organizational structure to achieve their strategic goals—only now the focus is on the people.[34]

employee training
A learning experience that seeks a relatively permanent change in employees by improving their ability to perform on the job

WHEN is training needed?

The questions in Exhibit 8–6 suggest the kinds of signals that can warn a manager when training may be necessary. The more obvious ones are related directly to productivity. Indications that job performance is declining include decreases in production numbers, lower quality, more accidents, and higher scrap or rejection rates. Any of these outcomes

Exhibit 8–6 Determining Whether Training Is Needed

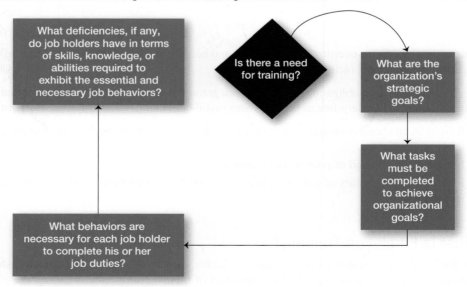

might suggest that worker skills need to be fine-tuned. Of course, we're assuming that an employee's performance decline is in no way related to lack of effort. Managers, too, must also recognize that training may be required because the workplace is constantly evolving. Changes imposed on employees as a result of job redesign or a technological breakthrough also require training.

HOW ARE EMPLOYEES TRAINED?   Most training takes place on the job. Why? It's simple and it usually costs less. However, on-the-job training can disrupt the workplace and result in an increase in errors while learning takes place. Also, some skill training is too complex to learn on the job and must take place outside the work setting.

Many different types of training methods are available. For the most part, we can classify them as traditional and technology-based. (See Exhibit 8–7.)

HOW CAN MANAGERS ENSURE THAT TRAINING IS WORKING?   It's easy to generate a new training program, but if training efforts aren't evaluated, it may be a waste of resources. It would be nice if all companies could boast the returns on investments in training that Neil Huffman Auto Group executives do; they claim they receive $230 in increased productivity for every dollar spent on training.[35] But to make such a claim, training must be properly evaluated.

Exhibit 8–7 Training Methods

TRADITIONAL TRAINING METHODS

On-the-job—Employees learn how to do tasks simply by performing them, usually after an initial introduction to the task.

Job rotation—Employees work at different jobs in a particular area, getting exposure to a variety of tasks.

Mentoring and coaching—Employees work with an experienced worker who provides information, support, and encouragement; also called apprenticeships in certain industries.

Experiential exercises—Employees participate in role-playing, simulations, or other face-to-face types of training.

Workbooks/manuals—Employees refer to training workbooks and manuals for information.

Classroom lectures—Employees attend lectures designed to convey specific information.

TECHNOLOGY-BASED TRAINING METHODS

CD-ROM/DVD/videotapes/audiotapes/podcasts—Employees listen to or watch selected media that convey information or demonstrate certain techniques.

Videoconferencing/teleconferencing/satellite TV—Employees listen to or participate as information is conveyed or techniques demonstrated.

E-learning—Employees participate in Internet-based learning, including simulations or other interactive modules.

Mobile learning—Employees participate in learning activities delivered via mobile devices.

Keeping Great People:
Two Ways Organizations Do This

8-4 Describe strategies for retaining competent, high-performing employees.

1

Performance Management System

- *Desired* employee performance levels determined by organizations and managers
- *Actual* employee performance levels measured/appraised by managers
- *AKA* **performance management system**

61 percent of office workers feel their manager plays favorites on performance reviews.[37]

Should people be **compared to one another** or **against a set of standards?**

Chris Zuppz/ZUMAPress/Newscom

performance management system
A system that establishes performance standards that are used to evaluate employee performance

Exhibit 8–8 Specific Performance Appraisal Methods

Method	Advantage	Disadvantage
(A) WRITTEN ESSAY—descriptions of employee's strengths and weaknesses	Simple to use	More a measure of evaluator's writing ability than of employee's actual performance
(B) CRITICAL INCIDENTS—examples of critical behaviors that were especially effective or ineffective	Rich examples; behaviorally based	Time-consuming; lack quantification
(C) ADJECTIVE RATING SCALES—lists descriptive performance factors (work quantity and quality, knowledge, cooperation, loyalty, attendance, honesty, initiative, and so forth) with numerical ratings	Provide quantitative data; less time-consuming than others	Do not provide depth of job behavior assessed
(D) BARS—rating scale + examples of actual job behaviors[38,39]	Focus on specific and measurable job behaviors	Time-consuming; difficult to develop measures
(E) MBO—evaluation of accomplishment of specific goals	Focuses on end goals; results oriented	Time-consuming
(F) 360-degree appraisal [40]—feedback from full circle of those who interact with employee	More thorough	Time-consuming
(G) MULTIPERSON—evaluation comparison of work group	Compares employees with one another	Unwieldy with large number of employees

- **(a)** through **(f)** (see Exhibit 8–8) are ways to evaluate employee performance against a set of established standards or absolute criteria.

- **(g)** (see Exhibit 8-8) is a way to compare one person's performance with that of one or more individuals and is a relative, not absolute, measuring device.

Three approaches to multiperson comparison:

1 Group-order ranking

Evaluator places employees into a particular classification ("top fifth," "second fifth," etc.; "top third," "middle third," "bottom third"; or whatever classification is desired). Note: Number of employees placed in each classification must be as equal as possible.

2 Individual ranking approach

Evaluator lists employees in order from highest to lowest performance levels. Note: Only one can be "best." In the appraisal of whatever number of employees, the difference between the first and second employee is the same as that between any other two employees. And no "ties" allowed.

3 Paired comparison approach

Each employee is compared with every other employee in the comparison group and rated as either the superior or weaker member of the pair. Note: Each employee is assigned a summary ranking based on the number of superior scores he or she achieved. Each employee is compared against every other employee—an arduous task when assessing large numbers of employees.

360-degree appraisal
An appraisal device that seeks feedback from a variety of sources for the person being rated

TRADITIONAL MANAGER-EMPLOYEE PERFORMANCE EVALUATION SYSTEMS MAY BE OUTDATED DUE TO:[41]

— **Downsizing**—supervisors may have more employees to manage, making it difficult to have extensive knowledge of each one's performance.

— Project teams and employee involvement—others (not managers) may be better able to make accurate assessments.[42]

Lasse Kristensen/Alamy
Stock Photo

Trevor Chriss/Alamy Stock Photo

When Employee's Performance Is Not Up to Par...

WHY?

Job mismatch (hiring error)   ⟶

Inadequate training   ⟶

Lack of desire to do job
(**discipline** problem)   ⟶

WHAT TO DO

Reassign individual to better-matched job

Provide training

Try **employee counseling**, a process designed to help employees overcome performance-related problems; attempt to uncover why employee has lost his/her desire or ability to work productively and find ways to fix the problem; or take disciplinary/punitive action *(verbal and written warnings, suspension, and even termination)*.

2

Compensating Employees: Pay and Benefits

Compensation–Pay for doing a job

An **effective** and **appropriate** compensation system will:[43]
— Help attract and retain competent and talented individuals
— Impact strategic performance[44]
— Keep employees motivated

MOST of us work to
have money

---

employee counseling	**discipline**
A process designed to help employees overcome performance-related problems	Actions taken by a manager to enforce an organization's standards and regulations

Artpartner-images.com/Alamy Stock Photo

Determining Pay Levels

Who gets
$15.85
an hour?

Who gets
$325,000
a year?

A compensation system should reflect the changing nature of work and the workplace.

- Determining pay levels isn't easy, but employees expect appropriate compensation.

Different jobs require:

- Different kinds and levels of **knowledge, skills**, and **abilities (KSAs)** that have varying value to the organization
- Different levels of responsibility and authority

The **higher the KSAs** and the greater the authority and responsibility, **the higher the pay**.

Alternative approaches to determining compensation:

- **Skill-based pay systems**—reward employees for job skills and competencies they have. Job title doesn't define pay, skills do.[45] Usually more successful in manufacturing organizations than in service organizations or in organizations pursuing technical innovations.[46]

- **Variable pay systems**—individual's compensation is contingent on performance.

90%
of U.S. organizations use variable pay plans[47]

As shown in Exhibit 8–9, *other **factors influencing compensation** and **benefit packages*** include:

Primary determinant of pay: the kind of job an employee performs

skill-based pay
A pay system that rewards employees for the job skills they demonstrate

variable pay
A pay system in which an individual's compensation is contingent on performance

Exhibit 8–9 What Determines Pay and Benefits?

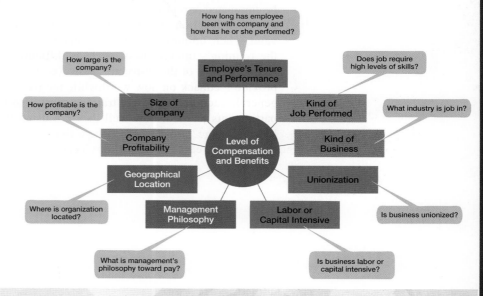

301

Compensation–Employee Benefits: Non-cash compensation from employers

- Compensation package is > just hourly wage or annual salary

- Also includes **employee benefits**—important and varied nonfinancial rewards designed to enrich employees' lives

- Benefit packages can vary widely and often reflect efforts to provide something that each employee values

- Some benefits—Social Security, workers' and unemployment compensation—are legally required, but organizations may provide others such as paid time off from work, life and disability insurance, retirement programs, and health insurance.[48]

employee benefits
Membership-based rewards designed to enrich employees' lives

J.R. Bale/Alamy Stock Photo

How can training programs be evaluated? Usually several managers, representatives from HRM, and a group of workers who have recently completed a training program are asked for their opinions. If the comments are generally positive, the program may get a favorable evaluation and it's continued until someone decides, for whatever reason, that it should be eliminated or replaced.

Such reactions from participants or managers, while easy to acquire, are the least valid. Their opinions are heavily influenced by factors that may have little to do with the training's effectiveness, such as difficulty, entertainment value, or the personality characteristics of the instructor. However, trainees' reactions to the training may, in fact, provide feedback on how worthwhile the participants viewed the training to be. Beyond general reactions, however, training must also be evaluated in terms of how much the participants learned, how well they are using their new skills on the job (did their behavior change?), and whether the training program achieved its desired results (reduced turnover, increased customer service, etc.).[36]

What Contemporary HRM Issues Face Managers?

8-5 Discuss contemporary issues in managing human resources.

HR issues that face today's managers include downsizing, workforce diversity, sexual harassment, and HR costs.

How Can Managers Manage Downsizing?

downsizing
The planned elimination of jobs in an organization

layoff-survivor sickness
A set of attitudes, perceptions, and behaviors of employees who survive layoffs

Downsizing is the planned elimination of jobs in an organization. Because downsizing typically involves shrinking the organization's workforce, it's an important issue in HRM. When an organization has too many employees—which may happen when it's faced with an economic crisis, declining market share, overly aggressive growth, or when it's been poorly managed—one option for improving profits is to eliminate excess workers. Over the last few years, many well-known companies have gone through several rounds of downsizing—AmEx, Boeing, McDonald's, Volkswagen, IBM, AT&T, Walmart, Ford Motor Co., PepsiCo, JCPenney, Amazon, and Comcast, among others. How can managers best manage a downsized workforce?

After downsizing, disruptions in the workplace and in employees' personal lives are to be expected. Stress, frustration, anxiety, and anger are typical reactions. And it may surprise you to learn that *both* victims and survivors experience those feelings.[49] Many organizations have helped layoff victims by offering a variety of job-help services, psychological counseling, support groups, severance pay, extended health insurance benefits, and detailed communications. Although some individuals react negatively to being laid off (the worst cases involve individuals returning to their former organization and committing a violent act), offers of assistance reveal that an organization does care about its former employees. While those being laid off get to start over with a clean slate and a clear conscience, survivors don't. Unfortunately, the "survivors" who retain their jobs and have the task of keeping the organization going or even of revitalizing it seldom receive attention. One negative consequence appears to be what is being called **layoff-survivor sickness**, a set of attitudes, perceptions, and behaviors of employees who survive involuntary staff reductions.[50] Symptoms include job insecurity, perceptions of unfairness, guilt, depression, stress from increased workload, fear of change, loss of loyalty and commitment, reduced effort, and an unwillingness to do anything beyond the required minimum.

To show concern for job survivors, managers may want to provide opportunities for employees to talk to counselors about their guilt, anger, and anxiety.[51] Group discussions can be a way for the survivors to vent their feelings. Some organizations have used downsizing as the spark to implement increased employee participation programs such as empowerment and self-managed work teams. In short, to keep morale and productivity high, managers should make every attempt to ensure that those individuals still working in the organization know that they're valuable and much-needed resources. Exhibit 8–10 summarizes some ways that managers can reduce the trauma associated with downsizing.

Exhibit 8–10 Tips for Managing Downsizing

- Communicate openly and honestly:
  - Inform those being let go as soon as possible
  - Tell surviving employees the new goals and expectations
  - Explain impact of layoffs
- Follow any laws regulating severance pay or benefits
- Provide support/counseling for surviving employees
- Reassign roles according to individuals' talents and backgrounds
- Focus on boosting morale:
  - Offer individualized reassurance
  - Continue to communicate, especially one-on-one
  - Remain involved and available

What Is Sexual Harassment?

Sexual harassment *is* a serious issue.

Several allegations against high-profile individuals in both public and private-sector organizations recently highlighted how prevalent sexual harassment is. The #MeToo movement took many by surprise because sexual harassment is an issue that's more pervasive than many thought.[52] Now, leaders in many organizations are reviewing their strategies for preventing and addressing sexual harassment.

Despite the apparent frequency of sexual harassment, only between 6,500 and 8,000 complaints are filed with the Equal Employment Opportunity Commission (EEOC) each year,[53] with more than 16 percent of those filed by males.[54] Settlements in some of these cases incurred a substantial cost to the companies in terms of litigation. It's estimated that sexual harassment is the single largest financial risk facing companies today—and can result in decreases (sometimes greater than 30 percent) in a company's stock price.[55] At Mitsubishi, for example, the company paid out more than $34 million to 300 women for the rampant sexual harassment to which they were exposed.[56] But it's more than just jury awards. Sexual harassment results in millions lost in absenteeism, low productivity, and turnover.[57] Sexual harassment, furthermore, is not just a U.S. phenomenon. It's a global issue. For instance, nearly 10 percent of workers responding to a global survey reported that they had been harassed sexually or physically at work. The survey covered countries such as India, China, Saudi Arabia, Sweden, France, Belgium, Germany, Great Britain, and Poland, among others.[58] Even though discussions of sexual harassment cases often focus on the large awards granted by a court, employers face other concerns. Sexual harassment creates an unpleasant work environment for organization members and undermines their ability to perform their jobs. But just what is sexual harassment?

Any unwanted action or activity of a sexual nature that explicitly or implicitly affects an individual's employment, performance, or work environment can be regarded as **sexual harassment**. It can occur between members of the opposite or of the same sex—between employees of the organization or between employee and nonemployee.[59] Although such an activity has been generally prohibited under Title VII (sex discrimination) in the United States, in recent years this problem has gained more recognition. By most accounts, prior to the mid-1980s, occurrences were generally viewed as isolated incidents, with the individual committing the act being solely responsible (if at all) for his or her actions.[60] Today, charges of sexual harassment continue to appear in the headlines on an almost regular basis.

---

48 percent of women report having been sexually, verbally, or physically harassed at work.[61]

Most of the challenges associated with sexual harassment involve determining what constitutes this illegal behavior.[62] The EEOC explains that it is unlawful to harass a person because of that person's sex. Harassment can include sexual harassment or unwelcome sexual advances, requests for sexual behavior, and other verbal or physical harassment of a sexual nature. However, harassment does *not* have to be of a sexual nature and can include offensive remarks about a person's sex. Simple teasing, offhand comments, or isolated incidents that are not serious are not prohibited by the law *unless* it becomes so frequent or so severe that it creates a hostile or offensive work environment or it results in an adverse employment decision (such as being demoted or fired).[63]

You gotta be attuned to what makes fellow **employees uncomfortable.**

---

sexual harassment
Any unwanted action or activity of a sexual nature that explicitly or implicitly affects an individual's employment, performance, or work environment

For many organizations, it's the offensive or hostile environment issue that's problematic.[64] Managers need to know what constitutes such an environment. How do you determine whether something is offensive? For instance, do off-color jokes in the office create a hostile environment? How about classical artwork that shows nude men or women? The answer is it very well could! It depends on the people in the organization and the environment in which they work. The key is knowing what makes fellow employees uncomfortable—and if we don't know, we should ask![65] Also, managers must understand that the victim doesn't necessarily have to be the person harassed but could be *anyone* affected by the offensive conduct.[66]

Organizational success will, in part, reflect how sensitive each employee is toward another in the company. At DuPont, for example, the corporate culture and diversity programs are designed to eliminate sexual harassment through awareness and respect for all individuals.[67] It means understanding one another and, most importantly, respecting others' rights. Similar programs exist at FedEx, General Mills, and Levi-Strauss, among other companies.

If sexual harassment carries with it potential costs to the organization, what can a company do to protect itself?[68] The courts want to know two things: (1) Did the organization know about, or should it have known about, the alleged behavior? (2) What did managers do to stop it?[69] With the number and dollar amounts of the awards today, it's even more important for organizations and managers to educate all employees on sexual harassment matters and to have mechanisms available to monitor employees. In addition, organizations need to ensure that no retaliatory actions—such as cutting back hours, assigning back-to-back work shifts without a rest break, etc.—are taken against a person who has filed harassment charges, especially in light of a U.S. Supreme Court ruling that broadened the definition of retaliation.[70]

---

98 percent of U.S. organizations have a sexual harassment policy. The problem is not not having a policy . . . it's the culture.[71]

Finally, in a sexual harassment matter, managers must remember that the harasser may have rights, too.[72] No action should be taken against someone until a thorough investigation has been conducted. Furthermore, the results of the investigation should be reviewed by an independent and objective individual before any action against the alleged harasser is taken. Even then, the harasser should be given an opportunity to respond to the allegation and have a disciplinary hearing if desired. Additionally, an avenue for appeal should also exist for the alleged harasser—an appeal heard by someone at a higher level of management who is not associated with the case.

How Are Organizations and Managers Adapting to a Changing Workforce?

Because organizations wouldn't be able to do what they're in business to do without employees, managers have to adapt to the changes taking place in the workforce. They're responding with workforce initiatives such as work/life balance programs and contingent jobs.

WORK/LIFE BALANCE PROGRAMS. The typical employee in the 1960s or 1970s showed up at the workplace Monday through Friday and did his or her job in eight- or nine-hour chunks of time. The workplace and hours were clearly specified. That's not the case anymore for a large segment of the workforce. Employees are increasingly

Employees at Citrix Systems, a leading provider of virtualization, networking, and cloud computing technologies, enjoy flexible work schedules that help them balance their work and home life. Citrix gives employees the freedom to determine how, when, and where their work gets done and allows them to use their own devices for working at home or at the office.

Charles Trainor Jr./Miami Herald/MCT/Newscom

complaining that the line between work and nonwork time has blurred, creating personal conflicts and stress.[73] Several factors have contributed to this blurring between work and personal life. One is that in a world of global business, work never ends. At any time and on any day, for instance, thousands of Caterpillar employees are working somewhere in the company's facilities. The need to consult with colleagues or customers 8 or 10 time zones away means that many employees of global companies are "on call" 24 hours a day. Another factor is that communication technology allows employees to do their work at home, in their cars, or on the beach in Tahiti. Although this capability allows those in technical and professional jobs to do their work anywhere and at any time, it also means there's no escaping from work. Another factor is that as organizations have had to lay off employees during the economic downturn, "surviving" employees find themselves working longer hours. It's not unusual for employees to work more than 45 hours a week, and some work more than 50. Finally, fewer families today have a single wage earner. Today's married employee is typically part of a dual-career couple, which makes it increasingly difficult for married employees to find time to fulfill commitments to home, spouse, children, parents, and friends.[74]

More and more, employees recognize that work is squeezing out their personal lives, and they're not happy about it. Today's progressive workplaces must accommodate the varied needs of a diverse workforce. In response, many organizations are offering **family-friendly benefits**: benefits that provide a wide range of scheduling options that allow employees more flexibility at work, accommodating their need for work/life balance. They've introduced programs such as onsite child care, summer day camps, flextime, job sharing, time off for school functions, telecommuting, and part-time employment. Organizations such as Microsoft, Blackstone Group LP, and Credit Suisse Group AG, for example, have added generous paid-leave policies to give employees time off to bond with their newborns.[75] Younger people, particularly, put a higher priority on family and a lower priority on jobs and are looking for organizations that give them more work flexibility.[76] How about an employer that gives employees paid paid vacations...no, that's not an editing error! Each employee at Moz, a Seattle software company, receives three weeks of paid time off, but also receives $3,000 a year to spend on vacation-related expenses.[77] This is a company that recognizes the importance of work/life balance.

CONTINGENT JOBS.   We discussed the concept of flexible work and contingent jobs in the last chapter as we looked at designing efficient and effective flexible work arrangements. We saw that the labor force has been shifting away from traditional full-time jobs toward a contingent workforce—part-time, temporary, and contract workers who are available for hire on an as-needed basis. Many organizations have converted full-time permanent jobs into contingent jobs. It is one way that organizations can control the supply and demand for labor.

What are the HRM implications for managers and organizations? Because contingent employees are not "employees" in the traditional sense of the word, managing them has its own set of challenges and expectations. Managers must recognize that because contingent workers lack the stability and security of permanent employees, they may not identify with the organization or be as committed or motivated. Managers may need to treat contingent workers differently in terms of practices and policies. However, with good communication and leadership, an organization's contingent employees can be just as valuable a resource to an organization as permanent employees are. Today's managers must recognize that it will be their responsibility to motivate their entire workforce, full-time and contingent, and to build their commitment to doing good work!

family-friendly benefits
Benefits that provide a wide range of scheduling options and allow employees more flexibility at work, accommodating their needs for work/life balance

How Can Workforce Diversity and Inclusion Be Managed?

8-6 Explain what workforce diversity and inclusion are and how they affect the HRM process.

> It's amazing all the different languages you can hear in **the lobby of one of MGM Mirage's hotels**. Because guests come from all over the world, the company is committed to reflecting that diversity in its workplace.

MGM Mirage has implemented a program that is devoted to making sure that everyone in the organization feels included.[78] Such diversity can be found in many organizational workplaces domestically and globally, and managers in those workplaces are looking for ways to value and develop that diversity.

What Is Workforce Diversity?

Look around your classroom (or your workplace). You're likely to see young/old, male/female, tall/short, blonde/brunette, blue-eyed/brown-eyed, any number of races, and any variety of dress styles. You'll see people who speak up in class and others who are content to keep their attention on taking notes or daydreaming. Have you ever noticed your own little world of diversity where you are right now? Many of you may have grown up in an environment that included diverse individuals, while others may not have had that experience. We want to focus on *workplace* diversity, so let's look at what it is.

Diversity has been "one of the most popular business topics over the last two decades. It ranks with modern business disciplines such as quality, leadership, and ethics. Despite this popularity, it's also one of the most controversial and least understood topics."[79] With its basis in civil rights legislation and social justice, the word "diversity" often invokes a variety of attitudes and emotional responses in people. Diversity has traditionally been considered a term used by human resources departments, associated with fair hiring practices, discrimination, and inequality. But diversity today is considered to be so much more.

We're defining **workforce diversity** as the ways in which people in an organization are different from and similar to one another. Notice that our definition not only focuses on the differences but also the similarities of employees, reinforcing our belief that managers and organizations should view employees as having qualities in common as well as differences that separate them. It doesn't mean that those differences are any less important, but rather that our focus as managers is in finding ways to develop strong relationships with and engage our entire workforce.

workforce diversity
Ways in which people in a workforce are similar and different from one another in terms of gender, age, race, sexual orientation, ethnicity, cultural background, and physical abilities and disabilities

What Types of Diversity Are Found in Workplaces?

Diversity is a big issue, and an important issue, in today's workplaces. What types of diversity do we find in those workplaces? Exhibit 8-11 lists several types of workplace diversity.

$12 million...that's the amount Texas Roadhouse paid to settle an age discrimination lawsuit.[80]

AGE.   The aging of the population is a major critical shift taking place in the workforce. With many of the nearly 85 million Baby Boomers still employed and active in the workforce, managers must ensure that those employees are not discriminated against because of age. Both Title VII of the Civil Rights Act of 1964 and the Age Discrimination in Employment Act of 1967 prohibit age discrimination. The Age Discrimination Act also restricts mandatory retirement at specific ages. In addition to complying with these laws, organizations need programs and policies in place that provide for fair and equal treatment of their older employees.

GENDER.   Women (46.8 percent) and men (53.2 percent) each make up almost half of the workforce.[81] However, gender diversity issues are still quite prevalent in organizations. These issues include the gender pay gap, career start and progress, and misconceptions about whether women perform their jobs as well as men do. It's important for managers and organizations to explore the strengths that both women and men bring to an organization and the barriers they face in contributing fully to organizational efforts.

RACE AND ETHNICITY.   There's a long and controversial history in the United States and in other parts of the world over race and, as recent events have shown, how people react to and treat others of a different race. Race and ethnicity are important types of diversity in organizations. We're going to define **race** as the biological heritage (including physical characteristics such as one's skin color and associated traits) that people use to identify themselves. Most people identify themselves as part of a racial group, and such racial classifications are an integral part of a country's cultural, social, and legal environments. **Ethnicity** is related to race, but it refers to social traits—such as one's cultural background or allegiance—that are shared by a human population.

race
The biological heritage (including physical characteristics, such as one's skin color and associated traits) that people use to identify themselves

ethnicity
Social traits, such as one's cultural background or allegiance, that are shared by a human population

Exhibit 8-11 Types of Diversity Found in Workplaces

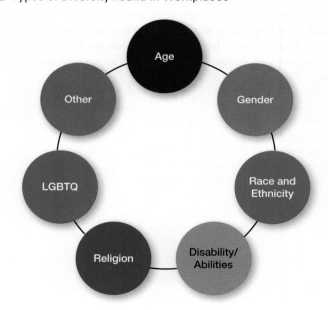

The racial and ethnic diversity of the U.S. population is increasing and at an exponential rate. We're also seeing this same effect in the composition of the workforce. Most of the research on race and ethnicity as they relate to the workplace has looked at hiring decisions, performance evaluations, pay, and workplace discrimination. Managers and organizations need to make race and ethnicity issues a key focus in effectively managing workforce diversity.

DISABILITY/ABILITIES.   For persons with disabilities, 1990 was a watershed year—the year the Americans with Disabilities Act (ADA) became law. ADA prohibits discrimination against persons with disabilities and also requires employers to make reasonable accommodations so their workplaces are accessible to people with physical or mental disabilities and enable them to effectively perform their jobs. With the law's enactment, individuals with disabilities became a more representative and integral part of the U.S. workforce.

In effectively managing a workforce with disabled employees, managers need to create and maintain an environment in which employees feel comfortable disclosing their need for accommodation. Those accommodations, by law, enable individuals with disabilities to perform their jobs, but they also need to be perceived as equitable by those not disabled. It's the balancing act that managers face.

RELIGION.   Hani Khan, a college sophomore, had worked for three months as a stock clerk at a Hollister clothing store in San Francisco.[82] One day, she was told by her supervisors to remove the head scarf that she wears in observance of Islam (known as a *hijab*) because it violated the company's "look policy" (which instructs employees on clothing, hair styles, makeup, and accessories they may wear to work). She refused on religious grounds and was fired one week later. Like a number of other Muslim women, she filed a federal job discrimination complaint. A spokesperson for Abercrombie & Fitch (Hollister's parent company) said that, "If any Abercrombie associate identifies a religious conflict with an Abercrombie policy . . . the company will work with the associate in an attempt to find an accommodation."

Title VII of the Civil Rights Act prohibits discrimination on the basis of religion (as well as race/ethnicity, country of origin, and sex). However, you'd probably not be surprised to find out that the number of religious discrimination claims has been growing in the United States.[83] In accommodating religious diversity, managers need to recognize and be aware of different religions and their beliefs, paying special attention to when certain religious holidays fall. Businesses benefit when they can accommodate, if possible, employees who have special needs or requests in a way that other employees don't view it as "special treatment."

LGBTQ—SEXUAL ORIENTATION AND GENDER IDENTITY.   The acronym LGBTQ—which refers to lesbian, gay, bisexual, transgender, and queer people—is being used more frequently and relates to the diversity of sexual orientation and gender identity.[84] Sexual orientation has been called the "last acceptable bias."[85] We want to emphasize that we're not condoning this perspective; what this comment refers to is that most people understand that racial and ethnic stereotypes are "off-limits." Unfortunately, it's not unusual to hear derogatory comments about gays or lesbians. How many LGBT people are there in the overall population? It's difficult to know exactly. Some governments are trying to find out by including questions about sexual identity on national census forms. Some estimates are already becoming available. For instance, the Office for National Statistics reports that 1.7 percent of the UK population identifies as lesbian, gay, or bisexual; of those people, most of them were in the age category of 16 to 24.[86]

Rohini Anand is the global chief diversity officer for Sodexo, a global food and facilities services management firm. She is responsible for directing and implementing Sodexo's diversity and inclusion initiatives to ensure that all employees are provided with the best possible work-life experience regardless of their age, gender, nationality, culture, or personal characteristics such as gender orientation, religion, and abilities or disabilities.

Mark Kauzlarich/Bloomberg/Getty Images

Charles Rex Arbogast/AP Images

Diversity management at Target includes developing employee talent through mentoring. Target offers employees, such as executive team leader Chenille English-Boswell, shown here, group, virtual, and peer mentoring, as well as skip mentoring, whereby a senior leader mentors a team member several pay grades below the mentor.

A growing number of nations are adopting laws banning discrimination against LGBT people. For example, in the European Union, the Employment Equality Directive requires all member states to introduce legislation making it unlawful to discriminate on grounds of sexual orientation.[87] Despite the progress, much more needs to be done. One study found more than 40 percent of gay and lesbian employees indicated they had been unfairly treated, denied a promotion, or pushed to quit their job because of their sexual orientation.[88] Another study found that "closeted" LGBTs who felt isolated at work were 73 percent more likely to leave their job within three years than "out" workers.[89] This statistic is not surprising based on the results of a third study: More than one-third of LGBT workers felt they had to lie about their personal lives at work, and about the same percentage felt exhausted from the time and energy needed to hide their gender identity.[90]

Employers take differing approaches to employing LGBT people. Sometimes companies band together to push for change as a group, as happened recently in Japan. Thirty businesses, including Panasonic, Sony, and Dai-ichi Life Insurance, jointly developed standards that individual firms can copy or adapt as policies for making LGBT employees more welcome in Japanese workplaces.[91] Another approach is to take the initiative by setting goals for increasing the number of LGBT people employed as part of the drive for diversity and inclusion in the workplace. The British Broadcasting Corporation (BBC), for example, has pledged to meet a target of having LGBT employees comprise 8 percent of its workforce within a few years. The BBC's other diversity targets include increasing the percentage of women to 50 percent of its workforce and the percentage of disabled people to 8 percent.[92] Other businesses are showing support for LGBT employees through personnel policies and practices. Not only does the Swedish communications tech giant Ericsson promote equal opportunity in employment and professional development for LGBT people, but it also encourages the formation of LGBT networking groups to foster a deeper sense of connection. The company has a global diversity council with representatives from each geographic region, plus local diversity councils in each area where Ericsson operates. These councils include LGBT employees in programs aimed at improving inclusion and understanding as well as reducing unconscious biases within the workforce.[93]

OTHER TYPES OF DIVERSITY. As we said earlier, diversity refers to *any* dissimilarities or differences that might be present in a workplace.

Other types of workplace diversity that managers might confront and have to deal with include socioeconomic background (social class and income-related factors), team members from different functional areas or organizational units, physical attractiveness, obesity/thinness, job seniority, or intellectual abilities. Each of these types of diversity also can affect how employees are treated in the workplace. Again, managers need to ensure that all employees—no matter the similarities or dissimilarities—are treated fairly and given the opportunity and support to do their jobs to the best of their abilities.

How Does Workforce Diversity and Inclusion Affect HRM?

Achieving workforce diversity and inclusion encompasses such basic HRM activities as recruitment, selection, orientation, training, performance management, and compensation/benefits.[94]

Improving workforce diversity requires managers to widen their recruiting net. For example, the popular practice of relying on current employee referrals as a source of new job applicants tends to produce candidates who have similar characteristics to those of present employees. So managers have to look for applicants in places where they haven't typically looked before. To increase diversity, managers are increasingly turning to nontraditional recruitment sources such as women's job networks, over-50 clubs, urban job banks, disabled people's training centers, ethnic newspapers, and gay rights organizations. This type of outreach should enable an organization to broaden its pool of applicants.

Once a diverse set of applicants exists, efforts must be made to ensure that the selection process does not discriminate. Moreover, applicants need to be made comfortable with the organization's culture and be made aware of management's desire to accommodate their needs. For instance, at TGI Friday's, company managers work diligently to accommodate differences and create workplace choices for a diverse workforce; so, too, do companies such as Sodexo, Johnson & Johnson, EY, Mastercard Worldwide, and Procter & Gamble.[95]

Orientation is often difficult for women and minorities. Many organizations, such as Lotus Development and Hewlett-Packard, provide special workshops to raise diversity consciousness among current employees as well as programs for new employees that focus on diversity issues. The thrust of these efforts is to increase individual understanding of the differences each of us brings to the workplace. A number of companies also have special mentoring programs to deal with the reality that lower-level female and minority managers have few role models with whom to identify.[96]

Finally, organizations must be aware of providing appropriate training, performance management choices, and compensation/benefits to its diverse workforce. Obviously, this does not mean that everyone be treated equally, but instead that the needs of diverse employees are considered.

What about Inclusion?

Achieving workforce diversity is only part of the picture for managers. As one HR expert described, diversity is similar to finding people for a choir who have different musical backgrounds, vocal talents, and abilities. To make that choir the best it can be, however, you have to "make sure that those different voices are heard and valued and that they contribute to the performance."[97] That's the idea behind D&I—diversity *and* inclusion. **Inclusion** is defined as "the achievement of a work environment in which all individuals are treated fairly and respectfully, have equal opportunities and resources, and can contribute fully to the organization's success.[98] So, it's not just a matter of getting diverse people in the organization, it's giving them the opportunities to contribute and show that their contributions are valued and important to the organization. And that's an important responsibility for organizational leaders.[99]

inclusion
The achievement of a work environment in which all individuals are treated fairly and respectfully, have equal opportunities and resources, and can contribute fully to the organization's success

CHAPTER SUMMARY BY LEARNING OUTCOME

8-1 Describe the key components of the human resource management process and the important influences on that process.

The HRM process consists of eight activities that will staff an organization with competent, high-performing employees who are capable of sustaining their performance level over the long term. The first three HR activities involve employment planning and include recruitment, downsizing, and selection. The next two steps involve helping employees adapt to the organization and ensuring that their skills and knowledge are kept current, and include the HR activities of orienting and training. The last steps involve identifying performance goals, correcting performance problems, and helping employees sustain high levels of performance. These are done using the HR activities of performance appraisal, compensation and benefits, and safety and health. The main influences on the HRM process are legal, although other environmental conditions such as restructuring, downsizing, diversity, and so forth can impact it as well.

8-2 Discuss the tasks associated with identifying and selecting competent employees.

The first task is employment planning, which involves job analysis and the creation of job descriptions and job specifications. Then, if job needs are indicated, recruitment involves attempts to develop a pool of potential job candidates. Downsizing is used to reduce the labor supply. Selection involves determining who is best qualified for the job. Selection devices need to be both reliable and valid. Managers may want to give potential employees a realistic job preview.

8-3 Explain how employees are provided with needed skills and knowledge.

New hires must be acclimated to the organization's culture and be trained and given the knowledge to do the job in a manner consistent with the organization's goals. Orientation—job, work unit, and organizational—provides new employees with information to introduce them to the job. Training is used to help employees improve their ability to perform on the job.

8-4 Describe strategies for retaining competent, high-performing employees.

Two HRM activities that play a role in this are managing employee performance and developing an appropriate compensation and benefits program. Managing employee performance involves establishing performance standards and then appraising performance to see if those standards have been met. There are various performance appraisal techniques managers can use. If an employee's performance is not up to par, managers need to assess why and take action. Compensation and benefits programs can help attract and retain competent and talented individuals. Managers have to determine who gets paid what and what benefits will be offered.

8-5 Discuss contemporary issues in managing human resources.

Downsizing is the planned elimination of jobs and must be managed from the perspective of layoff victims and job survivors. Workforce diversity must be managed through HRM activities including recruitment, selection, and orientation. Sexual harassment is a significant concern of organizations and managers, which means programs and mechanisms must be in place to educate all employees about it.

8-6 Explain what workforce diversity and inclusion are and how they affect the HRM process.

Workforce diversity is the ways in which people in a workforce are similar and different from one another in terms of gender, age, race, sexual orientation, ethnicity, cultural background, and physical abilities and disabilities. Inclusion is the achievement of a work environment in which all individuals are treated fairly and respectfully, have equal opportunities and resources, and can contribute fully to the organization's success. Both diversity and inclusion affect the HRM process, especially in basic activities such as recruitment, selection, orientation, performance management, and compensation/benefits.

DISCUSSION QUESTIONS

8-1 How does HRM affect all managers?

8-2 Discuss the external environmental factors that most directly affect the HRM process.

8-3 Some critics claim that corporate HR departments have outlived their usefulness and are not there to help employees but to shield the organization from legal problems. What do you think? What benefits are there to having a formal HRM process? What are the drawbacks?

8-4 Do you think it's ethical for a prospective employer to delve into an applicant's life by means of interviews, tests, and background investigations? What if those investigations involved looking at your Facebook page or personal blogs? Explain your position.

8-5 Discuss the advantages and drawbacks of the various recruiting sources.

8-6 Are selection devices biased? Explain why or why not. Identify the pros and cons of such devices.

8-7 What are the benefits and drawbacks of realistic job previews? (Consider this question from both the perspective of the organization *and* the perspective of a potential employee.)

8-8 What strategies can companies apply to retain competent employees?

8-9 What, in your view, constitutes sexual harassment? Describe how companies can minimize sexual harassment in the workplace.

8-10 Describe the six types of diversity found in organizations and how organizations should approach HR activities with a diverse workforce.

Applying: Getting Ready for the Workplace

Management Skill Builder | PROVIDING GOOD FEEDBACK

Everyone needs feedback! If you want people to do their best, they need to know what they're doing well and what they can do better. That's why providing feedback is such an important skill to have. But being effective at giving feedback is tricky! That's why we often see managers either (1) not wanting to give feedback or (2) giving feedback in such a way that it doesn't result in anything positive.

MyLab Management

PERSONAL INVENTORY ASSESSMENT

Go to **www.pearson.com/mylab/management** to complete the Personal Inventory Assessment related to this chapter.

Skill Basics

You can feel more comfortable with and be more effective at providing feedback if you use the following specific suggestions:

1. *Be straightforward by focusing on specific behaviors.* Feedback should be specific rather than general. Avoid such statements as "You have a bad attitude" or "I'm re-ally impressed with the good job you did." They're vague and although they provide information, they don't tell the recipient enough to correct the "bad attitude" or on what basis you concluded that a "good job" had been done so the person knows what behaviors to repeat or to avoid.

2. *Be realistic.* Focus your feedback on what can be changed. When people get comments on things over which they have no control, it can be frustrating.

3. *Keep feedback impersonal.* Feedback, particularly the negative kind, should be descriptive rather than judgmental or evaluative. No matter how upset you are, keep the feedback focused on job-related behaviors and never criticize someone personally because of an inappropriate action.

4. *Keep feedback goal oriented.* Feedback should not be given primarily to "blow off steam" or "unload" on another person. If you have to say something negative, make sure it's directed toward the recipient's goals. Ask yourself whom the feedback is supposed to help. If the answer is *you*, bite your tongue and hold the comment. Such feedback undermines your credibility and lessens the meaning and influence of future feedback.

5. *Know when to give feedback—make it well timed.* Feedback is most meaningful to a recipient when there's a very short interval between his or her behavior and the receipt of feedback about that behavior. Moreover, if you're particularly concerned with changing behavior, delays in providing feedback on the undesirable actions lessen the likelihood that the feedback will be effective in bringing about the desired change. Of course, making feedback prompt merely for the sake of promptness can backfire if you have insufficient information, if you're angry, or if you're otherwise emotionally upset. In such instances, "well timed" could mean "somewhat delayed."

6. *Ensure understanding.* Make sure your feedback is concise and complete so that the recipient clearly and fully understands the communication. It may help to have the recipient rephrase the content of your feedback to find out whether it fully captured the meaning you intended.

7. *Watch your body language, tone of voice, and facial expressions.* Your body language and tone of voice can speak louder than words. Think about what you want to communicate and make sure your body language supports that message.

Based on A. Tugend, "You've Been Doing a Fantastic Job. Just One Thing…," *New York Times Online*, April 5, 2013; C. R. Mill, "Feedback: The Art of Giving and Receiving Help," in L. Porter and C. R. Mill (eds.), The Reading Book for Human Relations Training (Bethel, ME: NTL Institute for Applied Behavioral Science, 1976), pp. 18–19; and S. Bishop, The Complete Feedback Skills Training Book (Aldershot, UK: Gower Publishing, 2000).

Practicing the Skill

Read through this scenario and follow the directions at the end of it.

Craig is an excellent employee whose expertise and productivity have always met or exceeded your expectations. But recently he's been making work difficult for other members of your advertising team. Like his coworkers, Craig researches and computes the costs of media coverage for your advertising agency's clients. The work requires laboriously leafing through several large reference books to find the correct base price and add-on charges for each radio or television station and time slot, calculating each actual cost, and compiling the results in a computerized spreadsheet. To make things more efficient and convenient, you've always allowed your team members to bring the reference books they're using to their desks while they're using them. Lately, however, Craig has been piling books around him for days and sometimes weeks at a time. The books interfere with the flow of traffic past his desk and other people have to go out of their way to retrieve the books from Craig's pile. It's time for you to have a talk with Craig.

Prepare an outline of how you will address this issue with Craig. Using the suggestions in the Skill Basics, be as specific as possible in terms of what you will say and how you will approach this. If your professor chooses, be prepared to do some role-playing in class.

Experiential Exercise

For this chapter's experiential exercise, we could have had you do something fairly simple like find the most common interviewer questions and practice your responses to those questions. (And who knows … you might want to do that on your own). But no! We decided to have you focus on something a little more challenging, and equally—if not more—important: the realities of office romances. Yes, it happens. After all, most employees spend a lot of hours every week at work. In fact, 25 percent of respondents to a survey on office romances said that they had been romantically involved with a coworker.[100] However, workplace relationships are increasingly being scrutinized as companies have concerns about power issues and potential sexual harassment charges.[101]

Have fun with this assignment, but also be serious! You're likely to have to deal with this issue, either as a participant or as a manager or both, sometime during your work career. In your assigned group, discuss and answer the following:

(1) What potential issues could arise when coworkers are romantically involved? (Think this through from relationship to potential break-up.)

(2) Should an organization prohibit coworker relationships? How about relationships between manager and subordinate? Explain.

(3) What should an organizational dating policy include? Create broad guidelines that you think might be important, especially in light of your discussions in Questions 1 and 2. If you're currently employed, you might want to check with your employer to see what guidelines might be in place.

CASE APPLICATION #1

Race Relations
Topic: Unconscious (implicit) bias, racial-bias training

After decades of affirmative action, diversity training, and inclusion practices, you'd think that bias (racial, gender, age, you-name it) wouldn't be an issue. But almost everyone has observed bias in the workplace ... jokes about a particular group of people, how men or coworkers who are friends with the boss seem to get the most important projects to work on, etc. Both overt workplace bias (which still does happen, unfortunately, probably on a daily basis in organizations) and unconscious bias, which can be more subtle and difficult to recognize in ourselves and others, create problems for organizations.[102] You're aware of the overt bias problems, but what about unconscious bias? Have you, for instance, wrongly judged someone by their weight (well, they don't look the part of a manager, so they wouldn't be a good candidate for a management training program) or by the school they attended (well, their degree is from a small, regional college, so they can't possibly know the most current techniques or have the best education) or by their introverted nature (well, they never speak up in meetings, so they obviously don't have an opinion)? Starbucks Corp. was about to get a wake-up call in both respects.

Recently, in downtown Philadelphia, two young black men met at a Starbucks store to discuss a real estate transaction they'd been working on for months. One of the young men asked to use the restroom and was told by the manager that the restrooms were only for paying customers. After being approached by the manager to see if they wanted to order drinks and them declining to do so, police were called and the two men were arrested on suspicion of trespassing. Starbucks did not press charges, and they were released. A customer's cell phone video posted online showed several police officers responding and handcuffing the two young men even with other customers saying that the two had done nothing wrong and

Anti-bias training. Will it WORK?

questioning why they were being arrested.[103] After a social-media outcry, Starbucks CEO Kevin Johnson apologized for the incident on Twitter and on television news programs. And the employee who called the police no longer works there. The CEO also said that it was his "responsibility to understand what happened and what led to that, and ensure that we fix it."[104]

So, how is Starbucks "fixing" it? One step was a review of company guidelines, which differ among its 28,000 stores found worldwide. Another, the most dramatic step, was an investment in unconscious bias training.[105] To implement this training, Starbucks closed all its more than 8,000 domestic stores for one day to conduct anti-bias training. Some 175,000 Starbucks U.S. employees were trained on unconscious or implicit bias, in which "people make decisions based partly on stereotypes without being aware that the stereotype has influenced them."[106] Academic researchers who've studied unconscious bias, say training can help individuals recognize it and identify ways they can minimize it. Other experts say that anti-bias training can either be effective or flop altogether. However, "training by itself won't put a stop to the problem of implicit bias," noted one HR expert.[107]

Discussion Questions

8-11 What is the focus of the training for Starbucks employees? Why is this training important?

8-12 What is unconscious (implicit) racial bias? Why is it a problem for organizations?

8-13 Beyond this intensive in-store training, what other things could Starbucks do to create a more sensitive, in-store experience?

8-14 What can you learn from this story that will benefit you (a) personally and (b) professionally?

8-15 Is implicit bias an ethical/social responsibility issue? Make a decision and defend your position. If so, explain why. If not, why not?

CASE APPLICATION #2

Résumé Regrets
Topic: Candidate Selection Dilemma

Protiviti is a global business consulting and internal audit firm specializing in risk, advisory, and organizational transformation and in human capital consultancy. Protiviti advises its clients on selecting the right talent for the right position as part of its advisory services.[108]

In one such assignment, the client faced challenges in selecting the right candidate for a key leadership position. The client was a newly established insurance company based in Oman and had aggressive growth plans. The client wanted to differentiate itself by using technology to provide convenient services that would allow its customers to carry out their transactions from the comfort of their home. Being in its nascent stage, the company did not have a clearly laid out IT strategy to support this vision.

The existing IT department consisted of a fairly qualified team, some of whom had been with the organization since its inception three years ago; however, the team was driven largely by day-to-day operations, query resolution, and gathering of business requirements for system enhancements. There was a general perception that the IT function was not responsive enough to cater to the dynamic nature of the evolving insurance industry landscape and the needs of consumers within it. The teams were process-oriented and felt that requests from customer-facing departments were coming in an *ad hoc* manner.

In this context, the client now wanted to fill a key leadership position, that of a chief information officer (CIO). It appointed Protiviti to assist them in evaluating and identifying the best candidate for the position; the bank then shortlisted four candidates. Protiviti studied the business context, identified the job specifications, and conducted preliminary assessment covering technical and leadership skills. The following were the observations on the top two candidates:

Candidate A is a very confident and assertive individual currently heading the IT department of a very large, well-established, and old insurance company in the country. He leads a team of more than 100 staff and is actively involved in the development of the IT strategy as a mandate from the board; however, he has only three years of experience in the insurance industry, the other 12 years being in the telecom and the oil-and-gas industries. He looks at the big picture and prefers to delegate a lot of tasks to the team. He is comfortable in stakeholder management and confident in resolving situations where there are disagreements. This candidate is very well read and follows the latest global trends in the insurance, banking, technology, and related industries.

Candidate B is an internal candidate leading one of the teams in the IT department. He is a structured, planned, and organized individual. He has been with the company since its inception three years ago and has more than 14 years of experience in the insurance industry. He is well aware of the work environment, leadership expectations, growth plans, and operational aspects of IT in an insurance company in addition to the regulatory and compliance requirements. Being an internal candidate, he knows all the challenges the department is currently facing and has a clear, well-laid out plan for the IT function if he were offered the CIO position. His communication skills are satisfactory, but he shows signs that he need to polish his capabilities in managing stakeholder demands and expectations.

Discussion Questions

8-16 What are some of the technical and leadership skills that you feel should be assessed at the recruitment stage and why?

8-17 Which candidate do you think should be offered the position and why?

8-18 What impact would Candidate A have on the team if selected for the position? Please provide reasons.

8-19 What impact would Candidate B have on the team if selected for the position? Please provide reasons.

CASE APPLICATION #3

Spotting Talent
Topic: HRM in the Hong Kong Police Force

The Hong Kong Police Force (HKPF), established in 1841, currently has a workforce of around 40,000 personnel. The organization's policy is to recruit throughout the year and looks at hiring "high caliber" individuals for the roles of inspectors and constables. The Hong Kong Police College, which was established in January 2006, is designed to run nine-month courses to provide comprehensive training for inspector-level candidates.[109]

Despite the need for more officers and the continuous recruitment, it isn't very easy to join—the HKPF is extremely selective. It believes that its people are its greatest asset, so an officer's access to professional development programs increases during their service in the force as well as after receiving promotions. Officers at the middle-management level are trained in leadership and commanding during critical incidents. Officers in the Force are only granted increments if their performance is considered satisfactory or better.

Based on the belief that every individual is a big asset to the organization, the HKPF expends considerable resources and effort in acquisition and training. It also adopts and implements sophisticated human resources management (HRM) practices to give them an edge over private employers.

Acquisition of the right people begins with recruitment and selection for entry-level posts, mostly police constables and police inspectors. The human resources branch, under the personnel wing, is actively engaged in publicizing the recruitment program through various media and organizations, including schools and universities. The Hong Kong Police Mentorship Program (PMP) looks for interested undergraduate students and enrolls them in a mentor-mentee program with members of the Force; the mentors serve as role models to the prospective recruits. PMP participants usually have a higher success rate in securing full-time posts in the Force after graduation than those acquired through other recruitment channels.

The selection process for police officers tries to identify various core competencies in each candidate, like communication, judgment, confidence, and leadership. Candidates who apply for the post of police inspector have to pass a written examination, which includes English and Chinese language proficiency tests, an aptitude test, and the Basic Law (BL) test. In 2010, a psychometric test was introduced to assess candidates' personalities. An extended interview (or assessment center) that requires group discussion, presentation, and management and leadership exercises is also conducted to gauge competencies such as communication, judgment, confidence, leadership, and staff and resource management. Then, a panel interview, physical fitness test, as well as an integrity check and a medical examination are organized.

The Police College is responsible for training and developing the new recruits. Its Foundation Training Centre organizes stringent training programs for recruits with a focus on foundational knowledge and skills. The programs cover law and procedures, practical exercises, police tactics, weaponry, parades, first aid, and public order. The training programs also lay out the vision, common purpose, and values of the force. In addition to these programs, a variety of development training courses are organized by the college's Professional Development Learning Centre specifically for junior police officers, inspectors, and superintendents after they complete a specified number of years of service or have received a promotion. Overseas development opportunities may also be provided.

As the work is quite demanding, police officers in Hong Kong are paid a little more than the civil servants in other departments. Newly recruited constables are paid between HKD31,000 and HKD34,000 (around $3,999–$4,387) while new inspectors and senior inspectors receive between HKD67,000 and HKD76,000 (around $8,645–$9,806) upon successful completion of standardized police examinations.

After graduation, the police officers are assigned to a specific unit or formation for a few years. Then they regularly rotate through posts in different units or districts. This rotation is believed to benefit the individual officers as well as the organization as they can gain more experience in policing, administration, and human resource issues, thus getting a better and more rounded career development opportunity. Each officer builds more relationships, develops greater confidence in their job-performance, and gains a holistic view of the force. This also enables the police organization to achieve better coordination and succession planning and be less susceptible to corruption in the local communities.

As a result, a learning culture is developed that constitutes a vital part of the HKPF's strategic human resource management framework.

Discussion Questions

8-20 Identify the environmental forces that affect the current development of various HRM activities in the HKPF.

8-21 What are the advantages or disadvantages of the police mentoring program for the force and prospective candidates?

8-22 Evaluate the reliability and validity of written tests being used in the selection of the police officers.

8-23 The HKPF successfully nurtures a learning culture in the organization. Identify various training and development activities that help shape the culture.

Endnotes

1. B. Busteed and Z. Auter, "Why College Should Make Internships a Requirement," *Gallup News Online*, November 27, 2017; and K. Gee, "Landing A Job After College," *Wall Street Journal*, October 5, 2017, p. B6.

2. NACE Job Outlook 2018, National Association of Colleges and Employers, www.naceweb .org, November 2017.

3. H. Haddon, "Kroger to Bulk Up Store Staffing," *Wall Street Journal*, April 11, 2018, p. B3.

4. Classic Concepts in Today's Workplace box based on D. A. Wren and A. G. Bedeian, *The Evolution of Management Thought*, 6th ed. (Hoboken, NJ: John Wiley & Sons, 2009), pp. 198–200; "Building Better Organizations: Industrial-Organizational Psychology in the Workplace," *Society for Industrial and Organizational Psychology*, www.siop.org, July 13, 2009; M. Munsterberg, *Hugo Munsterberg: His Life and Work* (New York: Appleton-Century-Crofts, 1922); and H. Munsterberg, *Psychology and Industrial Efficiency* (Boston: Houghton Mifflin Company, 1913).

5. Chris Cook, "Global Employers: Can an Employer Choose Which Country's Laws Apply to Its Employment Contracts?" *Personnel Today*, December 4, 2014, http://www.personneltoday.com/hr/global-employers-can-employer-choose-countrys-laws-apply-employment-contracts/ (accessed January 11, 2017); Carol Matlack, "Ryanair Clashes with Denmark over Labor Laws," *Bloomberg*, June 22, 2015, https://www.bloomberg.com (accessed January 11, 2017); Marcus Hoy, "Sweden: New Law Strengthens Hand of Whistleblowers," *Bloomberg BNA*, July 22, 2016, https://www.bna.com/sweden-new-law-n7301 4445180?programid=2054&arti kel=6507934 (accessed January 11, 2017); Maddy Savage, "The Truth about Sweden's Short Working Hours," *BBC News*, November 2, 2015, http://www.bbc.com (accessed January 11, 2017); "Swedish Fathers to Get Third Month of Paid Paternity Leave," *The Guardian*, May 28, 2015, https://www.theguardian.com; and Felicity Alexander, "Singapore Employment Law: What Changes Are Coming in 2017?" *Personnel Today* (accessed January 11, 2017).

6. Being Ethical: A Critical 21st-Century Skill box based on "State Marijuana Laws in 2018 Map," www.governing.com, April 16, 2018; and L. Nagele-Piazza, "The Haze of Marijuana Laws," *HR Magazine*, February 2017, pp. 69–70.

7. L. Nagele-Piazza, "Marijuana Laws, Opioid Crisis Prompt Workplace Policy Updates," *SHRM Online*, March 13, 2018.

8. J. Levitz, "Factories Tap Parents to Recruit Workers," *Wall Street Journal*, December 18, 2017, p. A3.

9. P. W. Tam and S. Woo, "Talent War Crunches Start-Ups," *Wall Street Journal*, February 28, 2011, pp. B1+; and C. Tuna, "Many Companies Hire as They Fire," *Wall Street Journal*, May 11, 2009, p. B6.

10. J. J. Salopek, "Employee Referrals Remain a Recruiter's Best Friend," *Workforce Management Online*, December 2010; L. G. Klaff, "New Internal Hiring Systems Reduce Cost and Boost Morale," *Workforce Management*, March 2004, pp. 76–79; M. N. Martinez, "The Headhunter Within," *HR Magazine*, August 2001, pp. 48–55; "Even Non-Recruiting Companies Must Maintain Hiring Networks," *HR Focus*, November 2001, p. 8; and L. Greenhalgh, A. T. Lawrence, and R. I. Sutton, "Determinants of Work Force Reduction Strategies in Declining Organizations," *Academy of Management Review*, April 1988, pp. 241–54.

11. Salopek, "Employee Referrals Remain a Recruiter's Best Friend"; "Employee Referral Programs: Highly Qualified New Hires Who Stick Around," *Canadian HR Reporter*, June 4, 2001, p. 21; and C. Lachnit, "Employee Referral Saves Time, Saves Money, Delivers Quality," *Workforce*, June 2001, pp. 66–72.

12. Aon Hewitt Stat of the Week, February 28, 2017.

13. B. Horovitz, "Layoffs Sting Icons Coca-Cola and McDonalds," *USA Today*, January 9, 2015, p. 5B.

14. B. Tuttle, "Why These 5 Companies Are Laying Off Thousands of Workers," http://time.com/money/3678511/ebay-amex-baker-hughes-layoffs/, January 22, 2015.

15. Ibid.

16. J. Mooney, "Pre-Employment Testing on the Internet: Put Candidates a Click Away and Hire at Modem Speed," *Public Personnel Management*, Spring 2002, pp. 41–52.

17. L. Weber and E. Dwoskin, "As Personality Tests Multiply, Employers Are Split," *Wall Street Journal*, September 30, 2014, pp. A1+.

18. See, for instance, R. D. Arvey and J. E. Campion, "The Employment Interview: A Summary and Review of Recent Research," *Personnel Psychology*, Summer 1982, pp. 281–322; M. M. Harris, "Reconsidering the Employment Interview: A Review of Recent Literature and Suggestions for Future Research," *Personnel Psychology*, Winter 1989, pp. 691–726; J. H. Prager, "Nasty or Nice: 56-Question Quiz," *Wall Street Journal*, February 22, 2000, p. A4; and M. K. Zachary, "Labor Law for Supervisors," *Supervision*, March 2001, pp. 23–26.

19. See, for instance, G. Nicholsen, "Screen and Glean: Good Screening and Background Checks Help Make the Right Match for Every Open Position," *Workforce*, October 2000, p. 70.

20. R. A. Posthuma, F. P. Morgeson, and M. A. Campion, "Beyond Employment Interview Validity: A Comprehensive Narrative Review of Recent Research and Trends Over Time," *Personnel Psychology*, Spring 2002, pp. 1–81.

21. A. I. Huffcutt, J. M. Conway, P. L. Roth, and N. J. Stone, "Identification and Meta-Analysis Assessment of Psychological Constructs Measured in Employment Interviews," *Journal of Applied Psychology*, October 2001, pp. 897–913; and A. I. Huffcutt, J. A. Weekley, W. H. Wiesner, T. G. Degroot, and C. Jones, "Comparison of Situational and Behavioral Description Interview Questions for Higher-Level Positions," *Personnel Psychology*, Autumn 2001, pp. 619–44.

22. See C. H. Middendorf and T. H. Macan, "Note-Taking in the Employment Interview: Effects on Recall and Judgments," *Journal of Applied Psychology*, April 2002, pp. 293–303; D. Butcher, "The Interview Rights and Wrongs," *Management Today*, April 2002, p. 4; P. L. Roth, C. H. Can Iddekinge, A. I. Huffcutt, C. E. Eidson, and P. Bobko, "Corrections for Range Restriction in Structured Interview Ethnic Group Differences: The Value May Be Larger Than Researchers Thought," *Journal of Applied Psychology*, April 2002, pp. 369–76; and E. Hermelin and I. T. Robertson, "A Critique and Standardization of Meta-Analytic Coefficients in Personnel Selection," *Journal of Occupational and Organizational Psychology*, September 2001, pp. 253–77.

23. See J. Merritt, "Improv at the Interview," *BusinessWeek*, February 3, 2003, p. 63; P. J. Taylor and B. Small, "Asking Applicants What They Would Do versus What They Did Do: A Meta-Analysis Comparison of Situation and Past Behavior Employment Interview Questions," *Journal of Occupational and Organizational Psychology*, September 2002, pp. 277–95; S. D. Mauer, "A Practitioner-Based Analysis of Interviewer Job Expertise and Scale Format as Contextual Factors in Situational Interviews," *Personnel Psychology*, Summer 2002, pp. 307–28; and J. M. Barclay, "Improving Selection Interviews with Structure: Organizations' Use of Behavioral Interviews," *Personnel Review* 30, no. 1 (2001), pp. 81–95.

24. Merritt, "Improv at the Interview," 63.

25. S. H. Applebaum and M. Donia, "The Realistic Downsizing Preview: A Management Intervention in the Prevention of Survivor Syndrome (Part II)," *Career Development International*, January 2001, pp. 5–19.

26. D. Zielinski, "Effective Assessments," *HRMagazine*, January 2011, pp. 61–64; W. L. Gardner, B. J. Reithel, R. T. Foley, C. C. Cogliser, and F. O. Walumbwa, "Attraction to Organizational Culture Profiles: Effects of Realistic Recruitment and Vertical and Horizontal Individualism-Collectivism," *Management Communication Quarterly*, February 2009, pp. 437–72; and S. L. Premack and J. P. Wanous, "A Meta-Analysis of Realistic Job Preview Experiments," *Journal of Applied Psychology*, November 1985, pp. 706–20.

27. C. Garvey, "The Whirlwind of a New Job," *HR Magazine*, June 2001, pp. 110–18.

28. B. P. Sunoo, "Results-Oriented Customer Service Training," *Workforce*, May 2001, pp. 84–90.

29. Managing Technology in Today's Workplace based on D. Zielinski, "Is HR Ready for Blockchain?" *HR Magazine*, March 2018, pp. 62–63; S. F. Gale, "Robots Ratchet Up Recruiting Process," www.workforce.com, October 23, 2017; L. Dishman, "Can Gamifying the Hiring Process Make It More Effective?" *Fast Company Online*, May 19, 2017; D. Zielinski, "Referral Booster," *HR Magazine*, March 2013, pp. 63–65; B. Horovitz, "Tweet for This Job—And It Could Be Yours," *USA Today*, February 18, 2013, p. A 4; "Action Items," *HR Magazine*, January 2013, pp. 33–35; B. Roberts, "From E-Learning to Mobile Learning,"

HR Magazine, August 2012, v61–65; D. Zielinski, "Effective Assessments"; R. E. DeRouin, B. A. Fritzsche, and E. Salas, "E-Learning in Organizations," *Journal of Management*, December 2005, pp. 920–40; K. O'Leonard, *HP Case Study: Flexible Solutions for Multi-Cultural Learners* (Oakland: CA: Bersin & Associates, 2004); S. Greengard, "The Dawn of Digital HR," *Business Finance*, October 2003, pp. 55–59; and J. Hoekstra, "Three in One," *Online Learning* 5 (2001), pp. 28–32.

30. See, for instance, E. G. Tripp, "Aging Aircraft and Coming Regulations: Political and Media Pressures Have Encouraged the FAA to Expand Its Pursuit of Real and Perceived Problems of Older Aircraft and Their Systems. Operators Will Pay," *Business and Commercial Aviation*, March 2001, pp. 68–75.

31. "A&S Interview: Sully's Tale," *Air & Space Magazine*, www.airspacemag.com, February 18, 2009; A. Altman, "Chesley B. Sullenberger III," *Time*, www.time.com, January 16, 2009; and K. Burke, P. Donohue, and C. Siemaszko, "US Airways Airplane Crashes in Hudson River—Hero Pilot Chesley Sullenberger III Saves All Aboard," *New York Daily News*, www.nydailynews.com, January 16, 2009.

32. C. S. Duncan, J. D. Selby-Lucas, and W. Swart, "Linking Organizational Goals and Objectives to Employee Performance: A Quantitative Perspective," *Journal of American Academy of Business*, March 2002, pp. 314–18.

33. "Training Expenditures," *Training*, November–December 2010, p. 19.

34. R. Langlois, "Fairmont Hotels: Business Strategy Starts with People," *Canadian HR Reporter*, November 5, 2001, p. 19.

35. M. Dalahoussaye, "Show Me the Results," *Training*, March 2002, p. 28.

36. See, for example, R. E. Catalano and D. L. Kirkpatrick, "Evaluating Training Programs: The State of the Art," *Training and Development Journal*, May 1968, pp. 2–9.

37. J. Yang and V. Bravo, "Feeling Unfair," *USA Today-Springfield, Missouri News-Leader*, February 15, 2017, p. 4B.

38. A. Tziner, C. Joanis, and K. R. Murphy, "A Comparison of Three Methods of Performance Appraisal with Regard to Goal Properties, Goal Perception, and Rate Satisfaction," *Group and Organization Management*, June 2000, pp. 175–90; and T. W. Kent and T. J. Davis, "Using Retranslation to Develop Operational Anchored Scales to Assess the Motivational Context of Jobs," *International Journal of Management*, March 2002, pp. 10–16.

39. See also C. A. Ramus and U. Steger, "The Roles of Supervisory Support Behaviors and Environmental Policy in Employee 'Ecoinitiatives' at Leading-Edge European Companies," *Academy of Management Journal*, August 2000, pp. 605–26.

40. See R. de Andrés, J. L. Garcia-Lapresta, and J. GonzálezPachón, "Performance Appraisal Based on Distance Function Methods," *European Journal of Operational Research*, December 2010 pp. 1599–607; and L. Atwater and J. Brett, "Feedback Format: Does It Influence Manager's Reaction to Feedback," *Journal of Occupational and Organizational Psychology*, December 2006, pp. 517–32.

41. M. A. Peiperl, "Getting 360 Feedback Right," *Harvard Business Review*, January 2001, pp. 142–47.

42. T. J. Maurer, D. R. D. Mitchell, and F. G. Barbeite, "Predictors of Attitudes Toward a 360-Degree Feedback System and Involvement in Post-Feedback Management Development Activity," *Journal of Occupational and Organizational Psychology*, March 2002, pp. 87–107.

43. This section based on R. I. Henderson, *Compensation Management in a Knowledge-Based World*, 9th ed. (Upper Saddle River, NJ: Prentice Hall, 2003).

44. M. P. Brown, M. C. Sturman, and M. J. Simmering, "Compensation Policy and Organizational Performance: The Efficiency, Operational and Financial Implications of Pay Levels and Pay Structure," *Academy of Management Journal*, December 2003, pp. 752–62; J. D. Shaw, N. P. Gupta, and J. E. Delery, "Pay Dispersion and Workforce Performance: Moderating Effects of Incentives and Interdependence," *Strategic Management Journal*, June 2002, pp. 491–512; E. Montemayor, "Congruence between Pay Policy and Competitive Strategy in High-Performing Firms," *Journal of Management* 22, no. 6 (1996), pp. 889–908; and L. R. Gomez-Mejia, "Structure and Process of Diversification, Compensation Strategy, and Firm Performance," *Strategic Management Journal* 13 (1992), pp. 381–97.

45. J. D. Shaw, N. Gupta, A. Mitra, and G. E. Ledford Jr., "Success and Survival of Skill-Based Pay Plans," *Journal of Management*, February 2005, pp. 28–49; C. Lee, K. S. Law, and P. Bobko, "The Importance of Justice Perceptions on Pay Effectiveness: A Two-Year Study of a Skill-Based Pay Plan,"

Journal of Management 26, no. 6 (1999), pp. 851–73; G. E. Ledford, "Paying for the Skills, Knowledge and Competencies of Knowledge Workers," *Compensation and Benefits Review*, July–August 1995, pp. 55–62; and E. E. Lawler III, G. E. Ledford Jr., and L. Chang, "Who Uses Skill-Based Pay and Why," *Compensation and Benefits Review*, March–April 1993, p. 22.

46. Shaw, Gupta, Mitra, and Ledford Jr., "Success and Survival of Skill-Based Pay Plans."

47. Information from Hewitt Associates Studies: "As Fixed Costs Increase, Employers Turn to Variable Pay Programs as Preferred Way to Reward Employees," August 21, 2007; "Hewitt Study Shows Pay-for-Performance Plans Replacing Holiday Bonuses," December 6, 2005; "Salaries Continue to Rise in Asia Pacific, Hewitt Annual Study Reports," November 23, 2005; and "Hewitt Study Shows Base Pay Increases Flat for 2006 with Variable Pay Plans Picking up the Slack," Hewitt Associates, LLC, www.hewittassociates.com, August 31, 2005.

48. "Mandated Benefits: 2002 Compliance Guide," *Employee Benefits Journal*, June 2002, p. 64; and J. J. Kim, "Smaller Firms Augment Benefits, Survey Shows," *Wall Street Journal*, June 6, 2002, p. D2.

49. P. P. Shah, "Network Destruction: The Structural Implications of Downsizing," *Academy of Management Journal*, February 2000, pp. 101–12.

50. See, for example, K. A. Mollica and B. Gray, "When Layoff Survivors Become Layoff Victims: Propensity to Litigate," *Human Resource Planning*, January 2001, pp. 22–32.

51. S. Berfield, "After the Layoff, the Redesign," *Business Week*, April 14, 2008, pp. 54–56; L. Uchitelle, "Retraining Laid-off Workers, but for What?" *New York Times Online*, March 26, 2006; D. Tourish, N. Paulsen, E. Hobman, and P. Bordia, "The Downsides of Downsizing: Communication Processes and Information Needs in the Aftermath of a Workforce Reduction Strategy," *Management Communication Quarterly*, May 2004, pp. 485–516; J. Brockner, G. Spreitzer, A. Mishra, W. Hochwarter, L. Pepper, and J. Weinberg, "Perceived Control as an Antidote to the Negative Effects of Layoffs on Survivors' Organizational Commitment and Job Performance," *Administrative Science Quarterly*, 49 (2004), pp. 76–100; and E. Krell, "Defusing Downsizing," *Business Finance*, December 2002, pp. 55–57.

52. J. Kantor, "#MeToo Called for an Overhaul. Are Workplaces Really Changing?" *New York Times Online*, March 23, 2018.

53. U.S. Equal Employment Opportunity Commission, "Charges Alleging Sexual Harassment: FY 2010–FY 2017," www.eeoc.gov, April 18, 2018.

54. Ibid.

55. N. F. Foy, "Sexual Harassment Can Threaten Your Bottom Line," *Strategic Finance*, August 2000, pp. 56–57.

56. "Federal Monitors Find Illinois Mitsubishi Unit Eradicating Harassment," *Wall Street Journal*, September 7, 2000, pp. A8.

57. L. J. Munson, C. Hulin, and F. Drasgow, "Longitudinal Analysis of Dispositional Influences and Sexual Harassment: Effects on Job and Psychological Outcomes," *Personnel Psychology*, Spring 2000, p. 21.

58. B. Leonard, "Survey: 10% of Employees Report Harassment at Work," *HR Magazine*, October 2010, p. 18.

59. "Nichols v. Azteca Restaurant Enterprises," *Harvard Law Review*, May 2002, p. 2074; A. J. Morrell, "Non-Employee Harassment," *Legal Report*, January–February 2000, p. 1. See also S. Lim and L. M. Cortina, "Interpersonal Mistreatment in the Workplace: The Interface and Impact of General Incivility and Sexual Harassment," *Journal of Applied Psychology*, May 2005, pp. 483–96.

60. Although the male gender is referred to here, it is important to note that sexual harassment may involve people of either sex or the same sex. (See, for instance, *Oncale v. Sundowner Offshore Service, Inc.*, 118 S. Ct. 998.)

61. *HR Magazine*, December 2017/January 2018, p. 8.

62. See also A. M. O'Leary-Kelly, L. Bowes-Sperry, C. A. Bates, and E. R. Lean, "Sexual Harassment at Work: A Decade (Plus) of Progress," *Journal of Management*, June 2009, pp. 503–36; M. Rotundo, D. H. Nguyen, and P. R. Sackett, "A Meta-Analytic Review of Gender Differences in Perceptions of Sexual Harassment," *Journal of Applied Psychology*, October 2001, pp. 914–22.

63. "Sexual Harassment," http://www.eeoc.gov/laws/types/sexual_harassment.cfm, April 24, 2015.

64. R. L. Wiener and L. E. Hurt, "How Do People Evaluate Social Sexual Conduct at Work? A Psychological Model," *Journal of Applied Psychology*, February 2000, pp. 75.

65. A. R. Karr, "Companies Crack Down on the Increasing Sexual Harassment by E-Mail," *Wall Street Journal*, September 21, 1999, p. A1; and A. Fisher, "After All This Time, Why Don't People Know What Sexual Harassment Means?" *Fortune*, January 12, 1998, p. 68.

66. Ibid.
67. "You and DuPont: Diversity," DuPont Company Documents (1999–2000), http://www.dupont.com/careers/you/diverse.html; and "DuPont Announces 2000 Dr. Martin Luther King, Days of Celebration," DuPont Company Documents, http://www.dupont.com/corp/whats-news/releases/00/001111.html, January 11, 2000.
68. It should be noted here that under the Title VII and the Civil Rights Act of 1991, the maximum award that can be given, under the federal act, is $300,000. However, many cases are tried under state laws that permit unlimited punitive damages.
69. J. W. Janove, "Sexual Harassment and the Big Three Surprises," *HR Magazine*, November 2001, pp. 123–30; and L. A. Baar and J. Baar, "Harassment Case Proceeds Despite Failure to Report," *HR Magazine*, June 2005, p. 159.
70. S. Shellenbarger, "Supreme Court Takes on How Employers Handle Worker Harassment Complaints," *Wall Street Journal*, April 13, 2006, p. D1.
71. J. C. Taylor Jr., "#MeToo: Where Was HR?" *HR Magazine*, February 2018, p. 4.
72. See, for instance, P. W. Dorfman, A. T. Cobb, and R. Cox, "Investigations of Sexual Harassment Allegations: Legal Means Fair—Or Does It?" *Human Resources Management*, Spring 2000, pp. 33–39.
73. See, for instance, P. Cappelli, J. Constantine, and C. Chadwick, "It Pays to Value Family: Work and Family Trade-Offs Reconsidered," *Industrial Relations*, April 2000, pp. 175–98; R. C. Barnett and D. T. Hall, "How to Use Reduced Hours to Win the War for Talent," *Organizational Dynamics*, March 2001, p. 42; and M. A. Verespej, "Balancing Act," *Industry Week*, May 15, 2000, pp. 81–85.
74. M. Conlin, "The New Debate over Working Moms," *BusinessWeek*, November 18, 2000, pp. 102–03.
75. R. Feinzeig, "Paid Parental Leave Gains Momentum," *Wall Street Journal*, June 7, 2017, p. B7.

76. M. Elias, "The Family-First Generation," *USA Today*, December 13, 2004, p. 5D.
77. D. Braff, "Reimaging Time Off," *HR Magazine*, April 2018, pp. 46–53.
78. S. Caminiti, "The Diversity Factor," *Fortune*, October 19, 2007, pp. 95–105; and B. Velez, "People and Places," *DiversityInc Online*, www.diversityinc.com, October 2006.
79. R. Anand and M. Frances Winters, "A Retrospective View of Corporate Diversity Training from 1964 to the Present," *Academy of Management Learning & Education*, September 2008, pp. 356–72.
80. L. Nagele-Piazza, "Texas Roadhouse Agrees to $12 Million Age Bias Settlement," www.shrm.org., April 17, 2017.
81. R. Fry, "Women May Never Make Up Half of the U.S. Workforce," Pew Research Center, www.pewresearch.org, January 31, 2017.
82. M. Bello, *USA Today*, "Controversy Shrouds Scarves," *Springfield, Missouri News-Leader*, April 17, 2010, p. 8A.
83. "Facts & Figures: Number of Religious Discrimination Complaints Received," *DiversityInc*, November–December 2009, p. 52.
84. P. Wang and J. L. Schwartz, "Stock Price Reactions to GLBT Nondiscrimination Policies," *Human Resource Management*, March–April 2010, pp. 195–216.
85. L. Sullivan, "Sexual Orientation—The Last 'Acceptable' Bias," *Canadian HR Reporter*, December 20, 2004, pp. 9–11.
86. "Statistical Bulletin: Sexual Identity, UK: 2015," Office for National Statistics (UK), 2015, https://www.ons.gov.uk/peoplepopulationandcommunity/culturalidentity/sexuality/bulletins/sexualidentityuk/2015 (accessed December 15, 2016).
87. F. Colgan, T. Wright, C. Creegan, and A. McKearney, "Equality and Diversity in the Public Services: Moving Forward on Lesbian, Gay and Bisexual Equality?" *Human Resource Management Journal*, 19(3), 2009: 280–301.

88. J. Hempel, "Coming Out in Corporate America," *BusinessWeek*, December 15, 2003, pp. 64–72.
89. S.A. Hewlett and K. Sumberg, "For LGBT Workers, Being 'Out' Brings Advantages," *Harvard Business Review*, July–August 2011, https://hbr.org/2011/07/for-lgbt-workers-being-out-brings-advantages.
90. "The Cost of the Closet and the Rewards of Inclusion," Human Rights Campaign Foundation, www.hrc.org, May 2014.
91. Kentaro Todo and Kunio Endo, "Japanese Workplaces Inching toward LGBT Inclusion," *Nikkei Asian Review*, June 22, 2016, http://asia.nikkei.com/Business/Trends/Japanese-workplaces-inching-toward-LGBT-inclusion (accessed December 15, 2016).
92. "BBC Pledges Half of Workforce Will Be Women by 2020," *BBC*, April 23, 2016, www.bbc.com/news/entertainment-arts-36120246 (accessed December 15, 2016).
93. Namrata Singh, "We Are Trying to Get People to Think about Unconscious Bias: Maria Angelica Pérez," *The Times of India*, November 19, 2016, http://timesofindia.indiatimes.com/business/india-business/We-are-trying-to-get-people-to-think-about-unconscious-bias-Maria-Angelica-Prez/articleshow/55516351.cms (accessed December 15, 2016); www.ericsson.com.
94. A. Joshi, "Managing the Organizational Melting Pot: Dilemmas of Workplace Diversity," *Administrative Science Quarterly*, December 2001, pp. 783–84.
95. L. Dishman, "These Are the Companies Winning the Race to Increase Diversity," http://www.fastcompany.com/3045438/these-are-the-companies-winningthe-race-to-increase-diversity, April 25, 2015.
96. See, for instance, K. Iverson, "Managing for Effective Workforce Diversity," *Cornell Hotel and Restaurant Administration Quarterly*, April 2000, pp. 31–38.

97. K. Gurchiek, "Get D&I Right," *HR Magazine*, April 2018, p. 39.
98. SHRM, www.shrm.org, April 18, 2018.
99. Ibid.
100. J. Yang and P. Trap, "Romance At Workplace," *USA Today-Springfield, Missouri News-Leader*, July 23, 2017, p. 4B.
101. Y. Koh and R. Feintzeig, "Your Heart, Your Job, an Dating a Co-Worker," *Wall Street Journal*, February 7, 2018, pp. B1+.
102. D.Wilkie, "Hidden Bias More Subtle and Difficult to Recognize than Bias of Decades Past," www.shrm.org, April 25, 2017.
103. C. Hauser, "Men Arrested at Starbucks Hope to Ensure 'This Situation Doesn't Happen Again,'" *New York Times Online*, April 19, 2018; and J. Jargon and L. Weber, "Starbucks to Shut Stores for Antibias Training," *Wall Street Journal*, April 18, 2018, pp. B1+.
104. C. Hauser, "Starbucks Employee Who Called Police on Black Men No Longer Works There, Company Says," *New York Times Online*, April 16, 2018.
105. Ibid.
106. N. Scheiber and R. Abrams, "Can Training Eliminate Biases? Starbucks Will Test the Thesis," *New York Times Online*, April 18, 2018.
107. K. Gurchiek, "Experts Weigh In on Starbucks' Racial-Bias Training," www.shrm.org, April 19, 2018.
108. Protiviti website, www.protiviti.com.
109. Based on interviews with Hong Kong police officers; Hong Kong Police Force website; www.police.gov.hk; J. Brennan, "HK Police Force Seeks Recruits to Rise to the Challenge," http://www.cpjobs.com/hk/article/hk-police-force-seeks-recruits-to-rise-to-the-challenge, March 21, 2015; A. Y. Jiao, "The Police in Hong Kong: A Contemporary View," Lanham, University Press of America, November 27, 2006; Hong Kong Police Force, Police Mentorship Program, http://www.police.gov.hk/ppp_en/15_recruit/pmp.html.

Professionalism Module

What is Professionalism?

You've probably heard (from instructors, employers, family, and now us!) that it's important to behave "professionally" in the workplace. What does that mean? If you want to be taken seriously at work, have promotion opportunities, and have your boss view you as an asset to the team (and organization), then doing things in a professional way is critical! It's so critical that we're telling you what it means by sharing tips and ideas with you in this Module.

So, what is **professionalism**? Very simply, it's how you conduct yourself at work—your attitudes, your actions, and your behaviors. And, professionalism isn't just for "professionals"—doctors, lawyers, engineers—it's for anyone who's employed by someone else. It's not the job title that makes you professional, it's you and your behavior, actions, and demeanor at work and how you interact with colleagues and customers. Even employees in jobs such as cashiers, food service personnel, and maintenance workers can exhibit professionalism. As a new college graduate, you'll start off on a good foot if you approach your job (and career) with professionalism.

> **professionalism**
> How you conduct yourself at work—your attitudes, your actions, your behaviors

A study of professionalism and recent college graduates by the Center for Professional Excellence at York College of Pennsylvania highlighted some interesting points about the level of professionalism of young people.[1] First, survey respondents were more likely to think that younger employees were less likely than all employees to exhibit professionalism.[2] Another finding from the survey was that the professionalism qualities seen as most lacking in recent college graduates included social/communication skills, respect, and work ethic. Another finding of this survey looked at the qualities or behaviors most associated with being professional as an employee and the qualities or behaviors most associated with being unprofessional. Here's what respondents said:[3]

Qualities or Behaviors Most Associated with Being Professional:

- Focused
- Punctual/attentive
- Humble
- Diligent
- Communication skills

Qualities or Behaviors Most Associated with Being Unprofessional:

- Disrespectful
- Irresponsible
- Not ambitious
- Late/absent
- Lack of communication skills

Other areas reported in this particular study involved new college graduates' sense of entitlement, information technology etiquette, unfocused behavior, attire and appearance, dress codes, tattoos, and attitudes toward work. The report offers an eye-opening glimpse of how professionalism (and lack of professionalism) is viewed.

How Can I Show My Professionalism?

Exhibiting professionalism is more than avoiding being unprofessional. Your attitude might be that as long as you do your job well, who cares? However, if you're always finishing tasks or projects late; if you're unprepared when attending meetings; if you're treating people disrespectfully; if you're using others' ideas without giving them credit; if you're saying one thing and then doing completely the opposite; if you're breaking promises regularly—you're going to be labeled as unprofessional. Exhibiting professionalism is intentional. Acting professionally means doing what it takes to show others through your skills, your attitudes, and your behaviors that you're reliable, respectful, and competent.

Skills. What skills do employers say are important? Three skills that top most lists are communication, critical thinking, and ethics/integrity. That's why we've made employability skills a key focus in this text. We've expanded the skills to include not only critical thinking, communication, and social responsibility/ethics, but also collaboration and knowledge application and analysis. Arming yourself with these skills by practicing and using them while in school is one way to up your level of professionalism. But skills only get you so far. Being viewed as professional by your manager and your employer requires having appropriate attitudes and behaviors, as well.

Attitudes and Behaviors. What attitudes and behaviors are important to being professional? We're going to share several with you. While our list is by no means exhaustive, these are important steps toward showing your professionalism.

- *Be reliable.* Show others that they can depend on you to be there, to do what you say you're going to do, and that you are attentive to deadlines. Seventy-eight percent of HR professionals say that reliability is one of the most important behaviors.[4]

- *Be honest.* Tell the truth. Be upfront about things. If you're not going to make a deadline, be honest with your team leader or manager. If someone asks your opinion, be honest. Your colleagues will know they can trust you if you tell the truth.

- *Conduct yourself with integrity.* Be consistent in living your principles. Hopefully, you've "landed" in an organization where your principles are in alignment with organizational principles.

- *Have respect for others.* Treat all other people—inside and outside your workplace—with respect. People like to know that they matter. A big part of having respect is *making it a priority to be on time*. When you arrive late for work or for meetings, it gives people the impression that you don't care about your job or about their schedules.

- *Exhibit a good work ethic.* You're being paid to do a job and to do it well. So, do that! That doesn't mean that if you see something that could be improved that you just keep your mouth shut. Speak up! If your organization does well, you'll do well.

- *Don't deflect blame.* Don't be the person who's always saying "It's not my job." It IS your job! Take responsibility even if it's not literally in your job description. Be willing to step up and out to help your team and your organization. And if you have done something wrong or screwed up, admit it!

- *Be a good listener.* The ability to effectively listen and respond to others is crucial in developing good work relationships. And most of us have to work at being good listeners. We tend to be thinking of how we're going to reply to the other person rather than really listening to what he or she has to say.

- *Manage your emotions.* Handling pressure and functioning well in high-pressure situations requires an ability to manage your emotions. It's not easy, but someone with a high level of professionalism has learned how to be civil even during arguments and disagreements and, as we said earlier, to be respectful.

- *Don't have a bad attitude.* Yup, we all know someone who goes through life with a bad attitude. (Hopefully, this doesn't describe you!) An individual with a bad attitude is cynical and negative. These individuals tend to find fault with everyone and everything before looking for benefits or solutions.

- *Be willing to change.* Yes, we know change is hard! We like the comfort of the familiar. But sometimes, change is necessary. Don't expect others to just accept you as you are and drag your feet in trying new approaches.

- *Try not to be a grump!* Yes, we all have bad days when we're not feeling our best. But leave your bad mood at the door. Don't take it out on your coworkers, your boss, or especially, your customers. If the reason you're in a bad mood is because of your work, hmmmm. It might be time to think about finding a different job.

How Can I Have a Successful Career?

The term *career* has several meanings. In popular usage, it can mean advancement ("she is on a management career track"), a profession ("he has chosen a career in accounting"), or a lifelong sequence of jobs ("his career has included eight jobs in four organizations"). For our purposes, we define a **career** as the sequence of work positions held by a person during his or her lifetime. Using this definition, it's apparent that we all have, or will have, a career. Moreover, the concept is as relevant to unskilled laborers as it is to software designers or physicians. But career development isn't what it used to be!

Although career development has been an important topic in management courses for years, some dramatic changes have occurred in the concept. Career development programs used to be designed to help employees advance their work lives within a specific organization. The focus of such programs was to provide employees the information, assessment, and training needed to help them realize their career goals. Career development was also a way for organizations to attract and retain highly talented people. This approach has all but disappeared in today's workplace. Now, organizations that have such traditional career programs are few and far between. Downsizing, restructuring, and other organizational adjustments have brought us to one significant conclusion about career development: You—not the organization—will be responsible for designing, guiding, and developing your own career. This idea of increased personal responsibility for one's career has been described as a **boundaryless career**.[5] The challenge is that few hard-and-fast rules are available to guide you.

One of the first decisions you have to make is career choice. The optimum choice is one that offers the best match between what you want out of life and your interests, your abilities and personality, and market opportunities. Good career choices should result in a series of jobs that give you an opportunity to be a good performer, make you want to maintain your commitment to your career, lead to highly satisfying work, and give you the proper balance between work and personal life. A good career match, then, is one in which you are able to develop a positive self-concept, to do work that you think is important, and to lead the kind of life you desire. In a survey by Capital One Financial Corporation, 66 percent of college graduates said that a comprehensive benefits package (including, for example, health care, 401(k) program, child care, and domestic partner benefits) was the most important factor in their job search. Starting salary ranked second at 64 percent, with job location ranked third at 60 percent. Today's college grads are also looking to be rewarded or compensated (with comp time or matching donations, for instance) for their volunteer and philanthropic activities.[6]

Once you've identified a career choice, it's time to initiate the job search. However, we aren't going to get into the specifics of job hunting, writing a résumé, or interviewing successfully, although those things are important. Let's fast-forward through all that and assume that your job search was successful. It's time to go to work! How do you survive and excel in your career? Here are several tips.

Assess Your Personal Strengths and Weaknesses

Where do your natural talents lie? What can you do, relative to others, that gives you a competitive advantage? Are you particularly good with numbers? Have strong people skills? Good with your hands? Write better than most people? Everyone has some things that they do better than others and some areas where they're weak. Play to your strengths.

Identify Market Opportunities

Where are tomorrow's job opportunities? Regardless of your strengths, certain job categories are likely to decline in the coming decades—for instance, bank tellers, small farmers, movie projectionists, travel agents, and secretaries. In contrast, abundant opportunities are

career
The sequence of work positions held by a person during his or her lifetime

boundaryless career
When an individual takes personal responsibility for his or her own career

more likely to be created by an increasingly aging society, continued emphasis on technology, increased spending on education and training, and concern with personal security. These factors are likely to create excellent opportunities for jobs in gerontological counseling, network administration, training consultants, and security-alarm installers.

Take Responsibility for Managing Your Own Career

Historically, companies tended to assume responsibility for their employees' careers. Today, this is the exception rather than the rule. Employees are increasingly expected to take responsibility for their own careers.

Think of your career as your business and you're its CEO. To survive, you have to monitor market forces, head off competitors, and be ready to quickly take advantage of opportunities when they surface. You have to protect your career from harm and position yourself to benefit from changes in the environment.

Develop Your Interpersonal Skills

Interpersonal skills, especially the ability to communicate, top the list of almost every employer's "must have" skills. Whether it's getting a new job or a promotion, strong interpersonal skills are likely to give you a competitive edge.

Practice Makes Perfect

There's an increasing amount of evidence indicating that super-high achievers aren't fundamentally different from the rest of us. They just work harder and smarter. It's been found, based on studies of world-class performers in music, sports, chess, science, and business, that people like Oprah Winfrey, Mozart, and Bill Gates put in about 10,000 hours (or 10 years at 1,000 hours a year) of persistent, focused training and experience before they hit their peak performance level. If you want to excel in any field, you should expect to have to put in a lot of deliberate practice—consistently engaging in repeated activity specifically designed to improve performance beyond your current comfort and ability level.

Stay Up to Date

In today's dynamic world, skills can become obsolete quickly. To keep your career on track, you need to make learning a lifetime commitment. You should be continually "going to school"—if not taking formal courses, then reading books and journals to ensure that you don't get caught with obsolete skills.

Network

Networking refers to creating and maintaining beneficial relationships with others in order to accomplish your goals. It helps to have friends in high places. It also helps to have contacts who can keep you informed of changes that are going on in your organization and in your industry. Go to conferences. Maintain contact with former college friends and alumni. Get involved in community activities. Cultivate a broad set of relationships. And in today's increasingly interconnected world, join online business networking groups such as LinkedIn, Spoke, and Talkbiznow.

Stay Visible

Networking can increase your visibility. So, too, can writing articles in your professional journals, teaching classes or giving talks in your area of expertise, attending conferences and professional meetings, and making sure your accomplishments are properly promoted. You increase your mobility and value in the marketplace by keeping visible.

Seek a Mentor

Employees with mentors are likely to have enhanced mobility, increased knowledge of the organization's inside workings, greater access to senior executives, increased satisfaction, and increased visibility. For women and minorities, having mentors has been shown to be particularly helpful in promoting career advancement and success.

Leverage Your Competitive Advantage

Develop skills that will give you a competitive advantage in the marketplace. Especially focus on skills that are important to employers, skills that are scarce, and areas where you have limited competition. Try to avoid a worst-case scenario: You have a job that anyone can learn in 30 minutes. Remember that the harder it is for you to learn and develop a highly prized skill, the harder it'll also be for others to acquire it. Generally speaking, the more training necessary to do a job and the fewer people who have that training, the greater your security and influence.

Here's an insight from many years as a student and a professor: To succeed in school, you have to be a generalist and excel at everything. For instance, to earn a 4.0 GPA, you need to be a star in English, math, science, geography, languages, and so on. The "real world," on the other hand, rewards specialization. You don't have to be good at everything. You just need to be good at something that others aren't and that society values. You can be lousy in math or science and still be a very successful opera singer, artist, salesperson, or writer. You don't have to excel in English to be a computer programmer or electrician. The secret to life success is identifying your comparative advantage and then developing it. And as we've noted previously, you need to invest approximately 10,000 hours in honing your skills to achieve optimum proficiency.

Don't Shun Risks

Don't be afraid to take risks, especially when you're young and you don't have much to lose. Going back to school, moving to a new state or country, or quitting a job to start your own business can be the decision that will set your life in a completely new direction. Great accomplishments almost always require taking the path less traveled—and the road to nowhere is paved with fears of the unknown.

It's OK to Change Jobs

Past generations often believed "you don't leave a good job." That advice no longer applies. In today's fast-changing job market, staying put often only means that you're staying behind. Employers no longer expect long-term loyalty. And to keep your skills fresh, your income increasing, and your job tasks interesting, it will be increasingly likely that you'll need to change employers.

Opportunities, Preparation, and Luck = Success

Successful people are typically ambitious, intelligent, and hardworking. But they are also lucky. It's not by chance that many of the biggest technology success stories—Bill Gates and Paul Allen at Microsoft, Steve Jobs at Apple, Scott McNealy at Sun Microsystems, Eric Schmidt at Novell and Google—were born in a narrow three-year period between June 1953 and March 1956. They were smart. They were interested in computers and technology. But they were also lucky. They reached their teens and early 20s in 1975—at the dawn of the personal computer age. Those people with similar interests and talents but born in the mid-1940s were likely to have joined a firm like IBM out of college and been enamored with mainframe computers. Had they been born in the early 1960s, they would have missed getting in on the ground floor of the revolution.

Success is a matter of matching up opportunities, preparation, and luck. It's been suggested that few of us get more than a couple of special opportunities in our lifetime. If you're lucky, you will recognize those opportunities, have made the proper preparations, and then act on them.

You can't control when you were born, where you were born, your parents' finances, or the like. Those are the luck factors. But what you can control is your preparation and willingness to act when opportunity knocks.

Endnotes

1. 2015 National Professionalism Survey: Recent College Graduates Report, Center for Professional Excellence, York College of Pennsylvania, www.ycp.edu, 2015.

2. Ibid, p. 9.

3. Ibid, p. 12.

4. "The Numbers," *Relevant,* January–February 2017, p. 30.

5. M. B. Arthur and D. M. Rousseau, *The Boundaryless Career: A New Employment Principle for a New Organizational Era* (New York: Oxford University Press, 1996).

6. "Capital One Survey Highlights What Today's College Graduates Want from Employers," www.businesswire.com (June 10, 2008).

Managing Work Groups and Work Teams

9

Management Myth Teams almost always outperform employees working individually.

Management **DEBUNKED?** Myth

Based on news reports, you'd think that every organization has restructured itself around teams. And it's widely believed that team-based organizations will always outperform more traditional organizations structured around individual efforts. As you'll see in this chapter, teams **can** be very effective devices for accomplishing tasks. But not always or even almost always! For tasks that demand highly creative thinking, individuals often outperform teams. Additionally, teams can dilute responsibility, which can lead to taking outsized risks and allowing contributors to hide behind the work of others.

MANAGERS

today believe that the use of teams allows their organizations to increase sales or produce better products faster and at lower costs. Although the efforts to create teams aren't always successful, well-planned teams can reinvigorate productivity and better position an organization to deal with a rapidly changing environment. For example, at Braskem, the largest petrochemical company in the Americas, the polypropylene team was already high performing, but the team leader believed they could be even stronger as a team. The solution: ongoing specialized team building and training.[1] And the team became stronger because they were working *together*, not just working.

You've probably had a lot of experience working in groups—class project teams, maybe an athletic team, a fundraising committee, or even a sales team at work. Work teams are one of the realities—and challenges—of managing in today's dynamic global environment. Many organizations have made the move to restructure work around teams rather than individuals. Why? What do these teams look like? And how can managers build effective teams? These are some of the questions we'll be answering in this chapter. Before we can understand teams, however, we first need to understand some basics about groups and group behavior. ●

Learning Outcomes

What Is a Group and What Stages of Development Do Groups Go Through?

9-1 Define *group* and describe the stages of group development.

Each person in this group had his or her assigned role: the Spotter, the Back Spotter, the Gorilla, and the Big Player. For over 10 years, this group—former MIT students who were members of a secret Black Jack Club—used their extraordinary mathematical abilities, expert training, teamwork, and interpersonal skills to take millions of dollars from some of the major casinos in the United States.[2] Although most groups aren't formed for such dishonest purposes, the success of this group at its task was impressive. Managers would like their work groups to be successful at their tasks also. The first step is understanding what a group is and how groups develop.

group
Two or more interacting and interdependent individuals who come together to achieve specific goals

forming stage
The first stage of group development in which people join the group and then define the group's purpose, structure, and leadership

storming stage
The second stage of group development, which is characterized by intragroup conflict

What Is a Group?

A **group** is defined as two or more interacting and interdependent individuals who come together to achieve specific goals. *Formal groups* are work groups that are defined by the organization's structure and have designated work assignments and specific tasks directed at accomplishing organizational goals. Exhibit 9–1 provides some examples. *Informal groups* are social groups. These groups occur naturally in the workplace and tend to form around friendships and common interests. For example, five employees from different departments who regularly eat lunch together are an informal group.

What Are the Stages of Group Development?

Five Stages of Group Development

Research shows that groups develop through five stages.[3] As shown in Exhibit 9–2, these five stages are: *forming, storming, norming, performing,* and *adjourning.*

The **forming stage** has two phases. The first occurs as people join the group. In a formal group, people join because of some work assignment. Once they've joined, the second phase begins: defining the group's purpose, structure, and leadership. This phase involves a great deal of uncertainty as members "test the waters" to determine what types of behavior are acceptable. This stage is complete when members begin to think of themselves as part of a group.

The **storming stage** is appropriately named because of the intragroup conflict. There's conflict over who will control the group and what the group needs to be doing. When this

Exhibit 9–1 Examples of Formal Work Groups

- **Command groups**—Groups that are determined by the organization chart and composed of individuals who report directly to a given manager.
- **Task groups**—Groups composed of individuals brought together to complete a specific job task; their existence is often temporary because when the task is completed, the group disbands.
- **Cross-functional teams**—Groups that bring together the knowledge and skills of individuals from various departments or work areas.
- **Self-managed teams**—Groups that are essentially independent and that, in addition to their own tasks, take on traditional managerial responsibilities, such as hiring, planning and scheduling, and evaluating performance.

norming stage
The third stage of group development, which is characterized by close relationships and cohesiveness

performing stage
The fourth stage of group development, when the group is fully functional and works on the group task

adjourning stage
The final stage of group development for temporary groups, during which groups prepare to disband

Exhibit 9–2 Stages of Group Development

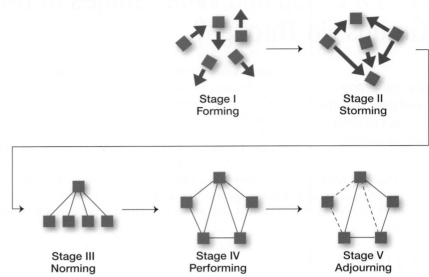

Stage I
Forming

Stage II
Storming

Stage III
Norming

Stage IV
Performing

Stage V
Adjourning

stage is complete, a relatively clear hierarchy of leadership and agreement on the group's direction will be evident.

The **norming stage** is one in which close relationships develop and the group becomes cohesive. The group now demonstrates a strong sense of group identity and camaraderie. This stage is complete when the group structure solidifies and the group has assimilated a common set of expectations (or norms) regarding member behavior.

The fourth stage is the **performing stage**. The group structure is in place and accepted by group members. Their energies have moved from getting to know and understand each other to working on the group's task. This is the last stage of development for permanent work groups. However, for temporary groups—project teams, task forces, or similar groups that have a limited task to do—the final stage is the **adjourning stage**. In this stage, the group prepares to disband. Attention is focused on wrapping up activities instead of task performance. Group members react in different ways. Some are upbeat, thrilled about the group's accomplishments. Others may be sad over the loss of camaraderie and friendships.

Think of a class project you've been involved in and you've probably experienced these stages firsthand. Group members are selected or assigned and then meet for the first time. There's a "feeling out" period to assess what the group is going to do and how it's going to be done. This is usually followed by a battle for control: Who's going to be in charge? Once this issue is resolved and a "hierarchy" agreed on, the group identifies specific work that needs to be done, who's going to do each part of the project, and dates by which the assigned work needs to be completed. General expectations are established. These decisions form the foundation for what you hope will be a coordinated group effort culminating in

Ashwini Asokan (right) is co-founder and CEO of Mad Street Den Systems, a computer visions and artificial intelligence firm launched in 2013 in Chennai, India. Now in the performing stage of development, Asokan and her employees are focused on the task of designing visual search technology and AI-assisted tools for on-line fashion retailers that analyze consumer data, predict consumer demand, and improve shopper's buying experiences.

Hemant Mishra/Mint/Hindustan Times/Getty Images

a project that's been done well. Once the project is complete and turned in, the group breaks up. Of course, some groups don't get much beyond the forming or storming stages. These groups may have serious interpersonal conflicts, turn in disappointing work, and get lower grades.

So, *does a group become more effective as it progresses through the first four stages?* Some researchers say yes, but it's not that simple.[4] That assumption may be generally true, but what makes a group effective is a complex issue. Here's why:

- Under some conditions, high levels of conflict are conducive to high levels of group performance; that is, there might be situations in which groups in the storming stage outperform those in the norming or performing stages.

- Groups don't always proceed sequentially from one stage to the next. Sometimes, groups are storming and performing at the same time. Groups even occasionally regress to previous stages.

- Don't assume all groups precisely follow this process or that performing is always the most preferable stage.

Think of this group stages model as a general framework that underscores the fact that *groups are dynamic entities* and *managers need to know the stage a group is in*. Why? So they can understand the problems and issues that are most likely to surface.

What else do you need to know about groups? Let's look at some important aspects of group behavior.

Making Ethical Decisions in Today's Workplace

When coworkers work closely on a team project, is there such a thing as TMI (too much information)?[5] At one company, a team that had just finished a major project went out to lunch to celebrate. During lunch, one colleague mentioned that he was training for a 20-mile bike race. In addition to a discussion of his new helmet and Lycra shorts, the person also described shaving his whole body to reduce aerodynamic drag. Afterward, another team member said that she didn't want to hear that type of information from someone who was a colleague not a friend and wasn't sure why this individual even wanted to share such information with the rest of the work team. At other companies, managers often hear awkward and questionable comments from their younger Gen Y employees about activities—like too much partying after work or on the weekend or that they're looking for another job at another company. At another company, an employee shared information about his pay increase with his coworkers, creating some serious morale issues on the team.[6]

Discussion Questions:

1 *Is* there such a thing as TMI on a team? Explain. What team benefits/drawbacks arise from sharing personal information like this?

2 What are the ethical implications of sharing personal information in the workplace? How can/should team leaders deal with this?

5 Major Concepts of Group Behavior

9-2 Describe the major concepts of group behavior.

1 Roles

Behavior patterns expected of someone who occupies a given position in a social unit

- We adjust our **roles** to the group we belong to at the time.
- Employees attempt to determine what behaviors are expected of them by: reading their job descriptions, getting suggestions from their bosses, *and* watching what their coworkers do.

—Role conflict happens when an employee has conflicting role expectations.

Kwest/Shutterstock

2ᵃ Norms

Acceptable standards shared by a group's members

*Each group has its own unique set of **norms**. Most organizations have common norms, which typically focus on:*

- Effort and performance
  —Probably most widespread norm
  —Can be extremely powerful in affecting an individual employee's performance
- Dress codes (what's acceptable to wear to work)

mogen creative/Shutterstock

role	norms
Behavior patterns expected of someone who occupies a given position in a social unit	Standards or expectations that are accepted and shared by a group's members

2b Conformity
Adjusting one's behavior to align with a group's norms

- We all want to be accepted by groups to which we belong, which makes us susceptible to conformity pressures.

- See the Classic Concepts from Today's Workplace box (p. 336) for more information on **Solomon Asch's classic studies on conformity**.[7]

35%
of participants in Asch's study would conform to group behavior or "follow the pack."

Kjpargeter/Shutterstock

3 Status Systems
A prestige grading, position, or rank within a group and an important factor in understanding behavior

- Human groupings have always had status hierarchies.

- A disparity between what individuals perceive their status to be and what others perceive it to be is a significant motivator with behavioral consequences.

- Anything can have status value if others in the group admire it.

- Group members have no problem placing people into status categories, and they usually agree about who's high, low, and in the middle.

- It's important for people to believe there's congruency (equity between perceived ranking of an individual and the status symbols he or she has) in an organization's status system to prevent disruptions to general "this is what I expect."

Vbar/Shutterstock

conformity	**status**
Adjusting one's behavior to align with a group's norms	A prestige grading, position, or rank within a group

4 Group Size

Group size affects a group's behavior, but the effect depends on what criteria you're using.[8]

Small Group Better At:

(5–7 members)  Lantapix/Shutterstock

- Completing tasks faster
- Figuring out what to do
- Getting job done

Large Group Better At:

(12 or more members)
Lantapix/Shutterstock

- Problem solving
- Finding facts
- Gaining diverse input

Drawbacks of Large Groups:

- Individual productivity of each group member declines as the group expands, which is known as **social loafing**[9]—reducing effort because dispersion of responsibility encourages individuals to slack off.

  —When a group's results can't be attributed to any single person, individuals may be tempted to become "free riders" and coast on the group's efforts because they think their contributions can't be measured.

When using large work groups, managers should **find a way to identify individual efforts**.

5 Group Cohesiveness

The degree to which members are attracted to one another and share the group's goals

- Groups that experience a lot of internal disagreement and lack of cooperation are less effective than are groups in which individuals generally agree, cooperate, and like each other.

- The more that members are attracted to one another and the more that a group's goals align with each individual's goals, the greater the group's cohesiveness.

- Highly cohesive groups are more effective than are those with less cohesiveness.

However, the **relationship between cohesiveness and effectiveness is more complex**.[10]

—A key moderating variable is the degree to which the group's attitude aligns with its formal goals or those of the larger organization.[11] See Exhibit 9–3, which tells us that:

Cohesiveness

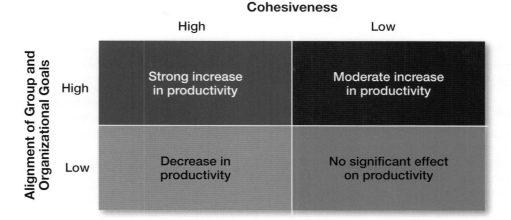

		High	**Low**
Alignment of Group and Organizational Goals	**High**	Strong increase in productivity	Moderate increase in productivity
	Low	Decrease in productivity	No significant effect on productivity

Exhibit 9–3 Group Cohesiveness and Productivity

—The more cohesive a group, the more its members will follow its goals. If these goals are favorable, a cohesive group is more productive than a less cohesive group.

—If cohesiveness is high and attitudes are unfavorable, productivity decreases.

—If cohesiveness is low and goals are supported, productivity increases, but not as much as when both cohesiveness and support are high.

—When cohesiveness is low and goals are not supported, cohesiveness has no significant effect on productivity.

social loafing
The tendency for individuals to expend less effort when working collectively than when working individually

group cohesiveness
The degree to which group members are attracted to one another and share the group's goals

◄◄◄ Classic Concepts in Today's Workplace ►►►

- *DOES* the desire to be accepted as a part of a group leave one susceptible to conforming to the group's norms?

- *WILL* a group exert pressure that's strong enough to change a member's attitude and behavior?

That's what Solomon Asch wanted to know, and according to his research, the answer appears to be yes.[12]

Asch's Research:

- Study involved groups of seven or eight people who sat in a classroom and were asked to compare two cards held by an investigator. The object was for each group member to announce aloud which of the three lines matched the single line.

- One card had one line; the other had three lines of varying length. One of the lines on the three-line card was identical to the line on the one-line card and the difference in line length was quite obvious. (See Exhibit 9–4.)

- Under ordinary conditions, subjects made errors of less than 1 percent.

BUT... what happens if members of the group begin to give incorrect answers?

Will the pressure to conform cause an unsuspecting subject (USS) to alter his or her answers to align with those of the others?

Exhibit 9–4 **Examples of Cards Used in Asch's Study**

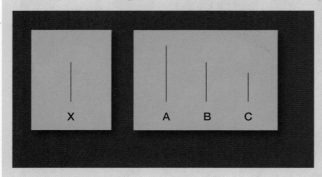

- The group was seated in a prearranged way so the USS was the last to announce his or her decision and so was unaware that the experiment was fixed.

- The experiment began with two sets of matching exercises in which all the subjects gave the right answers.

- On the third set, however, the first subject gave an obviously wrong answer—for example, saying C in Exhibit 9–4. The next subject gave the same wrong answer, and so did the others, until it was the unsuspecting subject's turn.

- The USS knew that "B" was the same as "X" but everyone else said "C".

> Have YOU ever been pressured by a group to conform?

- The decision confronting the USS was this: Do you publicly state a perception that differs from the preannounced position of the others? Or do you give an answer that you strongly believe to be incorrect in order to have your response agree with the other group members?

- Asch's subjects conformed—that is, gave answers they knew were wrong but were consistent with the replies of other group members—in about 35 percent of many experiments and many trials.

Implications for Managers:

- The Asch study provides considerable insight into group behaviors. The tendency, as Asch showed, is for individual members to go along with the pack. To diminish the negative aspects of conformity, managers should create a climate of openness in which employees are free to discuss problems without fear of retaliation.

Discussion Questions:

3 *Does* the desire to be accepted as a part of a group leave one susceptible to conforming to the group's norms? *Will* a group exert pressure that's strong enough to change a member's attitude and behavior? Discuss.

4 What can you use from this discussion to help you personally and professionally?

How Are Groups Turned into Effective Teams?

9-3 Discuss how groups are turned into effective teams.

work teams
Groups whose members work intensely on specific, common goals using their positive synergy, individual and mutual accountability, and complementary skills

When companies like W. L. Gore, Volvo, and Kraft Foods introduced teams into their production processes, it made news because no one else was doing it. Today, it's just the opposite—the organization that *doesn't* use teams would be newsworthy. It's estimated that some 80 percent of *Fortune* 500 companies have at least half of their employees on teams. In fact, more than 70 percent of U.S. manufacturers use work teams.[13] Teams are likely to continue to be popular. Why? Research suggests that teams typically outperform individuals when the tasks being done require multiple skills, judgment, and experience.[14] Organizations are using team-based structures because they've found that teams are more flexible and responsive to changing events than are traditional departments or other permanent work groups. Teams have the ability to quickly assemble, deploy, refocus, and disband. In this section, we'll discuss what a work team is, the different types of teams that organizations might use, and how to develop and manage work teams.

Work groups = Work teams?

Are Work Groups and Work Teams the Same?

At this point, you may be asking yourself: Are teams and groups the same thing? No. In this section, we clarify the difference between a work group and a work team.[15]

Most of you are probably familiar with teams especially if you've watched or participated in organized sports events. Work *teams* do differ from work *groups* and have their own unique traits (see Exhibit 9–5). Work groups interact primarily to share information and to make decisions to help each member do his or her job more efficiently and effectively. There's no need or opportunity for work groups to engage in collective work that requires joint effort. On the other hand, **work teams** are groups whose members work intensely on a specific, common goal using their positive synergy, individual and mutual accountability, and complementary skills.

These descriptions should help clarify why so many organizations have restructured work processes around teams. Managers are looking for that positive synergy that will help the organization improve its performance.[16] The extensive use of teams creates the potential for an organization to generate greater outputs with no increase in (or even fewer) inputs. For example, until the economic downturn hit, investment teams at Wachovia's Asset Management Division (which is now a part of Wells Fargo & Company) were able to significantly improve investment performance. As a result, these teams helped the bank improve its Morningstar financial rating.[17]

Exhibit 9–5 Groups versus Teams

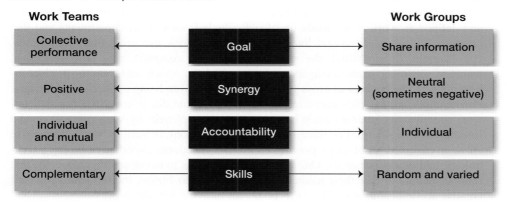

Team-based work is a key ingredient to the success of Google. Throughout the company, small teams that require multiple skills work on a specific common goal using their positive synergy. Shown here is Google's food preparation team in Toronto, whose goal is to plan and prepare nutritious and delicious meals for fellow workers.

Mark Blinch/Reuters

Recognize, however, that such increases are simply "potential." Nothing inherently magical in the creation of work teams guarantees that this positive synergy and its accompanying productivity will occur. Accordingly, merely calling a group a team doesn't automatically increase its performance.[18] As we show later in this chapter, successful or high-performing work teams have certain common characteristics. If managers hope to gain increases in organizational performance, they will need to ensure that the teams possess those characteristics.

What Are the Different Types of Work Teams?

Teams can do a variety of things. They can design products, provide services, negotiate deals, coordinate projects, offer advice, and make decisions.[19] For instance, at Rockwell Automation's facility in North Carolina, teams are used in work process optimization projects. At Arkansas-based Acxiom Corporation, a team of human resource professionals planned and implemented a cultural change. And every summer weekend at any NASCAR race, you can see work teams in action during drivers' pit stops.[20] The four most common types of work teams are problem-solving teams, self-managed work teams, cross-functional teams, and virtual teams.

1. When work teams first became popular, most were **problem-solving teams**, which are teams from the same department or functional area involved in efforts to improve work activities or to solve specific problems. Members share ideas or offer suggestions on how work processes and methods can be improved. However, these teams are rarely given the authority to implement any of their suggested actions.

2. Although problem-solving teams were helpful, they didn't go far enough in getting employees involved in work-related decisions and processes. This need led to another type of team, a **self-managed work team**, which is a formal group of employees who operate without a manager and are responsible for a complete work process or segment. A self-managed team is responsible for getting the work done *and* for managing themselves and usually includes planning and scheduling of work, assigning tasks to members, collective control over the pace of work, making operating decisions, and taking action on problems. For instance, teams at Corning have no shift supervisors and work closely with other manufacturing divisions to solve production-line problems and coordinate deadlines and deliveries. The teams have the authority to make and implement decisions, finish projects, and address problems.[21] Other organizations, such as Xerox, Boeing, PepsiCo, and Hewlett-Packard, also use self-managed teams. It's estimated that about 30 percent of U.S. employers now use this form of team; among large firms, the number is probably closer to 50 percent.[22] Most organizations that use self-managed teams find them to be effective.[23]

3. The third type of team is the **cross-functional team**, which we introduced in Chapter 7 and defined as work teams made up of individuals from various departments and that cross traditional departmental lines. Many organizations use cross-functional teams. For example, ArcelorMittal, the world's largest steel company, uses cross-functional teams of scientists, plant managers, and salespeople to review and monitor product innovations.[24] The concept of cross-functional teams is even being applied in health care. For example, global pharmaceutical giant Novartis introduces cross-functional teamwork to university students while inspiring its own employees by sponsoring an annual International BioCamp. For three days, 60 students from 18 nations work in teams to solve an assigned problem by pooling their cross-functional expertise in biology, technology, and other specialties. One recent challenge was to develop a digital device that reminds people to take their medicine on time. Novartis honors the top teams for their creative accomplishments and awards prizes for individual leadership.[25]

problem-solving teams
A team from the same department or functional area that's involved in efforts to improve work activities or to solve specific problems

self-managed work team
A type of work team that operates without a manager and is responsible for a complete work process or segment

cross-functional team
A work team made up of individuals from various departments and that cross traditional departmental lines

4. The final type of team is the **virtual team**, which is a team that uses technology to link physically dispersed members in order to achieve a common goal. For instance, a virtual team at Boeing-Rocketdyne played a pivotal role in developing a radically new product.[26] Another company, Decision Lens, uses a virtual team environment to generate and evaluate creative ideas.[27] In a virtual team, members collaborate online with tools such as wide-area networks, videoconferencing, fax, e-mail, or websites where the team can hold online conferences.[28] Virtual teams can do all the things that other teams can—share information, make decisions, and complete tasks; however, they lack the normal give-and-take of face-to-face discussions. That's why virtual teams tend to be more task-oriented, especially if the team members have never personally met.

| **virtual team** |
| A type of work team that uses technology to link physically dispersed members in order to achieve a common goal |

What Makes a Team Effective?

Making a Team Effective

Much research has been done on what it is that makes a team effective.[29] Out of these efforts, we now have a fairly focused model identifying those characteristics.[30] Exhibit 9–6 summarizes what we currently know about what makes a team effective. As we look at this model, keep in mind two things. ❶ Teams differ in form and structure. This model attempts to generalize across all teams, so you should only use it as a guide.[31] ❷ The model assumes that managers have already determined that teamwork is preferable to individual work. Creating "effective" teams in situations in which individuals can do the job better would be wasted effort.

One thing we need to clarify first before looking at the model is what we mean by team effectiveness. Typically, it includes:

- Objective measures of a team's productivity
- Managers' or team leaders' ratings of the team's performance
- Aggregate measures of member satisfaction

As you can see from the model, the four key components of effective teams include the context, the team's composition, work design, and process variables.

Managing Technology in Today's Workplace
KEEPING CONNECTED: IT AND TEAMS

Thirty percent of managers say their work teams are "digitally fluent" and communicate very well using new electronic channels.[32] Work teams need information to do their work. With work teams often being not just steps away, but continents away from each other, it's important to have a way for team members to communicate and collaborate. That's where IT comes in. Technology has enabled greater online communication and collaboration within teams of all types.[33]

The idea of technologically aided collaboration actually originated with online search engines. The Internet itself was initially intended as a way for groups of scientists and researchers to share information. Then, as more and more information was put "on the Web," users relied on a variety of search engines to help them find that information. Now, we see many examples of collaborative technologies such as wiki pages, blogs, and even multiplayer virtual reality games.

Today, online collaborative tools have given work teams more efficient and effective ways to get work done. For instance, engineers at Toyota use collaborative communication tools to share process improvements and innovations. These communication tools allow employees to collectively share common knowledge and innovate faster. Managers everywhere should look to the power of IT to help work teams improve the way work gets done.

Discussion Questions:

5 What challenges do managers face in managing teams that must rely on IT to communicate?

6 Using Exhibit 9–6, discuss how the four major components of team effectiveness would affect and be affected by a team's use of IT.

Exhibit 9–6 Team Effectiveness Model

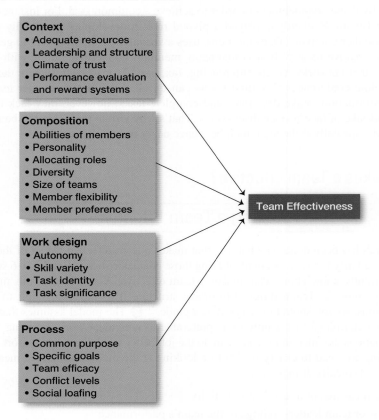

Source: Stephen P. Robbins and Timothy A. Judge, *Organizational Behavior*, 14th edition, © 2011, p. 319. Reprinted and electronically reproduced by permission of Pearson Education, Inc., New York, NY.

WHAT FACTORS IN THE CONTEXT APPEAR TO MAKE A TEAM EFFECTIVE? Four contextual factors appear to be most significantly related to team performance. These factors include adequate resources, leadership and structure, a climate of trust, and performance evaluation and reward systems.

As part of the larger organization system, a team relies on resources outside the group to sustain it. If it doesn't have *adequate resources*, the team's ability to perform its job effectively is reduced. This factor appears to be so important to team performance that one research study concluded that effective work groups must have support from the organization.[34] Resources can include timely information, proper equipment, encouragement, adequate staffing, and administrative assistance.

If a team can't agree on who is to do what or ensure that all members contribute equally in sharing the workload, it won't function properly. Agreeing on the specifics of work and how all the team members' individual skills fit together requires *team leadership and structure*. This aspect can come from the organization or from the team itself. Even in self-managed teams, a manager's job is to be more of a coach by supporting the team's efforts and managing outside (rather than inside) the team.

Members of effective teams *trust* each other. And they also trust their leaders.[35] Why is trust important? It facilitates cooperation, reduces the need to monitor each other's behavior, and bonds members around the belief that others on the team won't take advantage of them. Trusting the team leader is also important because it means the team is willing to accept and commit to the leader's goals and decisions.

The final contextual factor of an effective team is a *performance evaluation and reward system*. Team members have to be accountable both individually and jointly. So, in addition to evaluating and rewarding employees for their individual contributions, managers should consider group-based appraisals, profit-sharing, and other approaches that reinforce team effort and commitment.

WHAT TEAM COMPOSITION FACTORS LEAD TO EFFECTIVENESS?   Several team composition factors are important to a team's effectiveness. They include team member abilities, personality, role allocation, diversity, size of teams, member flexibility, and member preferences.

Part of a team's performance depends on its members' *knowledge, skills, and abilities*.[36] Research has shown that to perform effectively, a team needs three different types of skills. First, it needs people with technical expertise. Next, it needs members with problem-solving and decision-making skills. Finally, a team needs people with interpersonal skills. A team can't achieve its performance potential if it doesn't have or can't develop all these skills. And the right mix of these skills is also critical. Too much of one at the expense of another will lead to lower team performance. However, a team doesn't necessarily need all these skills immediately. It's not uncommon for team members to take responsibility for learning the skills in which the group is deficient. That way a team can achieve its full potential.

As we'll see in the next chapter, *personality* significantly influences individual behavior. It's also true for team behavior. Research has shown that three of the Big Five dimensions—a theory we'll discuss in Chapter 10—are relevant to team effectiveness.[37] For instance, high levels of both conscientiousness and openness-to-experience tend to lead to higher team performance. Agreeableness also appears to matter. And teams that had one or more highly disagreeable members performed poorly. Maybe you've had that not-so-good experience in group projects that you've been part of!

Nine potential team *roles* have been identified. (See Exhibit 9–7.) High-performing work teams have people who were selected to fulfill these roles based on their skills and preferences.[38] On many teams, individuals may play multiple roles. It's important for managers to understand the individual strengths a person will bring to a team and select team members with those strengths in mind to ensure that these roles are filled.

Team *diversity* is another factor that can influence team effectiveness. Although many of us hold the optimistic view that diversity is desirable, research seems to show the opposite. One review found that "Studies on diversity in teams from the last 50 years have shown that surface-level social-category differences such as race/ethnicity, gender, and age tend to . . . have negative effects" on the performance of teams.[39] Some evidence does show that the disruptive effects of diversity decline over time, but evidence does not confirm that diverse teams perform better eventually.

What *size* should a work team be in order to be effective? At Amazon, work teams have considerable autonomy to innovate and to investigate ideas. Jeff Bezos, founder and CEO, uses a "two-pizza" philosophy; that is, a team should be small enough that it can be fed with two pizzas. This "two-pizza" philosophy usually limits groups to five to seven people, depending, of course, on team member appetites![40] Generally speaking, the most effective teams have five to nine members. And experts suggest using the smallest number of people who can do the task.

Team *member preferences* need to be considered. Why? Some people just prefer not to work on teams. Given the

Creative director Shannon Washington (center) at New York City-based advertising agency Drago5 talks with members of the diverse CoverGirl ad campaign team. The team performed effectively in creating a successful cosmetics campaign due to the knowledge, skills, and abilities of all of its members including creative directors, copywriters, art director and artists, design director, and Web designers and developers.

Kathy Willens/AP Images

Exhibit 9–7 Team Member Roles

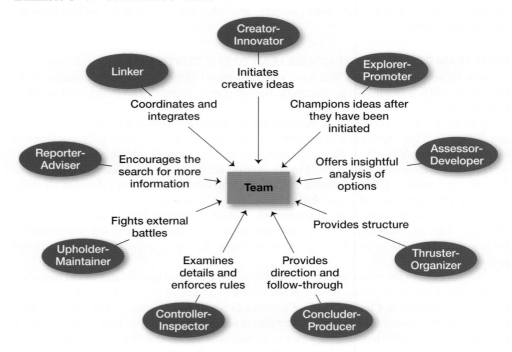

Source: Based on C. Margerison and D. McCann, *Team Management: Practical New Approaches* (London: Mercury Books, 1990).

option, many employees will opt not to be part of a team. When people who would prefer to work alone are forced on a team, it creates a direct threat to the team's morale and to individual member satisfaction.[41]

HOW DOES WORK DESIGN AFFECT TEAM EFFECTIVENESS? Effective teams need to work together and take collective responsibility for completing tasks. An effective team must be more than a "team in name only."[42] Important work design elements include *autonomy*, using a *variety of skills*, being able to complete a *whole and identifiable* task or product, and working on a task or project that has a *significant impact* on others. Research indicates that these characteristics enhance team member motivation and increase team effectiveness.[43]

WHAT TEAM PROCESSES ARE RELATED TO TEAM EFFECTIVENESS? Five team process variables have been shown to be related to team effectiveness. These include a common purpose, specific team goals, team efficacy, managed conflict, and minimal social loafing.

An effective team has a *common plan and purpose*. This common purpose provides direction, momentum, and commitment for team members.[44] Members of successful teams put a lot of time and effort into discussing, shaping, and agreeing on a purpose that belongs to them both individually and as a team.

Teams also need *specific goals*. Such goals facilitate clear communication and help teams maintain their focus on getting results.

Team efficacy emerges when teams believe in themselves and believe they can succeed.[45] Effective teams have confidence in themselves and in their members.

Of team managers, 63.5 percent say they are somewhat effective at resolving conflict.[46]

Effective teams need some *conflict*. Conflict on a team isn't necessarily bad and can actually improve team effectiveness.[47] But it has to be the right kind of conflict. Relationship conflicts—those based on interpersonal incompatibilities, tension, and autonomy toward others—are almost always dysfunctional. However, task conflicts—those based on disagreements about task content—can be beneficial because they may stimulate discussion, promote critical assessment of problems and options, and can lead to better team decisions.

Have you ever been part of a class group in which all teammates received the same grade, even though some team members didn't fulfill their responsibilities? How did that make you feel? Did it create conflict within the group, and did you feel that the process and outcome were unfair? Recent research also has shown that organizational justice or fairness is an important aspect of managing group conflict.[48] How group members feel about how they're being treated both by each other within the group and by outsiders can affect their work attitudes and behaviors. To promote the sense of fairness, it's important that group leaders build a strong sense of community based on fair and just treatment.

Finally, effective teams work to minimize the tendency for *social loafing*, which we discussed earlier in this chapter. Successful teams make members individually and jointly accountable for the team's purpose, goals, and approach.[49]

How Can a Manager Shape Team Behavior?

A manager can do several things to shape a team's behavior including proper selection, employee training, and rewarding the appropriate team behaviors. Let's look at each.

WHAT ROLE DOES SELECTION PLAY?   Some individuals already possess the interpersonal skills to be effective team players. When hiring team members, managers should check whether applicants have the technical skills required to successfully perform the job *and* whether they can fulfill team roles.

Some applicants may have been socialized around individual contributions and, consequently, lack team skills, which could also be true for some current employees being moved into teams due to organizational restructuring. When faced with this situation, a manager can do several things. First, and most obvious, if team skills are woefully lacking, don't hire the person. If successful performance is going to require interaction, not hiring the individual is appropriate. On the other hand, an applicant who has some basic skills can be hired on a probationary basis and be required to undergo training to shape him or her into a team player. If the skills aren't learned or practiced, then the individual may have to be let go.

The Container Store manager Jaimie Moeller (left) leads a team huddle with employees before they begin their work day. Because employees work as a team in serving customers, managers begin shaping team behavior when interviewing job candidates and hiring only a small percentage of applicants who are enthusiastic about working in a team-oriented environment.

Fifty-seven percent of team leaders said if someone on their team hated their job, they would encourage them to find another job. Only 7 percent said they would change their role to make them happy.[50]

CAN INDIVIDUALS BE TRAINED TO BE TEAM PLAYERS?   Performing well in a team involves a set of behaviors.[51] As we discussed in the preceding chapter, new behaviors *can* be

James Borchuck/Tampa Bay Times/ZUMAPRESS.com/ Alamy Live News/Alamy Stock Photo learned. Even people who feel strongly about the importance of individual accomplishment can be trained to become team players. Training specialists can conduct exercises so employees can experience what teamwork is all about. The workshops can cover such topics as team problem solving, communications, negotiations, conflict resolution, and coaching skills. In addition, it's not unusual for these individuals to be exposed to the five stages of team development that we discussed earlier.[52] At Verizon Communications, for example, trainers focus on how a team goes through various stages before it gels. And employees are reminded of the importance of patience, because teams take longer to do some things—such as make decisions—than do employees acting alone.[53]

WHAT ROLE DO REWARDS PLAY IN SHAPING TEAM PLAYERS? An organization's reward system needs to encourage cooperative efforts rather than competitive ones. For instance, Lockheed Martin's aeronautics division organized its some 20,000 employees into teams. Rewards are structured to return a percentage increase in the bottom line to the team members on the basis of achievements of the team's performance goals.

Promotions, pay raises, and other forms of recognition should be given to employees who are effective collaborative team members. Taking this approach doesn't mean that individual contribution is ignored, but rather that it's balanced with selfless contributions to the team. Examples of behaviors that should be rewarded include training new colleagues, sharing information with teammates, helping resolve team conflicts, and mastering new skills in which the team is deficient.[54] Finally, managers can't forget the inherent rewards that employees can receive from teamwork. Work teams provide camaraderie. It's exciting and satisfying to be an integral part of a successful team. The opportunity to engage in personal development and to help teammates grow can be a satisfying and rewarding experience for employees.[55]

What Current Issues Do Managers Face in Managing Teams?

9-4 Discuss contemporary issues in managing teams.

Few trends have influenced how work gets done in organizations as much as the use of work teams. The shift from working alone to working on teams requires employees to cooperate with others, share information, confront differences, and sublimate personal interests for the greater good of the team. Managers can build effective teams by understanding what influences performance and satisfaction. However, managers also face some current challenges in managing teams, including those associated with managing global teams and with understanding when teams aren't the answer.

What's Involved with Managing Global Teams?

Two characteristics of today's organizations are obvious: They're global and work is increasingly done by teams. Because of those reasons, any manager is likely to have to manage a global team. What do we know about managing global teams? We know there are both drawbacks and benefits in using global teams (see Exhibit 9–8). What are some of the challenges associated with managing global teams?

Exhibit 9–8 Global Teams

DRAWBACKS	BENEFITS
• Disliking team members	• Greater diversity of ideas
• Mistrusting team members	• Limited groupthink
• Stereotyping	• Increased attention on understanding
• Communication problems	others' ideas, perspectives, etc.
• Stress and tension	

Source: Based on N. Adler, *International Dimensions of Organizational Behavior*, 4th ed. (Cincinnati, OH: Southwestern Cengage Publishing, 2002), pp. 141–47.

HOW DO TEAM COMPOSITION FACTORS AFFECT MANAGING A GLOBAL TEAM? In global organizations, understanding the relationship between team effectiveness and team composition is more challenging because of the unique cultural characteristics represented by members of a global team. In addition to recognizing team members' abilities, skills, knowledge, and personality, managers need to be familiar with and clearly understand the cultural characteristics of the groups and the group members they manage.[56] For instance, is the global team from a culture in which uncertainty avoidance is high? If so, members will not be comfortable dealing with unpredictable and ambiguous tasks. Also, as managers work with global teams, they need to be aware of the potential for stereotyping, which can lead to problems.

HOW DOES TEAM STRUCTURE AFFECT MANAGING A GLOBAL TEAM? Some of the structural areas where we see differences in managing global teams include conformity, status, social loafing, and cohesiveness.

Are conformity findings generalizable across cultures? Research suggests that Asch's findings are culture-bound.[57] For instance, as might be expected, conformity to social norms tends to be higher in collectivistic cultures than in individualistic cultures. However, groupthink tends to be less of a problem in global teams because members are less likely to feel pressured to conform to the ideas, conclusions, and decisions of the group.[58]

Also, the importance of status varies among cultures. The French, for example, are extremely status conscious. Also, countries differ on the criteria that confer status. For instance, in Latin America and Asia, status tends to come from family position and formal roles held in organizations. In contrast, while status is important in countries like the United States and Australia, it tends to be less "in your face." And it tends to be given based on accomplishments rather than on titles and family history. Managers must understand who and what holds status when interacting with people from a culture different from their own. An American manager who doesn't understand that office size isn't a measure of a Japanese executive's position or who fails to grasp the importance the British place on family genealogy and social class is likely to unintentionally offend others and lessen his or her interpersonal effectiveness.

Social loafing has a Western bias. It's consistent with individualistic cultures, like the United States and Canada, which are dominated by self-interest. It's not consistent with collectivistic societies, in which individuals are motivated by group goals. For instance, teamwork is an integral element in Japan's corporate culture. The emphasis on group versus individual achievement begins in elementary school, where students in Japan learn to work collaboratively on projects that benefit the class and the school. In Japanese businesses, employees are expected to be active team members, and they get things done by group consensus.[59]

Cohesiveness is another group structural element that may create special challenges for

Karim Habib (left) is the executive design director of Infiniti, Nissan's luxury car brand. Based at Nissan's Global Design Center in Atsugi, Japan, Habib leads the design teams in Japan; Beijing, China; San Diego, California; and London, England. In managing the global team, Habib is challenged by the unique cultural traits of team members as he inspires them to create cars that expand Infiniti's share in the luxury market.

REUTERS/Toru Hanai

managers. In a cohesive group, members are unified and "act as one." There's a great deal of camaraderie and group identity is high. In global teams, however, cohesiveness is often more difficult to achieve because of higher levels of "mistrust, miscommunication, and stress."[60]

HOW DO TEAM PROCESSES AFFECT MANAGING A GLOBAL TEAM? The processes that global teams use to do their work can be particularly challenging for managers. For one thing, communication issues often arise because not all team members may be fluent in the team's working language, which can lead to inaccuracies, misunderstandings, and inefficiencies.[61] However, research has also shown that a multicultural global team is better able to capitalize on the diversity of ideas represented if a wide range of information is used.[62]

Managing conflict in global teams isn't easy, especially when those teams are virtual teams. Conflict can interfere with how information is used by the team. However, research shows that in collectivistic cultures, a collaborative conflict management style can be most effective.[63]

Some research has shown that using "multicultural brokers"—individuals who have experience in two or more cultures—can help global teams perform better.[64] Such individuals would bring a dimension to the ongoing work of global teams that could help minimize the barriers to effectiveness.

When Are Teams Not the Answer?

Teamwork takes more time and often more resources than does individual work.[65] Teams require managers to communicate more, manage conflicts, and run meetings. So, the benefits of using teams need to exceed the costs. And that's not always the case![66] In the rush to use teams, some managers have introduced them into situations in which it would have been better to have individuals do the work. So before implementing teams just because everyone's talking about their popularity, you should carefully evaluate whether the work requires or will benefit from a collective effort.

How do you know whether work is better done individually or by a group?

Three "tests" have been suggested.[67] First, can the work be done better by more than one person? Task complexity would be a good indicator of a need for different perspectives. Simple tasks that don't require diverse input are probably better done by individuals. Second, does the work create a common purpose or set of goals for the people in the group that's more than the sum of individual goals? For instance, many car dealerships use teams to link customer-service personnel, mechanics, parts specialists, and sales representatives. Such teams can better meet the goal of outstanding customer satisfaction. The final test to assess whether teams or individuals are better suited for doing work is to look at the interdependence of the individuals. Using teams makes sense when there's interdependence between tasks; that is, when the success of everyone depends on the success of each person *and* the success of each person depends on the others. For example, soccer is an obvious team sport. Success requires a lot of coordination between interdependent players. On the other hand, swim teams aren't really teams, except on relays. They're groups of individuals, performing individually, whose total performance is merely the sum of their individual performances.

CHAPTER SUMMARY BY LEARNING OUTCOME

9-1 Define *group* and describe the stages of group development.

A group is two or more interacting and interdependent individuals who come together to achieve specific goals. Formal groups are work groups that are defined by the organization's structure and have designated work assignments and specific tasks directed at accomplishing organizational goals. Informal groups are social groups.

The forming stage consists of two phases: joining the group and defining the group's purpose, structure, and leadership. The storming stage is one of intragroup conflict over who will control the group and what the group will be doing. The norming stage is when close relationships and cohesiveness develop as norms are determined. The performing stage is when group members work on the group's task. The adjourning stage happens when the group prepares to disband.

9-2 Describe the major concepts of group behavior.

A role refers to a set of behavior patterns expected of someone occupying a given position in a social unit. At any given time, employees adjust their role behaviors to the group of which they are a part. Norms are standards shared by group members. They informally convey to employees which behaviors are acceptable and which are unacceptable. Status is another factor to know because it can be a significant motivator and it needs to be congruent. Also, group size affects group behavior in a number of ways. Smaller groups are generally faster at completing tasks than are larger ones. However, larger groups are frequently better at fact finding because of their diversified input. As a result, larger groups are generally better at problem solving. Finally, group cohesiveness is important because of its impact on a group's effectiveness at achieving its goals.

9-3 Discuss how groups are turned into effective teams.

Effective teams have common characteristics. They have adequate resources, effective leadership, a climate of trust, and a performance evaluation and reward system that reflects team contributions. These teams have individuals with technical expertise as well as problem-solving, decision-making, and interpersonal skills and the right traits, especially conscientiousness and openness to new experiences. Effective teams also tend to be small, preferably of diverse backgrounds. They have members who fill role demands and who prefer to be part of a team. And the work that members do provides freedom and autonomy, the opportunity to use different skills and talents, the ability to complete a whole and identifiable task or product, and work that has a substantial impact on others. Finally, effective teams have members who believe in the team's capabilities and are committed to a common plan and purpose, specific team goals, a manageable level of conflict, and a minimal degree of social loafing.

9-4 Discuss contemporary issues in managing teams.

The challenges of managing global teams can be seen in team composition factors, especially the diverse cultural characteristics; in team structure, especially conformity, status, social loafing, and cohesiveness; in team processes, especially with communication and managing conflict; and in the manager's role in making it all work.

Managers also need to know when teams are not the answer. They can do this by assessing whether the work can be done better by more than one person; by whether the work creates a common purpose or set of goals for the members of the team; and by the amount of interdependence among team members.

DISCUSSION QUESTIONS

9-1 Think of a group to which you belong (or have belonged). Trace its development through the stages of group development as shown in Exhibit 9–2. How closely did its development parallel the group development model? How might the group development model be used to improve this group's effectiveness?

9-2 Contrast (a) self-managed and cross-functional teams, and (b) virtual and face-to-face teams.

9-3 How do you explain the popularity of work teams in countries such as the United States and Canada, whose national cultures place a high value on individualism?

9-4 "All work teams are work groups, but not all work groups are work teams." Do you agree or disagree with this statement? Discuss.

9-5 Would you prefer to work alone or as part of a team? Why?

9-6 "To have a successful team, first find a great leader." What do you think of this statement? Do you agree? Why or why not?

9-7 What traits do you think good team players have? Do some research to answer this question and write a short report detailing your findings using a bulleted list format.

9-8 Contrast the pros and cons of diverse teams.

9-9 How do you think scientific management theorists would react to the increased use of teams in organizations? How would behavioral science theorists react?

9-10 What challenges do managers face in managing global teams? How should those challenges be handled?

Applying: Getting Ready for the Workplace

Management Skill Builder | DEVELOPING YOUR COACHING SKILLS

Organizations have become increasingly structured around teams. Twenty years ago, the individual was the basic building block of an organization; today it's teams. As the manager, you need to be able to effectively lead and coach a team. Without those skills, you're likely to have a short tenure in your management position.

MyLab Management
PERSONAL INVENTORY ASSESSMENT

Go to **www.pearson.com/mylab/management** to complete the Personal Inventory Assessment related to this chapter.

 **P I A** PERSONAL INVENTORY ASSESSMENT

Skill Basics

Effective work team managers are increasingly being described as coaches rather than bosses. Just like coaches, they're expected to provide instruction, guidance, advice, and encouragement to help team members improve their job performance. You can learn to be a good team coach by practicing these behaviors:

• *Analyze ways to improve the team's performance and capabilities.* A coach looks for opportunities for team members to expand their capabilities and improve performance. How? You can use the following behaviors. Observe your team members' behaviors on a day-to-day basis. Ask questions of them: Why do you do a task this way? Can it be improved? What other approaches might be used? Show genuine interest in team members as individuals, not merely as employees. Respect them individually. Listen to each employee.

• *Create a supportive climate.* It's the coach's responsibility to reduce barriers to development and to facilitate a climate that encourages personal performance improvement. How? You can use the following behaviors. Create a climate that contributes to a free and open exchange of ideas. Offer help and assistance. Give guidance and advice when asked. Encourage your team. Be positive and upbeat. Don't use threats. Ask, "What did we learn from this that can help us in the future?" Reduce obstacles. Assure team members that you value their contribution to the team's goals. Take personal responsibility for the outcome, but don't rob team members of their full responsibility. Validate team members' efforts when they succeed. Point to what was missing when they fail. Never blame team members for poor results.

- *Influence team members to change their behavior.* The ultimate test of coaching effectiveness is whether an employee's performance improves. You must encourage ongoing growth and development. How can you do this? Try the following behaviors. Recognize and reward small improvements and treat coaching as a way of helping employees to continually work toward improvement. Use a collaborative style by allowing team members to participate in identifying and choosing among improvement ideas. Break difficult tasks down into simpler ones. Model the qualities you expect from your team. If you want openness, dedication, commitment, and responsibility from your team members, demonstrate these qualities yourself.

Practicing the Skill

Read through this scenario and follow the directions at the end of it:

You're the leader of a five-member project team that's been assigned the task of moving your engineering firm into the growing area of high-speed intercity rail construction. You and your team members have been researching the field, identifying specific business opportunities, negotiating alliances with equipment vendors, and evaluating high-speed rail experts and consultants from around the world. Throughout the process, Tonya, a highly qualified and respected engineer, has challenged a number of things you've said during team meetings and in the workplace. For example, at a meeting two weeks ago, you presented the team with a list of 10 possible high-speed rail projects and started evaluating your organization's ability to compete for them. Tonya contradicted virtually all of your comments, questioned your statistics, and was quite pessimistic about the possibility of getting contracts on these projects. After this latest display of displeasure, two other group members, Bryan and Maggie, came to you and complained that Tonya's actions were damaging the team's effectiveness. You originally put Tonya on the team for her unique expertise and insight. You'd like to find a way to reach her and get the team on the right track to its fullest potential.

Form three-member teams in class. Each team should analyze this leader's problem and suggest solutions for coaching Tonya (and other team members, if you feel it's important). Each class team should be prepared to present its conclusions to the class.

Experiential Exercise

Now, for a little fun! Organizations (work and educational) often use team-building exercises to help teams improve their performance. In your assigned group, *select two* of the characteristics of effective teams listed in Exhibit 9-6 and develop a team-building exercise for each characteristic. In developing your exercise, focus on helping a group improve that particular characteristic. Be creative! Write a group report describing your exercises, being sure to explain how your exercises will help a group improve or develop that characteristic. Be prepared to share your ideas with your class! OR, be prepared to demonstrate the team-building exercise!

Then, once you've concluded the assigned group work, you are to personally evaluate your "group" experience in working on this task. How did your group work together? What went "right?" What didn't go "right?" What could your group have done to improve its work performance and satisfaction with the group effort?

CASE APPLICATION #1

Rx: Teamwork
Topic: Team-based model

The health-care industry is the fastest growing sector of the U.S. economy, with annual revenues projected at over $1.6 trillion (that's 12 zeroes!).[68] And health care has surpassed manufacturing and retail as the largest source of jobs in the United States,[69] now employing more than 18 million workers.[70] Many challenges face the health-care industry, including changing laws/regulations, changing technologies, an aging population and increase in chronic disease, and labor shortages (physicians and nurses). But the goal is still the same—efficiently and effectively provide quality (appropriate and timely) health care to patients. Given the challenges, health-care organizations are looking for better ways to do this. And one way is through using a "team-based care" approach, which research studies have shown can improve patient outcomes and reduce costs.

Many hospitals, clinics, and medical practices have adopted this team-based care approach. What does that entail? A patient receives care from a team of medical professionals who divide up responsibilities for performing tasks that traditionally would have been done by a person's primary physician. Although supervising physicians still manage (oversee) patient care, tasks such as completing prescription refill requests, adjusting medication dosages, helping manage chronic diseases (e.g., teaching someone diagnosed with diabetes how to take blood sugar counts and to administer insulin), and other routine tasks are now done by a team of health-care providers. For instance, at Kaiser Permanente, one of the largest not-for-profit managed health-care companies in the United States, a new program model called "complete care" was designed to enable health-care staffers to work together to make sure that no patient concern, need, preventive action, or matter was missed or overlooked.[71] As one individual described, staffers often literally chased patients down hallways to get them to schedule needed screenings. But the team approach is working. After a number of years using this model, research on Kaiser's team model showed significant gains in patient medical care across a wide range of standardized measures. Getting to that outcome wasn't easy, however. Departments that were accustomed to working on their own now had to work together. Instead of focusing on their own specialties, a team of specialists now worked together to provide patients with a well-rounded health-care experience. Physicians had to be retrained to view themselves as part of a team, supported by other professionals such as nurses, assistants, and other staff. As the health-care environment continues to be challenging, is teamwork the Rx?

TEAMING UP for better outcomes

Discussion Questions

9-11 What challenges are managers of health-care organizations facing?

9-12 How would the way health-care organization managers manage be different in a team-based model?

9-13 Explain how roles, norms, status systems, and group cohesiveness might influence the success of a team-based model.

9-14 What are some reasons you think a team-based model has led to improved patient outcomes and reduced costs?

9-15 In the chapter, we brought up the idea of teams sharing too much information. Would this be a more serious ethical issue for teams in health-care organizations? Why or why not?

CASE APPLICATION #2

Building Better Software Build Teams

Topic: Team effectiveness

Microsoft Corp, quite often considered the granddaddy of the computer software industry, was founded in 1975 by childhood friends Bill Gates and Paul Allen. (Fun fact: The company was originally based in Albuquerque, New Mexico, not Seattle!) Since its founding, the company has been on the forefront of software development. From MS-DOS to Windows to Internet Explorer, Microsoft has pursued its mission to "empower every person and every organization on the planet to achieve more."[72] Although Microsoft's cloud-computing business continues to sizzle—growing by 93 percent in the most recent quarter—software development still plays an important role in the company's strategic revenue mix.[73] And software development is very much a team effort.

Build, which is the process of creating software from source code, is an essential activity in software development.[74] Any company in the software development business relies heavily on the effectiveness of its software build teams. And Microsoft has invested resources in making sure its build team effectiveness is solid. What is build team effectiveness? Microsoft defines it as "how reliably and efficiently the team produces builds."[75] The performance of company build teams leads to higher revenue, flawless product launches, higher customer satisfaction, and talent (employee) retention.[76] Now you see why it's so important for Microsoft to focus on build team effectiveness. So, how did it go about doing this? By researching impediments to build team effectiveness—which, by the way, have been found to be social, rather than technical—and creating ways for teams to work through those obstacles.

To understand how to make build teams more effective—that is, high performance—it was important to understand what went on as these teams did their work. Part of the process Microsoft used in ensuring that its build teams would be high-performance was researching what happened in build teams. That exploration of the process and the people provided

Microsoft with some very interesting insights, one of the most important which we just mentioned: impediments to team effectiveness were primarily social, not technical. The members of these build teams are intelligent, knowledgeable, and hard-working individuals who are very good at what they do. But in a team setting, those aspects don't always translate to high performance.

One other important thing that Microsoft did was to create a "Role Excellence (RolEx) function."[77] RolEx is part of the company's operational structure. It's not associated with the HR or talent management functions. If HR is having the right people in the right place at the right time (remember this from Chapter 8), then RolEx is making sure that those people are able to function at high levels of performance once they're in place. Team employees are given the integrated support they need to do what they were hired to do. What this means for software build teams is that they have the tools they need to contribute to releasing software on-time and on-budget. And that's what any team needs to be a high-performing work team.

Building high-performance work teams

Discussion Questions

9-16 Does a software build team meet the definition of a work team? (See Exhibit 9-5.) Explain.

9-17 Do you think a software build team goes through the stages of group development? Why or why not?

9-18 The chapter identified the four most common types of work teams. Which do you think probably best describes Microsoft's software build teams? Explain.

9-19 Using Exhibit 9-6 as your guide, discuss how Microsoft creates effective teams.

9-20 What could other organizations learn about building high-performance work teams from Microsoft's experiences? Prepare a list of three key points you would use in making a presentation about building high-performance work teams.

CASE APPLICATION #3

Employees Managing Themselves—Good Idea or Not?

Topic: Self-managed teams

Can employees really manage themselves? At W. L. Gore and Associates, self-managed teams have helped create a a thriving business that has operated profitably for more than 50 years.[78] Gore is a manufacturer that develops innovative solutions for demanding and extreme environments. Focusing primarily on protective fabrics, Gore products might be found in clothing worn by climbers tackling Mt. Everest or in medical implants for the human body. You may have used their best-known product, Gore-Tex fabric, in a pair of gloves that keep your hands warm even in the coldest temperatures.

Self-management is not new or not just a trend at Gore. It's a management structure that has been in place since the company was founded in 1958. The company has no titles, no bosses, and no hierarchy. Employees work in self-managed teams of 8 to 12 employees, and they make all of the decisions, including hiring and pay. This structure was created by company founders Wilbert "Bill" Lee and Genevieve Gore. In creating this type of structure, their goal was to combat traditional management practices and encourage innovative thinking. There is a CEO and some other respected leaders, but otherwise no clear management structure exists. The current CEO, Terri Kelly, stepped into the role in 2005 after 22 years with the company. While she's in charge, she was selected by a peer-driven process.

Why does it work? In this self-managed environment, employees are committed to make the organization a success, and everyone is working in the company's best interest. Employees are all partial owners of the company, which encourages them to focus on the company's success. Each employee has the freedom to decide what he or she will work on, but then also must make a commitment to deliver. There are leaders in the organization, but they are determined by who is willing to follow them. The test of leadership is this: If you call a meeting, does anyone show up?

Employee teams tackle **innovation challenge**

Self-management could easily turn into chaos, especially with more than 10,000 employees. However, Gore has a culture that reinforces the expectations for performance of the self-managed teams. The company has established norms of behavior and expected guidelines to follow. It often takes more time for decisions to be made because of the need for team buy-in when making the decision. But once decisions are made, actions are completed more quickly because the buy-in already exists. The self-managed teams at Gore aren't built easily. They spend a lot of time building relationships and building trust. This foundation of trust helps the team work better together, as everyone knows everyone else is working toward the same goals.

Could any company duplicate Gore's management practices? Probably not, say many management experts. Self-managed teams aren't effective in just any company. Self-managed teams are most appropriate in organizations where innovation is strategically important. They're also a useful structural approach in environments that change rapidly. Finally, in order for self-managed teams to be a success, a company must also have strongly shared values that direct work activities and employees.

Discussion Questions

9-21 Describe Gore's approach to self-managed teams.

9-22 Why is organizational culture so critical to the success of self-managed teams?

9-23 Using Exhibit 9-6, what characteristics of effective teams would these self-managed teams need? Explain.

9-24 Would you want to work at W.L. Gore and Associates? Why or why not?

9-25 Working in your assigned group, make a list of challenges that organizations with self-managed teams would face. Then, discuss ways that these challenges could be addressed.

Endnotes

1. V. Evangelista, "Are Your Team Members Working Together or Simply Working?" *TD*, April 2017, pp. 102–3.
2. B. Mezrich, *Bringing Down the House: The Inside Story of Six MIT Students Who Took Vegas for Millions* (New York: Free Press, 2002). The 2008 film *21* was a fictional work based loosely on the story.
3. B. W. Tuckman and M. C. Jensen, "Stages of Small-Group Development Revisited," *Group and Organizational Studies*, December 1977, pp. 419–27; and M. F. Maples, "Group Development: Extending Tuckman's Theory," *Journal for Specialists in Group Work*, Fall 1988, pp. 17–23.
4. L. N. Jewell and H. J. Reitz, *Group Effectiveness in Organizations* (Glenview, IL: Scott, Foresman, 1981); and M. Kaeter, "Repotting Mature Work Teams," *Training*, April 1994, pp. 54–56.
5. Making Ethical Decisions in Today's Workplace box based on R. Bellis, "How to Deal with a Chronic Oversharer at Work," *Fast Company Online*, February 28, 2018; S. Shellenbarger, "Office Oversharers: Don't Tell Us about Last Night," *Wall Street Journal*, June 25, 2014, p. D2; E. Bernstein, "Thank You for Not Sharing," *Wall Street Journal*, May 7, 2013, pp. D1+; P. Klaus, "Thank You for Sharing. But Why at the Office?" *New York Times Online*, August 18, 2012; K. McCullum, "Hush, Hush," *OfficePro*, March–April 2011, pp. 18–22; and E. Bernstein, "You Did What? Spare the Office the Details," *Wall Street Journal*, April 6, 2010, pp. D1+.
6. K. Brennan, "Can We Fire an Employee for Sharing His Pay Increase with Co-workers and Destroying Morale?" *HR Magazine*, March 2018, p. 14.
7. S. E. Asch, "Effects of Group Pressure upon the Modification and Distortion of Judgments," in H. Guetzkow (ed.), *Groups, Leadership, and Men* (Pittsburgh, PA: Carnegie Press, 1951), pp. 177–90.
8. See, for example, R. A. Henry, J. Kmet, and A. Landa, "Examining the Impact of Interpersonal Cohesiveness on Group Accuracy Interventions: The Importance of Matching versus Buffering," *Organizational Behavior and Human Decision Processes*, January 2002, pp. 25–43.
9. Asch, "Effects of Group Pressure upon the Modification and Distortion of Judgments."
10. O. A. Alnuaimi, L. P. Robert Jr., and L. M. Maruping, "Team Size, Dispersion, and Social Loafing in Technology-Supported Teams:

A Perspective on the Theory of Moral Disengagement," *Journal of Management Information Systems*, Summer 2010, pp. 203–30; C. Cheshire and J. Antin, "None of Us Is as Lazy as All of Us," *Information, Communication & Society*, June 2010, pp. 537–55; R. van Dick, J. Stellmacher, U. Wagner, G. Lemmer, and P. A. Tissington, "Group Membership Salience and Task Performance," *Journal of Managerial Psychology* 24, no. 7 (2009), pp. 609–26; A. Jassawalla, H. Sashittal, and A. Malshe, "Students' Perceptions of Social Loafing: Its Antecedents and Consequences in Undergraduate Business Classroom Teams," *Academy of Management Learning & Education*, March 2009, pp. 42–54; and R. Albanese and D. D. Van Fleet, "Rational Behavior in Groups: The Free Riding Tendency," *Academy of Management Review*, April 1985, pp. 244–55.
11. L. Berkowitz, "Group Standards, Cohesiveness, and Productivity," *Human Relations*, November 1954, pp. 509–19.
12. Classic Concepts in Today's Workplace box based on S. S. Wang, "Under the Influence: How the Group Changes What We Think," *Wall Street Journal*, May 3, 2011, pp. D1+; M. E. Shaw, *Group Dynamics: The Psychology of Small Group Behavior* (New York: McGraw-Hill, 1975); and E. J. Thomas and C. F. Fink, "Effects of Group Size," *Psychological Bulletin*, July 1963, pp. 371–84.
13. Cited in T. Purdum, "Teaming, Take 2," *Industry Week*, May 2005, p. 43; and C. Joinson, "Teams at Work," *HR Magazine*, May 1999, p. 30.
14. See, for example, S. A. Mohrman, S. G. Cohen, and A. M. Mohrman Jr., *Designing Team-Based Organizations* (San Francisco: Jossey-Bass, 1995); P. MacMillan, *The Performance Factor: Unlocking the Secrets of Teamwork* (Nashville, TN: Broadman & Holman, 2001); and E. Salas, C. A. Bowers, and E. Eden (eds.), *Improving Teamwork in Organizations: Applications of Resource Management Training* (Mahwah, NJ: Lawrence Erlbaum, 2002).
15. Information for this section is based on J. R. Katzenbach and D. K. Smith, *The Wisdom of Teams* (Boston: Harvard Business School Press, 1993), pp. 21, 45, 85; and D. C. Kinlaw, *Developing Superior Work Teams* (Lexington, MA: Lexington Books, 1991), pp. 3–21.
16. S. Adams and L. Kydoniefs, "Making Teams Work: Bureau

of Labor Statistics Learns What Works and What Doesn't," *Quality Progress*, January 2000, pp. 43–49.
17. D. Hoffman, "At Wachovia, Fund Teams Work: Bank's Buddy System Improves Performance," *Investment News*, February 2001, p. 8.
18. T. Capozzoli, "How to Succeed with Self-Directed Work Teams," *Supervision*, February 2002, pp. 25–27.
19. See, for instance, E. Sunstrom, DeMeuse, and D. Futrell, "Work Teams: Applications and Effectiveness," *American Psychologist*, February 1990, pp. 120–33.
20. J. S. McClenahen, "Bearing Necessities," *Industry Week*, October 2004, pp. 63–65; P. J. Kiger, "Acxiom Rebuilds from Scratch," *Workforce*, December 2002, pp. 52–55; and T. Boles, "Viewpoint—Leadership Lessons from NASCAR," *Industry Week*, www.industryweek.com, May 21, 2002.
21. M. Cianni and D. Wanuck, "Individual Growth and Team Enhancement: Moving Toward a New Model of Career Development," *Academy of Management Executive*, February 1997, pp. 105–15.
22. C. Joinson, "Teams at Work," 30; and "Teams," *Training*, October 1996, p. 69.
23. J. P. Millikin, P. W. Hom, and C. C. Manz, "Self-Management Competencies in Self-Managing Teams: Their Impact on Multi-Team System Productivity," *Leadership Quarterly*, October 2010, pp. 687–702; O. Turel and Y. Zhang, "Does Virtual Team Composition Matter? Trait and Problem-Solving Configuration Effects on Team Performance," *Behavior & Information Technology*, July–August 2010, pp. 363–75; J. S. Bunderson and P. Boumgarden, "Structure and Learning in Self-Managed Teams: Why 'Bureaucratic' Teams Can Be Better Learners," *Organization Science*, May–June 2010, pp. 609–24; and G. M. Spreitzer, S. G. Cohen, and G. E. Ledford Jr., "Developing Effective Self-Managing Work Teams in Service Organizations," *Group & Organization Management*, September 1999, pp. 340–66.
24. "Meet the New Steel," *Fortune*, October 1, 2007, pp. 68–71.
25. "Theresa Maier Wins Global Novartis International BioCamp," University of Cambridge, Department of Chemical Engineering and Biotechnology, September 8, 2016, http://www.ceb.cam.ac.uk/news/news-list/theresa-maier-novartis-sept16

(accessed December 23, 2016); "Students Take on the Challenges of Digital Medicine," Novartis, August 26, 2016, www.novartis.com (accessed December 23, 2016).
26. A. Malhotra, A. Majchrzak, R. Carman, and V. Lott, "Radical Innovation without Collocation: A Case Study at Boeing-Rocketdyne," *MIS Quarterly*, June 2001, pp. 229–49.
27. A. Stuart, "Virtual Agreement," *CFO*, November 2007, p. 24.
28. Managing Technology in Today's Workplace box based on K. Lee, "17 Tools for Remote Workers," http://www.fastcompany.com/3038333/17-tools-for-remote-workers, November 12, 2014; C. Mims, "Use of Voice Is Key to Managing Teams," *Wall Street Journal*, September 23, 2014, pp. B1+; "Virtual Team Collaboration and Innovation in Organizations," *Team Performance Management*, March 2011, pp. 109–19; M. Flammia, Y. Cleary, and D. M. Slattery, "Leadership Roles, Socioemotional Strategies, and Technology Use of Irish and US Students in Virtual Teams," *IEEE Transactions on Professional Communication*, June 2010, pp. 89–101; P. Evans, "The Wiki Factor," *BizEd*, January–February 2006, pp. 28–32; and M. McCafferty, "A Human Inventory," *CFO*, April 2005, pp. 83–85.
29. See, for instance, D. C. Jones and T. Kato, "The Impact of Teams on Output, Quality, and Downtime: An Empirical Analysis Using Individual Panel Data," *Industrial and Labor Relations Review*, January 2011, pp. 215–40; A. Gilley, J. W. Gilley, C. W. McConnell, and A. Veliquette, "The Competencies Used by Effective Managers to Build Teams: An Empirical Study," *Advances in Developing Human Resources*, February 2010, pp. 29–45; M. A. Campion, G. J. Medsker, and C. A. Higgs, "Relations between Work Group Characteristics and Effectiveness: Implications for Designing Effective Work Groups," *Personnel Psychology*, Winter 1993, pp. 823–50; and J. R. Hackman, "The Design of Work Teams," in J. W. Lorsch (ed.), *Handbook of Organizational Behavior* (Upper Saddle River, NJ: Prentice Hall, 1987), pp. 315–42.
30. This model is based on M. A. Campion, E. M. Papper, and G. J. Medsker, "Relations between Work Team Characteristics and Effectiveness: A Replication and Extension," *Personnel Psychology*, Summer 1996, pp.

429–52; D. E. Hyatt and T. M. Ruddy, "An Examination of the Relationship between Work Group Characteristics and Performance: Once More into the Breech," *Personnel Psychology*, Autumn 1997, pp. 553–85; S. G. Cohen and D. E. Bailey, "What Makes Teams Work: Group Effectiveness Research from the Shop Floor to the Executive Suite," *Journal of Management*, September 1997, pp. 239–90; L. Thompson, *Making the Team* (Upper Saddle River, NJ: Prentice Hall, 2000), pp. 18–33; and J. R. Hackman, *Leading Teams: Setting the Stage for Great Performance* (Boston: Harvard Business School Press, 2002).

31. See M. Mattson, T. V. Mumford, and G. S. Sintay, "Taking Teams to Task: A Normative Model for Designing or Recalibrating Work Teams," paper presented at the National Academy of Management Conference, Chicago, August 1999; and G. L. Stewart and M. R. Barrick, "Team Structure and Performance: Assessing the Mediating Role of Intrateam Process and the Moderating Role of Task Type," *Academy of Management Journal*, April 2000, pp. 135–48.

32. SmartPulse, "How Effectively Does Your Team Communicate Using New Electronic Channels?" Smart Brief on Leadership, www.smartbrief.com/leadership, October 7, 2014.

33. "Virtual Team Collaboration and Innovation in Organizations"; Flammia, Cleary, and Slattery, "Leadership Roles, Socioemotional Strategies, and Technology Use of Irish and U.S. Students in Virtual Teams"; A. Malhotra, A. Majchrzak, and B. Rosen, "Leading Virtual Teams," *Academy of Management Perspectives*, February 2007, pp. 60–70; B. L. Kirkman and J. E. Mathieu, "The Dimensions and Antecedents of Team Virtuality," *Journal of Management*, October 2005, pp. 700–18; J. Gordon, "Do Your Virtual Teams Deliver Only Virtual Performance?" *Training*, June 2005, pp. 20–25; L. L. Martins, L. L. Gilson, and M. T. Maynard, "Virtual Teams: What Do We Know and Where Do We Go from Here?" *Journal of Management*, December 2004, pp. 805–35; S. A. Furst, M. Reeves, B. Rosen, and R. S. Blackburn, "Managing the Life Cycle of Virtual Teams," *Academy of Management Executive*, May 2004, pp. 6–20; B. L. Kirkman, B. Rosen, P. E. Tesluk, and C. B. Gibson, "The Impact of Team Empowerment on Virtual Team Performance: The Moderating Role of Face-to-Face Interaction," *Academy of Management Journal*, April 2004, pp. 175–92; F. Keenan and S. E. Ante, "The New Teamwork," *Business Week e.biz*,

February 18, 2002, pp. EB12–EB16; and G. Imperato, "Real Tools for Virtual Teams," *Fast Company*, July 2000, pp. 378–87.

34. R. I. Sutton, "The Boss as Human Shield," *Harvard Business Review*, September 2010, pp. 106–09; and Hyatt and Ruddy, "An Examination of the Relationship between Work Group Characteristics and Performance," p. 577.

35. M. E. Palanski, S. S. Kahai, and F. J. Yammarino, "Team Virtues and Performance: An Examination of Transparency, Behavioral Integrity, and Trust," *Journal of Business Ethics*, March 2011, pp. 201–16; H. H. Chang, S. S. Chuang, and S. H. Chao, "Determinants of Cultural Adaptation, Communication Quality, and Trust in Virtual Teams' Performance," *Total Quality Management and Business Excellence*, March 2011, pp. 305–29; A. C. Costa and N. Anderson, "Measuring Trust in Teams: Development and Validation of a Multifaceted Measure of Formative and Reflective Indicators of Team Trust," *European Journal of Work & Organizational Psychology*, February 2011, pp. 119–54; M. Mach, S. Dolan, and S. Tzafrir, "The Differential Effect of Team Members' Trust on Team Performance: The Mediation Role of Team Cohesion," *Journal of Occupational and Organizational Psychology*, September 2010, pp. 771–94; B. A. DeJong and T. Elfring, "How Does Trust Affect the Performance of Ongoing Teams? The Mediating Role of Reflexivity, Monitoring, and Effort," *Academy of Management Journal*, June 2010, pp. 535–49; M. Williams, "In Whom We Trust: Group Membership as an Affective Context for Trust Development," *Academy of Management Review*, July 2001, pp. 377–96; and K. T. Dirks, "Trust in Leadership and Team Performance: Evidence from NCAA Basketball," *Journal of Applied Psychology*, December 2000, pp. 1004–12.

36. R. R. Hirschfeld, M. J. Jordan, H. S. Field, W. F. Giles, and A. A. Armenakis, "Becoming Team Players: Team Members' Mastery of Team Knowledge as a Predictor of Team Task Proficiency and Observed Teamwork Effectiveness," *Journal of Applied Psychology* 91, no. 2 (2006), pp. 467–74.

37. S. T. Bell, "Deep-Level Composition Variables as Predictors of Team Performance: A Meta-Analysis," *Journal of Applied Psychology* 92, no. 3 (2007), pp. 595–615; and M. R. Barrick, G. L. Stewart, M. J. Neubert, and M. K. Mount, "Relating Member Ability and Personality to

Work-Team Processes and Team Effectiveness," *Journal of Applied Psychology*, June 1998, pp. 377–91.

38. M. Costello, "Team Weaver," *People Management*, January 2011, pp. 26–27; and C. Margerison and D. McCann, *Team Management: Practical New Approaches* (London: Mercury Books, 1990).

39. K. H. T. Yu and D. M. Cable, "Unpacking Cooperation in Diverse Teams," *Team Performance Management*, March 2011, pp. 63–82; A. Nederveen Pieterse, D. van Knippenberg, and W. P. van Ginkel, "Diversity in Goal Orientation, Team Reflexivity, and Team Performance," *Organizational Behavior and Human Performance*, March 2011, pp. 153–64; M.-E. Roberge and R. van Dick, "Recognizing the Benefits of Diversity: When and How Does Diversity Increase Group Performance," *Human Resource Management Review*, December 2010, pp. 295–308; and E. Mannix and M. A. Neale, "What Differences Make a Difference: The Promise and Reality of Diverse Teams in Organizations," *Psychological Science in the Public Interest*, October 2005, pp. 31–55.

40. A. Deutschman, "Inside the Mind of Jeff Bezos," *Fast Company*, August 2004, pp. 50–58.

41. Hyatt and Ruddy, "An Examination of the Relationship between Work Group Characteristics and Performance"; J. D. Shaw, M. K. Duffy, and E. M. Stark, "Interdependence and Preference for Group Work: Main and Congruence Effects on the Satisfaction and Performance of Group Members," *Journal of Management*, June 2000, pp. 259–79; and S. A. Kiffin-Peterson and J. L. Cordery, "Trust, Individualism, and Job Characteristics of Employee Preference for Teamwork," *International Journal of Human Resource Management*, February 2003, pp. 93–116.

42. J. S. Bunderson and P. Boumgarden, "Structure and Learning in Self-Managed Teams: Why 'Bureaucratic' Teams Can Be Better Learners"; and R. Wageman, "Critical Success Factors for Creating Superb Self-Managing Teams," *Organizational Dynamics*, Summer 1997, p. 55.

43. Campion, Papper, and Medsker, "Relations between Work Team Characteristics and Effectiveness," p. 430; B. L. Kirkman and B. Rosen, "Powering Up Teams," *Organizational Dynamics*, Winter 2000, pp. 48–66; and D. C. Man and S. S. K. Lam, "The Effects of Job Complexity and Autonomy on Cohesiveness in Collectivist and Individualist Work Groups: A Cross-Cultural Analysis," *Journal*

of *Organizational Behavior*, December 2003, pp. 979–1001.

44. A. Mehta, H. Feild, A. Armenakis, and N. Mehta, "Team Goal Orientation and Team Performance: The Mediating Role of Team Planning," *Journal of Management*, August 2009, pp. 1026–46; K. Blanchard, D. Carew, and E. Parisi-Carew, "How to Get Your Group to Perform Like a Team," *Training and Development*, September 1996, pp. 34–37; K. D. Scott and A. Townsend, "Teams: Why Some Succeed and Others Fail," *HR Magazine*, August 1994, pp. 62–67; K. Hess, *Creating the High-Performance Team* (New York: Wiley, 1987); and Katzenbach and Smith, "The Wisdom of Teams," pp. 43–64.

45. H. van Emmerik, I. M. Jawahar, B. Schreurs, and N. de Cuyper, "Social Capital, Team Efficacy and Team Potency: The Mediating Role of Team Learning Behaviors," *Career Development International*, February 2011, pp. 82–99; T. Lewis, "Assessing Social Identity and Collective Efficacy as Theories of Group Motivation at Work," *International Journal of Human Resource Management*, February 2011, pp. 963–80; K. Tasa, G. J. Sears, and A. C. H. Schat, "Personality and Teamwork Behavior in Context: The Cross-Level Moderating Role of Collective Efficacy," *Journal of Organizational Behavior*, January 2011, pp. 65–85; J. A. Goncalo, E. Polman, and C. Maslach, "Can Confidence Come Too Soon? Collective Efficacy, Conflict and Group Performance Over Time," *Organizational Behavior & Human Decision Processes*, September 2010, pp. 13–24; K. Tasa, S. Taggar, and G. H. Seijts, "The Development of Collective Efficacy in Teams: A Multilevel and Longitudinal Perspective," *Journal of Applied Psychology*, January 2007, pp. 17–27; C. B. Gibson, "The Efficacy Advantage: Factors Related to the Formation of Group Efficacy," *Journal of Applied Social Psychology*, October 2003, pp. 2153–86; and D. I. Jung and J. J. Sosik, "Group Potency and Collective Efficacy: Examining Their Predictive Validity, Level of Analysis, and Effects of Performance Feedback on Future Group Performance," *Group & Organization Management*, September 2003, pp. 366–91.

46. SmartPulse, "How Effectively Do You Resolve Conflict with Others?" Smart Brief on Leadership, www.smartbrief.com, April 21, 2015.

47. K. C. Kostopoulos and N. Bozionelos, "Team Exploratory and Exploitative Learning: Psychological Safety, Task Conflict, and Team Performance," *Group & Organization*

Management, June 2011, pp. 385–415; K. J. Behfar, E. A. Mannix, R. S. Peterson, and W. M. Trochim, "Conflict in Small Groups: The Meaning and Consequences of Process Conflict," *Small Group Research*, April 2011, pp. 127–76; R. S. Peterson and K. J. Behfar, "The Dynamic Relationship between Performance Feedback, Trust, and Conflict in Groups: A Longitudinal Study," *Organizational Behavior and Human Decision Processes*, September–November 2003, pp. 102–12; and K. A. Jehn, "A Qualitative Analysis of Conflict Types and Dimensions in Organizational Groups," *Administrative Science Quarterly*, September 1997, pp. 530–57.

48. A. Li and R. Cropanzano, "Fairness at the Group Level: Justice Climate and Intraunit Justice Climate," *Journal of Management*, June 2009, pp. 564–99.

49. Alnuaimi, Robert Jr., and Maruping, "Team Size, Dispersion, and Social Loafing in Technology-Supported Teams: A Perspective on the Theory of Moral Disengagement"; Cheshire and Antin, "None of Us Is as Lazy as All of Us"; van Dick, Stellmacher, Wagner, Lemmer, and Tissington, "Group Membership Salience and Task Performance"; Jassawalla, Sashittal, and Malshe, "Students' Perceptions of Social Loafing: Its Antecedents and Consequences in Undergraduate Business Classroom Teams"; K. H. Price, D. A. Harrison, and J. H. Gavin, "Withholding Inputs in Team Contexts: Member Composition, Interaction Processes, Evaluation Structure, and Social Loafing," *Journal of Applied Psychology*, December 2006, pp.1375–84; and Albanese and Van Fleet, "Rational Behavior in Groups: The Free Riding Tendency."

50. SmartPulse, "If Someone on Your Team Hates Their Job, What Do You Do?" Smart Brief on Leadership, www.smartbrief.com/leadership, October 21, 2014.

51. "Helping Hands," *HR Magazine*, May 2011, p. 18; M. O'Neil, "Leading the Team," *Supervision*, April 2011, pp. 8–10; J. Beeson, "Build a Strong Team," *Leadership Excellence*, February 2011, p. 15; S. Brutus and M. B. L. Donia, "Improving the Effectiveness of Students in

Groups with a Centralized Peer Evaluation System," *Academy of Management Learning & Education*, December 2010, pp. 652–62; and N. H. Woodward, "Make the Most of Team Building," *HR Magazine*, September 2006, pp. 73–76.

52. R. M. Yandrick, "A Team Effort," *HR Magazine*, June 2001, pp. 136–41.

53. Ibid.

54. "How Should We Recognize Team Goals over Individual?" *Workforce Management Online*, February 2011; S. J. Goerg, S. Kube, and R. Zultan, "Treating Equals Unequally: Incentives in Teams, Workers' Motivation, and Production Technology," *Journal of Labor Economics*, October 2010, pp. 747–72; T. Taylor, "The Challenge of Project Team Incentives," *Compensation & Benefits Review*, September–October 2010, pp. 411–19; M. J. Pearsall, M. S. Christian, and A. P. J. Ellis, "Motivating Interdependent Teams: Individual Rewards, Shared Rewards, or Something in Between?" *Journal of Applied Psychology*, January 2010, pp. 183–91; M. A. Marks, C. S. Burke, M. J. Sabella, and S. J. Zaccaro, "The Impact of Cross-Training on Team Effectiveness," *Journal of Applied Psychology*, February 2000, pp. 3–14; and M. A. Marks, S. J. Zaccaro, and J. E. Mathieu, "Performance Implications of Leader Briefings and Team Interaction for Team Adaptation to Novel Environments," *Journal of Applied Psychology*, December 2000, p. 971.

55. C. Garvey, "Steer Teams with the Right Pay: Team-Based Pay Is a Success When It Fits Corporate Goals and Culture, and Rewards the Right Behavior," *HR Magazine*, May 2002, pp. 71–77.

56. F. Niederman and F. B. Tan, "Emerging Markets Managing Global IT Teams: Considering Cultural Dynamics," *Communications of the ACM*, April 2011, pp. 24–27; R. M. B. Boyle and S. Nicholas, "Cross-Cultural Group Performance," *The Learning Organization*, March 2011, pp. 94–101; G. K. Stahl, M. L. Maznevski, A. Voigt, and K. Jonsen, "Unraveling the Effects of Cultural Diversity in Teams: A Meta-Analysis of Research on Multicultural Work Groups," *Journal of International Business Studies*, May 2010, pp. 690–709; and M. R. Haas, "The p. d

Sword of Autonomy and External Knowledge: Analyzing Team Effectiveness in a Multinational Organization," *Academy of Management Journal*, October 2010, pp. 989-1008.

57. R. Bond and P. B. Smith, "Culture and Conformity: A Meta-Analysis of Studies Using Asch's [1952, 1956] Line Judgment Task," *Psychological Bulletin*, January 1996, pp. 111–37.

58. I. L. Janis, *Groupthink*, 2nd ed. (New York: Houghton Mifflin Company, 1982), 175.

59. Teru Clavel, "From Classroom to Boardroom: A Lesson in Business Practices from Japan's Elementary Schools," *Japan Today*, January 10, 2016, https://www.japanto-day.com/category/lifestyle/view/from-classroom-to-boardroom-a-lesson-in-business-practices-from-japans-elementary-schools (accessed December 23, 2016); Erin Meyer, "Managing Multi-cultural Teams," *HR Magazine* (UK), November 27, 2014, http://www.hrmagazine.co.uk/article-details/managing-multi-cultural-teams (accessed December 23, 2016).

60. N. J. Adler, *International Dimensions of Organizational Behavior*, 4th ed. (Cincinnati, OH: Southwestern, 2002), p. 142.

61. K. B. Dahlin, L. R. Weingart, and P. J. Hinds, "Team Diversity and Information Use," *Academy of Management Journal*, December 2005, pp. 1107–23.

62. Adler, *International Dimensions of Organizational Behavior*, p. 142.

63. S. Paul, I. M. Samarah, P. Seetharaman, and P. P. Mykytyn, "An Empirical Investigation of Collaborative Conflict Management Style in Group Support System-Based Global Virtual Teams," *Journal of Management Information Systems*, Winter 2005, pp. 185–222.

64. S. Jang, "Cultural Brokerage and Creative Performance in Multicultural Teams," *Organization Science*, December 2017, pp. 993–1009.

65. This section is based on S. P. Robbins and T. A. Judge, *Organizational Behavior*, 14th ed. (Upper Saddle River, NJ: Pearson Prentice Hall, 2011).

66. C. E. Naquin and R. O. Tynan, "The Team Halo Effect: Why Teams Are Not Blamed for Their Failures," *Journal of Applied Psychology*, April 2003, pp. 332–40.

67. A. B. Drexler and R. Forrester, "Teamwork—Not Necessarily the Answer," *HR Magazine*, January 1998, pp. 55–58. See also R. Saavedra, P. C. Earley, and L. Van Dyne, "Complex Interdependence in Task-Performing Groups," *Journal of Applied Psychology*, February 1993, pp. 61–72; and K. A. Jehn, G. B. Northcraft, and M. A. Neale, "Why Differences Make a Difference: A Field Study of Diversity, Conflict, and Performance in Work Groups," *Administrative Science Quarterly*, December 1999, pp. 741–63.

68. "43 Healthcare Industry Statistics and Trends," www.brandongaille.com, May 30, 2017.

69. D. Thompson, "Health Care Just Became the U.S.'s Largest Employer," *The Atlantic Online*, January 9, 2018.

70. "Health Care Industry Statistics," www.statisticbrain.com/health-care-industry-statistics/, February 3, 2015; and "Healthcare Workers," www.cdc.gov/niosh/topics/health-care, December 12, 2014.

71. L. Landro, "The Teamwork Approach to Medical Care," *Wall Street Journal*, June 9, 2014, p. R3.

72. Microsoft 2017 Annual Report, www.microsoft.com, April 27, 2018.

73. J. Greene, "Microsoft Buoyed by Cloud," *Wall Street Journal*, April 27, 2018, p. B4.

74. S. Phillips, T. Zimmermann, and C. Bird, "Understanding and Improving Software Build Teams," www.microsoft.com, February 2016.

75. Ibid.

76. C. Wilson and P. H. Elliott, "Helping Every Team Exceed Expectations," *TD*, May 2017, pp. 18–21.

77. Ibid.

78. D. Roberts, "At W. L. Gore, 57 Years of Authentic Culture," *Fortune Magazine Online*, March 5, 2015; T. Castille, "Hierarchy Is Overrated," *Harvard Business Review Online*, November 20, 2013; G. Hamel, "W. L. Gore: Lessons from a Management Revolutionary," *Wall Street Journal Online*, March 28, 2010; and C. Blakeman, "Why Self-Managed Teams Are the Future of Business," *Inc. Magazine Online*, November 24, 2014.

10

Management Myth
Myth
Myth

A good manager treats all employees the same.

Management Myth DEBUNKED!

One thing you've probably realized over the years is how differently you and your friends interact with and react to life's situations. Some friends are laid-back; others are more anxious. Some are good at reading emotional clues; others are, well, clueless. The same is true of the people a manager manages. **That's why a good manager works to get to know the unique individual characteristics of the people on his or her team to be able to effectively manage each of them.**

MOST organizations want to attract and retain employees with the right attitudes and personality. Even professional baseball teams! The Chicago Cubs, for instance, discovered that free agents appreciate the personal touch—especially information about what's going to help their families adjust.[1] Organizations want people who show up and work hard, get along with coworkers and customers, have good attitudes, and exhibit good work behaviors in other ways. But as you're probably already aware, people don't always behave like that "ideal" employee. They may job hop at the first opportunity or they may post critical comments in blogs. People differ in their behaviors and even the same person can behave one way one day and a completely different way another day. For instance, haven't you seen family members, friends, or coworkers behave in ways that prompted you to wonder: Why did they do that? In this chapter, we look at four psychological aspects—attitudes, personality, perception, and learning—and how these things can help managers understand the behavior of those people they work with. We conclude the chapter by looking at contemporary behavioral issues facing managers. •

Learning Outcomes

What Are the Focus and Goals of Organizational Behavior?

10-1 Identify the focus and goals of organizational behavior (OB).

Managers need good people skills.

The material in this and the next four chapters draws heavily on the field of study that's known as *organizational behavior (OB)*. It's concerned with the subject of **behavior**—that is, the actions of people—and **organizational behavior** is the study of the actions of people at work.

One of the challenges in understanding organizational behavior is that it addresses issues that aren't obvious. Like an iceberg, OB has a small visible dimension and a much larger hidden portion. (See Exhibit 10–1.) What we see when we look at an organization is its visible aspects: strategies, objectives, policies and procedures, structure, technology, formal authority relationships, and chain of command. But under the surface are other elements that managers need to understand—elements that also influence how employees behave at work. As we'll show, OB provides managers with considerable insights into these important, but hidden, aspects of the organization.

> **behavior**
> The actions of people
>
> **organizational behavior**
> The study of the actions of people at work

What Is the Focus of OB?

Organizational behavior focuses on three major areas:

1. *Individual behavior.* Based predominantly on contributions from psychologists, this area includes such topics as attitudes, personality, perception, learning, and motivation.
2. *Group behavior*, which includes norms, roles, team building, leadership, and conflict. Our knowledge about groups comes basically from the work of sociologists and social psychologists.
3. *Organizational* aspects, including structure, culture, and human resource policies and practices. We've addressed organizational aspects in previous chapters. In this chapter, we'll look at individual behavior, and in the following chapter we'll look at group behavior.

Exhibit 10 –1 Organization as Iceberg

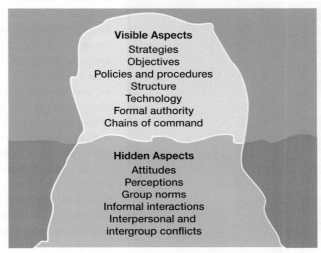

employee productivity
A performance measure of both work efficiency and effectiveness

absenteeism
The failure to show up for work

turnover
Voluntary and involuntary permanent withdrawal from an organization

organizational citizenship behavior
Discretionary behavior that's not part of an employee's formal job requirements, but that promotes the effective functioning of the organization

job satisfaction
An employee's general attitude toward his or her job

workplace misbehavior
Any intentional employee behavior that is potentially harmful to the organization or individuals within the organization

What Are the Goals of Organizational Behavior?

The goals of OB are to *explain*, *predict*, and *influence* behavior. Managers need to be able to *explain* why employees engage in some behaviors rather than others, *predict* how employees will respond to various actions and decisions, and *influence* how employees behave.

SIX important employee behaviors that managers are specifically concerned with explaining, predicting, and influencing include the following:

(1) **Employee productivity**—a performance measure of both work efficiency and effectiveness. Managers want to know what factors will influence the efficiency and effectiveness of employees.

(2) **Absenteeism**—the failure to show up for work. It's difficult for work to get done if employees don't show up. Studies have shown that the total of all major types of absences cost organizations an average 35 percent of payroll, with unscheduled absences costing companies around $660 per employee per year.[2] Although absenteeism can't be totally eliminated, excessive levels have a direct and immediate impact on the organization's functioning.

(3) **Turnover**—the voluntary and involuntary permanent withdrawal from an organization. It can be a problem because of increased recruiting, selection, training costs, and work disruptions. Just like absenteeism, managers can never eliminate turnover, but it is something they want to minimize, especially among high-performing employees.

(4) **Organizational citizenship behavior**—discretionary behavior that's not part of an employee's formal job requirements but that promotes the effective functioning of the organization.[3] Examples of good OCB include helping others on one's work team, volunteering for extended job activities, avoiding unnecessary conflicts, and making constructive statements about one's work group and the organization. Organizations need individuals who will do more than their usual job duties and the evidence indicates that organizations that have such employees outperform those that don't.[4] However, drawbacks to OCB arise if employees experience work overload, stress, and work/family conflicts.[5]

(5) **Job satisfaction**—an employee's general attitude toward his or her job. Although job satisfaction is an attitude rather than a behavior, it's an outcome that concerns many managers because satisfied employees are more likely to show up for work, have higher levels of performance, and stay with an organization.

(6) **Workplace misbehavior**—any intentional employee behavior that is potentially harmful to the organization or individuals within the organization. Workplace misbehavior shows up in organizations in four ways: deviance, aggression, antisocial behavior, and violence.[6] Such behaviors can range from playing loud music just to irritate coworkers, to verbal aggression, to sabotaging work—all of which can create havoc in any organization.

In the following discussion, you'll get a better understanding of how four psychological factors—employee attitudes, personality, perception, and learning—can help managers predict and explain these six employee behaviors.

Delta Air Line employees have a positive attitude toward their jobs that results in high work performance. Citing good pay and benefits, free travel, profit-sharing bonuses, and a professional and friendly work environment, employees say that Delta is a great place to work. Shown here are Delta employees having a good time as models during a fashion show launching the airline's new employee uniforms.

David Joles/ZUMA Press/Newscom

What Role Do Attitudes Play in Job Performance?

10-2 Explain the role that attitudes play in job performance.

You sure have an attitude!

Attitudes are evaluative statements, either favorable or unfavorable, concerning objects, people, or events. They reflect how an individual feels about something. When a person says, "I like my job," he or she is expressing an attitude about work.

What Are the Three Components of an Attitude?

An attitude is made up of three components: cognition, affect, and behavior.[7]

- The **cognitive component** of an attitude is made up of the beliefs, opinions, knowledge, and information held by a person. For example, Tenesha feels strongly that smoking is unhealthy.

- The **affective component** is the emotional or feeling part of an attitude. This component would be reflected in the statement by Tenesha, "I don't like Carlo because he smokes." Cognition and affect can lead to behavioral outcomes.

- The **behavioral component** of an attitude refers to an intention to behave in a certain way toward someone or something. So, to continue our example, Tenesha might choose to avoid Carlo because of her feelings about his smoking habit.

Looking at attitudes as being made up of three components—cognition, affect, and behavior—helps to illustrate their complexity and helps us better understand what "precedes" someone's response, reaction, or behavior. But keep in mind that when people use the term "attitude"—as in, "that person has a bad attitude" or "I'm glad your attitude towards this is positive"—they're usually referring only to the actual affective (emotional) component. Remember that managers are trying to explain, predict, and influence people's behavior, and knowing that there's more to "attitude" than just the emotional part helps us better know how to do just that.

What Attitudes Might Employees Hold?

Adobe Systems Inc. wanted to know what makes its 18,000 employees happy—and found out by surveying different segments of its workforce every quarter in 2017. These anonymous surveys asked employees questions such as whether they felt they could be themselves at work, whether they were encouraged to think creatively, whether they felt their work contributed to overall company goals, and whether they would recommend a job with Adobe to others.[8] With this information, managers are getting a feel for how employees view the company. (See Case Application #3 for more about Adobe's approach.)

Naturally, managers are not interested in every attitude an employee might hold. Rather, they're specifically interested in the following:[9]

Job-Related Attitudes

- Job satisfaction is an employee's general attitude toward his or her job. When people speak of employee attitudes, more often than not they mean job satisfaction.

- **Job involvement** is the degree to which an employee identifies with his or her job, actively participates in it, and considers his or her job performance important for self-worth.

- **Organizational commitment** represents an employee's orientation toward the organization in terms of his or her loyalty to, identification with, and involvement in the organization.

A concept associated with job attitudes generating widespread interest is **employee engagement**, which happens when employees are connected to, satisfied with, and enthusiastic about their jobs.[10] Highly engaged employees are passionate about and deeply connected to their work. Disengaged employees have essentially "checked out" and don't care. They show up

---

attitudes
Evaluative statements, either favorable or unfavorable, concerning objects, people, or events

cognitive component
The part of an attitude made up of the beliefs, opinions, knowledge, and information held by a person

affective component
The part of an attitude that's the emotional or feeling part

behavioral component
The part of an attitude that refers to an intention to behave in a certain way toward someone or something

job involvement
The degree to which an employee identifies with his or her job, actively participates in it, and considers his or her job performance important for self-worth

organizational commitment
An employee's orientation toward the organization in terms of his or her loyalty to, identification with, and involvement in the organization

employee engagement
When employees are connected to, satisfied with, and enthusiastic about their jobs

cognitive dissonance
Any incompatibility or inconsistency between attitudes or between behavior and attitudes

for work, but have no energy or passion for it. A global study of more than 12,000 employees found that the top five factors contributing to employee engagement were:[11]

1. Respect
2. Type of work
3. Work/life balance
4. Providing good service to customers
5. Base pay

Having highly engaged employees produces both benefits and costs. Highly engaged employees are two-and-a-half times more likely to be top performers than their less-engaged coworkers. In addition, companies with highly engaged employees have higher retention rates, which help keep recruiting and training costs low. And both of these outcomes—higher performance and lower costs—contribute to superior financial performance.[12]

Do Individuals' Attitudes and Behaviors Need to Be Consistent?

What I believe is what I do . . . I hope.

Did you ever notice how people change what they say so that it doesn't contradict what they do? Perhaps a friend of yours had consistently argued that American-manufactured cars were poorly built and that he'd never own anything but a foreign import. Then his parents gave him a late-model American-made car, and suddenly they weren't so bad. Or when going through sorority rush, a new freshman believes that sororities are good and that pledging a sorority is important. If she's not accepted by a sorority, however, she may say, "Sorority life isn't all it's cracked up to be anyway."

Research generally concludes that people seek consistency among their attitudes and between their attitudes and their behavior.[13] Individuals try to reconcile differing attitudes and align their attitudes and behavior so that they appear rational and consistent. How? By altering their attitudes or their behavior *or* by developing a rationalization for the discrepancy.

What Is Cognitive Dissonance Theory?

Can we assume from this consistency principle that an individual's behavior can always be predicted if we know his or her attitude on a subject? The answer isn't a simple "yes" or "no." Why? Cognitive dissonance theory.

Cognitive dissonance theory, proposed by Leon Festinger in the 1950s, sought to explain the relationship between attitudes and behavior.[14] **Cognitive dissonance** is any incompatibility or inconsistency between attitudes or between behavior and attitudes. The theory argued that inconsistency is uncomfortable and that individuals will try to reduce the discomfort and, thus, the dissonance.

People may believe they are safe drivers yet create potentially unsafe road conditions by driving and texting at the same time. To reduce this cognitive dissonance, they may stop their habit of driving and texting, or they may rationalize that it doesn't pose a threat to others' safety and that they are in control of the situation.

Of course, no one can avoid dissonance. You know you should floss your teeth every day, but don't do it. There's an inconsistency between attitude and behavior. How do people cope with cognitive dissonance? The theory proposed that how hard we try to reduce dissonance is determined by three things: (1) the *importance* of the factors creating the dissonance, (2) the degree of *influence* the individual believes he or she has over those factors, and (3) the *rewards* that may be involved in dissonance.

If the factors creating the dissonance are relatively unimportant, the pressure to correct the inconsistency will be low. However, if those factors are important, individuals may change their behavior, conclude that the dissonant behavior isn't so important, change their attitude, or identify compatible factors that outweigh the dissonant ones.

How much influence individuals believe they have over the factors also affects their re-action to the dissonance. If they perceive the dissonance is something about which they have no choice, they won't be receptive to attitude change or feel a need to do so. If, for example, the dissonance-producing behavior was required as a result of a manager's order, the pressure to reduce dissonance would be less than if the behavior had been performed voluntarily. Although dissonance exists, it can be rationalized and justified by the need to follow the manager's orders—that is, the person had no choice or control.

Finally, rewards also influence the degree to which individuals are motivated to reduce dissonance. Coupling high dissonance with high rewards tends to reduce the discomfort by motivating the individual to believe that there is consistency.

Let's look at an example. Tracey Ford, a corporate manager, believes strongly that no company should lay off employees. Unfortunately, Tracey has to make decisions that trade off her company's strategic direction against her convictions on layoffs. She knows that organizational restructuring means some jobs may no longer be needed. She also knows layoffs are in the best economic interest of her firm. What will she do? Undoubtedly, Tracey is experiencing a high degree of cognitive dissonance. Let's explain her behavior.

1. **Importance of factors.** Because of the *importance* of the issues in this example, she can't ignore the inconsistency. To deal with her dilemma, she can follow several steps. She can change her behavior (lay off employees). Or she can reduce dissonance by concluding that the dissonant behavior is not so important after all ("I've got to make a living, and in my role as a decision maker, I often have to place the good of my company above that of individual organizational members"). She might also change her attitude ("There is nothing wrong in laying off employees"). Finally, another choice would be to seek out more consonant elements to outweigh the dissonant ones ("The long-term benefits to the surviving employees from our restructuring more than offset the associated costs").

2. **Degree of influence.** The *degree of influence* that Tracey believes she has also impacts how she reacts to the dissonance. If she perceives the dissonance to be uncontrollable—something about which she has no choice—she's less likely to feel she needs to change her attitude. If, for example, her boss told her that she had to lay off employees, the pressure to reduce dissonance would be less than if Tracey was performing the behavior voluntarily. Dissonance would exist but it could be rationalized and justified. This tendency illustrates why it's critical in today's organizations for leaders to establish an ethical culture. With the leaders' influence and support, employees won't feel as much dissonance when faced with decisions of whether to act ethically or unethically.[15]

3. **Rewards.** Finally, *rewards* also influence how likely Tracy is to reduce dissonance. High dissonance, when accompanied by high rewards, tends to reduce the tension inherent in the dissonance. The reward reduces dissonance by adding to the consistency side of the individual's balance sheet. Tracey might feel because she is well compensated in her job that she sometimes has to make hard decisions, such as laying off employees.

So, what can we say about dissonance and employee behavior? These moderating factors suggest that although individuals experience dissonance, they won't necessarily move toward consistency, that is, toward reducing the dissonance. If the issues underlying the dissonance are of minimal importance, if an individual perceives that the dissonance is externally imposed and is substantially uncontrollable, or if rewards are significant enough to offset the dissonance, the individual will not be under great tension to reduce the dissonance.[16]

Making Ethical Decisions in Today's Workplace

Have you ever faked a smile or pretended to be happy and positive? All of us have sometime, somewhere. Now research has shown that employees "fake a positive outlook when the boss is around."[17] Being ambivalent (or even negative) about your work or about working for your organization can be a definite detriment. Employers want to see passion. They want you to love your job and be excited about coming to work and about doing your job. And when you don't? If you want to keep your job, you fake it. But all that faking takes a toll.

Discussion Questions:

1 What ethical issues might arise under these circumstances for both employees and for managers? Explain how "faking" might affect other stakeholders.

2 In your assigned group, talk about your work experiences where you felt you had to fake a positive outlook. Then, come up with ideas about how managers could create an environment where employees don't have to fake a positive outlook. Be prepared to share these with your class.

How Can an Understanding of Attitudes Help Managers Be More Effective?

Managers should be interested in their employees' attitudes because they influence behavior in the following ways:

1. *Satisfied and committed employees have lower rates of turnover and absenteeism.* If managers want to keep resignations and absences down—-especially among their more productive employees—they'll want to do things that generate positive job attitudes.

2. Whether satisfied workers are productive workers is a debate that's been going on for almost 80 years. After the Hawthorne studies (see p. 57 in the History Module), managers believed that happy workers were productive workers. Because it's not easy to determine whether job satisfaction "caused" job productivity or vice versa, some management researchers felt that the belief was generally wrong. However, we can say with some certainty that the correlation between satisfaction and productivity is fairly strong.[18] *Satisfied employees do perform better on the job.* So managers should focus on those factors that have been shown to be conducive to high levels of employee job satisfaction: making work challenging and interesting, providing equitable rewards, and creating supportive working conditions and supportive colleagues.[19] These factors are likely to help employees be more productive.

3. Managers should also survey employees about their attitudes. As one study put it, "*A sound measurement of overall job attitude is one of the most useful pieces of information an organization can have about its employees.*"[20] However, research has also shown that attitude surveys can be more effective at pinpointing employee dissatisfaction if done multiple times rather than just at one point in time.[21]

4. Managers should know that *employees will try to reduce dissonance.* If employees are required to do things that appear inconsistent to them or that are at odds with their attitudes, managers should remember that pressure to reduce the dissonance is not as strong when the employee perceives that the dissonance is externally imposed and uncontrollable. It's also decreased if rewards are significant enough to offset the dissonance. So the manager might point to external forces such as competitors, customers, or other factors when explaining the need to perform some work that the individual may have some dissonance about. Or the manager can provide rewards that an individual desires.

What Do Managers Need to Know About Personality?

10-3 Describe different personality theories.

Many colleges use roommate compatibility tests to assign rooms in on-campus housing.[22] If you've ever shared a living space with someone else (family or nonfamily), you know how important it can be for roommates to be compatible and to get along with each other. This compatibility is affected and influenced by our own and by other people's personalities.

Some of us are quiet and passive; others are loud and aggressive. When we describe people using terms such as *quiet, passive, loud, aggressive, ambitious, extroverted, loyal, tense, introverted,* or *sociable,* we're describing their personalities. An individual's **personality** is a unique combination of emotional, thought, and behavioral patterns that affect how a person reacts to situations and interacts with others. Personality is most often described in terms of measurable traits that a person exhibits. We're interested in looking at personality because just like attitudes, it affects how and why people behave the way they do.

personality
A unique combination of emotional, thought, and behavioral patterns that affect how a person reacts to situations and interacts with others

---

78 percent of employers say that personality is the most important attribute in a job candidate.[23]

How Can We Best Describe Personality?

Your personality is your natural way of doing things and relating to others. *Your personality traits influence, among other things, how you interact with others and how you solve problems.* Literally dozens of behaviors are attributed to an individual's personality traits. But how can we best describe personality? Over the years, researchers have attempted to focus specifically on which personality traits and personality types would describe an individual's personality. Two widely recognized personality research efforts are the Myers-Briggs Type Indicator® and the Big Five model. In addition, we can't possibly describe personality and behavior without looking at emotions and specifically, emotional intelligence.

Myers-Briggs Type Indicator (MBTI)
A personality assessment that uses four dimensions of personality to identify different personality types

WHAT IS THE MYERS-BRIGGS TYPE INDICATOR?   One of the more widely used methods of identifying personalities is the **Myers-Briggs Type Indicator (MBTI)**. The MBTI® assessment uses four dimensions of personality to identify 16 different personality types based on the responses to an approximately 100-item questionnaire. The MBTI personality assessment is used by some 80 percent of *Fortune* 1000 companies.[24]

The 16 personality types are based on four dimensions:

- *Extraversion versus Introversion (EI)*
  - The EI dimension describes an individual's orientation toward the external world of the environment (E) or the inner world of ideas and experiences (I).
- *Sensing versus Intuition (SN)*
  - The SN dimension indicates an individual's preference for gathering data while focusing on a standard routine based on factual data (S) to focusing on the big picture and making connections among the facts (N).
- *Thinking versus Feeling (TF)*
  - The TF dimension reflects one's preference for making decisions in a logical and analytical manner (T) or on the basis of values and beliefs and the effects the decision will have on others (F).
- *Judging versus Perceiving (JP)*
  - The JP dimension reflects an attitude toward how one deals with the external world—either in a planned and orderly way (J) or preferring to remain flexible and spontaneous (P).[25]

Let's give you some examples:

- ISTJ (Introversion Sensing Thinking Judging)—quiet, serious, dependable, practical, and matter-of-fact
- ESFP (Extraversion Sensing Feeling Perceiving)—outgoing, friendly, spontaneous, enjoys working with others, and learns best by trying a new skill with other people
- INFP (Introversion Intuition Feeling Perceiving)—idealistic, loyal to personal values, and seeks to understand people and help them fulfill their potential
- ENTJ (Extraversion Intuition Thinking Judging)—frank, decisive, and will assume leadership roles; also enjoys long-term planning and goal setting and is forceful in presenting ideas[26]

How can the MBTI assessment help managers? Proponents believe that it's important to know these personality types because they influence the way people interact and solve problems.[27] For example, if your boss prefers Intuition and you're a Sensing type, you'll deal with information in different ways. An Intuition preference indicates your boss is one who prefers gut reactions, whereas you, as a Sensing type, prefer to deal with the facts. To work well with your boss, you have to present more than just facts about a situation—you'll also have to discuss your gut feeling about the situation. The MBTI assessment has also been found to be useful in focusing on growth orientations for entrepreneurial types as well as profiles supporting emotional intelligence (something we'll look at shortly).[28]

Big Five model
A personality trait model that examines five traits: extraversion, agreeableness, conscientiousness, emotional stability, and openness to experience

emotional intelligence (EI)
The ability to notice and to manage emotional cues and information

WHAT IS THE BIG FIVE MODEL OF PERSONALITY? Another way of viewing personality is through a five-factor model of personality—more typically called the **Big Five model**.[29] The Big Five factors are:

1 Extraversion — A personality dimension that describes the degree to which someone is sociable, talkative, and assertive.

2 Agreeableness — A personality dimension that describes the degree to which someone is good-natured, cooperative, and trusting.

3 Conscientiousness — A personality dimension that describes the degree to which someone is responsible, dependable, persistent, and achievement oriented.

4 Emotional stability — A personality dimension that describes the degree to which someone is calm, enthusiastic, and secure (positive) or tense, nervous, depressed, and insecure (negative).

5 Openness to experience — A personality dimension that describes the degree to which someone is imaginative, artistically sensitive, and intellectual.

The Big Five model provides more than just a personality framework. Research has shown that important relationships exist between these personality dimensions and job performance.[30] For example, one study reviewed five categories of occupations: professionals (e.g., engineers, architects, attorneys), police, managers, sales, and semiskilled and skilled employees. Job performance was defined in terms of employee performance ratings, training competency, and personnel data such as salary level. The results of the study showed that conscientiousness predicted job performance for all five occupational groups.[31] Predictions for the other personality dimensions depended on the situation and the occupational group. For example, extraversion predicted performance in managerial and sales positions, in which high social interaction is necessary.[32] Openness to experience was found to be important in predicting training competency. Ironically, emotional security was not positively related to job performance. Although it would seem logical that calm and secure workers would be better performers, that wasn't the case. Perhaps it's a function of the likelihood that emotionally stable workers often keep their jobs and emotionally unstable people may not. Given that all those participating in the study were employed, the variance on that dimension was probably small.

The personality dimension of extraversion of the Big Five model applies to entrepreneur Sara Blakely, founder of Spanx. Being sociable, talkative, and assertive contributed to Blakely's launch and development of her enormously successful undergarment venture. Blakely (at left) is shown here introducing her employee team to shoppers at a new Spanx store in Tampa.

Will Vragovic/Tampa Bay Times/ZUMAPRESS.com/Alamy Live News/Alamy Stock Photo

WHAT IS EMOTIONAL INTELLIGENCE? *People who understand their own emotions and are good at reading others' emotions may be more effective in their jobs.* That, in essence, is the theme of the underlying research on emotional intelligence.[33]

Emotional intelligence (EI) refers to an assortment of noncognitive skills, capabilities, and competencies that influences a person's ability to cope with environmental demands and pressures.[34] It's composed of five dimensions:

- *Self-awareness.* Being aware of what you're feeling.
- *Self-management.* Managing your own emotions and impulses.
- *Self-motivation.* Persisting in the face of setbacks and failures.
- *Empathy.* Sensing how others are feeling.
- *Social skills.* Adapting to and handling the emotions of others.

Managing Technology in Today's Workplace

INCREASED RELIANCE ON EMOTIONAL INTELLIGENCE

Even as technology allows more and more employees to move to offsite work arrangements, that doesn't mean that they won't be interacting with others. Nope...they'll still have ongoing contact with colleagues and customers. And whether it goes by the name of emotional intelligence, social intelligence, or something else, the ability to understand yourself and others will be a skill that organizations will seek when hiring employees. **The ability to get along with others—coworkers, colleagues, team members, bosses, and customers—will be critical to success in most jobs.** Those employees who have strong technical skills but are weak on emotional intelligence will find it increasingly difficult to find and hold a job.

Discussion Questions:

3 Why do you think the ability to get along with others is so critical?

4 How can you develop this ability? Come up with some ideas on your own. Then, in your assigned group, compare your ideas and compile a list of ways to develop emotional intelligence in each of the five dimensions of emotional intelligence. Be prepared to share with your classmates.

Several studies suggest that EI may play an important role in job performance.[35] For instance, one study looked at the characteristics of Bell Lab engineers who were rated as stars by their peers. The scientists concluded that these stars were better at relating to others. That is, it was EI, not academic IQ, that characterized high performers. A second study of Air Force recruiters generated similar findings: Top-performing recruiters exhibited high levels of EI. Using these findings, the Air Force revamped its selection criteria. A follow-up investigation found that future hires who had high EI scores were 2.6 times more successful than those with low scores. Organizations such as American Express have found that implementing emotional intelligence programs has helped increase its effectiveness; other organizations also found similar results showing that emotional intelligence contributes to team effectiveness.[36] For instance, at Cooperative Printing in Minneapolis, a study of its 45 employees concluded that EI skills were twice as important in "contributing to excellence as intellect and expertise alone."[37] A poll of human resources managers asked this question: How important is it for your workers to demonstrate EI to move up the corporate ladder? Forty percent of the managers replied "very important." Another 16 percent said moderately important. Other studies also indicated that emotional intelligence can be beneficial to quality improvements in contemporary organizations.[38]

The implication is that employers should consider emotional intelligence as a criterion in their selection process—especially for those jobs that demand a high degree of social interaction.[39]

Can Personality Traits Predict Practical Work-Related Behaviors?

In a word, "YES!" Five specific personality traits have proven most powerful in explaining individual behavior in organizations. Let's take a look.

1. Who has control over an individual's behavior? Some people believe that they control their own fate. Others see themselves as pawns of fate, believing that what happens to them in their lives is due to luck or chance. The **locus of control** in the first case is internal. In the second case, it is external; these people believe that their lives are controlled by outside forces.[40] A manager might also expect to find that externals blame a poor performance evaluation on their boss's prejudice, their coworkers, or other events outside their control, whereas "internals" explain the same evaluation in terms of their own actions.

2. The second characteristic is called **Machiavellianism ("Mach")**, after Niccolo Machiavelli, who provided instruction in the sixteenth century on how to gain and manipulate power. An individual who is high in Machiavellianism is pragmatic, maintains emotional distance, believes that ends can justify the means,[41] and may have beliefs that are less ethical.[42] The philosophy "if it works, use it" is consistent with a high Mach perspective. Do high Machs make good employees? That answer depends on the type of job and

locus of control
The degree to which people believe they control their own fate

Machiavellianism ("Mach")
A measure of the degree to which people are pragmatic, maintain emotional distance, and believe that ends justify means

self-esteem (SE)
An individual's degree of like or dislike for himself or herself

self-monitoring
A personality trait that measures the ability to adjust behavior to external situational factors

whether you consider ethical implications in evaluating performance. In jobs that require bargaining skills (a labor negotiator) or that have substantial rewards for winning (a commissioned salesperson), high Machs are productive. In jobs in which ends do not justify the means or that lack absolute standards of performance, it's difficult to predict the performance of high Machs.

3. People differ in the degree to which they like or dislike themselves. This trait is called **self-esteem (SE)**.[43] The research on SE offers some interesting insights into organizational behavior. For example, SE is directly related to expectations for success. High SEs believe that they possess the ability to succeed at work. Individuals with high SE will take more risks in job selection and are more likely to choose unconventional jobs than are people with low SE.[44] The most common finding on self-esteem is that low SEs are more susceptible to external influence than are high SEs. Low SEs are dependent on positive evaluations from others. As a result, they're more likely to seek approval from others and more prone to conform to the beliefs and behaviors of those they respect than are high SEs. In managerial positions, low SEs will tend to be concerned with pleasing others and, therefore, will be less likely to take unpopular stands than will high SEs. Not surprisingly, self-esteem has also been found to be related to job satisfaction. A number of studies confirm that high SEs are more satisfied with their jobs than are low SEs.

4. Another personality trait researchers have identified is called **self-monitoring**.[45] Individuals high in self-monitoring can show considerable adaptability in adjusting their behavior to external, situational factors.[46] They're highly sensitive to external cues and can behave differently in different situations. High self-monitors are capable of presenting striking contradictions between their public persona and their private selves. Low self-monitors can't alter their behavior. They tend to display their true dispositions and attitudes in every situation; hence, they exhibit high behavioral consistency between who they are and what they do. Evidence suggests that high self-monitors tend to pay closer attention to the behavior of others and are more capable of conforming than are low self-monitors.[47] We might also hypothesize that high self-monitors will be more successful in managerial positions that require individuals to play multiple, and even contradicting, roles.

5. The final personality trait influencing worker behavior reflects the willingness to take chances—the propensity for *risk taking*. A preference to assume or avoid risk has been shown to have an impact on how long it takes individuals to make a decision and how much information they require before making their choice. For instance, in one classic study, 79 managers worked on a simulated human resources management exercise that required them to make hiring decisions.[48] High-risk-taking managers made more rapid decisions and used less information in making their choices than did the low-risk-taking managers. Interestingly, the decision accuracy was the same for both groups.

Although it's generally correct to conclude that managers in organizations are risk averse, especially in large companies and government agencies,[49] individual differences are still found on this dimension.[50] As a result, it makes sense to recognize these differences and even to consider aligning risk-taking propensity with specific job demands. For instance, a high-risk-taking propensity may lead to effective performance for a stock trader in a brokerage firm since this type of job demands rapid decision making. The same holds true for the entrepreneur.[51] On the other hand, this personality characteristic might prove a major obstacle to accountants performing auditing activities, which might be better done by someone with a low-risk-taking propensity.

In this photo, entrepreneur Elon Musk is applauded by employees during his presentation of a new Tesla model. Musk's high risk-taking propensity has resulted in his successful job performance in launching firms in different industries: PayPal, an Internet payment firm; Tesla Motors, maker of electric vehicles and batteries; Space Exploration Technologies (SpaceX), maker of rockets and spacecraft; and Solar City, producer of solar panels.

Andrej Sokolow/dpa picture alliance/Alamy Stock Photo

How Do We Match Personalities and Jobs?

We all want a job that **fits our personality.**

"What if you're not happy in your job? Is it possible that you're in the wrong career entirely?"[52] As you do your job day by day, you may realize that your tasks don't mesh well with your personality or talents. Wouldn't it seem to make more sense to strive for a match between your personality and your chosen job or career path?

Obviously, individual personalities differ. So, too, do jobs. How do we match the two? The best-documented personality–job fit theory was developed by psychologist John Holland.[53] His theory states that an employee's satisfaction with his or her job, as well as his or her likelihood of leaving that job, depends on the degree to which the individual's personality matches the job environment. Holland identified six basic personality types, as shown in Exhibit 10–2.

Holland's theory proposes that satisfaction is highest and turnover lowest when personality and occupation are compatible.[54] Social individuals should be in "people-type" jobs, and so forth. The key points of this theory include the following: (1) there do appear to be intrinsic differences in personality among individuals, (2) there are different types of jobs, and (3) people in job environments compatible with their personality types should be more satisfied and less likely to resign voluntarily than people in incongruent jobs.

Exhibit 10–2 Holland's Personality-Job Fit

TYPE	PERSONALITY CHARACTERISTICS	SAMPLE OCCUPATIONS
Realistic. Prefers physical activities that require skill, strength, and coordination	Shy, genuine, persistent, stable, conforming, practical	Mechanic, drill press operator, assembly-line worker, farmer
Investigative. Prefers activities involving thinking, organizing, and understanding	Analytical, original, curious, independent	Biologist, economist, mathematician, news reporter
Social. Prefers activities that involve helping and developing others	Sociable, friendly, cooperative, understanding	Social worker, teacher, counselor, clinical psychologist
Conventional. Prefers rule-regulated, orderly, and unambiguous activities	Conforming, efficient, practical, unimaginative, inflexible	Accountant, corporate manager, bank teller, file clerk
Enterprising. Prefers verbal activities that offer opportunities to influence others and attain power	Self-confident, ambitious, energetic, domineering	Lawyer, real estate agent, public relations specialist, small business manager
Artistic. Prefers ambiguous and unsystematic activities that allow creative expression	Imaginative, disorderly, idealistic, emotional, impractical	Painter, musician, writer, interior decorator

Source: Robbins, Stephen P., Coulter, Mary, *Management*, 13th Ed., © 2016, p. 444. Reprinted and electronically reproduced by permission of Pearson Education, Inc., New York, NY.

Jean-Paul Pelissier/Reuters

Understanding the differences in the emphasis countries place on personality dimensions helps managers of global companies. For example, knowing that the trait of conscientiousness is a valid predictor of performance in European Community nations helps U.S.-based Burger King manage employees such as this BK employee in France.

Do Personality Attributes Differ Across Cultures?

Do personality frameworks, like the Big Five model, transfer across cultures? Are dimensions like locus of control relevant in all cultures? Let's try to answer these questions.

The five personality factors studied in the Big Five model appear in almost all cross-cultural studies.[55] A wide variety of diverse cultures—such as China, Israel, Germany, Japan, Spain, Nigeria, Norway, Pakistan, and the United States—have been the setting for these studies. Differences are found in the emphasis on dimensions. The Chinese, for example, use the category of conscientiousness more often and use the category of agreeableness less often than do Americans. But a surprisingly high amount of agreement is found, especially among individuals from developed countries. As a case in point, a comprehensive review of studies covering people from the European Community found that conscientiousness was a valid predictor of performance across jobs and occupational groups.[56] U.S. studies found the same results.

We know that there are certainly no common personality types for a given country. You can, for instance, find high risk takers and low risk takers in almost any culture. Yet a country's culture influences the *dominant* personality characteristics of its people. We can see this effect of national culture by looking at one of the personality traits we just discussed: locus of control.

National cultures differ in terms of the degree to which people believe they control their environment. For instance, North Americans believe that they can dominate their environment; other societies, such as those in Middle Eastern countries, believe that life is essentially predetermined. Notice how closely this distinction parallels the concept of internal and external locus of control. On the basis of this particular cultural characteristic, we should expect a larger proportion of internals in the U.S. and Canadian workforces than in the workforces of Saudi Arabia or Iran.

As we have seen throughout this section, personality traits influence employees' behavior. For global managers, understanding how personality traits differ takes on added significance when looking at it from the perspective of national culture.

How Can an Understanding of Personality Help Managers Be More Effective?

Managers should be interested in their employees' personalities because those personalities influence their behavior in the following ways:

1. **Job–person compatibility.** Some 62 percent of companies are using personality tests when recruiting and hiring.[57] And that's where the major value in understanding personality differences probably lies. Managers are likely to have higher-performing and more-satisfied employees if consideration is given to matching personalities with jobs.

2. **Understanding different approaches to work.** By recognizing that people approach problem solving, decision making, and job interactions differently, a manager can better understand why, for instance, an employee is uncomfortable with making quick decisions or why an employee insists on gathering as much information as possible before addressing a problem. For instance, managers can expect that individuals with an external locus of control may be less satisfied with their jobs than those with an internal locus and also that they may be less willing to accept responsibility for their actions.

3. **Being a better manager.** Being a successful manager and accomplishing goals means working well together with others both inside and outside the organization. In order to work effectively together, you need to understand each other. This understanding comes, at least in part, from an appreciation of personality traits and emotions. Also, one of the

skills you have to develop as a manager is learning to fine-tune your emotional reactions according to the situation. In other words, you have to learn to recognize "when you have to smile and when you have to bark."[58]

What Is Perception and What Influences It?

10-4 Describe perception and the factors that influence it.

We interpret what we see and call it reality.

"L ke y ur b ain, the n w L nd Rov r autom tic lly adj sts to anyth ng."[59] This advertisement for a Land Rover SUV illustrates the perceptual process at work. You were likely able to read the sentence even with the missing letters because you recognized the word patterns and organized and interpreted them in a way that made sense.

Perception is a process by which we give meaning to our environment by organizing and interpreting sensory impressions. Research on perception consistently demonstrates that individuals may look at the same thing yet perceive it differently. One manager, for instance, can interpret the fact that her assistant regularly takes several days to make important decisions as evidence that the assistant is slow, disorganized, and afraid to make decisions. Another manager with the same assistant might interpret the same tendency as evidence that the assistant is thoughtful, thorough, and deliberate. The first manager would probably evaluate her assistant negatively; the second manager would probably evaluate the person positively. The point is that none of us see reality. *We interpret what we see and call it reality.* And, of course, as the example shows, we behave according to our perceptions.

What Influences Perception?

How do we explain the fact that Moranda, a marketing supervisor for a large commercial petroleum products organization, age 52, noticed Ambrose's nose ring during his employment interview, and Sean, a human resources recruiter, age 23, didn't? A number of factors operate to shape and sometimes distort perception. These factors can reside in (1) the perceiver, (2) the object or target being perceived, or (3) the context of the situation in which the perception is made.

1. When an individual looks at a target and attempts to interpret what he or she sees, that individual's personal characteristics will heavily influence the interpretation. These personal characteristics include attitudes, personality, motives, interests, past experiences, and expectations.

2. The characteristics of the target being observed can also affect what is perceived. Loud people are more likely than quiet people to be noticed in a group. So, too, are extremely attractive or unattractive individuals. Because targets are not looked at in isolation, the relationship of a target to its background also influences perception (see Exhibit 10–3 for an example), as does our tendency to group close things and similar things together.

perception
A process by which we give meaning to our environment by organizing and interpreting sensory impressions

Exhibit 10–3 Perceptual Challenges—What Do You See?

Old woman or young woman?   Two faces or an urn?   A knight on a horse?

3. The context in which we see objects or events is also important. The time at which an object or event is seen can influence attention, as can location, lighting, temperature, and any number of other situational factors.

How Do Managers Judge Employees?

Much of the research on perception is directed at inanimate objects. Managers, though, are more concerned with people. Our perceptions of people differ from our perceptions of such inanimate objects as computers, robots, or buildings because we make inferences about the actions of people that we don't, of course, make about inanimate objects. When we observe people, we attempt to develop explanations of why they behave in certain ways. Our perception and judgment of a person's actions, therefore, will be significantly influenced by the assumptions we make about the person's internal state. Many of these assumptions have led researchers to develop attribution theory.

WHAT IS ATTRIBUTION THEORY?   **Attribution theory** has been proposed to explain how we judge people differently depending on what meaning we attribute to a given behavior.[60] Basically, the theory suggests that when we observe an individual's behavior, we attempt to determine whether it was internally or externally caused. *Internally caused behavior* is believed to be under the control of the individual. *Externally caused behavior* results from outside causes; that is, the person is seen as having been forced into the behavior by the situation. That determination, however, depends on three factors: (1) distinctiveness, (2) consensus, and (3) consistency.

1. *Distinctiveness* refers to whether an individual displays a behavior in many situations or whether it is particular to one situation. Is the employee who arrived late to work today also the person coworkers see as a goof-off? What we want to know is whether this behavior is unusual. If it is, the observer is likely to give the behavior an external attribution. If this action is not unique, it will probably be judged as internal.

2. If everyone who is faced with a similar situation responds in the same way, we can say the behavior shows *consensus*. Our tardy employee's behavior would meet this criterion if all employees who took the same route to work today were also late. If consensus is high, you would be expected to give an external attribution to the employee's tardiness, whereas if other employees who took the same route made it to work on time, you would conclude the reason to be internal.

3. Finally, a manager looks for *consistency* in an employee's actions. Does the individual engage in the behaviors regularly and consistently? Does the employee respond the same way over time? Coming in 10 minutes late for work is not perceived in the same way if, for one employee, it represents an unusual case (she hasn't been late for several months), but for another it is part of a routine pattern (he is late two or three times a week). The more consistent the behavior, the more the observer is inclined to attribute it to internal causes.

Exhibit 10–4 summarizes the key elements in attribution theory. It would tell us, for instance, that if an employee, Mr. Black, generally performs at about the same level on other related tasks as he does on his current task (low distinctiveness), if other employees frequently perform differently—better or worse—than Mr. Black does on that current task (low consensus), and if Mr. Black's performance on this current task is consistent over time (high

Exhibit 10–4 Attribution Theory

OBSERVATION	INTERPRETATION	ATTRIBUTION OF CAUSE
Does person behave this way in other situations?	**YES:** Low distinctiveness **NO:** High distinctiveness	Internal attribution External attribution
Do other people behave the same way in similar situations?	**YES:** High consensus **NO:** Low consensus	External attribution Internal attribution
Does person behave this way consistently?	**YES:** High consistency **NO:** Low consistency	Internal attribution External attribution

Source: Robbins, Stephen P., Coulter, Mary, *Management*, 13th Ed., © 2016, p. 447. Reprinted and electronically reproduced by permission of Pearson Education, Inc., New York, NY.

fundamental attribution error
The tendency to underestimate the influence of external factors and overestimate the influence of internal factors when making judgments about the behavior of others

self-serving bias
The tendency for individuals to attribute their successes to internal factors while putting the blame for failures on external factors

selective perception
The tendency for people to only absorb parts of what they observe, which allows us to "speed read" others

consistency), his manager or anyone else who is judging Mr. Black's work is likely to hold him primarily responsible for his task performance (internal attribution).

CAN ATTRIBUTIONS BE DISTORTED?   One of the more interesting findings drawn from attribution theory is that errors or biases distort attributions. For instance, substantial evidence supports the hypothesis that when we make judgments about the behavior of other people, we have a tendency to underestimate the influence of external factors and overestimate the influence of internal or personal factors.[61] This **fundamental attribution error** can explain why a sales manager may be prone to attribute the poor performance of her sales agents to laziness rather than to the innovative product line introduced by a competitor. Individuals also tend to attribute their own successes to internal factors such as ability or effort while putting the blame for failure on external factors such as luck (or an "unfair" test). This **self-serving bias** suggests that feedback provided to employees in performance reviews will be predictably distorted by them, whether it is positive or negative.

WHAT PERCEPTUAL SHORTCUTS DO WE USE?   All of us, managers included, use a number of shortcuts to judge others. Perceiving and interpreting people's behavior is a lot of work, so we use shortcuts to make the task more manageable.[62] Such shortcuts can be valuable when they let us make accurate perceptions quickly and provide valid data for making predictions. However, they aren't perfect. They can and do get us into trouble. What are these perceptual shortcuts? (See Exhibit 10–5 for a summary.)

Individuals can't assimilate all they observe, so they're selective in their perception. They absorb bits and pieces. These bits and pieces are not chosen randomly; rather, they're selectively chosen depending on the interests, background, experience, and attitudes of the observer. **Selective perception** allows us to "speed read" others—but not without the risk of drawing an inaccurate picture.

Stereotyping generalizes that women lack the technical skills and emotional and physical strength required to succeed in auto racing. In announcing the formation of Grace Autosport, the first all-female IndyCar racing team, British race car driver Katherine Legge (right) purports that gender should not be a barrier to pursuing a successful career in motorsports.

Michael Conroy/AP Images

assumed similarity
An observer's perception of others influenced more by the observer's own characteristics than by those of the person observed

stereotyping
When we judge someone on the basis of our perception of a group to which that person belongs

halo effect
When we form a general impression of a person on the basis of a single characteristic

Exhibit 10-5 Perceptual Shortcuts

SHORTCUT	WHAT IT IS	DISTORTION
Selectivity	People assimilate certain bits and pieces of what they observe depending on their interests, background, experience, and attitudes	"Speed reading" others may result in an inaccurate picture of them
Assumed similarity	People assume that others are like them	May fail to take into account individual differences, resulting in incorrect similarities
Stereotyping	People judge others on the basis of their perception of a group to which the others belong	May result in distorted judgments because many stereotypes have no factual foundation
Halo effect	People form an impression of others on the basis of a single trait	Fails to take into account the total picture of what an individual has done

It's easy to judge others if we assume that they're similar to us. In **assumed similarity**, or the "like me" effect, the observer's perception of others is influenced more by the observer's own characteristics than by those of the person observed. For example, if you want challenges and responsibility in your job, you'll assume that others want the same. People who assume that others are like them can, of course, be right, but not always.

When we judge someone on the basis of our perception of a group he or she is part of, we're using the shortcut called **stereotyping**. For instance, "Married people are more stable employees than single persons" or "Older employees are absent more often from work" are examples of stereotyping. To the degree that a stereotype is based on fact, it may produce accurate judgments. However, many stereotypes aren't factual and distort our judgment.

When we form a general impression about a person on the basis of a single characteristic, such as intelligence, sociability, or appearance, we're being influenced by the **halo effect**. This effect frequently occurs when students evaluate their classroom instructor. Students may isolate a single trait such as enthusiasm and allow their entire evaluation to be slanted by the perception of this one trait. If an instructor who is quiet, assured, knowledgeable, and highly qualified has a classroom teaching style that lacks enthusiasm, that instructor might be rated lower on a number of other characteristics.

How Can an Understanding of Perception Help Managers Be More Effective?

Managers should be interested in perception because it helps them understand employee behavior in the following ways:

1. Managers need to recognize that their employees react to perceptions, not to reality. So whether a manager's appraisal of an employee's performance is actually objective and unbiased or whether the organization's wage levels are among the highest in the community is less relevant than what employees perceive them to be. If individuals perceive appraisals to be biased or wage levels as low, they'll behave as if those conditions actually exist.

2. Employees organize and interpret what they see, so there is always the potential for perceptual distortion. The message is clear: Pay close attention to how employees perceive both their jobs and management actions. Remember, the valuable employee who quits because of an inaccurate perception is just as great a loss to an organization as the valuable employee who quits for a valid reason.

How Do Learning Theories Explain Behavior?

Almost all behavior is learned.

 10-5 Discuss learning theories and their relevance in shaping behavior.

What Is **Learning**?

- Considerably broader than average person's view that "it's what you do in school."
- Occurs all the time as we continually learn from our experiences.

1 **Operant conditioning**—behavior is a function of its consequences.

- People learn to behave to get something they want or to avoid something they don't want.
- Voluntary or learned behavior, not reflexive or unlearned behavior.
- Tendency to repeat learned behavior is influenced by:

  - Reinforcement → strengthens a behavior and increases the likelihood it will be repeated.

  - Lack of reinforcement → weakens a behavior and lessens the likelihood it will be repeated.

- Examples of operant conditioning are everywhere—in any situation where *(explicitly or implicitly)* reinforcement *(rewards)* are contingent on some action on your part.

  - For more information on operant conditioning, see the Classic Concepts in Today's Workplace box on p. 378.

learning
A relatively permanent change in behavior that occurs as a result of experience

operant conditioning
A theory of learning that says behavior is a function of its consequences

Andres Rodriguez/Alamy

2 Social learning theory—learning both through observation and direct experience.[63]

- Influence of models, such as parents, teachers, peers, celebrities, managers, and so forth, is central to social learning.
- Four processes determine the amount of influence these models have:

1 Attentional processes. People learn from a model when they recognize and pay attention to its critical features.

2 Retention processes. A model's influence will depend on how well the individual remembers the model's action, even after the model is no longer readily available.

3 Motor reproduction processes. After a person has seen a new behavior by observing the model, the watching must become doing.

4 Reinforcement processes. Individuals will be motivated to exhibit the modeled behavior if positive incentives or rewards are provided. Reinforced behaviors will be given more attention, learned better, and performed more often.

Shaping Behavior
Putting Learning Theory into Practice

WHY
- Managers can teach employees to behave in ways that most benefit the organization.[64]

HOW
- Guide learning in graduated steps, that is, **shaping behavior**.

Vladimir Nenov/Alamy Stock Photo

---

social learning theory
A theory of learning that says people can learn through observation and direct experience

shaping behavior
The process of guiding learning in graduated steps, using reinforcement or lack of reinforcement

Four ways to shape behavior:

1 **Positive reinforcement:** Follow a desired behavior with something pleasant—a manager praising an employee for a job well done.

2 **Negative reinforcement:** Follow a desired behavior by terminating or withdrawing something unpleasant—a manager telling an employee he won't dock her pay if she starts coming to work on time. The only way for the employee to not have her pay docked is to come to work on time, which is the behavior the manager wants.

3 **Punishment** penalizes undesirable behavior—suspending an employee for two days without pay for showing up drunk.

4 **Extinction** is not reinforcing (ignoring) a behavior, making it gradually disappear.

Both punishment and extinction also result in learning; however, they weaken behavior and tend to decrease its subsequent frequency.

Both positive and negative reinforcement result in learning. They strengthen a desired response and increase the probability of repetition.

How Can an Understanding of Learning Help Managers Be More Effective?

Manage Employees' Learning

Employees are going to learn on the job. Are managers going to manage their learning through **(1)** the rewards they allocate and the examples they set, or **(2)** allow it to occur haphazardly?

Watch What You Reward:

If managers want behavior A, but reward behavior B, they shouldn't be surprised to find employees learning to engage in behavior B.

Watch What You Do:

Managers should expect that employees will look to them as models and do what they do.

Carlos's Pemium Images/Alamy Stock Photo

◄◄◄ Classic Concepts in Today's Workplace ►►►

To better understand operant conditioning, we need to first look at a different perspective on learning—classical conditioning theory. In classical conditioning, something happens, and we react in a specific way. As such, it can explain simple reflexive behavior. For instance, classical conditioning can explain why a scheduled visit by the "top brass" brings flurried activities of cleaning, straightening, and rearranging at a local outlet of a major retail company. However, most behavior by people at work is voluntary rather than reflexive; that is, employees choose to arrive at work on time, ask their boss for help with some problem, or "goof off" when no one is watching.

A better explanation for behavior is operant conditioning, which says that people behave the way they do so they can get something they want or avoid something they don't want. It's voluntary or learned behavior, not reflexive or unlearned behavior. Harvard psychologist B. F. Skinner first identified the process of operant conditioning and his research widely expanded our knowledge of it.[65] He argued that creating pleasing consequences to follow specific forms of behavior would increase the frequency of that behavior. Skinner demonstrated that people will most likely engage

in desired behaviors if they're positively reinforced for doing so, that rewards are most effective if they immediately follow the desired response (behavior), and that behavior that is not rewarded or is punished is less likely to be repeated. For example, a professor places a mark by a student's name each time the student makes a contribution to class discussions. Operant conditioning would argue that this practice is motivating because it conditions a student to expect a reward (earning class credit) each time she demonstrates a specific behavior (speaking up in class). Operant conditioning can be seen in work settings as well. And smart managers quickly recognize that they can use operant conditioning to shape employees' behaviors to get work done in the most effective and efficient manner possible.

> Learn how to **SHAPE SOMEONE'S BEHAVIOR!**

Discussion Questions:

5 How do classical conditioning and operant conditioning differ?

6 Might ethical concerns arise in "shaping" someone's behavior? Explain.

What Contemporary OB Issues Face Managers?

10-6 Discuss contemporary issues in OB.

By this point, you're probably well aware of why managers *need to understand* how *and* why *employees behave the way they do*. We conclude this chapter by looking at two OB issues having a major influence on managers' jobs today.

How Do Generational Differences Affect the Workplace?

In today's workplace, Baby Boomers, Generation X, Generation Y, and now, Generation Z are working side-by-side. Anecdotal and empirical evidence suggests that members of these four generational groups have significantly different attitudes on a range of work-related issues, including communication, uses of technology, work/life balance and preferred leadership styles. Attitudinal differences can cause conflicts and resentment to arise, making it important for managers to help coworkers understand the causes and consequences of different perspectives. Differing priorities and preferences mean managers need to be flexible and accommodating about work and work arrangements but also ensure equity and fairness. That's why it's important to understand how the generational groups differ and how generational differences can be managed.

WHAT ARE THE GENERATIONAL GROUPS? Members of each generation develop their work perspectives, attitudes, and behaviors from the influence of: their educational environment; their family situation; and the cultural, social, economic, and political conditions that they experienced when their impressions of what work is and how they're supposed to approach work were being formed. Common experiences cause members of a generational group to develop similar attitudes, which then distinguish them from members of other generational groups. Each generational group has a lot to offer organizations in terms of their knowledge, passions, and abilities. Managers, however, have to recognize and understand the behaviors of each group in order to create an environment in which work can be accomplished efficiently, effectively, and without disruptive conflict.

Baby Boomers, born between 1945 and 1964, grew up post–World War II in relative prosperity and safety but have experienced significant social and technological change over their lifetime, including the first explorations of space, the development of television and the contraceptive pill, and events such as the Vietnam War and Woodstock. Boomers tend to embrace growth and change and to be competitive and goal-oriented. Boomers—the generation that saw a vast number of women enter the workforce—pushed the working week from 40 hours up to 60 to 70 hours which, combined with single-parent households, aging parents, demanding jobs and approaching retirement, makes them susceptible to burn-out and stress-related illness.

Generation X, born between 1965 and 1977, grew up as the children of divorce and single-parent Boomer families, meaning many Gen Xers were raised as "latch-key" kids whose parents worked outside the home. Consequently, Gen Xers tend to be very independent, adaptable, and resilient, but also tend to feel very overlooked and unappreciated. As the first generation to use personal computers, they are technologically savvy. But having grown up during the AIDS epidemic and having seen their parents work hard only to be downsized, they also tend to be cynical and question authority. They prioritize career security rather than job security, focusing on building skills and experience to stay employable. They see job instability as part of employment and also tend to prioritize family over work. They're loyal to immediate supervisors and peers rather than to an organization, and if dissatisfied with a job, will simply leave.

Generation Y (Millennials), born between 1978 and 1994, are considered the most educated, traveled, and technologically proficient generation ever. Having grown up with the Internet, mobile phones, and DVDs, they are very comfortable using and communicating with technology. Like Gen Xers, they are independent, entrepreneurial, confident, prone to question, and seek immediate results for their efforts. They also share with Gen Xers a desire to live rather than live to work, to ensure that life is fun, and to win. They value work opportunities for creativity and personal growth and like to have strong personal connections to their immediate boss. However, they also see employment as a contract rather than a vocation and will sacrifice income and promotion for better work/life balance.

Generation Z, born between 1995 and 2010, is the most recent wave to hit the workforce. This group has grown up during a fairly prosperous period. Their parents have been involved in every aspect of their lives, providing direction, support, and coaching. This group also has never known a world without individually customized technology everywhere. They have only known "smart" phones and have had any bit or type of information available 24/7 at a touch. This post-millennial smartphone generation views the workplace as inclusive, and they're very comfortable working with people from different backgrounds and cultures. Gen Z employees very much want employers whose values reflect their own and will seek out a good match. Having a purpose in their work also is extremely important.

Apple Inc. describes itself as "an intergenerational company with employees from 18 to 85." Shown here is Apple CEO Tim Cook (center) with high school students attending the company's Worldwide Developers Conference. With their knowledge of and reliance on technology, Apple embraces this young, diverse Generation Z group as a major source of ideas and catalysts of innovation.

Bloomberg/Getty Images

Gen Z is an optimistic group who has a strong affinity for technology and its power to change things.

DEALING WITH THE MANAGERIAL CHALLENGES. Managing generational differences in the workplace presents some unique challenges. Conflicts and resentment can arise over issues such as different concepts of "professionalism" and ideas about what constitutes "appropriate" presentation—appearance, dress, and language; communication style—media used, forms of address, timeliness, and comprehensiveness; work ethic and time management—managing deadlines, face-time, time off, flexibility, and spending office time on personal activities; and management style. For example, Gen X and Gen Y often think Boomers overemphasize explanations and face-to-face meetings, taking up time that could be used for other purposes. Boomers perceive that Gen X and Gen Y over-rely on e-mail, instant messaging, and texting when communicating via phone or in-person would be more effective. Boomers believe that being a team player means that everyone on the team, whatever their role, should contribute until the task is completed. Gen Xers believe that each team member should have a unique role to execute, and they consider that their contribution is finished once they have completed their individual assignment. Gen Ys prefer to work in groups and teams but, before joining, want to know why contributing to the team is meaningful and worth their while. What about Gen Z, the newest age group to be joining the workforce? This generation is ambitious and wants to prove themselves immediately. They want flexibility and responsibility...right now. They're confident and extremely tech savvy. Their reliance on technology can be a significant advantage, however, as can Gen Z's comfort levels with diverse groups and opinions. On the other hand, they often have unrealistic expectations about organizational rules, procedures, and policies.

There are several approaches that managers can use to accommodate generational differences in their workplaces. First, managers can review traditional assumptions and ways of working. For example, reviewing assumptions about when face time is and isn't necessary might shift the organization's focus from where work is done to the results that are produced, creating more flexibility for all employees to determine where and how they do their jobs. Second, managers can help employees learn what is expected and appropriate by articulating expectations during orientation training and by teaching staff how to read and adapt to different behavioral and communication styles. Third, managers can help employees understand and appreciate the contributions that each generation can make. For example, arranging a regular weekly meeting at which staff can contribute ideas, ask questions and get answers signals to Gen Xers, Gen Ys, and Gen Zs that they are being listened to and taken seriously and helps Boomers understand the insights and understandings that younger generations can offer. Ongoing opportunities—such as workplace bonding activities—to communicate and learn from one another will build greater awareness, understanding, and appreciation of other generational groups. Finally, understanding and tapping into the assets that each generation brings to the workplace can give an organization a significant competitive advantage useful for customer insights as well as behavioral insights. And, as Gen Y and Gen Z move into organizational leadership positions, especially when managing individuals from an "older" generation, it's important to maintain an attitude of openness for ideas and approaches.

How Do Managers Deal with Negative Behavior in the Workplace?

Jerry notices the oil is low in his forklift but continues to drive it until it overheats and can't be used. After enduring 11 months of repeated insults and mistreatment from her supervisor, Maria quits her job. An office clerk slams her keyboard and then shouts profanity whenever her computer freezes up. Rudeness, hostility, aggression, and other forms of workplace negativity have become all too common in today's organizations. In a survey of U.S. employees, 10 percent said they witnessed rudeness daily within their workplaces, and 20 percent said that they personally were direct targets of incivility at work at least once a week. In a survey of Canadian workers, 25 percent reported seeing incivility daily, and 50 percent said they were the direct targets at least once per week.[66] And it's been estimated that negativity costs the U.S. economy some $300 billion a year.[67] As if these statistics aren't enough to get your attention, here's another one: One in three people may be looking to leave an organization because of a coworker they can't stand.[68] What can managers do to manage negative behavior in the workplace?

The main thing is to recognize that it's there. Pretending that negative behavior doesn't exist or ignoring such misbehaviors will only confuse employees about what is expected and acceptable behavior. Although researchers continue to debate about the preventive or responsive actions to negative behaviors, in reality, both are needed.[69] Preventing negative behaviors by carefully screening potential employees for certain personality traits and responding immediately and decisively to unacceptable negative behaviors can go a long way toward managing negative workplace behaviors. But it's also important to pay attention to employee attitudes since negativity will show up there as well. As we said earlier, when employees are dissatisfied with their jobs, they *will* respond somehow.

CHAPTER SUMMARY BY LEARNING OUTCOME

10-1 Identify the focus and goals of organizational behavior (OB).

OB focuses on three areas: individual behavior, group behavior, and organizational aspects. The goals of OB are to explain, predict, and influence employee behavior. Six important employee behaviors are as follows: Employee productivity is a performance measure of both efficiency and effectiveness. Absenteeism is the failure to report to work. Turnover is the voluntary and involuntary permanent withdrawal from an organization. Organizational citizenship behavior (OCB) is discretionary behavior that's not part of an employee's formal job requirements, but it promotes the effective functioning of an organization. Job satisfaction is an individual's general attitude toward his or her job. Workplace misbehavior is any intentional employee behavior that's potentially harmful to the organization or individuals within the organization.

10-2 Explain the role that attitudes play in job performance.

Attitudes are evaluative statements concerning people, objects, or events. The cognitive component of an attitude refers to the beliefs, opinions, knowledge, or information held by a person. The affective component is the emotional or feeling part of an attitude. The behavioral component refers to an intention to behave in a certain way toward someone or something.

Four job-related attitudes include job satisfaction, job involvement, organizational commitment, and employee engagement. Job satisfaction refers to a person's general attitude toward his or her job. Job involvement is the degree to which an employee identifies with his or her job, actively participates in it, and considers his or her job performance to be important to his or her self-worth. Organizational commitment is the degree to which an employee identifies with a particular organization and its goals and wishes to maintain membership in that organization. Employee engagement is when employees are connected to, satisfied with, and enthusiastic about their jobs.

According to cognitive dissonance theory, individuals try to reconcile attitude and behavior inconsistencies by altering their attitudes, altering their behavior, or rationalizing the inconsistency.

10-3 Describe different personality theories.

The MBTI measures four dimensions: social interaction, preference for gathering data, preference for decision making, and style of making decisions. The Big Five model consists of five personality traits: extraversion, agreeableness, conscientiousness, emotional stability, and openness to experience. Another way to view personality is through the five personality traits that help explain individual behavior in organizations: locus of control, Machiavellianism, self-esteem, self-monitoring, and risk taking.

Finally, how a person responds emotionally and how they deal with their emotions is a function of personality. A person who is emotionally intelligent has the ability to notice and to manage emotional cues and information.

10-4 Describe perception and the factors that influence it.

Perception is how we give meaning to our environment by organizing and interpreting sensory impressions.

Attribution theory helps explain how we judge people differently. It depends on three factors. Distinctiveness is whether an individual displays different behaviors in different situations (i.e., is the behavior unusual). Consensus is whether others facing a similar situation respond in the same way. Consistency is when a person engages in behaviors regularly and consistently. Whether these three factors are high or low helps managers determine whether employee behavior is attributed to external or internal causes.

The fundamental attribution error is the tendency to underestimate the influence of external factors and overestimate the influence of internal factors. The self-serving bias is the tendency to attribute our own successes to internal factors and to put the blame for personal failure on external factors. Shortcuts used in judging others are selective perception, assumed similarity, stereotyping, and the halo effect.

10-5 Discuss learning theories and their relevance in shaping behavior.

Operant conditioning argues that behavior is a function of its consequences. Social learning theory says that individuals learn by observing what happens to other people and by directly experiencing something.

Managers can shape behavior by using positive reinforcement (reinforcing a desired behavior by giving something pleasant), negative reinforcement (reinforcing a desired response by withdrawing something unpleasant), punishment (eliminating undesirable behavior by applying penalties), or extinction (not reinforcing a behavior to eliminate it).

10 -6 Discuss contemporary issues in OB.

The challenge of managing different generations in the workplace is that each group has significantly different attitudes on a range of work-related issues, including communication, uses of technology, work/life balance and preferred leadership styles. Attitudinal differences can cause conflicts and resentment to arise, making it important for managers to help co-workers understand the causes and consequences of different perspectives. Differing priorities and preferences mean managers need to be flexible and accommodating about work and work arrangements but also ensure equity and fairness.

Workplace misbehavior can be dealt with by recognizing that it's there; carefully screening potential employees for possible negative tendencies; and most importantly, by paying attention to employee attitudes through surveys about job satisfaction and dissatisfaction.

DISCUSSION QUESTIONS

10-1 How is an organization like an iceberg? Use the iceberg metaphor to describe the field of organizational behavior.

10-2 Does the importance of knowledge of OB differ based on a manager's level in the organization? If so, how? If not, why not? Be specific.

10-3 Define the six important employee behaviors.

10-4 Clarify how individuals reconcile inconsistencies between attitudes and behaviors.

10-5 Describe what is meant by the term *emotional intelligence*. Provide an example of how it's used in contemporary organizations.

10-6 "Instead of worrying about job satisfaction, companies should be trying to create environments where performance is enabled." What do you think this statement means? Explain. What's your reaction to this statement? Do you agree? Disagree? Why?

10-7 How might a manager use personality traits to improve employee selection in his or her department? Emotional intelligence? Discuss.

10-8 Discuss the benefits of using social learning to manage a diversified workforce in an organization.

10-9 A Gallup Organization survey shows that most workers rate having a caring boss even higher than they value money or fringe benefits. How should managers interpret this information? What are the implications?

10-10 Identify and discuss the three components of work-related attitude.

Applying: Getting Ready for the Workplace

Management Skill Builder | UNDERSTANDING EMPLOYEE EMOTIONS

Employees bring their emotions with them to work every day. Although managers would like to think that employees are always rational, they aren't. And any manager who deals with people by ignoring how emotions—such as fear, anger, love, hate, joy, and grief—shape employees' day-to-day behavior isn't likely to be very effective.

MyLab Management

PERSONAL INVENTORY ASSESSMENT

Go to **www.pearson.com/mylab/management** to complete the Personal Inventory Assessment related to this chapter.

Skill Basics

Understanding another person's felt emotions is a difficult task. But we *can* learn to read others' emotions. How? By focusing on actual behaviors as well as verbal, nonverbal, and paralinguistic cues.[70]

- *Assess others' emotional intelligence (EI).* Some people are more in touch with their emotions than others. Those who understand and can manage their emotions are said to be high in EI. When people exhibit the following behaviors, you should find that they have less variance in their emotions and are easier to read. People high in EI understand the way they feel (self-aware), are sensitive to the feelings of others (empathetic), voluntarily help others (socially responsible), see things the way they are rather than the way they wish them to be (reality-oriented), reach out to others and show concern for others' interests (sociable), and manage their frustrations and anger (impulse control).

- *Ask about emotions.* The easiest way to find out what someone is feeling is to ask them. Saying something as simple as "Are you OK? What's the problem?" can frequently provide you with the information to assess an individual's emotional state. But relying on a verbal response has two drawbacks. First, almost all of us conceal our emotions to some extent for privacy and to reflect social expectations. So we might be unwilling to share our true feelings. Second, even if we want to convey our feelings verbally, we may be unable to do so. Some people have difficulty understanding their own emotions and, hence, are unable to express them verbally. So, at best, verbal responses provide only partial information.

- *Look for nonverbal cues.* You're talking with a coworker. Does the fact that his back is rigid, his teeth clenched, and his facial muscles tight tell you something about his emotional state? It probably should. Facial expressions, gestures, body movements, and physical distance are nonverbal cues that can provide additional insights into what a person is feeling. Facial expressions, for instance, are a window into a person's feelings. Notice differences in facial features: the height of the cheeks, the raising or lowering of the brow, the turn of the mouth, the positioning of the lips, and the configuration of muscles around the eyes. Even something as subtle as the distance at which someone chooses to position him- or herself from you can convey their feelings, or lack, of intimacy, aggressiveness, repugnance, or withdrawal.

- *Look for how things are said.* As Janet and I talked, I noticed a sharp change in the tone of her voice and the speed at which she spoke. I was tapping into the third source of information on a person's emotions—*paralanguage*. This is communication that goes beyond the specific spoken words. It includes pitch, amplitude, rate, and voice quality of speech. Paralanguage reminds us that people convey their feelings not only in *what* they say, but also in *how* they say it.

Practicing the Skill

Do the following:

Part A. Form groups of two. Each person is to spend a couple of minutes thinking (without sharing with the other person) of a time in the past when he or she was emotional about something. Examples might include being upset with a parent, sibling, or friend; being excited or disappointed about an academic or athletic achievement; being angry with someone over an insult or slight; being disgusted by something someone has said or done; or being happy because of something good that happened.

Part B. Now you'll conduct two role plays. Each will be an interview. In the first, one person will play the interviewer and the other will play the job applicant. The job is for a summer management internship with a large retail chain. Each role play will last no longer than 10 minutes. The interviewer is to conduct a normal job interview, except you are to continually rethink the emotional episode you envisioned in Part A. Try hard to convey this emotion while, at the same time, being professional in interviewing the job applicant.

Part C. Now reverse positions for the second role play. The interviewer becomes the job applicant, and vice versa. The new interviewer will conduct a normal job interview, except that he or she will continually rethink the emotional episode chosen in Part A.

Part D. Spend 10 minutes deconstructing the interview, with specific attention focused on what emotion(s) you think the other was conveying? What cues did you pick up? How accurate were you in reading those cues?

Continue to practice these skills in your everyday interactions with others. Pretty soon, you'll feel more competent at reading others' emotional cues.

Experiential Exercise

Emotional intelligence (EI). You read in the chapter what it is and why it's important. What would you say your level of EI is? There's a very simple online tool that gives you a quick assessment of your level of EI. Visit *https://www.mindtools.com/pages/article/ei-quiz.htm* and take the brief assessment on "How Emotionally Intelligent Are You?" Once you've done this, calculate your total score. Look at the discussion of your score that follows the assessment. Compile a brief report that includes:

1. Your prior knowledge, if any, of emotional intelligence.
2. Your EI score from this quick Mindtools assessment. Discuss if you were surprised by your score and why or why not?
3. Using the score discussion section from the assessment, make a bulleted list of each dimension of EI and some suggestions that are given for improving that dimension.

In your assigned group, share your information. As a group, come up with a list of five suggestions for improving emotional intelligence. Be prepared to share these with your class.

CASE APPLICATION #1

Alibaba: Motivation for the Long Haul
Topic: Motivating Employees the Right Way

The Alibaba Group is China's largest e-commerce company. Its main platforms—Taobao, Tmall, and Alipay—offer the largest online marketplace for Chinese businesses and consumers to connect. Alibaba has evolved into a business giant with company acquisitions reaching into a range of industries such as entertainment, real estate, mobile technology, and finance. Its recent IPO on the New York Stock Exchange (NYSE) reflects its dominance in the area; it made Wall Street history when the company raised $25 billion as capital. No longer confined to the emerging online markets of China, Alibaba now plays on an international level, with plans to compete for customers from around the world.[71]

Jack Ma, Alibaba's founder and executive chairman, fuels the motivation and inspiration for the company's competitive spirit. Alibaba's bedrock rests in Ma's enthusiasm for fulfilling dreams and creating a lively atmosphere in which employees strive for success as a family. These ideals can be traced back to the company's roots. Ma and 17 other co-founders launched the Alibaba website from his humble six-room apartment. In his living room, the determined group set out to not only become one of the world's top Internet companies but to also be one that will survive for 102 years. Ma and his team believed that together they could achieve the extraordinary by valuing the customer and focusing on the future. The company now has over 34,000 employees and continues to grow, and Ma's motto of "customer first, employee second, and shareholder third" guides the company even today.

Alibaba's leaders try hard to maintain the culture that was established during those first days in Ma's apartment. Despite having offices worldwide and a 17.2-acre campus for its headquarters, the company seeks to maintain a transparent environment where employees are encouraged to challenge ideas at all levels. Each employee adopts a nickname to help reduce a sense of hierarchy and spur innovative dialogue. Annual events like Alifest celebrate employees and customer unity. During these celebrations, Ma has been known to wear dazzling costumes and sing. Employees are taken care of beyond their paychecks through access to benefits like iHome, Alibaba's own mortgage fund, which is used to fund interest-free loans for employees.

Despite such motivators, the company faces challenges to its retention. Losing employees who possess critical knowledge threaten its long-term vision despite it continuously attracting new talent. Over a quarter of its employees own company shares, so the temptation to cash out and walk away is common as the company rides the waves of the Wall Street.

In response, Ma has penned letters to employees exhorting them to remember the company's ideal of keeping the customer first and to consider the longer journey. Ma cautions employees to be wary of the temptation of easy wealth and to keep the greater good at heart. Such talk is reflected in Ma's actions and statements.

Now one of the world's leading billionaires, Ma focuses on motivations beyond just money. He has set up numerous charities focusing on education, the environment, and health. In a recent presentation to the Economic Club of New York, he reflected on how happiness does not always come with money; some of his happiest moments were when he was making $12 a month as an English school teacher. The question that remains is whether these ideals will keep Alibaba on its path toward its 102 years.

Discussion Questions

10-11 Alibaba has a vision to be a 102-year-old company. How can a manager motivate an employee to stay and effectively contribute for more than 30 years? Consider Alibaba's founding ideals.

10-12 How would you retain employees who are sitting on lucrative stock options and could walk out the door tomorrow knowing that they would never have to work another day in their life? Use various motivation theories to support your answer.

10-13 Explain Jack Ma's statement that he was happier earning $12 a month as a school teacher using motivational theories.

10-14 Where would equity theory be relevant in Alibaba's history?

10-15 Having read this case, which motivational theory do you feel best represents Ma's ability to lead his team to overcome all odds?

CASE APPLICATION #2

Putting Customers Second
Topic: Employee-first culture, employee engagement surveys

The Virgin Group Ltd. has succeeded with a simple plan—don't put customers first! The British multinational holding company that has businesses ranging from an airline to a media company follows founder Sir Richard Branson's strategy instead—put employees first.[72]

Virgin started as a mail-order record business in 1970, with its first retail location opening a year later, and soon after, adding a record label. The entrepreneurial-minded Branson surprised his business partners about 10 years later when he announced he wanted to expand into the airline industry. From there, the company has continued to grow, with currently more than 60 companies under the Virgin brand employing more than 71,000 employees in 35 countries.

Branson describes himself as customer-centric but knows that the success of his businesses depends on the people who are hired to run things. The company works to create a healthy and happy culture where employees can thrive. Their general rule is to treat the staff as you would want to be treated. The company knows that one size does not fit all, and it offers a variety of resources to its diverse staff to create a supportive work environment.

The company offers flexible work options, including the option to work from home. Employees have unlimited leave and access to many programs to improve health and well-being. The bottom line is Virgin treats its employees like adults. As a result, employees are generally more productive because they have a healthy balance between their work and their private lives. How does this help the customer? The company knows that one unsatisfied employee can create a bad experience for many customers, while happy employees will provide service with a smile.

Employees first?... Isn't that supposed to be customers first?

How does the company know if employees are engaged and happy? Put simply, it asks them! Richard Branson sets the example, taking time during flights on Virgin Airlines to walk around and talk to staff. He has also been known to personally call individuals who took the initiative to make a good customer experience even better and gather feedback from them. More formally, Virgin conducts an annual employee engagement survey to check in on job satisfaction across the company.

Discussion Questions

10-16 What is your impression of an "employees first" culture? Would this work in other organizations? Why or why not? What would it take to make it work?

10-17 Do satisfied employees provide better customer service? What has been your experience? Do employees that seem happy at work provide better customer service? Discuss.

10-18 What personality traits would be most needed for this type of employee-first organizational culture? Discuss

10-19 Why is it important for Virgin to offer a variety of resources to create a supportive work environment?

10-20 What kind of questions *should* Virgin ask in its annual employee engagement survey? Discuss this in your assigned group. (*Hint:* Look at the chapter section that lists what employee engagement is based on. How can these be measured?)

CASE APPLICATION #3

Adobe's Advantage

Topic: Employee satisfaction, employee surveys

Adobe Systems is one of the largest and most diversified software companies in the world. It is headquartered in San Jose, California, in the heart of Silicon Valley. Its 18,000 plus employees are a core asset and the key to the company's success. And the company's managers are constantly probing employees' attitudes to see what makes them happy and what they could be doing better. And Adobe Systems must be doing something right! It was the fourth-highest rated company in the employee engagement and development category on the Drucker Institute's Management Top 250 list in 2017. That's quite an honor since it indicates the company is one of the most effectively managed companies in the United States.[73]

In 2012, the company was at a crossroads of transforming its business dramatically. It was moving from its traditional desktop software business to a new cloud-based model. Not only was this a massive strategic change, employees would find themselves adapting to a whole new way of working. One of the initial actions that Adobe's "People Resources" leaders did was to change—reinvent—the annual performance review. Instead, of the once-a-year check-up that was time-consuming, negative, and slow, the company moved to a "Check-In"…an ongoing, two-way dialogue between managers and their employees. This led to dramatic efficiency gains, more effective performance management, and higher employee engagement and retention.[74]

From that time forward, Adobe's commitment has been to engaging and developing its employees. And a big part of that process is measuring employee attitudes. During each quarter in 2017, Adobe managers e-mailed surveys to a segment of its workforce. These anonymous surveys asked employees about various aspects of how they felt the company treated them. One of the most interesting questions on the survey was one that asked if they would recommend a job with Adobe to others. The answers to that would be quite revealing as to whether employees were happy with the company.

So, with all these surveys, what did the company find out? Well, one important thing they discovered was that four employee engagement surveys in a year was too many. Preparing, administering, and compiling results from that many surveys was quite repetitive and demanding. In 2018, only two employee engagement surveys were scheduled. However, the company remains committed to connecting with employees and finding out what they have to say, especially in light of how important it is to attract and retain technical talent. As we saw in the chapter, companies want employees to be engaged in their work and to feel that they are appreciated and valued for their efforts.

In additional to surveying its employees, Adobe's customer and employee experience team monitors what is being posted on sites like Glassdoor, where employees can post comments about their employers. The team even checks apps such as Blind, which people use to discuss jobs anonymously. The challenge for any company that wants to up its employee engagement efforts is that each employee has a different perspective on what an "engaging" work environment looks like. Keeping employee engagement rates high requires understanding the unique needs of different generations and groups of employees. And being engaged with their work isn't just for nonmanagerial employees, it's also for managers and team leaders.

> # A top company for **employee engagement and development!**

Discussion Questions

10-21 How can an understanding of employee attitudes help Adobe's managers and leaders be more effective?

10-22 How might an understanding of organizational behavior help Adobe's CEO Shantanu Narayen lead his company? Be specific. How about first-line team leaders? Again, be specific.

10-23 Would personality affect an individual's job satisfaction? If so, how? If not, why not?

10-24 Adobe is a tech company and likely has employees from all different age groups. Would Adobe have to change its employee engagement surveys for different generations that might be in its workforce? Explain.

10-25 In your assigned group, come with arguments supporting (a) why employee engagement surveys are useful and (b) why employee engagement surveys are not useful. Be prepared to "argue" for either.

Endnotes

1. J. Diamond, "The Art of Pitching Free Agents," *Wall Street Journal,* March 2, 2018, p. A16.

2. "Survey on the Total Financial Impact of Employee Absences," *Medical Benefits,* November 30, 2010, p. 9; and K. M. Kroll, "Absence-Minded," *CFO Human Capital,* 2006, pp. 12–14.

3. D. W. Organ, *Organizational Citizenship Behavior: The Good Soldier Syndrome* (Lexington, MA: Lexington Books, 1988), p. 4. See also J. L. Lavell, D. E. Rupp, and J. Brockner, "Taking a Multifoci Approach to the Study of Justice, Social Exchange, and Citizenship Behavior: The Target Similarity Model," *Journal of Management,* December 2007, pp. 841–66; and J. A. LePine, A. Erez, and D. E. Johnson, "The Nature and Dimensionality of Organizational Citizenship Behavior: A Critical Review and Meta-Analysis," *Journal of Applied Psychology,* February 2002, pp. 52–65.

4. J. R. Spence, D. L. Ferris, D. J. Brown, and D. Heller, "Understanding Daily Citizenship Behaviors: A Social Comparison Approach," *Journal of Organizational Behavior,* May 2011, pp. 547–71; L. M. Little, D. L. Nelson, J. C. Wallace, and P. D. Johnson, "Integrating Attachment Style, Vigor at Work, and Extra-Role Performance," *Journal of Organizational Behavior,* April 2011, pp. 464–84; N. P. Podsakoff, P. M. Podsakoff, S. W. Whiting, and P. Mishra, "Effects of Organizational Citizenship Behavior on Selection Decisions in Employment Interviews," *Journal of Applied Psychology,* March 2011, pp. 310–26; T. M. Glomb, D. P. Bhave, A. G. Miner, and M. Wall, "Doing Good, Feeling Good: Examining the Role of Organizational Citizenship Behaviors in Changing Mood," *Personnel Psychology,* Spring 2011, pp. 191–223; T. P. Munyon, W. A. Hochwarter, P. L. Perrewé, and G. R. Ferris, "Optimism and the Nonlinear Citizenship Behavior—Job Satisfaction Relationship in Three Studies," *Journal of Management,* November 2010, pp. 1505–28; R. Ilies, B. A. Scott, and T. A. Judge, "The Interactive Effects of Personal Traits and Experienced States on Intraindividual Patterns of Citizenship Behavior," *Academy of Management Journal,* June 2006, pp. 561–75; P. Cardona, B. S. Lawrence, and P. M. Bentler, "The Influence of Social and Work Exchange Relationships on Organizational Citizenship Behavior," *Group & Organization Management,* April 2004, pp. 219–47; M. C.

Bolino and W. H. Turnley, "Going the Extra Mile: Cultivating and Managing Employee Citizenship Behavior," *Academy of Management Executive,* August 2003, pp. 60–73; M. C. Bolino, W. H. Turnley, and J. J. Bloodgood, "Citizenship Behavior and the Creation of Social Capital in Organizations," *Academy of Management Review,* October 2002, pp. 505–22; and P. M. Podsakoff, S. B. MacKenzie, J. B. Paine, and D. G. Bachrach, "Organizational Citizenship Behaviors: A Critical Review of the Theoretical and Empirical Literature and Suggestions for Future Research," *Journal of Management* 26, no. 3 (2000), pp. 543–48.

5. M. C. Bolino and W. H. Turnley, "The Personal Costs of Citizenship Behavior: The Relationship between Individual Initiative and Role Overload, Job Stress, and Work-Family Conflict," *Journal of Applied Psychology,* July 2005, pp. 740–48.

6. This definition adapted from R. W. Griffin and Y. P. Lopez, "Bad Behavior in Organizations: A Review and Typology for Future Research," *Journal of Management,* December 2005, pp. 988–1005.

7. S. J. Becker, "Empirical Validation of Affect, Behavior, and Cognition as Distinct Components of Behavior," *Journal of Personality and Social Psychology,* May 1984, pp. 1191–1205.

8. K. Gee and S. Nassauer, "At Adobe, a Satisfied Workforce," *Wall Street Journal,* December 6, 2017, p. R3.

9. S. P. Robbins and T. A. Judge, *Essentials of Organizational Behavior,* 11th ed. (Upper Saddle River, NJ: Prentice Hall, 2010).

10. M. S. Christian, A. S. Garza, and J. E. Slaughter, "Work Engagement: A Quantitative Review and Test of Its Relations with Task and Contextual Performance," *Personnel Psychology,* Spring 2011, pp. 89–136; V. T. Ho, S-S Wong, and C. H. Lee, "A Tale of Passion: Linking Job Passion and Cognitive Engagement to Employee Work Performance," *Journal of Management Studies,* January 2011, pp. 26–47; D. R. May, R. L. Gilson, and L. M. Harter, "The Psychological Conditions of Meaningfulness, Safety and Availability and the Engagement of the Human Spirit at Work," *Journal of Occupational and Organizational Psychology,* March 2004, pp. 11–37; R. T. Keller, "Job Involvement and Organizational Commitment as Longitudinal Predictors of Job Performance: A Study of Scientists and Engineers,"

Journal of Applied Psychology, August 1997, pp. 539–45; W. Kahn, "Psychological Conditions of Personal Engagement and Disengagement at Work," *Academy of Management Journal,* December 1990, pp. 692–794; and P. P. Brooke Jr., D. W. Russell, and J. L. Price, "Discriminant Validation of Measures of Job Satisfaction, Job Involvement, and Organizational Commitment," *Journal of Applied Psychology,* May 1988, pp. 139–45. Also, see, for example, J. Smythe, "Engaging Employees to Drive Performance," *Communication World,* May–June 2008, pp. 20–22; A. B. Bakker and W. B. Schaufeli, "Positive Organizational Behavior: Engaged Employees in Flourishing Organizations," *Journal of Organizational Behavior,* February 2008, pp. 147–54; U. Aggarwal, S. Datta, and S. Bhargava, "The Relationship between Human Resource Practices, Psychological Contract, and Employee Engagement—Implications for Managing Talent," *IIMB Management Review,* September 2007, pp. 313–25; M. C. Christian and J. E. Slaughter, "Work Engagement: A Meta-Analytic Review and Directions for Research in an Emerging Area," *AOM Proceedings,* August 2007, pp. 1–6; C. H. Thomas, "A New Measurement Scale for Employee Engagement: Scale Development, Pilot Test, and Replication," *AOM Proceedings,* August 2007, pp. 1–6; A. M. Saks, "Antecedents and Consequences of Employee Engagement," *Journal of Managerial Psychology* 21, no. 7 (2006), pp. 600–19; and A. Parsley, "Road Map for Employee Engagement," *Management Services,* Spring 2006, pp. 10–11.

11. Mercer, *IndustryWeek,* April 2008, p. 24.

12. J. M. George, "The Wider Context, Costs, and Benefits of Work Engagement," *European Journal of Work & Organizational Psychology,* February 2011, pp. 53–59; and "Employee Engagement Report 2011," Blessing White Research, http://www.blessingwhite.com/eee__report.asp, January 2011, pp. 7–8.

13. A. J. Elliott and P. G. Devine, "On the Motivational Nature of Cognitive Dissonance: Dissonance as Psychological Discomfort," *Journal of Personality and Social Psychology,* September 1994, pp. 382–94.

14. L. Festinger, *A Theory of Cognitive Dissonance* (Stanford, CA: Stanford University Press, 1957); C. Crossen, "Cognitive Dissonance Became a Milestone

in 1950s Psychology," *Wall Street Journal,* December 4, 2006, p. B1; and Y. "Sally" Kim, "Application of the Cognitive Dissonance Theory to the Service Industry," *Services Marketing Quarterly,* April–June 2011, pp. 96–112.

15. H. C. Koh and E. H. Y. Boo, "The Link between Organizational Ethics and Job Satisfaction: A Study of Managers in Singapore," *Journal of Business Ethics,* February 15, 2001, p. 309.

16. See, for example, W. D. Crano and R. Prislin, "Attitudes and Persuasion," *Annual Review of Psychology,* 2006, pp. 345–74; and J. Jermias, "Cognitive Dissonance and Resistance to Change: The Influence of Commitment Confirmation and Feedback on Judgment Usefulness of Accounting Systems," *Accounting, Organizations, and Society,* March 2001, p. 141.

17. Z. Wang, S. N. Singh, Y. J. Li, S. Mishra, M. Ambrose, and M. Biernat, "Effects of Employees' Positive Affective displays on Customer Loyalty Intentions: An Emotions-As-Social-Information Perspective," *Academy of Management Journal,* February 2017, pp. 109–29; P. Jaskunas, "The Tyranny of the Forced Smile," *New York Times Online,* February 14, 2015; and R. E. Silverman, "Workers Really Do Put on a Happy Face for the Boss," *Wall Street Journal,* January 29, 2015, p. D4.

18. T. A. Judge, C. J. Thoresen, J. E. Bono, and G. K. Patton, "The Job Satisfaction–Job Performance Relationship: A Qualitative and Quantitative Review," *Psychological Bulletin,* May 2001, pp. 376–407.

19. L. Saari and T. A. Judge, "Employee Attitudes and Job Satisfaction," *Human Resource Management,* Winter 2004, pp. 395–407; and T. A. Judge and A. H. Church, "Job Satisfaction: Research and Practice," in C. L. Cooper and E. A. Locke (eds.), *Industrial and Organizational Psychology: Linking Theory with Practice* (Oxford, UK: Blackwell, 2000).

20. D. A. Harrison, D. A. Newman, and P. L. Roth, "How Important Are Job Attitudes?: Meta-Analytic Comparisons of Integrative Behavioral Outcomes and Time Sequences," *Academy of Management Journal,* April 2006, pp. 305–25.

21. G. Chen, R. E. Ployhart, H. C. Thomas, N. Anderson, and P. D. Bliese, "The Power of Momentum: A New Model of Dynamic Relationships between Job Satisfaction Change and Turnover Intentions," *Academy of Management Journal,* February 2011, pp. 159–81.

22. I. Arnsdorf, "No More New Kid on Campus," *Wall Street Journal*, August 5, 2010, pp. D1+.

23. "Personality Is More Important Than Hard Skills, Managers Say," *T&D*, July 2014, p. 19.

24. L. Evans, "Do You Have the Right Personality to Work from Home?" http://www.fastcompany.com/3046450/how-to-be-a-success-at-everything/do-you-have-the-right-personality-to-work-from-home, May 26, 2015.

25. CPP Inc., Myers-Briggs Type Indicator® (MBTI®), http://www.cpp.com/products/mbti/index.asp (2011); and J. Llorens, "Taking Inventory of Myers-Briggs," *T&D*, April 2010, pp. 18–19.

26. Ibid.

27. See, for instance, J. Overbo, "Using Myers-Briggs Personality Type to Create a Culture Adapted to the New Century," *T&D*, February 2010, pp. 70–72; and K. Garrety, R. Badham, V. Morrigan, W. Rifkin, and M. Zanko, "The Use of Personality Typing in Organizational Change: Discourse, Emotions, and the Reflective Subject," *Human Relations*, February 2003, pp. 211–35.

28. P. Moran, "Personality Characteristics and Growth-Orientation of the Small Business Owner Manager," *Journal of Managerial Psychology*, July 2000, p. 651; and M. Higgs, "Is There a Relationship between the Myers-Briggs Type Indicator and Emotional Intelligence?" *Journal of Managerial Psychology*, September–October 2001, pp. 488–513.

29. J. M. Digman, "Personality Structure: Emergence of the Five Factor Model," in M. R. Rosenweig and L. W. Porter (eds.), *Annual Review of Psychology*, vol. 41 (Palo Alto, CA: Annual Reviews, 1990), pp. 417–40; O. P. John, "The Big Five Factor Taxonomy: Dimensions of Personality in the Natural Language and in Questionnaires," in L. A. Pervin (ed.), *Handbook of Personality Theory and Research* (New York: Guilford Press, 1990), pp. 66–100; and M. K. Mount, M. R. Barrick, and J. P. Strauss, "Validity of Observer Ratings of the Big Five Personality Factors," *Journal of Applied Psychology*, April 1996, pp. 272–80.

30. See, for example, T. W. Yiu and H. K. Lee, "How Do Personality Traits Affect Construction Dispute Negotiation: Study of Big Five Personality Model," *Journal of Construction Engineering & Management*, March 2011, pp. 169–78; H. J. Kell, A. D. Rittmayer, A. E. Crook, and S. J. Motowidlo, "Situational Content Moderates the Association between the Big Five Personality Traits and Behavioral Effectiveness," *Human Performance*, February 2010, pp. 213–28; R. D. Meyer, R. S. Dalal, and S. Bonaccio, "A Meta-Analytic Investigation into the Moderating Effects of Situational Strength on the Conscientiousness–Performance Relationship," *Journal of Organizational Behavior*, November 2009, pp. 1077–102; G. Vittorio, C. Barbaranelli, and G. Guido, "Brand Personality: How to Make the Metaphor Fit," *Journal of Economic Psychology*, June 2001, p. 377; G. M. Hurtz and J. J. Donovan, "Personality and Job Performance: The Big Five Revisited," *Journal of Applied Psychology*, December 2000, p. 869; W. A. Hochwarter, L. A. Witt, and K. M. Kacmar, "Perceptions of Organizational Politics as a Moderator of the Relationship between Conscientiousness and Job Performance," *Journal of Applied Psychology*, June 2000, p. 472; and M. R. Barrick and M. K. Mount, "The Big Five Personality Dimensions and Job Performance: A Meta-Analytic Study," *Personnel Psychology* 44 (1991), pp. 1–26.

31. M. R. Barrick and M. K. Mount, "Autonomy as a Moderator of the Relationship between the Big Five Personality Dimensions and Job Performance," *Journal of Applied Psychology*, February 1993, pp. 111–118.

32. See also M. R. Furtner and J. F. Rauthmann, "Relations between Self-Leadership and Scores on the Big Five," *Psychological Reports*, October 2010, pp. 339–53; R. Barrick, M. Piotrowski, and G. L. Stewart, "Personality and Job Performance: Test of the Mediating Effects of Motivation Among Sales Representatives," *Journal of Applied Psychology*, February 2002, pp. 43–52; and I. T. Robertson, H. Baron, P. Gibbons, R. MacIver, and G. Nyfield, "Conscientiousness and Managerial Performance," *Journal of Occupational and Organizational Psychology*, June 2000, pp. 171–78.

33. See, for example, J. L. Kisamore, I. M. Jawahar, E. W. Liguori, T. L. Mharapara, and T. H. Stone, "Conflict and Abusive Workplace Behaviors: The Moderating Effects of Social Competencies," *Career Development International*, October 2010, pp. 583–600; P. S. Mishra and A. K. Das Mohapatra, "Relevance of Emotional Intelligence for Effective Job Performance: An Empirical Study," *Vikalpa: The Journal for Decision Makers*, January–March 2010, pp. 53–61; T-Y. Kim, D. M. Cable, S-P. Kim, and J. Wang, "Emotional Competence and Work Performance: The Mediating Effect of Proactivity and the Moderating Effect of Job Autonomy," *Journal of Organizational Behavior*, October 2009, pp. 983–1000; J. M. Diefendorff and G. J. Greguras, "Contextualizing Emotional Display Rules: Examining the Roles of Targets and Discrete Emotions in Shaping Display Rule Perceptions," *Journal of Management*, August 2009, pp. 880–98; J. Gooty, M. Gavin, and N. M. Ashkanasy, "Emotions Research in OB: The Challenges That Lie Ahead," *Journal of Organizational Behavior*, August 2009, pp. 833–38; N. M. Ashkanasy and C. S. Daus, "Emotion in the Workplace: The New Challenge for Managers," *Academy of Management Executive*, February 2002, pp. 76–86; N. M. Ashkanasy, C. E. J. Hartel, and C. S. Daus, "Diversity and Emotions: The New Frontiers in Organizational Behavior Research," *Journal of Management* 28, no. 3 (2002), pp. 307–38; S. Fox, "Promoting Emotional Intelligence in Organizations: Make Training in Emotional Intelligence Effective," *Personnel Psychology*, Spring 2002, pp. 236–40; B. E. Ashforth, "The Handbook of Emotional Intelligence: Theory, Development, Assessment, and Application at Home, School, and in the Work Place: A Review," *Personnel Psychology*, Autumn 2001, pp. 721–24; and R. Bar-On and J. D. A. Parker, *The Handbook of Emotional Intelligence: Theory, Development, Assessment, and Application at Home, School, and in the Work Place* (San Francisco, CA: Jossey-Bass, 2000).

34. See, for instance, C. S. P. Fernandez, "Emotional Intelligence in the Workplace," *Journal of Public Health Management and Practice*, February 2007, pp. 80–82.

35. R. Pearman, "The Leading Edge: Using Emotional Intelligence to Enhance Performance," *T&D*, March 2011, pp. 68–71; C. Prentice and B. King, "The Influence of Emotional Intelligence on the Service Performance of Casino Frontline Employees," *Tourism & Hospitality Research*, January 2011, pp. 49–66; E. H. O'Boyle Jr., R. H. Humphrey, J. M. Pollack, T. H. Hawver, and P. A. Story, "The Relation between Emotional Intelligence and Job Performance: A Meta-Analysis," *Journal of Organizational Behavior Online*, www.interscience.wiley.com, June 2010; and P. J. Jordan, N. M. Ashkanasy, and C. E. J. Hartel, "Emotional Intelligence as a Moderator of Emotional and Behavioral Reactions to Job Insecurity," *Academy of Management Review*, July 2002, pp. 361–72.

36. C. Cherniss and R. D. Caplan, "A Case Study of Implementing Emotional Intelligence Programs in Organizations," *Journal of Organizational Excellence*, Winter 2001, pp. 763–86; and S. B. Vanessa-Urch and W. Deuskat, "Building the Emotional Intelligence of Groups," *Harvard Business Review*, March 2001, pp. 81–91.

37. "Can't We All Just Get Along," *BusinessWeek*, October 9, 2000, p. 18.

38. C. Moller and S. Powell, "Emotional Intelligence and the Challenges of Quality Management," *Leadership and Organizational Development Journal*, July–August 2001, pp. 341–45.

39. See L. A. Downey, V. Papageorgiou, and C. Stough, "Examining the Relationship between Leadership, Emotional Intelligence, and Intuition in Female Managers," *Leadership & Organization Development Journal*, April 2006, pp. 250–64.

40. See, for instance, J. Silvester, F. M. Anderson-Gough, N. R. Anderson, and A. R. Mohamed, "Locus of Control, Attributions and Impression Management in the Selection Interview," *Journal of Occupational and Organizational Psychology*, March 2002, pp. 59–77; D. W. Organ and C. N. Greene, "Role Ambiguity, Locus of Control, and Work Satisfaction," *Journal of Applied Psychology*, February 1974, pp. 101–02; and T. R. Mitchell, C. M. Smyser, and S. E. Weed, "Locus of Control: Supervision and Work Satisfaction," *Academy of Management Journal*, September 1975, pp. 623–31.

41. I. Zettler, N. Friedrich, and B. E. Hilbig, "Dissecting Work Commitment: The Role of Machiavellianism," *Career Development International*, February 2011, pp. 20–35; S. R. Kessler, A. C. Bandelli, P. E. Spector, W. C. Borman, C. E. Nelson, and L. M. Penney, "Re-Examining Machiavelli: A Three-Dimensional Model of Machiavellianism in the Workplace," *Journal of Applied Social Psychology*, August 2010, pp. 1868–96; W. Amelia, "Anatomy of a Classic: Machiavelli's Daring Gift," *Wall Street Journal*, August 30–31, 2008, p. W10; S. A. Snook, "Love and Fear and the Modern Boss," *Harvard Business Review*, January 2008, pp. 16–17; and R. G. Vleeming, "Machiavellianism: A Preliminary Review," *Psychology Reports*, February 1979, pp. 295–310.

42. P. Harris, "Machiavelli and the Global Compass: Ends and Means in Ethics and Leadership," *Journal of Business Ethics*, (June 2010, pp. 131–38; and P. Van Kenhove, I. Vermeir, and S. Verniers, "An Empirical Investigation of the Relationship between Ethical Beliefs, Ethical Ideology, Political Preference and Need for Closure," *Journal of Business Ethics*, August 15, 2001, p. 347.

43. Based on J. Brockner, *Self-Esteem at Work: Research, Theory, and Practice* (Lexington, MA: Lexington Books, 1988), chs. 1–4.

44. See, for instance, R. Vermunt, D. van Knippenberg, B. van Knippenberg, and E. Blaauw, "Self-Esteem and Outcome Fairness: Differential Importance of Procedural and Outcome Considerations," *Journal of Applied Psychology*, August 2001, p. 621; T. A. Judge and J. E. Bono, "Relationship of Core Self-Evaluation Traits—Self-Esteem, Generalized Self Efficacy, Locus of Control, and Emotional Stability—With Job Satisfaction and Job Performance," *Journal of Applied Psychology*, February 2001, p. 80; and D. B. Fedor, J. M. Maslyn, W. D. Davis, and K. Mathieson, "Performance Improvement Efforts in Response to Negative Feedback: The Roles of Source Power and Recipient Self-Esteem," *Journal of Management*, January–February 2001, pp. 79–97.

45. M. Snyder, *Public Appearances, Private Realities: The Psychology of Self-Monitoring* (New York: W. H. Freeman, 1987).

46. See, for example, D. U. Bryant, M. Mitcham, A. R. Araiza, and W. M. Leung, "The Interaction of Self-Monitoring and Organizational Position on Perceived Effort," *Journal of Managerial Psychology* 26, no. 2 (2011), pp. 138–54; B. Vilela and J. A. V. González, "Salespersons' Self-Monitoring: Direct, Indirect, and Moderating Effects on Salespersons' Organizational Citizenship Behavior," *Psychology & Marketing*, January 2010, pp. 71–89; and P. M. Fandt, "Managing Impressions with Information: A Field Study of Organizational Realities," *Journal of Applied Behavioral Science*, June 2001, pp. 180–205.

47. Ibid.

48. R. N. Taylor and M. D. Dunnette, "Influence of Dogmatism, Risk Taking Propensity, and Intelligence on Decision Making Strategies for a Sample of Industrial Managers," *Journal of Applied Psychology*, August 1974, pp. 420–23.

49. I. L. Janis and L. Mann, *Decision Making: A Psychological Analysis of Conflict, Choice, and Commitment* (New York: Free Press, 1977).

50. See, for instance, C. P. Cross, L. T. Copping, and A. Campbell, "Sex Differences in Impulsivity: A Meta-Analysis," *Psychological Bulletin*, January 2011, pp. 97–130; A. A. Schooler, K. Fujita, X. Zou, and S. J. Stroessner, "When Risk Seeking Becomes a Motivational Necessity," *Journal of Personality and Social Psychology*, August 2010, pp. 215–31; A. Chatterjee and D. C. Hambrick, "Executive Personality,

Capability Cues, and Risk-Taking: How Narcissistic CEOs React to Their Successes and Stumbles," *Academy of Management Proceedings*, www.aomonline.org, 2010; E. Soane, C. Dewberry, and S. Narendran, "The Role of Perceived Costs and Perceived Benefits in the Relationship between Personality and Risk-Related Choices," *Journal of Risk Research*, April 2010, pp. 303–18; and N. Kogan and M. A. Wallach, "Group Risk Taking as a Function of Members' Anxiety and Defensiveness," *Journal of Personality*, March 1967, pp. 50–63.

51. H. Zhao, S. E. Seibert, and G. T. Lumpkin, "The Relationship of Personality to Entrepreneurial Intentions and Performance: A Meta-Analytic Review," *Journal of Management*, March 2010, pp. 381–404; and K. Hyrshy, "Entrepreneurial Metaphors and Concepts: An Exploratory Study," *Journal of Managerial Psychology*, July 2000, pp. 653; and B. McCarthy, "The Cult of Risk Taking and Social Learning: A Study of Irish Entrepreneurs," *Management Decision*, August 2000, pp. 563–75.

52. M. Goldman, "A Journey into Personality Self-Discovery, Vol. 2," *Bloomberg BusinessWeek Online*, March 22, 2011; M. Goldman, "A Journey into Personality Self-Discovery, Vol. 1," *Bloomberg BusinessWeek Online*, February 15, 2011; and P. Korkki, "The True Calling That Wasn't," *New York Times Online*, July 16, 2010.

53. J. L. Holland, *Making Vocational Choices: A Theory of Vocational Personalities and Work Environments* (Odessa, FL: Psychological Assessment Resources, 1997).

54. S. Bates, "Personality Counts: Psychological Tests Can Help Peg the Job Applicants Best Suited for Certain Jobs," *HR Magazine*, February 2002, pp. 28–38; and K. J. Jansen and A. K. Brown, "Toward a Multi-Level Theory of Person Environment Fit," Academy of Management Proceedings from the Fifty-Eighth Annual Meeting of the Academy of Management, San Diego, CA (August 7–12, 1998), HR: FR1–FR8.

55. See, for instance, G. W. M. Ip and M. H. Bond, "Culture, Values, and the Spontaneous Self-Concept," *Asian Journal of Psychology* 1 (1995), pp. 30–36; J. E. Williams, J. L. Saiz, D. L. FormyDuval, M. L. Munick, E. E. Fogle, A. Adom, A. Haque, F. Neto, and J. Yu, "Cross-Cultural Variation in the Importance of Psychological Characteristics: A Seven-Year Country Study," *International Journal of Psychology*, October 1995, pp. 529–50; V. Benet and N. G. Walker, "The Big Seven Factor

Model of Personality Description: Evidence for Its Cross-Cultural Generalizability in a Spanish Sample," *Journal of Personality and Social Psychology*, October 1995, pp. 701–18; R. R. McCrae and P. To. Costa Jr., "Personality Trait Structure as a Human Universal," *American Psychologist*, 1997, pp. 509–16; and M. J. Schmit, J. A. Kihm, and C. Robie, "Development of a Global Measure of Personality," *Personnel Psychology*, Spring 2000, pp. 153–93.

56. J. F. Salgado, "The Five Factor Model of Personality and Job Performance in the European Community," *Journal of Applied Psychology*, February 1997, pp. 30–43. Note: This study covered the 15-nation European community and did not include the 10 countries that joined in 2004.

57. G. Kranz, "Organizations Look to Get Personal in '07," *Workforce Management*, www.workforce.com, June 19, 2007.

58. A. O'Connell, "Smile, Don't Bark in Tough Times," *Harvard Business Review*, November 2009, p. 27; and G. A. Van Kleef et al., "Searing Sentiment or Cold Calculation? The Effects of Leader Emotional Displays on Team Performance Depend on Follower Epistemic Motivation," *Academy of Management Journal*, June 2009, pp. 562–80.

59. Reprinted by permission from Land Rover North America LLC.

60. H. H. Kelley, "Attribution in Social Interaction," in E. Jones et al. (eds.), *Behavior* (Morristown, NJ: General Learning Press, 1972).

61. G. Miller and T. Lawson, "The Effect of an Informational Option on the Fundamental Attribution Error," *Personality and Social Psychology Bulletin*, June 1989, pp. 194–204. See also G. Charness and E. Haruvy, "Self-Serving Bias: Evidence from a Simulated Labour Relationship," *Journal of Managerial Psychology*, July 2000, pp. 655; and T. J. Elkins, J. S. Phillips, and R. Konopaske, "Gender-Related Biases in Evaluations of Sex Discrimination Allegations: Is Perceived Threat a Key?" *Journal of Applied Psychology*, April 2002, pp. 280–93.

62. S. T. Fiske, "Social Cognition and Social Perception," *Annual Review of Psychology*, 1993, pp. 155–94; G. N. Powell and Y. Kido, "Managerial Stereotypes in a Global Economy: A Comparative Study of Japanese and American Business Students' Perspectives," *Psychological Reports*, February 1994, pp. 219–26; and J. L. Hilton and W. von Hippel, "Stereotypes," in J. T. Spence, J. M. Darley, and D. J. Foss (eds.), *Annual Review of Psychology*, vol. 47 (Palo Alto, CA: Annual Reviews Inc., 1996), pp. 237–71.

63. A. Bandura, *Social Learning Theory* (Upper Saddle River, NJ: Prentice Hall, 1977).

64. For an interesting article on the subject, see D. Nitsch, M. Baetz, and J. C. Hughes, "Why Code of Conduct Violations Go Unreported: A Conceptual Framework to Guide Intervention and Future Research," *Journal of Business Ethics*, April 2005, pp. 327–41.

65. B. F. Skinner, *Contingencies of Reinforcement* (East Norwalk, CT: Appleton-Century-Crofts, 1971).

66. C. M. Pearson and C. L. Porath, "On the Nature, Consequences, and Remedies of Workplace Incivility: No Time for Nice? Think Again," *Academy of Management Executive*, February 2005, pp. 7–18.

67. J. Robison, "Be Nice: It's Good for Business," *Gallup Brain*, http://brain.gallup.com, August 12, 2004.

68. "There's A Good Chance Your Coworkers Hate You," *Fast Company Online*, August 4, 2017.

69. M. Sandy Hershcovis and J. Barling, "Towards a Multi-Foci Approach to Workplace Aggression: A Meta-Analytic Review of Outcomes from Different Perpetrators," *Journal of Organizational Behavior*, January 2010, pp. 24–44; R. E. Kidwell and S. R. Valentine, "Positive Group Context, Work Attitudes, and Organizational Behavior: The Case of Withholding Job Effort," *Journal of Business Ethics*, April 2009, pp. 15–28; P. Bordia and S. L. D. Resubog, "When Employees Strike Back: Investigating Mediating Mechanisms between Psychological Contract Breach and Workplace Deviance," *Journal of Applied Psychology*, September 2008, pp. 1104–17; and Y. Vardi and E. Weitz, *Misbehavior in Organizations* (Mahwah, NJ: Lawrence Erlbaum Associates, 2004), pp. 246–47.

70. Based on V. P. Richmond, J. C. McCroskey, and S. K. Payne, *Nonverbal Behavior in Interpersonal Relations*, 2nd ed. (Englewood Cliffs, NJ: Prentice Hall, 1991), pp. 117–38; R. Bar-On, *The Emotional Intelligence Inventory (EQ-I): Technical Manual* (Toronto: Multi-Health Systems, 1997); L. A. King, "Ambivalence over Emotional Expression and Reading Emotions in Situations and Faces," *Journal of Personality and Social Psychology*, March 1998, pp. 753–62; and M. Lewis, J. M. Haviland-Jones, and L. F. Barrett (eds.), *Handbook of Emotions*, 3rd ed. (New York: Guilford Press, 2011).

71. J. D'Onfro, "How Jack Ma Went from Being a Poor School Teacher to Turning Alibaba into a $168 Billion Behemoth," *Business Insider*, May 7, 2014; Z. Soo,

"Jack Ma—Happier Making US$12 a Month Than Living as a Billionaire," *South China Morning Post*, June 10, 2015; H. H. Wang, "Why Amazon Should Fear Alibaba," *Forbes*, www.forbes.com, July 8, 2015; "Alibaba Unveiled: Inside China's E-Commerce Giant," *The Politic*, October 17, 2014; W. Fick, "The Secret to Alibaba's Culture Is Jack Ma's Apartment," *Harvard Business Review*, June 19, 2014; "China 'Unparalleled Ruthlessness' Awaits Jack Ma's

Letter to Alibaba Employees," *The Wall Street Journal*, May 7, 2014; H. Shao, "A Peek inside Alibaba's Corporate Culture," *Forbes Asia*, May 13, 2014; Alibaba Group 2015 Annual Report, http://ar.alibabagroup.com/2015/letter.html; Ryan Mac, "As Alibaba IPO Approaches, Founder Jack Ma Pens Letter to Potential Investors," *Forbes*, September 5, 2014; He Wei, "Alibaba Ponders Ways to Keep Flock Together," *China Daily*, June

6, 2014; "China's Carnegie," *The Economist*, May 3, 2014.

72. O. Raymond, "Richard Branson: Companies Should Put Empl oyees First," *Inc. Magazine Online*, October 28, 2014; C. Gallo, "How Southwest and Virgin American Win by Putting People Before Profit," *Forbes Online*, September 10, 2016; M. Fling and E. Vinberg Hearn, "6 Companies That Get Employee Engagement and What They Do Right," *Chartered Management*

Institute, www.managers.org.uk, December 11, 2015; and O. Thomas, "Why Virgin Media Prioritises Employee Engagement," *Workplace Savings and Benefits Online*, April 15, 2015.

73. Gee and Nassauer, 2017.

74. D. Morris, "Death to the Performance Review: How Adobe Reinvented Performance Management and Transformed Its Business," WorldAtWork, www.worldatwork.org, 2016.

Motivating and Rewarding Employees

Management
Myth
Myth

Motivation is all about "show me the money."

Management
DEBUNKED?
Myth

Maybe the greatest fallacy about motivation is that everyone is motivated by money. **Many ineffective or inexperienced managers naively believe that money is a prime motivator.** Then they proceed to ignore the many other actions and rewards they control that are as equally important as money, if not more so. As you'll see, one size doesn't fit all, and the secret to being an effective motivator is understanding each individual's unique needs.

SUCCESSFUL

managers need to understand that what motivates them personally may have little or no effect on others. Just because you're motivated by being part of a cohesive work team, don't assume everyone is. Or just because you're motivated by your job doesn't mean that everyone is. Or just because employees have access to free food, free massages, free laundry, and free M&Ms doesn't mean those extras are enough to keep them from looking elsewhere for career opportunities. Effective managers who get employees to put forth maximum effort know how and why those employees are motivated and tailor motivational practices to satisfy their needs and wants. Motivating and rewarding employees are some of the manager's most important and challenging activities. To get employees to put forth maximum work effort, managers need to know how and why they're motivated. ●

Learning Outcomes

What Is Motivation?

11-1 Define and explain motivation.

Several CEOs were attending a meeting where the topic was "What do employees want?"[1] Each CEO took turns describing the benefits they provided and how they gave out free M&Ms every Wednesday and offered their employees stock options and free parking spaces. However, the meeting's main speaker made the point that "employees don't want M&Ms; they want to love what they do." Half expecting his audience to laugh, the speaker was pleasantly surprised as the CEOs stood up one-by-one to agree. They all recognized that "the value in their companies comes from the employees who are motivated to be there."

These CEOs understand how important employee motivation is. Like them, all managers need to be able to motivate their employees, which requires understanding what motivation is. Let's begin by pointing out what motivation is not. Why? Because many people incorrectly view motivation as a personal trait; that is, they think some people are motivated and others aren't. Our knowledge of motivation tells us that we can't label people that way because individuals differ in motivational drive and their overall motivation varies from situation to situation. For instance, you're probably more motivated to work hard and do well in some classes than in others.

---

78 percent of managers say they do a fair job of motivating their people.[2]
21 percent of employees feel they're managed in a motivating way.[3]

It appears that managers may not be doing as good of a job at motivating as they believe they are. **Motivation** refers to the process by which a person's efforts are energized, directed, and sustained toward attaining a goal.[4] This definition has three key elements: energy, direction, and persistence.

The (1) *energy* element is a measure of intensity or drive. A motivated person puts forth effort and works hard. However, the quality of the effort must be considered as well as its intensity. High levels of effort don't necessarily lead to favorable job performance unless the effort is channeled in a (2) *direction* that benefits the organization. Effort that's directed toward, and consistent with, organizational goals is the kind of effort we want from employees. Finally, motivation includes a (3) *persistence* dimension. We want employees to persist in putting forth effort to achieve those goals.

Motivating high levels of employee performance is an important organizational concern and managers keep looking for answers. For instance, a recent Gallup poll found that a large majority of U.S. employees—some 64 percent—are not excited about their work.[5] This level of disengagement has been described by researchers: "These employees are essentially 'checked out.' They're sleepwalking through their workday, putting time, but not energy or passion, into their work."[6] It's no wonder, then, that both managers and academics want to understand and explain employee motivation.

Let's start by looking at several early theories of motivation.

motivation
The process by which a person's efforts are energized, directed, and sustained toward attaining a goal

4 Early Theories of Motivation (1950s & 1960s)

11-2 Compare and contrast early theories of motivation.

Know these early theories because they: ❶ *Represent the foundation from which contemporary theories grew*, and ❷ *Still are used by practicing managers to explain employee* **motivation**.

1 Maslow's Hierarchy of Needs Theory
(probably THE best-known motivation theory)[7]

- **Abraham Maslow**—a psychologist—proposed that within every person is a hierarchy of five needs:

Exhibit 11–1   Maslow's Hierarchy of Needs

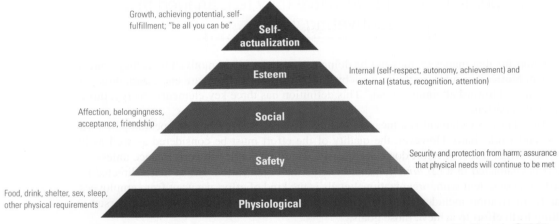

Growth, achieving potential, self-fulfillment; "be all you can be" — **Self-actualization**

Esteem — Internal (self-respect, autonomy, achievement) and external (status, recognition, attention)

Affection, belongingness, acceptance, friendship — **Social**

Safety — Security and protection from harm; assurance that physical needs will continue to be met

Food, drink, shelter, sex, sleep, other physical requirements — **Physiological**

Source: Maslow, Abraham H., Frager, Robert D., Fadiman, James, *Motivation and Personality*, 3rd ed., ©1987. Reprinted and electronically reproduced by permission of Pearson Education, Inc., New York, NY.

- Each level must be substantially satisfied before the next need becomes dominant; an individual moves up the hierarchy from one level to the next.
- *Lower-order needs* are satisfied predominantly externally, and *higher-order needs* are satisfied internally.

HOW is Maslow's hierarchy used to motivate employees?

- Managers will do things to satisfy employees' needs.
- **Remember:** Once a need is substantially satisfied, it no longer motivates.

hierarchy of needs theory
Maslow's theory that there is a hierarchy of five human needs: physiological, safety, social, esteem, and self-actualization

- Widely popular among practicing managers probably because it's easy to understand and intuitive.[8] HOWEVER...
- No empirical support provided for theory; other studies could not validate it.[9]

2

McGregor's Theory X and Theory Y

- Based on two assumptions about human nature.[10]

    - **Theory X**: a negative view of people that assumes workers have little ambition, dislike work, want to avoid responsibility, and need to be closely controlled to work effectively.

    - **Theory Y**: a positive view that assumes employees enjoy work, seek out and accept responsibility, and exercise self-direction.

- To maximize employee motivation, use Theory Y practices—allow employees to participate in decisions, create responsible and challenging jobs, and encourage good group relations.

- No evidence to confirm either set of assumptions or that being a Theory Y manager is the only way to motivate employees.

Marek/Fotolia

3

Herzberg's Two-Factor Theory

- **Frederick Herzberg's two-factor theory** (*also called motivation-hygiene theory*)—intrinsic factors are related to job satisfaction, while extrinsic factors are associated with job dissatisfaction.[11]

    - Popular theory from the 1960s to the early 1980s.
    - Criticized for being too simplistic.
    - Influenced today's approach to job design. (See Classic Concepts in Today's Workplace box on p. 402.)

Theory X	**Theory Y**	**two-factor theory**
The assumption that employees dislike work, are lazy, avoid responsibility, and must be coerced to work	The assumption that employees are creative, enjoy work, seek responsibility, and can exercise self-direction	Herzberg's motivation theory, which proposes that intrinsic factors are related to job satisfaction and motivation, whereas extrinsic factors are associated with job dissatisfaction

- **Research focus**: When people felt exceptionally good (satisfied—see left-hand side of Exhibit 11–2) *or* bad (dissatisfied—see right-hand side of exhibit) about their jobs.

- Replies showed these were *two different factors*!

  - When people felt good about their work, they tended to cite intrinsic factors arising from the *job content (job itself),* such as achievement, recognition, and responsibility.

  - When they were dissatisfied, they tended to cite extrinsic factors arising from the *job context,* such as company policy and administration, supervision, interpersonal relationships, and working conditions.

Andersphoto/Fotolia

Exhibit 11–2   Herzberg's Two-Factor Theory

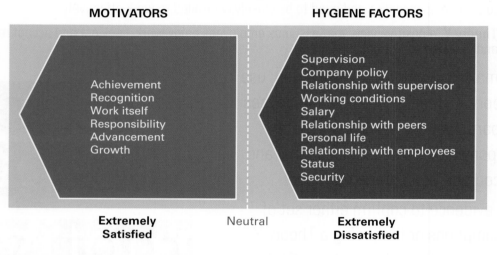

MOTIVATORS	HYGIENE FACTORS
Achievement Recognition Work itself Responsibility Advancement Growth	Supervision Company policy Relationship with supervisor Working conditions Salary Relationship with peers Personal life Relationship with employees Status Security
Extremely Satisfied	Neutral **Extremely Dissatisfied**

- Replies also gave us the new view of *Satisfaction vs. Dissatisfaction* (see Exhibit 11–3).

Exhibit 11–3   Contrasting Views of Satisfaction and Dissatisfaction

TRADITIONAL VIEW

Satisfied	Dissatisfied

HERZBERG'S VIEW

Motivators   *Hygiene Factors*

Satisfaction	No Satisfaction	No Dissatisfaction	Dissatisfaction

Source: Robbins, Stephen P., Coulter, Mary, *Management*, 13th Ed., © 2016, p. 465. Reprinted and electronically reproduced by permission of Pearson Education, Inc., New York, NY.

  - Herzberg concluded that the traditional view—*the opposite of satisfaction is dissatisfaction*—was wrong.

  - He believed that the factors that led to job satisfaction were separate and distinct from those that led to job dissatisfaction.

hygiene factors Factors that eliminate job dissatisfaction but don't motivate	**motivators** Factors that increase job satisfaction and motivation	**three-needs theory** McClelland's theory, which says that three acquired (not innate) needs—achievement, power, and affiliation—are major motives at work

- Removing dissatisfying characteristics from a job didn't necessarily make that job more satisfying (or motivating); it simply made you "less" dissatisfied.
- Proposed a dual continuum: The opposite of "satisfaction" is "no satisfaction," and the opposite of "dissatisfaction" is "no dissatisfaction."

Motivating Employees:

1 When **hygiene factors** are adequate, people won't be dissatisfied, but they won't be motivated, either.

2 To motivate people, use the **motivators**.

michael simons/Alamy Stock Photo

4 McClelland's Three-Needs Theory

- David McClelland and his associates proposed the **three-needs theory**, which says *three* acquired (not innate) needs are major motives in work, including:[12]

1 **need for achievement (nAch)**, which is the drive to succeed and excel in relation to a set of standards

2 **need for power (nPow)**, which is the need to make others behave in a way that they would not have behaved otherwise

3 **need for affiliation (nAff)**, which is the desire for friendly and close interpersonal relationships

- nAch has been researched the most:
  - People with a high nAch are striving for personal achievement rather than for the trappings and rewards of success.
  - They have a desire to do something better or more efficiently than it's been done before.[13]
  - They prefer **1** jobs that offer personal responsibility for finding solutions to problems, **2** receiving rapid and unambiguous feedback on their performance in order to tell whether they're improving, and **3** moderately challenging goals.
  - High achievers avoid what they perceive to be very easy or very difficult tasks.
  - A high nAch doesn't necessarily lead to being a good manager, especially in large organizations. Why? Because high achievers focus on their own accomplishments, while good managers emphasize helping others accomplish their goals.[14]
  - Employees can be trained to stimulate their nAch by being in situations where they have personal responsibility, feedback, and moderate risks.[15]

- The best managers tend to be high in nPow and low in nAff.[16]

need for achievement (nAch)	**need for power (nPow)**	**need for affiliation (nAff)**
The drive to succeed and excel in relation to a set of standards	The need to make others behave in a way that they would not have behaved otherwise	The desire for friendly and close interpersonal relationships

How Do the Contemporary Theories Explain Motivation?

11-3 Compare and contrast contemporary theories of motivation.

At Electronic Arts (EA), one of the world's largest video game designers, employees put in grueling hours developing games. However, EA takes care of its game developers by providing them with workday intramural sports leagues, pinball arcades, group fitness classes, and an open invite to pets at work.[17] With a little over 8,800 workers in more than 20 countries, EA's managers need to understand employee motivation.

The theories we look at in this section—goal-setting, job design, equity, and expectancy—represent current explanations of employee motivation. Although maybe not as well known as those we just discussed, these are backed by research.[18]

What Is Goal-Setting Theory?

Goals CAN be **powerful motivators!**

goal-setting theory
The proposition that specific goals increase performance and that difficult goals, when accepted, result in higher performance than do easy goals

Before a big assignment or major class project presentation, has a teacher ever encouraged you to "Just do your best"? What does that vague statement "do your best" mean? Would your performance on a class project have been higher had that teacher said you needed to score a 93 percent to keep your A in the class? Research on goal-setting theory addresses these issues, and the findings, as you'll see, are impressive in terms of the effect that goal specificity, challenge, and feedback have on performance.[19]

Substantial research support has been established for **goal-setting theory**, which says that specific goals increase performance and that difficult goals, when accepted, result in higher performance than do easy goals. *What does goal-setting theory tell us?*

(a) Working toward a goal is a major source of job motivation. Studies on goal setting have demonstrated that specific and challenging goals are superior motivating forces.[20] Such goals produce a higher output than does the generalized goal of "do your best." The specificity of the goal itself acts as an internal stimulus. For instance, when a sales rep commits to making eight sales calls daily, this intention gives him a specific goal to try to attain.

(b) Will employees try harder if they have the opportunity to participate in the setting of goals? Not always. In some cases, participatively set goals elicit superior performance; in other cases, individuals performed best when their manager assigned goals. However, participation is probably preferable to assigning goals when employees might resist accepting difficult challenges.[21]

(c) We know that people will do better if they get feedback on how well they're progressing toward their goals because feedback helps identify discrepancies between what they've done and what they want to do. But all feedback isn't equally effective. Self-generated feedback—where an employee monitors his or her own progress—has been shown to be a more powerful motivator than feedback coming from someone else.[22]

Three other contingencies besides feedback influence the goal-performance relationship: goal commitment, adequate self-efficacy, and national culture.

1. First, goal-setting theory assumes that an individual is committed to the goal. Commitment is most likely when goals are made public, when the individual has an internal locus of control, and when the goals are self-set rather than assigned.[23]

Working toward specific goals that are key to their company's growth and productivity is a major source of motivation for employees of The Motley Fool, a financial services company. Each year the firm's leaders create a road map for achieving goals and give all staff members a copy of the map. Employees are motivated to work towards the goals because the company bases its incentive programs on goal achievement.

Brooks Kraft LLC/Corbis/Getty Images

2. Next, **self-efficacy** refers to an individual's belief that he or she is capable of performing a task.[24] The higher your self-efficacy, the more confidence you have in your ability to succeed in a task. So, in difficult situations, we find that people with low self-efficacy are likely to reduce their effort or give up altogether, whereas those with high self-efficacy will try harder to master the challenge.[25] In addition, individuals with high self-efficacy seem to respond to negative feedback with increased effort and motivation, whereas those with low self-efficacy are likely to reduce their effort when given negative feedback.[26]

3. Finally, the value of goal-setting theory depends on the national culture. It's well adapted to North American countries because its main ideas align reasonably well with those cultures. It assumes that subordinates will be reasonably independent (not a high score on power distance), that people will seek challenging goals (low in uncertainty avoidance), and that performance is considered important by both managers and subordinates (high in assertiveness). Don't expect goal setting to lead to higher employee performance in countries where the cultural characteristics aren't like this.

Exhibit 11–4 summarizes the relationships among goals, motivation, and performance. Our overall conclusion: *The intention to work toward hard and specific goals is a powerful motivating force.* Under the proper conditions, it can lead to higher performance. However, there's no evidence that such goals are associated with increased job satisfaction.[27]

How Does Job Design Influence Motivation?

Yes—you *can* **design jobs** that motivate!

Because managers want to motivate individuals on the job, we need to look at ways to design motivating jobs. If you look closely at what an organization is and how it works, you'll find that it's composed of thousands of tasks. These tasks are, in turn, aggregated into jobs. We use the term **job design** to refer to the way tasks are combined to form complete jobs. The jobs that people perform in an organization should not evolve by chance. Managers should design jobs deliberately and thoughtfully to reflect the demands of the changing environment, the organization's technology, and employees' skills, abilities, and preferences.[28] When jobs are designed like that, employees are motivated to work hard. What are the ways that managers can design motivating jobs? We can answer that with the **job characteristics model (JCM)**, developed by J. Richard Hackman and Greg R. Oldham.[29]

self-efficacy
An individual's belief that he or she is capable of performing a task

job design
The way tasks are combined to form complete jobs

job characteristics model (JCM)
A framework for analyzing and designing jobs that identifies five primary core job dimensions, their interrelationships, and their impact on outcomes

Exhibit 11–4   Goal-Setting Theory

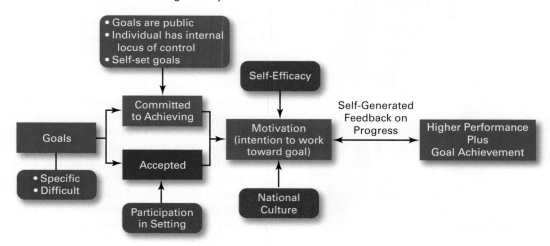

◀◀◀ **Classic Concepts in Today's Workplace** ▶▶▶

Deciding how work tasks should be performed has long been of interest to managers.[30] From scientific management's attempts to find the "one best way" to do work to the Hawthorne Studies that attempted to unravel patterns of human behavior at work, researchers have been curious about the ideal approach to work design. In the 1950s, Frederick Herzberg and his associates began research to "discover the importance of attitudes toward work and the experiences, both good and bad, that workers reported." He wanted to know the kinds of things that made people at their work happy and satisfied or unhappy and dissatisfied. What he discovered changed the way we view job design. The fact that job dissatisfaction and job satisfaction were the results of different aspects of the work environment was an important finding. Herzberg's two-factor theory gave practicing managers insights into both job context and job content. And if you

> ## Job Design: How *should* work tasks get done?

wanted to motivate employees, you'd better focus more on the job content aspects (the motivators) than on the job context aspects (the hygiene factors).

In addition, Herzberg's research stimulated additional interest in work design. The Job Characteristics model, for one, built upon Herzberg's findings in identifying the five core job dimensions, especially autonomy. As managers and organizations continue to search for work designs that will energize and engage employees, Herzberg's study of when people felt good and felt bad at work continues as a classic.

Discussion Questions:

1 Why do you think jobs need to be "designed"?

2 How can job design contribute to employee motivation?

According to Hackman and Oldham, any job can be described in terms of the following five core job dimensions:

1. ***Skill variety.*** The degree to which the job requires a variety of activities so the worker can use a number of different skills and talents
2. ***Task identity.*** The degree to which the job requires completion of a whole and identifiable piece of work
3. ***Task significance.*** The degree to which the job affects the lives or work of other people
4. ***Autonomy.*** The degree to which the job provides freedom, independence, and discretion to the individual in scheduling the work and in determining the procedures to be used in carrying it out
5. ***Feedback.*** The degree to which carrying out the work activities required by the job results in the individual's obtaining direct and clear information about the effectiveness of his or her performance

The job of this pediatric nurse caring for newborn babies at a children's hospital in Germany scores high on task significance as she uses her specialized knowledge and skills in caring for children, from infancy through the late teen years, and their families. Task significance contributes to the meaningfulness of her job and high internal work motivation.

Ulrich Baumgarten/Getty Images

Exhibit 11–5 presents the model. Notice how the first three dimensions—skill variety, task identity, and task significance—combine to create meaningful work. What we mean is that *if these three characteristics exist in a job, we can predict that the person will view his or her job as being important, valuable, and worthwhile.* Notice, too, that jobs that possess autonomy give the job incumbent a feeling of personal responsibility for the results and that, if a job provides feedback, the employee will know how effectively he or she is performing.

From a motivational point of view, the JCM suggests that internal rewards are obtained when an employee *learns* (knowledge of results through feedback) that he or she *personally* (experienced responsibility through autonomy of work) has performed well on a task that he or she *cares* about (experienced

Exhibit 11–5 Job Characteristics Model

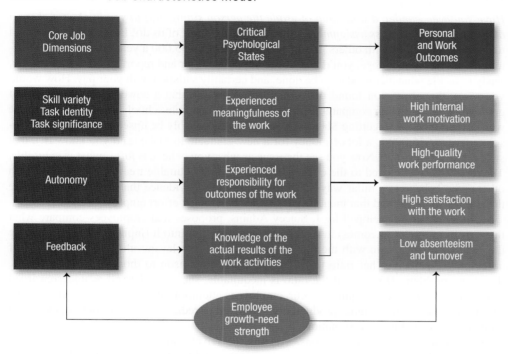

Source: See J. R. Hackman and G. R. Oldham, "Motivation Through the Design of Work: Test of a Theory," *Organizational Behavior and Human Performance*, August 1976, 250–79. Reprinted by permission from Judith D. Hackman (w/o) J. Richard Hackman.

meaningfulness through skill variety, task identity, and/or task significance). The more these three conditions characterize a job, the greater the employee's motivation, performance, and satisfaction and the lower his or her absenteeism and the likelihood of resigning. As the model shows, the links between the job dimensions and the outcomes are moderated by the strength of the individual's growth need (the person's desire for self-esteem and self-actualization). Individuals are more likely to experience the critical psychological states and respond positively when their jobs include the core dimensions than are individuals with a low growth need. This distinction may explain the mixed results with **job enrichment** (vertical expansion of a job by adding planning and evaluation responsibilities): Individuals with low growth need don't tend to achieve high performance or satisfaction by having their jobs enriched.

The JCM provides significant guidance to managers for job design for both individuals and teams.[31] The suggestions shown in Exhibit 11–6, which are based on the JCM, specify the types of changes in jobs that are most likely to improve each of the five core job dimensions.

job enrichment
The vertical expansion of a job by adding planning and evaluation responsibilities

Exhibit 11–6 Guidelines for Job Redesign

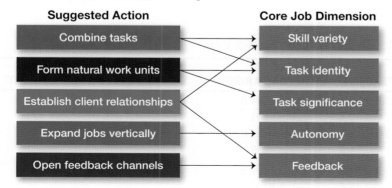

Source: J. R. Hackman and G. R. Oldham, "Motivation Through the Design of Work: Test of a Theory," *Organizational Behavior and Human Performance*, August 1976, 250–79. Reprinted by permission from Judith D. Hackman (w/o) J. Richard Hackman.

equity theory
The theory that an employee compares his or her job's input-to-outcome ratio with that of relevant others and then corrects any inequity

referent
The persons, systems, or selves against which individuals compare themselves to assess equity

distributive justice
Perceived fairness of the amount and allocation of rewards among individuals

procedural justice
Perceived fairness of the process used to determine the distribution of rewards

What Is Equity Theory?

Have you ever wondered what kind of grade the person sitting next to you in class makes on a test or on a major class assignment? Sure you have—most of us do! Being human, we tend to compare ourselves with others. If someone offered you $55,000 a year on your first job after graduating from college, you'd probably jump at the offer and report to work enthusiastic, ready to tackle whatever needed to be done, and certainly satisfied with your pay. How would you react, though, if you found out a month into the job that a coworker—another recent graduate, your age, with comparable grades from a comparable school, and with comparable work experience—was getting $60,000 a year? You'd probably be upset! Even though in absolute terms, $55,000 is a lot of money for a new graduate to make (and you know it!), that suddenly isn't the issue. Now you see the issue as what you believe is *fair*—what is *equitable*. The term *equity* is related to the concept of fairness and equitable treatment compared with others who behave in similar ways. There's considerable evidence that employees compare themselves to others and that inequities influence how much effort employees exert.[32]

Equity theory, developed by J. Stacey Adams, proposes that employees compare what they get from a job (outcomes) in relation to what they put into it (inputs) and then compare their input-outcome ratio with the input-outcome ratios of relevant others (Exhibit 11–7). If an employee perceives her ratio to be equitable in comparison to those of relevant others, there's no problem. However, if the ratio is inequitable, she views herself as underrewarded or overrewarded. When inequities occur, employees attempt to do something about it.[33] The result might be lower or higher productivity, improved or reduced quality of output, increased absenteeism, or voluntary resignation.

The **referent**—the other persons, systems, or selves individuals compare themselves against in order to assess equity—is an important variable in equity theory.[34] Each of the three referent categories is important. (1) The "persons" category includes other individuals with similar jobs in the same organization but also includes friends, neighbors, or professional associates. Based on what they hear at work or read about in newspapers or trade journals, employees compare their pay with that of others. (2) The "system" category includes organizational pay policies, procedures, and allocation. (3) The "self" category refers to inputs-outcomes ratios that are unique to the individual. It reflects past personal experiences and contacts and is influenced by criteria such as past jobs or family commitments.

Originally, equity theory focused on **distributive justice**, which is the perceived fairness of the amount and allocation of rewards among individuals. More recent research has focused on looking at issues of **procedural justice**, which is the perceived fairness of the process used to determine the distribution of rewards. This research shows that distributive justice has a greater influence on employee satisfaction than procedural justice, while procedural justice tends to affect an employee's organizational commitment, trust in his or her boss, and intention to quit.[35] What are the implications for managers? They should consider openly sharing information on how allocation decisions are made, follow consistent and unbiased procedures, and engage in similar practices to increase the perception of procedural justice. By increasing the perception of procedural justice, employees are likely to view their bosses and the organization as positive even if they're dissatisfied with pay, promotions, and other personal outcomes.

Exhibit 11–7 Equity Theory Relationships

PERCEIVED RATIO COMPARISON*	EMPLOYEE'S ASSESSMENT
$\dfrac{\text{Outcomes A}}{\text{Inputs A}} = \dfrac{\text{Outcomes B}}{\text{Inputs B}}$	Inequity (underrewarded)
$\dfrac{\text{Outcomes A}}{\text{Inputs A}} = \dfrac{\text{Outcomes B}}{\text{Inputs B}}$	Equity
$\dfrac{\text{Outcomes A}}{\text{Inputs A}} > \dfrac{\text{Outcomes B}}{\text{Inputs B}}$	Inequity (overrewarded)

*Person A is the employee, and Person B is a relevant other or referent.

Exhibit 11–8 Expectancy Model

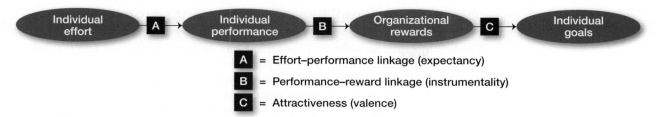

A = Effort–performance linkage (expectancy)

B = Performance–reward linkage (instrumentality)

C = Attractiveness (valence)

How Does Expectancy Theory Explain Motivation?

- How hard do I have to work to achieve a certain level of performance?
- Can I actually do that?
- What reward will I get for reaching it?
- How much do I want that reward?

The most comprehensive explanation of how employees are motivated is Victor Vroom's **expectancy theory**. Although the theory has its critics,[36] most research evidence supports it.[37]

Expectancy theory states that an individual tends to act in a certain way based on the expectation that the act will be followed by a given outcome and on the attractiveness of that outcome to the individual. It includes three variables or relationships (see Exhibit 11–8):

1. *Expectancy or effort-performance linkage* is the probability perceived by the individual that exerting a given amount of effort will lead to a certain level of performance.
2. *Instrumentality or performance-reward linkage* is the degree to which the individual believes that performing at a particular level is instrumental in attaining the desired outcome.
3. *Valence or attractiveness of reward* is the importance that the individual places on the potential outcome or reward that can be achieved on the job. Valence considers both the goals and needs of the individual.

This explanation of motivation might sound complicated, but it really isn't. It can be summed up in the questions: How hard do I have to work to achieve a certain level of performance, and can I actually achieve that level? What reward will performing at that level get me? How attractive is the reward to me, and does it help me achieve my own personal goals? Whether you are motivated to put forth effort (i.e., to work hard) at any given time depends on your goals and your perception of whether a certain level of performance is necessary to attain those goals. Let's look at an example. Many years ago, when a woman went to work for IBM as a sales rep, her favorite work "reward" became having an IBM corporate jet fly to pick up her best customers and her and take them for a weekend of golfing at some fun location. But to get that particular "reward," she had to achieve at a certain level of performance, which involved exceeding her sales goals by a specified percentage. How hard she was willing to work (i.e., how motivated she was to put forth effort) was dependent on the level of performance that had to be met and the likelihood that if she achieved at that level of performance she would receive that reward. Because she "valued" that reward, she always worked hard to exceed her sales goals. And the performance-reward linkage was clear because her hard work and performance achievements were always acknowledged by the company with the reward she valued (access to a corporate jet).

This employee of Tiens Group, a Chinese direct seller of healthcare products, carries a large plate of paella as part of a traditional Spanish meal during an all-expense-paid trip to Madrid that included a bullfight and a tour of King Felipe VI's Royal Palace. Rewarding employees with trips is a powerful motivator for Tiens salespeople because they appreciate the opportunity of traveling to other countries and learning about their people, culture, and traditions.

Paul White/AP Images

Career Advice: "Always go above and beyond because then your managers will have no choice but to reward you."[38]

The key to expectancy theory is understanding an individual's goal and the linkage between effort and performance, between performance and rewards, and finally, between rewards and individual goal satisfaction. It emphasizes payoffs, or rewards. As a result, we have to believe that the rewards an organization offers align with what the individual wants. Expectancy theory recognizes that no universal principle explains what motivates individuals and thus stresses that managers understand why employees view certain outcomes as attractive or unattractive. After all, we want to reward individuals with those things they value positively. Also, expectancy theory emphasizes expected behaviors. Do employees know what is expected of them and how they'll be evaluated? Finally, the theory is concerned with perceptions. Reality is irrelevant. An individual's own perceptions of performance, reward, and goal outcomes, not the outcomes themselves, will determine his or her motivation (level of effort).

How Can We Integrate Contemporary Motivation Theories?

Many of the ideas underlying the contemporary motivation theories are complementary, and you'll understand better how to motivate people if you see how the theories fit together.[39] Exhibit 11–9 presents a model that integrates much of what we know about motivation. Its basic foundation is the expectancy model. Let's work through the model, starting on the left.

Exhibit 11–9 Integrating Contemporary Theories of Motivation

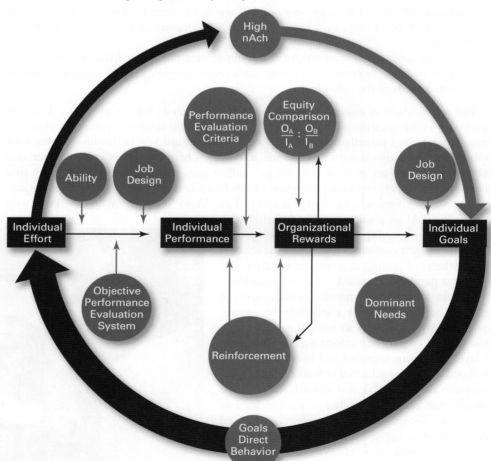

The individual effort box has an arrow leading into it. This arrow flows from the individual's goals. Consistent with *goal-setting theory*, this goals-effort link is meant to illustrate that goals direct behavior.

- *Expectancy theory* predicts that an employee will exert a high level of effort if he or she perceives a strong relationship between effort and performance, performance and rewards, and rewards and satisfaction of personal goals. Each of these relationships is, in turn, influenced by certain factors. You can see from the model that the level of individual performance is determined not only by the level of individual effort, but also by the individual's ability to perform and by whether the organization has a fair and objective performance evaluation system. The performance-reward relationship will be strong if the individual perceives that it is performance (rather than seniority, personal favorites, or some other criterion) that is rewarded. The final link in expectancy theory is the rewards-goal relationship.

- The *traditional need theories* come into play at this point. Motivation would be high to the degree that the rewards an individual received for his or her high performance satisfied the dominant needs consistent with his or her individual goals.

A closer look at the model also shows that it considers other theories.

- *Achievement-need* is seen, in that the high achiever isn't motivated by the organization's assessment of his or her performance or organizational rewards, hence the jump from effort to individual goals for those with a high nAch. Remember that high achievers are internally driven as long as the jobs they're doing provide them with personal responsibility, feedback, and moderate risks. They're not concerned with the effort-performance, performance-reward, or rewards-goals linkages.

- *Reinforcement theory* is seen in the model by recognizing that the organization's rewards reinforce the individual's performance. If managers have designed a reward system that is seen by employees as "paying off" for good performance, the rewards will reinforce and encourage continued good performance.

- Rewards also play a key part in *equity theory*. Individuals will compare the rewards (outcomes) they have received from the inputs or efforts they made with the inputs-outcomes ratio of relevant others. If inequities exist, the effort expended may be influenced.

- Finally, the *JCM* is seen in this integrative model. Task characteristics (job design) influence job motivation at two places. First, jobs that are designed around the five job dimensions are likely to lead to higher actual job performance because the individual's motivation will be stimulated by the job itself—that is, they will increase the linkage between effort and performance. Second, jobs that are designed around the five job dimensions also increase an employee's control over key elements in his or her work. Therefore, jobs that offer autonomy, feedback, and similar task characteristics help to satisfy the individual goals of employees who desire greater control over their work.

What Current Motivation Issues Do Managers Face?

11-4 Discuss current issues in motivating employees.

Understanding and predicting employee motivation is one of the most popular areas in management research. We've introduced you to several motivation theories. However, even current studies of employee motivation are influenced by some significant workplace issues—motivating in tough economic circumstances, managing cross-cultural challenges, motivating unique groups of workers, and designing appropriate rewards programs.

How Can Managers Motivate Employees When the Economy Stinks?

Zappos, the quirky Las Vegas–based online shoe retailer (now a part of Amazon.com), has always had a reputation for being a fun place to work.[40] However, during the economic recession, it, like many companies, had to cut staff—124 employees in total. CEO Tony Hsieh wanted to get out the news fast to lessen the stress for his employees. So he announced the layoff in an e-mail, on his blog, and on his Twitter account. Although some might think these are terrible ways to communicate that kind of news, most employees thanked him for being so open and so honest. The company also took good care of those being laid off. Laid-off employees with less than two years of service were paid through the end of the year. Longer-tenured employees got four weeks' severance pay for every year of service. All got six months of continued paid health coverage and, at the request of the employees, got to keep their 40 percent merchandise discount through the Christmas season. Zappos had always been a model of how to nurture employees in good times; now it showed how to treat employees in bad times.

When the economy is good and organizations aren't feeling the pinch of meeting performance goals, financial and other incentives are more readily available. However, economic recessions can be difficult for many organizations, especially when it comes to their employees. Layoffs, tight budgets, minimal or no pay raises, benefit cuts, no bonuses, long hours doing the work of those who had been laid off—this can be the reality that many employees face. As conditions deteriorate, employee confidence, optimism, and job engagement plummet as well. As you can imagine, it isn't an easy thing for managers to keep employees motivated under such challenging circumstances.

In an uncertain economy, managers have to be creative in keeping their employees' efforts energized, directed, and sustained toward achieving goals. They are forced to look at ways to motivate employees that don't involve money or that are relatively inexpensive.[41] So they use actions such as holding meetings with employees to keep the lines of communication open and to get their input on issues; establishing a common goal, such as maintaining excellent customer service, to keep everyone focused; creating a community feel so employees could see that managers cared about them and their work; and giving employees opportunities to continue to learn and grow. And, of course, an encouraging word always goes a long way, as well.

How Does Country Culture Affect Motivation Efforts?

The desire for **interesting work** seems to be global.

In today's global business environment, managers can't automatically assume that motivational programs that work in one geographic location are going to work in others. Most current motivation theories were developed in the United States by Americans and about Americans.[42] Maybe the most blatant pro-American characteristic in these theories is the strong emphasis on individualism and achievement. For instance, both goal-setting and expectancy theories emphasize goal accomplishment as well as rational and individual thought. Let's look at the cross-cultural transferability of the motivation theories.

Maslow's need hierarchy argues that people start at the physiological level and then move progressively up the hierarchy in order. This hierarchy, if it has any application at all, aligns with American culture. In countries such as Japan, Greece, and Mexico, where uncertainty avoidance characteristics are strong, security needs would be on top of the need hierarchy. Countries that score high on nurturing characteristics—Denmark, Sweden, Norway, the Netherlands, and Finland—would have social needs on top.[43] We would predict, for instance, that group work will be more motivating when the country's culture scores high on the nurturing criterion.

Like workers in most cultures, the desire for interesting work motivates Japan's Shigeru Miyamoto, the creator of many of Nintendo's characters including Mario, shown here. As a video game designer and producer, Miyamoto has also been motivated to achieve his goal of creating unique games that offer fun and joy to people of all ages throughout the world.

Jae C. Hong/AP Images

Another motivation concept that clearly has an American bias is the achievement need. The view that a high achievement need acts as an internal motivator presupposes two cultural characteristics— a willingness to accept a moderate degree of risk (which excludes countries with strong uncertainty avoidance characteristics) and a concern with performance (which applies almost singularly to countries with strong achievement characteristics). This combination is found in the Anglo-American countries of the United States, Canada, and Great Britain.[44] On the other hand, these characteristics are relatively absent in countries such as Chile and Portugal.

Equity theory has a relatively strong following in the United States, which is not surprising given that U.S.–style reward systems are based on the assumption that workers are highly sensitive to equity in reward allocations. In the United States, equity is meant to closely link pay to performance. However, recent evidence suggests that in collectivist cultures, especially in the former socialist countries of Central and Eastern Europe, employees expect rewards to reflect their individual needs as well as their performance.[45] Moreover, consistent with a legacy of communism and centrally planned economies, employees exhibited a greater "entitlement" attitude—that is, they expected outcomes to be greater than their inputs.[46] These findings suggest that U.S.–style pay practices may need to be modified in some countries in order to be perceived as fair by employees.

Despite these cross-cultural differences in motivation, a number of cross-cultural consistencies can be found. For instance, the desire for interesting work seems important to almost all workers, regardless of their national culture. In a study of seven countries, employees in Belgium, Britain, Israel, and the United States ranked "interesting work" number one among 11 work goals. It was ranked either second or third in Japan, the Netherlands, and Germany.[47] Similarly, in a study comparing job-preference outcomes among graduate students in the United States, Canada, Australia, and Singapore, growth, achievement, and responsibility were rated the top three and had identical rankings.[48] Both studies suggest some universality to the importance of intrinsic factors identified by Herzberg in his two-factor theory. Another recent study examining workplace motivation trends in Japan also seems to indicate that Herzberg's model is applicable to Japanese employees.[49]

How Can Managers Motivate Unique Groups of Workers?

Motivating employees has never been easy! Employees come into organizations with different needs, personalities, skills, abilities, interests, and aptitudes. They have different expectations of their employers and different views of what they think their employer has a right to expect of them. And they vary widely in what they want from their jobs. For instance, some employees get more satisfaction out of their personal interests and pursuits and only want a weekly paycheck—nothing more. They're not interested in making their work more challenging or interesting or in "winning" performance contests. Others derive a great deal of satisfaction in their jobs and are motivated to exert high levels of effort. Given these differences, how can managers do an effective job of motivating the unique groups of employees found in today's workforce? One thing is to understand the motivational requirements of these groups including (1) diverse employees, (2) professionals, and (3) contingent workers.

Making Ethical Decisions in Today's Workplace

A scary thing is happening. Workers facing extraordinary work demands are turning to ADHD (attention deficit hyperactivity disorder) drugs to boost their energy. These pills are amphetamine-based stimulants that give users a boost of energy. Although some students may use these when studying for exams or putting the final touches on a research paper/presentation (and we are, by no means, condoning such practices), experts now say that stimulant abuse is moving into the workplace. Many young workers using the drugs to increase their productivity say that "these drugs are used not to get high, but hired." Such seemingly harmless abuse can lead to serious consequences.[50]

Discussion Questions:

3 What do you think? Is this a problem of/for employee motivation? Explain.

4 Why is this a potential ethical dilemma? (Think of the impact on various stakeholders.) In your assigned group, discuss how managers might address this.

(1) MOTIVATING A DIVERSE WORKFORCE. To maximize motivation among today's workforce, managers need to think in terms of *flexibility*. For instance, studies tell us that men place more importance on having autonomy in their jobs than do women. In contrast, the opportunity to learn, convenient and flexible work hours, and good interpersonal relations are more important to women.[51] Having the opportunity to be independent and to be exposed to different experiences is important to Gen Y employees, whereas older workers may be more interested in highly structured work opportunities.[52] Managers need to recognize that what motivates a single mother with two dependent children who's working full-time to support her family may be very different from the needs of a single part-time employee or an older employee who is working only to supplement his or her retirement income. A diverse array of rewards is needed to motivate employees with such diverse needs. Many of the work/life balance programs (see Chapter 8) that organizations have implemented are a response to the varied needs of a diverse workforce. In addition, many organizations have developed flexible work arrangements (see Chapter 7) that recognize different needs. These types of programs (including telecommuting, compressed workweeks, flextime, and job sharing) may become even more popular as employers look for ways to help employees cope with high fuel prices.

Do flexible work arrangements motivate employees? Although such arrangements might seem highly motivational, both positive and negative relationships have been found. For instance, one study of the impact of telecommuting on job satisfaction found that job satisfaction initially increased as the extent of telecommuting increased, but as the number of hours spent telecommuting increased, job satisfaction started to level off, decreased slightly, and then stabilized.[53]

(2) MOTIVATING PROFESSIONALS. In contrast to a generation ago, the typical employee today is more likely to be a professional with a college degree than a blue-collar factory worker. What special concerns should managers be aware of when trying to motivate a team of engineers at Intel's India Development Center, software designers at SAS Institute in North Carolina, or a group of consultants at Accenture in Singapore?

Professionals are different from nonprofessionals.[54] They have a strong and long-term commitment to their field of expertise. To keep current in their field, they need to regularly update their knowledge, and because of their commitment to their profession they rarely define their workweek as 8 A.M. to 5 P.M. five days a week.

What motivates professionals? Money and promotions typically are low on their priority list. Why? They tend to be well paid and enjoy what they do. In contrast, job challenge tends to be ranked high. They like to tackle problems and find solutions. Their chief reward is the work itself. Professionals also value support. They want others to think that what they're working on is important. That may be true for all employees, but professionals tend to be focused on their work as their central life interest, whereas nonprofessionals typically have other interests outside of work that can compensate for needs not met on the job.

(3) MOTIVATING CONTINGENT WORKERS. As full-time jobs have been eliminated through downsizing and other organizational restructurings, the number of openings for part-time, contract, and other forms of temporary work have increased. Contingent workers don't have the security or stability that permanent employees have, and they don't identify with the organization or display the commitment that other employees do. Temporary workers also typically get little or no benefits such as health care or pensions.[55]

There's no simple solution for motivating contingent employees. For that small set of individuals who prefer the freedom of their temporary status, the lack of stability may not be an issue. In addition, temporariness might be preferred by highly compensated physicians, engineers, accountants, or financial planners who don't want the demands of a full-time job. But these are the exceptions. For the most part, temporary employees are not temporary by choice.

What will motivate involuntarily temporary employees? An obvious answer is the opportunity to become a permanent employee. In cases in which permanent employees are selected from a pool of temps, the temps will often work hard in hopes of becoming permanent. A less obvious answer is the opportunity for training. The ability of a temporary employee to find a new job is largely dependent on his or her skills. If an employee sees that the job he or she is doing can help develop marketable skills, then motivation is increased. From an equity standpoint, when temps work alongside permanent employees who earn more and get benefits too for doing the same job, the performance of temps is likely to suffer. Separating such employees or perhaps minimizing interdependence between them might help managers counteract potential problems.[56]

How Can Managers Design Appropriate Rewards Programs?

As the Group Company approached its tenth anniversary of success in the travel business, founder Helen Bilton wanted to reward her workforce for outstanding performance. Rather than plan a huge party, she arranged for all 32 employees to visit Barbados on a luxurious, all-expenses-paid three-day holiday. Rewards like this play a powerful role in motivating employee behavior.[57] Some of the more popular rewards programs include open-book management, employee recognition, and pay-for-performance.

HOW CAN OPEN-BOOK MANAGEMENT PROGRAMS MOTIVATE EMPLOYEES?   Within 24 hours after managers of the Heavy Duty Division of Springfield Remanufacturing Company (SRC) gather to discuss a multipage financial document, every plant employee will have seen the same information. If the employees can meet shipment goals, they'll all share in a large year-end bonus.[58] Many organizations of various sizes involve their employees in workplace decisions by opening up the financial statements (the "books"). They share that information so that employees will be motivated to make better decisions about their work, be better able to understand the implications of what they do and how they do it, and see the ultimate impact on the bottom line. This approach is called **open-book management** and many organizations are using it.[59]

The goal of open-book management is to get employees to think like an owner by seeing the impact their decisions have on financial results. Because many employees don't have the knowledge or background to understand the financials, they have to be taught how to read and understand the organization's financial statements. Once employees have this knowledge, however, managers need to regularly share the numbers with them. By sharing this information, employees begin to see the link between their efforts, level of performance, and operational results.

HOW CAN MANAGERS USE EMPLOYEE RECOGNITION PROGRAMS?   **Employee recognition programs** consist of personal attention and expressions of interest, approval, and appreciation for a job well done.[60] They can take numerous forms. For instance, Kelly Services introduced a new version of its points-based incentive system to better promote productivity and retention among its employees. The program, called Kelly Kudos, gives employees more choices of awards and allows them to accumulate points over a longer time period.[61] And it's working. Participants generate three times more revenue and hours than employees not receiving points. Most managers, however, use a far more informal approach. For example, Marks & Spencer encourages spontaneous posts recognizing the extra efforts of employees and peers on the U.K. department store's internal social network. Every month, the store posts an award for the employee of the month, chosen from peer nominations. In Singapore, managers at the e-commerce firm ShopBack sometimes open a bottle

open-book management
A motivational approach in which an organization's financial statements (the "books") are shared with all employees

employee recognition programs
Programs that consist of personal attention and expressions of interest, approval, and appreciation for a job well done

The bakers at Zingerman's Deli in Ann Arbor, Michigan, are empowered with information that enables them to think and act like an owner. Embracing open-book management, Zingerman shares financial, product, customer service, and other information employees need to understand how the company works and how their decisions affect the company's profitability.

Susan Montgomery/Shutterstock

Managing Technology in Today's Workplace

INDIVIDUALIZED REWARDS

Organizations have historically assumed that "one size fits all" when it comes to allocating rewards. Managers typically assumed that everyone wants more money and more vacation time. But as organizations become less bureaucratic and more capable of differentiating rewards, managers will be encouraged to differentiate rewards among employees as well as for individual employees over time.

Organizations control a vast number of potential rewards that employees might find appealing. A partial list would include increased base pay, bonuses, shortened workweeks, extended vacations, paid sabbaticals, flexible work hours, part-time employment, guaranteed job security, increased pension contributions, college tuition reimbursement, personal days off, help in purchasing a home, recognition awards, paid club memberships, and work-from-home options. And the latest twist in employee rewards comes through the use of social networking, mobile accessibility, and **gamification**—that is, applying typical aspects of game playing to other areas of activity especially in a work setting—giving employees the opportunity to earn ongoing "badges" or "honors." These types of reward programs have the potential to engage and inspire employees. In the future, most organizations will structure individual reward packages in ways that will maximize employee motivation.

Discussion Questions:

5 What are the positive aspects of having individualized rewards? What are the negative aspects of having individualized rewards? (Think in terms of employees and managers.)

6 Write a summary about individualized rewards explaining the concept to someone that isn't familiar with the concept of employee motivation.

---

gamification
Applying typical aspects of game playing to other areas of activity especially in a work setting

of champagne during informal celebrations of employee accomplishments such as clearing all outstanding customer service inquiries. At other times, managers surprise high-performing employee teams with free zoo tickets. ShopBack's human resources manager explains the reasoning behind this approach: "Cash rewards connote a transactional relationship, while non-cash rewards are powerful in building team relationships." The restaurant chain PizzaExpress Singapore has a "golden ticket" reward system, with tickets representing travel or shopping vouchers. When senior managers make unscheduled visits to the restaurants, they give away golden tickets to employees who have performed exceptionally well. "Our employees are what make the brand so successful, and we want to give back in more personal ways," said the general manager. Employee recognition is very important, but so is a tangible follow-up reward, he added—"More often than not, an actual gift means more than words."[62]

A survey of organizations found that **84 percent had some type of program to recognize worker achievements.**[63]

And do employees think these programs are important? You bet! A survey of a wide range of employees asked them what they considered the most powerful workplace motivator. Their response? Recognition, recognition, and more recognition![64]

Consistent with reinforcement theory (see Chapter 9), rewarding a behavior with recognition immediately following that behavior is likely to encourage its repetition. And recognition can take many forms. You can personally congratulate an employee in private for a good job. You can send a handwritten note or e-mail message acknowledging something positive that the employee has done. For employees with a strong need for social acceptance, you can publicly recognize accomplishments. To enhance group cohesiveness and motivation, you can celebrate team successes. For instance, you can do something as simple as throw a pizza party to celebrate a team's accomplishments. Some of these things may seem simple, but they can go a long way in showing employees they're valued.

HOW CAN MANAGERS USE PAY-FOR-PERFORMANCE TO MOTIVATE EMPLOYEES?

Here's a survey statistic that may surprise you: 40 percent of employees see no clear link between performance and pay.[65] You have to think: What are the companies where these employees work paying for? They're obviously not clearly communicating performance expectations.[66] **Pay-for-performance programs** are variable compensation plans that pay employees on the basis of some performance measure.[67] Piece-rate pay plans, wage incentive plans, profit-sharing, and lump-sum bonuses are examples. What differentiates these forms of pay from more traditional compensation plans is that instead of paying a person for time on the job, pay is adjusted to reflect some performance measure. These performance measures might include such things as individual productivity, team or work group productivity, departmental productivity, or the overall organization's profit performance.

> **pay-for-performance programs**
> Variable compensation plans that pay employees on the basis of some performance measure

Pay-for-performance is probably most compatible with expectancy theory. Individuals should perceive a strong relationship between their performance and the rewards they receive for motivation to be maximized. If rewards are allocated only on nonperformance factors—such as seniority, job title, or across-the-board pay raises—then employees are likely to reduce their efforts. From a motivation perspective, making some or all of an employee's pay conditional on some performance measure focuses his or her attention and effort toward that measure, then reinforces the continuation of the effort with a reward. If the employee, team, or organization's performance declines, so does the reward. Thus, there's an incentive to keep efforts and motivation strong.

Pay-for-performance programs are popular. Some 80 percent of large U.S. companies have some form of variable pay plan.[68] These types of pay plans have also been tried in other countries such as Canada and Japan. About 30 percent of Canadian companies and 22 percent of Japanese companies have company-wide pay-for-performance plans.[69]

Do pay-for-performance programs work? For the most part, studies seem to indicate that they do. For instance, one study found that companies that used pay-for-performance programs performed better financially than those that did not.[70] Another study showed that pay-for-performance programs with outcome-based incentives had a "positive impact on sales, customer satisfaction, and profits."[71] If an organization uses work teams, managers should consider group-based performance incentives that will reinforce team effort and commitment. But whether these programs are individual based or team based, managers need to ensure that they're specific about the relationship between an individual's pay and his or her expected level of appropriate performance. Employees must clearly understand exactly how performance—theirs and the organization's—translates into dollars on their paychecks.[72]

A FINAL NOTE ON EMPLOYEE REWARDS PROGRAMS. During times of economic and financial uncertainty, managers' abilities to recognize and reward employees are often severely constrained. It's hard to keep employees productive during challenging times, even though it's especially critical. It's not surprising, then, that employees feel less connected to their work. In fact, a recent study by the Corporate Executive Board found that declining employee engagement has decreased overall productivity by 3 to 5 percent.[73] But there are actions managers can take to maintain and maybe even increase employees' motivation levels. One is to clarify each person's role in the organization. Show them how their efforts are contributing to improving the company's overall situation. It's also important to keep communication lines open and use two-way exchanges between top-level managers and employees to soothe fears and concerns. The key with taking any actions is continuing to show workers that the company cares about them. As we said at the beginning of the chapter, the value in companies comes from employees who are motivated to be there. Managers have to give employees a reason to want to be there.

CHAPTER SUMMARY BY LEARNING OUTCOME

11-1 Define and explain motivation.

Motivation is the process by which a person's efforts are energized, directed, and sustained toward attaining a goal.

The *energy* element is a measure of intensity or drive. The high level of effort needs to be *directed* in ways that help the organization achieve its goals. Employees must *persist* in putting forth effort to achieve those goals.

11-2 Compare and contrast early theories of motivation.

Individuals move up the hierarchy of five needs (physiological, safety, social, esteem, and self-actualization) as needs are substantially satisfied. A need that's substantially satisfied no longer motivates.

A Theory X manager believes that people don't like to work, or won't seek out responsibility, so they have to be threatened and coerced to work. A Theory Y manager assumes that people like to work and seek out responsibility, so they will exercise self-motivation and self-direction.

Herzberg's theory proposed that intrinsic factors associated with job satisfaction were what motivated people. Extrinsic factors associated with job dissatisfaction simply kept people from being dissatisfied.

Three-needs theory proposed three acquired needs that are major motives in work: need for achievement, need for affiliation, and need for power.

11-3 Compare and contrast contemporary theories of motivation.

Goal-setting theory says that specific goals increase performance, and difficult goals, when accepted, result in higher performance than do easy goals. Important points in goal–setting theory include intention to work toward a goal as a major source of job motivation; specific hard goals to produce higher levels of output than generalized goals; participation in setting goals as preferable to assigning goals, but not always; feedback to guide and motivate behavior, especially self-generated feedback; and contingencies that affect goal setting, such as goal commitment, self-efficacy, and national culture.

The job characteristics model is based on five core job dimensions (skill variety, task identity, task significance, autonomy, and feedback) that are used to design motivating jobs.

Equity theory focuses on how employees compare their inputs-outcomes ratios to relevant others' ratios. A perception of inequity will cause an employee to do something about it. Procedural justice has a greater influence on employee satisfaction than does distributive justice.

Expectancy theory says that an individual tends to act in a certain way based on the expectation that the act will be followed by a desired outcome. Expectancy is the effort-performance linkage (how much effort do I need to exert to achieve a certain level of performance); instrumentality is the performance-reward linkage (achieving at a certain level of performance will get me what reward); and valence is the attractiveness of the reward (Is the reward what I want?).

11-4 Discuss current issues in motivating employees.

During rough economic conditions, managers must look for creative ways to keep employees' efforts energized, directed, and sustained toward achieving goals.

Most motivational theories were developed in the United States and have a North American bias. Some theories (Maslow's need hierarchy, achievement need, and equity theory) don't work well for other cultures. However, the desire for interesting work seems important to all workers and Herzberg's motivator (intrinsic) factors may be universal.

Managers face challenges in motivating unique groups of workers. A diverse workforce is looking for flexibility. Professionals want job challenge and support, and are motivated by the work itself. Contingent workers want the opportunity to become permanent or to receive skills training.

Open-book management is when financial statements (the books) are shared with employees who have been taught what that information means. Employee recognition programs consist of personal attention, approval, and appreciation for a job well done. Pay-for-performance programs are variable compensation plans that pay employees on the basis of some performance measure.

DISCUSSION QUESTIONS

11-1 Most of us have to work for a living, and a job is a central part of our lives. So why do managers have to worry so much about employee motivation issues?

11-2 What is motivation? Explain the three key elements of motivation.

11-3 Contrast lower-order and higher-order needs in Maslow's needs hierarchy.

11-4 What role would money play in (a) the hierarchy of needs theory, (b) two-factor theory, (c) equity theory, (d) expectancy theory, and (e) motivating employees with a high nAch?

11-5 What are some of the possible consequences of employees perceiving an inequity between their inputs and outcomes and those of others?

11-6 What are some advantages of using pay-for-performance programs to motivate employee performance? Are there drawbacks? Explain.

11-7 Many job design experts who have studied the changing nature of work say that people do their best work when they're motivated by a sense of purpose rather than by the pursuit of money. Do you agree? Explain your position. What are the implications for managers?

11-8 As a manager, what will you need to know about goal-setting theory as a motivation tool?

11-9 Can an individual be too motivated? Discuss.

11-10 What challenges do managers face in motivating today's workforce?

Applying: Getting Ready for the Workplace

Management Skill Builder | BEING A GOOD MOTIVATOR

Great managers are great motivators. They're able to find the magic "potion" that stimulates employees to reach their full potential. The fact that there are hundreds of business books on motivation and dozens of experts who make a living by putting on motivation seminars only confirms the importance of this topic to managerial effectiveness.

MyLab Management

PERSONAL INVENTORY ASSESSMENT

Go to **www.pearson.com/mylab/management** to complete the Personal Inventory Assessment related to this chapter.

PERSONAL INVENTORY ASSESSMENT

Skill Basics

Attempting to motivate others is a complex task. Unfortunately, no universal motivators are available that are guaranteed to work on anyone, anywhere. That said, we do know a lot about what works and doesn't work in terms of motivating others. The following suggestions summarize the essence of what we know is likely to be effective.[74]

*   *Recognize individual differences.* People have different needs. Don't treat them all alike. Moreover, spend the time

necessary to understand what's important to each person. This will allow you to individualize goals, level of involvement, and rewards to align with individual needs.

*   *Use goals and feedback.* People prefer to have goals. If you're in a position to assign or participate in setting goals for others, help them to set hard and specific goals. These are most likely to motivate. In addition, individuals are most likely to be motivated when they get feedback on how well they are faring in the pursuit of their goals.

- *Allow people to participate in decisions that affect them.* If you are in a position to influence the level of participation, actively seek input from the person you seek to motivate. Employees are especially likely to respond positively when allowed to participate in setting work goals, choosing their benefit packages, solving productivity and quality problems, and the like.

- *Link rewards to unsatisfied needs.* Recommendations 2 and 3 apply most directly to managers or team leaders trying to motivate their employees or team members. Effectively linking rewards to unsatisfied needs is a more generalizable action: It applies to motivating colleagues, friends, spouses, customers—as well as employees and team members. It builds on recommendation 1 and individual differences.

  Depending on your position in an organization and your resources, the rewards you control will vary. For example, senior-level executives typically can control pay increases, bonuses, promotion decisions, job assignments, and training decisions. They also can usually control job design such as allowing employees more freedom and control over their work, improving working conditions, increasing social interactions in the workplace, or modifying the workload. But everyone can offer others rewards such as recognition or providing sympathetic and sensitive help with problems. The key is identifying what needs are dominant and unsatisfied, then choosing rewards that will help satisfy those needs.

- *Link rewards to performance.* The rewards you choose should be allocated so as to be contingent on performance. Importantly, the person you're trying to motivate must perceive a clear linkage. Regardless of how closely rewards are actually correlated to performance criteria, it's perception that counts. If individuals perceive this relationship to be low, motivation and performance will suffer.

- *Maintain equity.* Rewards should be perceived by people in the organization as equating with the inputs they bring to their job. At a simplistic level, it means that experience, skills, abilities, effort, and other obvious inputs should explain differences in performance and, hence, pay, job assignments, and other obvious rewards.

Practicing The Skill

Read through this scenario and follow the directions at the end of it:

Sean's first job out of college is as a supervisor for Lyle's Catering Services. One of Lyle's main businesses is managing the food service operations at colleges and hospitals.

Sean has been given responsibility for the cafeteria at St. Paul College. He has a staff of approximately 12 full-time and 15 part-time workers. The cafeteria is open 7 days a week, from 6:30 A.M. until 8 P.M.

Sean has been in the job eight months and has become frustrated by the high employee turnover. Just since he's been on the job, three full-time and six part-time people have quit. Sean went back and looked at the personnel records for the past five years and this pattern has been a constant. He's frustrated by the cost and time involved in continually hiring and training new people. He's decided he needs to do something.

Sean has begun informally talking to employees. None seem particularly enthusiastic about their jobs. Even some of the "old timers"—who've worked in the cafeteria for six years or more—have little enthusiasm for their work. In fact, the part-timers seem more motivated than the full-timers even though the average part-timer makes only $11.50 an hour versus the full-timers' $15.00.

The class should form into small groups. Assume you are Sean. How can you improve the staff's motivation and reduce the turnover rate?

Experiential Exercise

After reading and studying this chapter, you're well aware of how important employee motivation is. You're also aware that showing employees they're appreciated can have a positive impact on morale and motivation. According to a CareerBuilder survey, 50 percent of employees said they believed turnover would decrease if managers simply recognized their efforts more frequently. On the other hand, 40 percent of employees said they were *unlikely to go above and beyond in work efforts* if their managers took their efforts for granted.[75] But recognition doesn't only need to come from managers. It can come from others, such as coworkers, as well. So, in this experiential exercise, you're going to do some brainstorming in your assigned group. Brainstorming about what, you ask? The Top 25 Compliments for Coworkers! Come up with a list of compliments you could give your coworkers for working hard and for good work! Here are a couple of examples:

- Fantastic work!
- Even when things get crazy around here, you continue to have the best attitude!

Have fun with this! And remember that giving compliments—sincere compliments—is a wonderful way to show your coworkers how much you appreciate them! Who knows? Maybe someone will compliment your hard work, too!

CASE APPLICATION #1

One for the Money...
Topic: The Real Living Wage

In 1999, the United Kingdom introduced the National Minimum Wage, requiring employers to pay a minimum hourly rate regardless of the size of the organization or the nature of the role. Reviewed by an independent body, this minimum rate has increased every year. The campaign for a living wage started in 2001 and was aimed at ensuring that wages were at levels that allowed workers to meet living costs, not just the government minimum. The campaign gained cross-party support, and in 2016, the government introduced the National Living Wage for workers over 25.

Both these policies were intended to help workers maintain a basic standard of living, and organizations seen to be breaking the rules faced government investigation and, in rare cases, prosecution.[76] With these legal requirements in place, why are some companies choosing to pay more?

The Living Wage Foundation aims to persuade organizations to pay employees more than the legal mandate to help them to afford what they need for a decent standard of living, which involves things like healthier food. At the beginning of January 2019, they had over 4,700 accredited living-wage employers, including a third of the FTSE 100.[77] One of these companies, IKEA UK, introduced the real living wage in April 2016, leading to a wage increase for 7,300 workers. Pernille Hagild, IKEA UK's Country HR Manager, said that the increase would help with the company's plans for growth in the United Kingdom and that it would lead to increased motivation and reduced staff turnover. Employees were reported to have said the changes in their lives would be quite significant, allowing them to apply for mortgages, pay their bills, and simply enjoy life more.[78]

Chelsea FC became the first premiership football club to sign up to the living wage in 2014. Chelsea's chairman, Bruce Buck, believed it showed a commitment to the staff, ensuring that hard work and dedication were rewarded fairly. It extended the hourly rate increase to include staff employed by external contractors at their training ground. The move was supported by the then Mayor of London, Boris Johnson, who felt this was a good example to set for the other clubs.[79]

The theme that this is simply the right thing to do is echoed by many of the accredited employers. Oxfam firmly believes that being able to work and earn a decent wage is fundamental to overcoming poverty. Nestlé see the commercial benefit, believing that being a Principal Partner of the Living Wage Foundation will help them influence the industry, but they also acknowledge that increased wages will have a positive impact on the wider community.

Has the move proved a success for Chelsea FC, IKEA, and the other 4,700 employers? Research carried out by the Living Wage Foundation does appear to support the decision. Surveying over 800 accredited real Living Wage businesses, the Foundation found that over half had seen improvements in both recruitment and retention. For example, Brewdog, a manufacturer and retailer of craft beer, saw staff turnover fall by 40 percent in the year after they introduced the living wage. Of the 800 businesses surveyed, 57 percent had seen an increase in the commitment and motivation of living wage employees (rising to 78 percent for larger employers). In addition, 86 percent believed that the decision to pay the real living wage had also enhanced the organization's reputation.

Discussion Questions

11-11 Does this case support the myth at the beginning of the chapter?

11-12 Do you think that the reported increase in motivation has to do with something apart from just the extra money?

11-13 Would these benefits to the organization be seen if middle or higher wage rates had been increased?

11-14 Do you see any long-term issues with this increase in wage levels?

CASE APPLICATION #2

Unlimited Vacation Time? Really?

Topic: Motivating professionals, expectancy theory

Would unlimited vacation time offered by an organization be important to you? Would it be an appealing enough benefit to attract you to an organization you might not have considered? Would it motivate you as an employee? Some businesses—Netflix, LinkedIn, Virgin America, Twitter, and BirchBox, among others—offer employees as much paid time off as they want. However, unlimited vacation policies continue to be rare in corporate America. Only 1 to 2 percent of companies offer this option according to the Society for Human Resource Management.[80] Technology has contributed to the impression that employees always feel like they need to be available, even while on vacation. And many employees don't even take the typical standard two-weeks' vacation time. In fact, a recent survey of more than 7,000 workers said that the average American employee earned 22.6 days of vacation in 2017, but only used 16.8 of those days.[81] Why have these atypical organizations chosen to offer employees unlimited vacation time, and what do employees think about it?

One of the reasons organizations choose to offer this option is because they feel their employees are overworked and stressed, with project deadlines, meetings, and unexpected crises. Even employees who are not in leadership positions may be "expected" to be available after business hours. But just because unlimited vacation is offered doesn't mean that employees are going to use it. Many employees are hesitant to take advantage of extensive time off because they feel that it sends a wrong message to their boss, especially if other employees—or even the managers—aren't taking off for vacation time.

Another reason that some organizations are offering this benefit is that they're having a difficult time attracting talented professionals. Kronos, a Massachusetts-based workplace management software company, was struggling to find qualified college-educated professionals because of its location in a tight labor market where professionals are in high demand.[82] The CEO directed the HR department to come up with strategies that could make the company more competitive in recruiting. One suggested strategy was an "open" vacation policy like the one pioneered by Netflix. After implementing a similar policy, Kronos found recruiting talented professionals not as challenging as it was without such a policy.

However, open vacation policies aren't without employee complaints. When Kronos implemented its open vacation policy, there were three major categories of complaints.[83] One of the major complaints came from managers who felt uncomfortable about the ambiguity created because there was no formal policy. These managers believed that they might have to deal with employees who wanted to take off excessive amounts of time or that they would have to mediate scheduling conflicts and juggle employees' work schedules. To address those concerns, the company provided individual training and coaching to managers and reassured them that HR would support them in whatever they needed.

Another major complaint came from employees who had been accruing their vacation time and who expected to get a cash reimbursement when they left the company. Because a company eliminates an accrued expense item, some critics of open vacation policies say that a company only does it to save money, not to improve employee morale. To address these concerns, Kronos' executives decided to reinvest any vacation accrual savings into other employee benefits, such as increased maternity leave, increased 401(k) match, a child-care assistance program, and contributing a set amount toward employees' student loans.

The final major complaint at Kronos came from employees who had been with the company for enough years to accumulate a significant amount of yearly vacation time. These employees felt it was unfair for new employees to get as much vacation time as they desired without having been there for years. Again, Kronos executives attempted to address these complaints in informal conversations with individual employees. The perception of inequity can be a challenge for managers.

As with any type of organizational change that impacts employees, managers at Kronos—and any company that has moved to or is contemplating moving to an open vacation policy—need to think through the change and how employees might be impacted.

How much vacation time is too much vacation time?

Discussion Questions

11-15 What are the pros and cons of unlimited vacation policies for both employees and for organizations?

11-16 Why do you think some companies are moving to unlimited vacation policies? Is it feasible in small companies? Discuss.

11-17 What impact might managers/team leaders have on whether employees actually take advantage of an unlimited vacation policy?

11-18 Do you think there might be generational differences in how employees feel about unlimited vacation? Explain your answer.

11-19 How might unlimited vacation affect employee motivation? In answering this question, discuss any relevant motivation theories (early and contemporary) as they relate to this organizational approach.

CASE APPLICATION #3

Passionate Pursuits
Topic: Motivating unique groups of workers, job design

At its headquarters in Ventura, California, Patagonia's office space feels more like a national park lodge than the main office of a $600 million retailer.[84] It has a Douglas fir staircase and a portrait of Yosemite's El Capitan. The company's café serves organic food and drinks. There's an infant and toddler child-care room for employees' children. An easy one-block walk from the Pacific Ocean, employees' surfboards are lined up by the cafeteria, ready at a moment's notice to catch some waves. (Current wave reports are noted on a whiteboard in the lobby.)

Motivating employees the **right way**

After surfing or jogging or biking, employees can freshen up in the showers found in the restrooms. And no one has a private office. If an employee doesn't want to be disturbed, he or she wears headphones. Visitors are evident by the business attire they wear. The company encourages celebrations to boost employee morale. For instance, at the Reno store, the "Fun Patrol" organizes parties throughout the year.

Patagonia has long been recognized as a great workplace for mothers. And it's also earned a reputation for loyal employees, something that many retailers struggle with. Its combined voluntary and involuntary turnover in its retail stores was around 25 percent, while it was only 7 percent at headquarters. (The industry average for retail is around 44 percent.) Patagonia's CEO Rose Marcario says the company's culture, camaraderie, and way of doing business is very meaningful to employees and they know that their work activities are helping protect and preserve

the outdoors that they all love and enjoy. Managers are coached to define expectations, communicate deadlines, and then let employees figure out the best way to meet those.

Founded by Yvon Chouinard, an avid advocate of the natural environment, Patagonia's first and strongest passion is for the outdoors and the environment. And that attracts employees who are also passionate about those things. But Patagonia's executives do realize that they are first and foremost a business and, even though they're committed to doing the right thing, the company needs to remain profitable to be able to continue to do the things it's passionate about. But that hasn't seemed to be an issue since the recession in the early 1990s, when the company had to make its only large-scale layoffs in its history.

Discussion Questions

11-20 What would it be like to work at Patagonia? (*Hint:* Go to Patagonia's website and find the section on Careers.) What's your assessment of the company's work environment?

11-21 Using what you've learned from studying the various motivation theories, what does Patagonia's situation tell you about employee motivation?

11-22 What do you think might be Patagonia's biggest challenge in keeping employees motivated?

11-23 In your assigned group, discuss this: If you were managing a team of Patagonia employees in the retail stores, how would you keep them motivated?

Endnotes

1. P. Bronson, "What Should I Do with My Life Now?" *Fast Company*, April 2009, pp. 35–37.
2. SmartPulse, "How Well Do You Motivate Your People?" Smart Brief on Leadership, www.smart-brief.com/leadership, January 20, 2015.
3. A. Adkins, "The Best Workplace Articles of 2017," *Gallup News Online*, December 13, 2017.
4. R. M. Steers, R. T. Mowday, and D. L. Shapiro, "The Future of Work Motivation Theory," *Academy of Management Review*, July 2004, pp. 379–87.
5. A. Adkins, "U.S. Employee Engagement Holds Steady at 31.7%," May 7, 2015, http://www.gallup.com/poll/183041/employee-engagement-holds-steady.aspx.
6. J. Krueger and E. Killham, "At Work, Feeling Good Matters," *Gallup Management Journal*, December 8, 2015, http://gmj.gallup.com.
7. "Maslow Motion," *New Statesman*, March 15, 2010, p. 37; "Dialogue," *Academy of Management Review*, October 2000, pp. 696–701; M. L. Ambrose and C. T. Kulik, "Old Friends, New Faces: Motivation Research in the 1990s," *Journal of Management* 25, no. 3 (1999), pp. 231–92; A. Maslow, D. C. Stephens, and G. Heil, *Maslow on Management* (New York: John Wiley & Sons, 1998); and A. Maslow, *Motivation and Personality* (New York: McGraw-Hill, 1954).
8. R. Coutts, "A Pilot Study for the Analysis of Dream Reports Using Maslow's Need Categories: An Extension to the Emotional Selection Hypothesis," *Psychological Reports*, October 2010, pp. 659–73; E. A. Fisher, "Motivation and Leadership in Social Work Management: A Review of Theories and Related Studies," *Administration in Social Work*, October–December 2009, pp. 347–67; and N. K. Austin, "The Power of the Pyramid: The Foundation of Human Psychology and, Thereby, of Motivation, Maslow's Hierarchy Is One Powerful Pyramid," *Incentive* (July 2002), p. 10.
9. See, for example, Ambrose and Kulik, "Old Friends, New Faces: Motivation Research in the 1990s"; J. Rowan, "Ascent and Descent in Maslow's Theory," *Journal of Humanistic Psychology*, Summer 1999, pp. 125–33; J. Rowan, "Maslow Amended," *Journal of Humanistic Psychology*, Winter 1998, pp. 81–92; R. M. Creech, "Employee Motivation," *Management Quarterly*, Summer 1995, pp. 33–39; E. E. Lawler III and J. L. Suttle, "A Causal Correlational Test of the Need Hierarchy Concept," *Organizational Behavior and Human Performance*, April 1972, pp. 265–87; and D. T. Hall and K. E. Nongaim, "An Examination of Maslow's Need Hierarchy in an Organizational Setting," *Organizational Behavior and Human Performance*, February 1968, pp. 12–35.
10. R. E. Kopelman, D. J. Prottas, and A. L. Davis, "Douglas McGregor's Theory X and Y: Toward a Construct-Valid Measure," *Journal of Managerial Issues*, Summer 2008, pp. 255–71; and D. McGregor, *The Human Side of Enterprise* (New York: McGraw-Hill, 1960). For an updated description of Theories X and Y, see an annotated edition with commentary of *The Human Side of Enterprise* (McGraw-Hill, 2006); and G. Heil, W. Bennis, and D. C. Stephens, *Douglas McGregor, Revisited: Managing the Human Side of Enterprise* (New York: Wiley, 2000).
11. F. Herzberg, B. Mausner, and B. Snyderman, *The Motivation to Work* (New York: John Wiley, 1959); F. Herzberg, *The Managerial Choice: To Be Effective or to Be Human*, rev. ed. (Salt Lake City, UT: Olympus, 1982); Creech, "Employee Motivation"; and Ambrose and Kulik, "Old Friends, New Faces: Motivation Research in the 1990s."
12. D. C. McClelland, *The Achieving Society* (New York: Van Nostrand Reinhold, 1961); J. W. Atkinson and J. O. Raynor, *Motivation and Achievement* (Washington, DC: Winston, 1974); D. C. McClelland, *Power: The Inner Experience* (New York: Irvington, 1975); and M. J. Stahl, *Managerial and Technical Motivation: Assessing Needs for Achievement, Power, and Affiliation* (New York: Praeger, 1986).
13. McClelland, *The Achieving Society*.
14. McClelland, *Power: The Inner Experience*; D. C. McClelland and D. H. Burnham, "Power Is the Great Motivator," *Harvard Business Review*, March–April 1976, pp. 100–10.
15. D. Miron and D. C. McClelland, "The Impact of Achievement Motivation Training on Small Businesses," *California Management Review*, Summer 1979, pp. 13–28.
16. "McClelland: An Advocate of Power," *International Management*, July 1975, pp. 27–29.
17. J. Flint, "How to Be a Player," *Bloomberg Businessweek*, January 24–30, 2011, pp. 108–09.
18. Steers, Mowday, and Shapiro, "The Future of Work Motivation Theory"; E. A. Locke and G. P. Latham, "What Should We Do about Motivation Theory? Six Recommendations for the Twenty-First Century," *Academy of Management Review*, July 2004, pp. 388–403; and Ambrose and Kulik, "Old Friends, New Faces: Motivation Research in the 1990s."
19. Ambrose and Kulik, "Old Friends, New Faces: Motivation Research in the 1990s."
20. J. C. Naylor and D. R. Ilgen, "Goal Setting: A Theoretical Analysis of a Motivational Technique," in B. M. Staw and L. L. Cummings (eds.), *Research in Organizational Behavior*, vol. 6 (Greenwich, CT: JAI Press, 1984), pp. 95–140; A. R. Pell, "Energize Your People," *Managers Magazine*, December 1992, pp. 28–29; E. A. Locke, "Facts and Fallacies about Goal Theory: Reply to Deci," *Psychological Science*, January 1993, pp. 63–64; M. E. Tubbs, "Commitment as a Moderator of the Goal-Performance Relation: A Case for Clearer Construct Definition," *Journal of Applied Psychology*, February 1993, pp. 86–97; M. P. Collingwood, "Why Don't You Use the Research?" *Management Decision*, May 1993, pp. 48–54; M. E. Tubbs, D. M. Boehne, and J. S. Dahl, "Expectancy, Valence, and Motivational Force Functions in Goal-Setting Research: An Empirical Test," *Journal of Applied Psychology*, June 1993, pp. 361–73; E. A. Locke, "Motivation through Conscious Goal Setting," *Applied and Preventive Psychology* 5 (1996), pp. 117–24; Ambrose and Kulik, "Old Friends, New Faces: Motivation Research in the 1990s; E. A. Locke and G. P. Latham, "Building a Practically Useful Theory of Goal Setting and Task Motivation: A 35-Year Odyssey," *American Psychologist*, September 2002, pp. 705–17; Y. Fried and L. H. Slowik, "Enriching Goal-Setting Theory with Time: An Integrated Approach," *Academy of Management Review*, July 2004, pp. 404–22; G. P. Latham, "The Motivational Benefits of Goal-Setting," *Academy of Management Executive*, November 2004, pp. 126–29; and G. Yeo, S. Loft, T. Xiao, and C. Kiewitz, "Goal Orientation and Performance: Differential Relationships Across Levels of Analysis and as a Function of Task Demands," *Journal of Applied Psychology*, May 2009, pp. 710–26.
21. J. A. Wagner III, "Participation's Effects on Performance and Satisfaction: A Reconsideration of Research and Evidence," *Academy of Management Review*, April 1994, pp. 312–30; J. George-Falvey, "Effects of Task Complexity and Learning Stage on the Relationship between Participation in Goal Setting and Task Performance," *Academy of Management Proceedings on Disk*, 1996; T. D. Ludwig and E. S. Geller, "Assigned versus Participative Goal Setting and Response Generalization: Managing Injury Control among Professional Pizza Deliverers," *Journal of Applied Psychology*, April 1997, pp. 253–61; and S. G. Harkins and M. D. Lowe, "The Effects of Self-Set Goals on Task Performance," *Journal of Applied Social Psychology*, January 2000, pp. 1–40.
22. J. M. Ivancevich and J. T. McMahon, "The Effects of Goal Setting, External Feedback, and Self-Generated Feedback on Outcome Variables: A Field Experiment," *Academy of Management Journal*, June 1982, pp. 359–72; and Locke, "Motivation Through Conscious Goal Setting."
23. J. R. Hollenbeck, C. R. Williams, and H. J. Klein, "An Empirical Examination of the Antecedents of Commitment to Difficult Goals," *Journal of Applied Psychology*, February 1989, pp. 18–23; see also, J. C. Wofford, V. L. Goodwin, and S. Premack, "Meta-Analysis of the Antecedents of Personal Goal Level and of the Antecedents and Consequences of Goal Commitment," *Journal of Management*, September 1992, pp. 595–615; Tubbs, "Commitment as a Moderator of the Goal-Performance Relation"; and J. W. Smither, M. London, and R. R. Reilly, "Does Performance Improve Following Multisource Feedback? A Theoretical Model, Meta-Analysis, and Review of Empirical Findings," *Personnel Psychology*, Spring 2005, pp. 171–203.
24. M. E. Gist, "Self-Efficacy: Implications for Organizational Behavior and Human Resource Management," *Academy of Management Review*, July 1987, pp. 472–85; and A. Bandura, *Self-Efficacy: The Exercise of Control* (New York: Freeman, 1997).
25. E. A. Locke, E. Frederick, C. Lee, and P. Bobko, "Effect of Self-Efficacy, Goals, and Task Strategies on Task Performance," *Journal of Applied Psychology*, May 1984, pp. 241–51; M. E. Gist

and T. R. Mitchell, "Self-Efficacy: A Theoretical Analysis of Its Determinants and Malleability," *Academy of Management Review*, April 1992, pp. 183–211; A. D. Stajkovic and F. Luthans, "Self-Efficacy and Work-Related Performance: A Meta-Analysis," *Psychological Bulletin*, September 1998, pp. 240–61; A. Bandura, "Cultivate Self-Efficacy for Personal and Organizational Effectiveness," in E. Locke (ed.), *Handbook of Principles of Organizational Behavior* (Malden, MA: Blackwell, 2004), pp. 120–36; and F. Q. Fu, K. A. Richards, and E. Jones, "The Motivation Hub: Effects of Goal Setting and Self-Efficacy on Effort and New Product Sales," *Journal of Personal Selling & Sales Management*, Summer 2009, pp. 277–92.

26. A. Bandura and D. Cervone, "Differential Engagement in Self-Reactive Influences in Cognitively Based Motivation," *Organizational Behavior and Human Decision Processes*, August 1986, pp. 92–113; and R. Ilies and T. A. Judge, "Goal Regulation across Time: The Effects of Feedback and Affect," *Journal of Applied Psychology* (May 2005): pp. 453–67.

27. See J. C. Anderson and C. A. O'Reilly, "Effects of an Organizational Control System on Managerial Satisfaction and Performance," *Human Relations*, June 1981, pp. 491–501; and J. P. Meyer, B. Schacht-Cole, and I. R. Gellatly, "An Examination of the Cognitive Mechanisms by Which Assigned Goals Affect Task Performance and Reactions to Performance," *Journal of Applied Social Psychology* 18, no. 5 (1988): pp. 390–408.

28. See, for example, R. W. Griffin, "Toward an Integrated Theory of Task Design," in L. L. Cummings and B. M. Staw (eds.), *Research in Organizational Behavior*, vol. 9 (Greenwich, CT: JAI Press, 1987), pp. 79–120; and M. Campion, "Interdisciplinary Approaches to Job Design: A Constructive Replication with Extensions," *Journal of Applied Psychology*, August 1988, pp. 467–81.

29. See J. R. Hackman and G. R. Oldham, "Motivation through the Design of Work: Test of a Theory," *Organizational Behavior and Human Performance*, August 1976, pp. 250–79; Y. Fried and G. R. Ferris, "The Validity of the Job Characteristics Model: A Review and Meta Analysis," *Personnel Psychology*, Summer 1987, pp. 287–322; S. J. Zaccaro and E. F. Stone, "Incremental Validity of an Empirically Based Measure of Job Characteristics," *Journal of Applied Psychology*, May 1988, pp. 245–52; and R. W. Renn and R. J. Vandenberg, "The Critical Psychological States: An Underrepresented Component in Job Characteristics Model Research," *Journal of Management*, February 1995, pp. 279–303.

30. Classic Concepts in Today's Workplace box based on C. M. Christensen, "How Will You Measure Your Life?" *Harvard Business Review*, July–August 2010, pp. 46–51; D. A. Wren and A. G. Bedeian, *The Evolution of Management Thought* (New York: John Wiley & Sons, Inc., 2009); F. Herzberg, *One More Time: How Do You Motivate Employees?* (Boston, MA: Harvard Business School Press, 2008); and Herzberg, Mausner, and Snyderman, *The Motivation to Work*.

31. G. Van Der Vegt, B. Emans, and E. Van Der Vliert, "Motivating Effects of Task and Outcome Interdependence in Work Teams," *Journal of Managerial Psychology*, July 2000, p. 829; and B. Bemmels, "Local Union Leaders' Satisfaction with Grievance Procedures," *Journal of Labor Research*, Summer 2001, pp. 653–69.

32. J. S. Adams, "Inequity in Social Exchanges," in L. Berkowitz (ed.), *Advances in Experimental Social Psychology*, vol. 2 (New York: Academic Press, 1965), pp. 267–300; and Ambrose and Kulik, "Old Friends, New Faces: Motivation Research in the 1990s."

33. See, for example, R. L. Bell, "Addressing Employees' Feelings of Inequity," *Supervision*, May 2011, pp. 3–6; P. S. Goodman and A. Friedman, "An Examination of Adams' Theory of Inequity," *Administrative Science Quarterly*, September 1971, pp. 271–88; M. R. Carrell, "A Longitudinal Field Assessment of Employee Perceptions of Equitable Treatment," *Organizational Behavior and Human Performance*, February 1978, pp. 108–18; E. Walster, G. W. Walster, and W. G. Scott, *Equity: Theory and Research* (Boston: Allyn & Bacon, 1978); R. G. Lord and J. A. Hohenfeld, "Longitudinal Field Assessment of Equity Effects on the Performance of Major League Baseball Players," *Journal of Applied Psychology*, February 1979, pp. 19–26; J. E. Dittrich and M. R. Carrell, "Organizational Equity Perceptions, Employee Job Satisfaction, and Departmental Absence and Turnover Rates," *Organizational Behavior and Human Performance*, August 1979, pp. 29–40; and J. Greenberg, "Cognitive Reevaluation of Outcomes in Response to Underpayment Inequity," *Academy of Management Journal*, March 1989, pp. 174–84.

34. P. S. Goodman, "An Examination of Referents Used in the Evaluation of Pay," *Organizational Behavior and Human Performance*, October 1974, pp. 170–95; S. Ronen, "Equity Perception in Multiple Comparisons: A Field Study," *Human Relations*, April 1986, pp. 333–46; R. W. Scholl, E. A. Cooper, and J. F. McKenna, "Referent Selection in Determining Equity Perception: Differential Effects on Behavioral and Attitudinal Outcomes," *Personnel Psychology*, Spring 1987, pp. 113–27; and C. T. Kulik and M. L. Ambrose, "Personal and Situational Determinants of Referent Choice," *Academy of Management Review*, April 1992, pp. 212–37.

35. See, for example, R. C. Dailey and D. J. Kirk, "Distributive and Procedural Justice as Antecedents of Job Dissatisfaction and Intent to Turnover," *Human Relations*, March 1992, pp. 305–16; D. B. McFarlin and P. D. Sweeney, "Distributive and Procedural Justice as Predictors of Satisfaction with Personal and Organizational Outcomes," *Academy of Management Journal*, August 1992, pp. 626–37; M. A. Konovsky, "Understanding Procedural Justice and Its Impact on Business Organizations," *Journal of Management* 26, no. 3 (2000), pp. 489–511; J. A. Colquitt, "Does the Justice of One Interact with the Justice of Many? Reactions to Procedural Justice in Teams," *Journal of Applied Psychology*, August 2004, pp. 633–46; J. Brockner, "Why It's So Hard to Be Fair," *Harvard Business Review*, March 2006, pp. 122–29; and B. M. Wiesenfeld, W. B. Swann Jr., J. Brockner, and C. A. Bartel, "Is More Fairness Always Preferred: Self-Esteem Moderates Reactions to Procedural Justice," *Academy of Management Journal*, October 2007, pp. 1235–53.

36. See, for example, H. G. Heneman III and D. P. Schwab, "Evaluation of Research on Expectancy Theory Prediction of Employee Performance," *Psychological Bulletin*, July 1972, pp. 1–9; and L. Reinharth and M. Wahba, "Expectancy Theory as a Predictor of Work Motivation, Effort Expenditure, and Job Performance," *Academy of Management Journal*, September 1975, pp. 502–537.

37. See, for example, V. H. Vroom, "Organizational Choice: A Study of Pre- and Postdecision Processes," *Organizational Behavior and Human Performance*, April 1966, pp. 212–25; L. W. Porter and E. E. Lawler III, *Managerial Attitudes and Performance* (Homewood, IL: Richard D. Irwin, 1968); W. Van Eerde and H. Thierry, "Vroom's Expectancy Models and Work-Related Criteria: A Meta-Analysis," *Journal of Applied Psychology*, October 1996, pp. 575–86; and Ambrose and Kulik, "Old Friends, New Faces: Motivation Research in the 1990s."

38. L. Bock, "My Smartest Employees Have Forced Me to Reward Them—Here's How," *Fast Company Online*, December 12, 2017.

39. See, for instance, M. Siegall, "The Simplistic Five: An Integrative Framework for Teaching Motivation," *The Organizational Behavior Teaching Review* 12, no. 4 (1987–1988), pp. 141–43.

40. "100 Best Companies to Work For," *Fortune*, February 7, 2011, pp. 91+; V. Nayar, "Employee Happiness: Zappos vs. HCL," *Businessweek.com*, January 5, 2011; D. Richards, "At Zappos, Culture Pays," *Strategy+Business Online*, Autumn 2010; T. Hseih, "Zappos's CEO on Going to Extremes for Customers," *Harvard Business Review*, July–August 2010, pp. 41–45; A. Perschel, "Work-Life Flow: How Individuals, Zappos, and Other Innovative Companies Achieve High Engagement," *Global Business & Organizational Excellence*, July 2010, pp. 17–30; and J. M. O'Brien, "Zappos Know How to Kick It," *Fortune*, February 2, 2009, pp. 54–60.

41. T. Barber, "Inspire Your Employees Now," *Bloomberg Businessweek Online*, May 18, 2010; D. Mattioli, "CEOs Welcome Recovery to Look after Staff," *Wall Street Journal*, April 5, 2010, B5; J. Sullivan, "How Do We Keep People Motivated Following Layoffs?" *Workforce Management Online*, March 2010; S. Crabtree, "How to Bolster Employees' Confidence," *Gallup Management Journal Online*, February 25, 2010; S. E. Needleman, "Business Owners Try to Motivate Employees," *Wall Street Journal*, January 14, 2010, p. B5; H. Mintzberg, "Rebuilding Companies as Communities," *Harvard Business Review*, July–August, 2009, pp. 140–43; and R. Luss, "Engaging Employees through Periods of Layoffs," *Towers Watson*, March 3, 2009, www.towerswatson.com.

42. N. J. Adler with A. Gundersen, *International Dimensions of Organizational Behavior*, 5th ed. (Cincinnati, OH: Thomson South-Western, 2008).

43. G. Hofstede, "Motivation, Leadership and Organization: Do American Theories Apply Abroad?" *Organizational Dynamics*, Summer 1980, p. 55.

44. Ibid.

45. J. K. Giacobbe-Miller, D. J. Miller, and V. I. Victorov, "A Comparison of Russian and U.S. Pay Allocation Decisions, Distributive Justice Judgments and Productivity under Different Payment Conditions," *Personnel Psychology*, Spring 1998, pp. 137–63.

46. S. L. Mueller and L. D. Clarke, "Political-Economic Context and Sensitivity to Equity: Differences between the United States and the Transition Economies of Central and Eastern Europe," *Academy of Management Journal*, June 1998, pp. 319–29.

47. I. Harpaz, "The Importance of Work Goals: An International Perspective," *Journal of International Business Studies*, First Quarter 1990, pp. 75–93.

48. G. E. Popp, H. J. Davis, and T. T. Herbert, "An International Study of Intrinsic Motivation Composition," *Management International Review*, January 1986, pp. 28–35.

49. R. W. Brislin, B. MacNab, R. Worthley, F. Kabigting Jr., and B. Zukis, "Evolving Perceptions of Japanese Workplace Motivation: An Employee-Manager Comparison," *International Journal of Cross-Cultural Management*, April 2005, pp. 87–104.

50. A. Schwartz, "Workers Seeking Productivity in a Pill Are Abusing ADHD Drugs," *New York Times Online*, April 18, 2015.

51. J. R. Billings and D. L. Sharpe, "Factors Influencing Flextime Usage among Employed Married Women," *Consumer Interests Annual*, 1999, pp. 89–94; and Harpaz, "The Importance of Work Goals: An International Perspective."

52. N. Ramachandran, "New Paths at Work," *U.S. News & World Report*, March 20, 2006, p. 47; S. Armour, "Generation Y: They've Arrived at Work with a New Attitude," *USA Today*, November 6, 2005, pp. B1+; and R. Kanfer and P. L. Ackerman, "Aging, Adult Development, and Work Motivation," *Academy of Management Review*, July 2004, pp. 440–58.

53. T. D. Golden and J. F. Veiga, "The Impact of Extent of Telecommuting on Job Satisfaction: Resolving Inconsistent Findings," *Journal of Management*, April 2005, pp. 301–18.

54. See, for instance, M. Alpert, "The Care and Feeding of Engineers," *Fortune*, September 21, 1992, pp. 86–95; G. Poole, "How to Manage Your Nerds," *Forbes ASAP*, December 1994, pp. 132–36; T. J. Allen and R. Katz, "Managing Technical Professionals and Organizations: Improving and Sustaining the Performance of Organizations, Project Teams, and Individual Contributors," *Sloan Management Review*, Summer 2002, pp. S4–S5; and S. R. Barley and G. Kunda, "Contracting: A New Form of Professional Practice," *Academy of Management Perspectives*, February 2006, pp. 45–66.

55. K. Bennhold, "Working (Part-Time) in the 21st Century," *New York Times Online*, December 29, 2010; and J. Revell, C. Bigda, and D. Rosato, "The Rise of Freelance Nation," *CNNMoney*, June 12, 2009, cnnmoney.com; and R. J. Bohner Jr. and E. R. Salasko, "Beware the Legal Risks of Hiring Temps," *Workforce*, October 2002, pp. 50–57.

56. H. G. Jackson, "Flexible Workplaces: The Next Imperative," *HR Magazine*, March 2011, p. 8; E. Frauenheim, "Companies Focus Their Attention on Flexibility," *Workforce Management Online*, February 2011; P. Davidson, "Companies Do More with Fewer Workers," *USA Today*, February 23, 2011, pp. 1B+; M. Rich, "Weighing Costs, Companies Favor Temporary Help," *New York Times Online*, December 19, 2010; P. Davidson, "Temporary Workers Reshape Companies, Jobs," *USA Today*, October 13, 2010, pp. 1B+; J. P. Broschak and A. Davis-Blake, "Mixing Standard Work and Nonstandard Deals: The Consequences of Heterogeneity in Employment Arrangements," *Academy of Management Journal*, April 2006, pp. 371–93; M. L. Kraimer, S. J. Wayne, R. C. Liden, and R. T. Sparrowe, "The Role of Job Security in Understanding the Relationship between Employees' Perceptions of Temporary Workers and Employees' Performance," *Journal of Applied Psychology*, March 2005, pp. 389–98; and C. E. Connelly and D. G. Gallagher, "Emerging Trends in Contingent Work Research," *Journal of Management*, November 2004, pp. 959–83.

57. Marianne Calnan, "The Group Company Rewards Staff with Trip to Barbados," *Employee Benefits* (UK), January 28, 2016, www.employeebenefits.

58. K. E. Culp, "Playing Field Widens for Stack's Great Game," *Springfield, Missouri, News-Leader*, January 9, 2005, pp. 1A+.

59. P. M. Buehler, "Opening Up Management Communication: Learning from Open Book Management," *Supervision*, August 2010, pp. 15–17; D. Drickhamer, "Open Books to Elevate Performance," *Industry Week*, November 2002, p. 16; J. Case, "Opening the Books," *Harvard Business Review*, March–April 1997, pp. 118–27; J. P. Schuster, J. Carpenter, and M. P. Kane, *The Power of Open-Book Management* (New York: John Wiley, 1996); and J. Case, "The Open-Book Revolution," *Inc.*, June 1995, pp. 26–50.

60. J. Singer, "Healing Your Workplace," *Supervision*, March 2011, pp. 11–13; P. Hart, "Benefits of Employee Recognition in the Workplace: Reduced Risk and Raised Revenues," *EHS Today*, February 2011, pp. 49–52; and F. Luthans and A. D. Stajkovic, "Provide Recognition for Performance Improvement," in E. A. Locke (ed.), *Principles of Organizational Behavior* (Oxford, UK: Blackwell, 2000), pp. 166–80.

61. C. Huff, "Recognition That Resonates," *Workforce Management Online*, April 1, 2008.

62. Kelvin Ong, "Small Gestures, Big Impacts," *HRM Asia*, November 3, 2016, www.hrmasia.com/content/small-gestures-big-impacts (accessed December 27, 2016); Marianne Calnan, "Marks and Spencer Takes a Mixed Approach to Staff Motivation," *Employee Benefits* (UK), May 15, 2015, www.employeebenefits.co.uk/issues/may-2015/marks-and-spencer-takes-a-mixed-approach-to-staff-motivation (accessed December 27, 2016).

63. K. J. Dunham, "Amid Sinking Workplace Morale, Employers Turn to Recognition," *Wall Street Journal*, November 19, 2002, p. B8.

64. See B. Nelson, "Try Praise," *Inc.*, September 1996, p. 115; and J. Wiscombe, "Rewards Get Results," *Workforce*, April 2002, pp. 42–48. Cited in S. Caudron, "The Top 20 Ways to Motivate Employees," *Industry Week*, April 3, 1995, pp. 15–16.

65. V. M. Barret, "Fight the Jerks," *Forbes*, July 2, 2007, pp. 52–54.

66. E. Krell, "All for Incentives, Incentives for All," *HR Magazine*, January 2011, pp. 35–38; and E. White, "The Best vs. the Rest," *Wall Street Journal*, January 30, 2006, pp. B1+.

67. R. K. Abbott, "Performance-Based Flex: A Tool for Managing Total Compensation Costs," *Compensation and Benefits Review*, March–April 1993, pp. 18–21; J. R. Schuster and P. K. Zingheim, "The New Variable Pay: Key Design Issues," *Compensation and Benefits Review*, March–April 1993, pp. 27–34; C. R. Williams and L. P. Livingstone, "Another Look at the Relationship between Performance and Voluntary Turnover," *Academy of Management Journal*, April 1994, pp. 269–98; A. M. Dickinson and K. L. Gillette, "A Comparison of the Effects of Two Individual Monetary Incentive Systems on Productivity: Piece Rate Pay versus Base Pay Plus Incentives," *Journal of Organizational Behavior Management*, Spring 1994, pp. 3–82; and C. B. Cadsby, F. Song, and F. Tapon, "Sorting and Incentive Effects of Pay for Performance: An Experimental Investigation," *Academy of Management Journal*, April 2007, pp. 387–405.

68. E. White, "Employers Increasingly Favor Bonuses to Raises," *Wall Street Journal*, August 28, 2006, p. B3.

69. "More Than 20 Percent of Japanese Firms Use Pay Systems Based on Performance," *Manpower Argus*, May 1998, p. 7; and E. Beauchesne, "Pay Bonuses Improve Productivity, Study Shows," *Vancouver Sun*, September 13, 2002, p. D5.

70. H. Rheem, "Performance Management Programs," *Harvard Business Review*, September–October 1996, pp. 8–9; G. Sprinkle, "The Effect of Incentive Contracts on Learning and Performance," *Accounting Review*, July 2000, pp. 299–326; and "Do Incentive Awards Work?" *HRFocus*, October 2000, pp. 1–3.

71. R.D. Banker, S.Y. Lee, G. Potter, and D. Srinivasan, "Contextual Analysis of Performance Impacts on Outcome-Based Incentive Compensation," *Academy of Management Journal*, August 1996, pp. 920–48.

72. S. A. Jeffrey and G. K. Adomza, "Incentive Salience and Improved Performance," *Human Performance* 24, no. 1 (2011), pp. 47–59; T. Reason, "Why Bonus Plans Fail," *CFO*, January 2003, p. 53; and "Has Pay for Performance Had Its Day?" *McKinsey Quarterly* 4 (2002), accessed at www.forbes.com.

73. E. Frauenheim, "Downturn Puts New Emphasis on Engagement," *Workforce Management Online*, July 21, 2009; S. D. Friedman, "Dial Down the Stress Level," *Harvard Business Review*, December 2008, pp. 28–29; and S. E. Needleman, "Allaying Workers' Fears During Uncertain Times," *Wall Street Journal*, October 6, 2008.

74. Based on V. H. Vroom, *Work and Motivation* (New York: John Wiley, 1964); J. S. Adams, "Inequity in Social Exchanges," in L. Berkowitz (ed.), *Advances in Experimental Social Psychology* (New York: Academic Press, 1965), pp. 267–300; and E. A. Locke and G. P. Latham, *A Theory of Goal Setting and Task Performance* (Upper Saddle River, NJ: Prentice Hall, 1990).

75. J. Reynolds, "The Top 50 Compliments for Coworkers," August 24, 2016, www.tinypulse.com.

76. "Minimum Wage Prosecutions Are Rare," Full Fact, April 18, 2015, https://fullfact.org/economy/minimum-wage-prosecutions-are-rare/.

77. "What Is the Real Living Wage," Living Wage Foundation, https://www.livingwage.org.uk/what-real-living-wage.

78. "IKEA UK Pays Living Wage to All UK Co-workers," Living Wage Foundation, March 30, 2016, https://www.livingwage.

org.uk/news/ikea-uk-pays-living-wage-all-uk-co-workers.

79. "Chelsea FC Makes Living Wage Commitment," *BBC News*, December 11, 2014, https://www.bbc.co.uk/news/uk-england-london-30414668.
80. D. Wilkie, "Unlimited Vacation: Is It about Morale or the Bottom Line?" SHRM Online, March 20, 2017.
81. F. Fontana, "Unlimited Vacation Time Is a Lot of Work," Wall Street Journal, August 29, 2017, p. B5.

82. A. Ain, "The CEO of Kronos on Launching an Unlimited Vacation Policy," *Harvard Business Review,* November–December 2017, pp. 37–42.
83. Ibid., pp. 40–41.
84. R. Bradley, "The Woman Driving Patagonia To Be (Even More) Radical, *Fortune Online,* September 14, 2015; B. Schulte, "A Company That Profits as It Pampers Workers," October 25, 2014, http://www.washingtonpost.com/business/a-company-that-profits

-as-it-pampers-workers/2014/10/22/d3321b34-4818-11e4-b72e-d60a9229cc10_story.html; D. Baer, "How Patagonia's New CEO Is Increasing Profits while Trying to Save the World," February 28, 2014, http://www.washingtonpost.com/business/a-company-that-profits-as-it-pampers-workers/2014/10/22/d3321b34-4818-11e4-b72e-d60a9229cc10_story.html; "Patagonia CEO & President Casey Sheahan Talks Business,

Conservation & Compassion," *offyonder.com*, February 13, 2012; T. Henneman, "Patagonia Fills Payroll with People Who Are Passionate," November 4, 2011, www.workforce.com; M. Hanel, "Surf's Up at Patagonia," *Bloomberg Businessweek,* September 5–11, 2011, pp. 88–89; J. Wang, "Patagonia, From the Ground Up," *Entrepreneur,* June 2010, pp. 26–32; and J. Laabs, "Mixing Business with Pleasure," *Workforce,* March 2000, pp. 80–85.

12

Leadership can't be taught.

Management Myth
Myth
Myth

Management DEBUNKED? Myth

Many people incorrectly assume that leaders are born. For example, they point to kids who, as early as four or five years old, are leading other kids around on the playground and displaying leadership qualities. The evidence suggests that while there are certainly personality traits associated with leadership and that these traits are more due to nature than nurture, **leadership *can* be taught**.

WHAT does it take to be an effective leader in today's organizations? It's important for managers in all organizations to be seen as effective leaders. One company that understands the importance of effective leadership and focuses on leadership development is Valvoline Inc., the automotive-maintenance company. Employees with leadership potential are groomed to take on increasing leadership responsibilities.[1] Why is leadership so important? Because it's the leaders in organizations who make things happen. But what makes leaders different from nonleaders? What's the most appropriate style of leadership? What makes leaders effective? Should the workplace environment be one in which employees feel like they're heard and trusted? These are just some of the topics we're going to address in this chapter. ●

Learning Outcomes

Who Are Leaders, and What Is Leadership?

12-1 Define *leader* and *leadership*.

Brian Chesky and Joe Gebbia, design school graduates in Silicon Valley, had a crazy idea after Gebbia's roommates suddenly moved out in 2008 and he needed people to fill the empty rooms. The crazy idea? A home-sharing platform now known as Air Bed and Breakfast (Airbnb). By 2017, the company had revenues over $2.6 billion (yes, billion!) and profits of $93 million.[2] Through the able leadership of Chesky, the company's CEO, the company is a success. In 2017, he was named one of *Fortune*'s World's Greatest Leaders.[3]

Let's begin by clarifying who leaders are and what leadership is. Our definition of a **leader** is someone who can influence others and who has managerial authority. **Leadership** is what leaders do; that is, it's a process of leading a group and influencing that group to achieve its goals.

Are all managers leaders? Because leading is one of the four management functions, ideally all managers *should* be leaders. Thus, we're going to study leaders and leadership from a managerial perspective.[4] However, even though we're looking at these from a managerial perspective, we're aware that groups often have informal leaders who emerge. Although these informal leaders may be able to influence others, they have not been the focus of most leadership research and are not the types of leaders we're studying in this chapter.

Leaders and leadership, like motivation, are organizational behavior topics that have been researched a lot. Most of that research has been aimed at answering the question: "What is an effective leader?" We'll begin our study of leadership by looking at some early leadership theories that attempted to answer that question.

leader
Someone who can influence others and who has managerial authority

leadership
The process of leading a group and influencing that group to achieve its goals

---

◄◄◄ Classic Concepts in Today's Workplace ►►►

Both the Ohio State and Michigan studies added a lot to our understanding of effective leadership.[5] Prior to the completion of these studies, it was widely thought by researchers and practicing managers that one style of leadership was good and another bad. However, as the research showed, both leader behavior dimensions—job-centered and employee-centered in the Michigan studies and initiating structure and consideration in the Ohio State studies—are necessary for effective leadership. That dual focus of "what" a leader does still holds today. Leaders are expected to focus on both the task and on the people he or she is leading. Even the later contingency leadership theories used the people/task distinction to define a leader's style. Finally, these early behavioral studies were important for the rigorous methodology they used and for increasing awareness of how important leader behavior is. Although the behavioral theories may not have been the final chapter in the book on leadership, they provided us with important insights that became the foundation of contingency leadership theories.

> ### People—Task: Both are important to leaders.

Dicussion Questions:

1 Is saying that the leader's "job" is to focus on the task and focus on the people too simplistic? Explain.

2 How did the behavioral theories serve as a springboard for the leadership research that followed?

What Do Early Leadership Theories Tell Us About Leadership?

12-2 Compare and contrast early leadership theories.

Leaders. Groups. Long History!

- Actual studies of leadership began in the twentieth century.

- Early leadership theories focused on:
  —The **person** (leader trait theories)
  —The **behaviors**—how the leader interacted with his or her group members (behavioral theories)

1 THE LEADER What Traits Do Leaders Have?

- **WHAT DO YOU KNOW ABOUT LEADERSHIP?** When asked that question, most people cite a list of qualities they admire in leaders—intelligence, charisma, decisiveness, enthusiasm, strength, bravery, integrity, self-confidence, and so forth.

- That's the **trait theories of leadership** in a nutshell—the search for traits or characteristics that differentiate leaders from nonleaders.

Sergiu Ungureanu/Shutterstock

- If this concept was valid, *all leaders would have to possess those unique and consistent characteristics*, making it easy to find leaders in organizations.

- But that's not going to happen: Despite the best efforts of researchers, they have yet to find a set of traits that would *always* differentiate a leader (the person) from a nonleader.

- Attempts to identify traits consistently associated with *leadership* (the process, not the person) have been more successful. See Exhibit 12–1 for those eight traits.[6]

> **trait theories of leadership**
> Theories that isolate characteristics (traits) that differentiate leaders from nonleaders

Exhibit 12–1 Traits Associated with Leadership

1 Drive. Leaders exhibit a high effort level. They have a relatively high desire for achievement, they are ambitious, they have a lot of energy, they are tirelessly persistent in their activities, and they show initiative.

2 Desire to lead. Leaders have a strong desire to influence and lead others. They demonstrate the willingness to take responsibility.

3 Honesty and integrity. Leaders build trusting relationships with followers by being truthful, or nondeceitful, and by showing high consistency between word and deed.

4 Self-confidence. Followers look to leaders who don't self-doubt. Leaders, therefore, need to show self-confidence in order to convince followers of the rightness of their goals and decisions.

5 Intelligence. Leaders need to be intelligent enough to gather, synthesize, and interpret large amounts of information, and they need to be able to create visions, solve problems, and make correct decisions.

6 Job-relevant knowledge. Effective leaders have a high degree of knowledge about the company, industry, and technical matters. In-depth knowledge allows leaders to make well-informed decisions and to understand the implications of those decisions.

7 Extraversion. Leaders are energetic, lively people. They are sociable, assertive, and rarely silent or withdrawn.

8 Proneness to guilt. Guilt proneness is positively related to leadership effectiveness because it produces a strong sense of responsibility for others.

Source: Based on S. A. Kirkpatrick and E. A. Locke, "Leadership: Do Traits Really Matter?" *Academy of Management Executive*, May 1991, pp. 48–60; and T. A. Judge, J. E. Bono, R. Ilies, and M. W. Gerhardt, "Personality and Leadership: A Qualitative and Quantitative Review," *Journal of Applied Psychology*, August 2002, pp. 765–80.

What Now?

- *Traits* alone were not sufficient for identifying effective leaders? Why? Explanations based solely on traits ignored the interactions of leaders and their group members as well as situational factors.

- Possessing the appropriate traits only made it *more likely* that an individual would be an effective leader.

- Leadership research from the late 1940s to the mid-1960s turned to finding preferred behavioral styles that leaders demonstrated.

Was there something unique in what leaders did—in other words, in their behavior?

Vege/Fotolia

429

THE BEHAVIORS What Behaviors Do Leaders Exhibit?

- Would **behavioral theories of leadership** provide more definitive answers about the nature of leadership?

- If behavioral theories could identify critical behavioral determinants of leadership, people could be trained to be leaders—the premise behind management development programs.

UNIVERSITY OF IOWA[7]

Behavioral Dimension

Democratic style: involving subordinates, delegating authority, and encouraging participation

Autocratic style: dictating work methods, centralizing decision making, and limiting participation

Laissez-faire style: giving group freedom to make decisions and complete work

CONCLUSION

Democratic style of leadership was most effective, although later studies showed mixed results.

OHIO STATE[8]

Behavioral Dimension

Consideration: being considerate of followers' ideas and feelings

Initiating structure: structuring work and work relationships to meet job goals

CONCLUSION

High–high leader (high in consideration and high in initiating structure) achieved high subordinate performance and satisfaction, but not in all situations.

UNIVERSITY OF MICHIGAN[9]

Behavioral Dimension

Employee oriented: emphasized interpersonal relationships and taking care of employees' needs

Production oriented: emphasized technical or task aspects of job

CONCLUSION

Employee-oriented leaders were associated with high group productivity and higher job satisfaction.

MANAGERIAL GRID[10]

Behavioral Dimension

Concern for people: measured leader's concern for subordinates on a scale of 1 to 9 (low to high)

Concern for production: measured leader's concern for getting job done on a scale 1 to 9 (low to high)

CONCLUSION

Leaders performed best with a 9,9 style (high concern for production and high concern for people).

What Now?

- Dual nature of leader behaviors—that is, focusing on the work to be done and focusing on the employees—is an important characteristic of each of these studies.

- Leadership researchers were discovering that predicting leadership success involved something more complex than isolating a few leader traits or preferable behaviors.

Coloures-pic/Fotolia

- They began looking at situational influences. *Specifically, which leadership styles might be suitable in different situations and what were these different situations?*

behavioral theories of leadership	**managerial grid**
Theories that isolate behaviors that differentiate effective leaders from ineffective leaders	A two-dimensional grid for appraising leadership styles

What Do the Contingency Theories of Leadership Tell Us?

12-3 Describe the four major contingency leadership theories.

"The corporate world is filled with stories of leaders who failed to achieve greatness because they failed to understand the context they were working in."[11] In this section, we examine four contingency theories—Fiedler, Hersey-Blanchard, leader-participation, and path-goal. Each looks at defining leadership style and the situation, and attempts to answer the *if-then* contingencies (i.e., *if* this is the context or situation, *then* this is the best leadership style to use). As an individual matures as a leader, it means being able to diagnose what type of leadership is needed in a particular situation. That's the premise behind contingency theories of leadership.

Fiedler contingency model
Leadership theory proposing that effective group performance depends on the proper match between a leader's style and the degree to which the situation allowed the leader to control and influence

least-preferred coworker (LPC) questionnaire
A questionnaire that measures whether a leader was task or relationship oriented

What Was the First Comprehensive Contingency Model?

The first comprehensive contingency model for leadership was developed by Fred Fiedler.[12] The **Fiedler contingency model** proposed that effective group performance depended on properly matching the leader's style and the amount of control and influence in the situation. The model was based on the premise that a certain leadership style would be most effective in different types of situations. The keys were:

1. define those leadership styles and the different types of situations, and then
2. identify the appropriate combinations of style and situation.

Fiedler proposed that a key factor in leadership success was an individual's basic leadership style, either task oriented or relationship oriented. To measure a leader's style, Fiedler developed the **least-preferred coworker (LPC) questionnaire**. This questionnaire contained 18 pairs of contrasting adjectives—for example, pleasant–unpleasant, cold–warm, boring–interesting, or friendly–unfriendly. Respondents were asked to think of all the coworkers they had ever had and to describe that one person they *least enjoyed* working with by rating him or her on a scale of 1 to 8 for each of the sets of adjectives (the 8 always described the positive adjective out of the pair and the 1 always described the negative adjective out of the pair).

If the leader described the least preferred coworker in relatively positive terms (in other words, a "high" LPC score—a score of 64 or above), then the respondent was primarily interested in good personal relations with coworkers and the style would be described as *relationship oriented*. In contrast, if you saw the least preferred coworker in relatively unfavorable terms (a low LPC score—a score of 57 or below), you were primarily interested in productivity and getting the job done; thus, your style would be labeled as *task oriented*. Fiedler did acknowledge that a small number of people might fall in between these two extremes and not have a cut-and-dried leadership style. One other important point is that Fiedler assumed a person's leadership style was fixed regardless of the situation. In other words, if you were a relationship-oriented leader, you'd always be one, and the same for task-oriented.

After an individual's leadership style had been assessed through the LPC, it was time to evaluate the situation in order to be able to match the leader with the situation. Fiedler's research uncovered three contingency dimensions that defined the key situational factors in leader effectiveness. These were:

- *Leader-member relations:* the degree of confidence, trust, and respect employees had for their leader; rated as either good or poor.
- *Task structure:* the degree to which job assignments were formalized and structured; rated as either high or low.
- *Position power:* the degree of influence a leader had over activities such as hiring, firing, discipline, promotions, and salary increases; rated as either strong or weak.

Richard Branson, founder and CEO of Virgin Group, is a relationship-oriented leader. Pictured here (center) starting the half marathon at the launch of Virgin Sport Hackney in London, Branson is fun loving, takes a personal interest in the needs of employees, emphasizes interpersonal relations, and accepts individual differences among workers.

Gareth Fuller/ZUMA Press/Newscom

Exhibit 12–2 The Fiedler Model

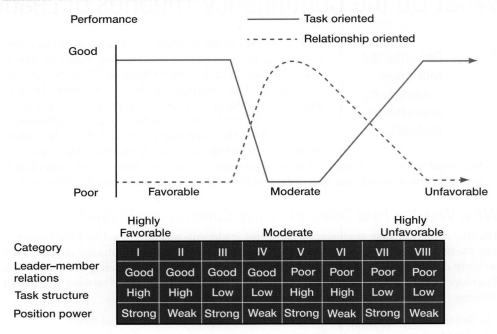

Category	I	II	III	IV	V	VI	VII	VIII
Leader–member relations	Good	Good	Good	Good	Poor	Poor	Poor	Poor
Task structure	High	High	Low	Low	High	High	Low	Low
Position power	Strong	Weak	Strong	Weak	Strong	Weak	Strong	Weak

Each leadership situation was evaluated in terms of these three contingency variables, which when combined produced eight possible situations that were either favorable or unfavorable for the leader. (See the bottom of the chart in Exhibit 12–2). Situations I, II, and III were classified as highly favorable for the leader. Situations IV, V, and VI were moderately favorable for the leader. And situations VII and VIII were described as highly unfavorable for the leader.

Once Fiedler had described the leader variables and the situational variables, he had everything he needed to define the specific contingencies for leadership effectiveness. To do so, he studied 1,200 groups where he compared relationship-oriented versus task-oriented leadership styles in each of the eight situational categories. He concluded that task-oriented leaders performed better in very favorable situations and in very unfavorable situations. (See the top of Exhibit 12–2, where performance is shown on the vertical axis and situation favorableness is shown on the horizontal axis.) On the other hand, relationship-oriented leaders performed better in moderately favorable situations.

Because Fiedler treated an individual's leadership style as fixed, there were only two ways to improve leader effectiveness. First, you could bring in a new leader whose style better fit the situation. For instance, if the group situation was highly unfavorable but was led by a relationship-oriented leader, the group's performance could be improved by replacing that person with a task-oriented leader. The second alternative was to change the situation to fit the leader. This could be done by restructuring tasks; by increasing or decreasing the power that the leader had over factors such as salary increases, promotions, and disciplinary actions; or by improving the leader-member relations. Research testing the overall validity of Fiedler's model has shown considerable evidence to support the model.[13] However, his theory wasn't without criticisms. The major one is that it's probably unrealistic to assume that a person can't change his or her leadership style to fit the situation. Effective leaders can, and do, change their styles. Another is that the LPC wasn't very practical. Finally, the situation variables were difficult to assess.[14] Despite its shortcomings, the Fiedler model showed that effective leadership style needed to reflect situational factors.

How Do Followers' Willingness and Ability Influence Leaders?

situational leadership theory (SLT)
A leadership contingency theory that focuses on followers' readiness

Paul Hersey and Ken Blanchard developed a leadership theory that has had a strong following among management development specialists.[15] This model, called **situational leadership theory (SLT)**, is a contingency theory that focuses on followers' readiness. Before we proceed, there are two points we need to clarify: Why a leadership theory focuses on the followers, and what is meant by the term *readiness*.

readiness
The extent to which people have the ability and willingness to accomplish a specific task

The emphasis on the followers in leadership effectiveness reflects the reality that it *is* the followers who accept or reject the leader. Regardless of what the leader does, the group's effectiveness depends on the actions of the followers. This is an important dimension that has been overlooked or underemphasized in most leadership theories. And **readiness**, as defined by Hersey and Blanchard, refers to the extent to which people have the ability and willingness to accomplish a specific task.

LEADER

SLT uses the same two leadership dimensions that Fiedler identified: task and relationship behaviors. However, Hersey and Blanchard go a step further by considering each as either high or low and then combining them into four specific leadership styles described as follows:

- *Telling* (high task–low relationship): The leader defines roles and tells people what, how, when, and where to do various tasks.
- *Selling* (high task–high relationship): The leader provides both directive and supportive behavior.
- *Participating* (low task–high relationship): The leader and followers share in decision making; the main role of the leader is facilitating and communicating.
- *Delegating* (low task–low relationship): The leader provides little direction or support.

FOLLOWERS

The final component in the model is the four stages of follower readiness:

- *R1:* People are both *unable and unwilling* to take responsibility for doing something. Followers aren't competent or confident.
- *R2:* People are *unable but willing* to do the necessary job tasks. Followers are motivated but lack the appropriate skills.
- *R3:* People are *able but unwilling* to do what the leader wants. Followers are competent, but don't want to do something.
- *R4:* People are both *able and willing* to do what is asked of them.

Now—let's put the **two together!**

SLT essentially views the leader-follower relationship as like that of a parent and a child. Just as a parent needs to relinquish control when a child becomes more mature and responsible, so, too, should leaders. As followers reach higher levels of readiness, the leader responds not only by decreasing control over their activities but also decreasing relationship behaviors. The SLT says:

- If followers are at R1 (*unable* and *unwilling* to do a task), the leader needs to use the *telling style* and give clear and specific directions.
- If followers are at R2 (*unable* and *willing*), the leader needs to use the *selling style* and display high task orientation to compensate for the followers' lack of ability and high relationship orientation to get followers to "buy into" the leader's desires.
- If followers are at R3 (*able* and *unwilling*), the leader needs to use the *participating style* to gain their support.
- If followers are at R4 (both *able* and *willing*), the leader doesn't need to do much and should use the *delegating style*.

French entrepreneur Bertin Nahum is the founder and CEO of Medtech, a firm that develops, designs, and markets computer-assisted neurosurgical robotics. With high follower readiness of being able and willing, Nahum's managers and staff have the skills and experience to innovate and provide superior technical support.

Alain Robert/APERCU/SIPA/Newscom

leader-participation model
A leadership contingency theory that's based on a sequential set of rules for determining how much participation a leader uses in decision making according to different types of situations

SLT has intuitive appeal. It acknowledges the importance of followers and builds on the logic that leaders can compensate for ability and motivational limitations in their followers. However, research efforts to test and support the theory generally have been disappointing.[16] Possible explanations include internal inconsistencies in the model as well as problems with research methodology. Despite its appeal and wide popularity, we have to be cautious about any enthusiastic endorsement of SLT.

How Participative Should a Leader Be?

Back in 1973, Victor Vroom and Phillip Yetton developed a **leader-participation model** that related leadership behavior and participation to decision making.[17] Recognizing that task structures have varying demands for routine and nonroutine activities, these researchers argued that leader behavior must adjust to reflect the task structure. Vroom and Yetton's model was normative. That is, it provided a sequential set of rules to be followed in determining the form and amount of participation in decision making in different types of situations. The model was a decision tree incorporating seven contingencies (whose relevance could be identified by making yes or no choices) and five alternative leadership styles.[18]

More recent work by Vroom and Arthur Jago has revised that model.[18] The new model retains the same five alternative leadership styles but expands the contingency variables to 12—from the leader's making the decision completely by himself or herself to sharing the problem with the group and developing a consensus decision. These variables are listed in Exhibit 12–3.

Research on the original leader-participation model was encouraging.[19] But unfortunately, the model is far too complex for the typical manager to use regularly. In fact, Vroom and Jago have developed a computer program to guide managers through all the decision branches in the revised model. Although we obviously can't do justice to this model's sophistication in this discussion, it has provided us with some solid, empirically supported insights into key contingency variables related to leadership effectiveness. Moreover, the leader-participation model confirms that leadership research should be directed at the situation rather than at the person. That is, it probably makes more sense to talk about autocratic and participative situations than autocratic and participative leaders. As House did in his path-goal theory, Vroom, Yetton, and Jago argue against the notion that leader behavior is inflexible. The leader-participation model assumes that the leader can adapt his or her style to different situations.[20]

Only 53 percent of leaders are willing to step outside their leadership comfort zone and try new techniques.[21]

Exhibit 12–3 Contingency Variables in the Revised Leader-Participation Model

> **1.** Importance of the decision
> **2.** Importance of obtaining follower commitment to the decision
> **3.** Whether the leader has sufficient information to make a good decision
> **4.** How well structured the problem is
> **5.** Whether an autocratic decision would receive follower commitment
> **6.** Whether followers "buy into" the organization's goals
> **7.** Whether there is likely to be conflict among followers over solution alternatives
> **8.** Whether followers have the necessary information to make a good decision
> **9.** Time constraints on the leader that may limit follower involvement
> **10.** Whether costs to bring geographically dispersed members together are justified
> **11.** Importance to the leader of minimizing the time it takes to make the decision
> **12.** Importance of using participation as a tool for developing follower decision skills
>
> *Source:* Stephen P. Robbins and Timothy A. Judge, *Organizational Behavior*, 13th ed., ©2009, p. 400. Reprinted and electronically reproduced by permission of Pearson Education, Inc., New York, NY.

How Do Leaders Help Followers?

Another approach to understanding leadership is **path-goal theory**, which states that the leader's job is to assist followers in attaining their goals and to provide direction or support needed to ensure that their goals are compatible with the goals of the group or organization. Developed by Robert House, path-goal theory takes key elements from the expectancy theory of motivation (see Chapter 10).[22] The term *path-goal* is derived from the belief that effective leaders clarify the path to help their followers get from where they are to the achievement of their work goals and make the journey along the path easier by reducing roadblocks and pitfalls.

House identified four leadership behaviors:

path-goal theory
A leadership theory that says the leader's job is to assist followers in attaining their goals and to provide direction or support needed to ensure that their goals are compatible with the organization's or group's goals

- *Directive leader:* Lets subordinates know what's expected of them, schedules work to be done, and gives specific guidance on how to accomplish tasks.
- *Supportive leader:* Shows concern for the needs of followers and is friendly.
- *Participative leader:* Consults with group members and uses their suggestions before making a decision.
- *Achievement-oriented leader:* Sets challenging goals and expects followers to perform at their highest level.

In contrast to Fiedler's view that a leader couldn't change his or her behavior, House assumed that leaders are flexible and can display any or all of these leadership styles depending on the situation. For instance, Bono, U2's leader, lead singer, and lyricist, uses the supportive and participative approaches of the path-goal theory. He includes band members in decision making, believing that their input is necessary to achieve excellence. And he supports them by expressing his appreciation for their talents in contributing to the band's success and for their role in helping achieve the band's goal of improving the world through its music and influence.[23]

As Exhibit 12–4 illustrates, path-goal theory proposes two situational or contingency variables that moderate the leadership behavior–outcome relationship:

1. those in the *environment* that are outside the control of the follower (factors including task structure, formal authority system, and the work group) and
2. those that are part of the personal characteristics of the *follower* (including locus of control, experience, and perceived ability).

Environmental factors determine the type of leader behavior required if subordinate outcomes are to be maximized; personal characteristics of the follower determine how the environment and leader behavior are interpreted. The theory proposes that a leader's behavior won't be effective if it's redundant with what the environmental structure is providing or is incongruent with follower characteristics. For example, some predictions from path-goal theory are:

Exhibit 12–4 Path-Goal Model

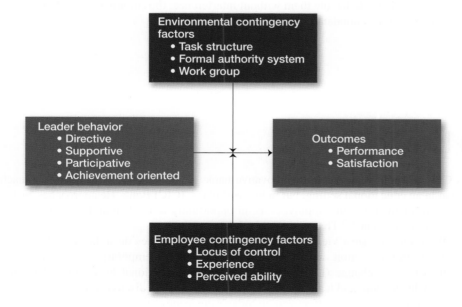

dpa picture alliance / Alamy Stock Photo

Mary Barra, CEO of General Motors, is a participative leader. She involves employees in the decision-making process by encouraging them to voice their opinions, and she holds town hall meetings to gather advice. Barra's participative style results in highly engaged employees, organizational commitment, and effective work teams.

- Directive leadership leads to greater satisfaction when tasks are ambiguous or stressful than when they are highly structured and well laid out. The followers aren't sure what to do, so the leader needs to give them some direction.
- Supportive leadership results in high employee performance and satisfaction when subordinates are performing structured tasks. In this situation, the leader only needs to support followers, not tell them what to do.
- Directive leadership is likely to be perceived as redundant among subordinates with high perceived ability or with considerable experience. These followers are quite capable so they don't need a leader to tell them what to do.
- The clearer and more bureaucratic the formal authority relationships, the more leaders should exhibit supportive behavior and deemphasize directive behavior. The organizational situation has provided the structure as far as what is expected of followers, so the leader's role is simply to support.
- Directive leadership will lead to higher employee satisfaction when there is substantive conflict within a work group. In this situation, the followers need a leader who will take charge.
- Subordinates with an internal locus of control will be more satisfied with a participative style. Because these followers believe that they control what happens to them, they prefer to participate in decisions.
- Subordinates with an external locus of control will be more satisfied with a directive style. These followers believe that what happens to them is a result of the external environment so they would prefer a leader who tells them what to do.
- Achievement-oriented leadership will increase subordinates' expectancies that effort will lead to high performance when tasks are ambiguously structured. By setting challenging goals, followers know what the expectations are.

Research findings on the path-goal model have been mixed because the theory has so many variables to examine. Although not every study has found support, we can still say that evidence supports the logic underlying the theory.[24] That is, an employee's performance and satisfaction are likely to be positively influenced when the leader chooses a leadership style that compensates for shortcomings in either the employee or the work setting. However, if the leader spends time explaining tasks that are already clear or when the employee has the ability and experience to handle them without interference, the employee is likely to see such directive behavior as redundant or even insulting.

What Is Leadership Like Today?

12-4 Describe modern views of leadership and the issues facing today's leaders.

As CEO of India's largest, most innovative bank, Kundapur Vaman Kamath is a teacher. Not at in an educational setting, but in his workplace, ICICI Bank. He approaches each day and each interaction with employees as an opportunity to explain and provide a "master class in management."[25] That's what great leaders do!

What are the latest views of leadership, and what issues do today's leaders have to deal with? In this section, we're going to look at four contemporary views of leadership: leader-member exchange (LMX), transformational-transactional leadership, charismatic-visionary leadership, and team leadership. In addition, we'll discuss some issues that leaders have to face in leading effectively in today's environment.

What Do the Four Contemporary Views of Leadership Tell Us?

Remember our discussion at the beginning of this chapter where we said that leadership studies have long had the goal of describing what it takes to be an effective leader? That goal hasn't changed! Even the contemporary views of leadership are interested in answering that question. These views of leadership have a common theme: leaders who interact with, inspire, and support followers.

HOW DO LEADERS INTERACT WITH FOLLOWERS?   Have you ever been in a group in which the leader had "favorites" who made up his or her in-group? If so, that's the premise behind leader-member exchange (LMX) theory.[26] **Leader-member exchange (LMX) theory** says that leaders create in-groups and out-groups and those in the in-group will have higher performance ratings, less turnover, and greater job satisfaction.

LMX theory suggests that early on in the relationship between a leader and a given follower, a leader will implicitly categorize a follower as an "in" or as an "out." That relationship tends to remain fairly stable over time. Leaders also encourage LMX by rewarding those employees with whom they want a closer linkage and punishing those with whom they do not.[27] For the LMX relationship to remain intact, however, both the leader and the follower must "invest" in the relationship.

It's not exactly clear how a leader chooses who falls into each category, but evidence indicates that in-group members have demographic, attitude, personality, and even gender similarities with the leader or they have a higher level of competence than out-group members.[28] The leader does the choosing, but the follower's characteristics drive the decision.

> Ninety-two percent of executives see favoritism in who gets job promotions.[29]

Research on LMX has been generally supportive. It appears that leaders do differentiate among followers; that these disparities are not random; and followers with in-group status will have higher performance ratings, engage in more helping or "citizenship" behaviors at work, and report greater satisfaction with their boss.[30] These findings probably shouldn't be surprising when leaders are most likely to invest their time and other resources in those whom they expect to perform best.

HOW DO TRANSACTIONAL LEADERS DIFFER FROM TRANSFORMATIONAL LEADERS?   Many early leadership theories viewed leaders as **transactional leaders**; that is, leaders who lead primarily by using social exchanges (or transactions). Transactional leaders guide or motivate followers to work toward established goals by exchanging rewards for their productivity.[31] But another type of leader—a **transformational leader**—stimulates and inspires (transforms) followers to achieve extraordinary outcomes. How? By paying attention to the concerns and developmental needs of individual followers; changing followers' awareness of issues by helping those followers look at old problems in new ways; and being able to excite, arouse, and inspire followers to exert extra effort to achieve group goals.

Transactional and transformational leadership shouldn't be viewed as opposing approaches to getting things done.[32] Transformational leadership develops from transactional leadership. Transformational leadership produces levels of employee effort and performance that go beyond what would occur with a transactional approach alone. Moreover, transformational leadership is more than charisma since the transformational leader attempts to instill in followers the ability to question not only established views but those views held by the leader.[33]

The evidence supporting the superiority of transformational leadership over transactional leadership is overwhelmingly impressive. For instance, studies that looked at managers in different settings, including the military and business, found that transformational leaders were evaluated as more effective, higher performers, more promotable than their transactional counterparts, and more interpersonally sensitive.[34] In addition, evidence indicates that transformational leadership is strongly correlated with lower

---

leader-member exchange (LMX) theory
A leadership theory that says leaders create in-groups and out-groups and those in the in-group will have higher performance ratings, less turnover, and greater job satisfaction

transactional leaders
Leaders who lead primarily by using social exchanges (or transactions)

transformational leaders
Leaders who stimulate and inspire (transform) followers to achieve extraordinary outcomes

charismatic leaders
Enthusiastic, self-confident leaders whose person-alities and actions influence people to behave in certain ways

visionary leadership
The ability to create and articulate a realistic, credible, and attractive vision of the future that improves on the present situation

turnover rates and higher levels of productivity, work engagement, employee satisfaction, creativity, goal attainment, and follower well-being.[35]

HOW DO CHARISMATIC LEADERSHIP AND VISIONARY LEADERSHIP DIFFER? Jeff Bezos, founder and CEO of Amazon.com, is a person who exudes energy, enthusiasm, and drive.[36] He's fun-loving (his legendary laugh has been described as a flock of Canada geese on nitrous oxide), but he has pursued his vision for Amazon with serious intensity and has demonstrated an ability to inspire his employees through the ups and downs of a rapidly growing company. Bezos is what we call a **charismatic leader**—that is, an enthusiastic, self-confident leader whose personality and actions influence people to behave in certain ways.

Several authors have attempted to identify personal characteristics of the charismatic leader.[37] The most comprehensive analysis identified five such characteristics: they have a vision, the ability to articulate that vision, willingness to take risks to achieve that vision, sensitivity to both environmental constraints and follower needs, and behaviors that are out of the ordinary.[38]

It's good to be **charismatic!**

An increasing body of evidence shows impressive correlations between charismatic leadership and high performance and satisfaction among followers.[39] Although one study found that charismatic CEOs had no impact on subsequent organizational performance, charisma is still believed to be a desirable leadership quality.[40]

If charisma is desirable, can people learn to be charismatic leaders? Or are charismatic leaders born with their qualities? Although a small number of experts still think that charisma can't be learned, most believe that individuals can be trained to exhibit charismatic behaviors.[41] For example, researchers have succeeded in teaching undergraduate students to "be" charismatic. How? They were taught to articulate a far-reaching goal, communicate high performance expectations, exhibit confidence in the ability of subordinates to meet those expectations, and empathize with the needs of their subordinates; they learned to project a powerful, confident, and dynamic presence; and they practiced using a captivating and engaging voice tone. The researchers also trained the student leaders to use charismatic nonverbal behaviors including leaning toward the follower when communicating, maintaining direct eye contact, and having a relaxed posture and animated facial expressions. In groups with these "trained" charismatic leaders, members had higher task performance, higher task adjustment, and better adjustment to the leader and to the group than did group members who worked in groups led by noncharismatic leaders.

One last thing we should say about charismatic leadership is that it may not always be necessary to achieve high levels of employee performance. It may be most appropriate when the follower's task has an ideological purpose or when the environment involves a high degree of stress and uncertainty.[42] This aspect may explain why, when charismatic leaders surface, it's more likely to be in politics, religion, or wartime; or when a business firm is starting up or facing a survival crisis. For example, Martin Luther King Jr. used his charisma to bring about social equality through nonviolent means, and the late Steve Jobs achieved unwavering loyalty and commitment from Apple's technical staff in the early 1980s by articulating a vision of personal computers that would dramatically change the way people lived.

Although the term *vision* is often linked with charismatic leadership, **visionary leadership** is different: It's the ability to create and articulate a realistic, credible, and attractive vision of the future that improves on the present situation.[43] This vision, if

Amazon.com founder and CEO Jeff Bezos is a charismatic leader. Described as energetic, enthusiastic, optimistic, and self-confident, Bezos has the drive to set and pursue goals for risky new ventures and uses his charisma to inspire his employees to work hard to achieve them. Bezos is shown here during the grand opening of the Spheres, plant-filled geodesic domes that serve as work and gathering places for employees.

Ted S. Warren/Ap Images

properly selected and implemented, is so energizing that it "in effect jump-starts the future by calling forth the skills, talents, and resources to make it happen."[44]

---

40 percent of employees are uninspired by leaders about the future.[45]
15 percent of employees strongly agreed that leadership at their companies makes them feel enthusiastic about the future.[46]

An organization's vision should offer clear and compelling imagery that taps into people's emotions and inspires enthusiasm to pursue the organization's goals. It should be able to generate possibilities that are inspirational and unique and offer new ways of doing things that are clearly better for the organization and its members. Visions that are clearly articulated and have powerful imagery are easily grasped and accepted. For instance, Michael Dell created a vision of a business that sells and delivers customized PCs directly to customers in less than a week. The late Mary Kay Ash's vision of women as entrepreneurs selling products that improved their self-image gave impetus to her cosmetics company, Mary Kay Cosmetics.

WHAT ABOUT LEADERS AND TEAMS?   Because leadership is increasingly taking place within a team context and more organizations are using work teams, the role of the leader in guiding team members has become increasingly important. The role of team leader *is* different from the traditional leadership role, as J. D. Bryant, a supervisor at Texas Instruments' Forest Lane plant in Dallas, discovered.[47] One day he was contentedly overseeing a staff of 15 circuit board assemblers. The next day he was told that the company was going to use employee teams and he was to become a "facilitator." He said, "I'm supposed to teach the teams everything I know and then let them make their own decisions." Confused about his new role, he admitted, "There was no clear plan on what I was supposed to do." What *is* involved in being a team leader?

Many leaders are not equipped to handle the change to employee teams. As one consultant noted, "Even the most capable managers have trouble making the transition because all the command-and-control type things they were encouraged to do before are no longer appropriate. There's no reason to have any skill or sense of this."[48] This same consultant estimated that "probably 15 percent of managers are natural team leaders; another 15 percent could never lead a team because it runs counter to their personality—that is, they're unable to sublimate their dominating style for the good of the team. Then there's that huge group in the middle: Team leadership doesn't come naturally to them, but they can learn it."[49]

The challenge for many managers is learning how to become an effective team leader. They have to learn skills such as patiently sharing information, being able to trust others and to give up authority, and understanding when to intervene. And effective team leaders have mastered the difficult balancing act of knowing when to leave their teams alone and when to get involved. New team leaders may try to retain too much control at a time when team members need more autonomy, or they may abandon their teams at times when the teams need support and help.[50]

Making Ethical Decisions in Today's Workplace

After a year-long investigation, the CEO of British banking giant Barclays, Jes Staley, was hit by U.K. regulators with financial penalties (a fine of $1.5 million) for his efforts to unmask a whistleblower.[54] The incident started with the hiring of a former colleague of Mr. Staley's and two anonymous letters written outlining "erratic behavior" observed when this individual was at another financial firm. The initial letter, received in June 2016 by a member of Barclay's board, was written by an individual identifying himself as "John Q Public" and a long-term shareholder of Barclays. The letter made personal allegations about the individual and questioned Barclay's hiring process. Later that month, another letter was delivered to Barclay's office in New York expressing similar concerns. In a letter written to employees, Mr. Staley explained that "the intent of the correspondents in airing all of this was, in my view, to maliciously smear this person."[55] He also called on the bank's internal security team to uncover the identity of the whistleblower. This triggered the regulatory investigation by the Financial Conduct Authority (FCA) into Mr. Staley's behavior. Mr. Staley told the FCA that he believed that the senders of the letters didn't work at Barclays but were from someone at another financial firm where Staley and the other individual had worked together so it didn't count as a whistleblower. In its report, FCA said that Mr. Staley failed to recognize that the letters "could have been written" by insiders at the bank and so whistleblowing regulations did apply to both incidents.

Dicussion Questions:

3 What ethical issue(s) do you see in this story? Why is unmasking a whistleblower a problem? What and how stakeholders might be affected by Staley's actions?

4 In your assigned group, discuss the ethical responsibilities of leaders and how Barclay's might use this incident as an ethics lesson.

empowerment
The act of increasing the decision-making discretion of workers

Four common traits of best team leaders:[51]

- Models collaborative action
- Builds strong employee networks
- Encourages collaboration across functions and departments
- Structures work effectively

One study looking at organizations that had reorganized themselves around employee teams found certain common responsibilities of all leaders. These responsibilities included coaching, facilitating, handling disciplinary problems, reviewing team and individual performance, training, and communication.[52] However, a more meaningful way to describe the team leader's job is to focus on two priorities: (1) managing the team's external boundary and (2) facilitating the team process.[53] These priorities entail four specific leadership roles, as shown in Exhibit 12–5.

What Issues Do Today's Leaders Face?

It's not easy being a chief information officer (CIO) today. A person responsible for managing a company's information technology activities faces a lot of external and internal pressures. Technology changes rapidly—almost daily, it sometimes seems. Business costs continue to rise. Competitors develop new strategies. Economic conditions continue to confound even the experts. Rob Carter, CIO and executive vice president of FedEx Information Services, is on the hot seat facing such challenges.[56] He's responsible for all the computer and communication systems that provide around-the-clock and around-the-globe support for FedEx's products and services. If anything goes wrong, you know who takes the heat. However, Carter has been an effective leader in this seemingly chaotic environment.

Leading effectively in today's environment is likely to involve such challenges for many leaders. Twenty-first-century leaders face some important leadership issues. In this section, we look at these issues, including empowering employees, cross-cultural leadership, emotional intelligence and leadership, and toxic bosses.

Say What? Lead by NOT Leading

WHY DO LEADERS NEED TO EMPOWER EMPLOYEES? As we've described in different places throughout the text, managers are increasingly leading by not leading—that is, by empowering their employees. **Empowerment** involves increasing the decision-making discretion of workers. Millions of individual employees and employee teams are making the key operating decisions that directly affect their work. They're developing budgets, scheduling workloads, controlling inventories, solving quality problems, and engaging in similar activities that until very recently were viewed exclusively as part of the manager's job.[57] For instance, at The Container Store, any employee who gets a customer request has permission to take care of it. The company's chairman emeritus Garret Boone says, "Everybody we hire, we hire as a leader. Anybody in our store can take an action that you might think of typically being a manager's action."[58]

Exhibit 12–5 Team Leader Roles

Managing Technology in Today's Workplace
VIRTUAL LEADERSHIP

How do you lead people who are physically separated from you and with whom your interactions are primarily written digital communications?[59] That's the challenge of being a virtual leader. And unfortunately, leadership research has been directed mostly at face-to-face and verbal situations. But we can't ignore the reality that today's managers and their employees are increasingly being linked by technology rather than by geographic proximity. So what guidance would be helpful to leaders who must inspire and motivate dispersed employees?

It's easy to soften harsh words in face-to-face communication with nonverbal action. A smile or a comforting gesture can go a long way in lessening the blow behind strong words like *disappointed, unsatisfactory, inadequate*, or *below expectations*. That nonverbal component doesn't exist in online interactions. The *structure* of words in a digital communication also has the power to motivate or demotivate the receiver. A manager who inadvertently sends a message in short phrases or in ALL CAPS may get a very different response than if the message had been sent in full sentences using appropriate punctuation.

To be an effective virtual leader, managers must recognize that they have choices in the words and structure of their digital communications. They also need to develop the skill of "reading between the lines" in the messages they receive. It's important to try and decipher the emotional content of a message as well as the written content. Also, virtual leaders need to think carefully about what actions they want their digital messages to initiate. Be clear about what's expected and follow up on messages.

For an increasing number of managers, good interpersonal skills may include the abilities to communicate support and leadership through digital communication and to read emotions in others' messages. In this "new world" of communication, writing skills are likely to become an extension of interpersonal skills.

Dicussion Questions:

5 What challenges does a "virtual" leader face?

6 How can virtual leaders use technology to help them be more effective leaders?

One reason more companies are empowering employees is the need for quick decisions by those people who are most knowledgeable about the issues—often those at lower organizational levels. If organizations want to successfully compete in a dynamic global economy, employees have to be able to make decisions and implement changes quickly. Another reason is that organizational downsizings left many managers with larger spans of control. In order to cope with the increased work demands, managers had to empower their people. Although empowerment is not a universal answer, it can be beneficial when employees have the knowledge, skills, and experience to do their jobs competently.

Technology also has contributed to the increases in employee empowerment. Managers face unique challenges, especially in leading empowered employees who aren't physically present in the workplace as the Managing Technology in Today's Workplace discusses.

DOES NATIONAL CULTURE AFFECT LEADERSHIP? One general conclusion that surfaces from leadership research is that effective leaders do not use a single style. They adjust their style to the situation. Although not mentioned explicitly, national culture is certainly an important situational variable in determining which leadership style will be most effective. What works in China isn't likely to be effective in France or Canada. For instance, one study of Asian leadership styles revealed that Asian managers preferred leaders who were competent decision makers, effective communicators, and supportive of employees.[60] Another study of leadership in sub-Saharan Africa found that charismatic leaders can help overcome cultural problems of corruption, poverty, tribalism, and violence.[61]

In China, the cultural value of collectivism affects the relationship between leaders and followers such as Yuki Tan, president of fashion retailer Folli Follie China, and store employees. During store visits, Tan displays her effective paternalistic leadership style of caring for her loyal, dependable, and hard-working employees.

Ton Koene/ZUMApress/Newscom

National culture affects leadership style because it influences how followers will respond. Leaders can't (and shouldn't) just choose their styles randomly. They're constrained by the cultural conditions their followers have come to expect. Exhibit 12–6 provides some findings from selected examples of cross-cultural leadership studies. Because most leadership theories were developed in the United States, they have an American bias. They emphasize follower responsibilities rather than rights; assume self-gratification rather than commitment to duty or altruistic motivation; assume centrality of work and democratic value orientation; and stress rationality rather than spirituality, religion, or superstition.[62] However, the GLOBE research program, which we first introduced in Chapter 4, is the most extensive and comprehensive cross-cultural study of leadership ever undertaken. The GLOBE study has found that there are some universal aspects to leadership. Specifically, a number of elements of transformational leadership appear to be associated with effective leadership regardless of what country the leader is in.[63] These elements include vision, foresight, providing encouragement, trustworthiness, dynamism, positiveness, and proactiveness. The results led two members of the GLOBE team to conclude that "effective business leaders in any country are expected by their subordinates to provide a powerful and proactive vision to guide the company into the future, strong motivational skills to stimulate all employees to fulfill the vision, and excellent planning skills to assist in implementing the vision."[64] Some people suggest that the universal appeal of these transformational leader characteristics is due to the pressures toward common technologies and management practices, as a result of global competitiveness and multinational influences.

HOW DOES EMOTIONAL INTELLIGENCE AFFECT LEADERSHIP?   We introduced emotional intelligence (EI) in our discussion of emotions in Chapter 9. We revisit the topic here because of recent studies indicating that EI—more than IQ, expertise, or any other single factor—is the best predictor of who will emerge as a leader.[65]

Becoming a STAR ★ leader

As we said in our earlier discussion of trait research, leaders need basic intelligence and job-relevant knowledge. But IQ and technical skills are "threshold capabilities." They're necessary but not sufficient requirements for leadership. It's the possession of the five components of emotional intelligence—self-awareness, self-management, self-motivation, empathy, and social skills—that allows an individual to become a star performer. Without EI, a person can have outstanding training, a highly analytical mind, a long-term vision, and an endless supply of terrific ideas but still not make a great leader, especially as individuals

Exhibit 12–6 Cross-Cultural Leadership

- Korean leaders are expected to be paternalistic toward employees.
- Arab leaders who show kindness or generosity without being asked to do so are seen by other Arabs as weak.
- Japanese leaders are expected to be humble and speak frequently.
- Scandinavian and Dutch leaders who single out individuals with public praise are likely to embarrass, not energize, those individuals.
- Effective leaders in Malaysia are expected to show compassion while using more of an autocratic than a participative style.
- Effective German leaders are characterized by high performance orientation, low compassion, low self-protection, low team orientation, high autonomy, and high participation.

Sources: Based on J.-H. Shin, R. L. Heath, and J. Lee, "A Contingency Explanation of Public Relations Practitioner Leadership Styles: Situation and Culture," *Journal of Public Relations Research*, April 2011, pp. 167–90; J. C. Kennedy, "Leadership in Malaysia: Traditional Values, International Outlook," *Academy of Management Executive*, August 2002, pp. 15–17; F. C. Brodbeck, M. Frese, and M. Javidan, "Leadership Made in Germany: Low on Compassion, High on Performance," *Academy of Management Executive*, February 2002, pp. 16–29; M. F. Peterson and J. G. Hunt, "International Perspectives on International Leadership," *Leadership Quarterly*, Fall 1997, pp. 203–31; R. J. House and R. N. Aditya, "The Social Scientific Study of Leadership: Quo Vadis?" *Journal of Management* 23, no. 3 (1997), p. 463; and R. J. House, "Leadership in the Twenty-First Century," in A. Howard (ed.), *The Changing Nature of Work* (San Francisco: Jossey-Bass, 1995), p. 442.

move up in an organization. The evidence indicates that the higher the rank of a person considered to be a star performer, the more that EI capabilities surface as the reason for his or her effectiveness. Specifically, when star performers were compared with average ones in senior management positions, nearly 90 percent of the difference in their effectiveness was attributable to EI factors rather than basic intelligence.

EI has been shown to be positively related to job performance at all levels. But it appears to be especially relevant in jobs that demand a high degree of social interaction. And of course, that's what leadership is all about. Great leaders demonstrate their EI by exhibiting all five of its key components: self-awareness, self-management, self-motivation, empathy, and social skills (see pp. 366–367).

Although there has been some controversy about the role of EI in leadership,[66] most research makes a case for concluding that EI is an essential element in leadership effectiveness.[67] As such, it could be added to the list of traits associated with leadership that we described earlier in the chapter.

Donald Heupel/Reuters

PepsiCo CEO Indra Nooyi is a leader with high emotional intelligence. Shown here listening to an employee at the firm's yogurt plant, Nooyi possesses the five EI components that have contributed to her excellent performance in jobs that demand a high degree of social interaction with workers, customers, and business leaders throughout the world.

WHAT ABOUT TOXIC BOSSES AND LEADERSHIP? Building, maintaining, and even repairing healthy working relationships on a team or in an organization are important skills for leaders. When it's done right, leaders are more effective. Feedback is better received, delegating is more straightforward, and coaching is more useful. But when it goes wrong, watch out! Destructive, toxic boss-employee relationships can lead to serious repercussions.[68] Increased absenteeism, higher turnover, an increase in ethical lapses, and drops in productivity can all be signs that a leader is abusive, ineffective, and toxic. And that's only the work-related problems. Rude, unpleasant, manipulative, demeaning, disrespectful, and unrelentingly demanding bosses also can lead to employee personal problems—stress, anxiety, and physical ailments. So, how can leaders not be toxic and instead build a culture of good working relationships with their team? It all boils down to being emotionally intelligent, setting appropriate boundaries, and making expectations clear from the start. Like any relationship, there are likely to be misunderstandings, but in the end, having strong, effective working relationships benefits individuals, teams, and the organization.

Why Is Trust the Essence of Leadership?

12-5 Discuss trust as the essence of leadership.

84 percent of Millennials say that trustworthiness is their primary leadership concern at work.[69]

One of the retired founders of the Ritz-Carlton hotel chain was a great example of a trust-building leader. Horst Schulze provided every employee with orientation and extensive training, and each was given a $2,000 discretionary fund he or she could use to solve a customer problem without checking with anyone first. One story is told of an employee who flew to Hawaii with a customer's laptop he'd forgotten that was critically needed for a presentation he was making. Yup, it might have been tempting to stay on a little vacation, but the employee took the next flight back home after delivering the customer's laptop. Why didn't the employee just overnight the laptop? Because she didn't want to take a chance that the customer would not get his much-needed laptop! That's the type of trusting culture a leader should be creating![70]

credibility
The degree to which followers perceive someone as honest, competent, and able to inspire

trust
The belief in the integrity, character, and ability of a leader

Trust, or lack of trust, is an increasingly important issue in today's organizations.[71] In today's uncertain environment, leaders need to build, or even rebuild, trust and credibility. Before we can discuss ways leaders can do that, we have to know what trust and credibility are and why they're so important.

The main component of credibility is honesty. Surveys show that honesty is consistently singled out as the number one characteristic of admired leaders. "Honesty is absolutely essential to leadership. If people are going to follow someone willingly, whether it be into battle or into the boardroom, they first want to assure themselves that the person is worthy of their trust."[72] In addition to being honest, credible leaders are competent and inspiring. They are personally able to effectively communicate their confidence and enthusiasm. Thus, followers judge a leader's **credibility** in terms of his or her honesty, competence, and ability to inspire.

Trust is closely entwined with the concept of credibility, and, in fact, the terms are often used interchangeably. **Trust** is defined as the belief in the integrity, character, and ability of a leader. Followers who trust a leader are willing to be vulnerable to the leader's actions because they are confident that their rights and interests will not be abused.[73] Research has identified five dimensions that make up the concept of trust:

- *Integrity:* honesty and truthfulness
- *Competence:* technical and interpersonal knowledge and skills
- *Consistency:* reliability, predictability, and good judgment in handling situations
- *Loyalty:* willingness to protect a person, physically and emotionally
- *Openness:* willingness to share ideas and information freely[74]

Of these five dimensions, integrity seems to be the most critical when someone assesses another's trustworthiness.[75] Both integrity and competence were seen in our earlier discussion of leadership traits found to be consistently associated with leadership.

Workplace changes have reinforced why such leadership qualities are important. For instance, trends of employee empowerment and self-managed work teams have reduced many of the traditional control mechanisms used to monitor employees. If a work team is free to schedule its own work, evaluate its own performance, and even make its own hiring decisions, trust becomes critical. Employees have to trust managers to treat them fairly, and managers have to trust employees to conscientiously fulfill their responsibilities.

Also, leaders have to increasingly lead others who may not be in their immediate work group or even may be physically separated—members of cross-functional or virtual teams, individuals who work for suppliers or customers, and perhaps even people who represent other organizations through strategic alliances. These situations don't allow leaders the luxury of falling back on their formal positions for influence. Many of these relationships, in fact, are fluid and fleeting. So the ability to quickly develop trust and sustain that trust is crucial to the success of the relationship.

Marc Benioff, co-founder and CEO of Salesforce and pioneer of cloud computing, has the leadership qualities that exemplify trust—honesty, competency, consistency, loyalty, and openness to sharing ideas and information. He believes that success is built on trust and that trust needs to be the highest value in every business venture and relationship with employees, customers, and other stakeholders.

Mike Blake/Reuters

Why is it important that followers trust their leaders?

Research has shown that trust in leadership is significantly related to positive job outcomes including job performance, organizational citizenship behavior, job satisfaction, and organizational commitment.[76] Given the importance of trust to effective leadership, leaders need to build trust with their followers. Some suggestions are shown in Exhibit 12–7.

Now, more than ever, managerial and leadership effectiveness depends on the ability to gain the trust of followers.[77] Downsizing, corporate financial misrepresentations, and the increased use of temporary employees have undermined employees' trust in their leaders and shaken the confidence of investors, suppliers, and customers. Today's leaders are faced with the challenge of rebuilding and restoring trust with employees and with other important organizational stakeholders.

Exhibit 12–7 Suggestions for Building Trust

1. **Practice openness.** Mistrust comes as much from what people don't know as from what they do know. Openness leads to confidence and trust. So keep people informed; make clear the criteria on how decisions are made; explain the rationale for your decisions; be candid about problems; and fully disclose relevant information.

2. **Be fair.** Before making decisions or taking actions, consider how others will perceive them in terms of objectivity and fairness. Give credit where credit is due; be objective and impartial in performance appraisals; and pay attention to equity perceptions in reward distributions.

3. **Speak your feelings.** Leaders who convey only hard facts come across as cold and distant. When you share your feelings, others will see you as real and human. They will know who you are and their respect for you will increase.

4. **Tell the truth.** If honesty is critical to credibility, you must be perceived as someone who tells the truth. Followers are more tolerant of being told something they "don't want to hear" than of finding out that their leader lied to them.

5. **Be consistent.** People want predictability. Mistrust comes from not knowing what to expect. Take the time to think about your values and beliefs. Then let them consistently guide your decisions. When you know your central purpose, your actions will follow accordingly, and you will project a consistency that earns trust.

6. **Fulfill your promises.** Trust requires that people believe that you're dependable. So you need to keep your word. Promises made must be promises kept.

7. **Maintain confidences.** You trust those whom you believe to be discreet and whom you can rely on. If people make themselves vulnerable by telling you something in confidence, they need to feel assured that you won't discuss it with others or betray that confidence. If people perceive you as someone who leaks personal confidences or someone who can't be depended on, you won't be perceived as trustworthy.

8. **Demonstrate confidence.** Develop the admiration and respect of others by demonstrating technical and professional ability. Pay particular attention to developing and displaying your communication, negotiating, and other interpersonal skills.

Sources: Based on P. S. Shockley-Zalabak and S. P Morreale, "Building High-Trust Organizations," *Leader to Leader*, Spring 2011, pp. 39–45; J. K. Butler Jr., "Toward Understanding and Measuring Conditions of Trust: Evolution of a Condition of Trust Inventory," *Journal of Management*, September 1991, pp. 643–63; and F. Bartolome, "Nobody Trusts the Boss Completely—Now What?" *Harvard Business Review*, March–April 1989, pp. 135–42.

A Final Thought Regarding Leadership

Despite the belief that some leadership style will always be effective regardless of the situation, *leadership may not always be important*! Research indicates that, in some situations, any behaviors a leader exhibits are irrelevant. In other words, certain individual, job, and organizational variables can act as "substitutes for leadership," negating the influence of the leader.[78]

For instance, follower characteristics such as experience, training, professional orientation, or need for independence can neutralize the effect of leadership. These characteristics can replace the employee's need for a leader's support or ability to create structure and reduce task ambiguity. Similarly, jobs that are inherently unambiguous and routine or that are intrinsically satisfying may place fewer demands on the leadership variable. Finally, such organizational characteristics as explicit formalized goals, rigid rules and procedures, or cohesive work groups can substitute for formal leadership.

CHAPTER SUMMARY BY LEARNING OUTCOME

12-1 Define *leader* and *leadership*.

A leader is someone who can influence others and who has managerial authority. Leadership is a process of leading a group and influencing that group to achieve its goals. Managers should be leaders because leading is one of the four management functions.

12-2 Compare and contrast early leadership theories.

Early attempts to define leader traits were unsuccessful, although later attempts found seven traits associated with leadership.

The University of Iowa studies explored three leadership styles. The only conclusion was that group members were more satisfied under a democratic leader than under an autocratic one. The Ohio State studies identified two dimensions of leader behavior—initiating structure and consideration. A leader high in both those dimensions at times achieved high group task performance and high group member satisfaction, but not always. The University of Michigan studies looked at employee-oriented leaders and production-oriented leaders. They concluded that leaders who were employee oriented could get high group productivity and high group member satisfaction. The Managerial Grid looked at leaders' concern for production and concern for people and identified five leader styles. Although it suggested that a leader who was high in concern for production and high in concern for people was the best, there was no substantive evidence for that conclusion.

As the behavioral studies showed, a leader's behavior has a dual nature: a focus on the task and a focus on the people.

12-3 Describe the four major contingency leadership theories.

Fiedler's model attempted to define the best style to use in particular situations. He measured leader style—relationship oriented or task oriented—using the least-preferred coworker questionnaire. Fiedler also assumed a leader's style was fixed. He measured three contingency dimensions: leader-member relations, task structure, and position power. The model suggests that task-oriented leaders performed best in very favorable and very unfavorable situations, and relationship-oriented leaders performed best in moderately favorable situations.

Hersey and Blanchard's situational leadership theory focused on followers' readiness. They identified four leadership styles: telling (high task–low relationship), selling (high task–high relationship), participating (low task–high relationship), and delegating (low task–low relationship). They also identified four stages of readiness: unable and unwilling (use telling style); unable but willing (use selling style); able but unwilling (use participative style); and able and willing (use delegating style).

The leader-participation model relates leadership behavior and participation to decision making. It uses a decision tree format with seven contingencies and five alternative leadership styles.

The path-goal model developed by Robert House identified four leadership behaviors: directive, supportive, participative, and achievement-oriented. He assumes that a leader can and should be able to use any of these styles. The two situational contingency variables were found in the environment and in the follower. Essentially the path-goal model says that a leader should provide direction and support as needed; that is, structure the path so the followers can achieve goals.

12-4 Describe modern views of leadership and the issues facing today's leaders.

Leader-member exchange (LMX) theory says that leaders create in-groups and out-groups and those in the in-group will have higher performance ratings, less turnover, and greater job satisfaction.

A transactional leader exchanges rewards for productivity where a transformational leader stimulates and inspires followers to achieve goals.

A charismatic leader is an enthusiastic and self-confident leader whose personality and actions influence people to behave in certain ways. People can learn to be charismatic. A visionary leader is able to create and articulate a realistic, credible, and attractive vision of the future.

A team leader has two priorities: manage the team's external boundary and facilitate the team process. Four leader roles are involved: liaison with external constituencies, troubleshooter, conflict manager, and coach.

The issues facing leaders today include employee empowerment, national culture, emotional intelligence, and toxic bosses. As employees are empowered, the leader's role tends to be one of not leading. As leaders adjust their style to the situation, one of the most important situational characteristics is national culture. EI is proving to be an essential element in leadership effectiveness. Finally, since toxic bosses can be detrimental to an organization, it's important for leaders to watch themselves for toxic behaviors and instead focus on building strong, effective work relationships.

12-5 Discuss trust as the essence of leadership.

The five dimensions of trust include integrity, competence, consistency, loyalty, and truthfulness. Integrity refers to one's honesty and truthfulness. Competence involves an individual's technical and interpersonal knowledge and skills. Consistency relates to an individual's reliability, predictability, and good judgment in handling situations. Loyalty is an individual's willingness to protect and save face for another person. Openness means that you share ideas and information freely and provide the whole truth.

DISCUSSION QUESTIONS

12-1 Define *leader* and *leadership*, and discuss why managers should be leaders.

12-2 Based on the behavioral theory of leadership, how does the behavior of one leader differ from that of other leaders?

12-3 "Leaders are born, not made." Do you agree with this statement? Why or why not?

12-4 "A leader's effectiveness depends on their followers' ability." Which theory claims this, and why?

12-5 Do you think that most managers in real life use a contingency approach to increase their leadership effectiveness? Discuss.

12-6 Does management style affect the way leaders lead? Consider McGregor's Theory X-Y and explain whether or not the leadership styles of a Theory X manager and a Theory Y manager would differ.

12-7 Do you think trust evolves out of an individual's personal characteristics or out of specific situations? Explain.

12-8 Do you think trustworthy leaders are more effective in getting results from followers? Explain.

12-9 How can organizations develop effective leaders?

12-10 When might leaders be irrelevant?

Applying: Getting Ready for the Workplace

Management Skill Builder | BEING A GOOD LEADER

The terms *management* and *leadership* are frequently used interchangeably. That's a misnomer. The two aren't the same but they are related. Although you don't need to hold a management position to be a leader, you're unlikely to be an effective manager if you can't be an effective leader.

MyLab Management

PERSONAL INVENTORY ASSESSMENT

Go to **www.pearson.com/mylab/management** to complete the Personal Inventory Assessment related to this chapter.

Skill Basics

Simply put, leadership style can be categorized as task- or people-oriented. Neither one is right for all situations. Although a number of situational variables influence the choice of an effective leadership style, four variables seem most relevant:[79]

- *Task structure.* Structured tasks have procedures and rules that minimize ambiguity. The more structured a job is, the less need there is for a leader to provide task structure.

- *Level of stress.* Situations differ in terms of time and performance stress. High-stress situations favor leaders with experience. Low stress favors a leader's intelligence.

- *Level of group support.* Members of close-knit and supportive groups help each other out. They can provide both task support and relationship support. Supportive groups make fewer demands on a leader.

- *Follower characteristics.* Personal characteristics of followers—such as experience, ability, and motivation—influence which leadership style will be most effective. Employees with extensive experience, strong abilities, and high motivation don't require much task behavior. They will be more effective with a people-oriented style. Conversely, employees with little experience, marginal abilities, and low motivation will perform better when leaders exhibit task-oriented behavior.

Practicing the Skill

Read through this scenario and follow the directions at the end of it:

You recently graduated from college with your degree in business administration. You've spent the past two summers working at Connecticut Mutual Insurance (CMI), filling in as an intern on a number of different jobs while employees took their vacations. You have received and accepted an offer to join CMI full-time as supervisor of the policy renewal department.

CMI is a large insurance company. In the headquarters office alone, where you'll be working, there are more than 1,500 employees. The company believes strongly in the personal development of its employees. This belief translates into a philosophy, emanating from the top executive offices, of trust and respect for all CMI employees. The company is also regularly atop most lists of "best companies to work for," largely due to its progressive work/life programs and strong commitment to minimizing layoffs.

In your new job, you'll direct the activities of 18 policy-renewal clerks. Their jobs require little training and are highly routine. A clerk's responsibility is to ensure that renewal notices are sent on current policies, to tabulate any changes in premiums, to advise the sales division if a policy is to be canceled as a result of nonresponse to renewal notices, and to answer questions and solve problems related to renewals.

The people in your work group range in age from 19 to 62, with a median age of 25. For the most part, they are high school graduates with little prior working experience. They earn between $2,350 and $3,200 a month. You will be replacing a long-time CMI employee, Jan Allison. Jan is retiring after 37 years with CMI, the past 14 spent as a policy-renewal supervisor. Because you spent a few weeks in Jan's group last summer, you're familiar with Jan's style and are acquainted with most of the department members. But people don't know you very well and are suspicious of the fact that you're fresh out of college and have little experience in the department. The reality is that you got this job because management wanted someone with a college degree to oversee the department. Your most vocal critic is Lillian Lantz. Lillian is well into her 50s, has been a policy-renewal clerk for over a dozen years, and—as the "grand old lady" of the department—carries a lot of weight with group members. You know that it'll be very hard to lead this department without Lillian's support.

Using your knowledge of leadership concepts, which leadership style would you choose? And why?

Experiential Exercise

We've spent the entire chapter talking about leadership. You should have a fairly good handle on what leading and leadership is all about by now. But, we want to "throw" one more thing at you.

In your assigned group, you are to discuss the following:

Is leadership a quality, an attribute, an attitude, or a job title? Come up with an answer and why you chose what you did. You could choose more than one of these, but explain your rationale for each. Also, explain why you didn't choose the others. Finally, be prepared to present your conclusion(s) to the class orally and written in an Executive Summary–type format.

CASE APPLICATION #1

"Success Theater" at General Electric
Topic: Football Focus

If trust is a fundamental part of leadership, how does an organization recover when the trust is lost? This is a question Fédération Internationale de Football Association (FIFA) recently had to ask itself after a series of scandals rocked it to its foundations.

Football is not just a sport; it is very big business. Deloitte estimated the revenue for the UK premiership alone for the 2016–17 season at $4.5 billion and expected this to rise to $5 billion for 2018–2019.[81] Founded in 1904, FIFA is the governing body responsible for running world football. One of its most important responsibilities is managing the bidding process for countries wishing to host the World Cup, the most-watched sporting event in the world. Countries spend millions of dollars preparing their bids and expect a fair, transparent process.

Long before FIFA President Sepp Blatter declared Russia the host of the 2018 World Cup and the small Gulf state of Qatar winner of the next in 2022, questions were being asked about the bidding process. For these two latest events, allegations were made that countries had colluded to trade votes, which Blatter confirmed in 2011, promising an internal investigation.

In July 2012, after further allegations were made, Blatter and FIFA tried to answer their critics by employing Michael J. Garcia, an American attorney. His job was to investigate corruption at FIFA, and he took a good look at the 2018 and 2022 World Cup bids. By September 2014, Garcia had compiled a comprehensive, 350-page report. However, FIFA's own ethics committee refused to publish the complete document, preferring instead a much shorter summary, casting more doubt on FIFA and ultimately leading to Garcia's resignation after he claimed the facts had been misrepresented.[82]

Things went from bad to worse for FIFA at the 2015 FIFA annual meeting in Zurich, Switzerland, when a number of dawn raids were carried out by U.S. federal authorities and seven FIFA officials were arrested in what was the culmination of an investigation lasting several years. In total, 14 people were detained over corruption allegedly involving more than $150 million worth of bribes dating back 24 years.[83] Sepp Blatter was re-elected as President that same year; however, this was to be short-lived. After only four days, he announced his intention to resign, asking the congress to appoint a successor as soon as possible. In the September of the same year, Swiss prosecutors opened proceedings against Blatter over a number of financial irregularities, including a "disloyal payment" to Michel Platini, his possible replacement as President. In December 2015, the FIFA ethics committee banned both Blatter and Platini from all football-related activity for eight years.

The year 2016 saw the appointment of a new president, Gianni Infantino, but more importantly the passing of a number of reforms focused on accountability and transparency within the organization and aimed at repairing FIFA's tarnished reputation. It is now Infantino's role to preside over this new FIFA and rebuild trust with clubs, countries, players, and fans.

Discussion Questions

12-11 What does the number of senior FIFA executives being investigated say about the culture at FIFA?

12-12 Of the 8 suggestions for building trust, which do you think should have been the focus for FIFA? Think about Michael J. Garcia's report.

12-13 What does the case say about Blatter's style of leadership?

12-14 In 2011, when asked about the crisis at FIFA around the rumors of financial irregularities, Blatter downplayed the allegations dismissively. Which of the 5 dimensions of trust do you think Blatter was failing to demonstrate here?

12-15 For Infantino to succeed, what style of leadership do you think would be most effective?

CASE APPLICATION #2

Developing Gen Y Leaders
Topic: Serving Up Leaders

Manchester United Football Club, a professional football club based in Old Trafford, England, enjoyed great success between 1986 and 2013, as evidenced by their 38 domestic and non-domestic trophies.

With the trophies came scrutiny. The British and world media were fascinated by the leadership at Manchester United. There were tales of the manager shouting at players in the dressing room with such ferocity that it was referred to as the "hairdryer treatment." One journalist stated from personal experience that this treatment was not reserved just for the players. High expectations were not restricted to the football pitch. When the captain openly criticized his teammates in an interview, his contract was terminated. While these make for good headlines, they do not reveal the whole story.

Is it really possible to lead an organization effectively for over a quarter of a century just by having the loudest voice and a fearsome reputation? How did Alex Ferguson, the manager of Manchester United FC for those 26 years lead his team so effectively?

When Ferguson joined Manchester United in 1986, he had very definite ideas about how he was going to build his club. Planning for long-term success, he set about changing the very culture of the club—which was no small task. He tackled a damaging drinking culture head-on and encouraged a strong work ethic of being the first into the office and last to leave. To increase the players' feeling of commitment and belonging, he insisted that they should dress as Manchester United, wearing blazers displaying the club badge, when representing the club. These all contributed to his vision.

David Gill, the club's former chief executive, has compared Alex Ferguson to Steve Jobs. There are some obvious similarities: both men were driven, determined, often terrifying, and ultimately extremely successful leaders in highly competitive arenas. However, while Jobs had an unapologetically blunt and aggressive approach, Ferguson would vary his managing style, shouting at some players and taking a different approach with others. This approach could seem arbitrary and inconsistent but was actually a conscious choice made by a manager who really knew his players and understood how to get the best out of each one. When it was necessary to instill discipline in players to ensure a positive working relationship, Ferguson would deal with the issue immediately and move on.

Ferguson knew the importance of detail. As a manager, knowing the names of your team is obviously essential, but he understood that the organization was bigger than the team, so he learned the names of all the support staff and took time to talk to them. One interviewer commented that by the end of a filming session Ferguson had learned the name of the film crew and was happy to converse with them while sharing a bottle of champagne.

In 2014, Ferguson took up a teaching post in executive education with Harvard Business School, and his book *Leading* was published in 2015.[84]

Discussion Questions

12-16 What leadership theories do you feel Ferguson's actions support?

12-17 What leadership traits do you see being demonstrated in the case?

12-18 To what degree has emotional intelligence played a part in Alex Ferguson's success?

12-19 What do you see as the possible problems of varying the leadership approach with different players?

CASE APPLICATION #3

Investing in Leadership

Topic: Leadership development, cross-cultural leadership, mentors

Jean Paul Agon, the president and CEO of L'Oreal, joined the company right after his university graduation in 1978 and has continued to grow as a leader over his more than 40 years with the company. Headquartered in France with more than 80,000 employees around the globe, L'Oreal is the world's largest cosmetic company. Today L'Oreal management still believes leadership development starts at the beginning of your career.

Each year, almost 650 recent university graduates join one of L'Oreal's management training programs.[85] The format of each program varies on geographic location, with trainees spending between 6 and 18 months taking on different missions throughout the organization to learn the business. Each trainee has a personal development plan that includes learning about the organization, understanding the business models utilized by the different brands, and developing relationships throughout the organization. The program immerses the trainee into the organizational culture, and the trainee learns what it takes to succeed in the work environment. Most trainees are also connected with a mentor to answer questions and provide guidance.

A significant contributor to L'Oreal's overall success is the cross-cultural awareness of managers who often lead diverse teams developing customized products for different regions of the world. While some of these leaders are recruited externally, many are developed through a specific international management training program that includes a 12-month rotation through Paris, New York, Singapore, and Rio de Janeiro. This program seeks out graduates from international business schools who are curious and able to adapt to other cultures, knowing this skill set is important to help tailor international brands to local markets.

When does leadership development start?

Doing business globally also requires ethical leadership, which is an important component of the firm's leadership development. L'Oreal has been recognized for its efforts on the ethical front. In 2016, the Ethics & Compliance Initiative recognized L'Oreal's innovation in ethical leadership. The company was also named as one of the World's Most Ethical Companies by Ethisphere.[86]

L'Oreal's leadership development efforts do not stop with recent graduates. In fact, managers at all levels of the organization have the opportunity to further develop their leadership ability through a variety of programs. These programs are primarily based on coaching leaders and are offered with the belief that an investment in leaders goes farther as those leaders then develop their own teams. Managers throughout the organization are held accountable for the development of their employees. Those that fail at developing their own teams, even if they meet business goals, lose out on performance awards. All this emphasizes this important point: Leadership matters at L'Oreal.

Discussion Questions

12-20 Why do you think L'Oreal invests so much in leadership development?

12-21 What role can a mentor play in leadership development?

12-22 Why is cross-cultural awareness important for leaders at a company such as L'Oreal?

12-23 Why is ethical leadership important for leaders at a company such as L'Oreal?

12-24 Do you think a management training program would be a good way to start a career with a company? Why or why not? Think about *your* answer to this question, and then, in your assigned group, discuss this question. Then, suppose you were mentoring a younger student, what would you tell them about leadership development and management training programs?

Endnotes

1. K. Gee, "Valvoline Sets Clear Path Up the Ladder," *Wall Street Journal*, February 1, 2018, p. B5.

2. J. Bort, "Airbnb Made $93 Million in Profit on $2.6 Billion in Revenue," *Business Insider Online*, February 6, 2018.

3. L. Gallagher, "Why Airbnb CEO Brian Chesky Is among the World's Greatest Leaders," *Fortune Online*, March 24, 2017.

4. Most leadership research has focused on the actions and responsibilities of managers and extrapolated the results to leaders and leadership in general.

5. Classic Concepts in Today's Workplace box based on D. S. Derue, J. D. Nahrgang, N. Wellman, and S. E. Humphrey, "Trait and Behavioral Theories of Leadership: An Integration and Meta-Analytic Test of Their Relative Validity," *Personnel Psychology*, Spring 2011, pp. 7–52; and D. A. Wren and A. G. Bedeian, *The Evolution of Management Thought*, 6th ed. (Hoboken, NJ: John Wiley & Sons, 2009), pp. 345–46.

6. See D. S. Derue, J. D. Nahrgang, N. Wellman, and S. E. Humphrey, "Trait and Behavioral Theories of Leadership: An Integration and Meta-Analytic Test of Their Relative Validity," *Personnel Psychology*, Spring 2011, pp. 7–52; T. A. Judge, J. E. Bono, R. Ilies, and M. W. Gerhardt, "Personality and Leadership: A Qualitative and Quantitative Review," *Journal of Applied Psychology*, August 2002, pp. 765–80; and S. A. Kirkpatrick and E. A. Locke, "Leadership: Do Traits Matter?" *Academy of Management Executive*, May 1991, pp. 48–60.

7. K. Lewin and R. Lippitt, "An Experimental Approach to the Study of Autocracy and Democracy: A Preliminary Note," *Sociometry* 1 (1938), pp. 292–300; K. Lewin, "Field Theory and Experiment in Social Psychology: Concepts and Methods," *American Journal of Sociology* 44 (1939), pp. 868–96; K. Lewin, R. Lippitt, and R. K. White, "Patterns of Aggressive Behavior in Experimentally Created Social Climates," *Journal of Social Psychology* 10 (1939), pp. 271–301; and R. Lippitt, "An Experimental Study of the Effect of Democratic and Authoritarian Group Atmospheres," *University of Iowa Studies in Child Welfare* 16 (1940), pp. 43–95.

8. R. M. Stodgill and A. E. Coons (eds.), *Leader Behavior: Its Description and Measurement*, Research Monograph No. 88 (Columbus: Ohio State University, Bureau of Business Research, 1951). See also S. Kerr, C. A. Schriesheim, C. J. Murphy, and R. M. Stodgill, "Toward a Contingency Theory of Leadership Based upon the Consideration and Initiating Structure Literature," *Organizational Behavior and Human Performance*, August 1974, pp. 62–82; and B. M. Fisher, "Consideration and Initiating Structure and Their Relationships with Leader Effectiveness: A Meta Analysis," in F. Hoy (ed.), *Proceedings of the 48th Annual Academy of Management Conference* (Anaheim, CA, 1988), pp. 201–05.

9. R. Kahn and D. Katz, "Leadership Practices in Relation to Productivity and Morale," in D. Cartwright and A. Zander (eds.), *Group Dynamics: Research and Theory*, 2nd ed. (Elmsford, NY: Pow, Paterson, 1960).

10. R. R. Blake and J. S. Mouton, *The Managerial Grid III* (Houston: Gulf Publishing, 1984).

11. W. G. Bennis, "The Seven Ages of the Leader," *Harvard Business Review*, January 2004, p. 52.

12. F. E. Fiedler, *A Theory of Leadership Effectiveness* (New York: McGraw-Hill, 1967).

13. R. Ayman, M. M. Chemers, and F. Fiedler, "The Contingency Model of Leadership Effectiveness: Its Levels of Analysis," *Leadership Quarterly*, Summer 1995, pp. 147–67; C. A. Schriesheim, B. J. Tepper, and L. A. Tetrault, "Lease Preferred Co-Worker Score, Situational Control, and Leadership Effectiveness: A Meta-Analysis of Contingency Model Performance Predictions," *Journal of Applied Psychology*, August 1994, pp. 561–73; and L. H. Peters, D. D. Hartke, and J. T. Pholmann, "Fiedler's Contingency Theory of Leadership: An Application of the Meta-Analysis Procedures of Schmidt and Hunter," *Psychological Bulletin*, March 1985, pp. 274–85.

14. See B. Kabanoff, "A Critique of Leader Match and Its Implications for Leadership Research," *Personnel Psychology*, Winter 1981, pp. 749–64; and E. H. Schein, *Organizational Psychology*, 3rd ed. (Upper Saddle River, NJ: Prentice Hall, 1980), pp. 116–17.

15. P. Hersey and K. H. Blanchard, *Management of Organizational Behavior: Leading Human Resources*, 8th ed. (Englewood Cliffs, NJ: Prentice Hall, 2001); and P. Hersey and K. Blanchard, "So You Want to Know Your Leadership Style?" *Training and Development Journal*, February 1974, pp. 1–15.

16. See, for instance, E. G. Ralph, "Developing Managers' Effectiveness: A Model with Potential," *Journal of Management Inquiry*, June 2004, pp. 152–63; C. L. Graeff, "Evolution of Situational Leadership Theory: A Critical Review," *Leadership Quarterly* 8, no. 2 (1997), pp. 153–70; and C. F. Fernandez and R. P. Vecchio, "Situational Leadership Theory Revisited: A Test of an Across-Jobs Perspective," *Leadership Quarterly* 8, no. 1 (1997), pp. 67–84.

17. V. H. Vroom and P. W. Yetton, *Leadership and Decision Making* (Pittsburgh: University of Pittsburgh Press, 1973).

18. V. H. Vroom and A. G. Jago, *The New Leadership: Managing Participation in Organizations* (Upper Saddle River, NJ: Prentice Hall, 1988). See especially Chapter 8.

19. See, for example, R. H. G. Field and R. J. House, "A Test of the Vroom Yetton Model Using Manager and Subordinate Reports," *Journal of Applied Psychology*, June 1990, pp. 362–66; J. T. Ettling and A. G. Jago, "Participation Under Conditions of Conflict: More on the Validity of the Vroom Yetton Model," *Journal of Management Studies*, January 1988, pp. 73–83; C. R. Leana, "Power Relinquishment versus Power Sharing: Theoretical Clarification and Empirical Comparison of Delegation and Participation," *Journal of Applied Psychology*, May 1987, pp. 228–33; and R. H. G. Field, "A Test of the Vroom Yetton Normative Model of Leadership," *Journal of Applied Psychology*, October 1982, pp. 523–32.

20. For additional information about the exchanges that occur between the leader and the follower, see A. S. Phillips and A. G. Bedeian, "Leader Follower Exchange Quality: The Role of Personal and Interpersonal Attributes," *Academy of Management Journal* 37, no. 4 (1994), pp. 990–1001; and T. A. Scandura and C. A. Schriesheim, "Leader Member Exchange and Supervisor Career Mentoring as Complementary Constructs in Leadership Research," *Academy of Management Journal* 37, no. 6 (1994), pp. 1588–602.

21. SmartPulse, "How Willing Are You to Step Outside Your Leadership Style 'Comfort Zone' and Try New Techniques?" December 10, 2013, www.smartbrief.com/leadership.

22. R. J. House, "Path-Goal Theory of Leadership: Lessons, Legacy, and a Reformulated Theory," *Leadership Quarterly*, Fall 1996, pp. 323–52; R. J. House and T. R. Mitchell, "Path-Goal Theory of Leadership," *Journal of Contemporary Business*, Autumn 1974, p. 86; and R. J. House, "A Path-Goal Theory of Leader Effectiveness," *Administrative Science Quarterly*, September 1971, pp. 321–38.

23. E. McGirt, "Why U2's Bono Is One of the World's Greatest Leaders," *Fortune Online*, March 24, 2016.

24. A. Sagie and M. Koslowsky, "Organizational Attitudes and Behaviors as a Function of Participation in Strategic and Tactical Change Decisions: An Application of Path-Goal Theory," *Journal of Organizational Behavior*, January 1994, pp. 37–47; and J. C. Wofford and L. Z. Liska, "Path-Goal Theories of Leadership: A Meta-Analysis," *Journal of Management*, Winter 1993, pp. 857–76.

25. S. Finkelstein, "The Best Leaders Are Great Teachers," *Harvard Business Review*, January–February 2018, pp. 142–45.

26. L. Ma and Q. Qu, "Differentiation in Leader-Member Exchange: A Hierarchical Linear Modeling Approach," *Leadership Quarterly*, October 2010, pp. 733–44; C. P. Schriesheim, S. L. Castro, X. Zhou, and F. J. Yamarinno, "The Folly of Theorizing 'A' but Testing 'B': A Selective Level-of-Analysis Review of the Field and a Detailed Leader-Member Exchange Illustration," *Leadership Quarterly*, Winter 2001, pp. 515–51; R. C. Liden, R. T. Sparrowe, and S. J. Wayne, "Leader-Member Exchange Theory: The Past and Potential for the Future," in G. R. Ferris (ed.), *Research in Personnel and Human Resource Management*, vol. 15 (Greenwich, CT: JAI Press, 1997), pp. 47–119; G. B. Graen and M. Uhl-Bien, "Relationship-Based Approach to Leadership: Development of Leader-Member Exchange (LMX) Theory of Leadership Over 25 Years: Applying a Multi-Domain Perspective," *Leadership Quarterly*, Summer 1995, pp. 219–47; and R. M. Dienesch and R. C. Liden, "Leader-Member Exchange Model of Leadership: A Critique and Further Development," *Academy of Management Review*, July 1986, pp. 618–34.

27. J. B. Wu, A. S. Tsui, and A. J. Kinicki, "Consequences of Differentiated Leadership in Groups," *Academy of Management Journal*, February 2010, pp. 90–106; S. S. Masterson, K. Lewis, and B. M. Goldman, "Integrating Justice and Social Exchange: The Differing Effects of Fair Procedures and Treatment on

Work Relationships," *Academy of Management Journal*, August 2000, pp. 738–48; S. J. Wayne, L. J. Shore, W. H. Bommer, and L. E. Tetrick, "The Role of Fair Treatment and Rewards in Perceptions of Organizational Support and Leader-Member Exchange," *Journal of Applied Psychology*, June 2002, pp. 590–98; R. C. Liden, S. J. Wayne, and D. Stilwell, "A Longitudinal Study of the Early Development of Leader-Member Exchanges," *Journal of Applied Psychology*, August 1993, pp. 662–74; and R. C. Liden and G. Graen, "Generalizability of the Vertical Dyad Linkage Model of Leadership," *Academy of Management Journal*, September 1980, pp. 451–65.

28. V. L. Goodwin, W. M. Bowler, and J. L. Whittington, "A Social Network Perspective on LMX Relationships: Accounting for the Instrumental Value of Leader and Follower Networks," *Journal of Management*, August 2009, pp. 954–80; R. Vecchio and D. M. Brazil, "Leadership and Sex-Similarity: A Comparison in a Military Setting," *Personnel Psychology*, vol. 60 (2007), pp. 303–35; M. Uhl-Bien, "Relationship Development as a Key Ingredient for Leadership Development," in S. E. Murphy and R. E. Riggio (eds.), *Future of Leadership Development* (Mahwah, NJ: Lawrence Erlbaum, 2003), pp. 129–47; Liden, Wayne, and Stilwell, "A Longitudinal Study of the Early Development of Leader-Member Exchanges"; and D. Duchon, S. G. Green, and T. D. Taber, "Vertical Dyad Linkage: A Longitudinal Assessment of Antecedents, Measures, and Consequences," *Journal of Applied Psychology*, February 1986, pp. 56–60.

29. P. Drexler, "The Upside of Favoritism," *Wall Street Journal*, June 8–9, 2013, p. C3.

30. See, for instance, R. Cropanzano, M. T. Dasborough, and H. M. Weiss, "Affective Events and the Development of Leader-Member Exchange," *Academy of Management Review*, April 2017, pp. 233–58; F. O. Walumbwa, D. M. Mayer, P. Wang, H. Wang, K. Workman, and A. L. Christensen, "Linking Ethical Leadership to Employee Performance: The Roles of Leader-Member Exchange Theory, Self-Efficacy, and Organizational Identification," *Organizational Behavior & Human Decision Processes*, July 2011, pp. 204–13; K. J. Harris, A. R. Wheeler, and K. M. Kacmar, "The Mediating Role of Organizational Embeddedness in the LMX-Outcomes Relationship," *Leadership Quarterly*, April 2011, pp. 271–81; W. M. Bowler, J. R. B.

Halbesleben, and J. R. B. Paul, "If You're Close with the Leader, You Must Be a Brownnose: The Role of Leader-Member Relationships in Follower, Leader, and Coworker Attributions of Organizational Citizenship Behavior Motives," *Human Resource Management Review*, December 2010, pp. 309–16; G. Sears and C. Holmvall, "The Joint Influence of Supervisor and Subordinate Emotional Intelligence on Leader-Member Exchange," *Journal of Business & Psychology*, December 2010, pp. 593–605; V. Venkataramani, S. G. Green, and D. J. Schleicher, "Well-Connected Leaders' Social Network Ties on LMX and Members' Work Attitudes," *Journal of Applied Psychology*, November 2010, pp. 1071–84; Z. Chen, W. Lam, and J. A. Zhong, "Leader-Member Exchange and Member Performance: A New Look at Individual-Level Negative Feedback-Seeking Behavior and Team-Level Empowerment Culture," *Journal of Applied Psychology*, January 2007, pp. 202–12; R. Ilies, J. D. Nahrgang, and F. P. Morgeson, "Leader-Member Exchange and Citizenship Behaviors: A Meta-Analysis," *Journal of Applied Psychology*, January 2007, pp. 269–77; and C. R. Gerstner and D. V. Day, "Meta-Analytic Review of Leader-Member Exchange Theory: Correlates and Construct Issues," *Journal of Applied Psychology*, December 1997, pp. 827–44.

31. B. M. Bass and R. E. Riggio, *Transformational Leadership*, 2d ed. (Mahwah, NJ: Lawrence Erlbaum Associates, Inc., 2006), p. 3.

32. J. Seltzer and B. M. Bass, "Transformational Leadership: Beyond Initiation and Consideration," *Journal of Management*, December 1990, pp. 693–703; and B. M. Bass, "Leadership: Good, Better, Best," *Organizational Dynamics*, Winter 1985, pp. 26–40.

33. B. J. Avolio and B. M. Bass, "Transformational Leadership, Charisma, and Beyond," working paper, School of Management, State University of New York, Binghamton, 1985, 14.

34. R. S. Rubin, D. C. Munz, and W. H. Bommer, "Leading from Within: The Effects of Emotion Recognition and Personality on Transformational Leadership Behavior," *Academy of Management Journal*, October 2005, pp. 845–58; T. A. Judge and J. E. Bono, "Five-Factor Model of Personality and Transformational Leadership," *Journal of Applied Psychology*, October 2000, pp. 751–65; B. M. Bass and B. J. Avolio, "Developing Transformational Leadership: 1992 and Beyond," *Journal of*

European Industrial Training, January 1990, p. 23; and J. J. Hater and B. M. Bass, "Supervisors' Evaluation and Subordinates' Perceptions of Transformational and Transactional Leadership," *Journal of Applied Psychology*, November 1988, pp. 695–702.

35. M. Tims, A. B. Bakker, and D. Xanthopoulou, "Do Transformational Leaders Enhance Their Followers' Daily Work Engagement?" *Leadership Quarterly*, February 2011, pp. 121–31; X.-H. (Frank) Wang and J. M. Howell, "Exploring the Dual-Level Effects of Transformational Leadership on Followers," *Journal of Applied Psychology*, November 2010, pp. 1134–44; A. E. Colbert, A. L. Kristof-Brown, B. H. Bradley, and M. R. Barrick, "CEO Transformational Leadership: The Role of Goal Importance Congruence in Top Management Teams," *Academy of Management Journal*, February 2008, pp. 81–96; R. F. Piccolo and J. A. Colquitt, "Transformational Leadership and Job Behaviors: The Mediating Role of Core Job Characteristics," *Academy of Management Journal*, April 2006, pp. 327–40; O. Epitropaki and R. Martin, "From Ideal to Real: A Longitudinal Study of the Role of Implicit Leadership Theories on Leader-Member Exchanges and Employee Outcomes," *Journal of Applied Psychology*, July 2005, pp. 659–76; J. E. Bono and T. A. Judge, "Self-Concordance at Work: Toward Understanding the Motivational Effects of Transformational Leaders," *Academy of Management Journal*, October 2003, pp. 554–71; T. Dvir, D. Eden, B. J. Avolio, and B. Shamir, "Impact of Transformational Leadership on Follower Development and Performance: A Field Experiment," *Academy of Management Journal*, August 2002, pp. 735–44; N. Sivasubramaniam, W. D. Murry, B. J. Avolio, and D. I. Jung, "A Longitudinal Model of the Effects of Team Leadership and Group Potency on Group Performance," *Group and Organization Management*, March 2002, pp. 66–96; J. M. Howell and B. J. Avolio, "Transformational Leadership, Transactional Leadership, Locus of Control, and Support for Innovation: Key Predictors of Consolidated-Business-Unit Performance," *Journal of Applied Psychology*, December 1993, pp. 891–911; R. T. Keller, "Transformational Leadership and the Performance of Research and Development Project Groups," *Journal*

of Management, September 1992, pp. 489–501; and Bass and Avolio, "Developing Transformational Leadership."

36. M. Thompson and B. Tracy, "Building a Great Organization," *Leader to Leader*, Fall 2010, pp. 45–49; and F. Vogelstein, "Mighty Amazon," *Fortune*, May 26, 2003, pp. 60–74.

37. J. M. Crant and T. S. Bateman, "Charismatic Leadership Viewed from Above: The Impact of Proactive Personality," *Journal of Organizational Behavior*, February 2000, pp. 63–75; G. Yukl and J. M. Howell, "Organizational and Contextual Influences on the Emergence and Effectiveness of Charismatic Leadership," *Leadership Quarterly*, Summer 1999, pp. 257–83; and J. A. Conger and R. N. Kanungo, "Behavioral Dimensions of Charismatic Leadership," in J. A. Conger, R. N. Kanungo and Associates, *Charismatic Leadership* (San Francisco: Jossey-Bass, 1988), pp. 78–97.

38. J. A. Conger and R. N. Kanungo, *Charismatic Leadership in Organizations* (Thousand Oaks, CA: Sage, 1998).

39. F. Walter and H. Bruch, "An Affective Events Model of Charismatic Leadership Behavior: A Review, Theoretical Investigation, and Research Agenda," *Journal of Management*, December 2009, pp. 1428–52; K. S. Groves, "Linking Leader Skills, Follower Attitudes, and Contextual Variables via an Integrated Model of Charismatic Leadership," *Journal of Management*, April 2005, pp. 255–77; J. J. Sosik, "The Role of Personal Values in the Charismatic Leadership of Corporate Managers: A Model and Preliminary Field Study," *Leadership Quarterly*, April 2005, pp. 221–44; A. H. B. deHoogh, D. N. den Hartog, P. L. Koopman, H. Thierry, P. T. van den Berg, J. G. van der Weide, and C. P. M. Wilderom, "Leader Motives, Charismatic Leadership, and Subordinates' Work Attitudes in the Profit and Voluntary Sector," *Leadership Quarterly*, February 2005, pp. 17–38; J. M. Howell and B. Shamir, "The Role of Followers in the Charismatic Leadership Process: Relationships and Their Consequences," *Academy of Management Review*, January 2005, pp. 96–112; J. Paul, D. L. Costley, J. P. Howell, P. W. Dorfman, and D. Trafimow, "The Effects of Charismatic Leadership on Followers' Self-Concept Accessibility," *Journal of Applied Social Psychology*, September 2001, pp. 1821–44; J. A. Conger, R. N. Kanungo, and S. T. Menon, "Charismatic Leadership and Follower Effects," *Journal of Organizational Behavior*, vol.

21 (2000), pp. 747–67; R. W. Rowden, "The Relationship between Charismatic Leadership Behaviors and Organizational Commitment," *Leadership & Organization Development Journal*, January 2000, pp. 30–35; G. P. Shea and C. M. Howell, "Charismatic Leadership and Task Feedback: A Laboratory Study of Their Effects on Self-Efficacy," *Leadership Quarterly*, Fall 1999, pp. 375–96; S. A. Kirkpatrick and E. A. Locke, "Direct and Indirect Effects of Three Core Charismatic Leadership Components on Performance and Attitudes," *Journal of Applied Psychology*, February 1996, pp. 36–51; D. A. Waldman, B. M. Bass, and F. J. Yammarino, "Adding to Contingent-Reward Behavior: The Augmenting Effect of Charismatic Leadership," *Group & Organization Studies*, December 1990, pp. 381–94; and R. J. House, J. Woycke, and E. M. Fodor, "Charismatic and Noncharismatic Leaders: Differences in Behavior and Effectiveness," in Conger and Kanungo, *Charismatic Leadership*, pp. 103–04.

40. B. R. Agle, N J. Nagarajan, J. A. Sonnenfeld, and D. Srinivasan, "Does CEO Charisma Matter? An Empirical Analysis of the Relationships among Organizational Performance, Environmental Uncertainty, and Top Management Team Perceptions of CEO Charisma," *Academy of Management Journal*, February 2006, pp. 161–74.

41. R. Birchfield, "Creating Charismatic Leaders," *Management*, June 2000, pp. 30–31; S. Caudron, "Growing Charisma," *Industry Week*, May 4, 1998, pp. 54–55; and J. A. Conger and R. N. Kanungo, "Training Charismatic Leadership: A Risky and Critical Task," in Conger and Kanungo, *Charismatic Leadership*, pp. 309–23.

42. J. G. Hunt, K. B. Boal, and G. E. Dodge, "The Effects of Visionary and Crisis-Responsive Charisma on Followers: An Experimental Examination," *Leadership Quarterly*, Fall 1999, pp. 423–48; R. J. House and R. N. Aditya, "The Social Scientific Study of Leadership: Quo Vadis?" *Journal of Management* 23, no. 3 (1997), pp. 316–23; and R. J.House, "A 1976 Theory of Charismatic Leadership," Working Paper Series 76-06, Toronto University, October 1976."

43. This definition is based on M. Sashkin, "The Visionary Leader," in Conger and Kanungo et al., *Charismatic Leadership*, pp. 124–25; B. Nanus, *Visionary Leadership* (New York: Free Press, 1992), p. 8; N. H. Snyder and M. Graves, "Leadership and Vision," *Business Horizons*, January–February 1994, p. 1; and

J. R. Lucas, "Anatomy of a Vision Statement," *Management Review*, February 1998, pp. 22–26.

44. Nanus, *Visionary Leadership*, p. 8.

45. "Creating Visionary Leadership," AON Hewitt Stat of the Week, December 14, 2017.

46. A. Moore, "The Bedrock of Effective Leadership," *T&D*, May 2018, p. 62.

47. S. Caminiti, "What Team Leaders Need to Know," *Fortune*, February 20, 1995, pp. 93–100.

48. Ibid., p. 93.

49. Ibid., p. 100.

50. M. Brody, "Courageous Coaching Isn't Easy, But It's Your Job," *T&D*, November 2017, pp. 70–73; D. S. DeRue, C. M. Barnes, and F. M. Morgeson, "Understanding the Motivational Contingencies of Team Leadership," *Small Group Research*, October 2010, pp. 621–51; B. Meredith, "Leader Characteristics: Is There a Shift in Requirements?" *Leadership Excellence*, September 2010, p. 19; B. Neal, "Heroes and Sidekicks: Ensuring Proper Followership," *T&D*, September 2010, pp. 76–77; R. D. Ramsey, "Preparing to Be Tomorrow's Leader Today," *Supervision*, January 2010, p. 79; N. Steckler and N. Fondas, "Building Team Leader Effectiveness: A Diagnostic Tool," *Organizational Dynamics*, Winter 1995, p. 20.

51. F. Fontana, "Common Traits of Best Team Leaders," *Wall Street Journal Online,* September 19, 2017.

52. R. S. Wellins, W. C. Byham, and G. R. Dixon, *Inside Teams* (San Francisco: Jossey-Bass, 1994), p. 318.

53. Steckler and Fondas, "Building Team Leader Effectiveness," p. 21.

54. M. Colchester, "Barclays CEO Hit with Penalties of $1.5 Million," *Wall Street Journal,* May 12–13, 2018, pp. B1+.

55. K. Kelly and Chad Bray, "Barclay's CEO Investigated over Treatment of Whistle-Blower," *New York Times Online,* April 10, 2017.

56. "The 100 Most Creative People in Business 2010," *Fast Company,* June 2010, pp. 70–119; and G. Colvin, "The FedEx Edge," *Fortune,* April 3, 2006, pp. 77–84.

57. J. Fabre, "The Importance of Empowering Front-Line Staff," *Supervision*, December 2010, pp. 6–7; S. Raub and C. Robert, "Differential Effects of Empowering Leadership on In-Role and Extra-Role Employee Behaviors: Exploring the Role of Psychological Empowerment and Power Values," *Human Relations*, November 2010, pp. 1743–70; N. D. Cakar and A. Erturk, "Comparing Innovation Capability of Small and Medium-Sized Enterprises: Examining the Effects of Organizational Culture

and Empowerment," *Journal of Small Business Management*, July 2010, pp. 325–59; A. Srivastava, K. M. Bartol, and E. A. Locke, "Empowering Leadership in Management Teams: Effects on Knowledge Sharing, Efficacy, and Performance," *Academy of Management Journal*, December 2006, pp. 1239–51; P. K. Mills and G. R. Ungson, "Reassessing the Limits of Structural Empowerment: Organizational Constitution and Trust as Controls," *Academy of Management Review*, January 2003, pp. 143–53; W. A. Rudolph and M. Sashkin, "Can Organizational Empowerment Work in Multinational Settings?" *Academy of Management Executive*, February 2002, pp. 102–15; C. Gomez and B. Rosen, "The Leader-Member Link between Managerial Trust and Employee Empowerment," *Group & Organization Management*, March 2001, pp. 53–69; C. Robert and T. M. Probst, "Empowerment and Continuous Improvement in the United States, Mexico, Poland, and India," *Journal of Applied Psychology*, October 2000, pp. 643–58; R. C. Herrenkohl, G. T. Judson, and J. A. Heffner, "Defining and Measuring Employee Empowerment," *Journal of Applied Behavioral Science*, September 1999, 373; R. C. Ford and M. D. Fottler, "Empowerment: A Matter of Degree," *Academy of Management Executive*, August 1995, pp. 21–31; and W. A. Rudolph, "Navigating the Journey to Empowerment," *Organizational Dynamics*, Spring 1995, pp. 19–32.

58. T. A. Stewart, "Just Think: No Permission Needed," *Fortune*, January 8, 2001, pp. 190–92.

59. Managing Technology in Today's Workplace box based on K. D. Strang, "Leadership Substitutes and Personality Impact on Time and Quality in Virtual New Product Development Projects," *Project Management Journal*, February 2011, pp. 73–90; A. Rapp, M. Ahearne, J. Mathieu, and T. Rapp, "Managing Sales Teams in a Virtual Environment," *International Journal of Research in Marketing*, September 2010, pp. 213–24; M. Muethel and M. Hoegl, "Cultural and Societal Influences on Shared Leadership in Globally Dispersed Teams," *Journal of International Management*, September 2010, pp. 234–56; J. Grenny, "Virtual Teams," *Leadership Excellence*, May 2010, p. 20; L. A. Hambley, T. A. O'Neill, and T. J. B. Kline, "Virtual Team Leadership: The Effects of Leadership Style and Communication Medium on Team Interaction Styles and Outcomes," *Organizational Behavior and Human Decision Processes*, May 2007, pp. 1–20; and B. J. Avolio and S. S. Kahai, "Adding the 'E' to

E-Leadership: How It May Impact Your Leadership," *Organizational Dynamics*, January 2003, pp. 325–38.

60. I. Wanasika, J. P. Howell, R. Littrell, and P. Dorfman, "Managerial Leadership and Culture in Sub-Saharan Africa," *Journal of World Business*, April 2011, pp. 234–41.

61. F. W. Swierczek, "Leadership and Culture: Comparing Asian Managers," *Leadership & Organization Development Journal*, December 1991, pp. 3–10.

62. House, "Leadership in the Twenty-First Century," p. 443; M. F. Peterson and J. G. Hunt, "International Perspectives on International Leadership," *Leadership Quarterly*, Fall 1997, pp. 203–31; and J. R. Schermerhorn and M. H. Bond, "Cross-Cultural Leadership in Collectivism and High Power Distance Settings," *Leadership & Organization Development Journal* 18, no. 4/5 (1997), pp. 187–93.

63. Wanasika, Howell, Littrell, and Dorfman, "Managerial Leadership and Culture in Sub-Saharan Africa"; R. J. House, P. J. Hanges, S. A. Ruiz-Quintanilla, P. W. Dorfman, et al., "Culture Specific and Cross-Culturally Generalizable Implicit Leadership Theories: Are the Attributes of Charismatic/Transformational Leadership Universally Endorsed?" *Leadership Quarterly*, Summer 1999, pp. 219–56; and D. E. Carl and M. Javidan, "Universality of Charismatic Leadership: A Multi-Nation Study," paper presented at the National Academy of Management Conference, Washington, DC, August 2001.

64. D. E. Carl and M. Javidan, "Universality of Charismatic Leadership," p. 29.

65. This section is based on D. Goleman, R. E. Boyatzis, and A. McKee, *Primal Leadership: Realizing the Power of Emotional Intelligence* (Boston: Harvard Business School Press, 2002); D. R. Caruso, J. D. Mayer, and P. Salovey, "Emotional Intelligence and Emotional Leadership," in R. E. Riggio, S. E. Murphy, and F. J. Pirozzolo (eds.), *Multiple Intelligences and Leadership* (Mahwah, NJ: Lawrence Erlbaum, 2002), pp. 55–74; J. M. George, "Emotions and Leadership: The Role of Emotional Intelligence," *Human Relations*, August 2000, pp. 1027–55; D. Goleman, "What Makes a Leader?" *Harvard Business Review*, November–December 1998, pp. 93–102; and D. Goleman, *Working with Emotional Intelligence* (New York: Bantam, 1998).

66. F. Walter, M. S. Cole, and R. H. Humphrey, "Emotional Intelligence: Sine Qua Non of

Leadership or Folderol?" *Academy of Management Perspectives*, February 2011, pp. 45–59.

67. See Walter, Cole, and Humphrey, "Emotional Intelligence: Sine Qua Non of Leadership or Folderol"; L. A. Zampetakis and V. Moustakis, "Managers' Trait Emotional Intelligence and Group Outcomes: The Case of Group Job Satisfaction," *Small Group Research*, February 2011, pp. 77–102; H.-W. Vivian Tang, M.-S. Yin, and D. B. Nelson, "The Relationship between Emotional Intelligence and Leadership Practices," *Journal of Managerial Psychology* 25, no. 8 (2010), pp. 899–926; P. K. Chopra and G. K. Kanji, "Emotional Intelligence: A Catalyst for Inspirational Leadership and Management Excellence," *Total Quality Management & Business Excellence*, October 2010, pp. 971–1004; R. Boyatzis and A. McKee, "Intentional Change," *Journal of Organizational Excellence*, Summer 2006, pp. 49–60, and R. Kerr; J. Garvin, N. Heaton, and E. Boyle, "Emotional Intelligence and Leadership Effectiveness," *Leadership and Organizational Development Journal*, April 2006, pp. 265–79.

68. See, for example, M. C. Race, "Boss, Buddy, or Bully," *T&D*, February 2018, pp. 52–56; E. X. M. Wee, H. Liao, D. Liu, and J. Liu, "Moving from Abuse to Reconciliation: A Power-Dependence Perspective on When and How a Follower Can Break the Spiral of Abuse," *Academy of Management Journal*, December 2017, pp. 2352–80; A. Gannett, "The Incredibly Simple Way to Tell if You're Being Manipulative," *Fast Company Online*, November 28, 2017; R. Sutton, "How to Survive an Office Jerk," *Wall Street Journal*, August 14, 2017, p. R2; V. Fuhrmans, "Some Toxic Bosses Manage to Hang On," *Wall Street Journal*, May 31, 2017, p. B5; J. K. Oh and C. I. C. Farh, "An Emotional Response Process Theory of How Subordinates Appraise, Experience, and Respond to Abusive Supervision over Time," *Academy of Management Review*, April 2017, pp. 207–32; and S.

Shellenbarger, "How to Manage a Demanding Boss," *Wall Street Journal*, January 18, 2017, p. A13.

69. "Aon Hewitt Stat of the Week," February 7, 2017.

70. K. Blanchard, "How to Build a High Trust Workplace," *Chief Learning Officer*, March 2017, p. 14.

71. S. Simsarian, "Leadership and Trust Facilitating Cross-Functional Team Success," *Journal of Management Development*, March–April 2002, pp. 201–15.

72. J. M. Kouzes and B. Z. Posner, *Credibility: How Leaders Gain and Lose It, and Why People Demand It* (San Francisco: Jossey-Bass, 1993), p. 14.

73. Based on F. D. Schoorman, R. C. Mayer, and J. H. Davis, "An Integrative Model of Organizational Trust: Past, Present, and Future," *Academy of Management Review*, April 2007, pp. 344–54; G. M. Spreitzer and A. K. Mishra, "Giving Up Control without Losing Control," *Group & Organization Management*, June 1999, pp. 155–87; R. C. Mayer, J. H. Davis, and F. D. Schoorman, "An Integrative Model of Organizational Trust," *Academy of Management Review*, July 1995, p. 712; and L. T. Hosmer, "Trust: The Connecting Link between Organizational Theory and Philosophical Ethics," *Academy of Management Review*, April 1995, p. 393.

74. P. L. Schindler and C. C. Thomas, "The Structure of Interpersonal Trust in the Workplace," *Psychological Reports*, October 1993, pp. 563–73.

75. H. H. Tan and C. S. F. Tan, "Toward the Differentiation of Trust in Supervisor and Trust in Organization," *Genetic, Social, and General Psychology Monographs*, May 2000, pp. 241–60.

76. J. H. Cho and E. J. Ringquist, "Managerial Trustworthiness and Organizational Outcomes," *Journal of Public Administration Research and Theory*, January 2011, pp. 53–86; R. C. Mayer and M. B. Gavin, "Trust in Management and Performance: Who Minds the Shop

While the Employees Watch the Boss?" *Academy of Management Journal*, October 2005, pp. 874–88; and K. T. Dirks and D. L. Ferrin, "Trust in Leadership: Meta-Analytic Findings and Implications for Research and Practice," *Journal of Applied Psychology*, August 2002, pp. 611–28.

77. R. Zemke, "The Confidence Crisis," *Training*, June 2004, pp. 22–30; J. A. Byrne, "Restoring Trust in Corporate America," *BusinessWeek*, June 24, 2002, pp. 30–35; S. Armour, "Employees' New Motto: Trust No One," *USA Today*, February 5, 2002, p. 1B; J. Scott, "Once Bitten, Twice Shy: A World of Eroding Trust," *New York Times*, April 21, 2002, p. WK5; and J. Brockner, P. A. Siegel, J. P. Daly, T. Tyler, and C. Martin, "When Trust Matters: The Moderating Effect of Outcome Favorability," *Administrative Science Quarterly*, September 1997, p. 558.

78. S. Kerr and J. M. Jermier, "Substitutes for Leadership: Their Meaning and Measurement," *Organizational Behavior and Human Performance*, December 1978, pp. 375–403; J. P. Howell, P. W. Dorfman, and S. Kerr, "Leadership and Substitutes for Leadership," *Journal of Applied Behavioral Science* 22, no. 1 (1986), pp. 29–46; J. P. Howell, D. E. Bowen, P. W. Dorfman, S. Kerr, and P. M. Podsakoff, "Substitutes for Leadership: Effective Alternatives to Ineffective Leadership," *Organizational Dynamics*, Summer 1990, pp. 21–38; and P. M. Podsakoff, B. P. Niehoff, S. B. MacKenzie, and M. L. Williams, "Do Substitutes for Leadership Really Substitute for Leadership? An Empirical Examination of Kerr and Jermier's Situational Leadership Model," *Organizational Behavior and Human Decision Processes*, February 1993, pp. 1–44.

79. Based on House and Aditya, "The Social Scientific Study of Leadership: Quo Vadis?"; and G. A. Yukl, *Leadership in Organizations*, 7th ed. (Upper Saddle River, NJ: Prentice Hall, 2010).

80. K. O. Tshkay, R. Zhu, C. Zou, and N. Rule, "Charisma in Everyday Life: Validation of the General Charisma Inventory," *Journal of Personality and Social Psychology*, January 2018, pp. 131–52.

81. "Annual Review of Football Finance 2018," Deloitte UK, https://www2.deloitte.com/uk/en/pages/sports-business-group/articles/annual-review-of-football-finance.html#.

82. "Fifa Corruption Crisis: Key Questions Answered," *BBC News*, December 21, 2015, https://www.bbc.co.uk/news/world-europe-32897066.

83. Samuel Stevens, "Fifa Presidential Election: Reforms Offer Chance for Change, Not the Identity of Sepp Blatter's Successor," *The Independent*, February 26, 2016, https://www.independent.co.uk/sport/football/international/fifa-presidential-election-re-forms-offer-chance-for-change-not-the-identity-of-sepp-blat-ters-a6897941.html#r3z-addoor

84. D. Meek, "The Real Sir Alex Ferguson: Memories of His Ghost-Writer," *BBC Sport*, http://www.bbc.com/sport/0/football/22539385, May 18, 2013; A. Elberse, "Ferguson's Formula," *Harvard Business Review*, https://hbr.org/2013/10/fergusons-formula, October 2013; W. Isaacson, "The Real Leadership Lessons of Steve Jobs," *Harvard Business Review*, April 2012; N. Robinson, "Nick Robinson: What I Learned about Leadership from Sir Alex Ferguson," www.radiotimes.com, October 11, 2015; J. Aglionby, "Sir Alex Ferguson Signs for Harvard Business School," www.ft.com, April 4, 2014.

85. J. Faragher, "Get the Leader You Deserve," *People Management*, October 2014, pp. 22–26; T. Team, "The Secret Sauce for Success in the Aggressive Beauty Business," *Forbes Online*, April 13, 2015; and H. Hong and Y. Doz, "L'Oreal Masters Multiculturalism," *Harvard Business Review Online*, June 2013.

86. "ECI Honors L'Oreal's Top Ethics Officer for Leadership in Corporate Ethics," *ECI Connector Online*, January 21, 2016.

13

Management Myth

Myth

Managers should try to stifle the grapevine.

Management Myth

DEBUNKED?

The grapevine is a well-known source for organizational gossip and news. For the inexperienced manager, it's seen as a destructive element in an organization's communication network. But the grapevine isn't going away. It's as natural to an organization as water is to an ocean. **Astute managers acknowledge the existence of the grapevine and learn to use it in beneficial ways.**

WELCOME

to the world of communication! In this "world," managers are going to have to understand both the importance and the drawbacks of communication—all forms of communication, even the grapevine. Communication takes place every day in every organization. In all areas. By all organizational members. In many different forms. Most of that communication tends to be work related. But as we'll see, sometimes communication can cause some unintended consequences. For instance, on the eve of a leadership retreat, the 42-year-old CEO of a branding firm wanted to wish his employees a good night's sleep and decided to send a pajama-clad bitmoji of himself lifting sheets up over a teddy bear in a bed—with the caption "Sleep Well." Some of his employees did not find the cartoon message funny, but instead, creepy.[1] In this chapter, we're going to look at basic concepts of organizational and interpersonal communication. We'll explain the communication process, methods of communicating, barriers to effective communication, and ways to overcome those barriers. In addition, we'll look at communication issues that today's managers face. ●

Learning Outcomes

13-1 Describe what managers need to know about communicating effectively. p. 459

13-2 Explain how technology affects managerial communication. p. 467

13-3 Discuss contemporary issues in communication. p. 471

How Do Managers Communicate Effectively?

13-1 Describe what managers need to know about communicating effectively.

Poor communication can cost a business up to $5,200 per employee each year![2]

A survey of employees found that the skill managers most need to improve is communication.[3]

Another employee survey found that over half the respondents said their workplace communication was "less than great."[4]

The importance of effective communication for managers cannot be overemphasized for one specific reason: **EVERYTHING A MANAGER DOES INVOLVES COMMUNICATING.** Not *some* things but *everything*! A manager can't formulate strategy or make a decision without information. That information has to be communicated. Once a decision is made, communication must again take place. Otherwise, no one will know that a decision has been made. The best idea, the most creative suggestion, or the finest plan cannot take form without communication. Managers, therefore, need effective communication skills. We're not suggesting, of course, that good communication skills alone make a successful manager. We can say, however, that ineffective communication skills can lead to a continuous stream of problems for a manager.

How Does the Communication Process Work?

WHAT is communicated? The 3 I's: Information, Ideas, Instructions

Communication can be thought of as a process or flow. Communication problems occur when deviations or blockages disrupt that flow. Before communication can take place, a purpose, expressed as a message to be conveyed, is needed. It passes between a source (the sender) and a receiver. The message is encoded (converted to symbolic form) and is passed by way of some medium (channel) to the receiver, who retranslates (decodes) the message initiated by the sender. The result is **communication**, which is a transfer of understanding and meaning from one person to another.[5]

Exhibit 13–1 depicts the **communication process**. This model has seven parts: (1) the communication source or sender, (2) encoding, (3) the message, (4) the channel, (5) decoding, (6) the receiver, and (7) feedback.

1 and 2. The sender initiates a message by **encoding** a thought. Four conditions affect the encoded message: skill, attitudes, knowledge, and the social cultural system. Our message in our communication to you in this book depends on our writing *skills*; if we don't have the requisite writing skills, our message will not reach you in the form desired. Keep in mind that a person's total communicative success includes speaking, reading, listening, and reasoning skills as well. As we discussed in Chapter 10, our attitudes influence our behavior. We

communication
A transfer of understanding and meaning from one person to another

communication process
The seven-part process of transferring and understanding of meaning

encoding
Converting a message into symbolic form

Exhibit 13–1 The Communication Process

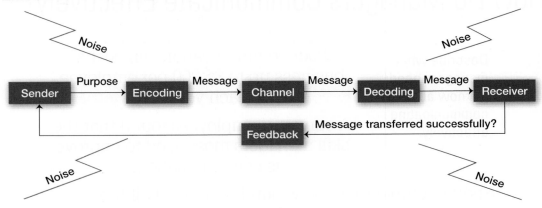

message
A purpose for communicating that's to be conveyed

channel
The medium by which a message travels

decoding
Translating a received message

feedback
Checking to see how successfully a message has been transferred

hold predisposed ideas on numerous topics, and our communications are affected by these *attitudes.* Furthermore, we're restricted in our communicative activity by the extent of our *knowledge* of the particular topic. We can't communicate what we don't know, and should our knowledge be too extensive, it's possible that our receiver will not understand our message. Clearly, the amount of knowledge the source holds about his or her subject will affect the message he or she seeks to transfer. And, finally, just as attitudes influence our behavior, so does our *position in the social cultural system* in which we exist. Your beliefs and values, all part of your culture, act to influence you as a communication source.

3. The **message** is the actual physical product from the source that conveys some purpose. When we speak, the words spoken are the message. When we write, the writing is the message. When we use a bitmoji, the character and words are the message. When we gesture, the movements of our arms and the expressions on our faces are the message.[6] Our message is affected by the code or group of symbols we use to transfer meaning, the content of the message itself, and the decisions that we make in selecting and arranging both codes and content.[7]

4. The **channel** is the medium through which the message travels. It's selected by the source, who must determine whether to use a formal or an informal channel. Formal channels are established by the organization and transmit messages that pertain to the job-related activities of members. They traditionally follow the authority network within the organization. Other forms of messages, such as personal or social, follow the informal channels in the organization.

5 and 6. The receiver is the person to whom the message is directed. However, before the message can be received, the symbols in it must be translated into a form that can be understood by the receiver—the **decoding** of the message. Just as the encoder was limited by his or her skills, attitudes, knowledge, and social cultural system, the receiver is equally restricted. Accordingly, the source must be skillful in writing or speaking; the receiver must be skillful in reading or listening; and both must be able to reason. A person's knowledge, attitudes, and cultural background influence his or her ability to receive, just as they do the ability to send.

7. The final link in the communication process is a feedback loop. "If a communication source decodes the message that he encodes, if the message is put back into his system, we have feedback."[8] **Feedback** is the check on how successful we've been in transferring our messages as originally intended. It determines whether understanding has been achieved. Given the cultural diversity that exists in our workforce today, the importance of effective feedback to ensure proper communications cannot be overstated.[9]

Participating in a meeting at company headquarters, these employees of Alibaba, China's largest e-commerce firm, illustrate the channel part of the communication process. The meeting is a formal channel established by Alibaba during which employees transmit messages that pertain to their job-related activities.

Steven Shi/Reuters

Are Written Communications More Effective Than Verbal Ones?

Written communications include memos, letters, e-mail and other forms of digital communication, organizational periodicals, bulletin boards, or any other device that transmits written words or symbols. Why would a sender choose to use written communications?

Advantages: Well, they're tangible, verifiable, and more permanent than oral communication. Typically, both sender and receiver have a record of the communication. The message can be stored for an indefinite period of time. If questions arise about the content of the message, it's physically available for later reference. This feature is particularly important for complex or lengthy communications. For example, the marketing plan for a new product is likely to contain a number of tasks spread out over several months. By putting it in writing, those who have to carry out the plan can readily refer to the document over the life of the plan. A final benefit of written communication comes from the process itself. Written communications are more likely to be well thought out, logical, and clear. Except in rare instances, such as when presenting a formal speech, more care is taken with the written word than with the spoken word. Having to put something in writing forces a person to think more carefully about what he or she wants to convey.

Drawbacks: Of course, written messages have their drawbacks. Writing may be more precise, but it also consumes a great deal of time. You could convey far more information to your college instructor in a one-hour oral exam than in a one-hour written exam. In fact, you could probably say in 10 to 15 minutes what it takes you an hour to write. The other major disadvantage is the lack of feedback. Oral communications allow receivers to respond rapidly to what they think they hear. However, written communications don't have a built-in feedback mechanism. Sending a memo is no assurance that it will be received and, if it is received, no guarantee that the recipient will interpret it as the sender meant. The latter point is also relevant in oral communication, but it's easier in such cases merely to ask the receiver to summarize what you have said. An accurate summary presents feedback evidence that the message has been received and understood.

Is the Grapevine an Effective Way to Communicate?

The **Grapevine**: Fruitful or Not?

The **grapevine** is the unofficial way that communication takes place in an organization. It's neither authorized nor supported by the organization. Rather, information is spread by word of mouth—and even through electronic means. Ironically, good information passes among us rapidly, but bad information travels even faster.[10] The grapevine gets information out to organizational members as quickly as possible.

The biggest question raised about the grapevine, however, focuses on the accuracy of the rumors. Research on this topic has found somewhat mixed results. In an organization characterized by openness, the grapevine may be extremely accurate. In an authoritative culture, the rumor mill may not be accurate. But even then, although the information flowing is inaccurate, it still contains some element of truth. Rumors about major layoffs, plant closings, and the like may be filled with inaccurate information regarding who will be affected or when it may occur. Nonetheless, the reports that something is about to happen are probably on target. (See the Classic Concepts in Today's Workplace box on p. 462 for more about the grapevine.)

How Do Nonverbal Cues Affect Communication?

Some of the most meaningful communications are neither spoken nor written. They are nonverbal communications. A loud siren or a red light at an intersection tells you something without words. A college instructor doesn't need words to know that students are bored; their eyes get glassy or they begin to read the school newspaper during class. Similarly, when papers start to rustle and notebooks begin to close, the message is clear: Class time is about over. The size of a person's office and desk or the clothes he or she wears also convey messages to others. However, the best-known areas of nonverbal communication are body language and verbal intonation.

grapevine
An unofficial channel of communication

◂◂◂ Classic Concepts in Today's Workplace ▸▸▸

One of the most famous studies of the grapevine was conducted by management researcher Keith Davis, who investigated the communication patterns among 67 managerial personnel.[11] The approach he used was to learn from each communication recipient how he or she first received a given piece of information and then trace it back to its source. It was found that, while the grapevine was an important source of information, only 10 percent of the executives acted as liaison individuals (i.e., passed the information on to more than one other person). For example, when one executive decided to resign to enter the insurance business, 81 percent of the executives knew about it, but only 11 percent transmitted this information to others. At the time, this study was interesting because of what it found, but more importantly because of what it showed about how the communication network worked.

Recent research by IBM and the Massachusetts Institute of Technology using a similar type of analysis focused more on

The Grapevine: An important source of information

people's social networks of contacts at work rather than on how information flowed through the organizational grapevine. However, what was noticeably interesting about this study was that it found that employees who have strong communication ties with their managers tend to bring in more money than those who steer clear of the boss.

What managers can learn from both of these studies is that *it's important to understand the social and communication networks that employees use as they do their work.* Know who the key contact points are so that if you ever need to find out or relay information, you know who to go to.

Discussion Questions:

1 Why is it important for managers to understand social and communication networks that employees use?

2 What have been your experiences with the grapevine and what did you learn from those experiences about dealing with the grapevine as a source of communication?

Body language refers to gestures, facial configurations, and other movements of the body.[12] A snarl, for example, says something different from a smile. Hand motions, facial expressions, and other gestures can communicate emotions or temperaments such as aggression, fear, shyness, arrogance, joy, and anger.[13]

It's not WHAT you say but **HOW you say it.**

Verbal intonation refers to the emphasis someone gives to words or phrases. To illustrate how intonations can change the meaning of a message, consider the student who asks the instructor a question. The instructor replies, "What do you mean by that?" The student's reaction will vary, depending on the tone of the instructor's response. A soft, smooth tone creates a different meaning from one that is abrasive with a strong emphasis on the last word. Most of us would view the first intonation as coming from someone who sincerely sought clarification, whereas the second suggests that the person is aggressive or defensive. The adage, "it's not what you say but how you say it," is something managers should remember as they communicate.

The fact that every oral communication also has a nonverbal message cannot be overemphasized.[14] Why? Because the nonverbal component is likely to carry the greatest impact. Research indicates that from 65 to 90 percent of the message of every face-to-face conversation is interpreted through body language. Without complete agreement between the spoken words and the body language that accompanies it, receivers are more likely to react to body language as the "true meaning."[15]

What Barriers Keep Communication from Being Effective?

A number of interpersonal and intrapersonal barriers affect why the message decoded by a receiver is often different from what the sender intended. We summarize the more prominent barriers to effective communication in Exhibit 13–2 and briefly describe them here.

body language
Nonverbal communication cues such as facial expressions, gestures, and other body movements

verbal intonation
An emphasis given to words or phrases that conveys meaning

HOW DOES FILTERING AFFECT COMMUNICATION?   **Filtering** refers to the way that a sender manipulates information so that it will be seen more favorably by the receiver. For example, when a manager tells his boss what he feels that boss wants to hear, he is filtering information. Does filtering happen much in organizations? Sure it does. As information is passed up to senior executives, it has to be condensed and synthesized by subordinates so upper management doesn't become overloaded with information. Those doing the condensing filter communications through their own personal interests and perceptions of what's important.

The extent of filtering tends to be the function of the organization's culture and number of vertical levels in the organization. More vertical levels in an organization mean more opportunities for filtering. As organizations become less dependent on strict hierarchical arrangements and instead use more collaborative, cooperative work arrangements, information filtering may become less of a problem. In addition, the ever-increasing use of e-mail to communicate in organizations reduces filtering because communication is more direct as intermediaries are bypassed. Finally, the organizational culture encourages or discourages filtering by the type of behavior it rewards. The more that organizational rewards emphasize style and appearance, the more managers will be motivated to filter communications in their favor.

Greeting customers with a handshake, a smile, and a warm welcome is a practice Apple stores adopted from Ritz-Carlton, the luxury hotel chain known as the gold standard of customer service. Apple benchmarked with Ritz-Carlton because it wants its employees to excel at customer service that leads to customer loyalty.

HOW DOES SELECTIVE PERCEPTION AFFECT COMMUNICATION?   The second barrier is **selective perception**. We've mentioned selective perception before in this book. We discuss it again here because the receivers in the communication process selectively see and hear based on their needs, motivations, experience, background, and other personal characteristics. Receivers also project their interests and expectations into communications as they decode them. The employment interviewer who expects a female job applicant to put

Exhibit 13–2 Barriers to Effective Communication

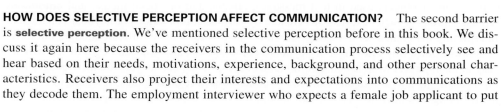

Barrier	Description
Filtering	The deliberate manipulation of information to make it appear more favorable to the receiver.
Selective perception	Receiving communications on the basis of what one selectively sees and hears depending on his or her needs, motivation, experience, background, and other personal characteristics.
Information overload	When the amount of information one has to work with exceeds one's processing capacity.
Emotions	How the receiver feels when a message is received.
Language	Words have different meanings to different people. Receivers will use their definition of words being communicated.
Gender	How males and females react to communication may be different, and they each have a different communication style.
National culture	Communication differences arising from the different languages that individuals use to communicate and the national culture of which they are a part.

filtering
Deliberately manipulating information to make it appear more favorable to the receiver

selective perception
Selectively perceiving or hearing a communication based on your own needs, motivations, experiences, or other personal characteristics

her family ahead of her career is likely to see that tendency in female applicants, regardless of whether the applicants would do so or not. As we said in Chapter 10, we don't see reality; rather, we interpret what we see and call it reality.

HOW DOES INFORMATION OVERLOAD AFFECT COMMUNICATION? Individuals have a finite capacity for processing data. For instance, consider an international sales representative who returns home to find that she has more than 600 e-mails waiting for her. It's not possible to fully read and respond to each one of those messages without facing **information overload**. Today's typical executive frequently complains of information overload.[16] The demands of keeping up with e-mail, phone calls, faxes, meetings, and professional reading create an onslaught of data that is nearly impossible to process and assimilate. What happens when you have more information than you can sort out and use? You're likely to select out, ignore, pass over, or forget information. Or you may put off further processing until the overload situation is over. In any case, the result is lost information and less effective communication.

HOW DO EMOTIONS AFFECT COMMUNICATION? How a sender or receiver feels when a message is sent or received influences how he or she interprets it. You'll often interpret the same message differently, depending on whether you're happy or distressed or angry. And extreme emotions are most likely to hinder effective communications. In such instances, we often disregard our rational and objective thinking processes and substitute emotional judgments. It's best to avoid sending or reacting to a message when you're upset or emotional because you're not likely to be thinking clearly.

Understanding how emotions can affect communication becomes even more important as more people communicate with abbreviations or slang (txt-speak or txt lingo, such as TTYL, SLAP, SMAM, BTW, LOL, etc.) or even with **emojis**, tiny drawings of facial expressions or objects used in text messages, emails, and on social media, and **emoticons**, representations of facial expressions created by various combinations of keyboard characters. Interpreting the content of a message when it's just words can be difficult enough, but throw in abbreviations, tiny drawings, or keyboard combinations and you can begin to see why it's easy to misinterpret what is being communicated. For instance, lawyers are increasingly finding that emojis and emoticons can lead to contention in legal disputes. It's hard to establish the meaning of a drawing, such as an "unamused face," especially in a legal situation.[17] And even when used in regular workplace communication, these types of communication choices can lead to confusion and misinterpretation.

HOW DOES LANGUAGE AFFECT COMMUNICATION? Words mean different things to different people. "The meanings of words are not in the words; they are in us."[18] Age, education, and cultural background are three of the more obvious variables that influence the language a person uses and the definitions he or she applies to words. Columnist George F. Will and rapper Iggy Azalea both speak English. But the language each one uses is vastly different from how the other speaks.

> Forty percent of employees say that buzzwords are very prevalent in normal conversations at work.[19]

In an organization, employees usually come from diverse backgrounds and, therefore, have different patterns of speech. Additionally, the grouping of employees into departments creates specialists who develop their own **jargon** or technical language.[20] The problem with jargon is that those who aren't familiar with the jargon are clueless as to what is being communicated.

> Eighty-eight percent of workers admit they pretend to understand office jargon even when they have no idea what it means.[21]

information overload
What results when information exceeds processing capacity

emojis
Tiny drawings of facial expressions or objects used in text messages, e-mails, and on social media

emoticons
Representations of facial expressions created by various combinations of keyboard characters

jargon
Technical language specific to a discipline or industry

In large organizations, members are also frequently widely dispersed geographically—even operating in different countries—and individuals in each locale will use terms and phrases that are unique to their area.[22] And the existence of vertical levels can also cause language problems. The language of senior executives, for instance, can be mystifying to regular employees not familiar with management jargon. Keep in mind that while we may speak the same language, our use of that language is far from uniform. Senders tend to assume that the words and phrases they use mean the same to the receiver as they do to them. This assumption, of course, is incorrect and creates communication barriers. Knowing how each of us modifies the language would help minimize those barriers.

HOW DOES GENDER AFFECT COMMUNICATION?   Effective communication between the sexes is important in all organizations if they are to meet organizational goals. But how can we manage the various differences in communication styles? To keep gender differences from becoming persistent barriers to effective communication, individuals must strive for acceptance, understanding, and a commitment to communicate adaptively with each other. Both men and women need to acknowledge differences are present in communication styles, that one style isn't better than the other, and that it takes real effort to talk successfully with each other.[23]

HOW DOES NATIONAL CULTURE AFFECT COMMUNICATION?   A $14-an-hour employee running Marriott International Inc.'s social media accounts used an official company account to like a post on Twitter from a Tibetan separatist group. The group had applauded the company for listing Tibet as a country rather than part of China. That tweet got the employee in hot water and eventually fired.[24] As this example shows, not only can communication differences arise from the different languages that individuals use to communicate, but also from the national culture and global politics of which they're a part.[25] For example, let's compare countries that place a high value on individualism (such as the United States) with countries where the emphasis is on collectivism (such as Japan).[26]

In the United States, communication patterns tend to be oriented to the individual and clearly spelled out. Managers in the United States rely heavily on memoranda, announcements, position papers, and other formal forms of communication to state their positions on issues. Supervisors here may hoard information in an attempt to make themselves look good (filtering) and as a way of persuading their employees to accept decisions and plans. And for their own protection, lower-level employees also engage in this practice.

In collectivist countries, such as Japan, there's more interaction for its own sake and a more informal manner of interpersonal contact. The Japanese manager, in contrast to the U.S. manager, engages in extensive verbal consultation with employees over an issue first and draws up a formal document later to outline the agreement that was made. The Japanese value decisions by consensus, and open communication is an inherent part of the work setting. Also, face-to-face communication is encouraged.[27]

Cultural differences can affect the way a manager chooses to communicate.[28] And these differences undoubtedly can be a barrier to effective communication if not recognized and taken into consideration.

How Can Managers Overcome Communication Barriers?

Given these barriers to communication, what can managers do to overcome them? The following suggestions should help make communication more effective (see also Exhibit 13–3).

WHY USE FEEDBACK?   Many communication problems are directly attributed to misunderstanding and inaccuracies. These problems are less likely to occur if the manager gets feedback, both verbal and nonverbal.

active listening
Listening for full meaning without making premature judgments or interpretations

Exhibit 13–3 Overcoming Barriers to Effective Communication

Use feedback	Check the accuracy of what has been communicated—or what you think you heard.
Simplify language	Use words that the intended audience understands.
Listen actively	Listen for the full meaning of the message without making premature judgment or interpretation—or thinking about what you are going to say in response.
Constrain emotions	Recognize when your emotions are running high. When they are, don't communicate until you have calmed down.
Watch nonverbal cues	Be aware that your actions speak louder than your words. Keep the two consistent.

A manager can ask questions about a message to determine whether it was received and understood as intended. Or the manager can ask the receiver to restate the message in his or her own words. If the manager hears what was intended, understanding and accuracy should improve. Feedback can also be more subtle as general comments can give a manager a sense of the receiver's reaction to a message.

Feedback doesn't have to be verbal. If a sales manager e-mails information about a new monthly sales report that all sales representatives will need to complete and some of them don't turn it in, the sales manager has received feedback. This feedback suggests that the sales manager needs to clarify the initial communication. Similarly, managers can look for nonverbal cues to tell whether someone's getting the message.

WHY SHOULD SIMPLIFIED LANGUAGE BE USED? Because language can be a barrier, managers should consider the audience to whom the message is directed and tailor the language to them. Remember, effective communication is achieved when a message is both received and *understood*. For example, a hospital administrator should always try to communicate in clear, easily understood terms and to use language tailored to different employee groups. Messages to the surgical staff should be purposefully different from those directed to the marketing team or office employees. Jargon can facilitate understanding if it's used within a group that knows what it means, but can cause problems when used outside that group.

Do you **really listen** OR do you just **hear?**

WHY MUST WE LISTEN ACTIVELY? When someone talks, we hear. But too often we don't listen. Listening is an active search for meaning, whereas hearing is passive. In listening, the receiver is also putting effort into the communication.

Many of us are poor listeners. Why? Because it's difficult, and most of us would rather do the talking. Listening, in fact, is often more tiring than talking. Unlike hearing, **active listening**, which is listening for full meaning without making premature judgments or interpretations, demands total concentration. The average person normally speaks at a rate of about 125 to 200 words per minute. However, the average listener can comprehend up to 400 words per minute.[29] The difference leaves lots of idle brain time and opportunities for the mind to wander.

Ana Botin, executive chairman of Spain's Banco Santander, is respected as an empathetic listener and a good communicator and consensus builder. Shown here communicating with employees at a bank in London, Botin asks questions and listens to feedback from employees, customers, and shareholders that helps her plan the company's strategy.

Anthony Devlin/Press Association/AP Images

(continues on p. 470)

Technology and Managerial Communication

IT is where it's at!

13-2 Explain how technology affects managerial communication.

- Information technology (IT) has radically changed the way organizational members work and communicate. How?

  — Improves a manager's ability to monitor individual and team performance

  — Allows employees to have more complete information to make faster decisions

  — Provides employees more opportunities to collaborate and share information

  — Allows employees to be fully accessible 24/7

Steven Senne/AP Images

2 IT developments have had a significant effect on organizational and interpersonal communication...

1 Networked Communication

In a networked communication system:

- Organizational computers are linked through compatible hardware and software, creating an integrated organizational network.

- Employees communicate with each other via networked computers

xstock/Shutterstock

467

Mobile Communication

In a mobile communication system:

- Employees can be connected without being physically "plugged in" at work!

- Mobile technology is extremely popular!

- Improving the way employees work is the payoff!

- People don't have to be physically "at the office" in order to communicate, collaborate, and share information with managers and colleagues.[30]

Fotolia

- Managers and employees "keep in touch" using smartphones, tablet computers, notebook computers, and mobile pocket communication devices.

- And mobile communication works—anywhere. People can send and receive information from the summit of Mt. Everest to the remotest locations on the planet.

Networked and Mobile Communication Applications

- **E-mail**—instantaneous transmission of messages on computers or mobile devices.

  ➕ Messages read at receiver's convenience   ➖ Slow and cumbersome

  ➕ Fast, cheap, efficient, and convenient

  ➕ Print documents, if needed

  Cemil Adakale/Fotolia

- **Workplace instant messaging (IM)** —interactive, real-time communication among coworkers who are logged on at the same time.

  ➕ Instantaneous communication without waiting for colleagues to read e-mail

  ➖ Users must be logged on at the same time

  ➖ Potential network and data security breaches

- **Voice mail**—a system that digitizes a spoken message, transmits it, and stores it for a receiver to retrieve later.[31]

  ➕ Information transmitted without receiver being physically present

  ➕ Message can be saved, deleted, or re-routed

  ➖ No immediate feedback

- **Teleconference and videoconference meetings**—confer simultaneously by phone, e-mail, or video screens.

  ➕ Participants don't need to be in same physical location to share information and collaborate

  ➕ Saves travel money

Arekmalang/Fotolia

- **Organizational intranet**—an organizational communication network that's accessible only to organizational employees.

  ➕ Share information and collaborate on documents and projects

  ➕ Access company policy manuals and employee-specific materials[32]

  ➖ Possible network and data security breaches

- **Organizational extranet**—an organizational communication network that allows authorized organizational users to communicate with certain outsiders such as customers or vendors.

  ➕ Faster and more convenient communication

  ➖ Concerns about network and data security breaches

- **Internet-based voice/video communication**—Internet based communication services (such as Skype, Viber, FaceTime, Vonage, Yahoo!).

  ➕ Fast and convenient communication

  ➖ Concerns about network and data security breaches

Managing Technology in Today's Workplace

OFFICE OF TOMORROW

The office of tomorrow is still likely to resemble in some ways the office of today. There probably won't be mail delivery by robots on hovercraft nor any teleportation devices. Most of the changes, however, will likely be in the *way* we communicate.[33] Employees will rely on multiple channels of communication with heavy reliance on social networks, text messaging, instant messaging, mobile technology, and dashboard apps that allow employees to message each other directly. Smartphones are as powerful as today's mainframes, meaning employees will be able to do heavy computing on the go. Software can track where employees are and blend that data with information about current projects and suggest potential collaborators. E-mail was thought to be likely to decline in popularity, largely because other channels are faster, more fluid, and more immediate, but that hasn't proved to be the case.

Accurately forecasting tomorrow's technology is not easy. But several patterns seem to be evolving. For instance, the combining of functions in a single device is likely to result in employees having a single product that will combine phone, text messaging, Internet access, video camera, teleconferencing, and language translator. It will allow people to read proposals, legal papers, news, or almost any document digitally. It won't need a keyboard and will operate via voice commands. It's also likely not to be handheld but rather something akin to combining reading glasses and an earpiece. These smart glasses will give workers all-in-one access to information or whatever they might need to perform work tasks efficiently and effectively. A number of companies already have smart glasses

> Over 83 percent of managers are using mobile technology to improve communication with employees.[34]

on the market. As this type of wearable technology becomes more common, organizations will have to address usage issues regarding information security and possible legal dilemmas.

Another tech development on the cusp of changing the way we communicate and interact with others is **augmented reality (AR)**, which is a technology that superimposes a computer-generated image on a user's view of the real world. The simulated reality offers users different experiences. If you've used any of Snapchat's filters, you've used AR. Or if you participated in the Pokemon Go phenomenon, you experienced AR. There are all kinds of scenarios in which you can see how organizational and interpersonal communication would be affected and changed by AR. The smart glasses we described in the previous paragraph use forms of AR.

Finally, another outcome made possible by technology will be a significant decrease in business travel. Improvements in computer-mediated groupware will allow individuals to conduct meetings in environments that closely simulate face-to-face interactions. In these settings, real-time translations will be transcribed and displayed on screen and teleconferencers will be able to hear and see the words.

Discussion Questions:

3 Do you view communicating using technology as more of a help or a hindrance? Explain.

4 What issues does wearable technology present in the workplace? What do you think managers will need to do to deal with these issues?

Wavebreakmedia Ltd PH85 / Alamy Stock Photo

Active listening is enhanced by developing empathy with the sender—that is, by putting yourself in the sender's position. Because senders differ in attitudes, interests, needs, and expectations, empathy makes it easier to understand the actual content of a message. An empathetic listener reserves judgment on the message's content and carefully listens to what is being said. The goal is to improve one's ability to get the full meaning of a communication without distorting it by premature judgments or interpretations. Other specific behaviors that active listeners use include making eye contact, exhibiting affirmative nods and appropriate facial expressions, avoiding distracting actions or gestures that suggest boredom, asking questions, paraphrasing using your own words, avoiding interrupting the speaker, not talking too much, and making smooth transitions between being a speaker and a listener.

> **augmented reality**
> A technology that superimposes a computer-generated image on a user's view of the real world

WHY MUST WE CONSTRAIN EMOTIONS?   It would be naïve to assume that managers always communicate in a rational manner. We know that emotions can cloud and distort communication. A manager who's upset over an issue is more likely to misconstrue incoming messages and fail to communicate his or her outgoing messages clearly and accurately. What to do? The simplest answer is to calm down and get emotions under control before communicating. Also, unless you know your audience (receivers) well, temper the use of texting abbreviations, emojis, and emoticons.

WHY THE EMPHASIS ON NONVERBAL CUES?   If actions speak louder than words, then it's important to make sure your actions align with and reinforce the words that go along with them. An effective communicator watches his or her nonverbal cues to ensure that they convey the desired message.

What Communication Issues Do Managers Face Today?

13-3 Discuss contemporary issues in communication.

"Pulse lunches." That's what managers at Citibank's offices throughout Malaysia used to address pressing problems of declining customer loyalty and staff morale and increased employee turnover. By connecting with employees and listening to their concerns—that is, taking their "pulse"—during informal lunch settings, managers were able to make changes that boosted both customer loyalty and employee morale by more than 50 percent and reduced employee turnover to nearly zero.[35]

Being an effective communicator in today's organizations means being connected—most importantly to employees and customers, but in reality, to any of the organization's stakeholders. In this section, we examine seven communication issues of particular significance to today's managers: managing communication in an Internet world, managing the organization's knowledge resources, communicating with customers, getting employee input, having civil conversations in the workplace, understanding the role of workplace design, and communicating ethically.

How Do We Manage Communication in an Internet World?

Lars Dalgaard, founder and chief executive of SuccessFactors, a human resource management software company, recently sent an e-mail to his employees banning in-house e-mail for a week. His goal? Getting employees to "authentically address issues amongst each other."[36] And he's not alone. Other companies have tried the same thing. As we discussed earlier, e-mail can consume employees, but it's not always easy for them to let go of it, even when they know it can be "intexticating." But e-mail is only one communication challenge in this Internet world. A recent survey found that 20 percent of employees at large companies say they contribute regularly to blogs, social networks, wikis, and other Web services.[37] Managers are learning, the hard way sometimes, that all this new technology has created special communication challenges. The two main ones are (1) legal and security issues and (2) lack of personal interaction.

This is BIG!

LEGAL AND SECURITY ISSUES. Chevron paid $2.2 million to settle a sexual harassment lawsuit stemming from inappropriate jokes being sent by employees over company e-mail. UK firm Norwich Union had to pay £450,000 in an out-of-court settlement after an employee sent an e-mail stating that its competitor, Western Provident Association, was in financial difficulties. Whole Foods Market was investigated by federal regulators and its board after CEO John P. Mackey used a pseudonym to post comments on a blog attacking the company's rival Wild Oats Markets.[38]

Although e-mail, blogs, tweets, and other forms of online communication are quick and easy ways to communicate, managers need to be aware of potential legal problems from inappropriate usage. Electronic information is potentially admissible in court. For instance, during the Enron trial, prosecutors entered into evidence e-mails and other documents they say showed that the defendants defrauded investors. Says one expert, "Today, e-mail and instant messaging are the electronic equivalent of DNA evidence."[39] But legal problems aren't the only issue; security concerns are an issue as well.

A survey addressing outbound e-mail and content security found that 26 percent of the companies surveyed saw their businesses affected by the exposure of sensitive or embarrassing information.[40] Managers need to ensure that confidential information is kept confidential. Employee e-mails and blogs should not communicate—inadvertently or purposely—proprietary information. Corporate computer and e-mail systems should be protected against hackers (people who try to gain unauthorized access to computer systems) and spam (electronic junk mail). These serious issues must be addressed if the benefits of communication technology are to be realized.

PERSONAL INTERACTION. It may be called social media, but another communication challenge posed by the Internet age we live and work in is the lack of personal interaction.[41] Even when two people are communicating face-to-face, understanding is not always achieved. However, it can be especially challenging to achieve understanding and collaborate on getting work done when communication takes place in a virtual environment. In response, some companies have banned e-mail on certain days, as we saw earlier. Others have simply encouraged employees to collaborate more in person. Yet, sometimes and in some situations, personal interaction isn't physically possible—your colleagues work across the continent or even across the globe. In those instances, real-time collaboration software (such as private workplace wikis, blogs, instant messengers, and other types of groupware) may be a better communication choice than sending an e-mail and waiting for a response.[42] Instead of fighting it, some companies are encouraging employees to utilize the power of social networks to collaborate on work and to build strong connections. This trend is especially appealing to younger workers who are comfortable with this communication medium. Some companies have gone as far as to create their own in-house social networks. For instance, employees at Starcom MediaVest Group tap into SMG Connected to find colleague profiles that outline their jobs, list the brands they admire, and describe their values. A company vice president says, "Giving our employees a way to connect over the Internet around the world made sense because they were doing it anyway."[43]

EMPLOYEES AND SOCIAL MEDIA

77 percent say they use social media to connect with colleagues.

35 percent say that social media has damaged a work relationship.

61 percent say that social media has led to new or better work relationships.

32 percent say they use social media to enhance work-related projects or solve problems.[44]

> **knowledge management**
> Cultivating a learning culture in which organizational members systematically gather knowledge and share it with others

> **communities of practice**
> Groups of people who share a concern, a set of problems, or a passion about a topic and who deepen their knowledge and expertise in that area by interacting on an ongoing basis

How Does Knowledge Management Affect Communication?

Part of a manager's responsibility in fostering an environment conducive to learning and effective communications is to create learning capabilities throughout the organization. These opportunities should extend from the lowest to the highest levels in all areas. How can managers create such an environment? An important step is recognizing the value of knowledge as a major resource, just like cash, raw materials, or office equipment. To illustrate the value of knowledge, think about how you register for your college classes. Do you talk to others who have had a certain professor? Do you listen to their experiences with this individual and make your decision based on what they have to say (their knowledge about the situation)? If you do, you're tapping into the value of knowledge. But in an organization, just recognizing the value of accumulated knowledge or wisdom isn't enough. Managers must deliberately manage that base of knowledge. **Knowledge management** involves cultivating a learning culture in which organizational members systematically gather knowledge and share it with others in the organization so as to achieve better performance.[45] For instance, accountants and consultants at Ernst & Young document best practices that they've developed, unusual problems they've dealt with, and other work information. This "knowledge" is then shared with all employees through computer-based applications and through community-of-interest teams that meet regularly throughout the company. Many other organizations, including General Electric, Toyota, and Hewlett-Packard, have recognized the importance of knowledge management within a learning organization (see Chapter 7, pp. 266–267). Today's technologies are helping improve knowledge management and facilitating organizational communications and decision making. So, what's involved with managing the organization's knowledge resources?

Kara Johnson, a materials expert at product design firm IDEO needed a system to make finding the right materials easier. So, she built a master library of samples linked to a database that explains their properties and manufacturing processes.[46] What she's doing is managing knowledge and making it easier for others at IDEO to learn and benefit from her knowledge. That's what today's managers need to do with the organization's knowledge resources—make it easy for employees to communicate and share their knowledge so they can learn from each other ways to do their jobs more effectively and efficiently. One way organizations can do this is to build online information databases that employees can access. For example, William Wrigley Jr. Co. launched an interactive website that allows sales agents to access marketing data and other product information. The sales agents can question company experts about products or search an online knowledge bank. In its first year, Wrigley estimates that the site cut research time of the sales force by 15,000 hours, making them more efficient and effective.[47] This one example, among many others, shows how managers can use communication tools to manage this valuable organizational resource called knowledge.

In addition to online information databases for sharing knowledge, companies can create **communities of practice**, which are groups of

Internal social media enable these IBM employees in Dublin, Ireland, to communicate and collaborate with colleagues at IBM offices throughout the world. They use IBM Connections, a social network platform, and Sametime 8.5.2, IBM's internal instant messaging system, to share knowledge, improve decision making, and accelerate innovation.

Artur Widak/ZUMA Press/Newscom

people who share a concern, a set of problems, or a passion about a topic, and who deepen their knowledge and expertise in that area by interacting on an ongoing basis. To make these communities of practice work, however, it's important to maintain strong human interactions through communication using such essential tools as interactive websites, e-mail, and video-conferencing. In addition, these groups face the same communication problems that individuals face—filtering, emotions, defensiveness, overdocumentation, and so forth. However, groups can resolve these issues by focusing on the same suggestions we discussed earlier.

What Role Does Communication Play in Customer Service?

You've been a customer many times; in fact, you probably find yourself in a customer service encounter several times a day. So what does a customer service encounter have to do with communication? As it turns out, a lot! *What* communication takes place and *how* it takes place can have a significant impact on a customer's satisfaction with the service and the likelihood of being a repeat customer. Managers in service organizations need to make sure that employees who interact with customers are communicating appropriately and effectively with those customers. How? By first recognizing the three components in any service delivery process: the customer, the service organization, and the individual service provider.[48] Each plays a role in whether communication is working. Obviously, managers don't have a lot of control over what or how the customer communicates, but they can influence the other two.

An organization with a strong service culture already values taking care of customers—finding out what their needs are, meeting those needs, and following up to make sure that their needs were met satisfactorily. Each of these activities involves communication, whether face-to-face, by phone or e-mail, or through other channels. In addition, communication is part of the specific customer service strategies the organization pursues. One strategy that many service organizations use is personalization. For instance, at Ritz-Carlton Hotels, customers are provided with more than a clean bed and room. Customers who have stayed at a location previously and indicated that certain items are important to them—such as extra pillows, hot chocolate, or a certain brand of shampoo—will find those items waiting in their room at arrival. The hotel's database allows service to be personalized to customers' expectations. In addition, all employees are asked to communicate information related to service provision. For instance, if a room attendant overhears guests talking about celebrating an anniversary, he or she is supposed to relay the information so something special can be done.[49] Communication plays an important role in the hotel's customer personalization strategy.

Communication also is important to the individual service provider or contact employee. The quality of the interpersonal interaction between the customer and that contact employee does influence customer satisfaction, especially when the service encounter isn't up to expectations.[50] People on the front line involved with those "critical service encounters" are often the first to hear about or notice service failures or breakdowns. They must decide *how* and *what* to communicate during these instances. Their ability to listen actively and communicate appropriately with the customer goes a long way in whether the situation is resolved to the customer's satisfaction or spirals out of control. Another important communication concern for the individual service provider is making sure that he or she has the information needed to deal with customers efficiently and effectively. If the service provider doesn't personally have the information, there should be some way to get the information easily and promptly.[51]

How Can We Get Employee Input and Why Should We?

Nokia's intranet soapbox, known as Blog-Hub, is open to employee bloggers around the world. There, employees have griped about their employer, but rather than shutting

Communication is an important part of the customer service strategy of Metro Bank in London. Recognizing that *how* communication takes place has a great impact on customer satisfaction, the bank expects all employees to greet guests with a smile and a friendly greeting and teaches them how to treat guests with warmth, courtesy, and respect.

Facundo Arrizabalaga/EPA/Newscom

it down, Nokia managers want them to "fire away." They feel that Nokia's growth and success can be attributed to a "history of encouraging employees to say whatever's on their minds, with faith that smarter ideas will result."[53]

In today's challenging environment, companies need to get input from their employees. Have you ever worked somewhere that had an employee suggestion box? When an employee had an idea about a new way of doing something—such as reducing costs, improving delivery time, and so forth—it went into the suggestion box, where it usually sat until someone decided to empty the box. Businesspeople frequently joked about the suggestion box and cartoonists lambasted the futility of putting ideas in the employee suggestion box. Unfortunately, this attitude about suggestion boxes still persists in many organizations, but it shouldn't. Managers do business in a world today where you can't afford to ignore such potentially valuable information. Companies need candor, even when the truth isn't easy to hear.[54] Managers need to be open to bad news and contrary opinions. Exhibit 13–4 lists some suggestions for letting employees know that their opinions matter.

Making Ethical Decisions in Today's Workplace

Want to vent about your boss or your company? Now, there are apps to do just that: Yik Yak, Whisper, and Memo, among others.[52] In these apps, users post anonymous messages about their employers. Giving and receiving feedback can be a significant challenge for employees and managers. Yes, providing the opportunity for employees to offer honest feedback about their managers and workplace is commendable. But are apps that provide a platform for employees to do just that, but anonymously, the answer?

Discussion Questions:

5 How do these apps that let employees post anonymous feedback benefit employees? Managers?

6 What ethical dilemmas might arise because of these apps?

How Do We Have Civil Conversations in the Workplace?

Tech giant Google has always encouraged a workplace where groups of employees who disagree can engage in debates about social and political beliefs. A healthy debate over issues can be a good way to figure out the best way to do things and to be creative and innovative. However, when coworkers have the perspective that "you're entitled to your opinion but my opinion is far more important than yours, especially if your opinion doesn't agree with mine," trouble is brewing. Although Google's organizational culture of "opinion entitlement" might be an important reflection of its corporate values, it has led to a workplace of nonstop, unhealthy, ineffective debate.[55] The "cacophony of voices" is consuming the company and creating a "war zone of debate."[56] And Google is not the only organization dealing with the reality. We've become a society of individuals who seemingly can't handle opinions that depart from their own "politically correct views."[57] Incivility and the need for civil conversations IS a topic that organizational managers need to address. A recent study documented how incivility diminishes collaboration and performance in medical teams.[58] There are very few jobs in an organization where employees work independently. In most organizations, work is done with the input, cooperation, and efforts of numerous individuals...whether on a team, in a department or across functional areas, or even outside the organizational boundary. And

Exhibit 13–4 How to Let Employees Know Their Input Matters

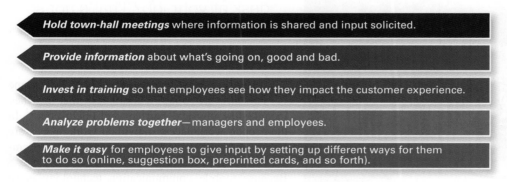

Hold town-hall meetings where information is shared and input solicited.

Provide information about what's going on, good and bad.

Invest in training so that employees see how they impact the customer experience.

Analyze problems together—managers and employees.

Make it easy for employees to give input by setting up different ways for them to do so (online, suggestion box, preprinted cards, and so forth).

Source: Robbins, Stephen P., Coulter, Mary, *Management*, 13th Ed., © 2016, p. 421. Reprinted and electronically reproduced by permission of Pearson Education, Inc., New York, NY.

open workplaces
Workplaces that have few physical barriers and enclosures

individuals, as we discussed in Chapter 8, come to the organization from and with diverse perspectives and characteristics. Working together to accomplish organizational goals is the "glue" that all should be working toward together. So, it seems, therefore, that the chapter on communication is the place, then, to discuss how coworkers can converse civilly. Somehow, somewhere, sometime, it seems we've forgotten how to do that.

Creating a culture of civility is the responsibility of an organization's leaders.[59] Respectful, civil conversations are modeled by leaders who set the example of how to be civil. Civil conversations and discussions are a matter of give and take. Talking and listening respectfully are paramount. Being civil doesn't mean that you have to agree with what the other person is saying or expressing. But it does mean that you listen and that you ask questions. It also means that you're able to separate facts from opinions. When opinions are mistaken as facts, it will be hard to have a civil conversation. All employees should strive to keep an open mind when exposed to another viewpoint. Keeping an open mind does not equal agreement; it simply means that you respect the other person enough to hear what he or she has to say. So, as we discussed earlier as we looked at the barriers to effective communication and how to overcome those barriers, coworkers need to be supportive of each other and reflect a more positive workplace culture in which rudeness and incivility are strongly discouraged. Building a culture of civility and respectfulness where coworkers can express differing opinions without fear of attack or intimidation or retribution is a goal that all organizational leaders should strive for.

How Does Workplace Design Affect Communication?

Another factor that affects organizational communication is workplace design. Despite all the information technology and employee mobility, much of an organization's communication still happens in the workplace. In fact, some 74 percent of an employee's average workweek is spent in an office.[60] How that office workspace is designed and configured can affect the communication that occurs as well as influence an organization's overall performance. In fact, in a survey of American workers, 90 percent believed that better workplace design and layout result in better overall employee performance.[61]

Research shows that a workplace design should successfully support four types of employee work: focused work, collaborative work, learning work, and socializing work.[62] *Focused work* is when an employee needs to concentrate on completing a task. *Collaborative work* is when employees need to work together to complete a task. *Learning work* is when employees are engaged in training or doing something new and could involve both focused and collaborative work. Finally, *socializing work* is when employees gather informally to chat or to exchange ideas. A survey found that when workers had these types of "oases" or informal meeting places nearby, they had 102 percent more face-to-face communication than people who had only minimal access to such spaces.[63] Because communication can and does take place in each of these settings, the workplace design needs to accommodate all directions and all types of organizational and interpersonal communications in order to be most effective.

Apple's new headquarters, known as Apple Park, accommodates 12,000 employees who work in an open space design where they can easily communicate to share ideas, learn, collaborate, and innovate. All employees, from the CEO to summer interns, work in pods designed to support the four different types of work: focused, collaborative, learning, and socializing.

Josh Edelson/AFP/Getty Images

Think you're gonna have your own desk at your job? That's not so likely in today's workplace! How do you feel about that?

Many organizational workplaces today—some 70 percent—are **open workplaces**; that is, they include few physical barriers and enclosures.[64] In these open workplaces, individual work spaces are being designed around the type of work an employee needs to do rather than an assigned place.[65] Because mobile communication technology is so widely available and powerful, some companies even are replacing the one-desk-per-employee workspace arrangements with first-come, first-served desks and then providing additional workspaces for team or one-one-one meetings.[66] For example, in Apple's new futuristic headquarters building, employees may be working at long tables with coworkers or working in "pods" made with a lot of glass (which has created a safety hazard, as distracted employees keep walking into them).[67] So, the point of all this attention on workplace design is that it can and does have an impact on how communication takes place and how effective that communication can be.

Why Should Managers Be Concerned with Communicating Ethically?

Fifteen percent of employees say they wish their managers would improve their communication skills, especially in clarity and transparency.[68]

It's particularly important today that a company's communication efforts be ethical. **Ethical communication** "includes all relevant information, is true in every sense, and is not deceptive in any way."[69] On the other hand, unethical communication often distorts the truth or manipulates audiences. What are some ways that companies communicate unethically? It could be by omitting essential information. For instance, not telling employees that an impending merger is going to mean some of them will lose their jobs is unethical. It's also unethical to plagiarize, which is "presenting someone else's words or other creative product as your own."[70] It would also be unethical communication to selectively misquote, misrepresent numbers, distort visuals, and fail to respect privacy or information security needs. For instance, although British Petroleum attempted to communicate openly and truthfully about the Gulf Coast oil spill, the public felt that much of the company's communication had some unethical elements to it.

So how can managers encourage ethical communications? One thing is to "establish clear guidelines for ethical behavior, including ethical business communication."[71] In a global survey by the International Association of Business Communicators, 70 percent of communication professionals said their companies clearly define what is considered ethical and unethical behavior.[72] If no clear guidelines exist, it's important to answer the following questions:

- Has the situation been defined fairly and accurately?
- Why is the message being communicated?
- How will the people who may be affected by the message or who receive the message be impacted?
- Does the message help achieve the greatest possible good while minimizing possible harm?
- Will this decision that appears to be ethical now seem so in the future?
- How comfortable are you with your communication effort? What would a person you admire think of it?[73]

Remember that as a manager, you have a responsibility to think through your communication choices and the consequences of those choices. If you always remember that, you're likely to have ethical communication.

ethical communication
Presented material that contains all relevant information, is true in every sense, and is not deceptive in any way

CHAPTER SUMMARY BY LEARNING OUTCOME

13-1 Describe what managers need to know about communicating effectively.

Communication is the transfer and understanding of meaning. The communication process consists of seven elements: First, a *sender* or source has a message. A *message* is a purpose to be conveyed. *Encoding* converts a message into symbols. A *channel* provides the medium along which a message travels. *Decoding* happens when the *receiver* retranslates a sender's message. Finally, *feedback* lets the sender know whether the communication was successful. The barriers to effective communication include filtering, emotions, information overload, defensiveness, language, and national culture. Managers can overcome these barriers by using feedback, simplifying language, listening actively, constraining emotions, and watching for nonverbal clues.

13-2 Explain how technology affects managerial communication.

Technology has radically changed the way organizational members communicate. It improves a manager's ability to monitor performance; it gives employees more complete information to make faster decisions; it provides employees more opportunities to collaborate and share information; and it makes it possible for people to be fully accessible, anytime anywhere. IT has affected managerial communication through the use of networked computer systems and wireless capabilities.

13-3 Discuss contemporary issues in communication.

The two main challenges of managing communication in an Internet world are the legal and security issues and the lack of personal interaction.

Organizations can manage knowledge by making it easy for employees to communicate and share their knowledge so they can learn from each other ways to do their jobs more effectively and efficiently. One way is through online information databases, and another way is through creating communities of practice.

Communicating with customers is an important managerial issue because *what* communication takes place and *how* it takes place can significantly affect a customer's satisfaction with the service and the likelihood of being a repeat customer.

It's important for organizations to get input from their employees. Such potentially valuable information should not be ignored.

Having civil conversations in the workplace is an important factor in managing organizational and interpersonal communication. Managers have to be the role models.

How an organization's workspace is designed and configured can affect the communication that occurs as well as influence an organization's overall performance. That's why it's important to make design choices that will enhance communication effectiveness..

Finally, it's important that a company's communication efforts be ethical. Ethical communication can be encouraged through clear guidelines and through answering questions that force a communicator to think through the communication choices made and the consequences of those choices.

DISCUSSION QUESTIONS

13-1 Explain why different types of communication are effective across an organization's hierarchy.

13-2 Why isn't effective communication synonymous with *agreement*?

13-3 Examine the communication process as illustrated in Exhibit 13-1. What constitutes noise? Do you think noise can be prevented? Explain the reasons for your answer

13-4 "Ineffective communication is the fault of the sender." Do you agree or disagree with this statement? Discuss.

13-5 What is your opinion on the possibility that information technology advancements in the future will cause information overload for managers?

13-6 How might a manager use the grapevine to his or her advantage? Support your response.

13-7 Research the characteristics of a good communicator. Write up your findings in a bulleted list report. Be sure to cite your sources.

13-8 Discuss the seven contemporary communication issues facing managers.

13-9 For one day, track nonverbal communication that you notice in others. What types did you observe? Was the nonverbal communication always consistent with the verbal communication taking place? Describe.

13-10 What purposes does communication serve?

13-11 Describe three barriers to communication and how managers can overcome those barriers.

13-12 MyLab Management only—additional assisted-graded writing assignment.

Applying: Getting Ready for the Workplace

Management Skill Builder | BEING A GOOD LISTENER

Most of us like to talk more than we like to listen. In fact, it's been facetiously said that listening is just the price we have to pay to get people to allow us to talk. Managers must be effective communicators if they are to do their job well. Part of effective communication is conveying clear and understandable messages. But it's also using active listening skills to accurately decipher others' messages.

MyLab Management
PERSONAL INVENTORY ASSESSMENT

Go to **www.pearson.com/mylab/management** to complete the Personal Inventory Assessment related to this chapter.

Skill Basics

Too many people take listening skills for granted. They confuse hearing with listening. Hearing is merely picking up sound vibrations. Listening is making sense out of what we hear; it requires paying attention, interpreting, and remembering. Active listening is hard work and requires you to "get inside" the speaker's head in order to understand the communication from his or her point of view.

Eight specific behaviors are associated with active listening. You can be more effective at active listening if you use these behaviors.[74]

- *Make eye contact.* We may listen with our ears, but others tend to judge whether we're really listening by looking at our eyes.

- *Exhibit affirmative nods and appropriate facial expressions.* The effective active listener shows interest in what's being said through nonverbal signals.

- *Avoid distracting actions or gestures.* When listening, don't look at your watch, shuffle papers, play with your pencil, or engage in similar distractions. They make the speaker feel that you're bored or uninterested.

- *Ask questions.* The critical listener analyzes what he or she hears and asks questions. This behavior provides clarification, ensures understanding, and assures the speaker that you're really listening.

- *Paraphrase.* Restate *in your own words* what the speaker has said. The effective active listener uses phrases such as "What I hear you saying is..." or "Do you mean...?" Paraphrasing is an excellent control device to check whether you're listening carefully and is also a control for accuracy of understanding.

- *Avoid interrupting the speaker.* Let the speaker complete his or her thoughts before you try to respond. Don't try to second-guess where the speaker's thoughts are going.

- *Don't overtalk.* Most of us would rather speak our own ideas than listen to what others say. Although talking might be more fun and silence might be uncomfortable, you can't talk and listen at the same time. The good active listener recognizes this fact and doesn't overtalk.

- *Make smooth transitions between the roles of speaker and listener.* In most work situations, you're continually shifting back and forth between the roles of speaker and listener. The effective active listener makes transitions smoothly from speaker to listener and back to speaker.

Practicing the Skill

Follow these directions:
Break into groups of two. This exercise is a debate. Person A can choose any contemporary issue. Some examples include business ethics, the value of unions, stiffer college grading policies, gun control, and money as a motivator. Person B then selects a position on this issue. Person A must automatically take the counterposition. The debate is to proceed for 8–10 minutes, with only one catch. Before each speaks, he or she must first summarize, in his or her own words and without notes, what the other has said. If the summary doesn't satisfy the speaker, it must be corrected until it does.

Experiential Exercise

Social media. For many of you, you've probably never known a time without social media. Logging on, checking your feed, posting photos and updates is now the norm for individuals in the United States and in other countries around the globe. Facebook, Twitter, Instagram... perhaps you use these or some other social media sites. And maybe in your younger days, before Facebook, Twitter, and Instagram, you used AOL Instant Messaging or Six Degrees or Friendster (considered the first real online connection of real-world friends) or even Myspace. Using social media in your personal life is one thing, but what about social media usage in the workplace? Should companies let employees use social media at work? In this Experiential Exercise, you're going to discuss the pros and cons of controlling social media usage in the workplace. In your assigned groups, discuss the following:

(1) Should organizations allow employees to use personal social media while at work? Defend your answer.
(2) Should organizations restrict the use of personal social media at work? Defend your answer.
(3) Make a list of the pros and cons of controlling social media usage in the workplace.
(4) Would you work for an organization that restricted social media usage in the workplace? Why or why not?

CASE APPLICATION #1

#AthletesusingTwitter

Topic: Social media, communicating ethically

Tweets. Twittering. Prior to 2006, the only definition we would have known for these words would have involved birds and the sounds they make. Now, practically everyone knows that Twitter is also an online platform—with 336 million monthly active users, 500 million tweets daily, and 1.6 billion daily search queries—used to trade short messages of 280 characters or less via the Web, cell phones, and other mobile devices.[75] According to its founders (Jack Dorsey, Biz Stone, and Evan Williams), Twitter is many things: a messaging service, a customer-service tool to reach customers, a real-time search tool, and microblogging. And as the numbers show, it's become quite popular!

The Good and the Bad of **TWITTER**

One place where Twitter has caught on is the sports world, especially in college sports. For instance, when Mike Riley was the head football coach at the University of Nebraska, he used Twitter to keep fans informed. Now at Oregon State, he continues to appreciate the power of instant communication. Hugh Freeze, former head football coach at the University of Mississippi, was an early adopter of social media to communicate recruitment news. He recognized that tweeting was an easy and fun way to communicate quick tidbits of information to fans, alumni boosters, and other interested people who subscribe to Twitter. And it's a convenient way for the football staff and football recruiting prospects to communicate with each other. There are pretty strict rules the NCAA has about contact allowed between potential recruits and coaches, but NCAA rules do allow unlimited direct messaging. However, coaches still are cautious about committing recruiting violations. So, using Twitter to announce their destinations on the recruiting trail, coaches can indirectly share their recruitment news without naming names.[76]

However, many universities and college coaches are monitoring and, in some cases, banning athletes' use of social media.[77] A potentially precarious issue can arise if an athlete tweets some comment that could put the university in a negative light, offend boosters, or possibly violate an NCAA regulation. Here are a couple of tweeting slip-ups: A Western Kentucky running back was suspended after he tweeted critical comments about the team's fans, the NCAA pulled 15 football scholarships after an investigation based on a player's tweet, and a Lehigh University wide receiver was suspended for retweeting a racial slur. We even saw how tweeting backfired at the London Olympics. The first "casualty"—a Greek triple jumper—was banned from the Games over some racially charged tweets. That seems to be good reason for the managers (i.e., coaches and administrators) of these programs to attempt to control the information flow. But is banning the answer? Some analysts say no. They argue that those setting up rules and regulations don't understand what social media is all about and the value it provides as a marketing and recruiting tool, and they argue that it's necessary to understand First Amendment rights (part of which includes freedom of speech). Rather than banning the use of social media, many universities are hiring companies to monitor athletes' posts. This, however, requires athletes to give access to their accounts, which some call an invasion of privacy. But as time goes on, social media conversations are becoming more common and more expected. Yet, caution is still needed. Harassment, sexism, and abuse continue to be common occurrences, despite Twitter's efforts to better police it.

Discussion Questions

13-13 What are the advantages and drawbacks of universities using social media to communicate with various stakeholders—students, potential students, alumni, donors, etc.?

13-14 Do you think there are more or fewer communication barriers when using social media? Discuss.

13-15 What should managers do to be sure they communicate effectively when using social media?

13-16 What have been your experiences—both positive and negative—with social media? From your experiences, what guidelines could you suggest for managers and organizations?

13-17 How do you balance an individual's "right" to use social media as he or she pleases, with the ethical challenges of being on social media? How does ethical communication come into play here? Think about your personal response to these questions and then discuss each person's answers in your assigned group.

CASE APPLICATION #2

Banning E-Mail. Banning Voice Mail.
Topic: Effective communication

It's estimated that the average corporate user sends and receives some 112 e-mails daily.[78] That's about 14 e-mails per hour, and even if half of those don't require a lot of time and concentration, that level of e-mail volume can be stressful and lead to unproductive time. Once imagined to be a time-saver, has the inbox become a burden? What about voice mails? Are phone messages even necessary for organizational communication? These and other concerns are forcing many organizations to take a closer look at how information is communicated.

What IS necessary for organizational communication?

Several years ago, U.S. Cellular's executive vice president implemented a ban on e-mail every Friday. In his memo announcing the change to employees, he told them to get out and meet the people they work with rather than sending an e-mail. That directive went over with a thud. One employee confronted him saying that Ellison didn't understand how much work had to get done and how much easier it was when using e-mail. Eventually, however, employees were won over. Forced to use the phone, one employee learned that a coworker he thought was across the country was, instead, across the hall. Now, other executives are discovering the benefits of banning e-mail.

Tom Gimbel, founder and CEO of LaSalle Network, instituted a "no e-mail day" once a quarter. By cutting back on some of the issues associated with email communications, he's found that his employees have gotten better at "live" communication, face-to-face conversations, and collaboration. Jessica Rovello, cofounder and president of Arkadium, which develops games, has described e-mail as "a form of business attention-deficit disorder." She found herself—and her employees—putting e-mail in the inbox ahead of everything else being worked on. What she decided to do was only check her e-mail four times a day and to turn off her e-mail notification. Another executive, Tim Fry of Weber Shandwick, a global public relations firm, spent a year preparing to "wean" his employees off their e-mail system. His goal: dramatically reduce how much e-mail employees send and receive. His approach started with the firm's interoffice communication system, which became an internal social network, with elements of Facebook, work group collaboration software, and an employee bulletin board. And then there's Thierry Breton, head of Europe's largest IT firm, Atos. He announced a "zero e-mail policy" to be replaced with a service more like Facebook and Twitter combined.

The latest casualty in organizational communication choices is voice mail. Under pressure to cut costs, several large financial institutions, including J.P. Morgan Chase & Co., Citigroup Inc., and Bank of America Corp., are deleting or cutting back on phone voice mail. Some company executives explaining their actions cite the reality that few people use voice mail anymore. The question remains, however, whether customers still expect to be able to maintain voice contact with their financial advisors.

Discussion Questions

13-18 What do you think of this? Do you agree that e-mail and voice mail can be unproductive in the workplace?

13-19 Were you surprised at the volume of e-mail an average employee receives daily? What are the challenges of dealing with this volume of e-mail? How much e-mail would you say you receive daily? Has your volume of e-mail increased? Have you had to change your e-mail habits?

13-20 What do you think of the e-mail "replacement" some businesses are using—more of a social media tool? In what ways might it be better? Worse?

13-21 What role should customer service play in choosing which organizational communication methods to use?

13-22 Write a memo that you would send to your employees telling them that you're declaring a no e-mail day once a month. In that memo, be sure to explain why you're doing it and what benefits you hope your employees will experience.

CASE APPLICATION #3

Using Social Media for Workplace Communication

Topic: Effective communication

Theories about communication should provide managers with the tools and information necessary to communicate more effectively and efficiently with members of the staff and avoid miscommunication. Nevertheless, there are numerous cases where a message was not received by staff or customers in the way it was intended. With the advent of social media, managers and businesses have new opportunities and methods to communicate with staff and customers. At the same time, messages that are transmitted via social media can lead to instances of miscommunication and confusion among recipients, with many often questioning whether managers have used the most appropriate channel of communication. Here are two examples.

- A cryptic Facebook post was how the staff of the Bank Café Bar, a popular Belfast restaurant, found out that they were to lose their jobs. Managers took the decision to announce the immediate closure of the restaurant to customers and staff in the same message, ending the message with "#nojob." Members of the staff had previously been told that the restaurant was facing some difficulties, but many had agreed to stay with the business nonetheless.[79]

- UK-based supermarket Morrisons fell victim to cybercrime and found that the personal data it had collected, including the bank details of 100,000 employees, had been stolen and uploaded to the Internet. They used social media platform Facebook to immediately announce the issue. Morrisons had also sent out notifications via email to managers within stores and requested that it be passed onto colleagues who did not have access to company email addresses. Many employees found out about the issue because of the announcement on Facebook long before any internal communication had reached them.[80]

Discussion Questions

13-23 Based on the two examples from the case, what do you think are the main communication issues? Did the managers of these organizations communicate effectively? Why or why not?

13-24 How would you feel if you were working in these organizations and were affected by such miscommunication through social media platforms?

13-25 What would you do differently if you were a manager for the companies mentioned in the examples?

13-26 What do you think other managers should learn from these examples of miscommunication?

Endnotes

1. S. E. Needleman, "The Pajama-Clad Bitmoji and the 'Creepy Boss,'" *Wall Street Journal*, February 18–19, 2017, pp. A1+.
2. D. Wilkie, "The 7 Deadliest Communication Sins," *SHRM Online*, April 26, 2017.
3. M. Cole, "Managing (Not) to Communicate," *TD*, June 2017, p. 12.
4. D. Wilkie, "Afraid to Speak Your Mind at Work? So Are Many of Your Colleagues," *SHRM Online*, September 25, 2017.
5. D. K. Berlo, *The Process of Communication* (New York: Holt, Rinehart & Winston, 1960), pp. 30–32.
6. Ibid., p. 54.
7. See, for instance, "Get the Message: Communication Is Key in Managing Change within Organizations—Yet Ensuring Its Effectiveness at Times of High Concerns Can Be Tricky," *Employee Benefits*, February 2002, pp. 58–60.
8. Ibid., p. 103.
9. L. R. Birkner and R. K. Birkner, "Communication Feedback: Putting It All Together," *Occupational Hazards*, August 2001, p. 9.
10. L. Hilton, "They Heard It through the Grapevine," *South Florida Business Journal*, August 18, 2000, p. 53.

11. Classic Concepts in Today's Workplace box based on S. Baker, "Putting a Price on Social Connections," *BusinessWeek Online*, April 8, 2009; and K. Davis, "Management Communication and the Grapevine," *Harvard Business Review*, September–October 1953, pp. 43–49.
12. L. Talley, "Body Language: Read It or Weep," *HR Magazine*, July 2010, pp. 64–65; and M. Fulfer, "Nonverbal Communication: How to Read What's Plain as the Nose…Or Eyelid…Or Chin…On Their Faces," *Journal of Occupational Excellence*, Spring 2001, pp. 19–38.
13. Ibid.; and T. Fernsler, "The Secrets and Science of Body Language," *Nonprofit World*, p. 25.
14. P. Mornell, "The Sounds of Silence," *Inc.*, February 2001, p. 117.
15. A. Warfield, "Do You Speak Body Language?" *Training and Development*, April 2001, p. 60.
16. S. Begley, "I Can't Think," *Newsweek*, March 7, 2011, pp. 28–33; D. Dean and C. Webb, "Recovering from Information Overload," *McKinsey Quarterly* 1 (2011), pp. 80–88; and "Information Overload," *Australian Business Intelligence*, April 16, 2002.

17. M. Cherney, "Lawyers Faced with Emojis and Emoticons Are -_("/)," *Wall Street Journal*, January 30, 2018, pp. A1+.
18. S. I. Hayakawa, *Language in Thought and Action* (New York: Harcourt Brace Jovanovich, 1949), p. 292.
19. SmartPulse, "How Prevalent Is the Use of Buzzwords in Your Organization?" Smart Brief on Leadership, www.smartbrief.com/leadership, July 29, 2014.
20. "Jargon Leaves Us Lost for Words," *Australian Business Intelligence*, August 23, 2002; and W. S. Mossberg, "A Guide to the Lingo You'll Want to Learn for Wireless Technology," *Wall Street Journal*, March 28, 2002, p. B1.
21. J. Yang and A. Gonzalez, "Jargon Junkies," *USA Today/Springfield, Missouri News-Leader*, August 5, 2017, p. 4B.
22. "Gobbledygook Be Gone," *Workforce*, February 2002, p. 12; and "Business-Speak," *Training and Development*, January 2002, pp. 50–52.
23. J. Langdon, "Differences between Males and Females at Work," *USA Today*, February 5, 2001, www.usatoday.com; J. Manion, "He Said, She Said," *Materials Management in Health Care*, November 1998, pp. 52–62; G.

Franzwa and C. Lockhart, "The Social Origins and Maintenance of Gender Communication Styles, Personality Types, and Grid-Group Theory," *Sociological Perspectives* 41, no. 1 (1998), pp. 185–208; and D. Tannen, *Talking From 9 to 5: Women and Men in the Workplace* (New York: Avon Books, 1995).
24. W. Ma, "Marriott Firing Tied to Error on Twitter," *Wall Street Journal*, March 5, 2018, pp. B1+.
25. See, for example, M. K. Kozan, "Subcultures and Conflict Management Styles," *Management International Review*, January 2002, pp. 89–106.
26. A. Mehrabian, "Communication without Words," *Psychology Today*, September 1968, pp. 53–55.
27. See also W. L. Adair, T. Okumura, and J. M. Brett, "Negotiation Behavior when Cultures Collide: The United States and Japan," *Journal of Applied Psychology*, June 2001, p. 371.
28. C. H. Tinsley, "How Negotiators Get to Yes: Predicting the Constellation of Strategies Used across Cultures to Negotiate Conflict," *Journal of Applied Psychology*, August 2001, p. 583.
29. See, for instance, S. P. Robbins and P. L. Hunsaker, *Training*

in Interpersonal Skills, 4th ed. (Upper Saddle River, NJ: Prentice Hall, 2006); M. Young and J. E. Post, "Managing to Communicate, Communicating to Manage: How Leading Companies Communicate with Employees," *Organizational Dynamics*, Summer 1993, pp. 31–43; J. A. DeVito, *The Interpersonal Communication Book*, 6th ed. (New York: HarperCollins, 1992); and A. G. Athos and J. J. Gabarro, *Interpersonal Behavior* (Upper Saddle River, NJ: Prentice Hall, 1978).

30. See, for instance, A. Cohen, "Wireless Summer," *Time*, May 29, 2000, pp. 58–65; and K. Hafner, "For the Well Connected, All the World's an Office," *New York Times*, March 30, 2000, p. D1.

31. See, for example, R. R. Panko, *Business Data Networks and Communications*, 4th ed. (Upper Saddle River, NJ: Prentice Hall, 2003).

32. "Virtual Paper Cuts," *Workforce*, July 2000, pp. 16–18.

33. S. Kessler, "Slack with Friends, Lovers and Geeks: How the Hot Workplace App Is Getting Personal," June 3, 2015, http://www.fastcompany.com/3046889/tech-forecast/slack-with-friends-lovers-and-geeks-how-the-hot-workplace-app-is-getting-perso; M. Ravindranath, "Slack Takes on Internal Communication for Small Teams and Startups," November 2, 2014, http://www.washingtonpost.com/business/on-it/slack-takes-on-internal-communication-for-small-teams-and-start-ups/2014/11/01/ab1ad5b4-5eed-11e4-8b9e-2ccdac31a031_story.html; and G. Colvin, "Brave New Work: The Office of Tomorrow," *Fortune*, January 16, 2012, pp. 49+.

34. SmartPulse, "Do You Use Emerging Mobile Technology…to Improve Your Communication with Your Employees?" Smart Brief on Exec Tech, February 22, 2015, www.smartbrief.com/exectech.

35. S. Luh, "Pulse Lunches at Asian Citibanks Feed Workers' Morale, Lower Job Turnover," *Wall Street Journal*, May 22, 2001, p. B11.

36. S. Shellenbarger, "Backlash against Email Builds," *Wall Street Journal*, April 29, 2010, p. D6.

37. H. Green, "The Water Cooler Is Now on the Web," *BusinessWeek*, October 1, 2007, pp. 78–79.

38. The Associated Press, "Whole Foods Chief Apologizes for Posts," *New York Times Online*, July 18, 2007; E. White, J. S. Lublin, and D. Kesmodel, "Executives Get the Blogging Bug," *Wall Street Journal*, July 13, 2007, pp. B1+; C. Alldred, "U.K. Libel Case Slows E-Mail Delivery," *Business Insurance*, August 4, 1997, pp. 51–53; and T. Lewin, "Chevron Settles Sexual Harassment Charges,"

New York Times Online, February 22, 1995.

39. J. Eckberg, "E-Mail: Messages Are Evidence," *Cincinnati Enquirer*, July 27, 2004, www.enquirer.com.

40. M. Scott, "Worker E-Mail and Blog Misuse Seen as Growing Risk for Companies," *Workforce Management*, July 20, 2007, www.workforce.com.

41. K. Byron, "Carrying Too Heavy a Load? The Communication and Miscommunication of Emotion by Email," *Academy of Management Review*, April 2008, pp. 309–27.

42. J. Marquez, "Virtual Work Spaces Ease Collaboration, Debate among Scattered Employees," *Workforce Management*, May 22, 2006, p. 38; and M. Conlin, "E-Mail Is So Five Minutes Ago," *BusinessWeek*, November 28, 2005, pp. 111–12.

43. Green, "The Water Cooler Is Now on the Web"; E. Frauenheim, "Starbucks Employees Carve Out Own 'Space,'" *Workforce Management*, October 22, 2007, p. 32; and S. H. Wildstrom, "Harnessing Social Networks," *BusinessWeek*, April 23, 2007, p. 20.

44. S. Castellano, "The Social Media Skills Gap," *T&D*, July 2014, p. 14.

45. J. S. Brown and P. Duguid, "Balancing Act: How to Capture Knowledge without Killing It," *Harvard Business Review*, May–June 2000, pp. 73–80; and J. Torsilieri and C. Lucier, "How to Change the World," *Strategy and Business*, October 2000, pp. 17–20.

46. J. Scanlon, "Woman of Substance," *Wired*, July 2002, p. 27.

47. H. Dolezalek, "Collaborating in Cyberspace," *Training*, April 2003, p. 33.

48. B. A. Gutek, M. Groth, and B. Cherry, "Achieving Service Success through Relationship and Enhanced Encounters," *Academy of Management Executive*, November 2002, pp. 132–44.

49. R. C. Ford and C. P. Heaton, "Lessons from Hospitality That Can Serve Anyone," *Organizational Dynamics*, Summer 2001, pp. 30–47.

50. M. J. Bitner, B. H. Booms, and L. A. Mohr, "Critical Service Encounters: The Employee's Viewpoint," *Journal of Marketing*, October 1994, pp. 95–106.

51. S. D. Pugh, J. Dietz, J. W. Wiley, and S. M. Brooks, "Driving Service Effectiveness through Employee-Customer Linkages," *Academy of Management Executive*, November 2002, pp. 73–84.

52. J. Mahler, "Who Spewed That Abuse? Anonymous Yik Yak App Isn't Telling," *New York Times Online*, March 8, 2015; L. Gellman, "App Lets Workers Vent Anonymously," *Wall Street Journal*, January 21, 2015, p. B7;

and K. Whitehouse, "Workplace Gossip App Draws Ire from Firms," *USA Today*, January 19, 2015, p. 3B.

53. J. Ewing, "Nokia: Bring on the Employee Rants," *BusinessWeek*, June 22, 2009, p. 50.

54. S. Shellenbarger, "Tell the Hard Truth at Work," *Wall Street Journal*, October 11, 2017, p. A15.

55. K. Grind and D. MacMillan, "Political Arguments Consume Google," *Wall Street Journal*, May 2, 2018, pp. A1+.

56. Ibid.

57. A. Wax, "The Closing of the Academic Mind," *Wall Street Journal*, February 17–18, 2018, pp. C1+.

58. C. Porath, "How Rudeness Stops People from Working Together," *SHRM Online*, February 16, 2017.

59. D. Meinert, "How to Create a Culture of Civility," *SHRM Online*, March 20, 2017.

60. Gensler, "The U.S. Workplace Survey, 2008," July 11, 2011, www.gensler.com.

61. Ibid, p. 11.

62. C.C. Sullivan and B. Horwitz-Bennett, "High-Performance Workplaces," *Building Design & Construction*, January 2010, pp. 22–26.

63. J. B. Stryker, "In Open Workplaces, Traffic and Head Count Matter," *Harvard Business Review*, December 2009, p. 24.

64. R. Feintzeig, "Study: Open Offices Are Making Us All Sick," *Wall Street Journal Online*, February 25, 2014.

65. G. Moran, "4 Ways Your Office May Change by 2025," *Fast Company Online*, January 27, 2016.

66. S. Shellenbarger, "Don't Get Too Used to Your Own Desk," *Wall Street Journal*, May 17, 2018, p. A14; and S. Lohr, "Don't Get Too Comfortable at That Desk," *New York Times Online*, October 6, 2017.

67. M. Bergen, "Apple's New Spaceship Campus Has One Flaw—and It Hurts," *Bloomberg Online*, February 16, 2018.

68. S. Vozza, "5 Things Your Employees Wish They Could Tell You," April 27, 2015, http://www.fastcompany.com/3045282/hit-the-ground-running/5-things-your-employees-wish-they-could-tell-you.

69. J. V. Thill and C. L. Bovee, *Excellence in Business Communication*, 9th ed. (Upper Saddle River, NJ: Prentice Hall, 2011), pp. 24–25.

70. Ibid.

71. Ibid.

72. Ibid.

73. Ibid.

74. Based on K. J. Murphy, *Effective Listening* (New York: Bantam Books, 1987); and T. Drollinger, L. B. Comer, and P. T. Warrington, "Development and Validation of the Active Empathetic Listening

Scale," *Psychology & Marketing*, February 2006, pp. 161–80.

75. E. Sherman, "Many Twitter Users Don't Tweet, Finds Report," April 14, 2014, http://www.cbsnews.com/news/many-twitter-users-dont-tweet-finds-report/; R. W. Ahrens, "Tweets Per Day," *USA Today*, March 20, 2013, p. 2A; M. Lopresti, "Elimination by Twitter," *USA Today*, July 26, 2012, p. 1C; K. Paulson, "College Athlete Tweet Ban? Free Speech Sacks That Idea," *USA Today*, April 16, 2012, p. 9A; L. East, "Les Miles' Tweets Entertain CWS Fans," July 12, 2012, theadvocate.com/sports; P. Thamel, "Tracking Twitter, Raising Red Flags," *New York Times Online*, March 30, 2012; L. Dugan, "Twitter to Surpass 500 Million Registered Users on Wednesday," February 21, 2012, www.mediabistro.com; C. Ho, "Companies Tracking College Athletes' Tweets, Facebook Posts Go after Local Universities," *Washington Post Online*, October 16, 2011; D. Rovell, "Coaches Ban of Twitter Proves College Sports Isn't about Education," *CNBC Sports Business Online*, August 8, 2011; Staff of Corporate Executive Board, "Corporate Confidential: How Twitter Changes Everything," *BusinessWeek Online*, September 4, 2009; S. Johnson, "How Twitter Will Change the Way We Live," *Time*, June 15, 2009, pp. 30–37; J. Swartz, "A World That's All a-Twitter," *USA Today*, May 26, 2009, pp. 1B+; and K. Whiteside, "College Coaches Are Chirping about Twitter!" *USA Today*, April 29, 2009, pp. 1C+.

76. G. Schroeder, "Coaches Using Twitter from Recruiting Trail," *USA Today*, February 2, 2015, p. 10C.

77. N. Best, "Twitter's Had a Huge Impact on Sports, But Not All Athletes, Media Members Are on Board," April 1, 2017, www.newsday.com.

78. T. Gimbel, "My Entire Company Avoids Email for One Full Day Every Quarter," *Fast Company Online*, July 5, 2017; M. Nalsky, "How Quitting Email Helped My Company Communicate Better," November 9, 2014, http://thenextweb.com/entrepreneur/2014/11/09/quitting-email-helped-company-team-communicate-better/; M. Prokopeak, "What If Email Got Pantsed?" October 14, 2013, www.workforce.com; C. Brown, A. Killick, and K. Renaud, "To Reduce E-mail, Start at the Top," *Harvard Business Review*, September 2013, p. 26; J. Wortham, "When E-Mail Turns from Delight to Deluge," *New York Times Online*, February 9, 2013; T. Provost, "Long Live E-Mail," *CFO*, January/February 2013, p. 29; M. V. Rafter, "Too Much Email on the Menu? Here

Are Five Tips to Curb Company Consumption," *Workforce Management Online*, April 24, 2012; M. V. Rafter, "If Tim Fry Has His Way, He'll Eradicate Email for Good," *Workforce Management Online*, April 24, 2012; M. A. Field, "Turning Off Email, Turning Up Productivity," *Workforce Management Online*, February 29, 2012; "Internet 2011 in Numbers," January 17, 2012, royalpingdom.com; "Should Workplaces Curtail Email?" *New York Times Online*, December 7, 2011; W. Powers, "The Phony 'Zero Email' Alarm," *New York*

Times Online, December 6, 2011; L. Suarez, "What We Would Miss," *New York Times Online*, December 5, 2011; P. Duncan, "Break Bad Habits," *New York Times Online*, December 5, 2011; N. Carr, "Put the Cost Back in Communication," *New York Times Online*, December 5, 2011; and P. Allen, "One of the Biggest Information Technology Companies in the World to Abolish E-mails," November 30, 2011, www.dailymail.com.

79. E. Reynolds, "How Facebook Could Cost You Your Job! One in Five Bosses Has Rejected a Job Applicant after Checking

Out Their Profile on Social Media Sites," *Mail Online*, http://www.dailymail.co.uk/news/article-2115927/How-Facebook-cost-job-One-applicants-rejected-bosses-check-profiles-social-media-sites.html, March 16, 2012; J. Beattie, "Staff at Popular East Belfast Restaurant Claim They Were Told They'd Lost Their Job via Facebook," Belfast Live, http://www.bel-fastlive.co.uk/news/belfast-news/staff-popular-east-belfast-restau-rant-10210444, October 6, 2015.

80. E. Simpson, "Wm Morrison Supermarket Suffers Payroll Data

Theft," *BBC News*, www.bbc.com, March 14, 2014; J. Davey, "UK Grocer Morrisons Suffers Payroll Data Theft," *Reuters*, www.reuters.com/article/uk-morrisons-data-theft-idUKBRE-A2D0O020140314, March 14, 2014; H. Gye, "Payroll Details of 100,000 Morrisons Staff Including Bank Account Numbers Leaked by Insider and Published on the Web," *Mail Online*, www.dailymail.co.uk, March 14, 2014.

14

A lack of employee turnover is a sign of a good manager.

Management Myth DEBUNKED?

While high employee turnover is almost always dysfunctional, low turnover is not necessarily the best goal. **An absence of turnover often can mean a complacent manager, one who's willing to accept mediocre employee performance**. In an effective organizational control system, managers are encouraged to identify and remove marginal employees. Low levels of employee turnover can be functional only *if* the right people—those who are the weakest performers—are the ones leaving.

CONTROLLING

is the final step in the management process. Managers must monitor whether goals that were established as part of the planning process are being accomplished efficiently and effectively. That's what they do when they control. Appropriate controls can help managers look for specific performance gaps and areas for improvement. Things don't always go as planned. But that's why controlling is so important! For instance, British Airways experienced a major global computer failure one weekend in 2017, causing the cancellation of hundreds of flights and affecting more than 75,000 passengers. Although the technical problem was resolved fairly quickly, flight crews were still in the wrong places instead of where they needed to be. The "fine-tuned system" was eventually restored.[1] In this chapter, we'll look at the fundamental elements of controlling, including the control process, the types of controls that managers can use, and contemporary issues in control. ●

Learning Outcomes

14-1 Explain the nature and importance of control. p. 489

14-2 Describe the three steps in the control process. p. 491

14-3 Discuss the types of controls organizations and managers use. p. 496

14-4 Discuss contemporary issues in control. p. 502

What Is Control and Why Is It Important?

14-1 Explain the nature and importance of control.

"Bailout" was the magic word that cost Domino's Pizza 11,000 free pizzas. The company had prepared an Internet coupon for an ad campaign that was considered but not approved. However, when someone apparently typed "bailout" into a Domino's promotional code window and found it was good for a free medium pizza, the word spread like wildfire on the Web. Somewhere, somehow, a lack of control cost the company big time.[2]

control
Management function that involves monitoring activities to ensure that they're being accomplished as planned and correcting any significant deviations

What Is Control?

How do you know a control system is effective? Look at whether **goals are being achieved!**

Control is the management function that involves monitoring activities to ensure that they're being accomplished as planned and correcting any significant deviations. Managers can't really know whether their units are performing properly until they've evaluated what activities have been done and have compared the actual performance with the desired standard. An effective control system ensures that activities are completed in ways that lead to the attainment of the organization's goals. The effectiveness of a control system is determined by how well it facilitates goal achievement. The more a control system helps managers achieve their organization's goals, the better it is.

Why Is Control Important?

- A press operator at the Denver Mint noticed a flaw—an extra up leaf or an extra down leaf—on Wisconsin state quarters being pressed at one of his five press machines. He stopped the machine and left for a meal break. When he returned, he saw the machine running and assumed that someone had changed the die in the machine. However, after a routine inspection, the machine operator realized the die had not been changed. The faulty press had likely been running for over an hour and thousands of the flawed coins were now commingled with unblemished quarters. As many as 50,000 of the faulty coins entered circulation, setting off a coin collector buying frenzy.[3]

- Northrop Grumman has implemented several major changes in its satellite production unit after serious slipups were discovered in the building of NASA's James Webb Space Telescope, the successor to the Hubble Space Telescope.[4]

- H&M, the Swedish fashion retailer has a problem: $4.3 billion of unsold inventory. For a competitor in fast fashion retailing, that's a pretty serious problem.[5]

- McDonald's Japan has apologized to customers and vowed to better control product safety after foreign objects—including a tooth and plastic—were found in food.[6]

- Hundreds of KFC stores in the United Kingdom had to close after a logistics error meant no chickens were on hand to cook and sell.[7]

- Hackers attacked a Saudi Arabian petrochemical plant and gained control over a safety shut-off system critical to defending against catastrophic events. The hackers would have had the ability to control what that safety system would do in the event of an emergency.[8]

- The 2017 Academy Awards were quite memorable...not for the emcee's lines or the clothing choices of the nominees, but for the Best Picture Award when the wrong envelope was handed to the presenters and the wrong picture announced as the winner, a mistake that had to be quickly corrected. A thorough review afterward by PricewaterhouseCoopers, the accounting firm in charge of the awards, of what went wrong led to revised protocols and "ambitious controls" to ensure it would not happen again.[9]

- No fast-food chain wants its employees doing gross stuff behind the scenes, but social media photos and videos of a Taco Bell employee licking a stack of taco shells, a Wendy's employee bending down under a Frosty machine with mouth wide open gobbling the treat, or a Domino's Pizza employee performing vulgar and unsanitary actions while preparing food have all shown up online.[10]

77 percent of executives say that the biggest threat to their organizations comes from within.[11]

Can you see now why controlling is such an important managerial function? Planning can be done, an organizational structure created to facilitate efficient achievement of goals, and employees motivated through effective leadership. But there's no assurance that activities are going as planned and that the goals employees and managers are working toward are, in fact, being attained. Control is important, therefore, because it's the only way that managers know whether organizational goals are being met and, if not, the reasons why. The value of the control function can be seen in three specific areas:

1. **Planning.** In Chapter 6, we described goals, which provide specific direction to employees and managers, as the foundation of planning. However, just stating goals or having employees accept goals doesn't guarantee that the necessary actions to accomplish those goals have been taken. As the old saying goes, "The best-laid plans often go awry." The effective manager follows up to ensure that what employees are supposed to do is, in fact, being done and goals are being achieved. As the final step in the management process, controlling provides the critical link back to planning. (See Exhibit 14–1.) If managers didn't control, they'd have no way of knowing whether goals and plans were being achieved and what future actions to take.

2. **Empowering employees.** The second reason controlling is important is because of employee empowerment. Many managers are reluctant to empower their employees because they fear something will go wrong for which they would be held responsible. But an effective control system can provide information and feedback on employee performance and minimize the chance of potential problems.

Exhibit 14–1 Planning–Controlling Link

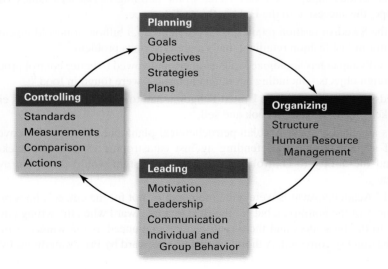

3. Protecting the workplace. The final reason that managers control is to protect the organization and its assets.[12] Organizations face threats from natural disasters, financial pressures and scandals, workplace violence, supply chain disruptions, security breaches, and even possible terrorist attacks. Managers must protect organizational assets in the event that any of these should happen. Comprehensive controls and backup plans will help minimize work disruptions.

John Jamason, media and public information manager, talks to employees working in the social media monitoring room at the Palm Beach County Emergency Operations Center. Social media such as Facebook and Twitter help the center track and monitor information during storm emergencies to get help to people in need.

What Takes Place as Managers Control?

14-2 Describe the three steps in the control process.

When Maggine Fuentes joined Ohio-based Core Systems as HR manager, she knew that her top priority was reducing the number of employee injuries, which was well above the industry average. The high frequency and severity of the company's injury rates not only affected employee morale, but also resulted in lost workdays and affected the bottom line.[13] Fuentes relied on the control process to turn this situation around.

The **control process** is a three-step process of (1) measuring actual performance, (2) comparing actual performance against a standard, and (3) taking managerial action to correct deviations or to address inadequate standards. (See Exhibit 14–2.) The control process assumes that performance standards already exist, and they do. They're the specific goals created during the planning process.

Specific goals ARE the performance standards.

---

1 What Is Measuring?

To determine actual performance, a manager must first get information about it. Thus, the first step in control is measuring.

HOW DO MANAGERS MEASURE? Four common sources of information frequently used to measure actual performance include personal observation, statistical reports, oral reports, and written reports. Each has its own particular strengths and weaknesses, but using a combination of them increases both the number of input sources and the probability of receiving reliable information.

Personal observation provides firsthand, intimate knowledge of the actual activity—information that is not filtered through others. It permits intensive coverage because minor as well as major performance activities can be observed, and it provides opportunities for the manager to read between the lines. **Management by walking around (MBWA)** is a phrase used to describe when a manager is out in the work area, interacting directly with employees and exchanging information about what's going on. Management by walking around can pick

control process
A three-step process of measuring actual performance, comparing actual performance against a standard, and taking managerial action to correct deviations

management by walking around (MBWA)
When a manager is out in the work area interacting with employees

up factual omissions, facial expressions, and tones of voice that may be missed by other sources. Unfortunately, in a time when quantitative information suggests objectivity, personal observation is often considered an inferior information source. It is subject to perceptual biases; what one manager sees, another might not. Personal observation also consumes a good deal of time. Finally, this method suffers from obtrusiveness. Employees might interpret a manager's overt observation as a lack of confidence or a sign of mistrust.

The widespread use of computers has led managers to rely increasingly on *statistical reports* for measuring actual performance. This measuring device, however, isn't limited to computer outputs. It also includes graphs, bar charts, and numerical displays of any form that managers can use for assessing performance. Although statistical information is easy to visualize and effective for showing relationships, it provides limited information about an activity. Statistics report on only a few key areas and may often ignore other important, often subjective, factors.

Information can also be acquired through *oral reports*—that is, through conferences, meetings, one-to-one conversations, or telephone calls. In employee-oriented organizations where employees work closely together, this approach may be the best way to keep tabs on work performance. For instance, at the Ken Blanchard Companies in Escondido, California, managers are expected to hold one-on-one meetings with each of their employees at least once every two weeks.[15] The advantages and disadvantages of this method of measuring performance are similar to those of personal observation. Although the information is filtered, it is fast, allows for feedback, and permits expression and tone of voice, as well as words themselves, to convey meaning. Historically, one of the major drawbacks of oral reports has been the problem of documenting information for later reference. However, our technological capabilities have progressed in the past couple of decades to the point where oral reports can be efficiently taped and become as permanent as if they were written.

Actual performance may also be measured by *written reports*. Like statistical reports, they are slower yet more formal than firsthand or secondhand oral measures. This formality also often gives them greater comprehensiveness and conciseness than found in oral reports. In addition, written reports are usually easy to catalog and reference.

Given the varied advantages and disadvantages of each of these four measurement techniques, managers should use all four for comprehensive control efforts.

Seventy-three percent of employers have taken efforts to address productivity killers at work.[16]

WHAT DO MANAGERS MEASURE? *What* managers measure is probably *more critical* to the control process than *how* they measure. Why? The selection of the wrong criteria can result in serious dysfunctional consequences. Besides, what we measure determines, to a great extent, what people in the organization will attempt to excel at.[17] For example, assume that your instructor has required a total of 10 writing assignments from the exercises at the end of each textbook chapter. But in the grade computation section of the syllabus, you notice that these assignments are not scored. In fact, when you ask your professor about this, she replies that these writing assignments are for your own enlightenment and do not affect your grade for the course; grades are solely a function of how well you perform on the three exams. We predict that you would, not surprisingly, exert most, if not all, of your effort toward doing well on the three exams.

Some control criteria are applicable to any management situation. For instance, because all managers, by definition, direct the activities of others, *criteria such as employee satisfaction or turnover and absenteeism rates* can be measured. Also, most managers have budgets for their area of responsibility set in monetary units (dollars, pounds, francs, lire, and so on).

Exhibit 14–2 The Control Process

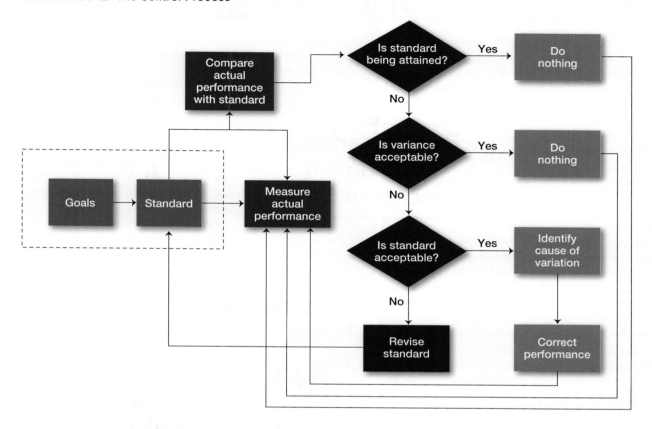

Keeping costs within budget is, therefore, a fairly common control measure. However, any comprehensive control system needs to recognize the diversity of activities among managers. For example, a production manager in a paper tablet manufacturing plant might use measures of the quantity of tablets produced per day, tablets produced per labor hour, scrap tablet rate, or percentage of rejects returned by customers. On the other hand, the manager of an administrative unit in a government agency might use number of document pages produced per day, number of orders processed per hour, or average time required to process service calls. Marketing managers often use measures such as percent of market held, number of customer visits per salesperson, or number of customer impressions per advertising medium.

As you might imagine, some activities are more difficult to measure in quantifiable terms. It is more difficult, for instance, for a manager to measure the performance of a medical researcher or a middle school counselor than of a person who sells life insurance. But most activities can be broken down into objective segments that allow for measurement. The manager needs to determine what value a person, department, or unit contributes to the organization and then convert the contribution into standards.

Most jobs and activities can be expressed in tangible and measurable terms. When a performance indicator cannot be stated in quantifiable terms, managers should look for and use subjective measures. Certainly, subjective measures have significant limitations. Still, they are better than having no standards at all and

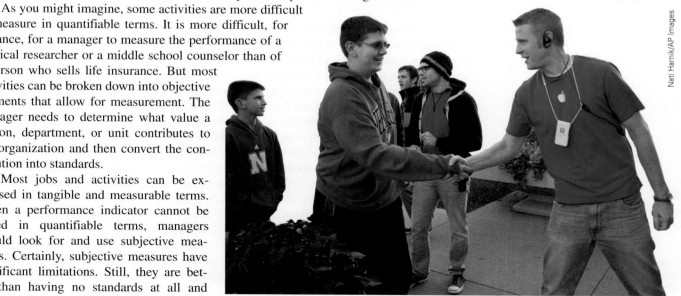

Greeting customers with a handshake, a smile, and a warm welcome is a practice Apple stores adopted from Ritz-Carlton, the luxury hotel chain known as the gold standard of customer service. Apple benchmarked with Ritz-Carlton because it wants its employees to excel at customer service that leads to customer loyalty.

Nati Harnik/AP Images

◄◄◄ Classic Concepts in Today's Workplace ►►►

Benchmarking: How do we measure up?

We introduced benchmarking in the planning chapter (Chapter 6) as a way for organizations to promote quality.[18] Not surprisingly, since planning and controlling are so closely linked, it also has implications for control. Benchmarking has been a highly utilized management tool. Although Xerox is often credited with the first wide-spread benchmarking effort in the United States, the practice can actually be traced back much further.

The benefits of benchmarking have long been recognized in the manufacturing industry. At the Midvale Steel Company plant where he was employed, Frederick W. Taylor (of scientific management fame) used concepts of benchmarking to find the "one best way" to perform a job and to find the best worker to perform the job. Even Henry Ford recognized the benefits. Based on the techniques used at Chicago slaughterhouses where carcasses were hung from hooks mounted on a monorail, with each man performing his job and then pushing the carcass to the next work station, Ford's assembly line used the same concept for producing cars, beginning in 1913. "The idea that revolutionized manufacturing was imported from another industry."

Today, managers in diverse industries such as health care, education, and financial services are discovering what manufacturers have long recognized—the benefits of benchmarking. For instance, the American Medical Association developed more than 100 standard measures of performance to improve medical care. When Carlos Ghosn was CEO of Nissan, he benchmarked against Walmart's operations in purchasing, transportation, and logistics. At its most basic, benchmarking means learning from others. However, as a tool for monitoring and measuring organizational and work performance, benchmarking can be used to identify specific performance gaps and potential areas of improvement.

Discussion Questions:

3 What are the benefits of benchmarking? What are the challenges in doing it?

4 In your "assigned" group, discuss whether benchmarking would be an appropriate activity for individuals. Explain your answer.

---

ignoring the control function. If an activity is important, the excuse that it's difficult to measure is inadequate. In such cases, managers should use subjective performance criteria. Of course, any analysis or decisions made on the basis of subjective criteria should recognize the limitations of the data.

2 How Do Managers Compare Actual Performance to Planned Goals?

The comparing step determines the variation between actual performance and the standard. Although some variation in performance can be expected in all activities, it's critical to determine an acceptable **range of variation** (see Exhibit 14–3). Deviations outside this range need attention. Let's work through an example.

Chris Tanner is a sales manager for Green Earth Gardening Supply, a distributor of specialty plants and seeds in the Pacific Northwest. Chris prepares a report during the first week of each month that describes sales for the previous month, classified by product line. Exhibit 14–4 displays both the sales goals (standard) and actual sales figures for the month of June. After looking at the numbers, should Chris be concerned? Sales were a bit higher than originally targeted, but does that mean there were no significant deviations? That depends on what Chris thinks is *significant*—that is, outside the acceptable range of variation. Even though overall performance was generally quite favorable, some product lines need closer scrutiny. For instance, if sales of heirloom seeds, flowering bulbs, and annual flowers continue to be over what was expected, Chris might need to order more product from nurseries to meet customer demand. Because sales of vegetable plants were 15 percent below goal, Chris may need to run a special on them. As this example shows, both overvariance and undervariance may require managerial attention, which is the third step in the control process.

range of variation
The acceptable parameters of variance between actual performance and a standard

Exhibit 14–3 Acceptable Range of Variation

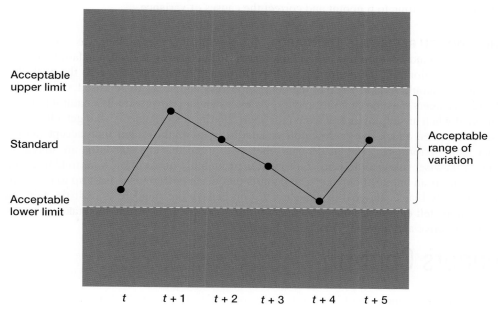

3 What Managerial Action Can Be Taken?

Managers can choose among **three possible courses of action**:

- Do nothing (self-explanatory)
- Correct actual performance
- Revise the standards

HOW DO YOU CORRECT ACTUAL PERFORMANCE? Depending on what the problem is, a manager could take different corrective actions. For instance, if unsatisfactory work is the reason for performance variations, the manager could correct it through training programs, disciplinary action, changes in compensation practices, and so forth. One decision that a manager must make is whether to take **immediate corrective action**, which corrects problems at once to get performance back on track, or to use **basic corrective action**, which looks at how and why performance deviated before correcting the source of deviation. It's not unusual for managers to rationalize that they don't have time to find the source of a problem (basic corrective action) and continue to perpetually "put out fires" with

immediate corrective action
Corrective action that addresses problems at once to get performance back on track

basic corrective action
Corrective action that looks at how and why performance deviated before correcting the source of deviation

Exhibit 14–4 Example of Determining Significant Variation: Green Earth Gardening Supply—June Sales

PRODUCT	STANDARD	ACTUAL	OVER (UNDER)
Vegetable plants	1,075	913	(612)
Perennial flowers	630	634	4
Annual flowers	800	912	112
Herbs	160	140	(20)
Flowering bulbs	170	286	116
Flowering bushes	225	220	(5)
Heirloom seeds	540	672	132
Total	3,600	3,777	177

immediate corrective action. Effective managers analyze deviations and, if the benefits justify it, take the time to pinpoint and correct the causes of variance.

HOW DO YOU REVISE THE STANDARD?   It's possible that the variance was a result of an unrealistic standard—too low or too high a goal. In such cases, it's the standard that needs corrective action, not the performance. If performance consistently exceeds the goal, then a manager should look at whether the goal is too easy and needs to be raised. On the other hand, managers must be cautious about revising a standard downward. It's natural to blame the goal when an employee or a team falls short. For instance, students who get a low score on a test often attack the grade cutoff standards as too high. Rather than accept the fact that their performance was inadequate, they will argue that the standards are unreasonable. Likewise, salespeople who don't meet their monthly quota often want to blame what they think is an unrealistic quota. The point is that when performance isn't up to par, don't immediately blame the goal or standard. If you believe the standard is realistic, fair, and achievable, tell employees that you expect future work to improve, and then take the necessary corrective action to help make that happen.

What Should Managers Control?

14-3 Discuss the types of controls organizations and managers use.

Cost efficiency. The length of time customers are kept on hold. Customers being satisfied with the service provided. These are just a few of the important performance indicators that executives in the intensely competitive call-center service industry measure. To make good decisions, managers in this industry want and need this type of information so they can control work performance.

How do managers know what to control? In this section, we're first going to look at the decision of *what* to control in terms of when control takes place. Then, we're going to discuss some different areas in which managers might choose to establish controls.

When Does Control Take Place?

Management can implement controls *before* an activity commences, *during* the activity, or *after* the activity has been completed. The first type is called feedforward control, the second is concurrent control, and the last is feedback control (see Exhibit 14–5).

WHAT IS FEEDFORWARD CONTROL?   The most desirable type of control—**feedforward control**—prevents problems because it takes place before the actual activity.[19] For instance, when McDonald's began doing business in Moscow, it sent company quality control experts to help Russian farmers learn techniques for growing high-quality potatoes and to help bakers learn processes for baking high-quality breads. Why? McDonald's demands consistent product quality no matter the geographical location. They want french fries in Moscow to taste like those in Omaha. Still another example of feedforward control is the scheduled preventive maintenance programs on aircraft done by the major airlines. These schedules are designed to detect and hopefully to prevent structural damage that might lead to an accident.

feedforward control
Control that takes place before a work activity is done

Exhibit 14–5 "When" Does Control Take Place?

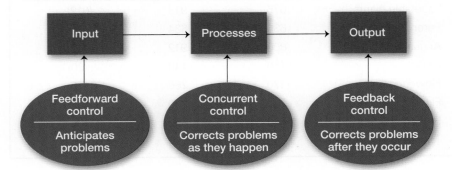

The key to feedforward controls is taking managerial action *before* a problem occurs. That way, problems can be prevented rather than having to correct them after any damage—poor-quality products, lost customers, lost revenue, etc.—has already been done. However, these controls require timely and accurate information that isn't always easy to get. Thus, managers frequently end up using the other two types of control.

WHEN IS CONCURRENT CONTROL USED? **Concurrent control**, as its name implies, takes place while a work activity is in progress. For instance, the director of business product management at Google and his team keep a watchful eye on one of Google's most profitable businesses—online ads. They watch "the number of searches and clicks, the rate at which users click on ads, the revenue this generates—everything is tracked hour by hour, compared with the data from a week earlier and charted."[20] If they see something that's not working particularly well, they fine-tune it.

Elaine Thompson/AP Images

Microsoft uses concurrent control to track its energy usage. Shown here at its operations center, control technician Ray Nichols monitors real-time data on heating, cooling, and other systems in the company's buildings that will help Microsoft achieve its goals of improving its carbon footprint and reducing its impact on the environment.

Fifty-five percent of employees say that micromanaging decreases their productivity.[21]

Technical equipment (such as computers and computerized machine controls) can be designed to include concurrent controls. For example, you've probably experienced this with word-processing software that alerts you to a misspelled word or incorrect grammatical usage. Also, many organizational quality programs rely on concurrent controls to inform workers whether their work output is of sufficient quality to meet standards.

The best-known form of concurrent control, however, is direct supervision. For example, Nvidia's CEO Jen-Hsun Huang had his office cubicle torn down and replaced with a conference table so he's now available to employees at all times to discuss what's going on.[22] All managers can benefit from using concurrent control because they can correct problems before they become too costly. MBWA, described earlier in this chapter, is a great way for managers to do this.

WHY IS FEEDBACK CONTROL SO POPULAR? The most popular type of control relies on feedback. In **feedback control**, the control takes place *after* the activity is done. For instance, remember our earlier Denver Mint example. The flawed Wisconsin quarters were discovered with feedback control. The damage had already occurred even though the organization corrected the problem once it was discovered. And that's the major problem with this type of control. By the time a manager has the information, the problems have already occurred, leading to waste or damage. However, in many work areas—the financial area being one example—feedback is the only viable type of control.

Managers should **develop goals for each of the four areas** and **then measure whether goals are being met**.

Feedback controls do have two advantages.[23] First, feedback gives managers meaningful information on how effective their planning efforts were. Feedback that shows little variance between standard and actual performance indicates that the planning was generally on target. If the deviation is significant, a manager can use that information to formulate new plans. Second, feedback can enhance motivation. People want to know how well they're doing, and feedback provides that information.

concurrent control
Control that takes place while a work activity is in progress

feedback control
Control that takes place after a work activity is done

KEEPING TRACK: What Gets Controlled?

Countless activities are taking place in different organizational locations and functional areas!

1 Keeping Track of an Organization's Finances

Want to earn a profit?
You need financial controls!

Traditional financial controls include:

- **Ratio analysis.** (See Exhibit 14–6.) Ratios are calculated using selected information from the organization's balance sheet and income statement.

Ekaterina Semenova/Fotolia

Exhibit 14–6 Popular Financial Ratios

OBJECTIVE	RATIO	CALCULATION	MEANING
Liquidity ratios: measure an organization's ability to meet its current debt obligations	Current ratio	$\dfrac{\text{Current assets}}{\text{Current liabilities}}$	Tests the organization's ability to meet short-term obligations
	Acid test	$\dfrac{\text{Current assets} - \text{Inventories}}{\text{Current liabilities}}$	Tests liquidity more accurately when inventories turn over slowly or are difficult to sell
Leverage ratios: examine the organization's use of debt to finance its assets and whether it's able to meet the interest payments on the debt	Debt to assets	$\dfrac{\text{Total debt}}{\text{Total assets}}$	The higher the ratio, the more leveraged the organization
	Times interest earned	$\dfrac{\text{Profits before interest and taxes}}{\text{Total interest charges}}$	Measures how many times the organization is able to cover its interest expenses
Activity ratios: assess how efficiently a company is using its assets	Inventory turnover	$\dfrac{\text{Sales}}{\text{Inventory}}$	The higher the ratio, the more efficiently inventory assets are being used
	Total asset turnover	$\dfrac{\text{Sales}}{\text{Total assets}}$	The fewer assets used to achieve a given level of sales, the more efficiently management is using the organization's total assets
Profitability ratios: measure how efficiently and effectively the company is using its assets to generate profits	Profit margin on sales	$\dfrac{\text{Net profit after taxes}}{\text{Total sales}}$	Identifies the profits that are being generated
	Return on investment	$\dfrac{\text{Net profit after taxes}}{\text{Total assets}}$	Measures the efficiency of assets to generate profits

- **Budget analysis.** Budgets are used for both planning and controlling.
  - ■ **Planning tool:** indicates which work activities are important and what and how much resources should be allocated to those activities.
  - ■ **Controlling tool:** provides managers with quantitative standards against which to measure and compare resource consumption. Significant deviations require action and a manager to examine what has happened and why and then take necessary action.

2 Keeping Track of Organization's Information

Ⓐ Information—*a critical tool for controlling other organizational activities*

(WHY) Managers need **RIGHT INFORMATION** at the **RIGHT TIME** and in the **RIGHT AMOUNT** to help them monitor and measure organizational activities:

- about what is happening within their area of responsibility.

- about the standards in order to be able to compare actual performance with the standard.

- to help them determine if deviations are acceptable.

- to help them develop appropriate courses of action.

Morena/Shutterstock

Information is important!

(HOW) A **management information system (MIS)**

Dusit/Shutterstock

- Can be manual or computer-based, although most organizational MIS are computer-supported applications.

- System in MIS implies order, arrangement, and purpose.

- Focuses specifically on providing managers with information (processed and analyzed data), not merely data (raw, unanalyzed facts).

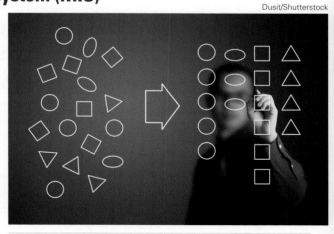

management information system (MIS)
A system used to provide management with needed information on a regular basis

B Information—*an organizational resource that needs controlling*

> **In 2017**—79,700 reported security incidents and 2,122 confirmed data breaches.[24]

- Information is critically important to everything an organization does—that information needs to be protected.

  - **Controls:** data encryption, system firewalls, data backups, and other techniques.[25]

  - Look for problems in places that might not even have been considered, like search engines.

  - Equipment such as laptop computers, tablets, and even RFID (radio-frequency identification) tags are vulnerable to viruses and hacking.

  - Monitor information controls regularly to ensure that all possible precautions are in place to protect important information.

Bedrin/Shutterstock

---

3 Keeping Track of Employee Performance

- Are employees doing their jobs as planned and meeting goals that have been set?

- If not, employee counseling or employee discipline may be needed.
  See p. 300 in Chapter 8.

Over 81 percent of managers say they don't do very well at giving difficult feedback.[26]

Mike Charles/Shutterstock

4 Keeping Track Using a Balanced Scorecard Approach

Balanced scorecard approach looks at more than the financial perspective[27] by typically looking at four areas that contribute to a company's performance:

❶ Financial

❷ Customer

❸ Internal processes

❹ People/innovation/ growth assets

Andriy Popov/Alamy Stock Photo

Managers should: **develop goals for each of the four areas** and **then measure whether goals are being met**.

balanced scorecard
A performance measurement tool that looks at more than just the financial perspective

What Contemporary Control Issues Do Managers Confront?

14-4 Discuss contemporary issues in control.

The employees of Integrated Information Systems Inc. didn't think twice about exchanging digital music over a dedicated office server they had set up. Like office betting on college and pro sports, it was technically illegal, but harmless—or so they thought. But after the company had to pay a $1 million settlement to the Recording Industry Association of America, managers wished they had controlled the situation better.[28] Control is an important managerial function. We're going to look at two control issues that managers face today: cross-cultural differences and workplace concerns.

Do Controls Need to Be Adjusted for Cultural Differences?

The concepts of control that we've discussed are appropriate for organizational units that aren't geographically distant or culturally distinct. But what about global organizations? Would control systems be different, and what should managers know about adjusting controls for national differences?

Methods of controlling employee behavior and operations can be quite different in different countries. In fact, the differences in organizational control systems of global organizations are primarily in the measurement and corrective action steps of the control process. In a global corporation, for instance, managers of foreign operations tend not to be closely controlled by the home office if for no other reason than that distance keeps managers from being able to observe work directly. Because distance creates a tendency for formalized controls, the home office of a global company often relies on extensive, formal reports for control. The global company may also use information technology to control work activities. For instance, Seven and i Holdings (Japan's biggest retail conglomerate and parent company of the 7-Eleven convenience store chain in the United States) uses automated cash registers not only to record sales and monitor inventory, but also to schedule tasks for store managers and to track their use of the built-in analytical graphs and forecasts. If managers don't use them enough, they're told to increase their activities.[29]

Technology's impact on control is most evident in comparisons of technologically advanced nations with countries that aren't as technologically advanced. Organizations in technologically advanced nations such as the United States, Japan, Canada, Great Britain, Germany, and Australia use indirect control devices—particularly computer-related reports and analyses—in addition to standardized rules and direct supervision to ensure that activities are going as planned. In less technologically advanced countries, direct supervision and highly centralized decision making are the basic means of control.

Also, constraints on what corrective action managers can take may affect managers in foreign countries because laws in some countries do not allow managers the option of closing facilities, laying off employees, or bringing in a new management team from outside the country. Finally, another challenge for global companies in collecting data is comparability. For instance, a company's manufacturing facility in Mexico might produce the same products as a facility in Scotland. However, the Mexican facility might be much more labor intensive than its Scottish counterpart (to take advantage of lower labor costs in Mexico). If top-level executives were to control costs by, for example, calculating labor costs per unit or output per worker, the figures would not be comparable. Managers in global companies must address these types of global control challenges.

These African railway attendants prepare to greet guests at the opening ceremony for a Chinese-built electric high-speed railway that connects Ethiopia and Djibouti. The technologically advanced Chinese staff who will initially manage the railway need to adjust their controls for cultural differences as they train local African counterparts how to operate and manage the rail system.

Qin bin/AP Images

Managing Technology in Today's Workplace
MONITORING EMPLOYEES

Technological advances have made the process of managing an organization much easier.[30] And technological advancements have also provided employers a means of sophisticated employee monitoring. Although most of this monitoring is designed to enhance worker productivity, it could, and has been, a source of concern over worker privacy. These advantages bring with them difficult questions regarding what managers have the right to know about employees and how far they can go in controlling employee behavior, both on and off the job. Consider the following:

- The mayor of Colorado Springs, Colorado, reads the e-mail messages that city council members send to each other from their homes. He defended his actions by saying he was making sure that e-mails to each other were not being used to circumvent the state's "open meeting" law that requires most council business to be conducted publicly.

- The U.S. Internal Revenue Service's internal audit group monitors a computer log that shows employee access to taxpayers' accounts. This monitoring activity allows management to check and see what employees are doing on their computers.

- American Express has an elaborate system for monitoring telephone calls. Daily reports provided to supervisors detail the frequency and length of calls made by employees, as well as how quickly incoming calls are answered.

- Employers in several organizations require employees to wear badges at all times while on company premises. These badges contain a variety of data that allow employees to enter certain locations in the organization. Smart badges, too, can transmit where the employee is at all times!

Just how much control a company should have over the private lives of its employees also becomes an issue. Where should an employer's rules and controls end? Does the boss have the right to dictate what you do on your free time and in your own home? Could your boss keep you from engaging in riding a motorcycle, skydiving, smoking, drinking alcohol, or eating junk food? Again, the answers may surprise you. Today many organizations, in their quest to control safety and health insurance costs, are delving into their employees' private lives.

Although controlling employees' behaviors on and off the job may appear unjust or unfair, nothing in our legal system prevents employers from engaging in these practices. Rather, the law is based on the premise that if employees don't like the rules, they have the option of quitting. Managers, too, typically defend their actions in terms of ensuring quality, productivity, and proper employee behavior. For instance, an IRS audit of its southeastern regional offices found that 166 employees took unauthorized looks at the tax returns of friends, neighbors, and celebrities.

Discussion Questions:

5 When does management's need for information about employee performance cross over the line and interfere with a worker's right to privacy?

6 Is any action by management acceptable as long as employees are notified ahead of time that they will be monitored? Discuss.

What Challenges Do Managers Face in Controlling the Workplace?

Today's workplaces present considerable control challenges for managers. From monitoring employees' computer usage at work to protecting the workplace against disgruntled employees intent on doing harm, managers need controls to ensure that work can be done efficiently and effectively as planned.

> Sixty-eight percent of employees admit to using company computers to check personal e-mail.[31]

IS MY WORK COMPUTER REALLY MINE?   If you work, do you think you have a right to privacy at your job? What can your employer find out about you and your work? You might be surprised at the answers! Employers can (and do), among other things, read your e-mail (even those marked "personal or confidential"), tap your telephone, monitor your work by computer, store and review computer files, monitor you in an employee bathroom or dressing room, and track your whereabouts in a company vehicle. And these actions aren't that uncommon. In fact, some 30 percent of companies have fired workers for misusing the Internet and another 28 percent have terminated workers for e-mail misuse.[32]

Charles Trainor Jr./Miami Herald/MCT/Newscom

At Citrix, a provider of virtualization, networking, and cloud technologies for businesses, employees are allowed to BYOD—bring your own device. Although more companies are adopting BYOD policies, the control risks are still very much the same. Even in a BYOD environment, workplace monitoring policies are very much needed.

Why do managers feel they need to monitor what employees are doing? A big reason is that employees are hired to work, not to surf the Web checking stock prices, watching online videos, playing fantasy baseball, or shopping for presents for family or friends. Recreational on-the-job Web surfing is thought to cost billions of dollars in lost work productivity annually. In fact, a survey of U.S. employers said that 87 percent of employees look at non-work-related websites while at work, and more than half engage in personal website surfing every day.[33] Watching online video has become an increasingly serious problem not only because of the time being wasted by employees, but also because it clogs already-strained corporate computer networks.[34] If you had to guess the video site viewed most often at work, what would you guess? If you said YouTube, you'd be absolutely correct![35] However, as innocent as it may seem (after all, it may be just a 30-second video), all this nonwork adds up to significant costs to businesses.

Another reason that managers monitor employee e-mail and computer usage is that they don't want to risk being sued for creating a hostile workplace environment because of offensive messages or an inappropriate image displayed on a coworker's computer screen. Concerns about racial or sexual harassment are one reason companies might want to monitor or keep backup copies of all e-mail. Electronic records can help establish what actually happened so managers can react quickly.[36]

Finally, managers want to ensure that company secrets aren't being leaked.[37] In addition to typical e-mail and computer usage, companies are monitoring instant messaging, blogs, and other social media outlets and are banning phone cameras in the office. Managers need to be certain that employees are not, even inadvertently, passing information on to others who could use that information to harm the company.

Because of the potentially serious costs and given the fact that many jobs now entail computers, many companies have workplace monitoring policies. Such policies should control employee behavior in a nondemeaning way, and employees should be informed about those policies.

IS EMPLOYEE THEFT ON THE RISE? Would you be surprised to find that up to 85 percent of all organizational theft and fraud is committed by employees, not outsiders?[38] And it's a costly problem—estimated to be about $4,500 per worker per year.[39] In a survey of U.S. companies, 20 percent said that workplace theft has become a moderate to very big problem.[40]

Employee theft is defined as any unauthorized taking of company property by employees for their personal use.[41] It can range from embezzlement to fraudulent filing of expense reports to removing equipment, parts, software, or office supplies from company premises. Although retail businesses have long faced serious potential losses from employee theft, loose financial controls at startups and small companies and the ready availability of information technology have made employee stealing an escalating problem in all kinds and sizes of organizations. It's a control issue that managers need to educate themselves about and be prepared to deal with it.[42]

employee theft
Any unauthorized taking of company property by employees for their personal use

Global employee fraud is estimated to cost organizations $3.7 trillion a year.[43]

Why do employees steal? The answer depends on whom you ask.[44] Experts in various fields—industrial security, criminology, clinical psychology—have different perspectives. The industrial security people propose that people steal because the opportunity presents itself through lax controls and favorable circumstances. Criminologists say that it's because people have financial-based pressures (such as personal financial problems) or vice-based pressures (such as gambling debts). And the clinical psychologists suggest that people steal because they can rationalize whatever they're doing as being correct and appropriate behavior ("everyone does it," "they had it coming," "this company makes enough money and they'll never miss anything this small," "I deserve this for all that I put up with," and so forth).[45] Although each approach provides compelling insights into employee theft and has been instrumental in attempts to deter it, unfortunately, employees continue to steal. What can managers do?

The concept of feedforward, concurrent, and feedback control is useful for identifying measures to deter or reduce employee theft.[46] Exhibit 14–7 summarizes several possible managerial actions.

WHAT CAN MANAGERS DO ABOUT WORKPLACE VIOLENCE? In January 2015, a cardiologist at Boston's Brigham and Women's Hospital was gunned down by a man whose mother had been operated on by the doctor and subsequently died. After killing the cardiologist, the man shot himself. In September 2014, a man who was recently fired walked into the UPS he had worked at and killed two individuals and then took his own life. In April 2014, an individual who worked as a baggage handler opened fire at a FedEx facility near Atlanta, injuring six employees. In August 2010, a driver about to lose his job at Hartford Distributors in Hartford, Connecticut, opened fire, killing eight other employees and himself. In July 2010, a former employee at a solar products manufacturer in Albuquerque, New Mexico, walked into the business and opened fire, killing two people

Exhibit 14–7 Controlling Employee Theft

FEEDFORWARD	CONCURRENT	FEEDBACK
Use careful prehiring screening.	Treat employees with respect and dignity.	Make sure employees know when theft or fraud has occurred—not naming names but letting people know this is not acceptable.
Establish specific policies defining theft and fraud and discipline procedures.	Openly communicate the costs of stealing.	Use the services of professional investigators.
Involve employees in writing policies.	Let employees know on a regular basis about their successes in preventing theft and fraud.	Redesign control measures.
Educate and train employees about the policies.	Use video surveillance equipment if conditions warrant.	Evaluate your organization's culture and the relationships of managers and employees.
Have a professional review of your internal security controls.	Install "lock-out" options on computers, telephones, and e-mail. Use corporate hotlines for reporting incidences. Set a good example.	

Source: Robbins, Stephen P., Coulter, Mary, *Management*, 13th Ed., © 2016, p. 541. Reprinted and electronically reproduced by permission of Pearson Education, Inc., New York, NY.

and wounding four others. On November 6, 2009, in Orlando, Florida, an engineer who had been dismissed from his job for poor performance returned and shot and killed one person while wounding five others. This incident happened only one day after a U.S. Army psychiatrist went on a shooting rampage at Fort Hood Army post, killing 13 and wounding 27.[47] These are just a few of the deadly workplace attacks in recent years. Is workplace violence really an issue for managers? Yes. Despite these examples, thankfully, the number of workplace shootings has decreased.[48] However, the U.S. National Institute of Occupational Safety and Health still says that each year, some 2 million American workers are victims of some form of workplace violence. In an average week, one employee is killed and at least 25 are seriously injured in violent assaults by current or former coworkers. And according to a Department of Labor survey, 58 percent of firms reported that managers received verbal threats from workers.[49] Anger, rage, and violence in the workplace are intimidating to coworkers and adversely affect their productivity. The annual cost to U.S. businesses is estimated to be between $20 billion and $35 billion.[50] And office rage isn't a uniquely American problem. A survey of aggressive behavior in Britain's workplaces found that 18 percent of managers say they have personally experienced harassment or verbal bullying, and 9 percent claim to have experienced physical attacks.[51]

What factors are believed to contribute to workplace violence? Undoubtedly, employee stress caused by job uncertainties, declining value of retirement accounts, long hours, information overload, other daily interruptions, unrealistic deadlines, and uncaring managers play a role. Even office layout designs with small cubicles where employees work amid the noise and commotion from those around them have been cited as contributing to the problem.[52] Other experts have described dangerously dysfunctional work environments characterized by the following as primary contributors to the problem:[53]

- Employee work driven by TNC (time, numbers, and crises)
- Rapid and unpredictable change where instability and uncertainty plague employees
- Destructive communication style where managers communicate in excessively aggressive, condescending, explosive, or passive-aggressive styles; excessive workplace teasing or scapegoating
- Authoritarian leadership with a rigid, militaristic mind-set of managers versus employees; employees not allowed to challenge ideas, participate in decision making, or engage in team-building efforts
- Defensive attitude with little or no performance feedback given; only numbers count; and yelling, intimidation, or avoidance as the preferred ways of handling conflict
- Double standards in terms of policies, procedures, and training opportunities for managers and employees
- Unresolved grievances due to an absence of mechanisms or only adversarial ones in place for resolving them; dysfunctional individuals protected or ignored because of long-standing rules, union contract provisions, or reluctance to take care of problems
- Emotionally troubled employees and no attempt by managers to get help for these people
- Repetitive, boring work and little chance for doing something else or for new people coming in
- Faulty or unsafe equipment or deficient training, which keeps employees from being able to work efficiently or effectively
- Hazardous work environment in terms of temperature, air quality, repetitive motions, overcrowded spaces, noise levels, excessive overtime, and so forth; to minimize costs, a failure to hire additional employees when workload becomes excessive, leading to potentially dangerous work expectations and conditions
- Culture of violence perpetuated by a history of individual violence or abuse, violent or explosive role models, or tolerance of on-the-job alcohol or drug abuse

Reading through this list, you surely hope that workplaces where you'll spend your professional life won't be like this. However, the competitive demands of succeeding in a 24/7 global economy put pressure on organizations and employees in many ways.

Exhibit 14–8 Controlling Workplace Violence

FEEDFORWARD	CONCURRENT	FEEDBACK
Ensure management's commitment to functional, not dysfunctional, work environments.	Use MBWA (managing by walking around) to identify potential problems; observe how employees treat and interact with each other.	Communicate openly about violent incidents and what's being done.
Provide employee assistance programs (EAPs) to help employees with behavioral problems.	Allow employees or work groups to "grieve" during periods of major organizational change.	Investigate incidents and take appropriate action.
Enforce organizational policy that any workplace rage, aggression, or violence will not be tolerated.	Be a good role model in how you treat others.	Review company policies and change, if necessary.
Use careful prehiring screening.	Use corporate hotlines or some other mechanism for reporting and investigating incidents.	
Never ignore threats.	Use quick and decisive intervention.	
Train employees about how to avoid danger if a situation arises.	Get expert professional assistance if violence erupts.	
Clearly communicate policies to employees.	Provide necessary equipment or procedures for dealing with violent situations (cell phones, alarm systems, code names or phrases, and so forth).	

Sources: Based on M. Gorkin, "Five Strategies and Structures for Reducing Workplace Violence," *Workforce Management Online,* December 3, 2000; "Investigating Workplace Violence: Where Do You Start?" *Workforce Management Online,* December 3, 2000; "Ten Tips on Recognizing and Minimizing Violence," *Workforce Management Online,* December 3, 2000; and "Points to Cover in a Workplace Violence Policy," *Workforce Management Online,* December 3, 2000.

What can managers do to deter or reduce possible workplace violence? Once again, the concept of feedforward, concurrent, and feedback control can help identify actions that managers can take.[54] Exhibit 14–8 summarizes several suggestions.

CHAPTER SUMMARY BY LEARNING OUTCOME

14-1 Explain the nature and importance of control.

Control is the management function that involves monitoring activities to ensure that they're being accomplished as planned and correcting any significant deviations.

As the final step in the management process, controlling provides the link back to planning. If managers didn't control, they'd have no way of knowing whether goals were being met.

Control is important because (1) it's the only way to know whether goals are being met and, if not, why; (2) it provides information and feedback so managers feel comfortable empowering employees; and (3) it helps protect an organization and its assets.

14-2 Describe the three steps in the control process.

The three steps in the control process are measuring, comparing, and taking action. Measuring involves deciding how to measure actual performance and what to measure. Comparing involves looking at the variation between actual performance and the standard (goal). Deviations outside an acceptable range of variation need attention.

Taking action can involve doing nothing, correcting the actual performance, or revising the standards. Doing nothing is self-explanatory. Correcting the actual performance can involve different corrective actions, which can either be immediate or basic. Standards can be revised by either raising or lowering them.

14-3 Discuss the types of controls organizations and managers use.

Feedforward controls take place before a work activity is done. Concurrent controls take place while a work activity is being done. Feedback controls take place after a work activity is done.

Financial controls that managers can use include financial ratios (liquidity, leverage, activity, and profitability) and budgets. One information control managers can use is an MIS, which provides managers with needed information on a regular basis. Others include comprehensive and secure controls, such as data encryption, system firewalls, data backups, and so forth, that protect the organization's information. Also, balanced scorecards provide a way to evaluate an organization's performance in four different areas rather than just from the financial perspective.

14-4 Discuss contemporary issues in control.

Adjusting controls for cross-cultural differences may be necessary, primarily in the areas of measuring and taking corrective actions.

Workplace concerns include workplace privacy, employee theft, and workplace violence. For each of these, managers need to have policies in place to control inappropriate actions and ensure that work is getting done efficiently and effectively.

DISCUSSION QUESTIONS

14-1 What is the role of control in management?

14-2 Describe four methods managers can use to acquire information about actual work performance.

14-3 Planning and controlling are the opposite sides of the same coin. Do you think this statement is true at all levels of the organizational hierarchy? Why or why not?

14-4 Contrast feedforward, concurrent, and feedback controls.

14-5 Feedback control is after the fact. Illustrate why its use may be perceived as a disadvantage for any organization.

14-6 In Chapter 5 we discussed the "white-water rapids" view of change. Do you think it's possible to establish and maintain effective standards and controls in this type of environment? Discuss.

14-7 Why is it that what is measured is more critical to the control process than how it is measured?

14-8 "Every individual employee in an organization plays a role in controlling work activities." Do you agree with this statement, or do you think control is something that only managers are responsible for? Explain.

14-9 What are some work activities in which the acceptable range of variation might be higher than average? What about lower than average? (*Hint:* Think in terms of the output from the work activities, whom it might affect, and how it might affect them.)

14-10 How could you use the concept of control in your personal life? Be specific. (Think in terms of feedforward, concurrent, and feedback controls as well as specific controls for the different aspects of your life—school, work, family relationships, friends, hobbies, etc.)

Applying: Getting Ready for the Workplace

Management Skill Builder | DISCIPLINING DIFFICULT EMPLOYEES

Almost all managers will, at one time or another, have to deal with employees who are difficult. There is no shortage of characteristics that can make someone difficult to work with. Some examples include being short-tempered, demanding, abusive, angry, defensive, complaining, intimidating, aggressive, narcissistic, arrogant, and rigid. Successful managers have learned how to cope with difficult people.

MyLab Management
PERSONAL INVENTORY ASSESSMENT

Go to **www.pearson.com/mylab/management** to complete the Personal Inventory Assessment related to this chapter.

Skill Basics

No single approach is always effective in dealing with difficult people. However, we can offer several suggestions that are likely to lessen the angst these people create in your life and may have some influence in reducing their difficult behavior.[55]

- *Don't let your emotions rule.* Our first response to a difficult person is often emotional. We get angry. We show frustration. We want to lash out at them or "get even" when we think they've insulted or demeaned us. This response is not likely to reduce your angst and may escalate the other person's negative behavior. So fight your natural tendencies and keep your cool. Stay rational and thoughtful. At worst, while this approach may not improve the situation, it is also unlikely to encourage and escalate the undesirable behavior.

- *Attempt to limit contact.* If possible, try to limit your contact with the difficult person. Avoid places where they hang out and limit nonrequired interactions. Also, use communication channels—like e-mail and text messaging—that minimize face-to-face contact and verbal intonations.

- *Try polite confrontation.* If you can't avoid the difficult person, consider standing up to them in a civil but firm manner. Let them know that you're aware of their behavior, that you find it unacceptable, and that you won't tolerate it. For people who are unaware of the effect their actions have on you, confrontation might awaken them to altering their behavior. For those who are acting purposefully, taking a clear stand might make them think twice about the consequences of their actions.

- *Practice positive reinforcement.* We know that positive reinforcement is a powerful tool for changing behavior. Rather than criticizing undesirable behavior, try reinforcing desirable behaviors with compliments or other positive comments. This focus will tend to weaken and reduce the exhibiting of the undesirable behaviors.

- *Recruit fellow victims and witnesses.* Finally, we know strength lies in numbers. If you can get others who are also offended by the difficult person to support your case, several positive things can happen. First, it's likely to lessen your frustrations because others will be confirming your perception and can offer support. Second, people in the organization with authority to reprimand are more likely to act when complaints are coming from multiple sources. And third, the difficult person is more likely to feel pressure to change when a group is speaking out against his or her specific behaviors than if the complaint is coming from a single source.

Practicing the Skill

Read through this scenario and follow the directions at the end of it:

Your career has progressed even faster than you thought possible. After graduating from college with an accounting degree, you passed your CPA exam and worked three years for a major accounting firm. Then you joined General Electric in its finance department. Two employers and four jobs later, you have just been hired by a *Fortune* 100 mining company as its vice president for finance. What you didn't expect in the new job was having to deal with Mark Hundley.

Mark is the vice president of company operations. He has been with the company for eight years. Your first impression of Mark was that he was a "know-it-all." He was quick to put you down and acted as if he was your superior rather than an equal. Based on comments you've heard around the offices, it seems you are not alone. Other executives all seemed to agree that Mark is a brilliant engineer and operations manager but very difficult to work with. Specific comments you've heard include "an abrasive attitude"; "talks down to people"; "arrogant"; "thinks everyone is stupid"; "poor listener."

In your short time in the new job, you've already had several run-ins with Mark. You've even talked to your boss, the company president, about him. The president's response wasn't surprising: "Mark isn't easy to deal with. But no one knows this company's operations like he does. If he ever leaves, I don't know how we'd replace him. But, that said, he gives me a lot of grief. Sometimes he makes me feel like I work for him rather than the other way around." Describe what you could do to improve your ability to work with Mark.

Experiential Exercise

In this Experiential Exercise, we're going to focus on some career dilemmas/advice as it relates to the control function. Read through the following list. Choose two that you're most interested in and come up with your response to each one. Then, after you've finished, get in your assigned group. Compare notes and discuss each person's answers. As a group, choose two of the shared answers that you'll share with the class.

(1) What would you do if you work for a boss who doesn't give you feedback?
(2) You're the boss. How will you give your employees constructive feedback?
(3) You get what you feel is an unfair performance review. What will you do next?
(4) You got blamed for your coworker's screw-up, what do you do now?
(5) You're the boss. How will you handle a problem employee?
(6) Your boss is a micromanager. How do you deal with/thrive with this kind of boss?
(7) You're the boss. One of your employees is terrible at managing her time. What do you do?

CASE APPLICATION #1

HealthyFast Food?

Topic: Control process, social responsibility

Non-GMO, organic, locally sourced…these terms are now a common part of our food vocabulary, although not typically associated with fast food. Chipotle entered the fast-food scene in the early 1990s with a seemingly impossible goal of creating a healthy fast-food alternative. Chipotle's promise of "food with integrity" includes fresh, locally sourced ingredients and naturally raised meats. They effectively met this promise for many years, but as the popular fast-food chain grew to more than 2,200 locations, the restaurant's ability to promise such quality while meeting food safety standards has become a challenge. Attempting to deliver on this promise on a national scale has created a complex and risky supply chain challenge.

Serving food with **integrity and safety!**

Chipotle's food contamination problems started with an *E. coli* outbreak in July 2015 in Seattle. Next was a norovirus outbreak in California, followed by a salmonella infection in Minnesota. Other foodborne illnesses emerged among Chipotle customers in nine more states. Over the course of a few months, more than 500 customers were sick from contaminated food in Chipotle stores across the country. Sales dropped 30 percent during the outbreak, and several stores closed for an extended period of time. The company's stock value dropped, and the company faced several lawsuits from customers who were sickened by food consumed at one of the stores.[56]

Most national fast-food restaurant chains control food quality by using a central source for ingredients, exposing the supply chain to fewer outside elements. Simply put, the more basic the food chain, the easier it is to control. To keep its fresh food promise, however, Chipotle sought to prepare as many foods as possible at the local stores. It also sourced ingredients locally wherever possible, creating relationships with hundreds of vendors. The complexity of its food sourcing, coupled with in-store food preparation, is most likely what caused the food contamination problem. There were no known specific negligent acts on the part of Chipotle; the problems occurred because offering fresh food on such a large scale creates a situation where quality control is difficult.

In most cases, Chipotle did not know which foods were contaminated, making the fix even more challenging. In response to the crisis, the company has implemented new controls to test for meat contamination and also changed some food-handling and preparation procedures. It has shifted much of its food preparation to centralized kitchens and started sourcing ingredients from fewer vendors, much like its fast-food competitors have done for years. To kick off its new standards, Chipotle closed all of its stores for an afternoon to train employees consistently on the new food-handling standards.[57] While it seems the company is moving in the right direction, critics suggest that a company that claims to focus so much on food quality should have done a better job focusing on food safety. The challenges for the company continue as it works to rebuild not only the company, but consumer trust. Meanwhile, founder and CEO Steve Ells has stepped away from the company he founded.[58] Under new management, it appears that the company's turnaround is working as it delivered better-than-expected sales numbers.

Discussion Questions

14-11 Why is it important for Chipotle to revise the company's food-handling and food supply standards?

14-12 Which controls would be more important to Chipotle: feedforward, concurrent, or feedback? Explain. Why is this level of managerial controls necessary?

14-13 How can Chipotle make sure that employees are following the new food-handling standards?

14-14 Explain the statement: "The more basic the food chain, the easier it is to control." Is there any managerial advice on control here? Explain.

14-15 What roles do social responsibility and ethical behavior play in ensuring that controls are appropriate and working?

CASE APPLICATION #2

If You Can't Say Something Nice, Don't Say Anything at All
Topic: Employee performance controls

Controlling employee performance is a vitally important responsibility of managers. After all, it's your employees who are working to accomplish established goals, and you want to see that those goals are being accomplished as planned. So wouldn't it seem that managing employees' performance would cover the good and the not-so-good? Well, some organizations are encouraging managers to lighten up on the harsh feedback and focus only on the positive.[59]

At consulting firm the Boston Consulting Group, managers now frequently praise employees, encourage them to celebrate even small victories, and conduct performance reviews focusing on an individual employee's strengths instead of

No Negativism Allowed!

any mistakes that may have happened. And managers are to bring up only one or two areas that require improvement and development. It never used to be this way. When employees didn't do a good job with a client's assignment, managers would focus on what went wrong and where and how the employee needed to improve and develop his or her skills. This shift toward more positive feedback occurred after the company noticed some employees leaving the company and other employees who were still upset for a period of time after a negative performance review. And BCG isn't the only company taking this approach. Others are increasing the use of positive feedback and minimizing any discussion of the areas that need improvement. At PricewaterhouseCoopers LLP, for instance, managers are asked to have discussions with employees about their future with the organization.

These "career outlook" discussions focus more on where an employee fits in, rather than on where they screwed up. The company also encourages its staff to send shout-outs via e-cards praising colleagues or subordinates for work done. Managers have also allocated money to further reward positive accomplishments.

But there are companies not following this positivism trend. These companies take a more "tough-love" approach and don't shy away from giving negative feedback. For instance, at Netflix, CEO Reed Hasting's view is that they're a "pro sports team, not a Little League squad," noting that "adequate performance gets a generous severance package." Not everyone in the company is going to get a trophy. There's little doubt as to what that company's performance expectations are.

Discussion Questions

14-16 Is controlling employee performance an important responsibility of managers? Discuss.

14-17 Should managers focus only on positive feedback? Explain.

14-18 What are the risks associated with providing employees only positive feedback and providing limited feedback on areas of improvement?

14-19 Where would you be more comfortable? An organization with a performance review approach more like the Boston Consulting Group or more like Netflix? Make a list of the pros and cons of both approaches before you make your choice. What career advice could you take away from this?

CASE APPLICATION #3

Goals and Controls
Topic: Role of goals in controlling, control process, efficiency and effectiveness

Tesla. Elon Musk. You've probably heard of both. Tesla was founded in 2003 by a group of engineers who wanted to prove that buyers didn't need to compromise looks and performance to drive electric—that electric cars

could be "better, quicker, and more fun to drive than gasoline cars."[60] Musk was not part of that original group but led the company's Series A investment (the name typically given to a company's first round of venture capital financing) and joined

Tesla's board of directors as chairman. He soon took an active role in the company and oversaw the design of Tesla's first car, the Roadster, which was launched in 2008. Next came the Model S, introduced in 2012 as the world's first premium all-electric sedan. The next product line expansion was the Model X in 2015, a sport utility vehicle, which achieved a 5-star safety rating from the National Highway Safety Administration. The Model 3 was introduced in 2016 and production began in 2017. From the beginning, Musk has maintained that Tesla's long-term strategic goal was to create affordable mass-market electric vehicles. And the Model 3 was intended to be that product. It represents Tesla's first attempt at manufacturing a mass-market car.[61] The company is, thus, at a critical juncture in its history…a make-or-break moment. And things aren't looking so good right now.

How hard can it be to make a car?

The company's long-term production goal was to increase production to 500,000 vehicles a year by 2018. Tesla's vehicles are produced at its Giga Factory in Fremont, California, as are most of its vehicles' components. Inside the factory, 1,068 robots weld, glue, or rivet parts together for the Model 3 sedans.[62] In April 2018, Tesla produced only 2,270 Model 3s, a far cry from the 5,000 cars a week that was its original goal for the end of 2017. So far, as of April 2018, only a total of 8,810 Model 3s have been delivered to customers since the beginning of the year. And there are 500,000 customers who have backorders on the car. During the first and second quarters of 2018, the company had to halt production to update some of its manufacturing lines. Musk himself says that the Model 3 is mired in what he calls "production hell."[63] A critical bottleneck? The production of batteries, which are made at its battery factory in Nevada.[64] It takes seven hours to product a battery pack. That's an eternity in an industry where production lines need to run continuously or risk burning through tons of cash. Musk sat down with workers and engineers, who had been discussing solutions for months, and worked to slash production time to 70 minutes. How? By completely reordering the flow of battery assembly.

So what's going on with the company's production processes? The company says that these downtimes are "planned" in that it gives company employees time to improve the automation and methodically tackle bottlenecks in order to increase production rates.[65] Tesla employs its own version of the Japanese principle of "kaizen" or "continuous improvement—something it calls 'continual disapproval' of its processes as it

looks for ways to be more efficient and effective."[66] However, although such adjustments and temporary shutdowns are nothing new in the automotive industry, Tesla is fighting to make a name for itself and production mishaps like this don't help that situation at all. One industry expert says that although Tesla may be a "pioneer in technology and a trailblazer in the electric vehicle market," those strategic capabilities and core competencies don't necessarily translate to knowledge of the manufacturing process.[67] Scaling up production has its own unique set of challenges, as Tesla and Musk are discovering. In addition to the production challenges, there's a financial roadblock. The company is burning through cash as it works through its production struggles. Other financial measures—including net working capital, market value of company stock, credit rating, and free cash flow—are also deteriorating.[68] Another challenge for Tesla is that two top key executives have "stepped away from" the company as it works to boost production of the Model 3.[69] One of those executives, according to a company spokesperson, is taking six weeks off to recharge and spend time with his family. The other executive has joined self-driving car company Waymo.

Epilogue: Tesla employees at the Fremont production facility met the 5,000 cars a week production goal the last week of June 2018…the final week of the second quarter. However, analysts now say that the true test is whether Tesla can maintain that aggressive rate without sacrificing quality.[70]

Discussion Questions

14-20 What type (or types) of control—feedforward, concurrent, or feedback—do you think would be helpful in this situation? Explain your choice.

14-21 Using Exhibit 14–2, discuss if and how this production nightmare could have been prevented.

14-22 Could Tesla's controls have been more effective? How? What about its goals? How?

14-23 In the text's first chapter, we introduced the concept of efficiency and effectiveness and how it's important to managers. Here in this story in the last chapter, we see how efficiency and effectiveness continue to be important to managers. Explain how.

14-24 Write an executive summary explaining what role information controls and financial controls could have played in this situation. What other controls do you think might have been useful?

Endnotes

1. P. Karasz, "After Technical Chaos, British Airways Looks to Restore Schedule," *New York Times Online*, May 29, 2017.
2. "Domino's Delivered Free Pizzas," *Springfield, Missouri News-Leader*, April 3, 2009, p. 3B.
3. B. Hagenbaugh, "State Quarters Extra Leaf Grew Out of Lunch Break," *USA Today*, January 20, 2006, 1B.
4. A. Pasztor, "Northrop Addresses Lapses," *Wall Street Journal*, March 31/April 1, 2018, p. B3.
5. E. Paton, "H&M, a Fashion Giant, Has a Problem: $4.3 Billion in Unsold Clothes," *New York Times Online*, March 27, 2018.
6. Reuters, "McDonald's Japan Apologizes after Tooth, Plastic Found in Food," *New York Times Online*, January 7, 2015.
7. C. Jasper, E. Pfanner, L. Patton, and R. Weiss, "At KFC, A Bucketful of Trouble," *Bloomberg BusinessWeek*, March 5, 2018, pp. 20–21.
8. R. McMillan, "Hack of Saudi Plant Targeted Safety System," *Wall Street Journal*, January 19, 2018, p. B4.
9. A. Mandell, "Academy Will Keep Accounting Firm PwC for Next Oscars," *USA Today-Springfield, Missouri News-Leader*, March 30, 2017, p. 7B.
10. B. Horovitz, "Gross Photo with Wendy's Frosty Is Latest to Go Viral," *USA Today*, June 14, 2013, p. 2B; and S. Clifford, "Video Prank at Domino's Taints Brand," *New York Times Online*, April 16, 2009.
11. SmartPulse, "Where Does the Biggest Threat to Your Organizations Come From?" www.smartbrief.com/leadership, May 12, 2015.
12. J. F. Van Niekerk and R. Von Solms, "Information Security Culture: A Management Perspective," *Computers & Security*, June 2010, pp. 476–86; T. Vinas and J. Jusko, "5 Threats That Could Sink Your Company," *Industry Week*, September 2004, pp. 52–61; "Workplace Security: How Vulnerable Are You?" special section in *Wall Street Journal*, September 29, 2003, pp. R1–R8; P. Magnusson, "Your Jitters Are Their Lifeblood," *Business Week*, April 14, 2003, p. 41; and T. Purdum, "Preparing for the Worst," *Industry Week*, January 2003, pp. 53–55.
13. A. Dalton, "Rapid Recovery," *Industry Week*, March 2005, pp. 70–71.
14. L. Dishman, "This New Platform Lets Your Coworkers Rate You Whether You Like It or Not," *Fast Company Online*, May 2, 2017.
15. B. Nelson, "Long-Distance Recognition," *Workforce*, August 2000, 50–52.
16. D. Auerbach, "Watch for Workplace Productivity Killers," *Springfield, Missouri, News-Leader*, July 13, 2014, p. 1G.
17. S. Kerr, "On the Folly of Rewarding A, While Hoping for B," *Academy of Management Journal*, December 1975, pp. 769–83; and N. F. Piercy, D. W. Cravens, N. Lane, and D. W. Vorhies, "Driving Organizational Citizenship Behaviors and Salesperson In-Role Behavior Performance: The Role of Management Control and Perceived Organizational Support," *Journal of the Academy of Marketing Science*, Spring 2006, pp. 244–62.
18. Classic Concepts in Today's Workplace box based on H. Min and H. Min, "Benchmarking the Service Quality of Fast-Food Restaurant Franchises in the USA," *Benchmarking: An International Journal*, April 2011, pp. 282–300; R. Pear, "A.M.A. to Develop Measure of Quality of Medical Care," *New York Times Online*, February 21, 2006; A. Taylor III, "Double Duty," *Fortune*, March 7, 2005, pp. 104–10; C. Bogan and D. Callahan, "Benchmarking in Rapid Time," *Industrial Management*, March–April 2001, pp. 28–33; and L. D. McNary, "Thinking about Excellence and Benchmarking," *Journal for Quality and Participation*, July–August 1994.
19. H. Koontz and R. W. Bradspies, "Managing through Feedforward Control," *Business Horizons*, June 1972, pp. 25–36.
20. M. Helft, "The Human Hands behind the Google Money Machine," *New York Times Online*, June 2, 2008.
21. J. Yang and S. Music, "Micromanaging," *USA Today*, August 8, 2014, 1B.
22. B. Caulfield, "Shoot to Kill," *Forbes*, January 7, 2008, pp. 92–96.
23. W. H. Newman, *Constructive Control: Design and Use of Control Systems* (Upper Saddle River, NJ: Prentice Hall, 1975), 33.
24. 2015 Data Breach Investigations Report, http://www.verizonenterprise.com/DBIR/2015/, May 31, 2015.
25. B. Grow, K. Epstein, and C.-C. Tschang, "The New E-Spionage Threat," *Business Week*, April 21, 2008, pp. 32–41; S. Leibs, "Firewall of Silence," *CFO*, April 2008, pp. 31–35; J. Pereira, "How Credit-Card Data Went out Wireless Door," *Wall Street Journal*, May 4, 2007, pp. A1+; and B. Stone, "Firms Fret as Office E-Mail Jumps Security Walls," *New York Times Online*, January 11, 2007.
26. SmartPulse, "How Well Do You Give Difficult Feedback?" Smart Brief on Leadership, www.smartbrief.`com/leadership, December 3, 2014.
27. E. R. Iselin, J. Sands, and L. Mia, "Multi-Perspective Performance Reporting Systems, Continuous Improvement Systems, and Organizational Performance," *Journal of General Management*, Spring 2011, pp. 19–36; L. Elmore, "The Balanced Business," *Women in Business*, Spring 2011, pp. 14–16; D. Agostino and M. Arnaboldi, "How the BSC Implementation Process Shapes Its Outcome," *International Journal of Productivity & Performance Management*, January 2011, pp. 99–114; R. S. Kaplan and D. P. Norton, "How to Implement a New Strategy without Disrupting Your Organization," *Harvard Business Review*, March 2006, pp. 100–09; L. Bassi and D. McMurrer, "Developing Measurement Systems for Managers in the Knowledge Era," *Organizational Dynamics*, May 2005, pp. 185–96; G. M. J. DeKoning, "Making the Balanced Scorecard Work (Part 1)," *Gallup Brain*, July 8, 2004, www.brain.gallup.com; G. M. J. DeKoning, "Making the Balanced Scorecard Work (Part 2)," *Gallup Brain*, August 12, 2004, www.brain.gallup.com; K. Graham, "Balanced Scorecard," *New Zealand Management*, March 2003, pp. 32–34; K. Ellis, "A Ticket to Ride: Balanced Scorecard," *Training*, April 2001, p. 50; and T. Leahy, "Tailoring the Balanced Scorecard," *Business Finance*, August 2000, pp. 53–56.
28. J. Yaukey and C. L. Romero, "Arizona Firm Pays Big for Workers' Digital Downloads," *Associated Press, Springfield, Missouri, News-Leader*, May 6, 2002, p. 6B.
29. Information on *Hoovers Online*, June 17, 2011, www.hoovers.com; and N. Shirouzu and J. Bigness, "7-Eleven Operators Resist System to Monitor Managers," *Wall Street Journal*, June 16, 1997, p. B1.
30. Managing Technology in Today's Workplace box based on C. A. Ciocchetti, "The Eavesdropping Employer: A Twenty-First-Framework for Employee Monitoring," *American Business Law Journal*, Summer 2011, pp. 285–369; G. M. Amsler, H. M. Findley, and E. Ingram, "Performance Monitoring: Guidance for the Modern Workplace," *Supervision*, January 2011, pp. 16–22; T. Harbert, "When IT Is Asked to Spy," *ComputerWorld Online*, October 11, 2010; D. Searcey, "Employers Watching Workers Online Spurs Privacy Debate," *Wall Street Journal*, April 23, 2009, p. A13; D. Darlin, "Software That Monitors Your Work, Wherever You Are," *New York Times Online*, April 12, 2009; S. Boehle, "They're Watching You," *Training*, September 2008, pp. 23+; S. Shellenbarger, "Work at Home? Your Employer May Be Watching You," *Wall Street Journal*, July 30, 2008, pp. D1+; J. Jusko, "A Watchful Eye," *Industry Week*, May 7, 2001, p. 9; "Big Brother Boss," *U.S. News and World Report*, April 30, 2001, p. 12; and L. Guernsey, "You've Got Inappropriate E-Mail," *New York Times*, April 5, 2000, pp. C1+.
31. A. R. Carey and P. Trap, "Wasting Work Time Online?" *USA Today*, October 18, 2014, p. 1A.
32. "2007 Electronic Monitoring & Surveillance Survey," *American Management Association*, www.amanet.org.
33. S. Armour, "Companies Keep an Eye on Workers' Internet Use," *USA Today*, February 21, 2006, p. 2B.
34. B. White, "The New Workplace Rules: No Video-Watching," *Wall Street Journal*, March 4, 2008, pp. B1+.
35. Ibid.
36. N. Lugaresi, "Electronic Privacy in the Workplace: Transparency and Responsibility," *International Review of Law, Computers, & Technology*, July 2010, pp. 163–73; P.-W. Tam, E. White, N. Wingfield, and K. Maher, "Snooping E-Mail by Software Is Now a Workplace Norm," *Wall Street Journal*, March 9, 2005, pp. B1+; D. Hawkins, "Lawsuits Spur Rise in Employee Monitoring," *U.S. News & World Report*, August 13, 2001, p. 53; and Guernsey, "You've Got Inappropriate Mail."
37. S. Armour, "More Companies Keep Track of Workers' E-Mail," *USA Today*, June 13, 2005, 4B; and E. Bott, "Are You Safe? Privacy Special Report," *PC Computing*, March 2000, pp. 87–88.
38. A. M. Bell and D. M. Smith, "Theft and Fraud May Be an Inside Job," *Workforce Online*, www.workforce.com (December 3, 2000).
39. C. C. Verschoor, "New Evidence of Benefits from Effective Ethics Systems," *Strategic Finance*, May 2003, pp. 20–21; and E. Krell, "Will Forensic Accounting Go Mainstream?" *Business Finance*, October 2002, pp. 30–34.
40. B. Mirza, "Combat Costly Discrimination, Employee Fraud, Theft," *HR Magazine*, February 2011, p. 14; and S. E. Needleman, "Businesses Say Theft by Their Workers Is Up," *Wall Street Journal*, December 11, 2008, p. B8.
41. J. Greenberg, "The STEAL Motive: Managing the Social

Determinants of Employee Theft," in R. Giacalone and J. Greenberg (eds.), *Antisocial Behavior in Organizations* (Newbury Park, CA: Sage, 1997), pp. 85–108.

42. M. S. Hershcovis, "Incivility, Social Undermining, Bullying... Oh My! A Call to Reconcile Constructs within Workplace Aggression Research," *Journal of Organizational Behavior*, April 2011, pp. 499–519; B. E. Litzky, K. A. Eddleston, and D. L. Kidder, "The Good, the Bad, and the Misguided: How Managers Inadvertently Encourage Deviant Behaviors," *Academy of Management Perspective*, February 2006, pp. 91–103; "Crime Spree," *BusinessWeek*, September 9, 2002, p. 8; B. P. Niehoff and R. J. Paul, "Causes of Employee Theft and Strategies That HR Managers Can Use for Prevention," *Human Resource Management*, Spring 2000, pp. 51–64; and G. Winter, "Taking at the Office Reaches New Heights: Employee Larceny Is Bigger and Bolder," *New York Times*, July 12, 2000, pp. C1+.

43. K. Aho, "A Highly Effective, Very Low-Tech Way to Stop Fraud," *Bloomberg*, August 11, 2014, http://www.bloomberg.com/bw/articles/2014-08-11/to-stop-fraud-employee-tip-hotlines-are-remarkably-effective.

44. This section is based on J. Greenberg, *Behavior in Organizations*, 10th ed. (Upper Saddle River, NJ: Prentice Hall, 2011).

45. A. H. Bell and D. M. Smith, "Why Some Employees Bite the Hand That Feeds Them," *Workforce Online*, December 3, 2000, www.workforce.com.

46. Litzky et al., "The Good, the Bad, and the Misguided"; A. H. Bell and D. M. Smith, "Protecting the Company against Theft and Fraud," *Workforce Online*, December 3, 2000; J. D. Hansen, "To Catch a Thief," *Journal of Accountancy*, March 2000, pp. 43–46; and J. Greenberg, "The Cognitive Geometry of Employee Theft," in *Dysfunctional Behavior in Organizations: Nonviolent and Deviant Behavior* (Stamford, CT: JAI Press, 1998), pp. 147–93.

47. T. K. Garrett, "Subduing Violence at Work: Setting Policies to Help Safeguard the Workplace," March 18, 2015, http://www.workforce.com/articles/21201-subduing-violence-at-work-setting-policies-to-help-safeguard-the-workplace; G. Botelho, "Workplace Violence: Know the Numbers, Risk Factors and Possible Warning Signs," September 28, 2014, http://www.cnn.com/2014/09/27/us/workplace-violence-questions-answers/; L. Copeland and D. Stanglin, "'Rambo' Gunman Injures 6 at FedEx Facility," *USA Today Online*, April 29, 2014; R. Rivera and L. Robbins, "Troubles Preceded Connecticut Workplace Killing," *New York Times Online*, August 3, 2010; J. Griffin, "Workplace Violence News," July 16, 2010, www.workplaceviolencenews.com; and J. Smerd, "Workplace Shootings in Florida, Texas Again Put Focus on Violence on the Job," *Workforce Management Online*, November 6, 2009.

48. "Workplace Homicides from Shootings," U.S. Bureau of Labor Statistics, January 2013, http://www.bls.gov/iif/oshwc/cfoi/osar0016.htm.

49. J. McCafferty, "Verbal Chills," *CFO*, June 2005, p. 17; S. Armour, "Managers Not Prepared for Workplace Violence," July 15, 2004, pp. 1B+; and "Workplace Violence," OSHA Fact Sheet, U.S. Department of Labor, Occupational Safety and Health Administration, 2002.

50. "Ten Tips on Recognizing and Minimizing Violence," *Workforce Management Online*, December 3, 2000.

51. "Bullying Bosses Cause Work Rage Rise," *Management Issues News*, January 28, 2003, www.management-issues.com.

52. C. Cosh, "Keep a Close Eye Out for the Signs," *Macleans*, December 27, 2010, p. 24; and R. McNatt, "Desk Rage," *BusinessWeek*, November 27, 2000, p. 12.

53. M. Gorkin, "Key Components of a Dangerously Dysfunctional Work Environment," *Workforce Online*, December 3, 2000, www.workforce.com.

54. L. D. Lieber, "HR's Role in Preventing Workplace Violence," *Employment Relations*, Winter 2011, pp. 83-88; Cosh, "Keep a Close Eye Out for the Signs"; "Ten Tips on Recognizing and Minimizing Violence," *Workforce Management Online*, December 3, 2000; A. C. Klotz and M. R. Buckley, "Where Everybody Knows Your Name: Lessons from Small Business about Preventing Workplace Violence," *Business Horizons*, November 2010, pp. 571–79; M. Gorkin, "Five Strategies and Structures for Reducing Workplace Violence," *Workforce Management Online*, December 3, 2000; "Investigating Workplace Violence: Where Do You Start?" *Workforce Management Online*, December 3, 2000; and "Points to Cover in a Workplace Violence Policy," *Workforce Management Online*, December 3, 2000.

55. Based on N. Pelusi, "Dealing with Difficult People," *Psychology Today*, September–October 2006, pp. 68–69; and R. I. Sutton, *The No Asshole Rule: Building a Civilized Workplace and Surviving One That Isn't* (New York: Business Plus, 2007).

56. A. Carr, "Chipotle Eats Itself," *Fast Company Online*, October 16, 2016; D. Alba, "Chipotle's Health Crisis Shows Fresh Food Comes at a Price," *Wired Magazine Online*, January 15, 2016; and S. Berfield, "Inside Chipotle's Contamination Crisis," *Bloomberg Online*, December 22, 2015.

57. E. Dockterman, "Chipotle Will Briefly Close All Its Restaurants to Address Food Safety Issue," *Time Magazine Online*, January 15, 2016.

58. J. Jargon, "Chipotle Founder to Step Down as CEO," *Wall Street Journal Online*, November 30, 2017.

59. R. Feintzeig, "Everything Is Awesome! Why You Can't Tell Employees They're Doing a Bad Job," *Wall Street Journal Online*, February 10, 2015; TciiStrategic and Management Consultants, "Why Positive Feedback Is Crucial to High Performance," May 13, 2013, http://www.businesszone.co.uk/blogs/tcii/tcii-strategic-and-management-consultants/why-positive-feedback-crucial-high-performance; and C. M. Phoel, "Feedback That Works," *Harvard Business Review*, April 27, 2009, https://hbr.org/2009/04/feedback-that-works/.

60. "About Tesla," June 8, 2018, www.tesla.com.

61. S.Banker, "Tesla's Disappointing Earnings Highlight Problems in Scaling Production," *Forbes Online*, May 3, 2018.

62. J. D. Stoll, "Tesla's Factory in a Fishbowl," *Wall Street Journal Online*, May 8, 2018.

63. L. Denning, "What If Tesla Runs Out of Gas?" *Bloomberg Businessweek*, April 23, 2018, pp. 17–19.

64. Stoll, "Tesla's Factory in a Fishbowl."

65. L. Poultney, "Hey, Tesla, How Hard Can It Be to Actually Make a Car?" *Wired UK Online*, April 22, 2018.

66. Stoll, "Tesla's Factory in a Fishbowl."

67. Ibid.; and Poultney, "Hey, Tesla, How Hard Can It Be to Actually Make a Car?"

68. C. Grant, "Tesla's Numbers Are More Dramatic than Its CEO," *Wall Street Journal*, May 7, 2018, p. B10.

69. T. Higgins and S. Goldfarb, "Big Test for Tesla as Officials Step Away," *Wall Street Journal*, May 14, 2018, pp. A1+.

70. N. Bomey, "Musk All Smiles After Tesla Model 3 Output Hits Target," *USA Today-Springfield, Missouri News-Leader*, July 3, 2018, p. 3B; T. Higgins, "Tesla Hits Model 3 Production Goal," *Wall Street Journal*, July 2, 2018, p. B2; and T. Higgins and S. Pulliam, "Deadline Places Musk In 'Production Hell,'" *Wall Street Journal*, June 28, 2018, pp. A1+.

Operations Module
MANAGING OPERATIONS

The steaming cup of coffee placed in a customer's hand at any Starbucks store location starts as coffee beans (berries) plucked from fields of coffee plants. From harvest to storage to roasting to retail to cup, Starbucks understands the important role each value chain participant plays.

Starbucks offers a selection of coffees from around the world, and its coffee buyers personally travel to the coffee-growing regions of Latin America, Africa/Arabia, and Asia/Pacific to select and purchase the highest-quality *arabica* beans. Once the beans arrive at any one of its five roasting facilities (in Washington, Pennsylvania, Nevada, South Carolina, or Amsterdam), Starbucks' master professional roasters do their "magic" in creating the company's rich signature roast coffees, a process that's the "cumulative result of expert roasters knowing coffee and bringing balance to all of its flavor attributes." There are many potential challenges in "transforming" the raw material into the quality product and experience that customers expect at Starbucks—weather, shipping and logistics, technology, political instability, and so forth. All could potentially affect the company. Although those operations management challenges are significant, the most challenging issue facing Starbucks today is balancing its vision of the uniquely Starbucks' coffee experience with the realities of selling a $4 latte in today's world.

Every organization produces something, whether it's a good or a service. Some, like Starbucks, produce both a good and a service. Technology has changed how production is done. This module focuses on how organizations manage operations and the important role that managers play in that process.

What Do I Need to Know about Operations Management?

You've probably never given much thought to how organizations "produce" the goods and services that you buy or use. But it's an important process. Without it, you wouldn't have a car to drive or McDonald's fries to snack on or even a hiking trail in a local park to enjoy. *Organizations need to have well-thought-out and well-designed operating systems, organizational control systems, and quality programs to survive in today's increasingly competitive global environment.* And ***it's the manager's job to manage those things***.

What Is Operations Management?

The term **operations management** refers to the design, operation, and control of the transformation process that converts such resources as labor and raw materials into goods and services that are sold to customers. Exhibit MOM–1 portrays a simplified overview of the transformation process of creating value by converting inputs into outputs. The system takes inputs—people, technology, capital, equipment, materials, and information—and transforms them through various processes, procedures, and work activities into finished goods and services. These processes, procedures, and work activities are found throughout the organization. For example, department members in marketing, finance, research and development, human resources, and accounting convert inputs into outputs such as sales, increased market share, high rates of return on investments, new and innovative products, motivated and committed employees, and accounting reports. As a manager, you'll need to be familiar with operations management concepts, regardless of the area in which you're managing, in order to achieve your goals more effectively and efficiently.

operations management
The study and application of the transformation process

Exhibit MOM–1 The Operations System

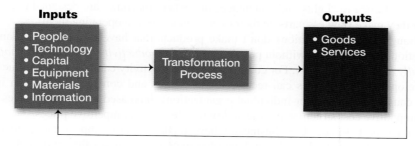

Why Is Operations Management Important?

1. It encompasses processes in services and manufacturing organizations.
2. It's important in effectively and efficiently managing productivity.
3. It plays a strategic role in an organization's competitive success.

1 How Do Service and Manufacturing Firms Differ?

With a menu that offers more than 250 items made fresh each day, The Cheesecake Factory restaurants rely on a finely tuned production system. One food-service consultant says, "They've evolved with this highly complex menu combined with a highly efficient kitchen."[1]

All organizations produce goods or services through the **transformation process**. Simply stated, every organization has an operations system that creates value by transforming inputs into finished goods and services outputs. For manufacturers, the products are obvious: cars, cell phones, or food products. After all, **manufacturing organizations** produce physical goods. It's easy to see the operations management (transformation) process at work in these types of organizations because raw materials are turned into recognizable physical products. But that transformation process isn't as readily evident in **service organizations** because they produce nonphysical outputs in the form of services. For instance, hospitals provide medical and health care services that help people manage their personal health; taxi companies provide transportation services that move people from one location to another; cruise lines provide vacation and entertainment services; residential plumbers and electricians ensure that we have electricity and running water where we live. All of these service organizations transform inputs into outputs. For example, look at your college. College administrators bring together inputs—instructors, books, multimedia classrooms, and similar resources—to transform students into educated and skilled individuals.

The reason we're making this point is that the U.S. economy—and, to a large extent, the global economy—is dominated by the creation and sale of services. Most of the world's developed countries are predominantly service economies.[2] In the United States, for instance, almost 78 percent of all economic activity is services, and in the European Union, it's nearly 73 percent. In lesser-developed countries, the services sector is less important. For instance, in Chad, it accounts for only 32 percent of economic activity; in Laos, only 44 percent; and in Bolivia, 48 percent.

2 How Do Businesses Improve Productivity?

One jetliner has some 4 million parts. Efficiently assembling such a finely engineered product requires intense focus. Boeing and Airbus, the two major global manufacturers, have copied techniques from Toyota. However, not every technique can be copied because airlines demand more customization than do car buyers, and there are significantly more rigid safety regulations for jetliners than for cars.[3] At the Evans Findings Company in East Providence, Rhode Island, which makes the tiny cutting devices on dental-floss containers, one production shift each day is run without people.[4] The company's goal is to do as much as possible with no labor. And it's not because they don't care about their employees. Instead, like many U.S. manufacturers,

transformation process
The process that converts resources into finished goods and services

manufacturing organizations
Organizations that produce physical goods

service organizations
Organizations that produce nonphysical products in the form of services

Evans needed to improve productivity in order to survive, especially against low-cost competitors. So they turned to "lights-out" manufacturing, where machines are designed to be so reliable that they make flawless parts on their own, without people operating them.

Although most organizations don't make products that have 4 million parts and most organizations can't function without people, *improving productivity has become a major goal in virtually every organization*. For countries, high productivity can lead to economic growth and development. Employees can receive higher wages and company profits can increase without causing inflation. For individual organizations, increased productivity gives them a more competitive cost structure and the ability to offer more competitive prices.

Over the past decade, U.S. businesses have made dramatic improvements to increase their efficiency. For example, at Latex Foam International's state-of-the-art digital facility in Shelton, Connecticut, engineers monitor all of the factory's operations. The facility boosted capacity by 50 percent in a smaller space and achieved a 30 percent efficiency gain.[5] And it's not just in manufacturing that companies are pursuing productivity gains. Pella Corporation's purchasing office improved productivity by reducing purchase order entry times anywhere from 50 percent to 86 percent, decreasing voucher processing by 27 percent, and eliminating 14 financial systems. Its information technology department slashed e-mail traffic in half and implemented work design improvements for heavy PC users such as call center users. The human resources department cut the time to process benefit enrollment by 156.5 days. And the finance department now takes two days, instead of six, to do its end-of-month closeout.[6]

Organizations that hope to succeed globally are looking for ways to improve productivity. For example, McDonald's Corporation drastically reduced the time it takes to cook french fries—65 seconds as compared to the 210 seconds it once took, saving time and other resources.[7] The Canadian Imperial Bank of Commerce, based in Toronto, automated its purchasing function, saving several million dollars annually.[8] And Skoda, the Czech car company, improved its productivity through an intensive restructuring of its manufacturing process.[9]

Productivity is a composite of people and operations variables. To improve productivity, managers must focus on both. The late W. Edwards Deming, a renowned quality expert, believed that managers, not workers, were the primary source of increased productivity. He outlined 14 points for improving management's productivity. Here's a quick overviewof his work:

William Edwards Deming was an American statistician, professor, author, lecturer, and consultant.[10] He is widely credited with improving production in the United States during World War II, although he's probably best known for his work in Japan. From 1950 onward, he taught Japanese top managers how to improve product design and product quality, testing, and sales, primarily through applying statistical methods. His philosophy has been summarized as follows: "Dr. W. Edwards Deming taught that by adopting appropriate principles of management, organizations can increase quality and simultaneously reduce costs (by reducing waste, rework, staff attrition and litigation while increasing customer loyalty). The key is to practice continual improvement and think of manufacturing as a system, not as bits and pieces."

Putting that philosophy into practice required following Deming's 14 points for improving management's productivity. These suggestions are as follows:

- Plan for the long-term future.
- Never be complacent concerning the quality of your product.
- Establish statistical control over your production processes and require your suppliers to do so as well.
- Deal with the best and fewest number of suppliers.
- Find out whether your problems are confined to particular parts of the production process or stem from the overall process itself.
- Train workers for the job that you are asking them to perform.
- Raise the quality of your line supervisors.
- Drive out fear.
- Encourage departments to work closely together rather than to concentrate on departmental or divisional distinctions.

- Do not adopt strictly numerical goals.
- Require your workers to do quality work.
- Train your employees to understand statistical methods.
- Train your employees in new skills as the need arises.
- Make top managers responsible for implementing these principles.

These principles have withstood the test of time and are still applicable for managers looking to improve productivity.

A close look at these suggestions reveals Deming's understanding of the interplay between people and operations. High productivity can't come solely from good "people management." The truly effective organization will maximize productivity by successfully integrating people into the overall operations system. For instance, at Simplex Nails Manufacturing in Americus, Georgia, employees were an integral part of the company's much-needed turnaround effort.[11] Some production workers were redeployed on a plant-wide cleanup and organization effort, which freed up floor space. The company's sales force was retrained and refocused to sell what customers wanted rather than what was in inventory. The results were dramatic. Inventory was reduced by more than 50 percent, the plant had 20 percent more floor space, orders were more consistent, and employee morale improved. Here's a company that understood the important interplay between people and the operations system.

3 What Role Does Operations Management Play in a Company's Strategy?

Modern manufacturing originated more than 110 years ago in the United States, primarily in Detroit's automobile factories. The success that U.S. manufacturers experienced during World War II led manufacturing executives to believe that troublesome production problems had been conquered. These executives focused, instead, on improving other functional areas such as finance and marketing and paid little attention to manufacturing.

However, as U.S. executives neglected production, managers in Japan, Germany, and other countries took the opportunity to develop modern, technologically advanced facilities that fully integrated manufacturing operations into strategic planning decisions. The competition's success realigned world manufacturing leadership. U.S. manufacturers soon discovered that foreign goods were being made not only less expensively but also with better quality. Finally, by the late 1970s, U.S. executives recognized that they were facing a true crisis and responded. They invested heavily in improving manufacturing technology, increased the corporate authority and visibility of manufacturing executives, and began incorporating existing and future production requirements into the organization's overall strategic plan. Today, successful organizations recognize the crucial role that operations management plays as part of the overall organizational strategy to establish and maintain global leadership.[12]

The strategic role that operations management plays in successful organizational performance can be seen clearly as more organizations move toward managing their operations from a value chain perspective.

What Is Value Chain Management and Why Is It Important?

It's 11 P.M., and you're reading a text message from your parents saying they want to buy you a laptop for your birthday this year and to order it. You log on to Dell's website and configure your dream machine. You hit the order button and within two to three days, your dream computer is delivered to your front door, built to your exact specifications, ready to set up and use immediately to finish that online management assignment due tomorrow. Or consider Siemens AG's Computed Tomography manufacturing plant in Forchheim, Germany, which has established partnerships with about 30 suppliers. These suppliers are partners in the truest sense because they share responsibility with the plant for overall process performance.

This arrangement has allowed Siemens to eliminate all inventory warehousing and has streamlined the number of times paper changes hands to order parts from 18 to one. At the Timken's plant in Canton, Ohio, electronic purchase orders are sent across the street to an adjacent "Supplier City" where many of its key suppliers have set up shop. The process takes milliseconds and costs less than 50 cents per purchase order. And when Black & Decker extended its line of handheld tools to include a glue gun, it totally outsourced the entire design and production to the leading glue gun manufacturer. Why? Because they understood that glue guns don't require motors, which was what Black & Decker did best.[13]

As these examples show, closely integrated work activities among many different players are possible. How? The answer lies in value chain management. The concepts of value chain management have transformed operations management strategies and turned organizations around the world into finely tuned models of efficiency and effectiveness strategically positioned to exploit competitive opportunities.

What Is Value Chain Management?

Every organization needs customers if it's going to survive and prosper. Even a not-for-profit organization must have "customers" who use its services or purchase its products. Customers want some type of value from the goods and services they purchase or use, and these customers decide what has value. Organizations must provide that value to attract and keep customers. **Value** is defined as the performance characteristics, features and attributes, and any other aspects of goods and services for which customers are willing to give up resources (usually money). For example, when you download Ariana Grande's new single on Amazon Music, buy a new pair of Australian sheepskin Ugg boots online at the company's website, purchase a Wendy's bacon cheeseburger at the drive-through location on campus, or get a haircut from your local hair salon, you're exchanging (giving up) money in return for the value you need or desire from these products—providing music during your evening study time, keeping your feet warm *and* fashionable during winter's cold weather, alleviating the lunchtime hunger pangs quickly since your next class starts in 15 minutes, or looking professionally groomed for the job interview you've got next week.

How *is* value provided to customers? Through transforming raw materials and other resources into some product or service that end users need or desire when, where, and how they want it. However, that seemingly simple act of turning varied resources into something that customers value and are willing to pay for involves a vast array of interrelated work activities performed by different participants (suppliers, manufacturers, and even customers)—that is, it involves the value chain. The **value chain** is the entire series of organizational work activities that add value at each step from raw materials to finished product. In its entirety, the value chain can encompass the supplier's suppliers to the customer's customer.[14]

Value chain management is the process of managing the sequence of activities and information along the entire value chain. In contrast to supply chain management, which is *internally* oriented and focuses on efficient flow of incoming materials (resources) to the organization, value chain management is *externally* oriented and focuses on both incoming materials and outgoing products and services. Although supply chain management is efficiency oriented (its goal is to reduce costs and make the organization more productive), value chain management is effectiveness oriented and aims to create the highest value for customers.[15]

What Are the Goals of Value Chain Management?

Who has the power in the value chain? Is it the supplier providing needed resources and materials? After all, suppliers have the ability to dictate prices and quality. Is it the manufacturer that assembles those resources into a valuable product or service? A manufacturer's contribution in creating a product or service is quite obvious. Is it the distributor that makes sure the product or service is available where and when the customer needs it? Actually, it's none of these. In value chain management, ultimately customers are the ones with the power.[16] They're the ones who define what value is and how it's created and provided. Using value chain management, managers seek to find that unique combination in which customers are offered solutions that truly meet their needs and at a price that can't be matched by competitors.[17]

For example, in an effort to better anticipate customer demand and replenish customer stocks, Shell Chemical Company developed a supplier inventory management order network. The software used in this network allows managers to track shipment status, calculate safety stock levels, and prepare resupply schedules.[18] With this capability, Shell Chemical enables its customers to purchase goods when desired and to receive them immediately.

A good value chain is one in which a sequence of participants works together as a team, each adding some component of value—such as faster assembly, more accurate information, or better customer response and service—to the overall process.[19] The better the collaboration among the various chain participants, the better the customer solutions. When value is created for customers and their needs and desires are satisfied, everyone along the chain benefits. For example, at Iomega Corporation, a manufacturer of personal computer storage devices, managing the value chain started first with improved relationships with internal suppliers, then expanded out to external suppliers and customers. As the company's experience with value chain management intensified and improved, so did its connection to customers, which ultimately paid off for all its value chain partners.[20]

How Does Value Chain Management Benefit Businesses?

Collaborating with external and internal partners in creating and managing a successful value chain strategy requires significant investments in time, energy, and other resources plus a serious commitment by all chain partners. Given this, why would managers ever choose to implement value chain management? A survey of manufacturers noted four primary benefits of value chain management: improved procurement, improved logistics, improved product development, and enhanced customer order management.[21]

How Is Value Chain Management Done?

The dynamic, competitive environment facing contemporary global organizations demands new solutions.[22] Understanding how and why value is determined by the marketplace has led some organizations to experiment with a new **business model**—that is, a strategic design for how a company intends to profit from its broad array of strategies, processes, and activities. For example, IKEA, the home furnishings manufacturer, transformed itself from a small, Swedish mail-order furniture operation into the world's largest retailer of home furnishings by reinventing the value chain in the home furnishings industry. The company offers customers well-designed products at substantially lower prices in return for the customers' willingness to take on certain key tasks traditionally done by manufacturers and retailers—such as getting the furniture home and assembling it.[23] The company's adoption of a unique business model and willingness to abandon old methods and processes have worked well. It also helped that IKEA recognized the importance of managing its value chain.

What Are the Requirements for Successful Value Chain Management?

So what does successful value chain management require? Exhibit MOM–2 summarizes the six main requirements. Let's look at each of these elements more closely.

1. COORDINATION AND COLLABORATION. For the value chain to achieve its goal of meeting and exceeding customers' needs and desires, comprehensive and seamless integration among all members of the chain is absolutely necessary. All partners in the value chain must identify things that they may not value but that customers do. Sharing information and being flexible as far as who in the value chain does what are important steps in building coordination and collaboration. This sharing of information and analysis requires open communication among the various value chain partners. For example, Furon Company, a manufacturer of specialty polymer products, believes that better communication with

business model
A strategic design for how a company intends to profit from its broad array of strategies, processes, and activities

Exhibit MOM–2 Requirements for Successful Value Chain Management

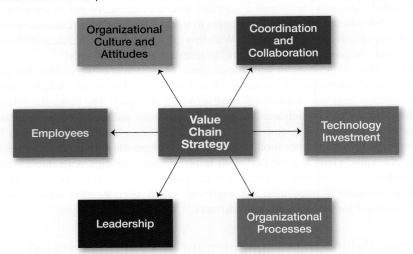

customers and with suppliers has facilitated timely delivery of goods and services and opened up additional business opportunities for all its value chain partners.[24]

2. TECHNOLOGY INVESTMENT. Successful value chain management isn't possible without a significant investment in information technology. The payoff from this investment is that information technology can be used to restructure the value chain to better serve end users.[25] For example, Rollerblade Inc., invested heavily in developing a website and used it to educate customers about its products. Although the company has chosen not to sell its products over the Web for fear of antagonizing its dealer network, managers remain flexible about the issue and would reconsider if they felt that value could be better delivered to customers by doing so.[26]

What types of technology are important? According to experts, the key tools include a supporting enterprise resource planning (ERP) software system that links all of an organization's activities, sophisticated work planning and scheduling software, customer relationship management systems, business intelligence capabilities, and e-business connections with trading network partners.[27] For instance, Dell Inc. manages its supplier relationships almost exclusively online. The company has one website for customers and one for suppliers. The supplier website is the primary mode of communication between Dell and its largest suppliers. The company's investment in this type of information technology allows it to meet customers' needs in a way that competitors haven't been able to match.[28]

3. ORGANIZATIONAL PROCESSES. Value chain management radically changes **organizational processes**—that is, the way organizational work is done.[29] Managers must critically evaluate all organizational processes from beginning to end by looking at core competencies—the organization's unique skills, capabilities, and resources—to determine where value is being added. Non-value-adding activities are eliminated. Questions such as "Where can internal knowledge be leveraged to improve flow of material and information?" "How can we better configure our product to satisfy both customers and suppliers?" "How can the flow of material and information be improved?" and "How can we improve customer service?" should be asked for each process. For example, when managers at Deere & Company implemented value chain management in its Worldwide Commercial and Consumer Equipment Division, a thorough process evaluation revealed that work activities needed to be better synchronized and interrelationships between multiple links in the value chain better managed. They changed numerous work processes division-wide in order to improve these relationships.[30]

organizational processes
The way organizational work is done

Three important conclusions can be made about how organizational processes must change:

- First, better demand forecasting is necessary and possible because of closer ties with customers and suppliers. For example, in an effort to make sure that Listerine was on the store shelves when customers wanted it, Walmart collaborated with product manufacturer Pfizer Consumer Healthcare on improving product demand forecast information. Through their mutual efforts, the partners boosted Walmart's sales of Listerine by $6.5 million. Customers also benefited because they were able to purchase the product when and where they wanted it.

- Second, selected functions may need to be done collaboratively with other partners in the value chain. This collaboration may even extend to sharing employees. For instance, Saint-Gobain Performance Plastics, headquartered in Northboro, Massachusetts, places its own employees in customer sites and brings employees of suppliers and customers to work on its premises. Saint-Gobain's CEO says this type of collaboration is essential.[31]

- Finally, new measures are needed for evaluating the performance of various activities along the value chain. Because the goal in value chain management is meeting and exceeding customers' needs and desires, managers need a better picture of how well value is being created and delivered to customers. For instance, when Nestlé USA implemented a value chain management approach, it redesigned its measurement system to focus on one consistent set of factors, including accuracy of demand forecasts and production plans, on-time delivery, and customer service levels. This redesign allowed management to more quickly identify problems and take actions to resolve them.[32]

4. LEADERSHIP. The importance of leadership to value chain management is plain and simple—successful value chain management isn't possible without strong and committed leadership.[33] From top organizational levels to lower levels, managers must support, facilitate, and promote the implementation and ongoing practice of value chain management. Managers must make a serious commitment to identifying what value is, how that value can best be provided, and how successful those efforts have been. That type of organizational atmosphere or culture, in which all efforts are focused on delivering superb customer value, isn't possible without a serious commitment on the part of the organization's leaders.

Also, it's important that leaders outline expectations for what's involved in the organization's pursuit of value chain management. Ideally, articulating expectations should start with a vision or mission statement that expresses the organization's commitment to identifying, capturing, and providing the highest possible value to customers. For example, when American Standard Companies began its pursuit of value chain management, the CEO attended dozens of meetings across the country explaining the changing competitive environment and why the company needed to create better working relationships with its value chain partners.[34] Throughout the organization, then, managers should clarify expectations regarding each employee's role in the value chain. Being clear about expectations also extends to partners. For example, managers at American Standard identified clear requirements for suppliers and were prepared to drop any that couldn't meet them. The company was so serious about its expectations that it did cut hundreds of suppliers from air-conditioning, bath and kitchen, and vehicle control systems businesses. The upside, though, was that those suppliers that met the expectations benefited from more business and American Standard had partners that could deliver better value to customers.

5. EMPLOYEES/HUMAN RESOURCES. We know from our discussions of management theories and approaches throughout this textbook that employees are the organization's most important resource. So, not surprisingly, employees play an important part in value chain management. Three main human resources requirements for value chain management are flexible approaches to job design, an effective hiring process, and ongoing training.

Flexibility is the key description of job design in a value chain management organization. Traditional functional job roles—such as marketing, sales, accounts payable, customer service representative, and so forth—are inadequate in a value chain management environment. Instead, jobs need to be designed around work processes that link all functions involved in creating and providing value to customers. This type of flexible job design supports the company's commitment to providing superb customer value.[35] In designing jobs for a value chain approach, the focus needs to be on how each activity performed by an employee can best contribute to the creation and delivery of customer value, which requires flexibility in what employees do and how they do it.

The fact that jobs in a value chain management organization must be flexible contributes to the second requirement: Flexible jobs require employees who are flexible. In a value chain organization, employees may be assigned to work teams that tackle a given process and are often asked to do different things on different days, depending on need. In an environment focusing on collaborative relationships that may change as customer needs change, employees' ability to be flexible is critical. Accordingly, the organization's hiring process must be designed to identify those employees who have the ability to quickly learn and adapt.

Finally, the need for flexibility also requires a significant investment in ongoing employee training. Whether the training involves learning how to use information technology software, how to improve the flow of materials throughout the chain, how to identify activities that add value, how to make better decisions faster, or how to improve any number of other potential work activities, managers must see to it that employees have the knowledge and tools they need to do their jobs. For example, at defense and electronics contractor Alenia Marconi Systems, based in Portsmouth, England, ongoing training is part of the company's commitment to efficiently and effectively meeting the needs of customers. Employees continually receive technical training as well as training in strategic issues, including the importance of emphasizing people and customers, not just sales and profits.[36]

6. ORGANIZATIONAL CULTURE AND ATTITUDES.   The last requirement for value chain management is having a supportive organizational culture and attitudes. Those cultural attitudes include sharing, collaborating, openness, flexibility, mutual respect, and trust. And these attitudes encompass not only the internal partners in the value chain, but external partners as well. For instance, American Standard has chosen to practice these attitudes the old-fashioned way—with lots of face time and telephone calls. However, as we mentioned earlier, Dell has taken a completely different approach becasue it works with its value chain partners almost exclusively through cyberspace.[37] Both approaches, however, reflect each company's commitment to developing long-lasting, mutually beneficial, and trusting relationships that best meet customers' needs.

What Are the Obstacles to Value Chain Management?

As desirable as value chain management may be, managers must tackle several obstacles in managing the value chain—organizational barriers, cultural attitudes, required capabilities, and people (see Exhibit MOM–3).

Exhibit MOM–3 Obstacles to Successful Value Chain Management

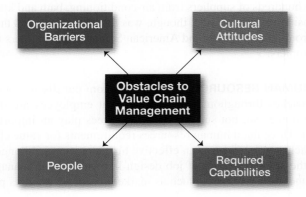

ORGANIZATIONAL BARRIERS. Organizational barriers are among the most difficult obstacles to handle. These barriers include refusal or reluctance to share information, reluctance to shake up the status quo, and security issues. Without shared information, close coordination and collaboration is impossible. And the reluctance or refusal of employees to shake up the status quo can impede efforts toward value chain management and prevent its successful implementation. Finally, because value chain management relies heavily on a substantial information technology infrastructure, system security and Internet security breaches are issues that need to be addressed.

CULTURAL ATTITUDES. Unsupportive cultural attitudes—-especially trust and control—also can be obstacles to value chain management. The trust issue is a critical one—both lack of trust and too much trust. To be effective, partners in a value chain must trust each other. There must be a mutual respect for, and honesty about, each partner's activities all along the chain. When that trust doesn't exist, the partners will be reluctant to share information, capabilities, and processes. But too much trust also can be a problem. Just about any organization is vulnerable to theft of intellectual property—that is, proprietary information that's critical to an organization's efficient and effective functioning and competitiveness. You need to be able to trust your value chain partners so your organization's valuable assets aren't compromised.[38] Another cultural attitude that can be an obstacle is the belief that when an organization collaborates with external and internal partners, it no longer controls its own destiny. However, this just isn't the case. Even with the intense collaboration that's important to value chain management, organizations still control critical decisions such as what customers value, how much value they desire, and what distribution channels are important.[39]

REQUIRED CAPABILITIES. We know from our earlier discussion of requirements for the successful implementation of value chain management that value chain partners need numerous capabilities. Several of these—coordination and collaboration, the ability to configure products to satisfy customers and suppliers, and the ability to educate internal and external partners—aren't easy. But they're essential to capturing and exploiting the value chain. Many of the companies we've described throughout this section endured critical, and oftentimes difficult, self-evaluations of their capabilities and processes in order to become more effective and efficient at managing their value chains.

PEOPLE. The final obstacles to successful value chain management can be an organization's people. Without their unwavering commitment to do whatever it takes, value chain management won't be successful. If employees refuse to be flexible in their work—how and with whom they work—collaboration and cooperation throughout the value chain will be hard to achieve. In addition, value chain management takes an incredible amount of time and energy on the part of an organization's employees. Managers must motivate those high levels of effort from employees, which isn't an easy thing to do.

What Contemporary Issues Do Managers Face in Managing Operations?

Redesigned milk jugs adopted by Walmart and Costco are cheaper to ship, better for the environment, cost less, and keep the milk fresher. Experts say this type of redesign is "an example of the changes likely to play out in the American economy over the next two decades. In an era of soaring global demand and higher costs for energy and materials, virtually every aspect of the economy needs to be re-examined and many products must be redesigned for greater efficiency."[40]

   If you somehow thought that managing operations didn't really matter in today's online 24/7 global economy, think again. It does matter . . . a lot. Managers face three contemporary issues in managing operations.

1 What Role Does Technology Play in Operations Management?

As we know from our previous discussion of value chain management, today's competitive marketplace has put tremendous pressure on organizations to deliver products and services that customers value in a timely manner. Smart companies are looking at ways to harness technology to improve operations management. Many fast-food companies are competing to see who can provide faster and better service to drive-through customers. With drive-through now representing a huge portion of sales, faster and better delivery can be a significant competitive edge. For instance, Wendy's added awnings to some of its menu boards and replaced some of the text with pictures. Others use confirmation screens, a technology that helped McDonald's boost accuracy by more than 11 percent. And technology used by two national chains tells managers how much food they need to prepare by counting vehicles in the drive-through line and factoring in demand for current promotional and popular staple items.[41]

Although an organization's production activities are driven by the recognition that the customer is king, managers still need to be more responsive. For instance, operations managers need systems that can reveal available capacity, status of orders, and product quality while products are in the process of being manufactured, not just after the fact. To connect more closely with customers, production must be synchronized across the enterprise. To avoid bottlenecks and slowdowns, the production function must be a full partner in the entire business system.

What's making such extensive collaboration possible is technology. Technology is also allowing organizations to control costs, particularly in the areas of predictive maintenance, remote diagnostics, and utility cost savings. For instance, Internet-compatible equipment contains embedded Web servers that can communicate proactively—that is, if a piece of equipment breaks or reaches certain preset parameters indicating that it's about to break, it asks for help. But technology can do more than sound an alarm or light up an indicator button. For instance, some devices have the ability to initiate e-mail or signal a pager at a supplier, the maintenance department, or contractor describing the specific problem and requesting parts and service. How much is such e-enabled maintenance control worth? It can be worth quite a lot if it prevents equipment breakdowns and subsequent production downtime.

Managers who understand the power of technology to contribute to more effective and efficient performance know that managing operations is more than the traditional view of simply producing the product. Instead, the emphasis is on working together with all the organization's business functions to find solutions to customers' business problems.

2 How Do Managers Control Quality?

Quality problems are expensive. For example, even though Apple has had phenomenal success with its iPod, the batteries in the first three versions died after four hours instead of lasting up to 12 hours, as buyers expected. Apple's settlement with consumers cost close to $100 million. At Schering-Plough, problems with inhalers and other pharmaceuticals were traced to chronic quality control shortcomings, for which the company eventually paid a $500 million fine. And the auto industry paid $14.5 billion to cover the cost of warranty and repair work in one year.[42]

Many experts believe that organizations unable to produce high-quality products won't be able to compete successfully in the global marketplace. What is quality? When you consider a product or service to have quality, what does that mean? Does it mean that the product doesn't break or quit working—that is, is it reliable? Does it mean that the service is delivered in a way that you intended? Does it mean that the product does what it's supposed to do? Or does quality mean something else? Exhibit MOM–4 provides a description of several quality dimensions. We're going to define quality as the ability of a product or service to reliably do what it's supposed to do and to satisfy customer expectations.

HOW IS QUALITY ACHIEVED?   How quality is achieved is an issue managers must address. A good way to look at quality initiatives is with the management functions—planning, organizing and leading, and controlling—that need to take place.

Exhibit MOM–4 What Is Quality?

PRODUCT QUALITY DIMENSIONS
1. Performance—Operating characteristics
2. Features—Important special characteristics
3. Flexibility—Meeting operating specifications over some period of time
4. Durability—Amount of use before performance deteriorates
5. Conformance—Match with preestablished standards
6. Serviceability—Ease and speed of repair or normal service
7. Aesthetics—How a product looks and feels
8. Perceived quality—Subjective assessment of characteristics (product image)

SERVICE QUALITY DIMENSIONS
1. Timeliness—Performed in promised period of time
2. Courtesy—Performed cheerfully
3. Consistency—Giving all customers similar experiences each time
4. Convenience—Accessibility to customers
5. Completeness—Full service, as required
6. Accuracy—Performed correctly each time

Sources: Based on J. W. Dean and J. R. Evans, *Total Quality: Management, Organization, and Society* (St. Paul, MN: West Publishing Company, 1994); H. V. Roberts and B. F. Sergesketter, *Quality Is Personal* (New York: The Free Press, 1993); D. Garvin, *Managed Quality: The Strategic and Competitive Edge* (New York: The Free Press, 1988); and M. A. Hitt, R. D. Ireland, and R. E. Hoskisson, *Strategic Management*, 4th ed. (Cincinnati: South-Western Publishing, 2001), p. 121.

When *planning for quality*, managers must have quality improvement goals and strategies and plans to achieve those goals. Goals can help focus everyone's attention toward some objective quality standard. For instance, Caterpillar's goal is to apply quality improvement techniques to help cut costs.[43] Although this goal is specific and challenging, managers and employees are partnering together to pursue well-designed strategies to achieve the goals, and are confident they can do so.

When *organizing and leading for quality*, it's important for managers to look to their employees. For instance, at the Moosejaw, Saskatchewan, plant of General Cable Corporation, every employee participates in continual quality assurance training. In addition, the plant manager believes wholeheartedly in giving employees the information they need to do their jobs better. He says, "Giving people who are running the machines the information is just paramount. You can set up your cellular structure, you can cross-train your people, you can use lean tools, but if you don't give people information to drive improvement, there's no enthusiasm." Needless to say, this company shares production data and financial performance measures with all employees.[44]

Organizations with extensive and successful quality improvement programs tend to rely on two important people approaches: cross-functional work teams and self-directed or empowered work teams. Because achieving product quality is something that all employees from upper to lower levels must participate in, it's not surprising that quality-driven organizations rely on well-trained, flexible, and empowered employees.

Finally, managers must recognize when *controlling for quality* that quality improvement initiatives aren't possible without having some way to monitor and evaluate their progress. Whether it involves standards for inventory control, defect rate, raw materials procurement, or other operations management areas, controlling for quality is important. For instance, at the Northrup Grumman Corporation plant in Rolling Meadows, Illinois, several quality controls have been implemented, such as automated testing and IT that integrates product design and manufacturing and tracks process quality improvements. Also, employees are empowered to make accept/reject decisions about products throughout the manufacturing process. The plant manager explains, "This approach helps build quality into the product rather than trying to inspect quality into the product." But one of the most important things they do is "go to war" with their customers—soldiers preparing for war or live combat situations. Again, the plant manager says, "What discriminates us is that we believe if we can understand our customer's mission as well as they do, we can help them be more effective. We don't wait for our customer to ask us to do something. We find out what our customer is trying to do and then we develop solutions."[45]

Quality improvement success stories can be found globally. For example, at a Delphi assembly plant in Matamoros, Mexico, employees worked hard to improve quality and made significant strides. For instance, the customer reject rate on shipped products is now 10 ppm (parts per million), down from 3,000 ppm—an improvement of almost 300 percent.[46] Quality initiatives at several Australian companies—including Alcoa of Australia, Wormald Security, and Carlton and United Breweries—have led to significant quality improvements.[47] At Valeo Klimasystemme GmbH of Bad Rodach, Germany, assembly teams build different climate-control systems for high-end German cars, including Mercedes and BMW. Quality initiatives by those teams have led to significant improvements.[48]

WHAT QUALITY GOALS MIGHT ORGANIZATIONS PURSUE?   To publicly demonstrate their commitment to quality, many organizations worldwide have pursued challenging quality goals. The two best-known are the following:

1. **ISO 9001** is a series of international quality management standards established by the International Organization for Standardization (www.iso.org), which sets uniform guidelines for processes to ensure that products conform to customer requirements. These standards cover everything from contract review to product design to product delivery. The ISO 9001 standards have become the internationally recognized standard for evaluating and comparing companies in the global marketplace. In fact, this type of certification can be a prerequisite for doing business globally. Achieving ISO 9001 certification provides proof that a quality operations system is in place.

2. More than 30 years ago, Motorola further popularized the use of stringent quality standards through a trademarked quality improvement program called **Six Sigma**.[49] Very simply, Six Sigma is a quality standard that establishes a goal of no more than 3.4 defects per million units or procedures. What does the name mean? Sigma is the Greek letter that statisticians use to define a standard deviation from a bell curve. The higher the sigma, the fewer the deviations from the norm—that is, the fewer the defects. At One Sigma, two-thirds of whatever is being measured falls within the curve. Two Sigma covers about 95 percent. At Six Sigma, you're about as close to defect-free as you can get.[50] It's an ambitious quality goal! Although it's an extremely high standard to achieve, many quality-driven businesses are using it and benefiting from it. For instance, General Electric estimates that it has saved billions since 1995 by using Six Sigma, according to company executives.[51] Other examples of companies pursuing Six Sigma include Amazon, Bank of America, Dow Chemical, 3M Company, American Express, Sony Corporation, Starwood Hotels & Resorts Worldwide, and Johnson & Johnson. Although manufacturers seem to make up the bulk of Six Sigma users, service companies such as financial institutions, retailers, and health-care organizations are beginning to apply it. What impact can Six Sigma have? Let's look at an example.

It used to take Wellmark Blue Cross and Blue Shield, a managed-care health-care company, 65 days or more to add a new doctor to its medical plans. Thanks to Six Sigma, the company discovered that half the processes they used were redundant. With those unnecessary steps gone, the job now gets done in 30 days or less and with reduced staff. The company also has been able to reduce its administrative expenses by $3 million per year, an amount passed on to consumers through lower health premiums.[52]

Although it's important for managers to recognize that many positive benefits come from obtaining ISO 9000 certification or Six Sigma, *the key benefit comes from the quality improvement journey itself*. In other words, the goal of quality certification should be having work processes and an operations system in place that enable organizations to meet customers' needs and employees to perform their jobs in a consistently high-quality way.

ISO 9001
A series of international quality standards that set uniform guidelines for processes to ensure that products conform to customer requirements

Six Sigma
A quality standard that establishes a goal of no more than 3.4 defects per million units or procedures

3 How Are Projects Managed?

As we discussed in Chapter 7, many organizations are structured around projects. A **project** is a one-time-only set of activities with a definite beginning and ending point.[53] Projects vary in size and scope, from a NASA space shuttle launch to a wedding. **Project management** is the task of getting the activities done on time, within budget, and according to specifications.

Project management has actually been around for a long time in industries such as construction and movie making, but now it has expanded into almost every type of business. What explains the growing popularity of project management? It fits well with a dynamic environment and the need for flexibility and rapid response. Organizations are increasingly undertaking projects that are somewhat unusual or unique, have specific deadlines, contain complex interrelated tasks requiring specialized skills, and are temporary in nature. These types of projects don't lend themselves well to the standardized operating procedures that guide routine and continuous organizational activities.[54]

In the typical project, team members are temporarily assigned to and report to a project manager who coordinates the project's activities with other departments and reports directly to a senior executive. The project is temporary: It exists only long enough to complete its specific objectives. Then it's wound down and closed up; members move on to other projects, return to their permanent departments, or leave the organization.

If you were to observe a group of supervisors or department managers for a few days, you would see them regularly detailing what activities have to be done, the order in which they are to be done, who is to do each, and when they are to be completed. The managers are doing what we call scheduling. The following discussion reviews some useful scheduling devices.

HOW DO YOU USE A GANTT CHART?   The **Gantt chart** is a planning tool developed around the turn of the century by Henry Gantt. The idea behind the Gantt chart is relatively simple. It's essentially a bar graph, with time on the horizontal axis and the activities to be scheduled on the vertical axis. The bars show output, both planned and actual, over a period of time. The Gantt chart visually shows when tasks are supposed to be done and compares the assigned date with the actual progress on each. This simple but important device allows managers to detail easily what has yet to be done to complete a job or project and to assess whether it's ahead of, behind, or on schedule.

Exhibit MOM–5 shows a Gantt chart that was developed for book production by a manager in a publishing firm. Time is expressed in months across the top of the chart. Major activities are listed down the left side. The planning comes in deciding what activities need to be done to get the book finished, the order in which those activities need to be done, and the time that should be allocated to each activity. The blue shading represents actual progress made in completing each activity.

A Gantt chart, then, actually becomes a managerial control device as the manager looks for deviations from the plan. In this case, most activities were completed on time. However, if you look at the "review first pages" activity, you will notice that it's actually almost two and a half weeks behind schedule. Given this information, the manager might want to take some

Exhibit MOM–5 A Sample Gantt Chart

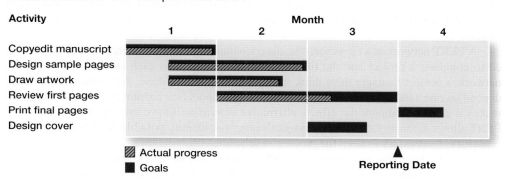

Exhibit MOM–6 A Sample Load Chart

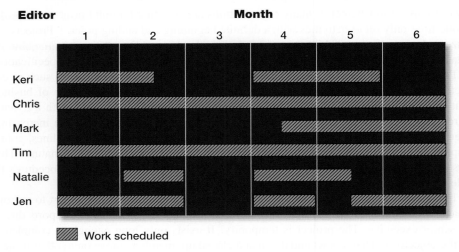

Work scheduled

corrective action to make up the lost time and to ensure that no further delays will occur. At this point, the manager can expect that the book will be published at least two weeks late if no corrective action is taken.

A modified version of the Gantt chart is a **load chart**. Instead of listing activities on the vertical axis, load charts list either whole departments or specific resources. This information allows managers to plan and control for capacity utilization. In other words, load charts schedule capacity by workstations. For example, Exhibit MOM–6 shows a load chart for six production editors at the same publishing firm. Each editor supervises the design and production of several books. By reviewing the load chart, the executive editor who supervises the six production editors can see who is free to take on a new book. If everyone is fully scheduled, the executive editor might decide not to accept any new projects, to accept some new projects and delay others, to ask the editors to work overtime, or to employ more production editors.

WHAT IS A PERT NETWORK ANALYSIS?   Gantt and load charts are helpful as long as the activities or projects being scheduled are few and independent of each other. But what if a manager had to plan a large project—such as a complex reorganization, the launching of a major cost-reduction campaign, or the development of a new product—that required coordinating inputs from marketing, production, and product design personnel? Such projects require coordinating hundreds or thousands of activities, some of which must be done simultaneously and some of which cannot begin until earlier activities have been completed. If you are constructing a shopping mall, you obviously cannot start erecting walls until the foundation has been laid. How, then, to schedule such a complex project? Use PERT.

PERT network analysis was originally developed in the late 1950s for coordinating the more than 3,000 contractors and agencies working on the Polaris submarine weapon system. This project was incredibly complicated, with hundreds of thousands of activities that had to be coordinated. PERT is reported to have cut two years off the completion date for the Polaris project.

A PERT network is a flowchart-like diagram that depicts the sequence of activities needed to complete a project and the time or costs associated with each activity. With a PERT network, a project manager must think through what has to be done, determine which events depend on one another, and identify potential trouble spots (see Exhibit MOM–7). PERT also makes it easy to compare the effects alternative actions will have on scheduling and costs. PERT allows managers to monitor a project's progress, identify possible bottlenecks, and shift resources as necessary to keep the project on schedule.

To understand how to construct a PERT network, you need to know three terms: *events, activities*, and *critical path*. Let us define these terms, outline the steps in the PERT process, and then develop an example.

load chart
A modified version of a Gantt chart that lists either whole departments or specific resources

PERT network analysis
A flowchart-like diagram that depicts the sequence of activities needed to complete a project and the time or costs associated with each activity

Exhibit MOM–7 Developing PERT Charts

Developing a PERT network requires the manager to identify all key activities needed to complete a project, rank them in order of dependence, and estimate each activity's completion time. This procedure can be translated into five specific steps:

1. Identify every significant activity that must be achieved for a project to be completed. The accomplishment of each activity results in a set of events or outcomes.

2. Ascertain the order in which these events must be completed.

3. Diagram the flow of activities from start to finish, identifying each activity and its relationship to all other activities. Use circles to indicate events and arrows to represent activities. The result is a flowchart diagram that we call the PERT network.

4. Compute a time estimate for completing each activity, using a weighted average that employs an optimistic time estimate (t_o) of how long the activity would take under ideal conditions, a most-likely estimate (t_m) of the time the activity normally should take, and a pessimistic estimate (t_p) that represents the time that an activity should take under the worst possible conditions. The formula for calculating the expected time (t_e) is then

$$t_e = \frac{t_o + 4t_m + t_p}{6}$$

5. Finally, using a network diagram that contains time estimates for each activity, the manager can determine a schedule for the start and finish dates of each activity and for the entire project. Any delays that occur along the critical path require the most attention because they delay the entire project. That is, the critical path has no slack in it; therefore, any delay along that path immediately translates into a delay in the final deadline for the completed project.

- **Events** are end points that represent the completion of major activities. Sometimes called milestones, events indicate that something significant has happened (such as receipt of purchased items) or an important component is finished. In PERT, events represent a point in time.

- **Activities**, on the other hand, are the actions that take place. Each activity consumes time, as determined on the basis of the time or resources required to progress from one event to another.

- The **critical path** is the longest or most time-consuming sequence of events and activities required to complete the project in the shortest amount of time.[55]

Let's apply PERT to a construction manager's task of building a 6,500-square-foot custom home.

As a construction manager, you recognize that time really is money in your business. Delays can turn a profitable job into a money loser. Accordingly, you must determine how long it will take to complete the house. You have carefully dissected the entire project into activities and events. Exhibit MOM–8 outlines the major events in the construction project and your estimate of the expected time required to complete each activity. Exhibit MOM–9 depicts the PERT network based on the data in Exhibit MOM–8.

HOW DOES PERT OPERATE? Your PERT network tells you that if everything goes as planned, it will take just over 32 weeks to build the house. This time is calculated by tracing the network's critical path: A B C D E I J K L M N P Q. Any delay in completing the events along this path will delay the completion of the entire project. For example, if it took six weeks instead of four to frame the house (event E), the entire project would be delayed by two weeks (or the time beyond that expected). But a one-week delay for installing the brick (event H) would have little effect because that event is not on the critical path. By using PERT, the construction manager would know that no corrective action would be needed. Further delays in installing the brick, however, could present

events
End points that represent the completion of major activities

activities
Actions that take place

critical path
The longest or most time-consuming sequence of events and activities required to complete a project in the shortest amount of time

Exhibit MOM–8 Major Activities in Building a Custom Home

Event	Description	Time (Weeks)	Preceding Activity
A	Approve design and get permits	3	None
B	Perform excavation/lot clearing	1	A
C	Pour footers	1	B
D	Erect foundation walls	2	C
E	Frame house	4	D
F	Install windows	0.5	E
G	Shingle roof	0.5	E
H	Install brick front and siding	4	F, G
I	Install electrical, plumbing, and heating and A/C rough-ins	6	E
J	Install insulation	0.25	I
K	Install sheetrock	2	J
L	Finish and sand sheetrock	7	K
M	Install interior trim	2	L
N	Paint house (interior and exterior)	2	H, M
O	Install all cabinets	0.5	N
P	Install flooring	1	N
Q	Final touch-up and turn over house to homeowner	1	O, P

problems—for such delays may, in actuality, result in a new critical path. Now back to our original critical path dilemma.

Notice that the critical path passes through N, P, and Q. Our PERT chart (Exhibit MOM–9) tells us that these three activities take four weeks. Wouldn't path N O Q be faster? Yes. The PERT network shows that it takes only 3.5 weeks to complete that path. So why isn't N O Q on the critical path? Because activity Q cannot begin until both activities O and P are completed. Although activity O takes half a week, activity P takes one full week. So, the earliest we can begin Q is after one week. What happens to the difference between the critical activity (activity P) time and the noncritical activity (activity O) time? The difference, in this case half a week, becomes slack time. **Slack time** is the time difference between the critical path and all other paths. What use is there for slack? If the project manager notices some slippage on a critical activity, perhaps slack time from a noncritical activity can be borrowed and temporarily assigned to work on the critical one.

As you can see, PERT is both a planning and a control tool. Not only does PERT help us estimate the times associated with scheduling a project, but it also gives us clues about where

slack time
The time difference between the critical path and all other paths

Exhibit MOM–9 A PERT Network for Building a Custom Home

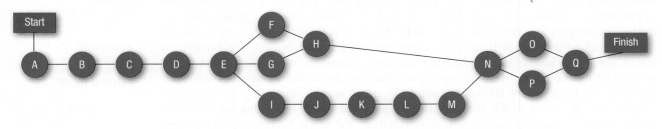

our controls should be placed. Because any event on the critical path that is delayed will delay the overall project (making us not only late but also probably over budget), our attention needs to be focused on the critical activities at all times. For example, if activity F (installing windows) is delayed by a week because supplies have not arrived, that is not a major issue. It's not on the critical path. But if activity P (installing flooring) is delayed from one week to two weeks, the entire project will be delayed by one week. Consequently, anything that has the immediate potential for delaying a project (critical activities) must be monitored closely.

Final Thoughts on Managing Operations

As we said earlier, it's the manager's job to manage the organization's operating systems, organizational control systems, and quality programs. That's the only way organizations will survive in today's increasingly competitive global economy.

Endnotes

1. D. Eng, "Cheesecake Factory's Winning Formula," *Fortune*, May 2, 2011, pp. 19–20; and D. McGinn, "Faster Food," *Newsweek*, April 19, 2004, pp. E20–E22.

2. All of the examples are from the *World Factbook 2015*, https://www.cia.gov/library/publications/the-world-factbook/geos/bl.html.

3. D. Michaels and J. L. Lunsford, "Streamlined Plane Making," *Wall Street Journal*, April 1, 2005, pp. B1+.

4. T. Aeppel, "Workers Not Included," *Wall Street Journal*, November 19, 2002, pp. B1+.

5. A. Aston and M. Arndt, "The Flexible Factory," *BusinessWeek*, May 5, 2003, pp. 90–91.

6. P. Panchak, "Pella Drives Lean throughout the Enterprise," *IndustryWeek*, June 2003, pp. 74–77.

7. J. Ordonez, "McDonald's to Cut the Cooking Time of Its French Fries," *Wall Street Journal*, May 19, 2000, p. B2.

8. C. Fredman, "The Devil in the Details," *Executive Edge*, April–May 1999, pp. 36–39.

9. http://new.skoda-auto.com/Documents/AnnualReports/skoda_auto_annual_report_2007_%20EN_FINAL.pdf (July 8, 2008); and T. Mudd, "The Last Laugh," *IndustryWeek*, September 18, 2000, pp. 38–44.

10. Based on "Honorary Members Form Impressive Lineup of Quality Thinkers," *Quality Progress*, March 2011, p. 17; "W. Edwards Deming," *Quality Progress*, November 2010, p. 17; R. Aguayo, *Dr. Deming: The American Who Taught the Japanese About Quality* (New York: Fireside Press, 1991); M. Walton, *The Deming Management Method* (New York: Penguin Group, 1986); and W. E. Deming, "Improvement of Quality and Productivity Through Action by Management," *National Productivity Review*, Winter 1981–1982, pp. 12–22.

11. T. Vinas, "Little Things Mean a Lot," *IndustryWeek*, November 2002, p. 55.

12. P. Panchak, "Shaping the Future of Manufacturing," *IndustryWeek*, January 2005, pp. 38–44; M. Hammer, "Deep Change: How Operational Innovation Can Transform Your Company," *Harvard Business Review*, April 2004, pp. 84–94; S. Levy, "The Connected Company," *Newsweek*, April 28, 2003, pp. 40–48; and J. Teresko, "Plant Floor Strategy," *IndustryWeek*, July 2002, pp. 26–32.

13. T. Laseter, K. Ramdas, and D. Swerdlow, "The Supply Side of Design and Development," *Strategy & Business*, Summer 2003, p. 23; J. Jusko, "Not All Dollars and Cents," *IndustryWeek*, April 2002, p. 58; and D. Drickhamer, "Medical Marvel," *IndustryWeek*, March 2002, pp. 47–49.

14. Q. H. Soon and Z. M. Udin, "Supply Chain Management from the Perspective of Value Chain Flexibility: An Exploratory Study," *Journal of Manufacturing Technology Management*, May 2011, pp. 506–26; G. Soni and R. Kodali, "A Critical Analysis of Supply Chain Management Content in Empirical Research," *Business Process Management*, April 2011, pp. 238–56; and J. H. Sheridan, "Managing the Value Chain," *IndustryWeek*, September 6, 1999, pp. 1–4, available online in archives at www.industryweek.com.

15. "Supply Chain Management: A New Narrative," *Strategic Direction*, March 2011, pp. 18–21; and Sheridan, "Managing the Value Chain."

16. S. Leibs, "Getting Ready: Your Suppliers," *IndustryWeek*, www.industryweek.com (September 6, 1999).

17. See, for example, J. Jusko, "Procurement—Not All Dollars and Cents," *IndustryWeek*, www.industryweek.com (April 4, 2002).

18. See "News Item Future Challenges for the Aromatics Supply Chain," speech given by Nancy Sullivan, Vice President Aromatics & Phenol, to the First European Aromatics and Derivatives Conference, London, UK (May 29, 2002), available online at http://www.shellchemicals.com/newsroom/1,1098.71.00.html.

19. D. Bartholomew, "The Infrastructure," *IndustryWeek*, September 6, 1999, p. 1.

20. G. Taninecz, "Forging the Chain," *IndustryWeek*, May 15, 2000, pp. 40–46.

21. T. Vinas, "A Map of the World: IW Value-Chain Survey," *IndustryWeek*, September 2005, pp. 27–34.

22. See J. H. Sheridan, "Now It's a Job for the CEO," *IndustryWeek*, March 20, 2000, pp. 22–30.

23. R. Norman and R. Ramirez, "From Value Chain to Value Constellation," *Harvard Business Review on Managing the Value Chain* (Boston: Harvard Business School Press, 2000), pp. 185–219.

24. S. Leibs, "Getting Ready: Your Customers," *IndustryWeek*, September 6, 1999, p. 4.

25. See, for example, C. Lunan, "Workers Doing More in Less Time," *Charlotte Observer*, June 1, 2002, p. D1.

26. Leibs, "Getting Ready: Your Customers," p. 3.

27. See, for instance, L. Harrington, "The Accelerated Value Chain: Supply Chain Management Just Got Smarter, Faster, and More Cost-Effective, Thanks to a Groundbreaking Alliance between Intel and Technologies," *IndustryWeek*, April 2002, pp. 45–51.

28. Ibid.

29. Ibid.; and Sheridan, "Managing the Value Chain."

30. Sheriden, "Managing the Value Chain," p. 3.

31. Leibs, "Getting Ready: Your Customers," p. 4.

32. Sheriden, "Managing the Value Chain," pp. 2–3; Leibs, "Getting Ready: Your Customers," 1, 4; and Bartholomew, "The Infrastructure," p. 6.

33. Taninecz, "Forging the Chain."

34. Ibid.

35. Ibid.

36. D. Drickhamer, "On Target," *IndustryWeek*, October 16, 2000, 111–12.

37. Ibid.

38. "Top Security Threats and Management Issues Facing Corporate America: 2003 Survey of Fortune 1000 Companies," ASIS International and Pinkerton, www.asisonline.org.

39. Sheridan, "Managing the Value Chain," p. 4.

40. S. Rosenbloom, "Solution, or Mess? A Milk Jug for a Green Earth," *New York Times Online*, June 30, 2008.

41. K. T. Greenfeld, "Taco Bell and the Golden Age of Drive-Thru," *Bloomberg BusinessWeek Online*, May 5, 2011; and S. Anderson, "Restaurants Gear Up for Window Wars," *Springfield, Missouri, News-Leader*, January 27, 2006, p. 5B.

42. D. Bartholomew, "Quality Takes a Beating," *IndustryWeek*, March 2006, pp. 46–54; J. Carey and M. Arndt, "Making Pills the Smart Way," *BusinessWeek*, May 3, 2004, pp. 102–03; and A. Barrett, "Schering's Dr. Feelbetter?" *BusinessWeek*, June 23, 2003, pp. 55–56.

43. T. Vinas, "Six Sigma Rescue," *IndustryWeek*, March 2004, p. 12.

44. J. S. McClenahen, "Prairie Home Companion," *IndustryWeek*, October 2005, pp. 45–46.

45. T. Vinas, "Zeroing In on the Customer," *IndustryWeek*, October 2004, pp. 61–62.

46. W. Royal, "Spotlight Shines on Maquiladora," *IndustryWeek*, October 16, 2000, pp. 91–92.

47. See B. Whitford and R. Andrew (eds.), *The Pursuit of Quality* (Perth: Beaumont Publishing, 1994).

48. D. Drickhamer, "Road to Excellence," *IndustryWeek*, October 16, 2000, pp. 117–18.

49. G. Hasek, "Merger Marries Quality Efforts," *IndustryWeek*, August 21, 2000, pp. 89–92.

50. J. Jusko, "An Elite Crew," *Industry Week*, March 2011, pp. 17–18; and M. Arndt, "Quality Isn't Just for Widgets," *Business Week*, July 22, 2002, pp. 72–73.

51. E. White, "Rethinking the Quality Improvement Program," *Wall Street Journal*, September 19, 2005, p. B3.

52. M. Arndt, "Quality Isn't Just for Widgets."

53. For a thorough overview of project management, see S. Berkun, *The Art of Project Management* (Upper Saddle River, NJ: Prentice Hall, 2005); or J. K. Pinto, *Project Management:* *Achieving Competitive Advantage and MS Project* (Upper Saddle River, NJ: Prentice Hall, 2007).

54. H. Maylor, "Beyond the Gantt Chart: Project Management Moving On," *European Management Journal*, February 2001, pp. 92–101.

55. For additional information on CPM, see W. A. Haga and K. A. Marold, "A Simulation Approach to the PERT/CPM Time-Cost Trade-Off Problem," *Project Management Journal*, June 2004, pp. 31–37.

Glossary

A

Absenteeism   The failure to show up for work

Active listening   Listening for full meaning without making premature judgments or interpretations

Activities   Actions that take place

Adjourning stage   The final stage of group development for temporary groups, during which groups prepare to disband

Affective component   The part of an attitude that's the emotional or feeling part

Affirmative action programs   Programs that ensure that decisions and practices enhance the employment, upgrading, and retention of members of protected groups

Assumed similarity   An observer's perception of others influenced more by the observer's own characteristics than by those of the person observed

Attitudes   Evaluative statements, either favorable or unfavorable, concerning objects, people, or events

Attribution theory   A theory used to explain how we judge people differently, based on what meaning we attribute to a given behavior

Augmented reality   A technology that superimposes a computer-generated image on a user's view of the real world

Authority   The rights inherent in a managerial position to give orders and expect the orders to be obeyed

B

Balanced scorecard   A performance measurement tool that looks at more than just the financial perspective

Basic corrective action   Corrective action that looks at how and why performance deviated before correcting the source of deviation

Behavior   The actions of people

Behavioral component   The part of an attitude that refers to an intention to behave in a certain way toward someone or something

Behavioral theories of leadership   Theories that isolate behaviors that differentiate effective leaders from ineffective leaders

Benchmarking   The search for the best practices among competitors or noncompetitors that lead to their superior performance

Big data   The vast amount of quantifiable information that can be analyzed by highly sophisticated data processing

Big Five Model   A personality trait model that examines five traits: extraversion, agreeableness, conscientiousness, emotional stability, and openness to experience

Board representatives   Employees who sit on a company's board of directors and represent the interest of employees

Body language   Nonverbal communication cues such as facial expressions, gestures, and other body movements

Boundaryless career   When an individual takes personal responsibility for his or her own career

Boundaryless organization   An organization whose design is not defined by, or limited to, boundaries imposed by a predefined structure

Bounded rationality   Making decisions that are rational within the limits of a manager's ability to process information

Brainstorming   An idea-generating process that encourages alternatives while withholding criticism

Break-even analysis   A technique for identifying the point at which total revenue is just sufficient to cover total costs

Business model   strategic design for how a company intends to profit from its broad array of strategies, processes, and activities

Business plan   A written document that summarizes a business opportunity and defines and articulates how the identified opportunity is to be seized and exploited

C

"Calm waters" metaphor   A description of organizational change that likens that change to a large ship making a predictable trip across a calm sea and experiencing an occasional storm

Capabilities   An organization's skills and abilities in doing the work activities needed in its business

Career   The sequence of work positions held by a person during his or her lifetime

Centralization   The degree to which decision making takes place at upper levels of the organization

Certainty   A situation in which a decision maker can make accurate decisions because all outcomes are known

Chain of command   The line of authority extending from upper organizational levels to lower levels, which clarifies who reports to whom

Change agents   People who act as change catalysts and assume the responsibility for managing the change process

Channel   The medium by which a message travels

Charismatic leaders   Enthusiastic, self-confident leaders whose personalities and actions influence people to behave in certain ways

Cloud computing   Storing and accessing data on the Internet rather than on a computer's hard drive or a company's network

Code of ethics   A formal document that states an organization's primary values and the ethical rules it expects managers and nonmanagerial employees

Cognitive component   The part of an attitude made up of the beliefs, opinions, knowledge, and information held by a person

Cognitive dissonance   Any incompatibility or inconsistency between attitudes or between behavior and attitudes

Commitment concept   The idea that plans should extend far enough to meet those commitments made when the plans were developed

Communication   A transfer of understanding and meaning from one person to another

Communication process   The seven-part process of transferring and understanding of meaning

Communities of practice   Groups of people who share a concern, a set of problems, or a passion about a topic and who deepen their knowledge and expertise in that area by interacting on an ongoing basis

Competitive advantage   What sets an organization apart; its distinctive edge

Competitive intelligence   A type of environmental scanning that gives managers accurate information about competitors

Competitive strategy   An organizational strategy for how an organization will compete in its business(es)

Compressed workweek   A workweek where employees work longer hours per day but fewer days per week

Conceptual skills   A manager's ability to analyze and diagnose complex situations

Concurrent control   Control that takes place while a work activity is in progress

Contingency approach (or situational approach)   An approach to management that says that individual organizations, employees, and situations are different and require different ways of managing

Contingent workers   Temporary, freelance, or contract workers whose employment is contingent upon demand for their services

Control   Management function that involves monitoring activities to ensure that they're being accomplished as planned and correcting any significant deviations

Control process   A three-step process of measuring actual performance, comparing actual performance against a standard, and taking managerial action to correct deviations

Controlling Monitoring activities to ensure that they are accomplished as planned

Core competencies The major value-creating capabilities of an Organization

Corporate strategy An organizational strategy that specifies what businesses a company is in or wants to be in and what it wants to do with those businesses

Cost leadership strategy When an organization competes on the basis of having the lowest costs in its industry

Creativity The ability to produce novel and useful ideas

Credibility The degree to which followers perceive someone as honest, competent, and able to inspire

Critical path The longest or most time-consuming sequence of events and activities required to complete a project in the shortest amount of time

Cross-functional team A work team made up of individuals from various departments and that cross traditional departmental lines

Cross-functional teams Teams made up of individuals from various departments and that cross traditional departmental lines

Customer departmentalization Grouping activities by customer

D

Decentralization The degree to which lower-level managers provide input or actually make decisions

Decision criteria Factors that are relevant in a decision

Decision implementation Putting a decision into action

Decision trees A diagram used to analyze a progression of decisions. When diagrammed, a decision tree looks like a tree with branches.

Decision-making process A set of eight steps that includes identifying a problem, selecting a solution, and evaluating the effectiveness of the solution

Decisional roles Entailing making decisions or choices

Decoding Translating a received message

Demographics The characteristics of a population used for purposes of social studies

Departmentalization How jobs are grouped together

Design thinking Approaching management problems as designers approach design problems

Differentiation strategy When an organization competes on the basis of having unique products that are widely valued by customers

Digital tools Technology, systems, or software that allow the user to collect, visualize, understand, or analyze data

Directional plans Plans that are flexible and set general guidelines

Discipline Actions taken by a manager to enforce an organization's standards and regulations

Disruptive innovation Innovations in products, services, or processes that radically change an industry's rules of the game

Distributive justice Perceived fairness of the amount and allocation of rewards among individuals

Division of labor (or job specialization) The breakdown of jobs into narrow repetitive tasks

Divisional structure An organizational structure made up of separate business units or divisions

Downsizing The planned elimination of jobs in an organization

E

Economic order quantity (EOQ) A model that seeks to balance the costs involved in ordering and carrying inventory, thus minimizing total costs associated with carrying and ordering costs

Effectiveness Doing the right things, or completing work activities so that organizational goals are attained

Efficiency Doing things right, or getting the most output from the least amount of inputs

Electronic meeting A type of nominal group technique in which participants are linked by computer

Emojis Tiny drawings of facial expressions or objects used in text messages, e-mails, and on social media

Emoticons Representations of facial expressions created by various combinations of keyboard characters

Emotional intelligence (EI) The ability to notice and to manage emotional cues and information

Employee assistance programs (EAPs) Programs offered by organizations to help employees overcome personal and health-related problems

Employee benefits Membership-based rewards designed to enrich employees' lives

Employee counseling A process designed to help employees overcome performance-related problems

Employee empowerment Giving employees the power to make decisions and take actions on their own

Employee engagement When employees are connected to, satisfied with, and enthusiastic about their jobs

Employee productivity A performance measure of both work efficiency and effectiveness

Employee recognition programs Programs that consist of personal attention and expressions of interest, approval, and appreciation for a job well done

Employee theft Any unauthorized taking of company property by employees for their personal use

Employee training A learning experience that seeks a relatively permanent change in employees by improving their ability to perform on the job

Employment planning The process by which managers ensure they have the right numbers and kinds of people in the right places at the right time

Empowerment The act of increasing the decision-making discretion of workers

Encoding Converting a message into symbolic form

Entrepreneur Someone who initiates and actively operates an entrepreneurial venture (EV)

Entrepreneurial ventures (EVs) Organizations that pursue opportunities, are characterized by innovative practices, and have growth and profitability as their main goals

Entrepreneurship The process of capitalizing on opportunities by starting new businesses for the purposes of changing, revolutionizing, transforming, or introducing new products or services

Environmental complexity The number of components in an organization's environment, how similar the components are, and the extent of knowledge that the organization has about those components

Environmental scanning An analysis of the external environment, which involves screening large amounts of information to detect emerging trends

Environmental uncertainty The degree of change, predictability of change, and complexity in an organization's environment

Equity theory The theory that an employee compares his or her job's input-to-outcome ratio with that of relevant others and then corrects any inequity

Escalation of commitment An increased commitment to a previous decision despite evidence that it may have been a poor decision

Ethical communication Presented material that contains all relevant information, is true in every sense, and is not deceptive in any way

Ethical culture A culture in which the shared concept of right and wrong behavior in the workplace reflects the organization's core values and influences employees' ethical decision making

Ethics A set of rules or principles that defines right and wrong conduct

Ethnicity Social traits, such as one's cultural background or allegiance, that are shared by a human population

Events End points that represent the completion of major activities

Expectancy theory The theory that an individual tends to act in a certain way based on the expectation that the act will be followed by a given outcome and on the attractiveness of that outcome to the individual

Exporting Making products domestically and selling them abroad

External environment Factors, forces, situations, and events outside the organization that affect its performance

F

Family-friendly benefits Benefits that provide a wide range of scheduling options and allow employees more flexibility at work, accommodating their needs for work/life balance

Feasibility study An analysis of the various aspects of a proposed entrepreneurial venture designed to determine its feasibility

Feedback Checking to see how successfully a message has been transferred

Feedback control Control that takes place after a work activity is done

Feedforward control Control that takes place before a work activity is done

Fiedler contingency model Leadership theory proposing that effective group performance depends on the proper match between a leader's style and the degree to which the situation allowed the leader to control and influence

Filtering Deliberately manipulating information to make it appear more favorable to the receiver

First-line managers Supervisors responsible for directing the day-today activities of non-managerial employees and/or team leaders

Fixed-point reordering system   A method for a system to "flag" the need to reorder inventory at some preestablished point in the process

Flextime (also known as flexible work hours)   A work scheduling system in which employees are required to work a specific number of hours per week but can vary when they work those hours within certain limits

Focus strategy   When an organization competes in a narrow segment or niche with either a cost focus or a differentiation focus

Foreign subsidiary   A direct investment in a foreign country that involves setting up a separate and independent facility or office

Formal planning department   A group of planning specialists whose sole responsibility is to help write the various organizational plans

Formalization   How standardized an organization's jobs are and the extent to which employee behavior is guided by rules and procedures

Forming stage   The first stage of group development in which people join the group and then define the group's purpose, structure, and leadership

Franchising   An agreement in which an organization gives another organization the right, for a fee, to use its name and operating methods

Functional departmentalization   Grouping activities by functions performed

Functional strategy   Strategy used in an organization's various functional departments to support the competitive strategy

Functional structure   An organizational design that groups similar or related occupational specialties together

Fundamental attribution error   The tendency to underestimate the influence of external factors and overestimate the influence of internal factors when making judgments about the behavior of others

G

Gamification   Applying typical aspects of game playing to other areas of activity especially in a work setting

Gantt chart   A planning tool that shows in bar graph form when tasks are supposed to be done and compares that with the actual progress on each

General administrative theory   Descriptions of what managers do and what constitutes good management practice

Global corporation   An MNC that centralizes management and other decisions in the home country

Global sourcing   Purchasing materials or labor from around the world, wherever it is cheapest

Global strategic alliance   A partnership between an organization and foreign company partner(s) in which both share resources and knowledge in developing new products or building production facilities

Global village   A boundaryless world where goods and services are produced and marketed worldwide

GLOBE   The Global Leadership and Organizational Behavior Effectiveness research program, a program that studies cross-cultural leadership behaviors

Goal-setting theory   The proposition that specific goals increase performance and that

difficult goals, when accepted, result in higher performance than do easy goals

Goals (objectives)   Desired outcomes or targets

Grapevine   An unofficial channel of communication

Group   Two or more interacting and interdependent individuals who come together to achieve specific goals

Group cohesiveness   The degree to which group members are attracted to one another and share the group's goals

Groupthink   When a group exerts extensive pressure on an individual to withhold his or her different views in order to appear to be in agreement

Growth strategy   A corporate strategy in which an organization expands the number of markets served or products offered either through its current business(es) or through new business(es)

H

Halo effect   When we form a general impression of a person on the basis of a single characteristic

Harvesting   Exiting a venture when an entrepreneur hopes to capitalize financially on the investment in the venture

Hawthorne studies   Research done in the late 1920s and early 1930s devised by Western Electric industrial engineers to examine the effect of different work environment changes on worker productivity, which led to a new emphasis on the human factor in the functioning of organizations and the attainment of their goals

Heuristics   Judgmental shortcuts or "rules of thumb" used to simplify decision making

Hierarchy of needs theory   Maslow's theory that there is a hierarchy of five human needs: physiological, safety, social, esteem, and self-actualization

Human resource inventory   A report listing important information about employees such as name, education, training, skills, languages spoken, and so forth

Human resource management (HRM)   The management function concerned with getting, training, motivating, and keeping competent employees

Hygiene factors   Factors that eliminate job dissatisfaction but don't motivate

I

Idea champions   Individuals who actively and enthusiastically support new ideas, build support for, overcome resistance to, and ensure that innovations are implemented

Immediate corrective action   Corrective action that addresses problems at once to get performance back on track

Importing   Acquiring products made abroad and selling them Domestically

Inclusion   The achievement of a work environment in which all individuals are treated fairly and respectfully, have equal opportunities and resources, and can contribute fully to the organization's success

Industrial Revolution   The advent of machine power, mass production, and efficient transportation beginning in the late eighteenth century in Great Britain

Information overload   What results when information exceeds processing capacity

Informational roles   Involving collecting, receiving, and disseminating information

Innovation   The process of taking a creative idea and turning it into a useful product, service, or method of operation

Intergroup development   Activities that attempt to make several work groups more cohesive

Interpersonal roles   Involving people (subordinates and persons outside the organization) and other duties that are ceremonial and symbolic in nature

Interpersonal skills   A manager's ability to work with, understand, mentor, and motivate others, both individually and in groups

Intuitive decision making   Making decisions on the basis of experience, feelings, and accumulated judgment

ISO 9001   A series of international quality standards that set uniform guidelines for processes to ensure that products conform to customer requirements

J

Jargon   Technical language specific to a discipline or Industry

Job analysis   An assessment that defines jobs and the behaviors necessary to perform them

Job characteristics model (JCM)   A framework for analyzing and designing jobs that identifies five primary core job dimensions, their interrelationships, and their impact on outcomes

Job description   A written statement that describes a job

Job design   The way tasks are combined to form complete jobs

Job enrichment   The vertical expansion of a job by adding planning and evaluation responsibilities

Job involvement   The degree to which an employee identifies with his or her job, actively participates in it, and considers his or her job performance important for self-worth

Job satisfaction   An employee's general attitude toward his or her job

Job sharing   When two or more people split a full-time job

Job specification   A written statement of the minimum qualifications that a person must possess to perform a given job successfully

Joint venture   A specific type of strategic alliance in which the partners agree to form a separate, independent organization for some business purpose

K

Karoshi   A Japanese term that refers to a sudden death caused by overworking

Knowledge management   Cultivating a learning culture in which organizational members systematically gather knowledge and share it with others

L

Layoff-survivor sickness   A set of attitudes, perceptions, and behaviors of employees who survive layoffs

Leader   Someone who can influence others and who has managerial authority

Leader-member exchange (LMX) theory   A leadership theory that says leaders create in-groups and out-groups and those in the in- group will have higher performance ratings, less turnover, and greater job satisfaction

Leader-participation model A leadership contingency theory that's based on a sequential set of rules for determining how much participation a leader uses in decision making according to different types of situations

Leadership The process of leading a group and influencing that group to achieve its goals

Leading Directing and coordinating the work activities of an organization's people

Learning A relatively permanent change in behavior that occurs as a result of experience

Learning organization An organization that has developed the capacity to continuously learn, adapt, and change

Least-preferred coworker (LPC) questionnaire A questionnaire that measures whether a leader was task or relationship oriented

Licensing An agreement in which an organization gives another the right, for a fee, to make or sell its products, using its technology or product specifications

Line authority Authority that entitles a manager to direct the work of an employee

Linear programming A mathematical technique that solves resource allocation problems

Load chart A modified version of a Gantt chart that lists either whole departments or specific resources

Locus of control The degree to which people believe they control their own fate

Long-term plans Plans with a time frame beyond three years

M

Machiavellianism ("Mach") A measure of the degree to which people are pragmatic, maintain emotional distance, and believe that ends justify means

Management The process of getting things done, effectively and efficiently, through and with other people

Management by objectives (MBO) A process of setting mutually agreed-upon goals and using those goals to evaluate employee performance

Management by walking around (MBWA) When a manager is out in the work area interacting with employees

Managerial grid A two-dimensional grid for appraising leadership styles

Managerial roles Specific categories of managerial behavior; often grouped around interpersonal relationships, information transfer, and decision making

Managers Individuals in an organization who direct and oversee the activities of others

Manufacturing organizations Organizations that produce physical goods

Mass production Large-batch manufacturing

Matrix structure A structure in which specialists from different functional departments are assigned to work on projects led by a project manager

Means-ends chain An integrated network of goals in which higher-level goals are linked to lower-level goals, which serve as the means for their accomplishment

Mechanistic organization A bureaucratic organization; a structure that's high in specialization, formalization, and centralization

Message A purpose for communicating that's to be conveyed

Middle managers Individuals who are typically responsible for translating goals set by top managers into specific details that lower-level managers will see get done

Mission A statement of an organization's purpose

MNC (multinational corporation) Any type of international company that maintains operations in multiple countries

Motivation The process by which a person's efforts are energized, directed, and sustained toward attaining a goal

Motivators Factors that increase job satisfaction and motivation

Multidomestic corporation An MNC that decentralizes management and other decisions to the local country where it's doing business

Myers-Briggs Type Indicator (MBTI) A personality assessment that uses four dimensions of personality to identify different personality types

N

Necessity entrepreneurs Individuals who start an EV out of necessity

Need for achievement (nAch) The drive to succeed and excel in relation to a set of standards

Need for affiliation (nAff) The desire for friendly and close interpersonal Relationships

Need for power (nPow) The need to make others behave in a way that they would not have behaved otherwise

Network organization An organization that uses its own employees to do some work activities and networks of outside suppliers to provide other needed product components or work processes

Nominal group technique A decision-making technique in which group members are physically present but operate independently

Nonmanagerial employees People who work directly on a job or task and have no responsibility for overseeing the work of others

Nonprogrammed decision A unique and nonrecurring decision that requires a custom-made solution

Norming stage The third stage of group development, which is characterized by close relationships and cohesiveness

Norms Standards or expectations that are accepted and shared by a group's members

O

Omnipotent view of management The view that managers are directly responsible for an organization's success or failure

Open systems Systems that dynamically interact with their environment

Open workplaces Workplaces that have few physical barriers and enclosures

Open-book management A motivational approach in which an organization's financial statements (the "books") are shared with all employees

Operant conditioning A theory of learning that says behavior is a function of its consequences

Operations management The study and application of the transformation process

Opportunities Positive trends in the external environment

Opportunity-based entrepreneurs Individuals who start an EV to pursue an opportunity

Organic organization A structure that's low in specialization, formalization, and centralization

Organization A deliberate collection of people brought together to accomplish some specific purpose

Organization design When managers develop or change the organization's structure

Organization development (OD) Efforts that assist organizational members with a planned change by focusing on their attitudes and values

Organizational behavior (OB) The field of study that researches the actions (behaviors) of people at work

Organizational change Any alteration of an organization's people, structure, or technology

Organizational citizenship behavior Discretionary behavior that's not part of an employee's formal job requirements, but that promotes the effective functioning of the organization

Organizational commitment An employee's orientation toward the organization in terms of his or her loyalty to, identification with, and involvement in the organization

Organizational processes The way organizational work is done

Organizational vision A broad comprehensive picture of what an entrepreneur wants his or her organization to become

Organizing The function of management in which the organization's structure is created by determining what needs to be done, how it will be done, and who is to do it

Orientation Introducing a new employee to the job and the Organization

P

Parochialism A narrow focus in which managers see things only through their own eyes and from their own perspective

Path-goal theory A leadership theory that says the leader's job is to assist followers in attaining their goals and to provide direction or support needed to ensure that their goals are compatible with the organization's or group's goals

Pay-for-performance programs Variable compensation plans that pay employees on the basis of some performance measure

Perception A process by which we give meaning to our environment by organizing and interpreting sensory impressions

Performance management system A system that establishes performance standards that are used to evaluate employee performance

Performance-simulation tests Selection devices based on actual job behaviors

Performing stage The fourth stage of group development, when the group is fully functional and works on the group task

Personality A unique combination of emotional, thought, and behavioral patterns that affect how a person reacts to situations and interacts with others

PERT network analysis A flowchart-like diagram that depicts the sequence of activities needed to complete a project and the time or costs associated with each activity

Planning Defining goals, establishing strategy, and developing plans to coordinate activities

Plans Documents that outline how goals are going to be met

Policy A guideline for making decisions

Political skills A manager's ability to build a power base and establish the right connections

Portfolio entrepreneur An individual who retains an original business and builds a portfolio of additional businesses through inheriting, establishing, or purchasing them

Power An individual's capacity to influence decisions

Principles of management Fayol's fundamental or universal principles of management practice

Proactive personality A personality trait describing those individuals who are more prone to take actions to influence their environment

Problem A discrepancy between an existing and a desired state of affairs to follow

Problem-solving teams A team from the same department or functional area that's involved in efforts to improve work activities or to solve specific problems

Procedural justice Perceived fairness of the process used to determine the distribution of rewards

Procedure A series of interrelated, sequential steps used to respond to a structured problem

Process consultation Using outside consultants to assess organizational processes such as workflow, informal intra-unit relationships, and formal communication channels

Process departmentalization Grouping activities on the basis of work or customer flow

Process production Continuous flow or process production

Product departmentalization Grouping activities by major product areas

Professionalism How you conduct yourself at work—your attitudes, your actions, your behaviors

Programmed decision A repetitive decision that can be handled using a routine approach

Project A one-time-only set of activities with a definite beginning and ending point

Project management The task of getting project activities done on time, within budget, and according to specifications

Project structure A structure in which employees continuously work on projects

Q

Quantitative approach The use of quantitative techniques to improve decision making

Queuing theory Also known as waiting line theory, it is a way of balancing the cost of having a waiting line versus the cost of maintaining the line. Management wants to have as few stations open as possible to minimize costs without testing the patience of its customers.

R

Race The biological heritage (including physical characteristics, such as one's skin color and associated traits) that people use to identify themselves

Range of variation The acceptable parameters of variance between actual performance and a standard

Rational decision making Describes choices that are consistent and value maximizing within specified constraints

Readiness The extent to which people have the ability and willingness to accomplish a specific task

Real goals Those goals an organization actually pursues as shown by what the organization's members are doing

Realistic job preview (RJP) A preview of a job that provides both positive and negative information about the job and the company

Recruitment Locating, identifying, and attracting capable Applicants

Referent The persons, systems, or selves against which individuals compare themselves to assess equity

Reliability The degree to which a selection device measures the same thing consistently

Remote work Doing work via virtual devices from any remote location

Renewal strategy A corporate strategy that addresses declining organizational performance

Resources An organization's assets that it uses to develop, manufacture, and deliver products to its customers

Responsibility An obligation to perform assigned duties

Rights view of ethics View that says ethical decisions are made in order to respect and protect individual liberties and privileges

Ringisei Japanese consensus-forming group decisions

Risk A situation in which a decision maker is able to estimate the likelihood of certain outcomes

Role Behavior patterns expected of someone who occupies a given position in a social unit

Rule An explicit statement that tells employees what can or cannot be done

S

Satisfice Accepting solutions that are "good enough"

Scientific management The use of scientific methods to define the "one best way" for a job to be done

Selection process Screening job applicants to ensure that the most appropriate candidates are hired

Selective perception (communication) Selectively perceiving or hearing a communication based on your own needs, motivations, experiences, or other personal characteristics

Selective perception (perceptual shortcuts) The tendency for people to only absorb parts of what they observe, which allows us to "speed read" others

Self-efficacy An individual's belief that he or she is capable of performing a task

Self-employment Individuals who work for profit or fees in their own business, profession, trade, or farm

Self-esteem (SE) An individual's degree of like or dislike for himself or herself

Self-managed work team A type of work team that operates without a manager and is responsible for a complete work process or segment

Self-monitoring A personality trait that measures the ability to adjust behavior to external situational factors

Self-serving bias The tendency for individuals to attribute their successes to internal factors while putting the blame for failures on external factors

Serial entrepreneur An individual who has sold or closed an original business, founded another business, sold or closed that business, and continues this cycle of entrepreneurial behavior

Service organizations Organizations that produce nonphysical products in the form of services

Sexual harassment Any unwanted action or activity of a sexual nature that explicitly or implicitly affects an individual's employment, performance, or work environment

Shaping behavior The process of guiding learning in graduated steps, using reinforcement or lack of reinforcement

Sharing economy An economic environment in which asset owners share with other individuals through a peer-to-peer service, for a set fee, their underutilized physical assets or their knowledge, expertise, skills, or time

Short-term plans Plans with a time frame of one year or less

Simple structure An organizational design with low departmentalization, wide spans of control, authority centralized in a single person, and little formalization

Single-use plan A one-time plan specifically designed to meet the needs of a unique situation

Situational leadership theory (SLT) A leadership contingency theory that focuses on followers' readiness

Six Sigma A quality standard that establishes a goal of no more than 3.4 defects per million units or procedures

Skill-based pay A pay system that rewards employees for the job skills they demonstrate

Skunk works A small group within a large organization, given a high degree of autonomy and unhampered by corporate bureaucracy, whose mission is to develop a project primarily for the purpose of radical innovation

Slack time The time difference between the critical path and all other paths

Small business An independent business having fewer than 500 employees that doesn't necessarily engage in any new or innovative practices and has relatively little impact on its industry

Social entrepreneur An individual or organization that seeks out opportunities to improve society by using practical, innovative, and sustainable approaches

Social learning theory A theory of learning that says people can learn through observation and direct experience

Social loafing The tendency for individuals to expend less effort when working collectively than when working individually

Social media Forms of electronic communication through which users create online communities to share ideas, information, personal messages, and other content

Social obligation When a business firm engages in social actions because of its obligation to meet certain economic and legal responsibilities

Social responsibility (corporate social responsibility, or CSR) A business firm's intention, beyond its legal and economic obligations, to do the right things and act in ways that are good for society

Social responsiveness When a business firm engages in social actions in response to some popular social need

Span of control The number of employees a manager can efficiently and effectively supervise

Specific plans Plans that are clearly defined and leave no room for interpretation

Stability strategy A corporate strategy in which an organization continues to do what it is currently doing

Staff authority Positions with some authority that have been created to support, assist, and advise those holding line authority

Stakeholders Any constituencies in an organization's environment that are affected by that organization's decisions and actions

Standing plans Plans that are ongoing and provide guidance for activities performed repeatedly

Stated goals Official statements of what an organization says, and wants its stakeholders to believe, its goals are

Status A prestige grading, position, or rank within a group

Status conformity Adjusting one's behavior to align with a group's norms. A prestige grading, position, or rank within a group

Stereotyping When we judge someone on the basis of our perception of a group to which that person belongs

Storming stage The second stage of group development, which is characterized by intragroup conflict

Strategic business units (SBUs) An organization's single businesses that are independent and formulate their own competitive strategies

Strategic management What managers do to develop an organization's strategies

Strategic management process A six-step process that encompasses strategy planning, implementation, and evaluation

Strategic plans Plans that apply to the entire organization and encompass the organization's overall goals

Strategies Plans for how the organization will do what it's in business to do, how it will compete successfully, and how it will attract its customers in order to achieve its goals

Strengths Any activities the organization does well or any unique resources that it has

Stress Response to anxiety over intense demands, constraints, or opportunities

Stressors Factors that cause stress

Strong cultures Cultures in which the key values are deeply held and widely shared

Structured problem A straightforward, familiar, and easily defined problem

Survey feedback A method of assessing employees' attitudes toward and perceptions of a change

Sustainability A company's ability to achieve its business goals and increase long-term shareholder value by integrating economic, environmental, and social opportunities into its business strategies

Sustaining innovation Innovations that represent small and incremental changes in established products rather than dramatic breakthroughs

SWOT analysis The combined external and internal analyses

Symbolic view of management The view that much of an organization's success or failure is due to external forces outside managers' control

Systems approach An approach to management that views an organization as a system, which is a set of interrelated and interdependent parts arranged in a manner that produces a unified whole

T

Tactical plans Plans that specify the details of how the overall goals are to be achieved

Team leaders Individuals who are responsible for leading and facilitating the activities of a work team

Team structure A structure in which the entire organization is made up of work teams

Team-building Using activities to help work groups set goals, develop positive interpersonal relationships, and clarify the roles and responsibilities of each team member

Technical skills Job-specific knowledge and techniques needed to perform work tasks

Technology Any equipment, tools, or operating methods that are designed to make work more efficient

Telecommuting A work arrangement in which employees work at home and are linked to the workplace by virtual device

Theory of justice view of ethics View that says ethical decisions are made in order to enforce rules fairly and impartially

Theory X The assumption that employees dislike work, are lazy, avoid responsibility, and must be coerced to work

Theory Y The assumption that employees are creative, enjoy work, seek responsibility, and can exercise self-direction

Threats Negative trends in the external environment

Three-needs theory McClelland's theory, which says that three acquired (not innate) needs—achievement, power, and affiliation—are major motives at work

360-degree appraisal An appraisal device that seeks feedback from a variety of sources for the person being rated

Top managers Individuals who are responsible for making decisions about the direction of the organization and establishing policies that affect all organizational members

Total quality management (TQM) A managerial philosophy devoted to continual improvement and responding to customer needs and expectations

Traditional goal setting Goals set by top managers flow down through the organization and become subgoals for each organizational area

Trait theories of leadership Theories that isolate characteristics (traits) that differentiate leaders from nonleaders

Transactional leaders Leaders who lead primarily by using social exchanges (or transactions)

Transformation process The process that converts resources into finished goods and services

Transformational leaders Leaders who stimulate and inspire (transform) followers to achieve extraordinary outcomes

Transnational (borderless) organization An MNC where artificial geographic boundaries are eliminated

Trust The belief in the integrity, character, and ability of a leader

Turnover Voluntary and involuntary permanent withdrawal from an organization

Two-factor theory Herzberg's motivation theory, which proposes that intrinsic factors are related to job satisfaction and motivation, whereas extrinsic factors are associated with job dissatisfaction

Type A personality People who have a chronic sense of urgency and an excessive competitive drive

Type B personality People who are relaxed and easygoing and accept change easily

U

Uncertainty A situation in which a decision maker has neither certainty nor reasonable probability estimates available

Unit production The production of items in units or small batches

Unity of command Structure in which each employee reports to only one manager

Unstructured problem A problem that is new or unusual for which information is ambiguous or incomplete

Utilitarian view of ethics View that says ethical decisions are made solely on the basis of their outcomes or consequences

V

Validity The proven relationship between a selection device and some relevant criterion

Value The performance characteristics, features and attributes, and any other aspects of goods and services for which customers are willing to give up resources

Value chain The entire series of organizational work activities that add value at each step from raw materials to finished product

Value chain management The process of managing the sequence of activities and information along the entire value chain

Variable pay A pay system in which an individual's compensation is contingent on performance

Verbal intonation An emphasis given to words or phrases that conveys meaning

Virtual organization An organization that consists of a small core of full-time employees and outside specialists temporarily hired as needed to work on projects

Virtual team A type of work team that uses technology to link physically dispersed members in order to achieve a common goal

Visionary leadership The ability to create and articulate a realistic, credible, and attractive vision of the future that improves on the present situation

W

Weaknesses Activities the organization doesn't do well or resources it needs but doesn't possess

Wellness programs Programs offered by organizations to help employees prevent health problems

"White-water rapids" metaphor A description of organizational change that likens that change to a small raft navigating a raging river

Work councils Groups of nominated or elected employees who must be consulted when management makes decisions involving personnel

Work specialization Dividing work activities into separate job tasks; also called division of labor

Work teams Groups whose members work intensely on specific, common goals using their positive synergy, individual and mutual accountability, and complementary skills

Workforce diversity Ways in which people in a workforce are similar and different from one another in terms of gender, age, race, sexual orientation, ethnicity, cultural background, and physical abilities and disabilities

Workplace misbehavior Any intentional employee behavior that is potentially harmful to the organization or individuals within the organization

Index